MW00758193

SEND FINAL MESSAGE ⟶

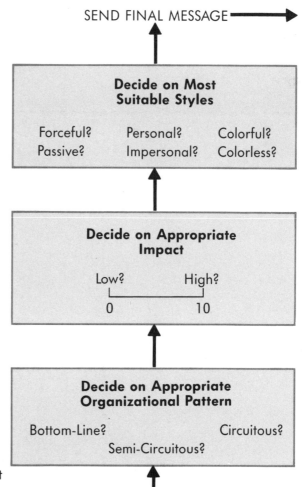

**Decide on Most
Suitable Styles**

Forceful?   Personal?   Colorful?
Passive?   Impersonal?   Colorless?

**Decide on Appropriate
Impact**

Low?   High?
0   10

**Decide on Appropriate
Organizational Pattern**

Bottom-Line?   Circuitous?
Semi-Circuitous?

Once you have decided on the appropriate message, you can proceed to make choices of organization, impact, and style best suited to producing the desired effect on the recipient.

ABOUT THE AUTHORS

Ronald E. Dulek, Ph.D., Professor of Management Communications, presently serves as interim Chairperson of the Management and Marketing Department at the University of Alabama. He is also coordinator of Management Communications, a position he has held since 1978. Dr. Dulek is a dedicated undergraduate and graduate teacher who has been selected as MBA Teacher of the Year twice in the past four years. He has published numerous academic and business-oriented articles in such journals as *Business Horizons*, IEEE *Transactions on Professional Communication*, *Personnel*, and *The Journal of Business Communication*.

John S. Fielden, Ph.D., University Professor of Management Communications at the University of Alabama, is an experienced teacher and administrator. Dr. Fielden served nine years as Dean of the College of Commerce and Business Administration at the University of Alabama and seven years as Dean of the School of Management at Boston University. While on the faculty of Harvard Business School, he served as Associate Editor of the *Harvard Business Review*. One of his articles, "What Do You Mean I Can't Write?" is included in the *Harvard Business Review*'s volume of all-time classics.

In addition to their academic and administrative experience, Drs. Dulek and Fielden have extensive experience as corporate and government consultants. Agencies and companies with which they have worked extensively include BellSouth, the Department of Health and Human Services, IBM, Kimberly-Clark Corporation, the National Science Foundation, and the Occupational Safety and Health Administration.

Most recently, Drs. Dulek and Fielden participated in a national OSHA Task Force that designed a simplified and consistent reporting procedure for safety and health reports throughout the United States. They also developed a written communication training program for IBM management personnel. This program is presently offered through IBM trainers to more than 35,000 IBM managers.

Prior to the development of the IBM program, Drs. Dulek and Fielden designed a written communication program for IBM support and field personnel. This highly successful program was offered to more than 10,000 IBM marketing representatives and systems engineers.

PRINCIPLES OF
BUSINESS COMMUNICATION

PRINCIPLES OF BUSINESS COMMUNICATION

RONALD E. DULEK

University of Alabama

JOHN S. FIELDEN

University of Alabama

Macmillan Publishing Company
New York

Collier Macmillan Publishers
London

Acquisition Editor: Charles E. Stewart, Jr.
Development Editor: Nancy Perry
Production Supervisor: Jennifer Carey
Production Manager: Richard C. Fischer
Text Designer: Eileen Burke
Cover Designer: Eileen Burke
Cover photograph: Slide Graphics

This book was set in Palatino by Waldman Graphics, Inc., printed and bound by Von Hoffmann Press, Inc. The cover was printed by Lehigh Press Lithographers.

Copyright © 1990, Macmillan Publishing Company, a division of Macmillan, Inc.

Printed in the United States of America

All rights reserved. No part of this book may be reproduced or transmitted in any form or by any means, electronic or mechanical, including photocopying, recording, or any information storage and retrieval system, without permission in writing from the publisher.

Macmillan Publishing Company
866 Third Avenue, New York, New York 10022

Collier Macmillan Canada, Inc.

Library of Congress Cataloging-in-Publication Data

Dulek, Ronald E.
    Principles of business communication / Ronald E. Dulek, John S. Fielden.
       p.   cm.
    Includes index.
    ISBN 0-02-330750-1
    1. Business communication.   2. Business writing.   I. Fielden,
John S.   II. Title.
HF5718.D83   1990
658.4′5—dc19   89-2351
                                                              CIP

Printing: 1 2 3 4 5 6 7 8   Year: 9 0 1 2 3 4 5 6 7 8

To Sally, Dan, and Laura
R.E.D.

To Jean
J.S.F.

Foreword

by Marvin L. Mann
IBM Vice President and General Manager, Services Industries

The need for effective communication is a reflection of the complexity of doing business in "the information age."

Not so many years ago, information was something of a luxury, as most people lived off the land or produced goods for a living. What has changed is that today information is a necessity, something we use to produce other things, and even to make products better. In fact, a lot of companies are using information effectively to gain a competitive edge.

Businesspeople need and work with information. But it's probable that just a tiny fraction of the information that we receive actually gets assimilated and acted upon. We are often overwhelmed by the streams of paper, facts, and data that flow through our offices. The challenge of *effective* business communication in one sense is that of the assembly line: to get the right information to the right people at the right time in usable form.

Electronic technology has created new delivery channels for information and speeded the process of information gathering, processing, and dissemination. Technology facilitates the delivery of business messages, resulting in an increased flow of information from many sources. Therefore, we must concentrate even harder on the messages to be delivered.

That's why the ability to communicate ideas effectively is essential for anyone who wants to be successful in business, and vital for anyone who aspires to business leadership. How vital? I am reminded of one top executive who was known to say to his staff, "The problem I have with writers is they always write what I say instead of what I am thinking."

My colleagues and I wish that more emphasis were placed on business communication training by our educational system. Every year, we at IBM spend considerable time and money teaching new employees how to write clear, to-the-point memos and reports. And we devote even greater resources to instructing our employees how to make effective presentations.

Effective business communication is different from reporting or other literary or academic forms of writing. Businesspeople don't have time to pore over the facts, to savor an idea or an expression. Precision, efficiency, and honesty are what's expected.

But that may not be enough to give what we have to say a hearing. Businesspeople spend long hours every day reading, listening, and talking. They may have no interest in our information and little time for it.

Our communications, therefore, need to be considerate of the audience and persuasive to gain acceptance. What we seek to communicate should be balanced carefully against the need to communicate tactfully with many different audiences. Such skills are the scope of this book.

Frank Cary, a former chief executive officer of the IBM Corporation, once said that the following qualities were required of top corporate executives: intelligence, integrity, empathy, and communication skills.

Skilled communicators make intelligence, integrity, and empathy apparent in every business communication. Those who learn how to present accurate, honest information and then shape that information tactfully to meet the needs of their audience, possess skills vital to success in today's "information age."

Preface

We consulted a number of different people before deciding to begin PRINCIPLES OF BUSINESS COMMUNICATION. The final decision to undertake the project came at the urging of

- Students who saw their communication skills improve dramatically because they had mastered the business communication system taught in this text.
- Business Communication instructors who wanted a text that provided realistic advice about business communications. "Texts should reflect the reality of the business world," one instructor told us, "and such reality comes best from writers who have been there!"
- Practicing businesspeople who noted that college students they hire often have little or no understanding of real business communication. "These students know how to write such things as direct mail advertisements and collection letters," one manager told us, "but they don't know how to do the type of writing that I do daily—brief memos and memo reports sent internally to other employees in my organization."

As academicians and consultants, we have had numerous opportunities to observe and study the way people communicate on the job. As administrators, we have had opportunities to practice what we have learned. In each situation we have seen the positive results of effective communication—organizations that developed teamwork and mutual trust through honest, candid dissemination of information to and among their employees at all levels.

The field research on which this book is based resembles that done by many social scientists. Academic institutions, businesses, and government agencies have provided living laboratories within which we could study business communications. We did our research by working beside, studying with, and learning from top businesspeople and top academic and government leaders. These leaders know and taught us that their professional survival depends greatly on their ability to communicate effectively on a daily basis.

KEY FEATURES

PRINCIPLES OF BUSINESS COMMUNICATION develops a commonsense, highly useful, and realistic business communication system. The system shows students the process they must go through in order to make intelligent, educated choices about the organizational pattern, level of impact, and styles appropriate for all the different types of business messages they will have to send on the job.

The Flow Chart found on the inside front cover of this book summarizes this system. We have located the Flow Chart in such a prominent position to show readers the text's overall direction and to provide them with easy access to the Chart. The Chart will help students cope intelligently with exercises, cases, and other assignments throughout the text.

Other important features of PRINCIPLES OF BUSINESS COMMUNICATION include

- *Simplified Terminology.* As PRINCIPLES OF BUSINESS COMMUNICATION explains its communication system, it develops an efficient, economical language for examining business messages. Messages are divided into two broad categories: non-sensitive (which convey unemotional facts); and sensitive (which impart information that elicits either a positive or a negative reaction on the part of the reader).

  Sensitive messages are further divided into positive, negative, positive-persuasive (which attempt to persuade readers to do what is clearly in their best interest) and negative-persuasive (in which readers see nothing of benefit in the requested action).

  This simple classification is economical because it eliminates the redundancies that result when letters "denying credit," "refusing adjustments," "rejecting job applicants," and so on are treated separately. Such letters are clearly all negative in terms of the readers' perceptions of their messages.

  Furthermore, the terminology used in PRINCIPLES OF BUSINESS COMMUNICATION avoids labeling messages based on their department of origin. What type of letter is an "adjustment letter," for example? By applying the text's classification system, you see that if an adjustment letter denies the reader's request, it is negative; if it grants the adjustment, it is positive; if it tries to get the customer to accept a compromise settlement favorable to the writer, it is negative-persuasive; if its goal is to persuade the customer that a compromise is really to his or her benefit, it is positive-persuasive.

- *Logical Order of Topics.* The text proceeds in orderly steps, first presenting non-sensitive messages then presenting sensitive messages. Since non-sensitive messages convey factual, unemotional information, students learn to construct these messages in a bottom-line or direct organizational pattern and in a way that gives them the highest possible level of impact. Sensitive messages are usually more difficult for students to handle. Students, therefore, learn to control organization, impact, and style in the process of learning how to handle these messages. Thus, by the end of the text, students are able to handle all types of business messages, from memorandums and letters to informal and formal reports.

- *Completeness.* The system the text teaches does not apply solely to written communication. It also applies to business presentations, the use of visuals and graphics, international communication, non-verbal communication, listening, and ethics. In addition, the text helps students become more sophisticated about the organizational structure of most enterprises. Students also learn how they, as individuals, are expected to behave and perform in such organizations. For example, what "reporting to" *really* means on the job is explored in depth, as is the importance of knowing what "reporting through channels" means.

- *Flexibility.* Different classrooms have different needs. The structure of this text meets the needs of these diverse groups by providing in-depth coverage of *every major topic* an instructor may want to cover.

Most teachers, we believe, will want their students to master the business communication system that unifies this text, and, therefore, will make assignments in the order we have presented the topics. Other teachers may feel that their students need a review of the basics prior to beginning to learn the system. Therefore, they may wish first to assign Special Features Unit B, a review of the basics of grammar and punctuation. Those instructors who base their teaching on cases may first assign Special Features Unit C, a discussion of how to analyze cases.

ORGANIZATION

The text is organized into ten main units and three supplementary units. Unit 1 introduces students to the communication system developed throughout the text and to the environment in which business communication occurs. Units 2 and 3 examine the organization of non-sensitive messages, with Unit 2 focusing on memos and letters and Unit 3 on long reports and the use of graphics in such reports. Unit 4 ends the discussion of non-sensitive messages by explaining how impact contributes to a message's effectiveness. High-impact word choice, sentence structure, and visual display are the areas covered within this unit.

Unit 5 examines the organization of sensitive messages, with attention focused on alternative organizational patterns that writers may choose. Unit 6 covers style, the final vital element of the text's communication system.

Unit 7 brings together the different elements studied separately throughout the text. This unit shows how organization, impact, and style interrelate and affect one another. Also introduced here is the Strategy Wheel, a valuable tool that helps readers remember and apply the advice offered throughout the text.

Units 8 and 9 examine other areas to which the text's communication system can be applied: business presentations, listening, non-verbal communication, and international communication, all areas of vital importance to practicing businesspeople. The communication system developed in this book clarifies these areas in interesting and useful ways.

Finally, Unit 10 examines ethical applications of the communication system used. Here students learn that honesty is not only the best policy in terms of business communication, it is the only policy that works.

Three important Special Features Units are found at the end of the text. Special Features Unit A examines the employment process and covers application letters, resumes, and how to conduct oneself at interviews. Special Features Unit B reviews the basics of business communication:

mechanics, punctuation, grammar, and format. Special Features Unit C thoroughly examines case analysis. Tips on how to read, analyze, and report on cases are all contained within this useful addition.

Two full-color photo essays expand the text's coverage by providing insight into technological developments in the modern office and in the field of computer graphics.

PEDAGOGICAL FEATURES

Years of experience have taught us that good teaching involves more than merely presenting information once and then moving forward to the next topic. Students need to know why a particular topic is important and must have an opportunity to see practical applications of all major points. Further, students need to have an opportunity to review chapters and units of books in as quick and efficient a manner as possible. Recognizing these needs, we have incorporated the following pedagogical features into PRINCIPLES OF BUSINESS COMMUNICATION:

- *Unit Memorandums.* Each unit begins with a memo written from the authors to the reader. This memo introduces topics that will be covered in the forthcoming chapters and shows readers how these topics fit into the overall communication system developed throughout the text.
- *Chapter Objectives.* Each chapter begins with concise statements that clarify what the student will learn in that chapter.
- *Margin Notes.* Notes provide students with a handy means for reviewing the text and for selecting areas that need additional review.
- *Highlighted Key Terms.* Important terms within the text are in bold type to call them to the reader's attention. Students can easily review them as they prepare assignments or for examinations.
- *Principles.* Throughout the text, principles summarize major points for students to study and learn. These principles are listed at the end of each unit for easy review.
- *Illustrations and Tables.* Graphs, charts, drawings, photographs, and tables supplement and reinforce major points throughout the text.
- *Summaries.* Each chapter concludes with a summary of the important concepts and terms of the chapter.
- *Review Questions.* Each chapter has a series of questions that enable students to check their understanding of the material covered within that chapter.
- *Discussion Questions.* Each chapter also has a series of discussion questions that challenge readers to consider important philosophical and/or psychological ramifications of the topics covered.
- *Unit Exercises.* Each unit includes a series of exercises that provide students with opportunities to practice and apply the information learned within that unit.

- *Realistic and "Teachable" Cases.* Each unit has a series of cases for students to analyze, discuss, and answer. These cases, based on real-life situations, provide an opportunity for students to apply the information they have just learned. Although realistic, these cases do not require teachers or students to have expertise in accounting, economics, finance, marketing, and statistics. The cases are instead designed for people who want realistic, business-oriented cases that cover a wide range of topics.
- *Unit References.* Each unit ends with a list of relevant articles, readings, or texts that students can research to find additional information on the unit's topic.
- *Glossary.* A glossary of key terms can be used for easy reference or review.
- *The Strategy Wheel.* This handy device, found in the inside back cover of the text, summarizes the text's advice on the appropriate organizational pattern, level of impact, and style for various business communication situations. Readers can use the Wheel to dial up advice about the appropriate strategies for any communication situation.

ANCILLARY PACKAGE

PRINCIPLES OF BUSINESS COMMUNICATION is supported by a full package of instructional materials:

- The *Instructor's Manual* contains an overview and a topical outline for each chapter of the text. It provides learning objectives and suggested course outlines as well as lecture topics and activities. The Instructor's Manual gives solutions to questions, exercises, and cases presented in the text and includes reproducible transparency masters and additional references. Additional cases, which can be assigned, are also included.
- The *Test Bank* contains over 1500 multiple-choice, true/false and fill-in questions. Items are referenced according to page number as well as type of question.
- The *Computerized Test Bank* provides the printed Test Bank on disk and allows for generation of varied tests and the addition of other questions. The Computerized Test Bank is available for MS-DOS machines (IBM PC and compatibles).
- *Software,* available free to adopters, is easy for students to use. It presents students with business communication situations and calls upon them to apply what they have learned in the text. The software is available for MS-DOS machines (IBM PC and compatibles).
- The *Transparency Package* contains 50 color acetates for overhead projection that allow you to illustrate important points.
- The *Study Guide* reviews the terms and content of each chapter of the text. It includes an outline and summary of each chapter as well as additional exercises, self-tests, and cases.

ACKNOWLEDGMENTS

Of course, a project such as this one depends upon the help of many different people. We must first of all thank the thousands of students who have taken our courses and helped us tailor the materials to their particular skills and needs.

The earliest drafts of this text were evaluated by a carefully selected Board of Reviewers, at which time we became keenly aware of the need to add specific chapters on international communication and ethics. The many subsequent reviews helped define for us even further the needs of the changing marketplace so that we could include all traditional as well as contemporary topics now required by our colleagues. The insights of the reviewers helped significantly to make this book more useful for students taking this course in a wide variety of departments.

We remain indebted to the following people who read various drafts of the text and provided intelligent and constructive suggestions:

Mary Ellen Adams   *Indiana State University*
Dorothy A. Arel   *Shasta College*
Vanessa Dean Arnold   *University of Mississippi*
John D. Beard   *Wayne State University*
Patty Glover Campbell   *University of Tennessee*
Marian Cox Crawford   *University of Arkansas—Little Rock*
Robert D. Gieselman   *University of Illinois—Urbana Champaign*
Maxine B. Hart   *Baylor University*
Thomas J. Housel   *University of Southern California*
Bonnie Bellamy Howard   *University of Georgia*
Frank Jaster   *Tulane University*
Joan M. Lally   *University of Utah*
Patricia Lehrling   *Kankakee Community College*
Donald Leonard   *Arizona State University*
Mohan Limaye   *Colorado State University*
Barbara Loush   *Oakland Community College*
Carol D. Lutz   *University of Texas—Austin*
Kenneth Mayer   *Cleveland State University*
Linda McCallister   *California State University—Long Beach*
Carolyn T. Murphree   *Ohio University—Athens*
Martha Nord   *Vanderbilt University*
Gerald M. Parsons   *University of Nebraska—Lincoln*
Leonard Robertson   *Portland State University*
Charlotte Rosen   *Cornell University*
Joan S. Ryan   *Lane Community College*
Grant T. Savage   *Texas Tech University*
Dwayne Schramm   *California State University—Fresno*
Goldie S. Sparger   *Surry Community College*
Larry R. Smeltzer   *Arizona State University*
Douglas C. Smith   *University of Kentucky*
Jim Stull   *San Jose State University*
James Suchan   *The Naval PostGraduate School*

Roberta M. Supnick *Western Michigan University*
John L. Waltman *Eastern Michigan University*

We express our highest level of appreciation and regard for Becky Payton, our staff assistant who made this project work. She is a dedicated professional whose organizational skills and patience far exceed those of either author.

Finally, we thank our friends at Macmillan Publishing Company. Charles Stewart supported us from the time he read the first draft. His encouragement and vision made major contributions to the overall quality of the project. It is only through his encouragement and hard work that it ever was born. Nancy Perry guided the project on a daily basis. She is the most intelligent, hardworking editor either of us has had the pleasure of working with. Peter Knapp provided diligent support. His efforts contributed significantly to the quality of the work. Jennifer Carey deserves praise for the excellent production. Even a cursory glance at the quality of this text demonstrates her professionalism. Finally, we thank Eileen Burke for her creative design and Rick Fischer for his painstaking care in manufacturing.

R.E.D.
J.S.F.

Brief Contents

SPECIAL FEATURES

Detailed Contents

Unit 1 INTRODUCTION

Unit 2 ORGANIZING NON-SENSITIVE MESSAGES

Unit 3 ORGANIZING NON-SENSITIVE LONG REPORTS

Unit 4 CONTROLLING IMPACT IN NON-SENSITIVE MESSAGES

Unit 5 ORGANIZING SENSITIVE MESSAGES

Unit 6 CONTROLLING STYLE IN NON-SENSITIVE AND SENSITIVE MESSAGES

Chapter 14 INTRODUCTION TO STYLE AND TONE

Unit 7 STYLE, ORGANIZATION, IMPACT, AND THE STRATEGY WHEEL

Unit 8 ORAL BUSINESS PRESENTATIONS

Unit 9 PRINCIPLES OF INTERNATIONAL COMMUNICATION

Unit 10 CONCLUSION

Chapter 24 THE ETHICS OF EFFECTIVE COMMUNICATION 452

SPECIAL FEATURES

Unit A THE APPLICATION PACKAGE

Chapter B-3 FORMATTING LETTERS, MEMOS, AND FORMAL REPORTS

Unit C HOW TO ANALYZE CASES

Chapter C-1 CASE ANALYSIS

PRINCIPLES OF
BUSINESS COMMUNICATION

Unit 1

INTRODUCTION

Chapter 1

Overview of an Effective Communication System

Chapter 2

Introduction to a Modern Business Office

INTRA-TEXT MEMORANDUM

TO: Readers

FROM: Authors

SUBJECT: Organization of the Text

Each unit in this text begins with a brief memo from the authors to the readers. These memos have two primary goals: (1) to show the overall direction the text is following and (2) to summarize briefly, and thereby prepare you for, the information you will be studying in the unit you are about to read.

Direction of the Text

This text divides communication into three components: **organization, impact,** and **style**. When you communicate, of course, organization, impact, and style all work together to influence how well a communication works. But for teaching purposes, we will deal at first with each component as if it were independent of the others. Through this process, you will be able to take an in-depth look at each topic and become proficient in each. Then, after you have studied and mastered all three—organization, impact, and style—we can put them back together and examine them as a whole.

The following diagram portrays the three components of communication we will be examining and includes basic information about what we will cover in each.

EFFECTIVE COMMUNICATION

ORGANIZATION		IMPACT		STYLE	
Bottom-Line	Circuitous	Word Choice	Visual Display	Forceful/Passive	Colorful/Colorless
	Semi-Circuitous		Sentence Structure		Personal/Impersonal

This diagram provides an overview of all of the text's key points. We will refer to this diagram in many of our unit memos to show you the particular aspect of the communication system we are exploring in that unit.

Summary of Unit 1

The purpose of Unit 1 is to provide a kind of road map that will guide you on your trip through the remainder of this text. Chapter 1, "Overview of an Effective Communication System," explains the text's purpose and tells you how the information in the book is organized and developed. This information is important for you to have so that you can understand the overall business communication system that the book develops.

Chapter 2, "Introduction to a Modern Business Office," describes the setting in which business communication takes place. Organizations have set structures within which communication occurs. Unless you are aware of these structures and abide by their norms and expectations, you may be forced to learn some costly but vital lessons about how to communicate in business. For many people, these lessons come at a price, a price that sometimes means damage to their corporate careers. The information in Chapter 2 will help protect you from such injury.

As one final preparatory note, let us point out a basic assumption made throughout this text. We have assumed that you want to do well in business. Doing well may mean that you become known as the best, most competent person ever to hold your particular job. Or, doing well may mean that you advance rapidly up the organization ladder to positions of higher and higher responsibility.

This text should help you accomplish either of these objectives. We hope that the information we provide will help you achieve whatever goals you set for yourself.

Chapter 1

OVERVIEW OF AN EFFECTIVE COMMUNICATION SYSTEM

OBJECTIVES

This chapter will help you to

•

Become acquainted with the communication system that will be developed throughout the text

•

See a relationship between this communication system and everyday business messages

•

Understand the overall organizational development of the text

The business communication system you will learn from this book is derived from what successful executives have learned through experience. The system will teach you to handle even the most complex communication situations with speed, ease, and efficiency. Some of you have already faced complex communication situations. Others will do so soon. Here are some examples of difficult writing situations common to most businesses:

This text teaches a communication system.

- Your immediate boss hands you a mound of data and asks you to summarize it in no more than two pages. Does the boss really mean to ask you to do the impossible? How can you meet the boss's request without running the risk of giving only superficial treatment to important facts because of the two-page limit? (You will learn precisely how to write that report in two pages, plus attachments.)

The system shows how to summarize information.

- An important customer demands that an adjustment be made to her bill because the supplies she ordered from your company arrived later than the contract stated. She demands a 15 percent discount. Your company's policy does not provide for discounts of that size for a few days delay in delivery. Yet, you are afraid that an outright refusal of her request may cause her to take her business elsewhere. How should you handle a touchy situation like this? (This book will teach you how to develop a strategy for determining what response is best, and then how best to organize and express that response.)

The system shows how to handle upset customers.

- A management consultant conducting a study of the morale in your department asks you to put in writing your frank opinion of your boss's competence. Your opinion of your boss is strongly negative. How can you express this opinion honestly yet safely? (You will learn how to tell the truth in ways that minimize the risk you run in doing so.)

The system shows how to express negative opinions.

- An influential state senator inquires as to why the state-funded agency you head refused to hire one of his constituents. The applicant, your interviewers felt, was arrogant and presumptuous, apparently believing that the senator's influence would guarantee his being hired. The senator's good will is critical to your agency receiving adequate funding in the upcoming state budget. What should you write to the senator? (This book will explain how to handle even the most delicate situations with tact, diplomacy, and honesty.)

The system shows how to handle powerful individuals.

A SYSTEMATIC APPROACH

You can see how difficult it would be for any textbook to give you pat answers to the questions raised by situations like these. So, don't look for formulas or checklists in this book. Instead, look for sound principles that tell you how experienced, practicing businesspeople handle situations like these every day.

How do we know that what we say truly reflects the advice businesspeople would give? We know because, for more than twenty years, we have worked closely with people in all types and levels of business. We have conducted field tests to discover how literally thousands of businesspeople would react to and deal with situations ranging from the simple to

The system you will learn has been field tested.

the highly complex. Furthermore, we have reduced this knowledge into a system, a simple step-by-step process that enables *you* to decide how to handle given communication situations.

Begin by Assessing Your Message

The flow chart at the front of this text illustrates the system you will learn. When you are faced with a situation requiring a response, you must begin by deciding what message you think you want to send. But the message you first think you want to send must be tempered by the realities of the communication situation. You must answer the following questions before you can be sure that the message you *think* you want to send is the one you actually can *risk* sending.

Consider key issues before you begin to write.

1. Is the message being sent internally within your own organization? Or is it going to someone in the external world?

   Is the message being sent internally or externally?

2. Is the recipient in a position of power over you? Or are you in the superior position? (You will soon see clearly what an important distinction this is.)

   Is the message going to a superior or to a subordinate?

3. What is your relationship with the recipient of your communication? Are you friends? Enemies? Complete strangers? (Again, this distinction makes a real difference in how you respond.)

   What is the writer/reader relationship?

4. Given the answers to these questions, how safe is it (both for you and your organization) to send the message you first choose? If you decide your message is too risky, you have to redefine realistically the message you *can* send to get the job at hand done without causing trouble.

   What risks are involved in the message?

This text will discuss each of these steps thoroughly and will teach you how to define your message. It will then give you advice on choosing for your message the organization, impact, and style that will have the highest probability of achieving the results you desire.

Applying the System

To get a glimpse of how the system works, let's go back to one of the complex communication problems we mentioned at the beginning of this chapter—the situation of the very important customer who is demanding a 15 percent discount because of your company's delay in delivering the supplies she ordered.

First you decide on your message. Since your company policy does not permit 15 percent discounts in this situation, the first message you might consider is to deny the customer's request. However, since she is a very important customer who is now quite angry and hostile, a negative message may cause your company to lose her business. Knowing this, you decide to consider sending a safer message. Since granting the customer's request flies in the face of company policy, you cannot send a positive message either. What should you do? One solution is to meet with your boss to devise a compromise adjustment and then write a letter attempting to persuade the customer to accept it. At least this message would be much less risky than bluntly telling the customer, "No."

The system helps you handle difficult adjustments.

This sensitive situation illustrates an important point. When we talk about communicating in business, we are talking about communicating to *get a job done*. And, in the process of communicating to get that job done, businesspeople make a strong effort to avoid negative fallout. Losing a good customer by sending a poorly thought-through message is a prime example of the type of fallout you want to avoid. The system you will learn will show you how successful businesspeople always communicate in ways that minimize or eliminate the possibility of unpleasant results. Our system will show you how to handle a communication efficiently, effectively, or, in many cases, tactfully.

DEVELOPMENT OF THE COMMUNICATION SYSTEM

Context of Business Communication

We begin by placing the communication system you have just sampled in a context, by introducing you to the **environment** in which businesspeople communicate. Businesspeople do not communicate in a vacuum; the environment in which they live and work significantly affects the way they communicate. You will be introduced to the factors within this environment that affect how businesspeople communicate.

Message Types

Once you understand the environment businesspeople communicate in, you need to be familiar with the types of messages they send. In business, people communicate orally much of the time. Because it is impossible for us to offer examples of oral communications, we must teach our system to you through examples of written business communications. We assure you, however, that the system applies equally to spoken communication, and that later chapters will be devoted to effective oral communication.

Business messages can be broadly classified as non-sensitive and sensitive.

Generally, both spoken and written business messages are one of two basic types: **non-sensitive** and **sensitive**. Although you must eventually be familiar with both types of messages, the text, for teaching purposes, examines each type separately, dealing first with non-sensitive messages.

Non-Sensitive Messages

Non-sensitive messages cause little or no emotional reaction.

A non-sensitive message causes little or no emotional reaction in the reader or listener. Because of this, non-sensitive messages are far easier to handle than sensitive messages. Also, the vast majority of business messages are non-sensitive. Thus, once you learn how to organize these messages and how to achieve the proper level of impact within them, you will have developed skills that will help you handle most of the messages you will send in business.

Organizing Non-Sensitive Messages

The key to the efficient handling of non-sensitive messages is learning how to organize them. Thus, we next take up the very important topic of the **bottom-line** or **direct** organizational pattern. **Bottom-lining** means organizing your thoughts so that they communicate directly, clearly, and forthrightly the gist, the very essence of what you have to say. In a non-sensitive message, you should write as forthrightly, as consistently, and as clearly as you possibly can. Bottom-lining does not just mean "Don't be wordy" (although being wordy wastes readers' time). It means being businesslike, directly stating your purpose for writing. Above all, it means organizing your message so that what is important to your reader (not to you, the writer) comes first. Bottom-lining, therefore, is honest, candid, and often brave. It is how all successful executives want people to write non-sensitive information to them.

The term *bottom line* is borrowed from accounting and finance. There, it essentially means this: When all the income and expenses of a company are taken into account, the company's bottom line will show whether it made a profit or sustained a loss. Businesspeople have borrowed the term and have applied it to communication. In effect, they mean, "Cut through all the time-wasting chitchat, all the justifications and alibis, and tell me right away exactly what the purpose of your communication is. If you want something, say so. If you want to tell me something, do so!"

Some businesspeople like the term bottom line because its meaning is immediately clear. Others think of the term as a cliché because it is used so frequently on television and in the business sections of newspapers and magazines. But we have found no other term that so completely describes what we mean and so effectively communicates that meaning to business-oriented students.

Controlling Impact

Once you have mastered the direct, bottom-line organization of non-sensitive messages, the text next introduces you to the topic of impact. By impact we mean the strength of the effect that a message exerts on a reader. You will learn what the terms **high-** and **low-impact messages** mean and when each type of impact is most appropriate. First, you will learn how to write in the high-impact fashion that is especially appropriate in non-sensitive messages as well as in some sensitive messages. You will learn how to control your word choice, sentence structure, and visual display to achieve the level of impact desirable in non-sensitive messages. Later, in the section on sensitive messages, you will see that low-impact writing has a surprisingly important place in the real business world, especially for defensive purposes.

Sensitive Messages

After you gain a detailed understanding of how to handle non-sensitive messages, you will learn about handling sensitive messages. Sensitive

Bottom-lining means direct presentation of what you have to say.

Top executives appreciate and practice a bottom-line approach.

Impact is controlled by words, sentence structure, and visual display.

Impact can be high or low.

messages evoke emotions, favorable or negative, on the part of the sender, the receiver, or both.

Since sensitive situations often carry with them a high degree of risk, you have to consider carefully the situational factors surrounding the message. Are you communicating internally or externally? With superiors or subordinates? What is your relationship with your readers and listeners? And, above all, how much risk is involved in sending a certain message in that situation?

Sensitive Organizational Patterns

After introducing you to the realities of life surrounding sensitive situations, the text shows you ways to organize your sensitive messages. You will learn about **circuitous** and **semi-circuitous** organizational patterns and when to use each in sensitive situations where bottom-lining is inappropriate—or too risky.

Controlling Style

The final part of the communication system you will learn deals with **style**. The word *style* has many dictionary definitions, but when businesspeople talk about writing style, they mean the *way* a person says things, as opposed to *what* he or she says (that is, the message being conveyed).

Once you learn what businesspeople mean by the term *style*, you will learn to master the six basic style choices that are available to businesspeople in their day-to-day writing. You will also learn how to judge which style is appropriate for the type of message being sent, after taking into account both your relationship with that person and whether the message is sent up to a superior or down to a subordinate.

PUTTING THE SYSTEM TOGETHER

Later chapters will fit all the pieces of the communication system together for you. The separately presented topics of environment, organization, impact, and style will be united and discussed in terms of how they interact and influence one another and the content of the message. These chapters also show you how to understand and use the Strategy Wheel, the device located in the back pocket of this book. The Strategy Wheel is a very handy memory aid that summarizes most of the points discussed throughout the text. It will help you remember the valuable guidance the book has offered about the organizational pattern, level of impact, and style most probably appropriate to the content of a given message.

The Strategy Wheel helps you
remember and apply the
system.

Whenever you use the Strategy Wheel, however, we encourage you to remember a point that we will make throughout the text: Communication is a complex activity. Many factors influence how you should handle a given situation. Some of these factors, such as the actual content of the message, are beyond a writer's control. For example, if your boss tells you to dismiss someone, you cannot change the message to a warning telling the person not to make any additional mistakes.

Other factors, however, *can* be controlled by a writer. The organizational pattern, the level of impact, and the style are all communication strategies that writers consciously select. These choices significantly influence the way readers interpret and respond to a message's content. In the vast majority of communication situations, the Strategy Wheel's advice will help you make the best conscious selection of each of these factors.

FURTHER APPLICATIONS

Oral Presentations

The text next applies the communication system you have learned to oral business presentations. You will find that the system enables you to decide the best strategy to use in making business presentations. We will also discuss topics valuable for oral presentations, including getting over stage fright, interacting with your audience, controlling your voice, and using visual aids.

The system can be applied to oral presentations.

International Applications

Finally, the system is applied to international communication, both written and oral. Here, you will be made more conscious of the cultural differences and sensitivities that make international communication so difficult. As U.S. business becomes more internationalized daily, the information you will obtain from this book will prove applicable and highly useful at some time in your career.

International communications require sensitivity to cultural differences.

Ethics and Communication

The presentation of the system concludes with a consideration of the ethics of effective communication. The chapter on ethics will convince you of a critical fact: In business interactions anywhere in the world, honesty is not only the best policy; it is, in the long run, the only policy. Just ask yourself whether you want to work for, work with, or do business with persons who are dishonest in their dealings with you. Can you work effectively with people who lie about what they tell you? Of course not. Only in the short run can people get away with being dishonest with you. In the long run, you will find them out, probably to your sorrow, and that will be the end of your trusting relationship with them.

Business communication must be ethical.

SPECIAL FEATURES

Several special topics—basics of writing, employment letters and resumes, and case analysis—make up the final chapters of the book. We have put these topics at the end only because discussion of them did not fit smoothly into our presentation of the system. Don't conclude, however, that the information covered in these chapters is unimportant. This information is vital for you to know and to master in order to be an effective communicator.

One unit covers employment-seeking letters and resumes.

For example, those who would like help in writing effective job-seeking letters and resumes will find these topics covered in Special Features. Help in obtaining work or a new job is valuable all throughout your career.

In addition, many of us can benefit from a review of the basics of writing. Those who need such a review of grammar, punctuation, and the format of business communications will find it in the Special Features section.

Another unit reviews grammar, punctuation, and format.

A final unit covers complex case analysis.

The Special Features section ends with a discussion of how to analyze complex business case situations. Business schools invariably require a course in business policy or strategy. The content of the section on logical case analysis will prove useful in these and other case-oriented courses you take. This knowledge will also be of great help to you as your business career progresses.

YOUR ABILITY TO COMMUNICATE REPRESENTS YOU

What you write and how you speak, especially the language you use, are, in effect, your calling cards. Often, one of your first opportunities to impress higher-ups in your company comes either from (a) the way you write an important memo, letter, or report that ends up on the desk of some superior many levels above you, or (b) the way you organize and use language within a business presentation attended by important superiors. Therefore, your future promotions may not hinge on how you demonstrate your knowledge and expertise in one-on-one situations. Nor may promotions depend, as others suggest, on how you dress or on your physical attractiveness. Instead, your success may depend on the impression made by the way you communicate information.

People judge you by the way you communicate.

Whether you like it or not, in business, superiors often make judgments about their subordinates based on the way the subordinates write and on the way they use language in general, especially in business presentations. Superiors judge their subordinates' intelligence, education, and social standing based on the words they use, how their sentences are constructed, and how their messages are organized. Furthermore, superiors judge their subordinates' diplomacy and tact by the way they use language to deal with sensitive situations. In short, the memo you send or the report you make to a superior contains many levels of messages about you and how effectively you can handle various kinds of business situations.

Therefore, we encourage you to read and study this book carefully. The business communication system developed and applied throughout this text will not only offer long-range business benefits to you, but it will also help you in your day-to-day communication activities, both in school and in your personal life. A full grasp of the system and its use will give you a knowledge of effective and efficient business communication that experienced, successful businesspeople have acquired only after years of hard work and hard knocks. Your advantage is that you will have this knowledge at the beginning of, or close to the beginning of, a successful business career.

REVIEW QUESTIONS

1. What does the business communication system you will learn enable successful executives to do?

2. What choices does the system you will learn within this book involve?

3. How will this text introduce you to the communication system?

4. How do successful businesspeople always try to communicate?

5. What is the difference between non-sensitive and sensitive messages?

6. What is the purpose of the Strategy Wheel? On what is it based?

DISCUSSION QUESTIONS

1. Why is effective communication important to your future business career?

2. Why can you not give "pat" answers to all communication situations?

3. What do you think are some of the goals of communicating in business?

INTRODUCTION TO A MODERN BUSINESS OFFICE

OBJECTIVES

This chapter will help you to

●

Understand the structure of organizations and their headquarters offices

●

Develop an awareness of electronic technology and its effect upon the skills you need to learn

●

Learn key office communication principles that will help you be successful on the job

Working in business does not necessarily mean working in the private sector. The public sector—including city and state governments, hospitals, and social service agencies—also employ millions of people in office settings. Regardless of which sector you work in, you are in a setting where the majority of American workers spend at least some, if not most, of their working lives. According to the latest U.S. Census data, over 50 percent of all U.S. workers are employed in white-collar positions. In such positions, people work in or, in the case of salespeople, report to branch or headquarters offices.

The American work force is largely "white-collar."

As an employee in such a setting, you have to communicate effectively. Clients, customers, and people in other parts of your own organization need to send information to you and obtain information from you. Information also flows internally from one part of the office to the other.

Effective communication is essential in all business offices.

To communicate effectively within an office environment, you have to understand how a sizable office functions. Therefore, we will first examine the traditional organizational structure of such an office. This structure is important to understand since the power and position of writers and receivers significantly affect how messages are written.

Once you understand how the office structure affects communication, we can then examine the type of communication support—technological and human—that will be provided in an office. Such support, whether provided by secretarial personnel or by a personal computer, has a significant influence upon our ability to communicate.

Office structure and communication support systems affect the quality of communication.

Finally, you will learn some guiding principles for communicating effectively within an office environment. These principles apply the information learned about office structure and office support, and offer practical tips for you to remember throughout your career.

ORGANIZATIONAL STRUCTURE OF A HEADQUARTERS OFFICE

If you have taken a course in organizational behavior, you have probably learned much about the various ways enterprises are organized. If you have worked or are now working in a small, medium, or large organization, you have seen this structure in action and you are undoubtedly already aware of its importance to effective communication. If you have not had such a course or such an experience, let us give you a brief overview.

The Organization Chart

The vast majority of organizations have a hierarchical structure. Those employees high in the organization have more power than do those at lower levels. It does not matter whether the place of employment is an army, a government agency, a hospital, or a religious organization. If it is organized (as in "organized religion" or a "sports organization"), it is hierarchical, and the structure and levels of that organization can be drawn on a chart. That chart, not surprisingly, is known as an **organization chart**. Figure 2.1 shows a typical business organization chart.

The organization chart shows how power flows.

FIGURE 2.1
Sample organization chart of a headquarters office.

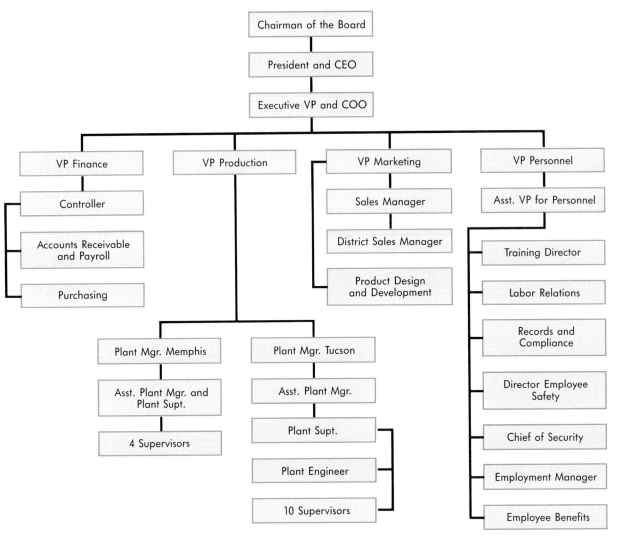

The source of all power in a business organization is the **Chief Executive Officer**, referred to by businesspeople as the **CEO**. The CEO's power is delegated downward in paths that are indicated in the chart by solid lines.[1] The CEO is invariably either the Chairman of the Board or the President. If the President is the CEO, then the Chairman of the Board is

---

[1]Bear in mind, however, that the officers of a company are responsible to that company's Board of Directors. The Board has the power to remove any officer. But the Board's exercise of its power is generally restricted to approving or disapproving recommendations made to it by the officers. If the Board does not like the actions or recommendations of those officers, the Board dismisses the officers and hires new leadership. In the private sector, most organizations have overseeing boards. Hospitals, universities, and many governmental units have boards of influential citizens (or legislators) overseeing the performance of those in charge.

quite possibly an older, semi-retired former CEO of the company, or an owner (or other large stockholder) who does not want responsibility for overseeing the company's performance. The CEO usually focuses on the long-range, not the day-to day, activities of the business.

Next in the chain of command is the **Chief Operating Officer**, the **COO**, who is responsible for the day-to-day operations of the company. The COO may be the President or an Executive Vice President, as is the case in Figure 2.1.

Line Responsibility

The lines on an organization chart indicate the downward flow of delegated authority. Persons whose positions lie in the direct line of delegated authority are called **line managers.** Line managers are people who have direct responsibility for implementing policies and plans that are sent down from above. If the Executive Vice President decides that all corporate personnel must receive two weeks of training in the operation of the latest electronic office equipment, this order will go to the Vice President of Personnel and from him or her down the line until it reaches the person who is to implement the training, most likely the Training Director.

Line managers receive power delegated down the line to them.

In most corporations, line managers' levels of authority are ranked by numbers. There are first-line managers (oddly enough, the lowest level), second-line, third-line, fourth-line, and sometimes fifth-line managers. The higher the number, the greater power the manager has. And, of course, the higher the level, the greater responsibility the manager has.

Power Down the Line

You will notice in Figure 2.1, the organization chart, that line responsibility, or power, branches as it flows downward into the various **functions**, or departments, of the organization. Each department is charged with responsibility for performing one of the business functions—Finance, Accounting, Production, Marketing, or Personnel.[2] However, each function, or department, is often tempted to operate much like an independent state. Headed by a powerful vice president, each function is jealous of its territory, its rights, and its duties. Each defends its own area (often known as *turf*) and its own people and tries to make certain that its responsibilities and duties are never usurped by another function.

Business functions are finance, accounting, marketing, personnel, and production.

A company's top executives alone have power across functions. One of their most important duties is to use their cross-functional authority to make the functions perform as a team instead of behaving parochially or selfishly.

Top executives have cross-functional authority.

Look at Figure 2.1. You see that purchasing in this company is centralized under the Finance function. Suppose the plant managers in Memphis and Tucson resent the fact that Finance has been given this power.

---

[2]If you are in a business school, your degree will require you to take certain "functional field courses" in Marketing, Finance, Accounting, Personnel, and Production Management. Each of these functional courses is usually housed in a department. Hence, your business school is probably organized essentially the same way most businesses are.

Corporate headquarters are the communication centers of large organizations. Clockwise from top left: Transamerica Corporation, San Francisco; ARCO, Los Angeles; IBM, Armonk, NY.

The plant managers believe that no one knows better than they what materials they need for their plant's production. They complain up the line to their vice president, the VP of Production. If the VP of Production tells them to go ahead and handle their own purchasing, the VP of Finance will quickly resent this seizure of turf by Production. The VP of Finance will immediately take these objections to the Executive VP and argue that uncoordinated purchasing by individual plants will waste money because purchases would be made in uneconomical, smaller lots. The Executive VP will have to rule on the situation and the VPs of Finance and Production will have to abide by that decision.

Staff Responsibility

Line officers in business are supported by **staff people**. This support may either be indirect or direct. **Indirect staff support** refers to work performed by departments, such as Accounting and Personnel, that provide centralized services for the entire organization. **Direct staff support** is the work performed by staff assistants who assist line managers, their bosses, in the performance of given tasks.

Staff people support line managers.

If you look at Figure 2.1, the sample organization chart, you will see that Production and Marketing are the primary line functions in this typical company and the company also has two large staff functions—Finance (including Accounting) and Personnel (or Human Resources). These staff functions offer centralized services for the entire company.[3]

Written Reporting Inescapable

Throughout your career, you will most likely move back and forth between line and direct staff supporting positions. Regardless of which position you have, you will be involved in communication. A great deal—almost all—of this communication will be internal. You will be writing memos and short reports to be sent up, down, and laterally within the corporation. Much of the information exchange will, of course, take the form of oral reports—some formal, most informal. But in the end, much of the oral communication will also appear in written form.

COMMUNICATION SUPPORT

With written communications proving so vital to your corporate career, it is logical for you to ask, "What kind of support will the company provide me? How about word processing? How about a secretary?" These two

[3]There is also the term **staff professional**, which usually refers to experts in various specialized areas who have been brought into headquarters to perform the complex, analytical work required as background for sound decisions. Although they do not usually show up on an organization chart, they are highly paid experts, offering high-level staff assistance to their manager and the function they support. In fact, frequently, such experienced expert analysts or strategists may receive higher pay than many personnel who carry managerial titles.

Computers dominate the modern office.

Computers dominate the modern office.

Businesses provide two types of support: technological and human.

types of support, generally labeled **technological** and **human support**, are important considerations for anyone involved in or entering the work force. Let's briefly examine each.

Technological Support

The business of writing constitutes a major expense for most offices. This expense is incurred whether one thinks about writing as words on a page or as words on a computer screen. The following facts demonstrate the volume and cost of writing in business:

1. U.S. businesses generate each workday:
   - 600 million pages of computer printout
   - 350 million copies for distribution
   - 200 million file copies
2. In total, businesses use more than one billion sheets of paper each day to keep their office force going. Furthermore, businesses publish 70 billion document pages a year.

Communication is costly to businesses.

3. The annual postage bill, through meters and permits alone, is over $10 billion. And, to speed delivery by overnight courier, businesses pay a $4 billion premium.

4. The cost of typing and mailing an average business letter is estimated to be $10. Between 20 and 30 million letters are written, typed, and mailed each day.[4]

Awareness of these costs has resulted in a concerted effort to bring these expenses under control. In offices of the past, managers dictated memos and letters, and secretaries typed them. More recently, businesses have developed word processing centers and relied on personal computers and even electronic mail in an effort to lessen the need for secretarial support. (For more information, also see Photo Essay 1: The Modern Office.)

Word Processing Centers   Word processing centers are areas in an office where highly skilled typists, operating the latest in electronic word processing equipment, process into final hard copy the content of documents created by managers or staff professionals. Content may be sent to the center in the form of handwritten copy, roughly typed copy on disks, or taped dictation for transcription. In some larger organizations, it may be dictated by telephone directly onto the word processing center's recording equipment. Word processing centers are usually able to return perfectly typed copy in a matter of hours, depending upon how many demands are made on their time at any given instant.

Word processing centers have skilled typists and modern equipment.

Personal Computers   Accompanying the efforts to reduce secretarial support has been the willingness of companies to provide personal computers (PC's) to managers and staff professionals. Often these PC's are similar to or the same as those many students use in day-to-day educational activities. These individual PC's may be connected to a far larger mainframe computer by means of telephone wires, microwaves, or cable TV wiring. Often PC's are linked together into networks so that what is stored in one station can be sent directly into the PC of anyone else linked to that network. Documents are, therefore, typed, edited, and corrected by managers themselves and then printed at any linked location.

Personal computers provide another form of technological support.

Three of the most popular types of computer software programs are **word processing programs**, which help you write and edit memos, letters, and reports; **data management programs** or **databases**, which help you manage and use long lists of data; and **spreadsheet programs**, which handle tables of numbers.

Telephone and Electronic Mail   In the most modern offices, the secretary who traditionally would take messages has been replaced by **telephone mail** and by **electronic mail (E-mail)**. Telephone mail operates somewhat like a home answering machine. You come back from lunch, for example, and note that a button on your telephone is lit. The light indicates that a message is waiting. You dial the appropriate number and the recorded voice of the person who called you tells you what he or she wanted.

Telephone mail and electronic mail have reduced the need for secretarial support.

To use electronic mail, the sender and receiver each need a PC, a modem (a device that changes data to a form that can be sent by telephone

---

[4]Data supplied by the AMTEL Consulting Group (a unit of American Telesystems Corporation, Atlanta, Georgia), a leading consulting company in the office automation field.

The Wang Freestyle™ personal computing system lets users turn any information on the PC screen into an electronic piece of paper. The user may add handwritten, typed, and spoken comments to send to all other Freestyle users in a network.

to any other computer), and an E-mail software program. Once the hardware and software are all in place, you keyboard your message on your PC, usually in the conventional To/From/Subject memo form. Then you press the appropriate transmit keys to send the memo to the PC of the person addressed. Messages received by that person—let's call her Mary Jones—are stored in her PC until she decides to see what E-mail awaits. Once she accesses a list of her incoming messages, Mary Jones then selects the message she wants to deal with first and displays it on her monitor. After reading the message, she can take the following actions:

1. Delete it.
2. Save it electronically.
3. Save it and print it.
4. Add her own commentary, and send it electronically or in print to someone else, perhaps her boss, for approval or instructions.

Or, if Jones wants to, she can keyboard an answer to the writer and send it off.

Human Support

Probably all students planning to go into business have fantasized about having a private secretary to do most of their writing for them. Anyone

High-tech teleconferencing: In business communications the future is now.

with actual experience knows, however, that almost no one today, except very senior executives, has a private secretary. Certainly, no one gets one at the beginning of a career. Yet, all who work for an organization will have to write numerous memos, reports, and letters. If a naive, uninformed, and probably unemployed person says, "I don't need to learn to write, or master grammar, or even know how to spell. I'll have a secretary who'll take care of that," the proper response is "Forget it. You will have to write and keyboard almost all your own communications."

Few businesspeople have private secretaries.

Middle-level managers, staff analysts, and staff assistants *share* secretaries. The lower the ranking of a manager or staff person, the higher the ratio between the number of managers sharing a secretary and the actual secretary. Figure 2.2 shows the average manager/secretary ratios at various levels of the corporate hierarchy.

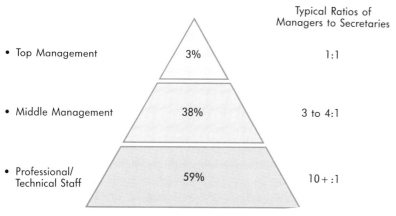

Typical Ratios of Managers to Secretaries

- Top Management   3%   1:1

- Middle Management   38%   3 to 4:1

- Professional/ Technical Staff   59%   10+:1

FIGURE 2.2

Distribution of managers by levels and their typical secretarial support ratios.

(*Source:* Richard W. Larson, from internal IBM Corporation studies.)

Top management of an organization (usually the level from Chief Executive Officer to Vice President) amounts to 3 percent of the white-collar force and enjoys a one-to-one support ratio in big organizations. In other words, only 3 percent of the workers have the private secretaries some students dream of. At the middle-manager levels, three, four, or slightly more managers will share the services of one secretary. At the professional staff level, ten or more professionals share a single secretary. At levels below the professional staff, fifty junior employees may share one secretary. Obviously, then, they will have to do most of their writing themselves on their PC's.

EFFECTIVE OFFICE COMMUNICATION

Once you understand the organization and the largely electronic support structures of the modern office, you can begin to communicate more realistically within a business environment. However, if you want to do so effectively, then you should be aware of three key communication principles. If you follow these principles, you will likely achieve early success in your career:

OFFICE COMMUNICATION PRINCIPLE 1:
Always remember that orders flow down through channels.

Every hierarchical organization has a defined reporting structure. People with work experience have already witnessed this structure, as have people with military experience and those who have participated in team sports. In an army, the general says, "Charge!" and the troops charge. That's all there is to it. If you don't follow orders, you are court-martialed.

Businesses, like the military and organized sports, are hierarchical. Orders are only given down, never up, and orders are obeyed—even when they are only implied. For example, if a superior says, "I think it would be nice if you got those letters out today," he or she means, "Do it! Even if you have to stay late!" In business, if you do not promptly do what you are told, and do it well, you will soon be replaced by someone who will.

Power only flows *down* within a given channel (or department). This is as true in a government agency, hospital, or university as it is in a corporation. Suppose a corporation has just employed an internationally recognized research scientist. Let's assume she becomes dissatisfied with the way her research budget is being handled. Instead of taking her complaint to the administrative head of Research and Development, she goes directly to the clerks in the accounting department and begins to berate them. Are they frightened? Not particularly. Why? Isn't this world-renowned scientist more important than they are? Doesn't she, therefore, have power over them? Of course not. More than likely, they will politely ignore her or refer her to their boss who will tell her to take matters up with the head of her function.

She will find out that she has no power whatsoever over the accounting clerks, although she has naively assumed that she does. She has power

Orders never flow up in an organization.

Power flows only within its assigned channels.

only in her own channel, not in any other. The accounting clerks know that the only person they report to is their manager. And their manager takes orders only from his or her manager, all the way up to the head of their function, the Vice President of Finance. The clerks have no intention of taking orders from a researcher who is not even in the financial function of the company. And if they did change their procedures on orders from the researcher, their boss would soon remind them whom they work for.

Remember this fact when you report to work in a large office: You work only for your immediate boss, and you must operate within your own functional reporting channel.

OFFICE COMMUNICATION PRINCIPLE 2:
Always remember you report up through channels.

On the job, you would be unwise to send memos off across functional lines of authority. If you did, you would probably receive the same treatment that our irritated research scientist received, and you would deserve it for being naive. Moreover, you would be very ill-advised to think you could send memos off to persons superior to your manager without receiving prior approval from your boss.

> Avoid communicating outside your assigned channels.

Suppose, for instance, you have what you think is a terrific idea about a new way to do your job. You know you ought to discuss this with your boss, Sarah Hendrix, but she is out of the country on a business trip and you will be unable to consult with her for two weeks. You are so enamored with your idea, however, that you can't wait for your boss to return. So you go to her manager, Walt Peters, with your idea.

What's wrong with that? Just this: Either way, you lose. If your idea is a good one, Walt Peters might recognize you for it, praise you for your ingenuity, and begin to implement it. But when your boss, Sarah Hendrix, returns, what does she think? She thinks you did something behind her back that made her look bad, just to make *you* look good. She'll have every reason to suspect that whenever you have a good idea you will go around her authority. Needless to say, you will have created an enemy in a position best held by a friend.

What will happen if Walt Peters thinks your idea is ridiculous? Perhaps it is an idea that the company has already tried with disastrous results. Peters is annoyed that you wasted his time. When Hendrix returns, he calls her in and asks, "Sarah, why did you send your subordinate to me to waste my time with such a stupid idea?"

"I didn't," says Hendrix. "I didn't even know someone had seen you!"

"Can't you control your own people?" Peters asks. "Don't you even know what they're doing?"

Hendrix can hardly wait to get back to her office, call you in, and say, "Don't you *ever* go over my head again! Once more and you're through!"

Remember, you report only upward and only to your immediate boss (unless that boss specifically tells you it is all right to report differently in a special case). In fact, that's what the term **report to** means—to be responsible to, and only to, your immediate superior.

> Report upward and within channels.

Never delegate tasks upward.

Not only do you report to your boss, you also work for him or her. Don't become confused and think your boss works for *you*. Avoid saying to your boss, "You've got a problem. What are *you* going to do about it?"

Don't say to your boss, "*You'd* better write a report on this." Instead of looking as if you're trying to delegate a task upward, you should say, "*This* had better be reported promptly. Is it okay if I work up a draft for you to sign if you think it covers the subject adequately?" Your job is not to remind the boss of what you think the boss should do. Instead, you should offer to do what you think needs to be done. The more you make your boss look good, the higher he or she will rate your performance. Those annual ratings will be critical to your future advancement.

Completed staff work means you—not your boss—do the job.

When you perform tasks rather than telling your boss to do them, you are practicing what is called completed staff work. Really first-rate subordinates cheerfully serve as extensions of the capabilities of the persons they report to. They work as a team, with the superior serving as the ultimate leader and decision maker. When faced with a serious problem, the subordinate should analyze various alternative courses of action, assess the assets and liabilities of each, and recommend one of these alternatives. But the actual decision would be made by the boss.

Completed staff work results in more work for the staff person, but it also results in more freedom for the manager. All organizations regard this as the way things should be. In business, remember that the final test of completed staff work is this:

1. If you were your own manager, would you be willing to sign the report you have prepared (or take the action you recommend) and stake your professional reputation on its being right?

2. If your answer to question 1 is no, then you should revise the report or recommendation because it is not yet completed staff work.

SUMMARY

All organizations are hierarchical. As such, they contain certain lines of authority that permit (a) information to flow up and down the organization's structure and (b) decisions, policies, and orders to flow down the lines. People in **line** positions have direct access to the flow of information moving up and down the organization that is relevant to their duties and responsibilities.

Two types of **staff** positions exist. Ones like Personnel and Accounting offer centralized services across the organization. Others offer direct staff assistance to particular line managers.

Whether you function in a staff or a line capacity, written reporting will be an essential part of your job. The main form of support you will have in this task will be either a centralized word processing staff or a personal computer. In either case, most of the responsibility for effective communication will fall upon your shoulders.

To carry out effectively your communication responsibilities, and to increase significantly your opportunities for rapid advancement within an organization, keep in mind the three basic Office Communication Principles developed in this chapter.

REVIEW QUESTIONS

1. What is an organization chart?

2. What is a CEO and for what is a CEO responsible?

3. What is a line manager? To whom does a line manager report?

4. What is meant by the terms *direct support* and *indirect support*?

5. What kind of technological and human support should you expect when you begin working for an organization?

6. What does staying in channels mean? What are the risks of *not* staying in channels?

7. What does the phrase *report to* mean?

8. Suppose you are a district sales manager for a large organization. You are having a problem with one of your customers, and it is a problem that you think the CEO should be aware of. How would you go about making the CEO aware of your problem?

9. Explain the concept of completed staff work.

10. What is the final test of completed staff work?

DISCUSSION QUESTIONS

1. What are the benefits of having an organization chart? How do you suppose the presence of such a chart influences the behavior of people within the company?

2. Assume you have a desire to become president of the company you work for. In your career to date, you have had both staff and line experience. How might each type of experience contribute toward your advancement? Which do you think would contribute more? Explain the reasons for your choice.

3. Name some ways that the business concept of completed staff work could prove beneficial within your academic career.

OFFICE COMMUNICATION PRINCIPLES
REVIEW LIST

1

Always remember that orders flow through channels.

2

Always remember that you report up through channels.

3

Never delegate upward. Instead, always practice completed staff work.

EXERCISES

Exercise 1

Draw an organization chart for a group, business, college, school, church, or other large organization with which you are familiar.

Exercise 2

Some new organizations have taken the traditional hierarchical organization chart and given it a 90-degree turn. As a result, the CEO position is centered at the left-hand margin and all positions develop to the right on the page. Explain why a company would want to make such a change and the symbolic implications that such a change implies. Be sure to include your own observations about whether you think such a shift is worth doing. Also include some observations about the risks and benefits of such a change.

Exercise 3

Call and ask permission to visit a modern office in your locality. (Or you can use the office where you are presently working.) If possible, try to observe an office that serves as a corporate or divisional headquarters. Interview workers in this office, from those at the secretarial level to those functioning in management positions. Ask how much time they spend on such activities as writing, meetings, and giving presentations. Ask how important they feel effective communication is to their positions. Be sure to prepare your questions in advance and jot down notes, or use a tape recorder, to keep records of the information you receive. Report on your findings.

Exercise 4

Conduct a brief study on recent advances in office automation. Information for this report can come not only from the library but also from computer centers, companies that specialize in office services and products, and any other source available to you. You may even choose to conduct interviews of certain departments or colleges on your campus or departments in your office that have recently introduced the newest office equipment into the work place. Try to learn how the equipment is being used, the adjustments that various people are having to make to the equipment, and the advantages and disadvantages that users of the equipment find.

CASE

Introduction to the Master Case

The Allgood Products, Inc. Master Case follows. This case presents all the details you need to know at this time about this fictional, but realistic, company. It tells you how the company is organized, who the important personnel are, and what types of business the company is engaged in.

In each subsequent unit, we will present cases that spin off from this master case. They will depict various communication problems faced by people at Allgood Products, Inc. In these cases, you will usually play the role of an assistant to an Allgood executive and apply what you have learned about business communication in order to complete certain tasks. Any additional information you need to perform the tasks will be provided in the spin-off cases. You should also refer to this master case to refresh your memory about how the executive in question wants memos and reports written. Be sure to consider the preferences of the receiver of the memos or reports you write.

There are several advantages to a master case approach. You do not have to learn about a different company and about different personnel each time you are assigned a new case. In addition, a master case resembles the type of experience people have in real life; that is, they work for one company for a certain period of time.

Furthermore, from the single company portrayed in the master case, you learn to ''interact'' with people who are different in personality, in sensitivity, in emotionality, and in their likes and dislikes about the way they want memos and reports written to them. In the spin-off cases, you are forced to work with and for people with whom you have a long-run ''relationship'' and who influence the progress of your career.

Your instructor may recommend that you now read Special Features Section C (''How to Analyze Cases''), p. 577. Some of the material in ''How to Analyze Cases'' is rather advanced and may be best left for later in the course. However, the beginning of Section C, which deals with how to play the ''case game,'' may prove helpful to you now.

The Master Case
Allgood Products, Inc.

Allgood Products, Inc. has been in business since 1915. At that time, Hiram P. Allgood, the proprietor of a small, local bakery, invented a packaging machine that would seal bakery products against air and, hence, would guard against staleness. Because of his invention, Hiram Allgood was able to close the bakery and establish a company that supplied shelf bakery products for the various corner groceries in and around Kansas City, Missouri, where the company's corporate headquarters are still located.

Hiram's son, Prentice Allgood, took over the active management of the company in 1935, and added a line of packaged dry food products to the Allgood line. These included dehydrated soups, potatoes, sauce mixes, instant rice, and various pasta mixes. The company grew remarkably, and its two lines of products were sold nationally in all major grocery chains.

Maxwell P. Allgood, Prentice's son, returned in 1946 from service in World War II, and rejoined the company. He became President and Chief Operating Officer in 1969 when his father semi-retired to the office of Chief Executive Officer. Because frozen food products had earned acceptance with the public, one of Maxwell Allgood's first moves was to enter into the frozen food business. Hence, the company soon produced and sold three lines of products. Upon Prentice Allgood's complete retirement in 1975, Maxwell Allgood became Chairman of the Board as well as Chief Executive Officer.

The top executives of the company currently are

- Maxwell P. Allgood, Chairman and CEO;
- Carl Hilton, President and COO;
- Cyrus Fine, Vice President of Product Marketing;
- Mary Lou Higgins, Vice President of Personnel;
- Samuel Potnick, Vice President of Finance and Controller; and
- Frank Finnegan, Vice President of Production

Carl Hilton joined the company as President after twenty years of service in various executive positions with a competitor. Hilton is fifty-three years old, very logical and analytical, a person who demands that all communications sent to him be as succinct and concise as possible. Like most top executives, he claims that he has sufficient control over his emotions to make it completely unnecessary for any subordinate to beat around the bush with him. His motto: "I want it straight, and to the point, and I want the truth, no matter who it makes angry!"

Although this is Carl Hilton's professed philosophy, the word around the office is that you had better take what he says with a grain of salt. He is widely judged to be a man of considerable pride and one who would not take kindly to being made to look bad publicly. Subordinates are constantly trying to figure out whether in their reports they should follow what Hilton *claims* he wants, or what they think he probably *actually* wants.

Cyrus Fine, Vice President of Product Marketing, is perfectly suited to his job, having served at various times in his career as Assistant Sales Manager for Bakery Products and Sales Manager for Instant Foods. Earlier in his career he worked at a low level in the frozen foods department, so he brings to his job a keen knowledge of every branch of Allgood Products. Fine is a friendly, affable man in his late forties. He is on very good terms with most of the movers and shakers in the large supermarket chains.

There is no conflict in Cyrus Fine's mind about how people should report to him. He knows he is a person of considerable sensitivity, and he expects people who report to him to do so with tact and diplomacy. "My job," he has said, "is getting along with people, making them like me, making them like our products, and persuading them to buy our products.

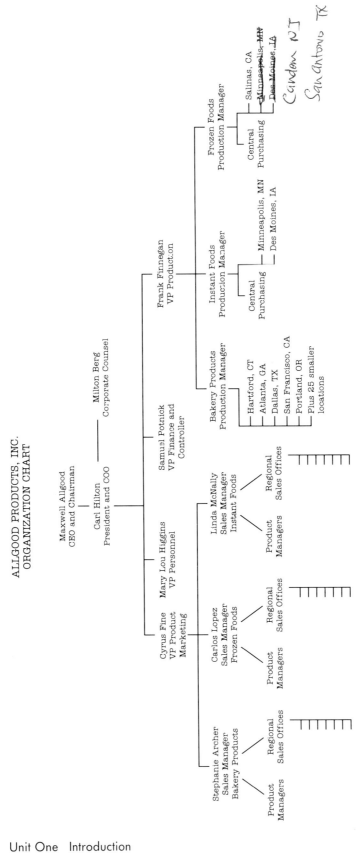

ALLGOOD PRODUCTS, INC.
ORGANIZATION CHART

Maxwell Allgood
CEO and Chairman

Carl Hilton
President and COO

Milton Berg
Corporate Counsel

Cyrus Fine
VP Product
Marketing

Mary Lou Higgins
VP Personnel

Samuel Potnick
VP Finance and
Controller

Frank Finnegan
VP Production

Stephanie Archer
Sales Manager
Bakery Products

Carlos Lopez
Sales Manager
Frozen Foods

Linda McNally
Sales Manager
Instant Foods

Bakery Products
Production Manager

Instant Foods
Production Manager

Frozen Foods
Production Manager

Product
Managers

Regional
Sales Offices

Product
Managers

Regional
Sales Offices

Product
Managers

Regional
Sales Offices

Hartford, CT
Atlanta, GA
Dallas, TX
San Francisco, CA
Portland, OR
Plus 25 smaller
locations

Central
Purchasing

Minneapolis, MN
Des Moines, IA

Central
Purchasing

Salinas, CA
Minneapolis, MN
Des Moines, IA

Camden NJ
San Antonio TX

I expect people to have the same attitude toward me. I want them to persuade me to do what they want; I simply do not take kindly to abrasive behavior or to being ordered about."

Consequently, those who report to Cyrus Fine only find difficulty in situations where they have to communicate something negative to him. In these instances, they have to search for a way to do so without offending his sensitivities. Reporting to Fine are the following executives:

- Stephanie Archer, 36, Sales Manager for Bakery Products. She is a graduate of Howard University in Washington, D.C., and an expert on nutrition and food chemistry. She rose quickly through the management ranks to her present position and is highly regarded in the company. She was appointed Sales Manager two years ago.

- Carlos Lopez, 41, Sales Manager for Frozen Foods. He began his career at the age of 14 working with his family as an itinerant laborer. Lopez earned his own way through high school and then through San Diego State College. He became a naturalized citizen before going to work for Allgood Products as a purchasing agent buying fresh farm products for flash freezing. His experience and his drive enabled him to rise quickly in the Frozen Foods Division. He was appointed Sales Manager three years ago.

- Linda McNally, 41, Sales Manager for Instant Foods. She has a background in nutrition and marketing. After earning her degree in Food Sciences from the University of Illinois, she obtained an MBA from Washington University. She has been with the company for seventeen years and was appointed Sales Manager five years ago.

Reporting to each sales manager are product managers who are responsible for the development, promotion, and sales of a single brand-name product. In this fashion, Allgood Products assures that each product in its line receives individual attention and management.

Allgood Products' Vice President of Personnel is Mary Lou Higgins. She is fifty-six years old and after some years working as a secretary, returned to college and graduated twenty years ago from Kent State University with a degree in personnel administration. Upon graduation, she joined Allgood Products and rose to a vice presidency seven years ago. She heads a staff that oversees the personnel needs of the total corporation.

Higgins is a stickler for policy and has made sure that the company has in place all policies necessary to deal with many of the problems, such as racial or sexual discrimination, that currently plague U.S. industry. She has worked very carefully in the labor relations area and has, much to Maxwell Allgood's pleasure, maintained a strike-free relationship with the unions in the various manufacturing departments.

Mary Lou Higgins is like Carl Hilton in that she requires people to report to her in a no-nonsense fashion. The only difference is that she is sufficiently secure to be able to accept from her subordinates reports that practice what she preaches. She does not wear her emotions on her sleeve, is slow to anger, and is highly analytical, intelligent, and very well organized.

Samuel Potnick, Vice President of Finance and Controller, has an MBA degree from the Wharton School and has been with Maxwell Allgood since they both joined the company after the war. Potnick, as his job requires, is very exact and extremely conservative about expenditures of money. Like most financial executives, he is regarded as a veritable dragon who stands before the company budget to guarantee that there is no waste.

Even though the organization chart does not show this to be the fact, Samuel Potnick actually reports directly to Maxwell Allgood. This situation reflects Maxwell Allgood's firm belief that he who controls the purse strings controls the company. Persons who seek approval from Potnick for programs they want funded had better be sure that they fully support their arguments with facts from which they have drawn absolutely logical and completely defensible inferences. Potnick is very intelligent, very tough, and completely humorless. He, like Maxwell Allgood, is in his late sixties.

Frank Finnegan, Vice President of Production, is a graduate of Lehigh University with a degree in Industrial Engineering. Upon graduating, he worked in the production end of the division and rose over the years to Production Manager and finally to Vice President ten years ago. Frank Finnegan is 52 and, like most engineers, prefers his subordinates to report to him in a straightforward, bottom-lined fashion.

The attached organization chart shows the parts of Allgood Products' operations that report to these officers of the company. In the Marketing function, product managers develop and supervise sales of their products. Actual sales of each of the three product lines are conducted by seven regional sales offices located in the heart of each main geographical market in the nation.

As for production, Allgood Products has always followed the sensible policy of placing purchasing and production operations geographically near to the source of raw food materials. Consequently, the Frozen Foods Division has three large operations near the produce farming areas of Salinas, California; Camden, New Jersey; and San Antonio, Texas.

Following the same logic, the Instant Foods Division placed its production operations in the Midwestern cities of Minneapolis, Minnesota, and Des Moines, Iowa, near the sources of grain products.

The Bakery Products Division, unlike the other two divisions, has no large central purchasing function and for the most part buys its raw materials from the Instant Foods Division. Bakery Products is divided into thirty main production areas where sizable automated bakeries serve large metropolitan markets. The largest of these production units are in Hartford, Connecticut; Atlanta, Georgia; Dallas, Texas; San Francisco, California; and Portland, Oregon, but smaller ones are dotted around the country in strategic locations.

REFERENCES

Bowman, G. W. (1964). What helps or harms promotability. *Harvard Business Review, 42,* 6–26; 184–196.

Cross, T. B. (1982). Computer conferencing via portable terminals solves many business communication problems. *Marketing News, 16* (Section 2), 12.

Fielden, J. S. (1964). What do you mean I can't write? *Harvard Business Review, 42,* 144–152.

Gilsdorf, J. (1987). Written corporate communication policy: Extent, coverage, cost, benefits. *The Journal of Business Communication, 24,* 35–52.

Hildebrandt, H. W., Bond, F. A., Miller, E. L., and Swinyard, A. W. (1982). An executive appraisal of courses which best prepare one for general management. *The Journal of Business Communication, 19,* 5–15.

Housel, T. J., and Housel, M. (1986). The role of business communications practitioners in the computer age. *The Journal of Business Communication, 23,* 5–12.

Hunter, M. (1986). Using the computer in business communication courses. *The Journal of Business Communication, 23,* 31–42.

Kaye, S. (1977). Why WP employees must know how to write letters. *Word Processing World, 4,* 53.

Langdon, J. A. (1986). Are our schools really teaching business basics? *Office, 103,* 72–73.

Lappington, J. (1986). ECHELON: A comprehensive technology for business communication. *Telecommunications, 20,* 86–96.

Mitchell, R. B., Crawford, M. C., and Madden, R. B. (1985). An investigation of the impact of electronic communication systems on organizational communication patterns. *The Journal of Business Communication, 22,* 9–16.

Mortimer, N. (1979). Write to be seen. *Supervisory Management, 24,* 19–22.

Myers, D. (1986). The forces shaping the industry's future. *Telephony, 210,* 64–65.

Otten, K. W. (1984). Changes in business communications: Innovative uses of new media and technologies. *Journal of Information and Image Management, 17,* 28–35.

Overnight delivery service has impact on business communications (1987). *Supervision, 49,* 12–13.

Penrose, J. (1984). Telecommunications, teleconferencing, and business communications. *The Journal of Business Communication, 21,* 93–111.

Penrose, J. M. (1976). A survey of the perceived importance of business communication and other business-related abilities. *The Journal of Business Communication, 13,* 17–24.

Penrose, J. M., Bowman, J. P., and Flatley, M. E. (1987). The impact of microcomputers on ABC with recommendations for teaching, writing, and research. *The Journal of Business Communication, 24,* 79–91.

Ramsey, R. D., Hammer, J., Lathan, M. G., Pearson, P., and White, K. (1987). How to teach supervisor-subordinate relationships in a basic business communication class. *The Journal of Business Communication, 24,* 35–46.

Renee, M. A. (1974). What business wants from beginners. *Administrative Management, 35,* 55–57.

Simons, R. H. (1960). Skills businessmen use most. *Nation's Business, 48,* 88.

Smeltzer, L. R., Glab, J., and Golen, S. (1983). Managerial communication: The merging of business communication, organizational communication, and management. *The Journal of Business Communication, 20,* 71–78.

Smith, F. E. (1985). Does your writing send the wrong signals? *Personnel Journal, 64,* 28–30.

Treece, M. C. (1972). Business communications practices and problems of professional secretaries. *The Journal of Business Communication, 9,* 25–32.

Unit 2

ORGANIZING NON-SENSITIVE MESSAGES

INTRA-TEXT MEMORANDUM

TO: Readers

FROM: Authors

SUBJECT: Unit 2

Unit 2 will

1. Define bottom-lining and show you how to apply this strategy to business situations;
2. Introduce you to the "So-what?" test, a handy tool for identifying whether a sentence is or is not a bottom-line sentence;
3. Explain why some people fail to bottom-line and teach you how to avoid their traps.

The highlighted parts of the Effective Communication diagram show the segment of the system that Unit 2 covers.

EFFECTIVE COMMUNICATION

ORGANIZATION		IMPACT		STYLE	
Bottom-Line	Circuitous	Word Choice	Visual Display	Forceful/ Passive	Colorful/ Colorless
	Semi-Circuitous		Sentence Structure		Personal/ Impersonal

In terms of its placement and proportion in the diagram, bottom-lining may seem a small, perhaps even an insignificant, part of the communication system. Nothing could be further from the truth! The concept of bottom-lining is vital to the vast majority of business messages.

Remember that to be labeled as an efficient and effective communicator you have to master the bottom-line concept. And labels such as efficient and effective can often speed your advancement within an organization.

Chapter 3

HOW TO ORGANIZE THE MAJORITY OF BUSINESS MEMOS

OBJECTIVES

This chapter will help you to

•

Distinguish between three key terms: *message, organization,* and *non-sensitive messages*

•

Understand the meaning of bottom-line reporting

•

Recognize immediate and long-range benefits of a bottom-line approach

This chapter teaches you how to organize non-sensitive messages as efficiently and effectively as successful executives do. To accomplish this task, we first need to agree on the meaning of a few basic terms. Once you have these definitions in mind, we can examine how best to organize most business messages.

THREE BASIC TERMS

Message

For the purposes of business communication, you need to think of the term **message** as meaning WHAT is said. In other words, a writer attempts to convey some piece or pieces of information to a particular reader. That information is the writer's message.

Message is "what" is said.

Organization

The term **organization** refers to WHEN something is said. More specifically, organization refers to *when* in the body of the message the writer chooses to reveal the message's purpose. In many instances, a writer may choose to reveal the purpose at the beginning of a memo, letter, or report. We will refer to such an approach as a direct or a bottom-line organizational pattern. At other times, a writer may choose to withhold the statement of purpose until the middle or end of the document. We will refer to such approaches as circuitous or semi-circuitous organizational patterns. Regardless of where he or she chooses to reveal the purpose, the writer is still making an organizational decision about *when* to reveal certain pieces of information.

Organization is "when" something is said.

Non-Sensitive Messages

Non-sensitive messages convey information that readers process and respond to intellectually but not emotionally. In fact, the message is so unemotional that readers will never become upset, disgruntled, or dismayed by the information. Likewise, they will not become pleased, overjoyed, or ecstatic.

Non-sensitive messages have few emotional overtones.

HOW TO ORGANIZE NON-SENSITIVE MESSAGES

Since non-sensitive situations are basically unemotional, writers do not need to beat around the bush in organizing a non-sensitive message. Therefore, the decision about when to reveal the purpose is really quite simple: Reveal your purpose at the very beginning of a non-sensitive message. When you organize the message in this direct way, you are doing what business people call bottom-lining.

As mentioned earlier, the term bottom-lining might sound colloquial, perhaps even like business jargon. But the word works because it accu-

State your purpose at the beginning of a non-sensitive message.

rately describes the concept you need to master. Bottom-line writers are efficient, effective communicators. They come to the point quickly, stating their purpose or purposes directly and immediately. By now everyone has probably heard someone say "What's the bottom line?"—meaning "What is your point or purpose?" That is the meaning we want you to remember as you begin to understand and master a bottom-line organizational approach to non-sensitive writing situations.

Bottom-Line Principle 1 introduces you to the bottom-line concept.

BOTTOM-LINE PRINCIPLE 1:

State your purpose first, unless you have overriding reasons for not doing so.

This principle is important to your success in business, particularly since the vast majority of all business messages are non-sensitive. In fact, this principle is so important that we are going to devote the remainder of this chapter—and most of Unit 2—to exploring its significance and its ramifications.

Non-Bottom-Lined Messages Waste Time

What happens when writers fail to obey Bottom-Line Principle 1 and don't state their purpose first? The answer is that their readers waste time trying to figure out *what* they are reading and *why* they are reading it.

Let's look at a hypothetical non-bottom-lined message. Suppose you come into work one morning and find the following message on your computer screen.

Screen 1: Northwestern
Harvard
Dartmouth
Wharton
Cornell

Screen 2: Michigan
Virginia
North Carolina
Stanford
Duke

Screen 3: Chicago
Indiana
Carnegie-Mellon
Columbia
MIT

"What is this about?" you wonder. Finally, you go to the last screen and find the following sentence:

These are the top MBA business schools according to a survey that appeared in <u>Business Week</u>.

"But I don't care about top MBA business schools," you say. "If this person had told me in the first sentence what he or she told me in the last, I wouldn't have wasted my time reading this useless information!"

The point is obvious. If writers directly state their purpose at the beginning, readers can immediately decide whether or not to read the message. Many writers do not give readers the choice. As a result, readers are forced to wade through the equivalent of the list of business schools until finally, at the end of the message, they are let in on the purpose the writer has kept secret until then. All too often, readers decide resentfully that they did not want to read the useless information in the first place.

Let's see what happens when Bottom-Line Principle 1 is applied to some actual business memos. (We have changed the names and facts in the memos.) Busy executives typically receive such memos every day on the job.

Bottom-lined messages let readers choose to continue reading.

I. Original

TO: Dorothy Johnson, Vice President, Manufacturing

FROM: T. R. Little, Staff Assistant

SUBJECT: Manufacturing Plan Review

DATE: May 16, 19——

As you know, I have been asked to coordinate the Manufacturing Plan Review effort. You have stated regularly that this planning effort should receive top priority.

Preplanning meetings will be held at various company sites:

- In Gastonville, July 1.
- In Charlottesburg, July 5.
- In Durbin, July 10.

At these meetings, all plant managers will discuss their views on:

1. Retooling progress for new products under development at each site.
2. Any needed extra financing for problems encountered in retooling.
3. Adequacy of each site's managerial structure and organization.
4. Input they would like to make to next year's manufacturing plan.

These discussions should make it possible for the resultant manufacturing plan to establish production schedules that complement our marketing strategy for all of our new and existing products. Also, these discussions will help Mike Montani to reassess our manufacturing organization and its effectiveness.

How did you react to this memo? Although the memo is visually attractive, didn't you find that you were jumping back and forth in search of a statement of purpose? If you were Dorothy Johnson, you would wonder just what T. R. Little was trying to tell you.

Now test your reaction to another memo.

II. Original

TO: Dorothy Johnson, Vice President, Manufacturing

FROM: G. H. Conrad, Staff Assistant

SUBJECT: Consolidating HQ Marketing

DATE: February 21, 19— —

I am working with our organization department on consolidating Headquarters Marketing functions into the new building at Pebble Brook. The new building will be ready for occupancy in September.

The following occupancy plan for the Pebble Brook building has been suggested:

1. Consolidation of all of the Marketing Communications people into this new building.
2. Relocation of our Advertising and Media people from Northside to this new building.
3. Centralization of the Procurement function entirely in the new building.

These new moves would consolidate all of Headquarters Marketing into the Pebble Brook location with the exception of Ron Reynolds and his Market Research people. They would remain in Building I because of their heavy utilization of our computer facilities. Suggested also is that we leave Market Research in its current location but provide it with additional space for expansion.

I have attached a preliminary building layout, floor by floor. If I don't hear any objections from you within the next week, I will assume the plan has your endorsement.

How would Dorothy Johnson react to this memo? She would scan it, looking for the writer's purpose. She would wonder at first why G. H. Conrad was telling her all this in the first place. Then, when she finally found the purpose in the last paragraph, she would recognize that she was being subtly manipulated into approving Conrad's plan. If she had refused to finish the memo, she would never have learned that she had better express any objections fast and in writing or her silence would be taken as tacit approval of the plan. Johnson would probably deeply resent such a tactic by Conrad.

Bottom-lined messages neither trick nor manipulate readers.

Bottom-Lined Messages Save
Readers' Time

Now let's organize the two memos in a direct, bottom-line fashion. Judge for yourself whether Johnson would like them much better.

I. Bottom-Lined

TO: Dorothy Johnson, Vice President, Manufacturing

FROM: T. R. Little, Staff Assistant

SUBJECT: Manufacturing Plan Review

DATE: May 16, 19— —

The Manufacturing Plan Review effort has been set in motion, as you requested.

Preplanning meetings have been set up for the purpose of discussing all factors necessary to a successful Manufacturing Plan Review. In brief, the purposes of these discussions are as follows:

1. To establish production schedules for all of our new and existing products that complement our marketing strategy.
2. To reassess our manufacturing organization and its effectiveness for Mike Montani.

Here are the details:
....
....

If Johnson wants to know the details of what will be covered in these meetings, she has the choice of reading further. She, the reader, is in control of her time; the writer is not in charge. See if you feel that a direct approach in Memo II also dramatically improves its effectiveness and eliminates its manipulativeness.

II. Bottom-Lined

TO: Dorothy Johnson, Vice President, Manufacturing

FROM: G. H. Conrad, Staff Assistant

SUBJECT: Consolidating HQ Marketing

DATE: February 21, 19— —

Please review the attached detailed occupany plan for the Pebble Brook building and let me know during the next week if you agree with it.

As you will see, it calls for a consolidation of all Headquarters Marketing (with the exception of Market Research) into our new building.

Occupancy is planned for September.

Now that Conrad has let her know the real purpose for writing—to ask her to agree or disagree with a proposed rearrangement of the Headquarters Marketing function in the new building—Johnson is alerted to read an attached plan carefully. The memo does not force her to read it twice; nor does it try to trick her. It alerts her right away that she is being asked to approve a plan involving the relocation of a lot of important people.

The revisions of Memos I and II exemplify the practicality of Bottom-Line Principle 1, which will invariably lead you to write effective bottom-lined messages.

Bottom-lined messages can be read once.

BENEFITS OF BOTTOM-LINED MESSAGES

Benefits to Your Employer

One of the reasons top executives urge employees to bottom-line is that bottom-lining saves not only time, but also money. An internal report in one large international corporation once estimated that the average cost for every memo or letter written in that corporation was more than $10.

Bottom-lining helps busy executives get the job done efficiently and effectively.

One division of the same corporation monitored the number of documents sent out by its divisional headquarters staff and found that the number exceeded nine million pieces in one year. Admittedly, some were multiple copies (in some instances, thousands of duplicate product and price announcements were sent to customers). Even if we assume that only 10 percent of these nine million letters and memos were individually composed, the cost of writing nine hundred thousand messages at $10 per copy was $9 million!

Writing is costly to American corporations.

Yet, the writing costs are only part of the picture. Reading costs, surprisingly, are significantly greater. Another large organization recently discovered through internal analysis that managers and professional staff personnel spend close to 60 percent of their time reading and writing. (*Automated Business Communications: The Management Workstation,* 21.) No wonder experts estimate that American industry spends over $1 billion annually in reading time. Imagine the savings that would result if reading time could be reduced by 10 percent, 20 percent, or even 30 percent. That's what bottom-line reporting can do.

Reading time is even more costly to American corporations.

Benefits to You

Long-Range Benefits to Bottom-Lining   One way to increase the likelihood of a rapid climb up the organizational ladder is for you to imitate the behavior of your superior. Not only do high-ranking executives voice their support for bottom-lining messages, they practice what they preach. High-level executives almost uniformly demonstrate the mastery of bottom-line skills in their messages—both oral and written.

We are not claiming that these executives got to the top *only* because they bottom-lined their communications. But it is clear that at some time in their careers, these corporate executives discovered that using a roundabout organizational pattern in their writing was not respected by their colleagues. Most successful executives have learned, probably in the school of hard knocks, to present their thoughts directly and efficiently. Somehow, they learned to bottom-line. And if bottom-lining has proved valuable to them, it certainly should to you.

Most high-level executives bottom-line their messages.

Immediate Benefits to Bottom-Lining   The benefits of a bottom-line approach are not limited to the business world. Bottom-lining can be used in many of the business courses you may be presently taking. Suppose you are taking a course that is case-oriented. Over the semester, you will have to write several written analyses of cases. Suppose, further, that your instructor is a very busy person with multiple demands upon his or her time.

A bottom-line approach works in school as well as business.

When your case analysis is graded, do you think the busy instructor will give extra points for long-windedness? Do you think the instructor wants to read a long history of company XYZ's problems—a history that probably is already stated (probably more succinctly) in the case itself? Do you think the instructor wants to read a restatement of case data describing what is wrong with XYZ's internal operations?

No! The instructor will certainly want to know immediately what you think the company's problems are and what you recommend to solve these problems. If you provide this information at the beginning of your report (and, of course, if what you say is logical and based on the facts of the case), you can be sure that you will impress the instructor and receive a higher grade for your efforts.

However, BE CAREFUL. A bottom-line statement of a problem and a succinct statement of recommended solutions do not make up the whole analytical report. Bottom-lining is not synonymous with superficiality. Both your professor and your boss on the job will want to receive a full and careful analysis of all pertinent aspects of a situation. But neither one will want to wade through to page fifteen before discovering the point of the report.

A bottom-line approach is not the same as being superficial or incomplete.

SUMMARY

We established the following definitions for three key terms:

- **Message** = WHAT is said
- **Organization** = WHEN something is said
- **Non-Sensitive Messages** = Communications that have few or no emotional overtones

In non-sensitive message situations, always apply Bottom-Line Principle 1: State your purpose first, unless you have overriding reasons for not doing so.

The benefit of using this approach is that it saves readers significant amounts of time by

- Allowing readers to determine immediately whether or not to read all of a given message.
- Helping readers to read a message with little or no rereading.

Saving readers' time ultimately translates into organizational benefits because the entire organization becomes more efficient, with readers spending less time wondering what writers have in mind and writers saving their own time by stating what they want without elaborate and useless preamble.

REVIEW QUESTIONS

1. What does the term *message* mean?

2. What does the term *organization* mean?

3. What is a non-sensitive message?

4. What is bottom-lining?

5. What happens when writers fail to state their purpose first?

6. Explain why Bottom-Line Principle 1 should be followed when writing a non-sensitive message.

7. How does your employer benefit from bottom-lining?

8. What is an effective strategy for moving up rapidly in any business?

9. Why is bottom-lining so important to high-level corporate executives?

10. How does bottom-lining benefit you in the long run?

DISCUSSION QUESTIONS

1. What are some possible reasons why businesspeople do not use a bottom-line approach?

2. Businesspeople sometimes note that a relationship exists between a person's being willing to bottom-line a message and that person's power within an organization. How would you define such a relationship? What do you think causes it?

3. What are the possible benefits of applying the bottom-line concept to business meetings, business presentations, and other communication activities conducted within a business environment?

Chapter 4

USING THE "SO-WHAT?" TEST TO RECOGNIZE BOTTOM-LINE STATEMENTS

OBJECTIVES

This chapter will help you to

•

Understand and apply the "So-what?" test

•

Distinguish between bottom-line and non-bottom-line sentences

•

Locate the bottom-line sentence in longer documents

Bottom-lining is the key to incisive thought. Unfortunately, neither the ability to bottom-line nor the ability to think incisively comes easy. Going right to the heart of a message may seem easy, but bottom-lining actually takes practice and a lot of thought.

The ability to bottom-line takes practice and hard work.

However, the rewards are great. Successful men and women of action are noted for their ability to cut through the non-essential to the necessary and to make crystal clear what they want and why. The purpose of this chapter is to help you develop that ability. The chapter begins by teaching you to distinguish bottom-line from non-bottom-line statements and then goes on to show you how to identify bottom-line statements in longer memos, letters, and reports.

Successful people quickly determine what is essential in a message.

RECOGNIZING A BOTTOM-LINE STATEMENT

Bottom-line writers need to be able to recognize a sentence containing the true bottom line or purpose of a message. If the message is non-sensitive, this bottom-line statement should usually appear in the first sentence or two.

The "So-what?" Test

The most effective way to separate a bottom-lined from a non-bottom-lined memo is to apply the **"So-what?" test** to its beginning. When you read a non-sensitive memo or letter, pause after the first two or three sentences and ask yourself, "So what? What's this all about?" If the writer has not made the answer to this question immediately clear, the message has not been bottom-lined.

The "So-what?" test helps you find the bottom line.

Look at the following three memo beginnings and ask "So what?" about each. Assume each example is the first sentence in an unsolicited memo or letter. Further, assume you have not requested the information conveyed.

Apply the "So-what?" test to unsolicited messages.

1. The price quotations from Jewel Mineral Castings arrived Thursday.
2. Employees are being trained in five areas.
3. On January 13, 198-, Mary Gobel represented XYZ Headquarters at the Fire Safety Task Force.

You are probably inclined to respond like this:

Non-Bottom-Lined Beginning	Likely Reader Response
1. The price quotations from Jewel Mineral Castings arrived Thursday.	So what? Why are you telling me this?
2. Employees are being trained in five areas.	That's nice, but what's that to me?
3. On January 13, 198-, Mary Gobel represented Agency Headquarters at the Fire Safety Task Force.	So what?

Each of these likely responses, showing irritation on the part of the reader, actually undercuts the significance of the message that follows.

Now look at what happens when these beginnings are recast into bottom-line statements:

Non-Bottom-Lined Beginning	Revised Bottom-Lined Beginning	Likely Reader Response to Revision
1. The price quotations from Jewel Mineral Castings arrived Thursday.	Unless you have objections, I plan to place an immediate order with Jewel Mineral Castings for twelve XYZ castings units at $1359.00 each.	Fine!
2. Employees are being trained in five areas.	If your employees haven't received training on the equipment they are assigned to operate, they should begin training immediately.	Will do!
3. On January 13, 198-, Mary Gobel represented Agency Headquarters at the Fire Safety Task Force.	Mary Gobel reports that Agency Headquarters is now in full compliance with federal fire-safety standards.	Excellent!

The "So-what?" test helps readers determine whether to read further.

With each bottom-lined beginning, readers can recognize the message's purpose and can read further if they desire additional information.

Applying the "So-what?" Test

Let's see if the "So-what?" test can help you distinguish bottom-line from non-bottom-line sentences. Read the following three sentences, again assuming all occur at the beginning of unsolicited memos or letters. Can you identify the bottom-line sentence in each set?

Set A
1. Program/Assistance is a program product for accessing technical information from 1234 Terminal.
2. Please install XYZ's software package and encourage all departments within your business units to install and use it.
3. System programmers have easy access to technical information.

Once you apply the "So-what?" test, sentence 2 stands out as the only sentence that states directly information the reader needs to know. Sentences 1 and 3 offer what may or may not end up being useful information.

Set B
4. As you are probably aware, this office is required to make a yearly report on the results of our negotiations.

5. I need to know the number of parcels acquired per professional grade ✓ employee as well as the percentage of tracts condemned.

6. We realize that you have had no work assigned other than your normal duties.

In set B, sentence 5 presents the bottom line by requesting specific information of the reader.

Set C

7. The financial coordinator is responsible for five separate activities.

8. The legal division is responsible for acquiring permission for building improvements.

9. The government's new policy on standardizing parts nomenclature will probably affect your operation.

In set C, sentence 9 quickly alerts the reader that the information that follows is of great relevance and should be digested carefully. The other sentences merely provide background information.

Once you become adept at spotting bottom-line sentences, you can carefully scrutinize your own non-sensitive letters and memos to make sure that they start off with the bottom line of your message. Decide for yourself whether you need more practice. If so, study the following three sets of opening sentences. Pick out the bottom line in each set.

Use the "So-what?" test to analyze your own messages.

Set D

10. The enclosed blueprints were completed last February.

11. Enclosed for your review and consideration are three blueprints of ✓ preliminary building layouts.

12. We submitted blueprints of the original layout on March 15.

Set E

13. Material costs now comprise 40 percent of the sales value of our product.

14. Some companies have proposed combining Production, Control, Purchasing, and Distribution into a single Materials Management department.

15. Please ask your staff to conduct an in-depth evaluation of our current ✓ materials organization and recommend changes that will improve our ability to control materials costs.

Set F

16. Please seriously consider making some personnel available for transfer ✓ on a permanent or temporary basis.

17. There are currently 2,336 people employed in this division.

18. The division office provides estimates of the cost of right-of-way, relocation assistance, and appraisal fees, broken down on a tract-by-tract basis.

In sets D, E, and F, sentences 11, 15, and 16 are the ones that pass the "So-what?" test.

Finding the Bottom Line in Longer Passages

The "So-what?" test helps you find the bottom line in longer passages.

Practice in identifying bottom-line sentences should help you spot them readily in longer passages. Test yourself. Can you quickly spot the only bottom-line sentence in the following passage?

> I'd like to express my concern regarding one of our customers, Charles Rourke, owner and operator of Techtonics, Inc.
>
> I continue to have difficulty collecting money he owes us for equipment delivered to his facilities. At present our records show three deliveries to Techtonics for which the firm owes us in excess of $5,000. Mr. Rourke has been billed monthly—since September—for this equipment, and I have talked to his assistant, Sheila Davis, by phone on three separate occasions. Ms. Davis claims Mr. Rourke travels a great deal, but she assures us he will pay us by the end of February.
>
> I plan to continue to try to contact Mr. Rourke, requesting his cooperation in resolving this matter. Based on his past behavior, I recommend we take legal action against Mr. Rourke.

The final clause—*I recommend we take legal action against Mr. Rourke*—is the bottom line. All the earlier details are essentially meaningless until we are given the bottom line.

Where is the bottom line in this second example?

> The use of external consultants has been considered on several occasions.
>
> In a memorandum dated October 25, 198—, XYZ issued guidelines for corporate use of external consultants. At that time, the company's first priority was getting internal consultants. Now we are genuinely concerned over the feasibility of finding external consultants to assist us in key areas.
>
> Aside from hiring two local consultants, headquarters has two objections to using externals for our purpose. The first concerns data reliability. Headquarters contends that external consultants do not have data as reliable as those of internal consultants. The second objection concerns their lack of specific expertise with XYZ, a problem that undercuts the validity of some of their suggestions. The attached memorandum provides statistical support for each of these objections.
>
> It is our opinion that aggressive recruitment of external consultants for XYZ would not be economically justified.

Again, the bottom line appears in the last sentence—*It is our opinion that aggressive recruitment of external consultants for XYZ would not be economically justified.*

Now let's make the tests a bit harder. Can you quickly spot the bottom-line sentence in this memo?

TO: XYZ HQ Managers

FROM: Purchasing Director

SUBJECT: Contact with Suppliers or Potential Suppliers

DATE: September 16, 19——

The XYZ policy on contacts with suppliers or potential suppliers is clearly outlined in the attached booklet, "Doing Business With Our Suppliers." All managers must recognize that when an employee's work requires oral or written communication with a supplier or potential supplier, authorization must be received from Purchasing prior to the employee contacting the supplier. This policy applies to employees' contacts relative to suppliers' (or potential suppliers') commercial product lines as well as to information, material, parts, equipment, services, and supplies.

This one is a little more difficult. However, a careful review shows that the bottom line is in the second sentence—*All managers must. . . .* This memo would have been much clearer if the writer had begun with a proper bottom-line statement like this:

Please obtain authorization from Purchasing when an employee's work requires oral or written communication with a supplier or potential supplier. This authorization must be received before the employee contacts the supplier.

Let's end by giving you one final, extremely difficult non-sensitive memo. Can you find the bottom line?

TO: R. H. Joyce

FROM: John Harris

SUBJECT: Recordkeeping

DATE: January 14, 19——

Recordkeeping can no longer be a function performed at the discretion and convenience of the responsible party. The addition of part 48 to the federal law, coupled with the demands already imposed by parts 70, 75, and 77, has made accurate, timely records mandatory. We are now subject to OSHA audits with citations being issued for ill-kept and inaccurate records.

Currently we are required to train all areas covered by state and federal laws, ABCD contracts, and company programs, and also participate in various outside programs. During 199—, we trained approximately 2,050 employees for a total of 16,700 hours. With this increasing demand for training, the trainers must utilize their time developing better methods, updating materials, and developing their own skills rather than record-keeping. Presently they are spending five to six days per month on recordkeeping.

More and more demands are being placed on the already over-loaded mine personnel supervisor. Currently, he takes care of all personnel-related matters for 606 employees—98 salaried and 508 ABCD. A standard work week for this individual is 50–60 hours, and approximately one half of this time is devoted to reports and recordkeeping necessary to meet require-ments of the various state and federal agencies, as well as our own needs. This activity includes all typing, filing, and clerical functions associated with maintaining a personnel office. With the many interruptions that are part of his daily functions, very little time is left to carry out and develop company pro-grams that would be beneficial to the operation. Your consider-ation, approval, and assistance in providing us with an addi-tional clerk position would be greatly appreciated.

I believe this change will allow both our trainers and the mine personnel supervisor the freedom and flexibility to develop pro-grams that will directly affect and improve employee—employer relations and the safety, production, and efficiency of the operation.

Some bottom lines mistakenly appear in the middle of non-sensitive messages.

If readers tried to skim this message they probably would conclude that there is no bottom line. But in fact there *is* a bottom-line statement; un-fortunately, it is hidden at the end of paragraph 3—"Your consideration, approval, and assistance in providing us with an additional clerk position would be greatly appreciated."

DEVELOP THE BOTTOM-LINE HABIT FOR EFFICIENCY

You must develop an ability to recognize bottom-line sentences.

The ability to recognize a bottom-line sentence is the key to becoming a bottom-line writer. As you become proficient at identifying bottom lines in others' messages, you likewise become proficient in identifying them in your own writing. Eventually, your ability to recognize the bottom line will eliminate your need to revise the organization of your messages. You will develop the habit of determining the following before you write:

1. What the bottom line or purpose of your message is.
2. Whether the message is non-sensitive; if it is, you will know to state the bottom line at the beginning.

Once you reach this stage, you will become an *efficient* writer, not only in organizing messages for your readers, but also in drastically reducing the amount of time you spend staring into space before you begin to write. Such a reduction in wasted time can be valuable to you both in college and in ascending the corporate ladder.

Bottom-line writers spend less time staring into space.

SUMMARY

Effective writers are constantly searching for a bottom line, both in their own writing and in that of others. The **"So-what?" test** is the best tool available to help effective writers conduct this search. Thus, the key question to ask in determining whether a statement is a bottom-line expression is "So what?" As you become proficient at applying this question to your own and to the messages of others, you will refine your ability to identify bottom-line statements. Even more importantly, you will develop the ability to cut through the non-essential to get to the necessary.

REVIEW QUESTIONS

1. What abilities are needed if you are to become an effective bottom-line writer?

2. What is the key question to ask to distinguish between a bottom-line and a non-bottom-line statement? *So-what*

3. What habit should you develop before you begin to write? *the habit of recognizing a bottom line sentence.*
   - content of memo
   - relationship [sensitive/non sen

DISCUSSION QUESTIONS

1. Why do successful men and women of action need to have the ability to cut through the non-essential to the necessary? Why do these same people need to be able to make crystal clear what they want and why they want it?

2. In what ways can the "So-what?" test help reduce the time a writer spends staring into space?

3. Name some additional business-communication situations in which the "So-what?" test can be used.

I
1. get to the point of the message
2. try to identify bottom

Chapter 5

FIVE MORE BOTTOM-LINE PRINCIPLES TO HELP YOU COMMUNICATE BETTER

OBJECTIVES

This chapter will help you to

●

Organize non-sensitive messages that have more than one purpose

●

Place background material after the statement of purpose

●

Distinguish between a message's subject and its purpose

●

Determine how to organize material based on its importance to the reader

Bottom-Line Principle 1 (State your purpose first unless you have overriding reasons for not doing so) and the "So-what?" test introduced you to the concept of bottom-lining. You learned that Bottom-Line Principle 1 is the foundation upon which all effective non-sensitive memos and reports rest. Moreover, Bottom-Line Principle 1 is a source from which other bottom-line principles can be derived. This chapter will develop five additional bottom-line principles that will help you to write more efficiently and effectively.

This chapter develops five additional bottom-line principles.

HANDLING NON-SENSITIVE MESSAGES WITH MORE THAN ONE PURPOSE

Let's begin our analysis of these principles by introducing Bottom-Line Principle 2:

BOTTOM-LINE PRINCIPLE 2:
When a message has more than one purpose, state all purposes at the beginning, or write additional memos.

If you have multiple purposes, don't bottom-line only one of them and bury the others. Most business readers read in hopes of finding out as quickly as possible what a message is all about. When readers think they have found the purpose, they are quick to stop reading. It seldom enters their minds to look for additional purposes.

Readers often stop reading after identifying one purpose.

As a student, you react similarly. If you are taking a test in which a professor poses many long, rambling questions, you read each question until you think you have discovered just what the professor wants you to answer. Then you start writing your answer. You have to react this way because most tests have time limitations imposed by class schedules. What happens if near the end of one question the professor slips in a second question? You may earn only half credit for your answer.

Business people are under time constraints similar to those of a test taker. Business people simply do not have time to read every memo word for word. Therefore, they pay close attention only to memos they decide deserve it, and merely skim the others—especially those memos that do not closely or obviously relate to their jobs or personal interests. What happens, then, when a memo begins with one bottom-line statement but then adds another in the middle of the third paragraph? In essence, this second statement says, "Oh, yes, I forgot to mention this, but I really think you ought to. . . ." The addition runs a good chance of being lost on the reader.

Key Words Indicate Bottom Lines

Think of how you and other practicing businesspeople read memos. Once you spot certain key words, you stop reading. One such key word is *recommendation*. At this word, you tend to stop reading and focus on whether to accept or reject the recommendation. A reader of Memo I would demonstrate this tendency.

Certain key words encourage you to read carefully or to stop reading.

TO: J. B. Alvarez

FROM: Susan Greenspan

SUBJECT: F-62 Line

DATE: January 24, 19— —

Jim, I recommend that we reduce the purchase price of the
F-62 line as soon as possible for the following reasons:

1. The entire line has had no significant....
2. Customer acceptances are off markedly....
3. We will not be able to achieve our....

I understand that some of our manufacturers' reps have proposed bonuses or rebates to help certain elements of the F-62
line. Also, some retailers are requesting that we reduce our
down payment requirement from 25 percent to 10 percent.
I recommend that we aggressively support both of these
proposals.

While our current sales plan has a 15 to 20 percent profit for
F-62 products, I believe 10 percent is a more realistic figure
since:

1. Our Commercial Analysis people believe....
2. With lower prices, the F-62 line would be positioned....

Notice that the first recommendation is made clearly in the first paragraph.
But a reader could be fooled into thinking that this is the sole recommendation being made. As a result, this memo is not very clear or effective.
In fact, it is unintentionally deceptive, because at the end of the second
paragraph the writer has hidden a second and equally important recommendation. If busy people would read this memo the way they read most
communications, they probably would miss the second recommendation.

Why run the risk of accidentally fooling a reader? This writer should
have begun by stating that the memo makes two recommendations. Something like the following would have done the job:

I. Bottom-Lined

TO: J. B. Alvarez

FROM: Susan Greenspan

SUBJECT: F-62 Line

DATE: January 24, 19— —

I have two recommendations about the F-62 line. Specifically:

1. We should reduce the purchase price on the F-62 line as
   soon as possible because:

Non-sensitive messages
should not have hidden
purposes.

a. The entire line has had significant....

b. Customer acceptances are off markedly....

c. We will not be able to achieve our....

2. We should aggressively support the following suggestions made by our manufacturing reps and our retailers for stimulating F-62 line sales:

a. Some manufacturers' reps have proposed....

b. Some retailers are requesting....

While our sales plan has a 15 to 20 percent profit for F-62 products, I believe....

THE PROPER PLACE FOR BACKGROUND INFORMATION

Now let's introduce Bottom-Line Principle 3.

BOTTOM-LINE PRINCIPLE 3:
State your purpose first, even if you know your readers need background information before they can fully understand the purpose of your communication.

This principle is perhaps the most difficult to follow of the bottom-line organizing principles. Writers often assume that managers are totally ignorant about a message's subject. As a result, upper-level managers often report that messages waste significant amounts of time briefing managers about things they already know.

The reasons subordinates feel a need to set the stage (by briefing or updating) before coming to the bottom line are understandable. People writing to powerful readers feel insecure about blurting out their purposes, even when the purpose is the core of a non-sensitive message. Beginning businesspeople, therefore, often succumb to the need to explain—in fact, to overexplain—what they have been doing and what factors or occurrences have led to their writing to their superior.

But how do the superiors feel? They get bored and annoyed at having to wade through paragraphs of information they already know! What these high-level executives want is first the bottom line and then (and only then) any background that the writer feels they might need. This way, the executives themselves can decide whether or not they need additional information. This decision to read the background material is a choice that upper-level managers feel *they* should make, not their subordinates.

Do not assume your superior is ignorant about your message's subject.

Let superiors decide whether they need additional information.

Applying Bottom-Line Principle 3

Let's look at a few typical situations where Bottom-Line Principle 3 can be applied.

Suppose a company plans to raise prices on October 1. The writer wants to urge important customers to place their orders before that date. But the writer does not know for certain whether these customers want to buy or not. For fear of appearing pushy, the writer doesn't want to bottom-line the purpose by beginning the letter with "Please get your order in before September 30." Frightened into believing a non-sensitive letter is sensitive, the writer feels the need to recount the history of price changes in the recent past before arriving at the fact, several paragraphs later, that there is going to be a price change on October 1. Only then does the writer feel safe enough to tell customers that they had better get their orders in before September 30 or face higher prices.

Instead, the writer should follow Bottom-Line Principle 3 and begin the letter with the real purpose. Why risk having important customers refuse to wade through several paragraphs of apparently irrelevant history, only to toss the letter into the wastebasket? Why risk that on October 1 they will become angry because they think they weren't warned?

Don't force readers to have to read background first.

Here is another example. Suppose you want your superior to approve a transfer of salary funds from an unfilled position so that the money can be used to hire a consultant to conduct a reorganization of your department. Suppose further that you know your boss neither favors nor opposes such expenditures. In essence, your boss has no particular emotions about such requests. Hence, the situation is again a non-sensitive one.

Inexperienced writers would begin by pointing out how understaffed their department is and how upsetting the proposed reorganization may be to many people. They would then identify several alternative courses of action that might be considered. Finally, only after going into extreme, boring, and perhaps confusing detail, these writers would dare to recommend hiring a consultant as the best available alternative.

Businesspeople are willing to make important decisions.

With such an approach, these writers not only delay stating their purpose, they also forget that businesspeople, especially high-level businesspeople, are used to making important decisions. All that needs to be explained are the recommendations and the reasons for the recommendations. Then, efficient superiors will rapidly decide whether to go along with or to reject the recommendations.

Your understanding of Bottom-Line Principle 3 would prevent you from making such an organizational mistake. Since the consultant situation is non-sensitive, you would recognize the obvious need to bottom-line the request. Thus, you would begin in a way similar to this:

TO: Superior

FROM: Subordinate

SUBJECT: Reorganization Support

DATE: June 6, 19——

Please approve the hiring of a consultant to accomplish the planned departmental reorganization. The consultant could be compensated from unspent salary funds in budget line 4783.

Beware of Appearing to "Con" Your Superiors

By following the advice of Bottom-Line Principle 3, you gain another advantage as well: You avoid appearing as though you are trying to manipulate your superior.

Background information can sometimes appear to be manipulative.

To help you appreciate this point, let's imagine that you are a busy executive sitting in your office in the middle of a typically busy day. You are putting the finishing touches on a presentation you have to give to your company's Board of Directors. There is a knock on the door. An obviously distraught staff assistant enters. Busy as you are, you invite the assistant to tell you what is bothering him. "Whew! I've been getting angry calls from customers for the last four days," he says. "It's brutal. . . ." The assistant continues to give a detailed description of all his calls, offering an analysis of what happened on each occasion.

You offer solace and encouragement to him. The assistant then talks about his immediate and long-range plans. You listen attentively, offering occasional advice. You console yourself over the loss of time, because you think the young man needs you as a sounding board. You also think the calls may have given the young assistant insights into a problem of which you were not aware.

But how do you feel when the staff assistant finally gets to the bottom line: "Well, what I *really* came to talk about is this. Can I have next week off? My parents are visiting, and I'd really like to have an opportunity to spend some time with them."

You feel insulted, as though the assistant thought you were a fool. And, worse, still, you acted like one. The assistant used a non-bottom-line organizational pattern to manipulate you at a very inopportune time. And you let him get away with it. Has the assistant's non-bottom-line approach proved effective? No, the assistant has harmed—perhaps irreparably—his image in your eyes.

That is why successful businesspeople have learned to resist attempts by subordinates to manipulate them and to waste their valuable time. A smart boss will say:

Successful executives ask for bottom lines, not background.

> You tell me first why you are writing to me, what your purpose is, and what you want me to do. Then offer your background briefing. If I need the briefing, I'll read it. If I don't, I won't. At least this way I'll know what you're talking about right away. This way we'll both save time.

Background Is Not the Bottom Line

We cannot overemphasize the need to maintain a clear understanding of the difference between a message's background and its bottom line.

Here is a memo that affords a classic illustration of subordinates' tendencies to give a detailed background briefing in messages sent to their superiors.

II. Original

TO: Division President

FROM: Sarah Schneider

SUBJECT: Energy Conservation

DATE: February 5, 19— —

Last year we set a goal to reduce energy usage by 7 percent. We have met that goal; actual energy expenditures amount to only 93 percent of last year's.

Furthermore, since A & B Corporation grew by 6 percent this year, the energy reduction actually exceeded our goal—probably in the range of a 10 percent to 13 percent reduction. A survey of all operations indicated that additional reductions in energy usage will be difficult. And considering the almost unpredictable but skyrocketing costs of energy, A & B faces a future energy conservation dilemma.

Energy usage will grow in Chicago because of increased computer utilization and additional automated production equipment. However, the solar project and the substitution of a small boiler for a large one in the cafeteria should increase energy conservation in Dallas. Also, in Palo Alto, several conservation projects, including weekend shutdown of air conditioning, will contribute to overall savings.

With this background in mind, would you please either convene a meeting yourself, or authorize me to convene one to discuss the impact of future energy conservation on A & B's operations? If you need any further information before making your decision, please let me know.

If you were the division president, would you think this background briefing was really necessary before Sarah Schneider told you the bottom line— that is, that a meeting needed to be called? We doubt that you would. But the writer's decision to offer the background before stating her purpose doesn't give you a choice. That choice should be made by you, the reader, not by the writer. According to Bottom-Line Principle 3, the memo should begin directly with a statement of purpose, not with a statement of background.

II. Bottom-Lined

TO: Division President

FROM: Sarah Schneider

SUBJECT: Energy Conservation

DATE: February 5, 19————

I am pleased to report that A & B Corporation is doing very well in conserving energy. On the other hand, we face a future energy conservation dilemma. Therefore, I request that you

1. Convene a meeting yourself, or
2. Authorize me to convene a meeting to discuss the impact of future energy conservation on A & B Corporation's operations.

Here is the background you may need to keep in mind as you consider this matter:

1. ....
2. ....
3. ....

REMEMBER TO STATE YOUR PURPOSE

Now let's take up Bottom-Line Principle 4.

BOTTOM-LINE PRINCIPLE 4:
Subject and purpose are not the same. Do not assume that once readers know a message's subject they automatically know your purpose for writing.

This principle derives from the fact that writers often make two faulty assumptions about their readers:

▪ Assumption 1: Writers convince themselves that, since they mentioned something in the subject line, they have actually told the reader their purpose.

▪ Assumption 2: Writers assume their reader already knows their purpose. Therefore, they don't state it. This forces the reader to infer what a message is really about.

Let's briefly examine each assumption.

Subject Is Not Purpose

A marked difference exists between a subject and a purpose. That is why subject lines in reports and memos usually do not do the job of stating the purpose. Subject lines are, for the most part, key words to be used in the filing of documents. For example, one writer relied on this subject line in a memo:

> Subject: Route 128

Imagine that you have received this memo. What does "Route 128" mean to you? You need a first-paragraph statement of purpose, like this:

> Route 128 has been eliminated by our real estate people as a potential site for the New England Headquarters building.

Moreover, stating the subject in the opening paragraph is usually a poor substitute for a bottom-line statement of your purpose. Consider this example:

> I am quite pleased about the revenue contribution made by the marketing support system Fred and Mary have been working on. Their system has evolved since they joined ABCD. . . .

The writer obviously thought the message did its job by stating promptly the subject to be discussed. But you wonder, "So he's pleased. So what? What does this have to do with me?" It would have been far more effective if the writer had made the purpose clear, like this:

> I would very much appreciate your authorizing an independent evaluation of the revenue contributions made by the marketing support system that Fred and Mary have been working on. I think you will find the results as interesting as I will.

"Okay," says the reader. "Tell me about it." The statement of purpose has set the stage for meaningful communication.

Writers Should Not Assume Readers Know the Purpose

Writers who violate Bottom-Line Principle 4 omit their purpose and go straight into the subject. In beginning this way, these writers do the exact opposite of those who violate Bottom-Line Principle 3 by providing background rather than purpose. Writers who violate Bottom-Line Principle 3 assume their readers are ignorant and need a thorough education before they can evaluate a message's purpose. Writers who violate Bottom-Line Principle 4 fall victim to the opposite assumption. These writers assume that, since they are tremendously involved in their own work, their readers will be equally knowledgeable about and interested in it.

Some writers mistakenly
assume readers know all
about their work.

Furthermore, these writers assume that readers are able (and eager) to infer (or guess) the purpose of the communication. Imagine that you are sitting in your office one morning when the mail arrives. You look at the first memo. It says essentially, "Myra Sandi passed her Certified Management Accountant examination." "That's nice," you think, "but so what?" Obviously, the writer felt that this information was something you wanted to know, but the importance of the statement completely escapes you. Either you throw the memo in the wastebasket, or you write back and say, "Why did you tell me that Myra Sandi passed her CMA exam?"

If the writer had stated the purpose, the memo might have looked like this:

> You asked me to let you know when Myra Sandi completed her CMA exam so that you could support the promotion I've promised her.
>
> I'm happy to tell you that Myra has indeed passed the exam and with very high grades. Therefore, I'd appreciate your writing an appropriate letter to recommend her promotion.

"Oh," you say, "that's right! I did promise. All right, I'll recommend her for promotion."

DECIDING WHAT IS IMPORTANT TO YOUR READER

Now let's move to Bottom-Line Principle 5.

BOTTOM-LINE PRINCIPLE 5:
Bottom-line non-sensitive information in order of importance to the reader.

Do not organize non-sensitive information based on your own interests. Organize each item in terms of its importance to your *reader*.

The Problem of Reporting History First

Unskilled writers tend to report the progress of their thoughts as they work their way through a problem. Here is an example of the steps almost everyone takes in approaching a problem. Suppose your boss asked you the following question: "Should we continue to do business with Smith and Brown? Research it for me, will you?" After you have completed your investigation and begun to write your report, you would most likely be tempted to organize it as follows:

Unskilled writers organize all materials in chronological order.

1. The question under consideration is whether we should continue to do business with Smith and Brown.
2. There are certain benefits to dealing with Smith and Brown.
3. There are certain disadvantages.
4. After weighing each, I conclude that the disadvantages outweigh the advantages.
5. Therefore, we should not do business with Smith and Brown.

If, like most people, you followed this procedure, you would end up writing a report that offered your boss a history of your thoughts.

A More Effective Organization

Ask yourself this, however: If you were the boss, how would you want to have this report organized? You would want to receive information in the following order:

1. First, you would want the bottom line, that is, this recommendation: "I recommend that we stop doing business with Smith and Brown."

2. Next, you would want to have that recommendation supported by solid evidence. The report should immediately state the following:
   Here are my reasons for making this recommendation:
   a. Smith and Brown's prices are high. . . .
   b. Their quality is only average. . . .
   c. Their service is poor. . . .

3. Now, if you, as the boss, are not entirely convinced by this quick summary of the recommendation and the evidence supporting it, what might help you become more convinced? You would expect a good assistant to say: "Attached is a detailed record of the analysis I undertook before arriving at my recommendation." Then, as the boss, you can now choose to examine all the details without being forced to wade through them.

After all, transmitting the recommendation is the *real* purpose in writing this report. The justification (or defense) of that recommendation should follow—not precede—the recommendation. If the details of your analysis are needed (as is often the case), they can be included later in the report or in an attachment or appendix.

Naturally, you must think a problem through step by step before you can arrive at the conclusion and/or the recommendation you want to communicate. But once the bottom line is known ("We should not do business with Smith and Brown"), you should place that bottom line of your analysis at the beginning of your report.

USING ATTACHMENTS

Let's move now to Bottom-Line Principle 6.

BOTTOM-LINE PRINCIPLE 6
Put information of questionable importance to the reader into an attachment. (This also applies to detailed information that probably will not be read in its entirety by the receiver.)

People who progress higher in their organization generally tend to be handed more and more material to read. It is only natural that since third-line managers have more people reporting up to them than do first-line managers, more information gets sent up to them. As a result of this ever-increasing load of information, successful businesspeople constantly have to make decisions about whether to read messages carefully, casually, or not at all. If a message is bottom-lined, the chances of its receiving the appropriate kind of attention from a higher-up increases significantly.

This situation of having ever-increasing information to process and digest is probably similar to what you have experienced throughout your education. Think of how your reading requirements have changed as your education has advanced. Think of the difference between the amount you had to read in junior high school, in high school, and now in college. What do you think will happen if you continue on to graduate school or law school? The answer is obvious: You will have more pages than ever to read.

Very few of us read every word that is put in front of us. As we read a chapter in a textbook, for example, the following questions are in the back of our minds:

> What kind of information does this chapter contain? Is this information important to me in terms of
> 1. my business career?
> 2. a final exam?
> 3. a midterm exam?
> 4. a pop quiz?
> 5. my personal life?

The answer to these questions has a significant effect upon the care with which you read the text.

Businesspeople are inundated with even more information than people in college. Businesspeople have to be highly selective about what they choose to read carefully and what they choose to skim. They, therefore, ask questions such as these:

> What kind of information does this report (memo, letter) contain? Is this information
> 1. important to me and/or my job?
> 2. of probable use to me?
> 3. of possible use to me?
> 4. of no relevance whatsoever to my personal or professional interests?

As a writer, you need to keep these questions in mind, especially when you are communicating with a superior. Information that is important to the reader and to his or her job (see Question 1) should be placed at the very beginning of a memo or report. Information of questionable or possible use (see Questions 2 and 3) should be placed later in the message—or perhaps in an attachment. Information that is irrelevant to a reader should not be sent at all. If you are not sure if the information is relevant or not, you can play it safe by putting it in an attachment.

Arrange information based on what the reader needs to know.

Applying Bottom-Line Principles 5 and 6

Let's see how Bottom-Line Principles 5 and 6 can be applied to the following memo, which informs branch personnel managers about a corporate founder's college scholarship award.

III. Original

TO:	Branch Personnel Managers
FROM:	Headquarters Personnel
SUBJECT:	Scholarship Qualifying Test
DATE:	June 18, 19——

The National Scholarship Qualifying Test (NSQT) will be given at selected overseas high schools on either October 23 or 27 (as determined by the individual schools).

Brochures describing the details of the program will be distributed by this office in August.

Students who are entering their junior year at an overseas location this fall should check now with their principals to see if the test will be administered at their school. If their school does not plan to give the test, the student or principal should write to NSQT, Box 123, New York, NY 10101, before July 6, to determine alternative testing locations.

If your location has employees on overseas assignments, you should pass this information along to them, since the NSQT is used as the basis for selecting A & B Founders' Award college scholarships.

Suppose some—or most—of the branches of the A & B Company do not have employees on overseas assignments. Why should the writer force *all* branch personnel managers to wade through information that is of no relevance whatsoever to them?

Let's look at this same memo organized according to Bottom-Line Principles 5 and 6:

III. Bottom-Lined

TO:	Branch Personnel Managers
FROM:	Headquarters Personnel
SUBJECT:	Scholarship Qualifying Test
DATE:	June 18, 19——

If your location has—or will have—employees on overseas assignment who have high-school age children, you should share the attached important information with them. It contains details of how these employees' children may compete while overseas for an A & B Founders' Award college scholarship.

Notice how much more considerate the revision is. If the branch personnel managers don't have overseas employees who have high-school-age children, they know immediately that they need read no further (Bottom-Line Principle 5). If they do have such employees, the details to be communicated are attached (Bottom-Line Principle 6).

SUMMARY

This chapter demonstrates that bottom-lining means more than merely identifying your purpose and stating it at the beginning. First of all, you must be certain to determine whether the message has more than one purpose. If it has more than one, you must state all of the purposes at the beginning or else prepare more than one document.

Effective writers also efficiently arrange detailed, complex material. They are careful to place background material in its appropriate position after the bottom line. And they make a conscious effort to distinguish between the subject of a message and its purpose.

Finally, bottom-line writers are <u>reader-based</u>. That is, they organize material according to its importance to the reader, not to themselves. And when material is of questionable importance to the reader, a bottom-line writer moves that information to a position of lesser importance in the message, most often to an appendix or attachment.

[handwritten margin note: Since something is mentioned in the subject, reader knows their purpose — assume reader already know purpose. It is not stated.]

REVIEW QUESTIONS

1. What is the risk of not following Bottom-Line Principle 2? *[handwritten: fooling of reader —]*

2. What bothers upper-level managers about the way people write to them? *[handwritten: out of background info that is presented before the bottom line]*

3. Why do subordinates, when reporting up to powerful superiors, set the stage before coming to the bottom line? *[handwritten: they feel insecure]*

[handwritten: ⨉] 4. What are two faulty assumptions that writers often make about their readers?

5. What are subject lines used for in reports and memos? *[handwritten: for purpose of filing]*

6. How do subject and purpose differ?

7. What do writers who violate Bottom-Line Principle 4 mistakenly assume? *[handwritten: readers are able to infer the purpose of the comm.]*

8. If you were a boss, in what order would you want to receive information?

9. What must you do before you arrive at a conclusion or recommendation? *[handwritten: Think through and bottom line]*

DISCUSSION QUESTIONS

1. State some reasons why people bury the purpose in a non-sensitive message.

2. Discuss the relationship between bottom-lining and the scientific method (i.e., recognition and formulation of a problem, collection of data, formulation and testing of hypotheses). What similarities exist between the two systems? What differences?

3. Discuss the organizational differences between non-sensitive business messages and other types of writing you have studied (e.g., essays, themes, short stories, novels). What are the reasons for these differences?

BOTTOM-LINE PRINCIPLES 1–6
REVIEW LIST

1

State your purpose first, unless you have overriding reasons for not doing so.

2

When a message has more than one purpose, state all purposes at the beginning, or write additional memos.

3

State your purpose first, even if you know your readers need background information before they can fully understand the purpose of your communication.

4

Subject and purpose are not the same. Do not assume that once readers know a message's subject they automatically know your purpose for writing.

5

Bottom-line non-sensitive information in order of importance to the reader.

6

Put information of questionable importance to the reader into an attachment. (This also applies to detailed information that probably will not be read in its entirety by the receiver.)

EXERCISES

Exercise 1
Identifying Bottom-Line Sentences

Identify the bottom-line sentence in each of the following sets and tell why you chose that sentence. Again assume that each of the following sentences occurs at the beginning of unsolicited letters and memos.

Set 1

a. Your present telephone service requires all calls to be handled by an operator.
b. Further efficiencies in operating costs can be made by utilizing the operator's time for other duties.
c. Here are the details that you need to know about the installation of your new telephone system.

Set 2

a. Early last winter I worked as an interviewer for a public health survey in the Green Springs area.
b. I would like to have a personal interview with you at your convenience.
c. As a major in marketing research, I believe I possess the qualifications needed for the position of part-time interviewer in your organization.

Set 3

a. Attached is a memo from the Director of Marketing in the central region.
b. Please develop a plan as soon as possible to address the affirmative action process before it develops into a major problem.
c. Customer confusion develops when multiple surveys are sent to one establishment.

Set 4

a. The Annual Report for the year ending December 31, 19— — is in its final stages of preparation.
b. I want to extend you a most cordial welcome into our family of shareholders and trust that your association with us will be pleasant.
c. I have been advised by our transfer agent that you are a registered holder of our common stock.

Set 5

a. This is to inform you that we have completed conversion of our shareholder records system to computer operation, as you requested last month.

b. The enclosed dividend check is the first to be issued utilizing the new system.
c. We are confident that conversion of our shareholder records system to computer operation will provide efficient, accurate service to our shareholders.

Set 6

a. I am sure you are well aware that we have consolidated most of our donations into two major contributions.
b. Our company has operations in more than twenty-five locations across the country.
c. We are unable to commit ourselves to a contribution to your organization since the funds we set aside for charitable contributions have already been expended.

Set 7

a. Since I believe participants would be better served with increased flexibility in the area of Employee Savings Plans, this memo suggests some changes for you to consider.
b. Several days ago, Joe Cook stopped by to discuss some concern he had with the Employee Savings Plan.
c. Participants may not be prepared to make an investment election.

Set 8

a. All of the employees of the service department are performing their work in a satisfactory manner.
b. As a result of the investigation of the bidding process, I believe that you can effect appreciable savings by adopting the following recommendations.
c. The work done by the service department could very well be restricted because of lack of proper equipment.

Set 9

a. There has been an abnormal increase in the daily number of absences among company employees.
b. I am concerned that the efficiency of our organization is being impaired.
c. Please conduct an investigation to determine the causes for employee absenteeism and make recommendations as to how this problem can be alleviated.

Exercise 2
Identifying Bottom-Line Statements in Messages

Identify the bottom line in each of the following memos and letters.

TO: James Miller

FROM: Ed Hoeppner

SUBJECT: Trip Evaluation/Report

DATE: October 1, 19— —

The Fire Prevention and Control Course that I attended September 20–24, 19— —, was very educational. Instructors James and Donner were very capable and equipped to provide basic knowledge about fire control and prevention.

Actual hands-on training cannot be overemphasized. I especially like the smoke-filled room exercise, although all phases of the training were well thought-out. I appreciated them also.

The school, as a whole, was very well presented and planned out, except for the delayed shipment. The handout material was well written and will serve as an excellent reference.

I appreciate the opportunity you gave me to attend a school of this nature and thank the company for offering such excellent opportunities.

Message B

TO: Wan Min Kim

FROM: Ann Krebs

SUBJECT: Attendance at an Internal Audit Course

DATE: March 22, 19— —

This course presented various techniques that are an essential part of effective supervision. The following topics were discussed:

1. The Supervisor's Role
2. Motivation
3. Fact Finding
4. Questioning and Listening Techniques
5. Communication Styles
6. Interpersonal Communication
7. Selling Your Message
8. Team Work
9. Delegation and On-the-Job Training
10. Time Management

Joe Sims was an excellent instructor. His presentation was very effective and included lecture, discussion, group exercises, and role plays for each topic.

In my opinion, this course was excellent and will benefit me in the future.

Insurance Office Management Association
150 Beverly Road, West Hartford, CT 06119

June 12, 19— —

Mr. David Hyche
Hyche and Associates
7186 South Cedar Street
Lansing, MI 48911

Dear Mr. Hyche:

At a district meeting of the Insurance Office Management Association, plans were made for the monthly meetings to be held during the coming year. The Association decided to devote one meeting to the problems of employment faced by insurance office managers. The value of vocational guidance is considered a point of interest.

I have been asked by the Directors of the Insurance Office Management Association to invite you to be a guest speaker at the monthly meeting on Thursday, February 13, 19— —. The meeting will be at 5:00 P.M., and dinner will be served afterwards. We hope it will be possible for you to speak at this meeting.

Please let us know if you would be available so we can plan an effective program for the coming year. I will contact you at a later date regarding further details of the meeting.

Sincerely,

Arthur Barrows

Arthur Barrows
Program Director

ALI, Incorporated
29000 Euclid Avenue, Cleveland, OH 44132

August 6, 19— —

Mr. Juan Mendoza
6010 Prospect Street
Cleveland, OH 44104

Dear Mr. Mendoza:

Welcome to ALI, Incorporated. Our employees feel a sense of pride in this company and in the high caliber of the employees now being hired.

Our employment supervisor, Ann Armond, will be glad to explain the company benefits such as insurance, sick pay, vacation, and holiday pay.

To enable you to become familiar with the scope of your duties and responsibilities, I will have one of your coworkers, Harold Franks, introduce you to the staff and outline what you will be doing.

Would you please contact my office to set up a meeting with Mr. Franks? I have the utmost confidence in your ability to do the work for which you have been selected and look forward to working with you.

Sincerely,

Jonathan Burns

Jonathan Burns
President

Exercise 3
Identifying Bottom-Line Principles and Writing Bottom-Line Beginnings

Reread the Bottom-Line Principles on page 72. Then read each of the following letters and memos and decide which of the Bottom-Line Principles have been violated in each letter or memo. After you have identified the appropriate principles, write new bottom-lined beginnings for each letter or memo.

Clark Consultants—for health and safety
11599 Wilshire Boulevard, Los Angeles, CA 90025

July 17, 19——

Mr. John Sparks
ALCO, Inc.
403 Hilgard Avenue
Los Angeles, CA 90024

Dear Mr. Sparks:

We have enjoyed being able to help you in your goal to reduce accidents and illness in your operation. Our consultant spoke very highly of your interest and attitude toward these goals, and we hope that our consultative inspection and the resultant recommendations have been instrumental in reducing your costs.

I would appreciate it if you would write me a letter. Do not refer to this correspondence but covering the following points:

1. Your opinion of the value of the consultative inspection.
2. A comment on the expertise and attitude of the consultant.
3. A comment on the approach used to reduce the chance for accidents and illness in the work place.

Again, it has been a pleasure to serve you. In addition to your letter, I would appreciate the names, addresses, and telephone numbers of any other business operations that you think could use our service. Thank you for your cooperation and the opportunity to serve you.

Sincerely,

Pete Benton

Pete Benton
Marketing Manager

Bottom-Line Principle(s) violated: # 1, 5, 7

TO: Fred Steinberger

FROM: Allyson Dean

SUBJECT: Special Services Training

DATE: March 14, 19— —

Joseph Stearn, Staff Manager, has asked me to respond to your letter of February 19, 19— —, concerning installation and repair of Special Services. This letter asked if ACME is providing training on either the 490-A or the 450-B multi-purpose test set.

This is to inform you that no training is being provided on either the 490-A or the 450-B multi-purpose test set in ACME. Also, we have been advised by our training organization in Stanton that installation and repair of Special Services training is no longer being offered due to lack of demand.

If you have any questions, or need further information, please let me know.

Bottom-Line Principle(s) violated: # _____3_____

LDS, Inc.
17532 Clayton Road, St. Louis, MO 63124

July 17, 19——

Ms. Susan France
Amstar Corporation
8154 Market Street, Suite 459
St. Louis, MO 63101

Dear Ms. France:

Over the past few days, we have made several changes regarding long-distance service affecting those extensions served off the present telephone system. A malfunction that allowed a number of calls to override automatically without the user's knowledge has been corrected. In addition, several extensions that were previously allowed override have had the feature removed. Those of you having the override feature have been notified concerning its correct usage.

Please advise your employees who have LDS (Long-Distance Saver) service but not the override feature of the following procedure for accessing long distance service. A list of your area telephones showing the features provided will be sent to you under separate cover within the next few days.

When you place a long distance call and all available LDS lines are busy, you will hear a fast busy signal. At this point you should activate the Ring Again feature to place you in queue for the appropriate LDS line. On an electronic set, press the Ring Again button; on a single line set, flash the switch hook and dial 31. The system will save your number and ring back when the LDS line is available.

Your cooperation in this matter is appreciated.

Sincerely,

Carl Martin

Carl Martin
Operations Assistant

Bottom-Line Principle(s) violated: # _____5_____

1,3,4

TO: All Employees

FROM: Julia Rossi

SUBJECT: Safety

DATE: February 2, 19——

Our objective in 19—— is to reduce our accident rate to zero, both here at work and when we are away from work. In order to do this, we want to raise everyone's awareness that safety is the number one priority so that, when we start every task or job, our first and foremost thought will be for the safety of ourselves, our fellow employees, our family members, and so on. In order to help accomplish this, we are increasing the number of visual safety reminders in our work areas and will provide additional safety literature.

Many of you have already participated in putting up safety labels on various pieces of equipment. Later this month, safety posters will be put up on the coffee room bulletin board. These posters will be changed at regular intervals. Enclosed with this memo is a booklet entitled Defensive Driving Tips. Other safety bulletins will follow.

Safety comes down to the individual, and all of us have to participate every minute of every day. Report anything that you think could be a safety hazard or lead to an unsafe condition. If you want safety information on any subject, please request it and we will provide it. Any suggestions for special topics for our safety meetings will be welcomed. Let us all join together and have a defect-free safety record for 19——.

Bottom-Line Principle(s) violated: # _1 3 4_

CASES

The following Allgood Products cases provide an opportunity for you to practice the bottom-line organizational skills you learned in this unit. Each of the three cases provides non-sensitive situations that can be bottom-lined.

Some of the cases have more than one assignment. Your instructor will choose which assignments to use, or he or she may modify, merge, delete, or change the assignments in ways to meet the needs of your particular class.

No matter what changes are made, however, one question should always guide your analysis of the case and your written answers to the assignments:

What is the message's bottom line?

This question serves as the guiding factor in all cases used in this text. In the following units, this question will serve as the first of many questions you can use as a guide in evaluating cases. However, no matter how many questions follow the bottom-line question, remember that the bottom-line question is always the most important. We, therefore, urge you to keep it in mind as you handle the cases assigned throughout this book.

Case 1
Time Management Analysis

Assume that you have been accepted into a management trainee program at Allgood Products, Inc. While you are still completing degree requirements at your college, you receive the following letter from James Holmay, a time management expert who works for Allgood Products, Inc.

Allgood Products, Inc.
1 Communications Circle, Kansas City, MO 64142

October 14, 19——

Mr. Robert Winters
12 Liberty Drive
Kansas City, MO 64111

Dear Management Trainee:

Congratulations on your appointment to a Management Trainee position at Allgood Products, Inc. You are coming to work for a fine company and should find the experience beneficial in a number of different ways.

I am writing to ask that you participate in a time-management study that we are currently conducting in the corporation. All current and future management personnel are being asked to keep a record of time spent on various activities during a three-day period. I realize that since you are a college student your daily activities will be far different than those of full-time Allgood employees; however, the results of the study will still be useful both for our purposes and for yours.

Here, specifically, is what I want you to do.

1. Create a chart for recording your daily activities—this chart should cover a full three-day time span in fifteen-minute increments.

2. Record on your chart your various activities during three typical days of your college life. This chart should include all activities, such as time spent in class and preparing for class; social, professional, civic, and athletic activities; work; and routine duties such as sleeping, eating, grooming.

When you have completed your chart, please make a copy and send it to us. Keep the original for follow-up questions.

Sincerely,

James Holmay

James Holmay
Time Management Expert

Pre-Assignment

Record your daily activities on a chart similar to that suggested in the case. Make sure your record covers a full three-day time span in fifteen-minute increments.

Assignment 1

You receive a call from James Holmay soon after you send your chart to him. He asks you to write a brief but complete report telling how you spend your time.

Write a bottom-lined response to Holmay.

Assignment 2

You receive a call from James Holmay. He asks you to evaluate and analyze how you spend your time. Specifically, he wants to know the following: (a) Do you use your time as efficiently as possible, and (b) Can you think of ways to use your time more effectively?

Write a bottom-lined response to Holmay.

Assignment 3

Holmay calls to ask you to develop three short-term and three long-term goals for yourself. A short-term goal, he says, is one you hope to accomplish within the next six months to a year. A long-term goal is one you hope to accomplish in the next one to five years.

He asks you to compare your goals with your analysis of how you spend your time (see Assignment 2). He now wants you to write him an evaluation of how effectively you are using your time to advance yourself toward your short- and long-term goals.

Write a bottom-lined evaluation to Holmay.

Case 2
Guidelines to Bottom-Lining
at Allgood Products

When you report to work at Allgood Products in the morning, Carl Hilton's secretary tells you to wait because Hilton, the President, and Maxwell Allgood, the CEO, want to meet with you. Five minutes later, Maxwell Allgood appears. "Come into Mr. Hilton's office with me," he says. "We've got a job for you."

Hilton is busy reading his way through a one-foot high pile of memos, reports, and letters. "I'll bet the guy who invented the word processor thought he was saving time for humanity," he grumbles.

"The greatest producer of waste in our country sits every day on your desk and mine," exclaims Allgood. "That computer, its disks, and its print-outs! They're all time wasters!" he shouts. "Of course," he goes on a bit more calmly, "it's not really the computer's fault. All it does is process information and order printers to type what others have written on it. The real problem is the people who use the computers."

"I agree completely," adds Hilton. "Most of the stuff I read is simply too long-winded to be believed. And new employees fresh from college are the worst," he growls, fixing you with a baleful stare.

"That's why we have decided to put you on this job," Allgood says. "We want somebody who understands what our new employees and management trainees know and don't know about corporate communication. We want you to go around and interview all our Vice Presidents. Collect everything you can about their likes and dislikes about written memos."

"All right, I'll do my best," you say. As you leave Carl Hilton's office, you are pleased and surprised that you could be called upon for such a task. And you are somewhat surprised that writing can play such an important part in a manager's job.

You hurry off to see Frank Finnegan, the Vice President of Production. You tell him about the assignment that Allgood and Hilton have given you.

Finnegan responds, "On this point, I'm with Hilton! I really feel exactly the way he does about people not getting to the point. There are too many people today who beat all around the darn bush and never say what they want. A communication is like one of the machines in a factory. If it just spins its wheels but doesn't produce anything but hot air, it just wastes everybody's time and money. I like people to come to the point, just the way Hilton does.

"There is another thing that bugs me," says Finnegan. "Too many people who write to me don't make clear what they want me to do. They bury whatever action they want in the middle of the third paragraph and make me look for it. If I'm in a hurry, I may not even recognize that I'm being asked to do something. The first thing people have got to remember when they are asking me to do something is to make it clear and make it simple. Just tell me what it is they expect me to know or do."

The next person on your list is Cyrus Fine, the Vice President of Marketing. He is delighted to meet with you. "Writing is extremely important in the business world," he says. "Here's something you may not know: there are only three types of people who *have* to write all the time. Fiction writers and reporters, that's one type. Advertising copy writers, that's two. And managers make three. The first two everybody recognizes. But most people don't know that managers are constantly writing letters and memos.

"Hey," says Fine, "what did Hilton and Finnegan tell you about reporting?"

You tell him briefly, keeping in mind what you've already learned about getting to the point.

Fine says, "Well, I certainly don't disagree with Hilton or Finnegan on the benefits of not wasting a reader's time. It's also a fact that 90 percent of the stuff you're going to write in a typical corporation isn't going to be particularly sensitive; it's not going to bother anybody. And with that 90 percent you certainly can—and ought to—come to the point and be direct.

"Of course, there are times when we have to send sensitive messages, and so we shouldn't lose sight of the fact that many people are really very sensitive and can get their feelings hurt very easily. In such cases, I'd rather waste a little time in a sensitive situation rather than bluntly get to the point and insult somebody. But I know what top management is upset about. Too many people reporting to them beat around the bush when a perfectly routine, non-sensitive message can be expressed in a direct straightforward way."

You thank Cyrus Fine for his help and head for your next appointment, which is with Mary Lou Higgins, the Vice President of Personnel. She says, "I'll be glad to talk with you. I really don't think of myself as a great writer, but you know I came up the way many women did in the old days, through the secretarial route. So I've had lots of experience, not only with my own writing but with typing and reading other people's memos. What did the others tell you about reporting?"

You tell her in reasonable detail.

"Well, I find it hard to disagree with anything they have said. Sounds like good advice to me. Let me see if I think they have forgotten anything. Well, yes; I guess it might be this. After having spent so many years as a subordinate, I guess I'm more sensitive to the problems a subordinate faces when reporting to a superior in a company.

"A man like Mr. Hilton may tell you that he wants a short report. But when you as a newcomer and a subordinate actually begin to write to him, you'll get nervous and be afraid *not* to write everything you know about the topic. The primary reason why overly long reports are written by subordinates stems from the fact that the writers are afraid to be succinct. I think that subordinates make a lot of incorrect assumptions when they have to write upwards in an organization.

"A lot of them think that the more important their reader is, the more thorough and detailed their report needs to be and that if they don't tell *everything* they know about the topic, their reader will be annoyed at having to request more information. So they go on and on giving details, and never make their point clearly.

"Others are timid and feel sure that their reader is not going to agree with them. Then they, too, bury the boss under a torrent of unfocused data. The less certain they are, the more they write, in order to sound convincing.

"Some other newcomers feel that this is their chance to show their superior just how thorough, conscientious, and hard working they are.

"In other words," Higgins continues, "based on what I've seen around this company over these past twenty-five years, the main reason for long reports is insecurity masquerading as thoroughness."

"That's very interesting, Ms. Higgins," you say. "But what can I do about it? I'm just as anxious as any other subordinate when I start writing reports that may be seen by top executives."

"Well, it's all right to be anxious," said Higgins, "but it's not all right to be stupid. So let me give you some good advice. Here's what subordinates should assume about the people they are writing to.

"Readers, especially if they are superiors, are extremely busy. You must not waste their time by making them read unnecessary or undigested detail, any more than you would waste their time chattering on in a face-to-face interview. You should make a judgment as to how much readers need to know in order to take the action required by their communication. And if you're in doubt as to whether specific information is necessary to your reader, you should either put that information in attachments or tell your reader that you stand ready to offer more information, if such is requested."

"You mean it's all right to put material in attachments or appendices?"

"It's not only all right, it's absolutely *necessary* in business. When you as a subordinate are anxious about how much detail your boss needs, you've got to hedge your bets by writing a direct statement in your first paragraph, putting any necessary supporting evidence next, and attaching any information that you are not sure the boss will need. Then, if the boss wants to read the attachment, he or she can. Or, the boss can quit after reading your brief memo and ignore the attachments."

"Yes, but, Ms. Higgins," you interject, "I think I'd be scared to write such a brief report to any of these top executives."

Mary Lou Higgins responds in a most forceful manner. "Let me tell you something. You are *not* writing a brief report. I never told you that. Too many people get the notion that coming to the point means someone has given them a license to be superficial and careless. I don't mean that at all. I mean organizing non-sensitive material in such a way that what is important to the reader is placed first.

"When I talk about using attachments, I mean that you should put in those attachments all the details that may or may not be important to your reader. If you fail to put those details into an appendix and it turns out that these details are important to your reader, you will receive just as bad a 'grade' on that report as you would if you were to simply put the answer to a mathematics question down on a test without showing how you arrived at that answer.

"Supporting detail is very, very important. But just because it is important doesn't mean that all the detail must come first, before you tell the boss just what it is you are talking about. In other words, in our mathematics-test analogy, you would say, 'The answer to the question is 22.4378. Here is how I arrived at this answer.' And then you give all the details. A poorly organized report would wade through all the details and then bury the 22.4378 somewhere in the middle of the fourth paragraph. That's what the other people you talked to are complaining about."

You thank Mary Lou Higgins and you go next to the last interview with Samuel Potnick, who is both Vice President of Finance and Controller.

Like the others, he asks for a brief summary of what the other Vice Presidents said. After you have told him, he says, "Well, there's not much left for me to add. Except, I do want to underscore how much I agree with what Ms. Higgins has said to you, that coming to the point is not a license to be superficial and careless. Especially in my line of work, where we are dealing with large sums of money that don't belong to us, but really to our shareholders, we have to make sure that everything we do is thoroughly documented.

"The kind of reports we write in Finance and Accounting are highly complex. It is of great benefit to the reader if writers learn to be clear in every section and sub-section of complex reports that they write.

"The people who write to me are usually logical people. The problem I have with new recruits is that they are used to putting the answer at the end, rather than at the beginning. I more or less tell them to go ahead and write the analytical report they are used to writing. But when they get to the end and are going to offer a specific conclusion—say, about which stocks we should buy and which we should sell—they should move that conclusion to the very beginning of their report. Then they can tell me the process of reasoning by which they arrived at that conclusion.

"I much prefer to read a report written this way, because they have told me what they are talking about and what they are recommending. Then, as I read their justification of their conclusions, I can determine whether I agree or not. If they put their conclusions at the end, I find myself reading pages of justification, but I have no idea *what* they are justifying!

"So, I think what all of them have said, and especially what Ms. Higgins has added, is very, very useful information. I know that I, for one, will look forward to reading what you put together, and I'll be happy to offer any constructive criticism I can."

You thank Samuel Potnick, and return to Carl Hilton's office.

Assignment 1

Write a bottom-lined memo to Hilton and Allgood that summarizes your findings. Assume that Hilton and Allgood have asked only for what you found—they do not want recommendations for improvement.

Assignment 2

Write a bottom-lined memo to Hilton and Allgood that summarizes your findings and makes recommendations for improvement.

Assignment 3

Hilton and Allgood were impressed by your findings and your recommendations. They now want you to write some guidelines for new employees and management trainees. These guidelines should capture and present your findings and include recommendations for ways Allgood can improve its memos and letters. Entitle your handout: "Guidelines for Effective Writing at Allgood Products, Inc."

These guidelines should

1. Provide specific advice for improving Allgood's messages.
2. Offer explanations about your source and/or authority for providing this advice.
3. Demonstrate a bottom-line organizational approach.

Case 3
Applying the Guidelines

Your manual entitled "Guidelines for Effective Writing at Allgood Products, Inc." has been in distribution for three months. (See Case 2, Assignment 3 for details about this manual.) Carl Hilton, the President of Allgood, calls you in and praises the work you did on the manual. He tells you he has heard many compliments about it from all levels of management.

"Unfortunately," Hilton goes on, "we still have not received all the benefits from the assignment that we had hoped for. Too many people are still not coming to the point in Allgood's memos and letters."

"I think we need to take one more step," Hilton notes. "We need to show managers and subordinates how to come to the point. Allgood employees need to see specific examples of what we are asking them to do. That's why I have asked you to come in today."

Assignment

Carl Hilton hands you Messages A–D that follow. He says they are typical of messages still being sent within or received by Allgood. Your assignment is to revise each message so that it is organized in a bottom-line fashion. After you complete your assignment, Hilton will send the messages to Allgood employees as examples for them to follow.

TO: Ralph Czaplewski

FROM: Arnold Watters

SUBJECT: Tasks

DATE: November 15, 19——

Next week I want you to visit with Lance Smithers, President of Smithers and Co., in Metro and see if you can revive his business. He was a regular customer until last May. Find out if something happened to displease him. Also, while you are in Metro, try to see Mr. Aames of ABC, Inc. Our company is running behind in its orders to Mr. Aames. Try to soothe him a little.

We are planning the regional sales convention for February 16. I'm sure you will enjoy attending this convention since it will be your first. If you want a reservation at the Harrison Hotel, don't forget to advise Ms. Amery so she can make your reservation.

Again, let me compliment you on the job you are doing. Please report to me on the matters I have mentioned.

TO: All Department Heads

FROM: Maintenance Services

SUBJECT: Underground Valves

DATE: July 17, 19——

As everyone by now knows, last month unauthorized persons closed the water valve at Hefflon Center and shut down water to several other administrative buildings that are also served by the main that feeds the Hefflon Center. This shut down all water services into these buildings—including bathrooms, boilers, water coolers, and cooling towers. Maintenance Services expended significant labor costs in locating and correcting the problems, including damage to air conditioning and plumbing systems, that resulted from this shut down. In addition, the City of Metropolis had to send a crew to the headquarters complex to locate the source of the shut down. Also, the interruptions to routine activities in these buildings and inconvenience to the occupants—combined with all the other problems—made this a very serious matter. There are several buildings in the headquarters complex where a similar shut down would cause irreversible and very costly damage to building equipment.

Operation of underground valves controlling water, natural gas, and steam is the responsibility of the Maintenance Department for Allgood-owned valves or the City of Metropolis for valves owned by the utility providers.

Any department at headquarters that needs to have a valve operated/opened/closed, etc., should call the Maintenance Department at 123-4567 for proper referral. Unauthorized operation is extremely dangerous and can also cause extensive property and equipment damage.

Message C

TO: All Employees

FROM: Amelia Bennett

SUBJECT: Retirement Benefits

DATE: August 3, 19— —

The current retirement plan has recently undergone some procedural changes. You will find an explanation of the amendments on pages 7 and 8 of the attached revised Employee Handbook. Examples are located in the back of the handbook.

For your convenience, a detailed explanation of the changes in the plan is also attached. Your attention should be directed to Section B on page 8 of the handbook, which refers to the provisions of the Survivor's Benefit. Please notice that your spouse must be your named beneficiary in order to receive this benefit.

To change the name of your survivor beneficiary, ask your supervisor for the appropriate form, fill it out, and return it to your supervisor. He or she will forward it to the proper department. Your beneficiary change will become effective when you return the filled-in form. This procedure can be used for all other benefit changes as well.

Message D

Boston Office Machines and Supplies
317 Oxford Street, Boston, MA 02140

July 12, 19——

Mr. Maxwell Allgood
Allgood Products, Inc.
1 Communications Circle
Kansas City, MO 64142

Dear Mr. Allgood:

For over sixty-five years we have established our reputation for product
quality and reliability under the name Courier Typewriters. We appreciate all our customers throughout the United States. Their support has
enabled us to grow. We will continue our efforts to warrant your
patronage.

Your business has helped us to progress and diversify our lines, so that
the name Courier Typewriters no longer fully describes what we manufacture and sell. We feel that our new name, Boston Office Machines and
Supplies, better describes our general operation without the limitations
of the old name.

We would be pleased to send you our new catalog that describes all of
our products.

Please adjust your records to reflect our new name.

Sincerely,

Al Courier

Al Courier
President

REFERENCES

Anderson, W. S. (1987). Process in business writing texts? *The Journal of Business Communication, 24*, 73–77.

Byrne, J. A. (1988). The best B-schools. *Business Week,* November 28, 76–80.

Columb, G. G., and Williams, J. M. (1985). Perceiving structure in professional prose: A multiply determined experience. In Odell, L. and Goswami, D. *Writing in nonacademic settings.* New York: The Guilford Press.

DeGise, R. F. (1980). A systems approach to business writing. IEEE *Transactions on Professional Communication, 23*, 77–78.

Dewey, J. (1933). *How we think.* Boston: Heath.

Fielden, J. S., and Dulek, R. D. (1984). How to use bottom-line writing in corporate communications. *Business Horizons, 27*, 24–30.

Housel, T. J., and Housel, M. (1986). The role of business communications practitioners in the computer age. *The Journal of Business Communication, 23*, 5–12.

Hulbert, J. E. (1980). Effective business writing. IEEE *Transactions on Professional Communication, PC-23*, 128–129.

Hunter, W. L. (1981). Eight steps to better communication. *Management World, 10*, 36–37.

International Data Corporation (1981). *Automated Business Communications: The Management Workstation.* Framingham, MA, 21.

Kent, J. L. (1982). Your business writing affects your success. IEEE *Transactions on Professional Communication, PC-25*, 220–221.

Kent, T. L. (1984). Paragraph production and the given—new—contract. *The Journal of Business Communication, 21*, 45–66.

Litterst, J. K., and Eyo, B. (1982). Gauging the effectiveness of formal communication programs: A search for the communication-productivity link. *The Journal of Business Communication, 19*, 15–26.

Locker, K. (1977). Patterns of organization for business writing. *The Journal of Business Communication, 14*, 35–45.

MacMillan, B. B. (1985). How to write to top management. *Business Marketing, 70*, 136–139.

Mitchell, R. E., Crawford, M. C., and Madden, R. B. (1985). An investigation of the impact of electronic communication systems on organizational communication patterns. *The Journal of Business Communication, 22*, 9–16.

Murphy, H. A. (1987). Process vs. product in freshman composition and business communication textbooks and in our teaching. *The Journal of Business Communication, 24*, 79–88.

Murray, M. H. (1975). If you have any questions, please do not hesitate to contact us. *Best's Review* (Prop/Casualty), *75*, 80–83.

Owens, E. L. (1987). Effective managerial communication skills increase productivity. *Data Management, 25*, 22–25.

Pinsker, S. (1986). Business and communicating: The case against chronology. *Business, 36,* 38–40.

Roundy, N., and Thralls, C. (1983). Modeling the communication context: A procedure for revision and evaluation in business writing. *The Journal of Business Communication, 20,* 27–46.

Rutkskie, A., and Murphree, C. (1982). *Effective writing for business: An analytical approach.* Columbus: Charles E. Merrill.

Sparrow, W., and Cunningham, D., eds. (1978). *The practical craft: Readings for business and technical writers.* Boston: Houghton Mifflin.

Sweetnam, S. (1986). How to organize your thoughts for better communication. *Personnel, 63,* 38–40.

Welter, T. R. (1987). Overwhelmed by info? *Industry Week, 235,* 30–32.

Unit 3

ORGANIZING NON-SENSITIVE LONG REPORTS

INTRA-TEXT MEMORANDUM

TO: Readers

FROM: Authors

SUBJECT: Unit 3

You have probably noticed that so far we have not distinguished between short and long reports. This omission has been intentional. No matter the length of a report, the principles of bottom-lining equally apply.

Chapter 6 will demonstrate to you how bottom-line principles can be applied to long reports. As shown in our diagram, this chapter also introduces you to two additional strategies, **contract sentences** or **statements** and **skeletal organization,** that are essential to the successful creation of clear, effective longer documents. (Details of report format and conventions are discussed in Special Features Chapter B-3.)

EFFECTIVE COMMUNICATION

ORGANIZATION		IMPACT		STYLE	
Bottom-Line	Circuitous	Word Choice	Visual Display	Forceful/Passive	Colorful/Colorless
	Semi-Circuitous		Sentence Structure		Personal/Impersonal

Contract Sentences   **Skeletal Organization**

Because long reports often contain significant amounts of supporting data that can best be expressed through graphs, charts, and tables, we thought it timely to deal with graphics in Chapter 7. Here you are introduced to the basic types of graphics available. You are also provided with guidelines about when and how to use each type of graphic. What you will learn about graphics in non-sensitive reports applies equally to graphics in sensitive reports.

Chapter 7 concludes by showing you how bottom-lining, contract sentences, skeletal organization, and graphics can work together to produce a tightly organized, highly efficient, and effective long report.

Chapter 6

USING BOTTOM-LINING, CONTRACT SENTENCES, AND SKELETAL ORGANIZATION IN LONG REPORTS

OBJECTIVES

This chapter will help you to

•

Make long, complex reports more easily understood

•

Understand the importance of bottom-lining and sub-bottom-lining in long reports

•

Use contract sentences when needed

•

Tie contract sentences to a report's skeletal organization

At some point in your career, your job may require you to write long, complex, analytical reports. Fortunately, the principles of bottom-lining apply equally to long as well as to short reports. If you understand how to apply the bottom-line principles to these reports, and if you are familiar with two related bottom-line techniques, **contract sentences** or **statements** and **skeletal organization,** you can organize long, complex reports in an efficient and effective manner that should prove beneficial to your career.

THE IMPORTANCE OF BOTTOM-LINING LONG REPORTS

Bottom-lining is even more important in long reports than in short memos, letters, or shorter reports. Many industries depend on long reports. For example, the main products of consulting companies are long reports that document detailed investigations of and solutions to problems faced by clients. The clients, of course, want the reports to be clear and easy to read. However, they also expect evidence of a lot of work for the fee they are charged. Hence, a long report evolves.

Long reports should be bottom-lined.

Accounting firms, also, are involved in offering clients written statements of professional opinions. These statements are often quite detailed and provide an interesting mix of numerical and verbal information. In marketing, sales proposals can be lengthy, depending on the situation and the product. These proposals can be more than a hundred pages long, with some of the material being written by the proposer and some of the material being boilerplate insertions. (*Boilerplate* refers to prewritten passages, usually stored in the computer, that can be inserted easily in the appropriate places in a report.)

Bottom-Lining a Sales Proposal

Let's see how bottom-line concepts apply to a long sales proposal. Suppose that you are employed as a marketing representative for a large computer company. You call on the key managers of ABC, Inc., a potential customer, in an attempt to persuade them to change over to your company's computer system. ABC, Inc. has a system, now outdated, that was installed by one of your competitors. Although the managers find the system less than ideally responsive to their needs, they are not totally displeased with it.

You do your best sales job, pointing out how your company's more modern system can perform more efficiently, effectively, and economically. As you leave, you are pleased that the key managers ask you to send them a formal sales proposal to consider.

Since ABC has asked you to present a sales proposal, there is no possible reason not to bottom-line it. But, suppose you forget for a moment that bottom-lining is not an excuse for being superficial. Therefore, you simply write:

> We recommend that you adopt our computer for your com-
> pany's use. We know we have the best computer, and after hav-
> ing studied your company carefully, we know that our system

is what your company needs. Please call us when you are ready for installation.

Of course, these three sentences would not get the job done. Confusing bottom-lining with superficiality can be dangerous. If the people reading your proposal had spent a great deal of their valuable time explaining their needs to you, your one-paragraph report would not make them feel that they had spent their time well. They would expect, instead, a detailed explanation of why they should adopt your system. They would expect—and rightfully so—a lengthy, in-depth sales proposal. And if that's what they expect, that's what you must give them.

But should your proposal be organized in the following way?

> On May 28, we visited your company's headquarters for the purpose of assessing your needs. We interviewed three of your management information specialists (John Brodus, Margaret Masterani, and David Chung) to obtain their perceptions of how your current computer system is responsive to your needs. Next, on May 29, we interviewed personnel at three levels—professional staff, middle management, and executive—to assess their perceived level of satisfaction with the current computer system.
>
> One week later, we did (this, that, and the other thing) ....
> ....
>
> Then, over the next month, we did (even more, etc.) ....
> ....
>
> (And so on) ....
> ....

How do you think the customer would react to the first non-bottom-lined paragraph? And how would the customer react to the writer's choice of a chronological organizational pattern that forces the reader to plow through a step-by-step history of the study that was conducted?

A wise marketing representative would bottom-line the opening of the proposal in this way:

> We recommend that your company adopt our ABC computer system for the following reasons:
>
> 1. Our system will solve the primary information problems hindering your management's decision-making capability. It will do the following:
>   a. ....
>   b. ....
>   c. ....
>
> 2. Savings of over $_____ will be made during each year of operation, thus offsetting the initial investment of $_____.
>
> In the detailed report that follows, we will thoroughly justify our reasons for this recommendation.

Bottom-lining is not a license to be superficial.

shallow
apparent rather than actual

Chronological organization is not effective in sales proposals.

This version bottom-lines the essence of the proposal, but it also leaves no doubt that all evidence gathered in support of the recommendation to adopt the ABC system will be made known to the reader.

Bottom-lining can be an effective sales tool.

Bottom-Lining in College Reports

Keep in mind always that you must not confuse bottom-lining with a license to be superficial. This advice is as true in college as in business.

Suppose your economics professor asks you to write a term paper about import quotas. The professor states that the report should be from six to eight typewritten pages. You go to the library, study diligently, and reach the conclusion that import quotas cause severe inflation within a nation's economy because domestic producers are free to sell domestic goods at prices higher than they would have been had cheaper foreign imports been allowed to compete. You write the following bottom-lined report:

> Import quotas should never be established. Such quotas artificially raise prices domestically and contribute significantly to a nation's inflationary spiral.

What kind of grade would this two-sentence report get? Even if your bottom-lined answer were absolutely correct, you would still receive an F, because you did not do the job as defined by the professor. For one thing, you did not follow the length requirements of six to eight pages prescribed by your professor. He or she wanted six to eight pages containing well-ordered facts. You were to analyze and support all conclusions thoroughly, while also applying the principles of bottom-lining. That is, you should have stated your conclusions at the beginning and then proceeded to justify them by presenting your research and analysis in the asked-for depth.

A bottom-line statement must be backed up by supporting information.

ORGANIZATION OF LONG REPORTS

Businesspeople in most jobs regard a long report as one that exceeds one or two pages. Longer reports had better have good reason for being so. If not, the writer will be told to stop wasting people's time.

However, some topics are so complex, and so involved, that it is impossible for even the best of writers to condense the information into one or two pages. The technique used by good business writers in such cases is to make the long report seem to the reader to be a series of short bottom-lined memos, easy to read and absorb. The way to achieve this goal is to use a **contract sentence** or **statement** and **skeletal organization.** Let us briefly explain what we mean by these strategies.

A long report should read like a series of brief bottom-lined memos.

Contract Sentences

The term **contract sentence** means a guiding statement that organizes, for both the reader and the writer, the direction a long document takes. For convenience, we use the term *contract sentence* even if some complex re-

Contract sentences
immediately follow the
bottom-line statement.

ports, as you will see, often require several sentences to convey the contract clearly and precisely to the reader. Contract sentences or statements are required only in long, complex documents. They usually follow immediately after the bottom-line sentence. Moreover, as you will see, in long documents they should also be placed at the beginning of important subsections.

The following paragraphs, typical of a sales proposal, contain a bottom-line statement (first paragraph) followed by a contract statement (second paragraph):

> This proposal recommends that you adopt the XYZ Mobilized Transfer System (MTS). MTS was developed to answer the needs of growing systems like yours for the distribution of data throughout a system.
>
> Let me explain in more detail the reasons in support of this recommendation. I will point out
>
> 1. The needs of your present environment, and
> 2. MTS's adaptability to that environment.

Contract sentences promise
future delivery of items
contracted for.

The reader is clearly led to expect the following discussion to deal with, first, the needs of the company's environment for MTS and, second, MTS's adaptability to that environment. That is the contract that the writer has made with the reader.

Here is another example of a bottom-line statement followed by a contract sentence:

> I recommend that we do not give our business to XYZ, Inc. There are three reasons for this negative recommendation:
>
> 1. Cost,
> 2. Quality, and
> 3. Service.
>
> Let me elaborate on each point.

Items contracted for must be
presented in the promised
sequence.

What should follow? The contract calls for a discussion of cost, quality, and service—in that order. Wouldn't all writers follow this sequence? Surprisingly, no! Many untrained writers will discuss service first, probably because service was the last item they thought of. Then they might discuss either cost or quality, or they might even forget to discuss either one of these factors.

Why do untrained writers do this? People tend to continue thinking about whatever is psychologically related to the last thought they have expressed. Therefore, for an untrained writer to continue to discuss service (or something related to service) immediately after writing "cost, quality, and service" is natural.

In a sense, then, the way we organize thoughts in writing is not natural; it is far more logical than our ordinary thought processes are. By forcing ourselves to follow the sequence announced in a contract sentence, we force ourselves to be logical and orderly. A good contract sentence organizes a document not only for the reader but for the writer as well.

For a final example of a contract sentence following a bottom-line statement, let's return to the sales proposal we began on page 97. We will add a contract sentence that will make clear to the reader the parts of the detailed, complex report being presented:

We recommend that your company adopt our ABC computer system for the following reasons:

1. Our system will solve the primary information problems hindering your management's decision-making capability. It will do the following:
   a. . . . .
   b. . . . .
   c. . . . .
2. Savings of over $_____ will be made during each year of operation, thus offsetting the initial investment of $_____.

In the detailed report that follows, we will thoroughly justify our reasons for this recommendation. Specifically this report will cover:

Part A. Problems occurring with the present system.

Part B. A needs assessment as reported by your managers and technical personnel.

Part C. A cost benefit analysis, assuming your purchase and installation of ABC equipment.

Part D. Full disclosure of costs, warranties, and other financial aspects of this proposal.

You should now be ready to organize your long reports following Bottom-Line Principle 7:

BOTTOM-LINE PRINCIPLE 7:
In long, complex, or analytical reports, begin by making a contract with your reader. Fulfill every clause of that contract in the same order as contracted.

Applying Bottom-Line Principle 7 to an Internal Sales Proposal

One common type of long internal report is written to seek additional funding from superiors. Such reports are essentially internal sales proposals. Since these reports are internal, superiors much prefer them to be bottom-lined. Compare the following two abbreviated versions of a long internal sales proposal and determine how the application of Bottom-Line Principle 7 would dramatically improve this complex report.

Original. No Contract Sentence or Skeletal Organization

TO: J. Lee

FROM: M. Watts

SUBJECT: Funding Allocations

DATE: September 28, 19— —

I should like at this time to request that corporate headquarters make an allocation to the Biloxi division in order that Biloxi may be able to handle local situations that, for the most part, are of an emergency nature.

All of the department's financial business is handled at our division office; we are allocated no funds for local situations in Biloxi. In order to respond to problems at the Biloxi facility, we need some local funds to ....
....
....

Internal Maintenance presently needs additional funds because of the recent flood. The flood shorted out our power station, and we are presently operating on temporary load borrowed from the city. Furthermore, ...

Version A. Includes Contract Sentence and
Derived Skeletal Organization

TO: J. Lee

FROM: M. Watts

SUBJECT: Funding Allocations

DATE: September, 28, 19— —

I am writing to request that corporate headquarters make an allocation to the Biloxi division in order that we may be able to handle local situations that, for the most part, are of an emergency nature.

Let me give you the background of our financial set-up and explain in some detail our present needs for additional funds.

A. Financial Set-Up

All of our department's financial business is handled at our division office; we are allocated no funds for local situations in Biloxi. In order to respond to problems at the Biloxi facility, we need some local funds to ....
....
....

Bottom-lining and contract sentences help make internal reports more persuasive.

B. <u>Additional Funds Needs</u>

Internal Maintenance presently needs additional funds because
of the recent flood. The flood shorted out our power station, and
we are presently operating on a temporary load borrowed from
the city. Furthermore, ...
....

Both versions of this internal sales proposal begin with a bottom-line sentence. But note in Version A how the contract sentence that immediately follows specifies what will be discussed. The underlined subheadings clarify and make obvious to the busy reader the report's skeletal organization.

Skeletal Organization

To define **skeletal organization,** let's take up an even more complicated report. (We will present just the skeletal organization of the report in order to show you how it derives from the items mentioned in the contract sentence.) The report begins with the bottom line, a series of recommendations to top management (not included here). The contract statement immediately follows:

These recommendations are based on a close analysis of
ACME's plant problems. This report discusses these problems
in two separate parts. The first part presents the results of my
investigation of the short-run problems in the plant: personnel
turnover and transportation deficiencies.

The second section deals with the results of an investigation
into the long-run problems of growth: expansion and new
products. In this section, I have implicitly accepted the idea
that we should first concentrate on solving our immediate
problems and, later, with an improved operating position,
worry about the longer term.

This necessarily lengthy contract statement has organized the report for both the reader and the writer. The skeletal framework of headings and subheadings deriving from this contract statement would be as follows:

Part I. SHORT-RUN PROBLEMS IN PLANT
   A. <u>Personnel turnover</u>
       ....
       ....
       ....
   B. <u>Transportation deficiencies</u>
       ....
       ....
       ....

Part II. LONG-RUN PROBLEMS OF GROWTH
   A. <u>Expansion</u>

      ....
      ....
      ....

   B. <u>New products</u>

      ....
      ....
      ....

The next Bottom-Line Principle summarizes these organization concepts:

BOTTOM-LINE PRINCIPLE 8:

In complex and/or lengthy reports, make your report's skeletal organization clear by

a. Using headings and subheadings to serve as guideposts for the reader.
b. Making sure that those headings and subheadings follow exactly the order of the items listed in the contract statement.

In the type of long, complex report we are discussing, another problem must be faced. A contract statement appearing on page one of, for example, a twenty-page report would be forgotten by the reader when he or she got to page ten. Therefore, we recommend the following:

BOTTOM-LINE PRINCIPLE 9:

In complex, multisection reports, write subcontract sentences for each subsection. The subcontract sentence does the following:

a. Bottom-lines what that subsection is about.
b. Makes a transition from previous subsections to the present subsection (if needed).
c. Specifies clearly the topics to be discussed in that particular subsection.

Thus, if a report is extremely complicated, not only should each of its subsections (e.g., I. A, I. B, I. C, II. A, and II. B) have a **sub-bottom-line statement** summarizing the information in that subsection, but any especially complex subsection should also have a new contract sentence. Let's take subsection I. B of our hypothetical report as an example. Notice how the writer presents a **subcontract sentence** to help the reader.

| Complex subsections of reports need subcontract sentences.

               I. B: <u>Transportation deficiencies</u>

Sub-bottom-line statement   Based on our study, we conclude that we must sharply reduce the problems our employees have getting to and from our satellite plant locations. Unless we do so, we can expect the unsatisfactory personnel turnover rate just described to increase. The

Subcontract sentence

basic aspects of the transportation problem discussed in this section are as follows:

1. Traffic problems associated with an 8 to 5 work schedulo.
2. Ever-escalating costs of gasoline and reliable vans and buses.
3. Unlikely prospects of future mass transportation being funded in plant areas.
4. Lack of success to date with employee carpooling.

Writers sometimes worry about whether such transitional contract sentences will seem labored and cumbersome to readers. The answer is no. Business readers won't think them cumbersome. They will like anything that helps them understand and follow the parts of a report written on a difficult and complex subject.

Readers like the organization of a long report to be simple and clear.

Subcontract sentences make your organizational pattern obvious. That is good. You should never force your reader to infer your organizational pattern. In fact, you should, in effect, lead your reader by the hand through the labyrinth of your analysis. [difficult to find one's way through] mace

The Highlighter Effect

Furthermore, the use of a bottom-line statement, a contract sentence, sub-bottom-line statements, subcontract sentences in subsections (as needed), and skeletal organization (headings and subheadings), all do more than just make it much easier for the reader to absorb your meaning. They serve to highlight the critical parts of a long report and make it possible for the reader to review quickly a complex document, perhaps even a week or more after the first reading. The reader does not have to use a marker to highlight important points of the report. The writer has, in effect, already done the highlighting. Now the reader can simply skip from the main bottom-line statement, to the bottom-line statements appearing in each subsection—right after each heading and subheading. Busy business-people like it if your reports show this built-in highlighter effect.

A built-in highlighter effect helps readers.

PUTTING IT ALL TOGETHER: AN INTERNAL SALES PROPOSAL

Let's examine a moderately long, complex internal sales proposal that is bottom-lined and that has an effective contract sentence. Notice how each subsection of this persuasive report is bottom-lined. Notice also how the skeletal framework guides your eye. If you had read this report and then were called away on a two-week business trip, you could easily, upon your return to the office, scan the first sentences of each section and recapture the gist of the report.

TO: Joseph Gaulesky, V.P. Personnel

FROM: Robin Baker, Plant Manager, River Division

SUBJECT: Additional Headcount Justification

DATE: June 18, 19——

General bottom-line statement

I am writing to request that River Division be permitted to add a Data Processing Supervisor to its staff. This addition is needed so that the division can continue to operate in the most efficient, effective manner possible. More specifically, this staff

Contract sentence

increase will enable us to handle the following five assignments we recently received:

1. To document and maintain existing plant systems.
2. To provide additional training to the computer operator.
3. To develop and test River Division's computer disaster plan.
4. To develop specialized reports from data provided by existing systems.
5. To support the implementation of new corporate systems.

The following will show how the Data Processing Supervisor would enable us to accomplish these five assignments.

Document and Maintain Existing Plant Systems

Skeletal organization begins with headings in the same sequence as contract sentence

Sub-bottom-line statement

The requested Data Processing Supervisor would alleviate current documentation problems. Specifically, River Division has many systems that were either not documented or for which the documentation has been lost. As a result, these systems have not been maintained. Many of the systems require manual adjustment to the output to make the reports useful. This manual manipulation decreases productivity and at month-end extends the time required to close the plant. The Data Processing Supervisor could meet with users to ensure that systems are working properly. This would drastically reduce the manual posting of computer reports and the time needed to close and would facilitate better analysis of data.

Provide Additional Training to the Computer Operator

Sub-bottom-line statement

If a Data Processing Supervisor were hired, he or she could provide training to our present Computer Operator. This would improve the efficiency of the Data Processing area and reduce down time. Presently, River Division has one non-exempt Computer Operator. She has no formal computer training. All of her knowledge has been gained through on-the-job training and trial and error. Although she has done an extremely good job, she could do even better with more training. She is presently supervised by the Cost Accountant. He has little or no computer knowledge.

Develop and Test River Division's Computer Disaster Plan

The addition of a Data Processing Supervisor would enable us to conform with the policy manual's specification that each division have a documented computer disaster plan. River Division does not have such a plan. This is partly due to a lack of knowledge of what is required. If the computer went down, the division could be in serious trouble. The Data Processing Supervisor would be knowledgeable about computers and would know what steps to take if a disaster were to occur.

Sub-bottom-line statement

Develop Specialized Reports from Data Provided by Existing Systems

The Data Processing Supervisor would write programs and specialized reports that would allow better use of the data already on the computer. These would include reports for Personnel, Planning, Operations, Engineering, Quality Control, and Finance. A lot of data on the mainframe cannot be used by the plant because we either cannot access them with the present programs or the programs do not present the data in a usable format. Specialized reports would provide management with more timely and better information. The reports would also reduce the amount of overtime required to provide this information.

Sub-bottom-line statement

Support the Implementation of New Corporate Systems

The Data Processing Supervisor would be extremely valuable during the installation phase of a whole series of new systems that Corporate is developing. He or she could ensure that the system was installed with minimal interruption of present plant systems and could also maintain these new systems. These new systems include Purchasing, Payables and Stores, MCIS, and the Maintenance Control System.

Sub-bottom-line statement

In conclusion, River Division definitely needs a Data Processing Supervisor if it is going to continue to operate in the most efficient and most effective manner possible. If you need any additional information, please contact me.

SUMMARY

Bottom-lining is as important in long reports as it is in short reports. A long, complex report should make its organizational pattern clear at the beginning. Each subsection should contain a **sub-bottom-line statement** of that subsection's purpose.

Contract sentences, statements that show the planned organizational pattern of the report, should be used at the beginning of a report to indicate the direction the total report is following. **Subcontract sentences**

should be used in highly complex subsections of the report. The contract sentence should make clear the **skeletal organization** of a long report. That skeletal organization should be obvious to the reader through headings and subheadings that follow exactly the order contracted for in the contract sentence.

REVIEW QUESTIONS

1. What two related techniques will help you organize long, complex reports efficiently and effectively? *Contract sentences + skeletal Organization.*

2. Name some of the jobs in business that require people to write long reports. *Marketing A/c Consultant*

3. With what is it dangerous to confuse bottom-lining? *Superficiality (shallowness)*

4. What is a contract sentence? *guiding state-directs doc + Specific points it will cover.*

5. When is a contract sentence required? *at b/l line or begin of ¶ subsects*

6. What do we force ourselves to do when we adhere to the sequence of factors announced in a contract sentence?

7. What is skeletal organization? *headings + sub that guide dev. of reports.*

8. What do subsections of complex, multisection reports need? *Subcontract Sentences.*

9. Explain the concept of the built-in highlighter effect. *highlight critical points it means reader can review quickly, saves time.*

DISCUSSION QUESTIONS

1. Why is the strict, logical order that we use in a report not the way we usually communicate—either when writing to friends or relatives or in casual conversation?

2. Does presenting a detailed contract statement, and then following (or fulfilling) it guarantee a coherent, logical organization of a report? Why or why not?

3. Examine some chapters of this book. Do they exhibit a built-in highlighter effect?

Chapter 7

USING GRAPHICS TO HELP PRESENT COMPLEX INFORMATION IN REPORTS

OBJECTIVES

This chapter will help you to

- Appreciate the ability of graphics to present complex data clearly

- Know which type of graphic best presents which type of data

- Understand the importance of honest presentation and interpretation of graphics

Graphics are a key way to present complex information clearly.

Computer software packages permit easy creation of graphics.

You need to choose the most effective type of graphic for your data.

Graphics are useful in the effective presentation of both non-sensitive and sensitive reports. Thanks to the advent of personal computers and the development of numerous software packages (often available even to the newest white-collar employees in a firm), you can produce high-quality graphs, charts, and tables from complex data with minimal effort.

Many computer graphics packages are available, each with its own distinct features. We have provided a description and examples of some in Photo Essay 2: Computer Graphics. However, before you can tell your computer how to present data graphically, you need to know the type of graphic that will best present your data. This is a decision the computer cannot make for you. This chapter will teach you about various types of graphics and the kind of data they most effectively communicate.

BOTTOM-LINING THROUGH GRAPHICS

Graphics are, in themselves, a form of bottom-lining. Properly used, graphics can often convey the bottom line of complex data far better than prose can.

Graphics Principle 1 presents advice about the three most frequently used types of graphs, or charts. Principle 1 also informs us about when it is appropriate to use each.

GRAPHICS PRINCIPLE 1:
Line, bar, and pie charts provide useful ways of summarizing complex data. Use them for the following purposes:

a. Line charts—to show trends.
b. Bar charts—to show comparisons among different sizes and different amounts.
c. Pie charts—to show comparisons among proportions or percentages.

Line Charts

Begin by considering the following listing of the closing prices of XYZ, Inc.'s stock over the past thirty days:

TABLE 7.1						
	6/1 37.2	6/6 38	6/11 39.5	6/16 41	6/21 44.5	6/26 47.5
	6/2 37.4	6/7 39	6/12 40	6/17 42	6/22 46	6/27 48
	6/3 37.2	6/8 39.5	6/13 41	6/18 42.5	6/23 46.5	6/28 50
	6/4 37	6/9 39	6/14 40.5	6/19 43	6/24 48	6/29 49.5
	6/5 37.5	6/10 39	6/15 40	6/20 45	6/25 47	6/30 50.5

This presentation does not lead to easy comprehension of the data. Suppose, instead, we display this information in the form of a **line chart** as in

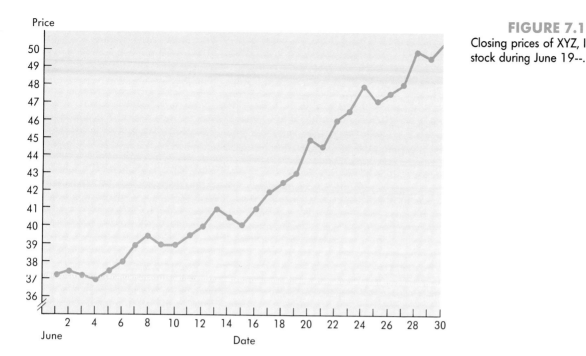

FIGURE 7.1
Closing prices of XYZ, Inc.'s
stock during June 19--.

Figure 7.1. If we do, the reader can clearly see the upward trend in the price of the stock.

Line charts show trends best.

Line charts can also be used to show multiple trends, such as in Figure 7.2, which compares XYZ's closing price with the closing price of ABC on the same days.

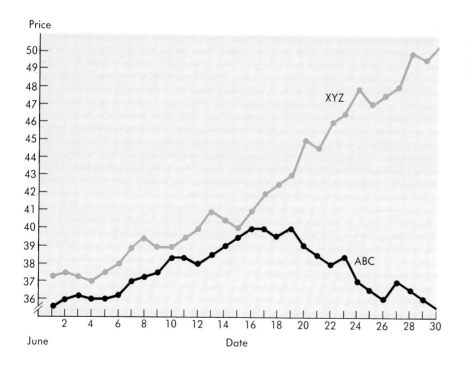

FIGURE 7.2
Comparative trends in stock
prices of XYZ, Inc. and ABC
Corp. for June 19--.

FIGURE 7.3
EXAMPLE OF AN OVERLY
COMPLEX GRAPHIC
Closing prices of XYZ, Inc.'s
stock during June 19--.

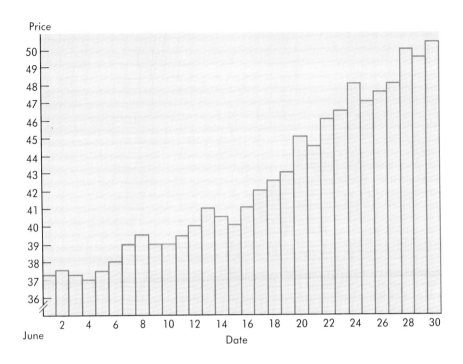

Bar Charts

Figure 7.3 takes the information about XYZ's closing stock prices presented in Figure 7.1 and presents it in a **bar chart.** It is still possible to note the upward trend of the stock in this bar chart, but the use of individual bars to present these data results in an overly complex picture. The line chart of Figure 7.1 presented the same data in a much more visually understandable way.

Pie Charts

Neither bar charts nor pie charts clearly communicate information with many data points.

A **pie chart** shows comparisons among proportions or percentages of a whole. Therefore, the information about XYZ's closing prices *cannot* be presented in the form of a pie chart. Also, a pie chart should not be used to present numerous points of data.

Figure 7.4 is an effective pie chart. Pie charts are best used when the percentages to be shown are so different from each other that the reader does not need to use calipers to measure the size of different slices or wedges. The pie chart shown in Figure 7.4 clearly shows that institutions and individual stockholders are the largest holders of XYZ, Inc. stock, and that more stock is held by internal personnel than by banks. However, you cannot tell exactly what the percentage held by each is. As you will see later, labeling each pie slice with its percentage will make the chart much more meaningful.

Pie charts best present percentages that differ significantly from each other.

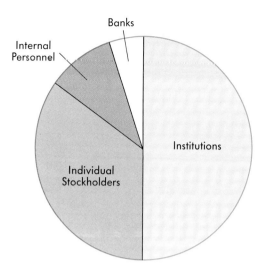

FIGURE 7.4
Major holders of XYZ, Inc.
stock.

Comparison of Line, Bar, and Pie Charts

Now let's suppose we had presented the data about the holders of XYZ stock as a line or a bar chart. Figure 7.5 shows that a bar chart could have worked as well as did the pie chart in presenting this information.

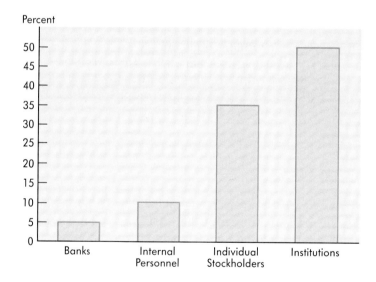

FIGURE 7.5
Major holders of XYZ, Inc.
stock.

Figure 7.6, by contrast, shows that an attempt to portray the same information in a line chart would misrepresent the data by suggesting a trend where it does not, and could not, logically exist. A line chart should be used only when *both* sets of information are numerical and/or sequential. In Figure 7.6, the types of major holders of XYZ, Inc. stock are neither numerical nor sequential. Hence, the line chart in Figure 7.6 is inappropriate.

Line charts require both sets of data to be numerical or sequential.

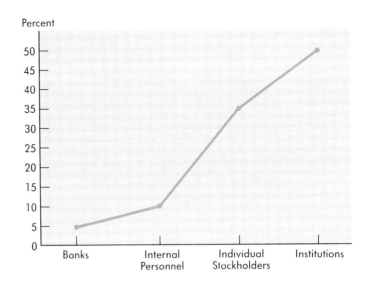

FIGURE 7.6
IMPROPER USE OF A LINE CHART
Major holders of XYZ, Inc. stock.

USING GRAPHICS EFFECTIVELY

Once you are familiar with the types of graphs available, you need to consider how to use them most effectively to clarify and simplify complex quantitative data. Graphics Principle 2 provides practical advice:

GRAPHICS PRINCIPLE 2:
Graphics should be used only if they help readers understand information more easily. When using graphics, remember that

a. Graphics should never be used to distort information or to mislead a reader.
b. Graphics should be introduced and interpreted for the reader.

Let's briefly examine the significance of Graphics Principle 2.

Never Use Graphics to Mislead

Most graphics that mislead readers probably do so by accident, not by intention. Often, the developer of the graphic is so familiar with the information and knows so well the material to be communicated, that he or she simply assumes the graphic's message is readily apparent to all readers. In many instances, this assumption proves to be invalid.

Suppose, in a report to top management, the members of Acme Chemicals, Inc., Research Department request that funding for basic chemical research be sharply increased. To support their argument, they include the following graph (Figure 7.7) to show how research funding as a percentage of total sales revenue has dwindled over the past ten years.

What is wrong with Figure 7.7? The size of the laboratory flasks is meant to convey the percentage of total sales revenue spent on basic research. However, the point being made is dramatically biased by the size of the flasks. As a result, the 13 percent funding of 1980 looks to be at

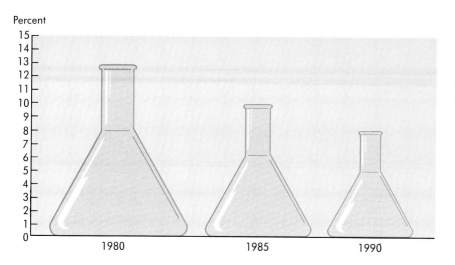

FIGURE 7.7
EXAMPLE OF A
MISLEADING GRAPHIC
Research funding as a
percentage of ACME's total
sales revenue.

least three to four times larger than the funding of 1990. Actually, of course, the difference is a fall of five percentage points, from 13 percent to 8 percent, as is shown more fairly by Figure 7.8.

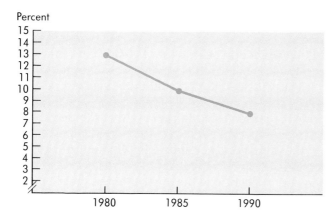

FIGURE 7.8
Research funding as a
percentage of ACME's total
sales revenue.

Accuracy in graphic presentation demands that you use a simple graphic form that conveys as accurately as possible both the content and the spirit of the data you are presenting. All that you should add to the graphic is information the readers need in order to appreciate fully what they see.

Introduce and Interpret Graphics

Readers are disturbed when they unexpectedly encounter a graphic that has not previously been introduced. Such insertions merely interrupt the flow of the text and often sidetrack the reader into wasted minutes spent puzzling over an out-of-context visual.

However, you must make sure that introductions to graphics do not mislead the reader. Here is a particularly interesting example of how a verbal lead-in, combined with a visual, can sharply influence a viewer's perspective of the graph shown in Figure 7.9.

FIGURE 7.9
My college should require all
undergraduates to take more
courses in:

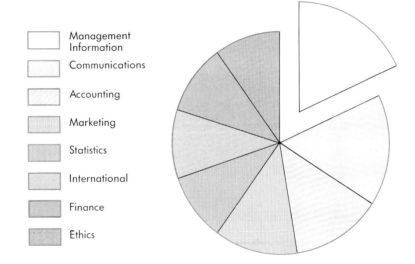

(*Source:* Adapted from Howard Wainer and David Thissen, "Plotting in the Modern World:
Statistics Packages and Good Graphics," *Chance*, 1:10–20, 1988.)

*Don't trick the reader with
your graphics.*

Assume that business school students in response to a survey were
asked which subject they wished their business school had required them
to take more courses in. Look at Figure 7.9. What are we led to believe by
the pie chart? We are led to believe that Management Information was by
far the most popular choice in the survey. However, if you look carefully
at Figure 7.9, you will see that the only thing you can be absolutely sure
about is that the section lifted out—an interesting visual trick—is the subject most students chose. You will also see that the demand for management information courses may not be so overwhelming as the chart implies. In fact, the demand may not be very different from the demand for
several other courses. Readers would have to use calipers to measure the
pie slices in order to determine the answer to the question in the survey.

FIGURE 7.10
My college should require all
undergraduates to take more
courses in:

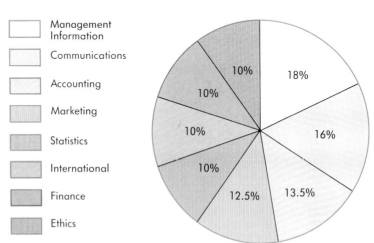

(*Source:* Adapted from Howard Wainer and David Thissen, "Plotting in the Modern World:
Statistics Packages and Good Graphics," *Chance*, 1:10–20, 1988.)

Furthermore, because of the similarity in size of the other sections, readers may not see any significant difference in the demand for the other subjects included in the chart.

To make the chart communicate more clearly, the writer could insert the percentages inside or beside each pie slice. The percentages would answer most, if not all, of the questions raised by Figure 7.9. Figure 7.10 shows how this visual would then appear.

USE OF TABLES

Not all information lends itself to being presented in a chart or graph. In such cases, writers need to present their information in tabular form.

Tables, like graphs, present numerical information in a compact, readable form. Graphics Principle 3 offers useful advice on the use of tables.

GRAPHICS PRINCIPLE 3:
Tables should be used when data contain so many points of information that a chart or graph of the data would be unreadable, confusing, or unwieldy in size.

A graph can be made from *any* table, but the resultant graph may be too complex. For example, information about the gross national product (GNP) of the fifty states in a given year could not be clearly presented in a bar chart with fifty bars nor in a pie chart with fifty slices.

Take as a further example the difficulties of presenting in a visual display the data gathered in the following research project. A study was made of the importance of different kinds of communication skills needed by three groups of accountants: corporate accountants, public accountants, and academic professors of accounting (Juchau and Galvin, 17–32). Each group was asked to rate the importance of the following list of skills from 1 (= least important) to 5 (= most important). Table 7.2 shows their average responses. You can readily see how impossible it would have been to present these data in any form other than a table.

Tables should be used whenever the amount of data would make charts too confusing.

Guidelines for Clear Table Presentation

Keep in mind the following guidelines for clear table presentation:

1. Introduce each table in your text and clearly explain the source and meaning of the numbers.
2. Give every row and column in the table a clear label.
3. Arrange the data in the rows and columns of the table to reflect the point you are trying to make about the numbers presented. (For example, in Table 7.2, the column on academic accountants clearly presents the writer's point about how this group of accountants ranked the various communication skills.)
4. Make sure your reader knows what the units of measurement are. You can describe them in the text, in the title of the table, in labels on the table, or in footnotes to the table.

Tables must be clearly introduced and labeled. Measurement units must be explicit.

TABLE 7.2

Perceptions of Importance of Various Communications Skills by Three Groups of Accountants

Communication Skill	Corporate	Public	Academic
Informal Oral Presentation	4.23	4.47	4.58
Clarity	4.42	4.54	4.58
Reading Comprehension	4.66	4.63	4.58
Outline Development	4.27	4.21	4.54
Coherence	4.44	4.58	4.50
Listening Attentiveness	4.59	4.55	4.44
Memos and Report Writing	4.60	4.50	4.44
Correct Spelling	4.40	4.50	4.41
Listening Responsiveness	4.39	4.51	4.36
Conciseness	4.48	4.42	4.35
Formal Report Writing	4.47	4.16	4.35
Correct Grammar	4.34	4.48	4.32
Correct Punctuation	4.19	4.25	4.32
Correspondence Writing	4.45	4.53	4.30
Inductive Reasoning	4.27	4.21	4.29
Deductive Reasoning	4.31	4.19	4.26
Formal Oral Presentation	3.87	3.69	4.05
Paragraph Development	3.95	4.16	4.00
Reading Speed	3.70	3.62	3.58
Use of Visual Aids	3.52	3.25	3.52

Adapted from R. Juchau and M. Galvin, "Communication Skills of Accountants in Australia," *Accounting and Finance*, 24(1), 1984.

PUTTING IT ALL TOGETHER:
A COMPLEX, ANALYTICAL REPORT

Let's show how what you have learned about bottom-lining, contract sentences, skeletal organization, and graphics can be used in a non-sensitive, complex analytical report. The report will be based on the following case, a realistic situation that businesspeople face frequently.

Sample Case: Productivity Opinion Survey

You are the assistant to Mary Lou Higgins, Vice President of Personnel of Allgood Products, Inc. She has asked you to analyze a recent Headquarters Opinion Survey that was given to all head office personnel.

Participants in the survey were asked to list things that wasted their time and reduced their productivity. Employees from a number of different levels answered the survey. You have literally hundreds of written comments to categorize, analyze, and evaluate. Attachment

A contains a small sample of typical comments made by principals (P),[1] executive secretaries (ES), secretaries (S), and Word Processing Center staff (WPC). Attachment B contains a tabulation of responses each group made to two questions on the 1990 Opinion Survey. Attachment C contains a tabulation of the responses principals have given to a survey question each year for five years.

Mary Lou Higgins tells you that she wants you to prepare a report for her signature summarizing the survey's findings for executive management. She tells you to do simple frequency distributions of the complaints of each level of employee shown in Attachment A, and to present the results in graphic form. Then she wants you to take the hard-to-grasp tables shown in Attachments B and C and present them in graphic forms more readily understandable to executives. Higgins tells you also to find a time and place for the management team to consider your report.

Fortunately for you, your message, although complicated, is nonsensitive. Consequently, you should bottom-line your report and present your analysis in as clear and as efficient a manner as possible.

ATTACHMENT A
SAMPLE OF TYPICAL CONCERNS ABOUT CAUSES OF
WASTED TIME AND LOWERED PRODUCTIVITY[2]

Unreasonable demands on turnaround time. There seems to be a great deal of procrastination and poor planning. This seems to be the norm rather than the exception. (WPC)

Duplication of work—two people doing basically the same thing. (P)

Copiers—too far away. Too many machine breakdowns. Bad enough I have to waste my time making copies. (P)

Poor planning leading to schedule conflicts. (S)

Too many unnecessary revisions. Principals must learn to collect thoughts first time around. Careful rereading by them of their rough drafts would help. (WPC)

Constant making and breaking of meetings. (ES)

Unnecessary, rude interruptions. I have an In-Basket. I don't need to be told every time something is put there. I will get to it—quicker without interruptions! (ES)

Copier has too many breakdowns. (S)

---

[1]The term **principal** is used in office-management research to refer to managers, staff professionals, and staff assistants.

[2]Note that the full list of complaints ran on for over twenty pages. Because of space limitations, only this brief sample is presented. It, at least, captures the flavor of all the complaints registered. Also note that the sample report that follows is based on *all* the complaints.

Unrealistic deadlines. (WPC)

Turnaround time too long for typing from WPC. Lose my chain of thought. (P)

No organization. (ES)

Lack of communication—I need to be told <u>exactly</u> what is expected of me by my principals. I don't want to find out at appraisal time that I am not doing something they want. Principals should spend a few minutes each day with their secretaries to discuss priorities, calendars, etc. It would help!! (ES)

Poor planning. (ES)

Last minute projects. (WPC)

Time spent making telephone calls for others. Lazy staff/managers; they can't make an outside telephone call without secretarial help. (S)

Too many revisions and unrealistic time to do work. (WPC)

Too much time spent on answering phones. (WPC)

Everyone wants their work done first, and you seem not to get anything done. (WPC)

ATTACHMENT B
TABULATION OF RESPONSES TO TWO
1990 OPINION SURVEY QUESTIONS

1. One of the questions asked on the 1990 Opinion Survey was: "To what extent is your productivity lowered unnecessarily?"

    1 = No extent   4 = Considerable extent
    2 = Little extent   5 = Very great extent
    3 = Some extent

Results:

	1	2	3	4	5
Principals	5%	15%	40%	25%	15%
Executive Secretaries	10%	20%	40%	20%	10%
Secretaries	0%	0%	20%	40%	40%
Word Processing Center Staff	0%	0%	10%	40%	50%

2. Another Opinion Survey question was: "If conditions were right, how much would you say you could increase your productivity?"

    1 = Not at all   4 = 16–25%
    2 = 1–5%   5 = 26–50%
    3 = 6–15%   6 = More than 50%

Results:

	1	2	3	4	5	6
Principals	5%	20%	30%	20%	15%	10%
Executive Secretaries	10%	25%	25%	20%	10%	10%
Secretaries	0%	0%	20%	40%	30%	10%
Word Processing Center Staff	0%	0%	0%	30%	40%	30%

ATTACHMENT C

TABULATION OF PRINCIPALS' RESPONSES TO AN OPINION
SURVEY QUESTION OVER FIVE YEARS

For each of the past five years, principals were asked the question, "If conditions were right, how much would you say you could increase your productivity?" Here is a summary of principals' responses over that period, rounded to the nearest 5 percent:

1 = Not at all	4 = 16–25%
2 = 1–5%	5 = 26–50%
3 = 6–15%	6 = More than 50%

	1	2	3	4	5	6
1986	25%	40%	25%	10%	0%	0%
1987	20%	30%	25%	15%	10%	0%
1988	15%	25%	35%	15%	10%	0%
1989	10%	20%	35%	20%	15%	0%
1990	5%	20%	30%	20%	15%	10%

Sample Report Using Graphics

The report that follows resembles the report you might write to top management in this case. We have interspersed comments on how organization of the report and the graphics contribute to the creation of an effective report to top management. (Remember, the frequency distributions shown in this report are based on the full twenty-page list of complaints expressed by all levels of employees.)

TO: Executive Management, Allgood Products, Inc.

FROM: Mary Lou Higgins, Vice President of Personnel

SUBJECT: Analysis of Annual Headquarters Opinion Survey

DATE: May 3, 19— —

We have completed the analysis you requested of the 1990 Headquarters Opinion Survey. Results of the survey indicate the following:

1. Wasted time has many different causes, varying with job level. A frequency distribution of concerns voiced by partici-

pants in the survey showed they thought the following areas were the major causes of lost time:

Principals
—Lack of communication
—Copier breakdowns

Executive Secretaries
—Poor planning
—Lack of communication

Secretaries
—Poor planning
—Copier breakdowns
—Phone calls

Word Processing Center Personnel
—Unrealistic deadlines
—Needless interruptions

2. All groups apparently agree that there are (a) unnecessary impediments to productivity and, hence, (b) many opportunities to improve office productivity.

3. Over the past five years, principals have tended to see an increased need for taking steps to improve productivity.

COMMENTARY

Notice that the report begins with a series of bottom-line statements that reveal (a) the purpose and (b) the major findings of the report. _____

I have reserved Conference Room A in the 2700 Building for all day on Tuesday, May 25, so that we can discuss these data, draw conclusions, and make action plans.

A detailed description of the results, including graphic illustrations of the findings, follows. The material is presented in three separate sections:

- Part I identifies causes of wasted time as reported by each group participating in the Opinion Survey.
- Part II examines participants' opinions on opportunities to improve office productivity.
- Part III discusses principals increasing awareness of the need for improved office productivity over the past five years.

COMMENTARY

Notice the detailed contract statement. Notice also how each item in the contract sentence is repeated as a major heading in the body of the report. _____

Part I. <u>Causes of Wasted Time</u>

Each group surveyed identified different causes of wasted time.

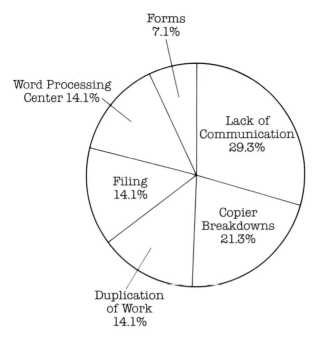

FIGURE 1

Principals' concerns (expressed as percentages of all complaints by that employee group).

Principals

Figure 1 shows that the area of greatest concern to principals is "Lack of communication" (29.3 percent). This concern is expected, given the pressures of daily business life. What is <u>not</u> expected is the percentage of concerns dealing with such matters as copying difficulties (21.3 percent), filing (14.1 percent), and forms (7.1 percent).

COMMENTARY

The pie chart used in Figure 1 proves to be a simple and clear way to show proportions. Notice that Figure 1 contains numbers showing the percentage of complaints that principals made about each of the various categories. These percentages save readers from the impossible task of determining visually whether complaints about the word processing center, filing, and duplication of work are identical or whether there are minute differences among them. Notice also that all relevant percentage numbers are also listed in the text and that unexpected concerns are pointed out.

Executive Secretaries

As Figure 2 shows, 36 percent of the concerns voiced by executive secretaries dealt with poor planning, especially in the

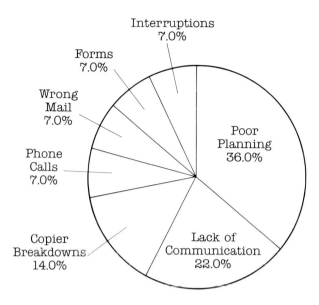

FIGURE 2

Executive secretaries' concerns (expressed as percentages of all complaints by that employee group).

scheduling of meetings and conferences. Executive secretaries also pointed out lack of communication concerning assignments given them. Executive secretaries would like the principals to tell them exactly what is expected of them and to give them information adequate for the completion of particular tasks.

Executive secretaries, like other employee groups, joined in expressing concern over the availability and reliability of copying equipment.

COMMENTARY

Figure 2 is actually rather simple to understand because indicating percentages on the chart again eliminates the problem of trying to show minute differences between and among similar pie slices.

Clear visual differences exist among "poor planning" (36 percent), "lack of communication" (22 percent), and "copier breakdowns" (14 percent). The pie chart makes these differences just about as clear as a bar chart would.

Secretaries

Figure 3 shows secretaries also believe their productivity is impeded by poor planning (28.7 percent), copying problems (18.8 percent), and shortcomings of our phone system (18.8 percent).

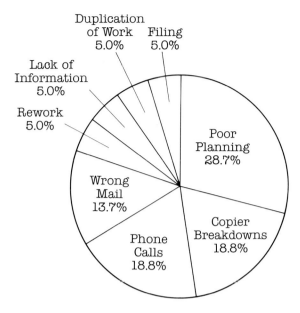

FIGURE 3

Secretaries' concerns (expressed as percentages of all complaints by that employee group).

COMMENTARY

Once again, labeling the percentages of each category of complaint makes clear the <u>differences that are not readily visible</u>.

Word Processing Center (WPC) Personnel

Figure 4 shows the problems perceived by word processing center personnel. It is important to recognize that these problems have a two-fold interpretation, one that relates to word processing personnel and one that relates to higher-level personnel.

From the perspective of the word processing personnel, it is interesting to note that 31 percent of their complaints deal with interruptions. Such interruptions undoubtedly make jobs in the word processing center frustrating and difficult to perform.

From the persepctive of higher-level Allgood Products personnel, two complaints expressed by word processing center personnel indicate a lack of communication and mutual understanding. Specifically, 46 percent of WPC personnel object to unrealistic deadlines set by principals. And 23% complain about "rework," that is, principals' revision of their work. These figures may show a lack of understanding on the part of WPC personnel about the difficulties principals have in writing analytical documents and the necessity of revising such documents several times. These figures also probably indicate that principals are not receiving typing back from the WPC as fast

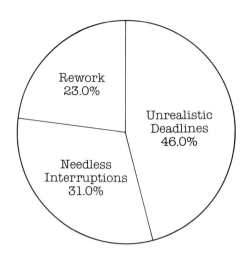

FIGURE 4

Word processing center personnel's concerns (expressed as percentages of all complaints by that employee group).

as they would like. This may be caused by understaffing of the WPC.

COMMENTARY

Figure 4 is a good example of a pie chart that the reader can readily understand. There are obvious differences in the sizes of the slices of the pie attributed to "unrealistic deadlines," "interruptions," and "rework." Including the percentages in this figure might not even have been necessary, although they certainly are helpful in presenting the evidence with greater completeness and accuracy.

Notice also that the lead-in to this chart cues the reader about inferences drawn from the data: how the concerns of word processing center personnel may point to a possibly greater issue, that of adequately meeting the needs of higher-paid principals.

Part II. <u>Opportunities to Improve Office Productivity</u>

In addition to collecting information about areas of concern affecting headquarters productivity, the Headquarters Opinion Survey gathered information about the benefits possible from addressing and correcting these concerns. Overall, the survey participants believe that many opportunities exist to make significant enhancements in office productivity.

<u>Possible Productivity Improvements</u>

The strongest evidence that opportunities to improve productivity exist is contained in the responses given to two questions:

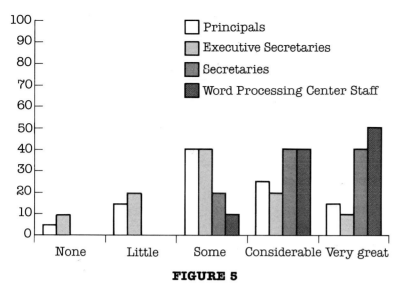

FIGURE 5
Extent of productivity interference.

1. "To what extent is your productivity lowered unnecessarily?"
   Respondents were asked to express their opinions ranging
   from (1) No extent to (5) Very great extent. As shown in
   Figure 5:
   —40 percent of the principals indicated at least a "considerable extent" (25 percent "considerable extent" + 15 percent "very great extent"), while 80% indicated at least
   "some extent."
   —30 percent of the executive secretaries indicated at least a
   "considerable extent," while 70 percent indicated at least
   "some extent."
   —80 percent of the secretaries and 90 percent of the WPC
   staff indicated at least a "considerable extent."

   COMMENTARY

   **Figure 5 uses a simple bar chart. This visual makes it easy
   to compare the responses given by the four categories of
   employees.**

   ———————

2. "If conditions were right, how much would you say you
   could increase your productivity?"
   Here respondents were asked to express their opinions in
   the following categories: (1) Not at all; (2) 1–5 percent;
   (3) 6–15 percent; (4) 16–25 percent; (5) 26–50 percent;
   (6) More than 50 percent. As Figure 6 shows:
   —45 percent of the principals indicated at least a 16–25
   percent increase in productivity, while 75 percent indicated at least a 6–15 percent increase.
   —40 percent of the executive secretaries indicated at least a
   16–25 percent increase, while 65 percent indicated at
   least a 6–15 percent increase.

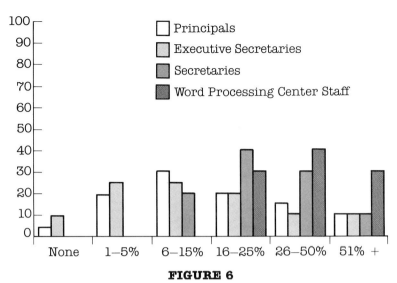

FIGURE 6

Increase productivity with improved conditions.

—80 percent of secretaries and 100 percent of the WPC staff indicated at least a 16–25 percent increase in productivity was possible.

COMMENTARY

Figure 6 uses a bar chart <u>for the same reasons that Figure 5 did</u>.

Part III. <u>Principals' Increasing Awareness of the Need for Improved Productivity</u>

The following question has been asked of principals for each of the past five years: "If conditions were right, how much would you say you could increase your productivity?" A comparison of principals' responses to this question shows that our highest salaried personnel have increasingly believed that if conditions were right, their productivity could be increased.

Figure 7 shows the trend in the average responses[3] given by principals over this five-year period. These averages are based on a 1–6 scale, with each number representing the previously mentioned category:

[3]To find the average scaled response per year, multiply each rating by the percentage of people who chose it, add the products, and divide by 100.

Example: 1986

$$
\begin{array}{rcl}
1 \times 25 &=& 25 \\
2 \times 40 &=& 80 \\
3 \times 25 &=& 75 \\
4 \times 10 &=& 40 \\
5 \times 0 &=& 0 \\
6 \times 0 &=& \underline{0} \\
& & 220 \div 100 = 2.2
\end{array}
$$

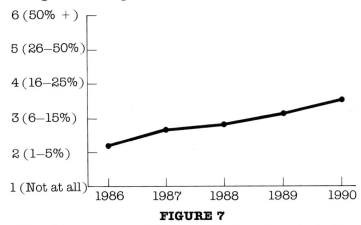

FIGURE 7

Trend in average scaled responses given by principals over the past five years.

1. Not at all
2. 1–5 percent
3. 6–15 percent
4. 16–25 percent
5. 26–50 percent
6. More than 50 percent

Notice that there is a steady increase over time from 2.2 to 3.5. At first glance this trend may not seem too dramatic; however, a more careful look shows that principals' perception of the productivity improvements possible has steadily risen from the 1–5 percent category to the 6–15 percent category.

COMMENTARY

Figure 7 uses a simple line chart because that type of chart best describes changes in principals' opinions over the five-year period.

Figure 8 compares the scores of principals in 1986 to those in 1990. It can be clearly seen how the opinions of principals have moved markedly toward the feeling that productivity could be dramatically improved if conditions were improved. It is also worthy of note in Figure 8 that the number of principals who believe their productivity could be improved more than 25 percent has jumped from 0 percent to 25 percent in the last five years. Even more worthy of concern is the fact that 10 percent of principals in 1990 believe their productivity could be raised more than 50 percent if conditions were right.

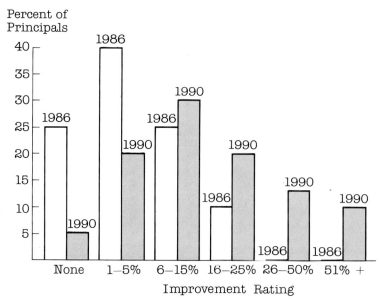

FIGURE 8

Five-year comparison of principals' opinions about possibility of productivity improvements.

COMMENTARY

Figure 8 uses bars to show a comparison between principals' responses in the year 1986 and the year 1990. It would be inefficient to communicate this information in numerical form since the bar chart clearly makes the point that principals seem to think more and more that changes in conditions could serve to increase their productivity.

Data from the analysis are available. In case anyone should want to see individual responses, I will bring them to the May 25 meeting.

SUMMARY

Graphics have always played an important role in conveying complex information visually. Today, software packages enable you to produce sophisticated graphics with relative ease.

Line charts are best for showing trends, **bar charts** for comparisons among different sizes and amounts, and **pie charts** for comparisons among proportions or percentages. When data are too complex or too great in amount, they are best presented in **table form**.

Graphics should not be used to mislead. And although graphics should be introduced in the text of a document, their introduction should not be used to bias the way a reader will interpret a graphic. Finally, all graphs presented in a document should be honestly interpreted in the text.

REVIEW QUESTIONS

1. When should you use graphics instead of or in support of prose? *In conveying complex info visually.*

2. What kind of information can a line chart convey better than any other visual? *trends*

3. When should a bar chart be used?

4. When should a pie chart be used, and when not?

5. How could Figure 7.4 (page 113) be improved? *by labeling each slice with its %*

6. What ethical considerations must you keep in mind when using graphics?

7. When should tables be used rather than charts? *amt of data would make charts too confusing & hard/ c used*

8. In the report analyzing the Headquarters Opinion Survey, beginning on page 121, where do references to graphics appear? *contract statement*

9. Why has the author of this report chosen to use a different kind of chart in Figures 5 and 6 from that in Figure 7? *before the graph*

10. Why has the author gone back to the bar chart in Figure 8? *the numerical form of the data*

DISCUSSION QUESTIONS

1. Do you think it is easier to distort data and mislead a reader by means of graphics or through prose?

2. In what way can an effective graphic represent the ultimate in bottom-lining?

To show

3. Comparisons among different sizes & amts. and proportions that are not close in numbers.

4. for comparisons among % or proportions and should not be used to present numerous points of data.

6. how they will help readers understand infor more easily without misleading them.

9. Figs 5 & 6 a bar chart is used making it easy to compare responses of the 4 divisions of employees, while Fig 7 shows the trends of principals

BOTTOM-LINE PRINCIPLES 7–9
REVIEW LIST

7

In long, complex, or analytical reports, begin by making a contract with your reader. Fulfill every clause of that contract in the same order as contracted.

8

In complex and/or lengthy reports, make your report's skeletal organization clear by
a. Using headings and subheadings to serve as guideposts for the reader.
b. Making sure that those headings and subheadings follow exactly the order of the items listed in the contract statement.

9

In complex, multisection reports, write subcontract sentences for each subsection. The subcontract sentence does the following:
a. Bottom-lines what that subsection is about.
b. Makes a transition from previous subsections to the present subsection (if needed).
c. Specifies clearly the topics to be discussed in that particular subsection.

GRAPHICS PRINCIPLES
REVIEW LIST

1

Line, bar, and pie charts provide useful ways of summarizing complex data. Use each for the following purposes:

a. Line charts—to show trends.
b. Bar charts—to show comparisons among different sizes and different amounts.
c. Pie charts—to show comparisons among proportions or percentages.

2

Graphics should be used only if they help readers understand information more easily. When using graphics, remember that

a. Graphics should never be used to distort information or to mislead a reader.
b. Graphics should be introduced and interpreted for the reader.

3

Tables should be used when data contain so many points of information that a chart or graph of the data would be unreadable, confusing, or unwieldy in size.

EXERCISES

PART A

Exercises 1 to 3 will help you learn to create contract sentences, headings, and subheadings appropriate in long reports. You will practice providing your reader with a clear skeletal organization of complex documents. For the purposes of these exercises, however, we are presenting you only with *summaries* of ideas discussed in the paragraphs of some long reports rather than with the full paragraphs themselves. We do this here so that you do not have to spend a considerable amount of time copying over so many words.

General Assignment

For each of the following summaries of long reports, write an appropriate contract sentence (or sentences) and all necessary headings and subheadings.

Exercise 1

The Sales Manager of your company has asked you to edit a report dealing with various types of consumers and their values.

Paragraph 1 is the introduction to the report, where the bottom line and the contract sentence belong.

Paragraph 2 deals with low-socioeconomic-level consumers who have the income only to purchase items needed for bare existence.

Paragraph 3 deals with blue-collar consumers who are in their later years and are primarily women. They tend to purchase goods traditionally, buying those that they have used in the past, rather than newly introduced or high-tech products.

Paragraph 4 deals with consumers who have the means to purchase luxury items. Most of this group is college-educated and hold high-level positions.

Paragraph 5 deals with groups of customers who are swayed by the latest social movements and are, hence, especially susceptible to advertising that focuses on newness and trends.

Exercise 2

The President of your company asks you to edit the following report to the Board of Directors. The report is about span of control.

Paragraph 1 explains that the term *span of control* pertains to the matter of how many subordinates a supervisor can effectively manage.

Paragraph 2 recognizes that the size of a span of control depends to a great extent upon the competence of both the supervisor and the subordinates.

Paragraph 3 states that the size of a span of control is also influenced by geographical location, that is, whether the subordinates are physically placed close or far from the supervisor.

Paragraph 4 explains that a span of control may also vary according to the type of managerial job required. An executive who has to interact hourly with subordinates might have difficulty in managing as few as three to five subordinates. By contrast, a top executive who is interested in knowing only whether preset sales goals have been met by each division manager could manage perhaps as many as twenty or thirty subordinates.

Exercise 3

The Vice President of Marketing asks you to edit the following report dealing with various advertising media.

Paragraph 1 points out that each medium has its particular assets and liabilities.

Paragraph 2 points out that an advantage of radio is that people can listen to it as they drive or work. Television does not share this advantage. Radio is also far less expensive than television, but its impact in advertising is considerably less.

Paragraph 3 points out that although television is commonly considered the most effective medium for getting messages across, it has the disadvantage of not reaching during the day the vast majority of people, both male and female, who work. Daily television does, however, effectively reach those people who are at home.

Paragraph 4 deals with direct mail. This advertising medium has the advantage of being able to be addressed to particular individuals. The costs of sending letters is so high, however, that the cost per person in direct mail can actually be much higher than in either television or radio.

Paragraph 5 deals with signs and billboards. Roadside signs are inexpensive and, in high traffic areas, reach many people. But their influence is fleeting, and the message they convey is necessarily very brief.

PART B

Exercises 4 to 7 ask you to apply the knowledge you have gained about graphics to the presentation of sets of complex data.

Exercise 4

You have been given the following figures on market shares of six brands of mouthwash. You need to present this information to your superiors in the clearest, most easily understood way possible.

Market Shares of Six Brands of Mouthwash

	Market Shares (%)					
Year	Brand A	Brand B	Brand C	Brand D	Brand E	Brand F
1985	30	29	25	5	5	6
1986	22	35	22	7	6	8
1987	25	25	30	10	5	5
1988	25	29	28	8	6	4
1989	28	30	25	6	6	5
1990	25	28	28	6	7	6
1991	22	30	29	6	6	7
1992	22	27	32	7	7	5
1993	20	29	33	5	7	6
1994	18	28	34	7	8	5

Assignment 1

What type of graphic would present these data most clearly? Why?

Assignment 2

Suppose you wanted to depict the market shares for 1994 only. What kind of chart should then be used?

Assignment 3

Suppose you wanted to compare the market shares held by these brands in the years 1985 and 1994. What kind of chart should you use then?

Exercise 5

As part of a study of the size of the businesses located in a particular city, a researcher collected the following information showing the average number of employees in certain categories of business.

Type of Business	Average Number of Employees
Employment	39
Consulting	10
Stock brokerage	75
Insurance	22
Law	9
Advertising	42
Medical	77
Real estate	35
Banking	60
Engineering	21

Assignment 1

How should these data be displayed? Why?

Assignment 2

Suppose you question whether a graphic is the best way to present these data. What other way could the data be arranged so as to be quickly comprehended by the reader?

Exercise 6

You have collected the following information about a sample of people's eating habits. The question was asked: "Which of the following foods do you have a clear preference for?"

	Males		Females	
	Whites	Non-Whites	Whites	Non-Whites
Beef	45%	25%	20%	10%
Chicken	10%	35%	35%	40%
Pork	20%	20%	15%	20%
Fish	25%	20%	40%	30%

Assignment

How should these data best be presented? Why?

Exercise 7

The dealers representing a popular automobile commissioned a consulting firm to project how new cars would sell during the next year. A large sample of respondents were asked by telephone to tell whether they intended to purchase an automobile within the next twelve months. The following data were collected:

Intend to Purchase Auto	Family Income (in dollars)					
	Under 30,000	30,000– 39,000	40,000– 49,000	50,000– 59,000	60,000– 69,000	Over 70,000
Definitely Yes	5%	7%	22%	24%	23%	40%
Probably Yes	7%	9%	26%	20%	26%	45%
Probably No	64%	43%	39%	30%	35%	5%
Definitely No	19%	28%	5%	18%	5%	5%
Uncertain	5%	13%	8%	8%	11%	5%
	100%	100%	100%	100%	100%	100%

Assignment

What are some of the various ways these data could be graphically displayed effectively? Which do you think would be most effective and why?

CASES

The next two Allgood Products cases present you with the challenge of putting into practice what you have learned about effective organization and proper use of graphics.

To develop effective reports in response to these cases, pay careful attention to the following steps and questions.

Step 1: Plan

What is the message's bottom line?

Is the message complex enough and/or long enough to need a contract sentence? Subcontract sentences? Skeletal organization? Graphics?

Step 2: Create

Compose a draft copy of the message.

Step 3: Review and Revise

Is the bottom-line statement made clearly and promptly?

If needed:

- Is a contract sentence clearly presented? Are subcontract sentences used? Does the skeletal organization follow the order of the contract sentence?
- Are graphics used to present and clarify complex data? Are the graphics properly introduced, appropriate for the information conveyed, and free of bias and distortion?

Case 1
Flavored Popcorn Product

You are a product manager at Allgood Products, Inc., reporting to Linda McNally, Sales Manager for Instant Foods. Under your direction, two new products have been tried out in four test markets: Minneapolis, Philadelphia, Atlanta, and Los Angeles.

The products being studied are Nacho-flavored Microwave Popcorn and Pizza-flavored Microwave Popcorn. Allgood Products already knows how well people have reacted to microwaveable products. The issue to investigate is whether people will like the taste of nacho-flavored popcorn and pizza-flavored popcorn.

In order to find out people's reactions, large supplies of already popped corn were supplied free for a two-week period to selected theaters and bars in each of the geographical areas. The owners of these establishments had previously agreed that they would offer these products for sale at a lower price than that charged for conventional buttered popcorn. The same two-week test was conducted in elementary schools, but in this test, children going through the school lunch line were given a choice of either free pizza-flavored or free nacho-flavored popcorn, but not both. To get a reaction of households to the product, smaller samples of microwave-ready popcorn of both flavors were sent to a sizable sample of homes in each of the four geographical test areas.

After the test period, researchers asked the proprietors of the theaters and bars to rate each product. They were asked to rate the product as excellent (they would definitely buy it regularly for the theater or bar); good (they would buy it sometimes); fair (they would rarely purchase it); or poor (they would definitely never buy it).

To get information from the elementary schools, interviewers asked the dietitians in each school to gather evidence of the acceptance of the products as shown by the amount of each flavor of popcorn left over at the end of the two-week period.

To determine how householders responded to the product, researchers followed up with in-depth phone interviews of a scientifically accurate sample of people. Respondents were asked to rate each product as excellent, good, fair, or poor. The householders' responses and the responses of the theater and bar proprietors were rounded off to the nearest full percentage.

The results obtained for nacho-flavored popcorn were as follows. Theaters and bars reported 73 percent, excellent; 20 percent, good; 7 percent, fair; 0 percent, poor. Householders reported 40 percent, excellent; 43 percent, good; 8 percent, fair; 9 percent, poor. Schools reported 10 percent, excellent; 15 percent, good; 35 percent, fair; 40 percent, poor.

The results obtained for pizza-flavored popcorn differed decidedly. Here, householders reported 50 percent, excellent; 40 percent, good; 5 percent, fair; 5 percent, poor. Theaters and bars reported 25 percent, excellent; 30 percent, good; 30 percent, fair; 15 percent, poor. Schools reported 75 percent, excellent; 15 percent, good; 10 percent, fair; 0 percent poor.

Assignment

Report the results of this market test to Linda McNally. Do not draw conclusions or make recommendations; just report the results and how the test was conducted. Use both prose and graphics to report your results.

Case 2
Dessert Pizza Product

You are a product manager at Allgood Products, Inc., reporting to Carlos Lopez, Sales Manager for Frozen Foods. You are responsible for determining public acceptance of a new line of very expensive dessert pizzas to be sold in the frozen foods section of stores. These dessert pizzas would be packaged in attractive cardboard cartons upon which glamorous and appetizing pictures of the contents would be printed.

Three products have been tested:

- Blueberry Bell Pizza, made with fresh blueberries, the most expensive cheeses (camembert, fontina, mozzarella), and spices. It is served on a sweetened crust advertised as being as light and flaky as strudel.
- Cherries Jubilee Pizza, made with fresh bing cherries and the same exotic cheeses and sweetened crust as in Blueberry Bell Pizza.
- Strawberry Real Shortcake Pizza, made with fresh strawberries and the same exotic cheeses, but served on a true shortcake dough in the shape of a pizza.

Arrangements for testing these products were made with a large supermarket chain. Tests were made in stores in two test markets: Dallas and Chicago. People were hired to offer free bite-sized samples to customers in the chains' supermarkets in these cities. They would tell customers of a special introductory offer enabling them to buy any of these new pizzas at half off the price printed on the box. Customers were also told about a mail-in order form on each box which they could fill out and send to Allgood Products, Inc., together with the UPC bar code (as proof of purchase), to receive a coupon entitling them to a free dessert pizza.

The mail-in order form instructed purchasers to fill out the following brief questionnaire in order to receive the free dessert pizza coupon. The questionnaire merely asked two questions:

1. How do you rate this product?
   Excellent   Good   Fair   Poor
   ____   ____   ____   ____

2. Do you intend to buy an Allgood dessert pizza again?
   Regularly   Frequently   Rarely   Almost Never   Never
   ____   ____   ____   ____   ____

The mail-in order forms were color-coded so that researchers knew which product had been sampled. On each form there was a small space left for comments. The results that were obtained from returns of the mail-in forms indicated that the products were rated very high in terms of customer acceptance. Blueberry Bell Pizza was regarded by 80 percent as excellent, 20 percent as good, and 0 percent as fair and poor. Cherries Jubilee Pizza was regarded by 70 percent as excellent, 25 percent as good, 5 percent as fair, and 0 percent as poor. Strawberry Real Shortcake Pizza was regarded by 75 percent as excellent, 25 percent as good, and 0 percent as fair and poor.

However, the results are deceptive, since the responses to the question "Do you intend to buy an Allgood dessert pizza?" showed that only 5 percent said regularly, 10 percent said frequently, 60 percent said rarely, 10 percent said almost never, and 15 percent said never. Furthermore, in the tiny space given for respondents to write in comments, the most common statements focused on the high regular price listed on the box. People wrote in such comments as "Too expensive" or "Can't afford it."

Since respondents had to give their names and addresses in order to receive the free coupon, Allgood's market researchers were able to conduct a telephone campaign with a sample of respondents. The results of these interviews were remarkably uniform. Almost all said the products were excellent and that they and their families really thoroughly enjoyed eating them. But it was the rare respondent who said that he or she could afford buying a ten-inch dessert pizza, serving four, for a retail price of $4.

Assignment

Report the facts of your market test to Carlos Lopez. Use both prose and graphics to report your results.

REFERENCES

Anderson, C., Saunder, A., and Weeks, F. (1957). *Business reports*. New York: McGraw-Hill.

Baxter, C. (1983). *Business report writing: A practical approach*. Boston: Kent.

Berenson, C., and Colton, R. (1971). *Research report writing for business and economics*. New York: Random House.

Bergwerk, R. J. (1970). Effective communication of financial data. *The Journal of Accountancy*.

Bertin, J. (1983). *Semiology of graphics*. Madison: University of Wisconsin Press.

Chambers, J., Cleveland, W., Kleiner, B., and Tukey, P. (1983). *Graphical methods for data analysis*. Boston: Duxbury Press.

Cleveland, W. (1985). *The elements of graphing data*. Monterey, CA: Wadsworth Press.

Juchau, R., and Galvin, M. (1984). Communications skills of accountants in Australia. *Accounting and Finance*, 24(1), 17–32.

Lewis, P. and Baker, W. (1978). *Business report writing*. Columbus, OH: Grid.

Peterson, B. K. (1983). Tables and graphs improve reader performance and reader reaction. *The Journal of Business Communication*, 20, 47–56.

Stout, V., and Perkins, E. (1987). *Practical management communication*. Cincinnati: South-Western Publishing.

Tufte, E. (1983). *The visual display of quantitative information*. Cheshire, CT: Graphics Press.

Wainer, H. (1984). How to display data badly. *American Statistician*, 38, 137–147.

Wainer, H., and Thissen, D. (1988). Plotting in the modern world: Statistics packages and good graphics. *Chance: New Directions for Statistics and Computing*, 1, 10–22.

Unit 4

CONTROLLING IMPACT IN NON-SENSITIVE MESSAGES

INTRA-TEXT MEMORANDUM

TO: Readers
FROM: Authors
SUBJECT: Unit 4

In Units 2 and 3, we thoroughly examined important techniques for organizing non-sensitive messages: bottom-lining, contract sentences, and skeletal organization. From the following diagram, you will notice there are two other organizational strategies that need to be considered: the circuitous and semi-circuitous patterns. These will be discussed when we examine effective organization of sensitive messages in Unit 5. For now, however, our focus remains on how to create effective non-sensitive messages. To achieve that end, we need to show you the importance of **impact.**

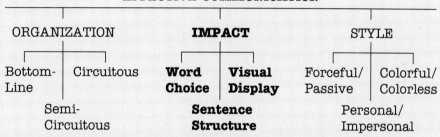

EFFECTIVE COMMUNICATION

ORGANIZATION		**IMPACT**		STYLE	
Bottom-Line	Circuitous	**Word Choice**	**Visual Display**	Forceful/ Passive	Colorful/ Colorless
	Semi-Circuitous		**Sentence Structure**		Personal/ Impersonal

Impact means the strength of the effect a message has on a reader. A message can have one of two kinds of impact—**high** or **low.** In non-sensitive messages, the impact should be as high as possible. (You will see later in Units 5 and 6 that high impact may or may not be appropriate for sensitive messages.)

In Unit 4, three factors contributing to high impact will be discussed, each in a separate chapter:

1. high-impact word choice
2. high-impact sentence structure
3. high-impact display

At the end of the unit you will see how these three factors can work together to create the impact appropriate for a non-sensitive message.

Chapter 8

NON-SENSITIVE MESSAGES AND HIGH-IMPACT WORD CHOICE

OBJECTIVES

This chapter will help you to

•

Distinguish between high-impact and
low-impact writing

•

Understand the main elements that affect
message impact

•

Choose high-impact words

•

Raise the impact of your
non-sensitive messages

Besides the bottom-line organizational principles you learned in Units 2 and 3, additional writing principles contribute significantly to the creation of effective non-sensitive messages. These principles are the basis for what we call high-impact writing.

HIGH-VERSUS LOW-IMPACT WRITING

By **high-impact messages,** we mean writing that is clear and easy to read. Words and sentences appear to leap off the page and demand the reader's attention. High-impact writing is essential for effective, non-sensitive messages.

Low-impact messages, by contrast, are difficult to read. The words are unfamiliar, and the sentences are complicated. Low-impact messages almost defy the reader to extract information from them. Boredom, fatigue, and monotony are what people feel while reading low-impact writing. Such responses are not the kind that writers seek for non-sensitive messages. Of course, as we shall see in Units 5 and 6, these low-impact responses may sometimes fit high-risk, sensitive situations.

Look at the following memo. Decide whether its effect on you is high or low impact:

Non-sensitive messages should be high impact.

Original

TO: H. B. Smith

FROM: R. L. Greene

SUBJECT: Management Conference

DATE: August 3, 19————

The Management Conference scheduled for August 29 has been terminated because of conflicts arising in the schedules of far too many of the would-be participants, many of whom are truly paramount to the success of the conference. Immediate re-scheduling is similarly encountering schedule impenetrability because of the exigent pressure on all branch managers to achieve sales quotas, which, of course, take primary priority in the minds of branch managers who are cognizant of the impor-tance of the conference but comprehend that they would set a reprehensible example in the eyes of subordinates by departing the branch at such an inopportune time.

Notice that although this memo is bottom-lined, it is still poorly written. The memo is so inappropriately low impact that it is laughable.

What would you do if you came to work one morning and found a copy of that memo and the following note from your boss on your electronic message board?

I scribbled off the attached memo late last night. I didn't even have a chance to proof it. How about cleaning up the memo, signing my name, and sending it off this afternoon? I'm off for a three-day trip to Boston.

At first glance, the assignment seems impossible. You cannot create a signable draft of this memo through one fast revision. However, if you approach this assignment step by step, you will quickly discover that your task is not as difficult as it first seemed. You can revise the memo by increasing the impact of its words, sentences, and paragraphs. Here, in brief, is what we mean by high-impact words, sentences, and paragraphs:

Three elements affect the impact of a message.

1. High-impact words are familiar and, hence, easy to understand.
2. High-impact sentences are easy to read and understand.
3. High-impact paragraphs are short and display ideas in small, manageable segments.

In Chapters 8 through 10, we will examine each of these techniques in detail. At the end of each chapter we will apply the strategies discussed to the sample memo you have just examined. This approach will help us to show how each technique affects the impact of a given message. Let's begin with word choice.

THE PROBLEM OF WORD CHOICE

You have undoubtedly noticed that one of the primary faults of the Management Conference memo lies in the words used. A number of them are showy and artificial. Words such as *terminate, paramount, impenetrability, cognizant, reprehensible,* and *inopportune* make the memo resemble a badly written government document.

Causes of Faulty Word Choice

People mistakenly use ornate words to impress others.

Why do some people want to use what are often called "ten-dollar words"? One possible reason is that these people are insecure and use words to impress rather than express. A second reason is that some people sincerely (but mistakenly) believe that good writers write this way. They associate competency with a showy display of vocabulary.

A third reason people often use ornate words is that they think doing so demonstrates their in-depth knowledge of and competence in a particular field. This tendency seems especially prevalent among people who are new to an organization. Often they parrot the shop talk or specialized jargon of their particular specialty in order to demonstrate that they truly are members of their particular field. Unfortunately, such people also tend to use shop talk outside the in-group of the "shop." Perhaps they generalize, "If I can impress my peers, why not impress everybody?" They

Photo Essay 1

THE MODERN OFFICE

A revolution in communication is occurring in offices throughout the industrialized world. The two forces motivating the changes are (1) the demand for more information and (2) the creation of new technologies for the development and transmittal of this information.

Information flows into, within, and out from business offices worldwide. It is more readily available, more current, and more abundant than ever before in history.

Equally important, however, is the realization that information comes in formats never before seen. The traditional typed business letter has been supplemented by computer screens, electronic mail, advanced printers, and various other forms of computer innovation.

Here, a typical businessperson is caught in the midst of this revolution. The notepad and pen are tools of the past still in use today; the computer screen, the printer, and the video

equipment—which can be used both for dictation purposes and to listen to audio feedback dealing with the computer display—are former tools of the future that are available today.

Historians studying the modern office will someday debate the causes of the office revolution. The debate will center on whether the need for more information led to the creation of advanced office equipment or whether new technologies made this information more readily available and, therefore, seemingly indispensable. Whichever side wins this argument, both sides will always agree that the modern business office has never since been the same.

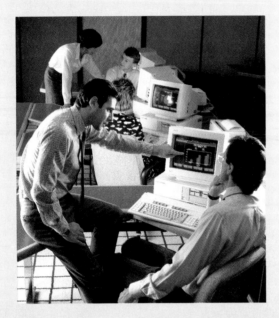

These scenes are witnessed daily in the modern business office. In both photos businesspeople are analyzing data, evaluating information, and making decisions based directly on information presented on computer screens.

Many offices are making a smooth transition from past to present technologies.

Many stockbrokers and financial institutions still keep teletrade boards visible while at the same time gathering more recent and relevant information from computer terminals linked directly to the stock exchanges.

Architects create designs on computer terminals but keep the traditional drawing tables available for specialized purposes.

Members of the medical community still hand record vital patient information but then transfer this information to computers for analysis and filing.

Two key pieces of equipment that have led the office revolution are mainframe computers and minicomputers.

Mainframe computers are general purpose computers that perform vast information processing needs for corporate headquarters, governmental agencies, and universities.

Minicomputers, smaller and less powerful than mainframes on the market today, are more powerful than mainframes manufactured ten years ago. Uses of minicomputers range from blood analysis and text editing to stand-alone computers for small businesses. As minicomputers become more and more powerful, the distinction between them and mainframes will become more and more blurred.

Two recent entries into the office revolution are the microcomputer and the laptop computer.

Microcomputers in the form of personal computers are found throughout modern offices and are used for accounting, inventory control, word processing, text editing, and a variety of other purposes.

Laptop computers, a portable form of the micro, enable businesspeople to extend the walls of the modern office. Airplanes, cars, homes, and hotel rooms convert instantly into traveling offices thanks to the availability of laptop computers.

The office revolution is changing the jobs done in the modern office.

With desktop publishing equipment and software, people in the modern office can publish, print, and produce pamphlets and other documents that previously had to be ordered from other companies.

Thanks to equipment such as IBM's InfoWindow, people with little or no computer or typing expertise can perform computer applications by merely touching the screen in the appropriate place.

Thanks to laser and color printers, business-people can produce typeset-quality documents that contain various types of color, type faces, and other forms of visual display.

The office revolution is even changing the way information arrives in the modern office.

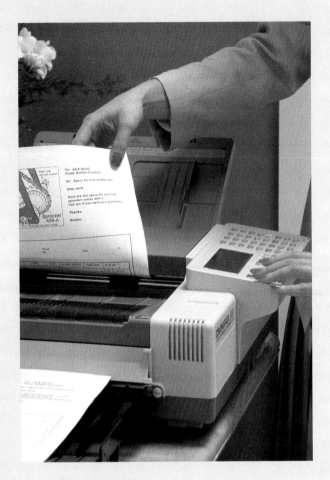

FAX machines transmit documents instantly from one office to another and allow a document to be printed exactly as it appears in the sender's office.

Electronic mail allows paperless communication to occur within and between business offices. When a formal document needs to be saved, it can either be saved in the computer's file or a copy can be printed.

Through teleconferencing businesspeople can exchange ideas and gain information from various far-away sources without even leaving the confines of their own office building.

are unaware that in most instances, the use of specialized jargon confuses the average person.

Jargon can confuse your reader.

For example, if you have ever talked with computer buffs, you may have heard a lot of specialized terms. The conversation probably included words such as *hard disk, boot, DOS, dump, download,* and *resident.* And unless you were computer literate, you didn't have any idea what they were talking about.

Therefore, if you do have specialized knowledge about a field, you must be considerate of your listeners' or readers' ability to receive and interpret the message you want to send. Shop talk is all right when it is used by people who share a common vocabulary, but be careful when you are talking or writing to non-specialists.

The Battle for Plain Language

The problem of inept word choice in business and government documents has become so serious that many people post wall placards expressing concern over or disapproval of poorly worded documents. Acronyms such as KISS (Keep It Simple, Stupid!) and posters that urge others to "Eschew Obfuscation" often decorate the walls of high-level business executives and government administrators.

Many states have gone so far as to pass laws to control the use of obscure English. More than 25 states have passed plain-language laws. These laws require that certain government documents and certain private business contracts, especially insurance contracts, be written with words and phrases that are understandable to the general public, not just to lawyers.

Laws require use of plain language in certain messages.

HIGH-IMPACT WORD CHOICE

Although it is easy to say, "Keep it simple," it is not so easy to put advice about word choice into practice. We are, therefore, going to show you how you can control word choice.

The English language is a mixture of many different words from many different languages. The English writer Daniel Defoe perhaps labeled it most accurately when he called it "your Roman-Saxon-Danish-Norman English." But not all words in English are equally effective; some work in one context while others function better in another context. That is why we advise you to apply High-Impact Principle 1 in business communications:

English words derive from several languages.

HIGH-IMPACT PRINCIPLE 1:
Words derived from Anglo-Saxon are high impact. Readers appreciate these words because they are readily understood, familiar, and clear.

A thumbnail sketch of the historical development of the English language will clarify this principle.

Wars, invasions, and domination often have significant influence upon languages, and that is especially true of English. The first invasion of England occurred in 449 A.D., when the Angles, Saxons, and Jutes moved into the British Isles from what is now Denmark and Germany. The result of this invasion was the formation of what is often considered the language upon which modern English is based—the Anglo-Saxon language.

Even to this day, most of our everyday words derive from Anglo-Saxon. Words like *dog, horse, cow, pig, earth, wood,* and *field* all come from Anglo-Saxon. In fact, the majority of the common English words, such as *the, is, you,* and *your,* also derive from this source. A recent analysis of the one hundred most commonly used words in English showed that *all one hundred* of these words derived from Anglo-Saxon roots (McCrum, Cran, and MacNeil, 61).

Latin Enters the Language   In 597 A.D., the Anglo-Saxon language, or Old English as it is also called, engaged in its first battle for supremacy: St. Augustine brought Christianity, with its gigantic Latin vocabulary, into England. This Latin invasion not only brought many new words into English, it also brought new kinds of words. Church words, such as *disciple, bishop,* and *monk,* came in, as did terms that gave the language the ability to express abstract thought—an immensely difficult, if not impossible, task for Anglo-Saxon words that were limited to common objects such as sun and moon, sea and land. The mingling of these two languages led towards an increasingly sophisticated, complex, dual-edged language, a language in which we have at least two words for almost everything.

The Norman Conquest   Other factors influenced the English language between 597 and 1066. The most notable was the invasion and settlement of England by the Vikings, which brought Old Norse into contact with English. But this influence pales when placed beside the event that has been described as having a greater effect on the English language than any other—the Norman Conquest.

The Norman Conquest, which began when William the Conqueror, Duke of Normandy, defeated the English king Harold at the Battle of Hastings in 1066, meant that suddenly three languages were interacting in one geographic area: Norman French, Latin, and Anglo-Saxon. French, itself derived from Latin, began to dominate Anglo-Saxon, becoming the language of culture and society, as many still think of it today. Latin became the language of religion and learning, as it still is for some today, although its use has diminished. Anglo-Saxon became the everyday language used in the speech of common people. In short, Anglo-Saxon suffered a loss of prestige.

Current Uses of Words Derived from Anglo-Saxon   Today, however, words derived from Anglo-Saxon are being used more and more. People recognize that these words enable them to communicate with clarity and high impact.

Think, for example, how over the past few decades many of our great English speeches, sayings, and slogans have derived from Anglo-Saxon, not from French or Latin. Was it a mistake for John F. Kennedy to ignite the American people with his famous inaugural statement, "Ask not what your country can do for you; ask what you can do for your country"? Did Franklin Roosevelt make a mistake when he told the depression-ridden American people, "All we have to fear is fear itself"? No. Each of these great communicators recognized that simple, common words, words derived largely from Anglo-Saxon, were words with which people could identify—they were words that could motivate the masses.

HOW TO CHOOSE HIGH-IMPACT WORDS

How can we distinguish Anglo-Saxon from Latinate and French words? Do we have to memorize the historical origins of thousands of words? The answer is given by High-Impact Principle 2:

HIGH-IMPACT PRINCIPLE 2:
When writing, use words you would use in normal business conversation.

If you write as you speak in normal business conversation, most of the words you automatically use will be of Anglo-Saxon origin rather than Latinate. Let's prove this statement. Examine the following words drawn from typical business memos. One set of words is derived from Latin, the other from Anglo-Saxon. Which words would you use in *conversation* in a normal business situation?

Normal business conversation is the key.

Latinate	Anglo-Saxon
pursuant	after
ascertain	find out
cognizant	know
objective	goal
advise	tell

Most likely, you would prefer the words in the Anglo-Saxon column. If a staff assistant asked you, "Will the sales proposal be shown to upper management?" how likely is it that you would answer, "I will ascertain that information and so advise you as soon as I am cognizant of the facts"?

In your likes and dislikes about words, you are no different from businesspeople. Look at the following memo written by the president of an international corporation.

TO: All Staff Members

FROM: Corporate President

SUBJECT: Word Choice

DATE: February 23, 19——

Thought for the day—I would very much appreciate in the letters you prepare for my signature your following an informal tone as much as possible.

In my terms, this simply means being as conversational as you can.

The advice that this corporate president has given is most useful. Do what he suggests. Use the same words in writing that you use in ordinary business conversation. If you do so, you will find you are primarily using familiar words derived from the Anglo-Saxon.

A word of warning concerning High-Impact Principle 2 is necessary. Notice that the principle suggests choosing words based on *normal* business conversation. *Normal*, in our terminology, does not apply to business terminology that is sometimes directed toward a specialized audience. Colloquial, profane, or even stilted, ornate language is sometimes used in special business settings. However, such conversation is not the usual practice and should not set the standard to be followed.

Beware of colloquial language.

INCREASING IMPACT
THROUGH CONCISENESS

High-Impact Principles 1 and 2 concentrate on word selection. The final high-impact principle relates to the number of words you use:

HIGH-IMPACT PRINCIPLE 3:
Control wordiness by avoiding empty phrases and unnecessary words.

Removing Empty Phrases

Increase impact by deleting absent subjects.

Empty phrases are words or groups of words that make no contribution to the overall thought of a sentence. Such phrases are known as "absent subjects." People use this label to describe sentence subjects that provide no relevant or useful information. *It is* and *There are* are the two most commonly used absent subjects.

Notice in the following sentences how the subjects have no purpose besides serving as subjects for the sentences.

It is entirely possible that we will need to extend Tuesday's meeting into the afternoon.

There are five computer terminals that the Manufacturing Division needs to have replaced.

Removing the absent subjects significantly increases the impact of both sentences.

> We will probably need to extend Tuesday's meeting into the afternoon.

> The Manufacturing Division needs to have five computer terminals replaced.

Eliminating Unnecessary Words

The second point in High-Impact Principle 3, "Avoid unnecessary words," always deserves mention in business. Unit 2 emphasized that business people prefer a direct, bottom-line organizational pattern for non-sensitive messages. This pattern is efficient, as it reduces the time it takes to read a message. Another way of saving your reader's time is to make sure your sentences contain only words that contribute to the message's purpose. Most writers use more words than they need to express an idea, especially in the first draft of a document when many different ideas are going through their minds at once.

For high impact, eliminate unnecessary words.

Editing Your Messages

Writers must make a conscious effort to eliminate unnecessary words in non-sensitive messages. However, few writers have the ability to phrase their ideas precisely and concisely in a first draft. Editing is always necessary. You must allow a draft of the message to "get cold" for awhile. Stop working temporarily on the message and perform some other task. Then, after a period of time has elapsed—a period that may range from a few minutes to a few days—you can reexamine the message to clarify vague ideas and eliminate excess words.

Take time to edit your work.

Fortunately, the modern office has made editing a much simpler process than it was in the past. Personal computers and word-processing software make it easy for writers to edit their own work on a terminal. Writers can now try out a variety of different phrases and never have to make someone type and retype a draft copy. Through a few strokes of highlight, delete, and insert keys, phrases such as those in the left-hand column of the following chart can gain the higher impact of those in the right-hand column:

Computers make rewriting easier.

Low Impact	Edit	High Impact
As per your request	~~As per~~	At your request
Please make every possible effort to attend	~~make every possible effort~~	Please try to attend
The central, key issue is a matter of whether	~~central, is a matter of whether~~	The key issue involves
Please find enclosed herewith	~~Please find, herewith~~	Enclosed is
All of the department heads who are concerned	~~of who are~~	All the concerned department heads

In short, writers' efforts at controlling wordiness result in more efficient, clearer, and higher-impact messages.

MEMO RESCUE ATTEMPT: STEP ONE

Let's see what happens if we apply the high-impact principles about word choice and wordiness to the Management Conference memo on page 147.

Version A. Familiar Words, Less Wordy

TO: H. B. Smith

FROM: R. L. Greene

SUBJECT: Management Conference

DATE: August 3, 19——

The Management Conference scheduled for August 29 has been canceled because of conflicts in the schedules of far too many of the people in attendance, many of whom are truly important to the success of the conference. Immediate rescheduling of the conference is impossible because of the pressure on branch managers to reach sales quotas which, of course, are of first importance in the minds of branch managers, who are aware of the importance of the conference but do not want to set a bad example for their subordinates by leaving their branch at this very busy time.

The message is clearer as a result of inserting familiar words. This memo still needs a lot of work on sentence and paragraph structure, but as poor as it still is, it now appears salvageable. To reach the next stage of improvement, we will have to revise its sentence structure. This is the subject of Chapter 9.

SUMMARY

Impact in messages is controlled through word selection, sentence structure, and paragraph display. **High-impact messages** contain familiar words and easy-to-read sentences that are displayed clearly. By contrast, **low-impact messages** have unfamiliar words and complicated sentences. In non-sensitive messages, the impact should be as high as possible.

High-impact word selection requires you to use familiar and easy-to-understand words, deriving from Anglo-Saxon rather than Latin. Since most of our conversational language comes from Anglo-Saxon, you can easily measure the impact of a word by deciding whether you would normally use it in a business conversation with your reader. If you would use the word in normal business conversation, then use the word in your message.

Impact is determined not only by the types of words you use but also by the number of words you use. Fewer words leads to a higher-impact message. Thus, good writers take time to edit their work, removing unnecessary and meaningless words before sending their messages to busy readers.

REVIEW QUESTIONS

1. What is high-impact writing?
2. What is low-impact writing?
3. What are three reasons people use ornate words?
4. When is it okay to use shop talk?
5. What kind of impact do words derived from Latin and French often have?
6. Where do many of our conversational words derive from?
7. Why do readers appreciate the use of Anglo-Saxon words?
8. When writing, what type of words should you use?

DISCUSSION QUESTIONS

1. Why does the text focus on high- versus low-impact word choice rather than on correct versus incorrect word choice?
2. Based on the types of words they use, what insights can we develop about people?
3. The following phrases are often heard in discussions about word selection:

- Be clear in your word selection.
- Always use the right word.
- Be precise.
- Keep It Simple, Stupid!

Discuss the advantages and disadvantages of such advice.

Chapter 9

HOW TO WRITE HIGH-IMPACT SENTENCES

OBJECTIVES

This chapter will help you to

●

Distinguish between the three basic types of sentences—simple, compound, and complex

●

Use each sentence type to change the impact of your message

●

Understand how sentence structure affects a message's impact

●

Use sentence voice to change the impact of your message

Businesspeople who understand sentence structure have information that is essential for controlling impact. Their knowledge of the basic types of sentences, the different ways that sentences can be structured, and the role of voice in sentence clarity permits them to use language to achieve their goals. In addition, a mastery of sentence structure helps business-people avoid punctuation problems, a topic examined in the Special Features section at the end of this text.

SENTENCE TYPE AND IMPACT

To understand the relationship between sentence structure and impact, we first need to examine how the three basic types of sentences affect impact. That is the topic of High-Impact Principle 4:

HIGH-IMPACT PRINCIPLE 4:
a. **Use simple sentences for maximum impact.**
b. **Use compound sentences to lower a message's impact.**
c. **Use a combination of complex and simple sentences for variety and high impact.**

This advice, much like the advice on word choice, may not be appropriate in a creative writing course. However, always bear in mind that our subject is business writing, not literary writing. Some of what students are taught about sophisticated prose in creative writing classes is inappropriate in business writing. Likewise, some aspects of writing taught in business communication classes are inappropriate in creative writing classes.

Why, then, do simple sentences work well in business? The answer is that when businesspeople read business prose, they have a different purpose in mind than when they read a work of literature. Businesspeople do not read memos for pleasure; they read them to get a job done. Hence, sentences that convey information in the clearest, simplest, easiest-to-read form are the best. For conveying information one idea at a time, simple sentences work fine.

Simple sentences convey information efficiently.

THREE TYPES OF SENTENCES

The three basic types of English sentences are the **simple,** the **compound,** and the **complex.** Here is a reminder of how each sentence type works:

Three types of sentences— simple, compound, complex.

1. *The Simple Sentence*

   I   ran   the meeting.
   Subject Verb   Object

2. *The Compound Sentence*

   I   ran   the meeting,   and   I
   Subject Verb   Object   Coordinating   Subject
                                  Conjunction

   wrote   the minutes.
   Verb   Object

3. *The Complex Sentence*
   After I read the contract,   I sent it to headquarters.
   Dependent Clause   Independent Clause

Simple Sentences

A **simple sentence** needs to contain a subject and a verb and needs to be able to stand by itself as an independent unit. A simple sentence may or may not also contain an object. Notice in sentence 1 that *I ran* and *I wrote* are just as much simple sentences as *I ran the meeting* and *I wrote the minutes*. *I ran* and *I wrote*, although short, are sentences because they contain the basic elements required of a sentence—a complete idea, a subject, and a verb. These two verbs—*ran* and *wrote*—do not need an object. However, since most sentences found in business writing will contain objects, it is not necessary to concern ourselves with such exceptional sentences as *I jumped, I slept,* or *You eat.*

Compound Sentences

A **compound sentence** is made up of two **independent clauses** (that is, sentences that can stand alone) joined together by a conjunction such as *and, or,* or *but.* Notice sentence 2, *I ran the meeting,* and *I wrote the minutes.* A compound sentence is just two simple sentences joined together.

Which sentence type is easier to read—simple or compound?

Compare the following two versions of the same memo. Version B changes Version A's compound sentences into simple sentences. Which version do you prefer?

Version A. Compound Sentences

All of you have been kept aware of the studies conducted by Corporate Personnel Research in 19—— and 19——, and many of you and your staff members assisted with them. These management effectiveness studies were presented to the President on March 28, 19——, and the attached letter contains a summary of the conclusions and actions being taken.

The seventh point in the summary states that appropriate guidelines are being developed to improve the management identification and selection process, and these identification and selection guidelines will be provided to the operating units in the third quarter of this year.

Version B. Simple Sentences

All of you have been kept aware of the studies conducted by Corporate Personnel Research in 19—— and 19——. Many of you and your staff members assisted with them. These management effectiveness studies were presented to the President on March 28, 19——. The attached letter contains a summary of the conclusions and actions being taken.

The seventh point in the summary states that appropriate guidelines are being developed to improve the management identification and selection process. These identification and selection guidelines will be provided to the operating units in the third quarter of this year.

Changing the sentences from compound to simple definitely raises the impact of the message.

Some of you will recall hearing a "rule" to the effect that "Thou shalt never begin a sentence with *and, but,* or *or.*" Nowadays this rule is only observed in the most formal writing. You can, therefore, begin a sentence with these conjunctions, as long as the sentence begins with a capital letter! (That is, you cannot begin a sentence with a figure, as in "8 people attended the meeting." Instead, spell the number out.) But we urge you to be cautious. If you have a boss who wants to follow the old "rule" and you are writing a memo for his or her signature, do not begin sentences with *and, or,* or *but.* However, when *you* are the boss, you can tell your subordinates to do as they wish. You can even encourage them to begin sentences with conjunctions so that they can break their compound sentences into simple ones.

You can begin a sentence with a conjunction—but be cautious!

Complex Sentences

A **complex sentence** consists of at least one independent clause and one or more **dependent clauses.** A dependent clause contains a subject and a verb but cannot stand alone. It must be joined to an independent clause— a true, stand-alone sentence. Sentence 3 illustrates a complex sentence. The dependent clause is *After I read the contract;* the independent clause is *I sent it to headquarters.*

To make sure you understand how a complex sentence works, let's see how a simple sentence—*I took the job*—can be turned into the dependent clause necessary in a complex sentence. Notice how simply an independent sentence can be subordinated and turned into a dependent clause:

After
When
Before   I took the job, . . .
Although
As soon as

By adding any of the subordinating words in the left column, you make the statement dependent: *After I took the job . . . ; When I took the job . . . ; Before I took the job . . . ; Although I took the job . . . ; As soon as I took the job. . . .* Basically, you simply have to trust your ear. When you hear *After I took the job,* you know that a second part has to fall in place for the sentence to be complete and not fragmentary. That second part is the independent sentence—*I selected my office.*

To make a complex sentence, you join the newly dependent clause to an independent clause, like this:

After I took the job,   I selected my office.
Dependent Clause   Independent Clause

Note that you could subordinate the second clause instead: *I took the job before I selected my office.* Or you could make both clauses dependent by writing the following: *After I took the job, but before I selected my office, I. . . .* Now both clauses leave us in suspense. In fact, you could keep adding dependent clauses until a convoluted sentence is created:

> When I arrived in Kansas City, after I took the job, but before I picked out my office (although it would be many weeks yet before I would appear for work). . . .

You could keep adding dependent clauses until finally you have mercy on the reader. Then you could conclude by adding an independent clause such as *I came down with the flu.*

Sentence Type, Impact, and Variety

Reminder: Sentence structure affects impact.

Add complex sentences for variety.

The important point to remember is that the kinds of sentences you use in your writing significantly affect your reader's ability to interpret your message. Since most businesspeople can interpret short sentences more readily than they can long ones, you should maximize your use of simple sentences. This advice is especially important when you deal with key ideas that you want to leap off the page into your reader's mind. When you want your message to have a little more variety, add some complex sentences to the mix of simple sentences. The inclusion of complex sentences will eliminate the possibility of your writing sounding choppy.

THE IMPORTANCE OF THE SENTENCE'S TOPIC

One of the most important points to be made about sentence structure is that in order to begin to process information, you need to know the topic of the sentence. The topic is essentially the bottom line of the sentence. The mind asks about *any* message, "What is the subject? What are you talking about?" Next, it asks, "What action is the subject taking?" (that is, "What is the verb?"). And, finally, the mind asks, "What is the object of this action?"

High-Impact Principle 5 is the building block on which you can base much of your understanding of how to communicate with people in non-sensitive situations.

HIGH-IMPACT PRINCIPLE 5:
Put the topic first as often as possible in sentences used in non-sensitive messages.

Imagine that you are standing in the hall one day and a fellow manager corners you and says, "The customer respects Joe," "We need the contract," "No one else is as persuasive," and "Joe always gets the job done."

Desperate, you hold up your hand, crying, "Stop! What are you talking about?"

"These are the reasons why we need to send Joe Brennon to San Francisco next week," the manager replies.

"Oh?" you say. "What were those reasons again?"

Your mind was asked to store up reasons when you did not even know what the topic was. The fact that you say, "Oh? What were those reasons again?" shows that you cannot be asked to store up a whole list of information on an unknown topic. You need to know what the topic is.

Readers encounter problems reading sentences that give them large amounts of information before they learn the topic. They get confused and frustrated while waiting to find out what the true purpose is. The result is much like a non-bottom-lined message—you have to read the sentence twice to understand the topic.

Stating the purpose at the end of the sentence is confusing.

Waiting for the Topic

Look at the following examples. As you read them, monitor your thought processes:

1. Assistance in designing a system tailored to a customer's needs provides. . . .
2. As I consider the discussion topics, the subject matter I am to address, and the divergent interests of the group. . . .

Are you ready to take an action? Are you comfortable as you read? Are you processing what you read? Or, rather, is your mind attempting to store this information until something happens, until you learn something? What is that something your mind is waiting for? Your mind is waiting to learn the topic of the sentence.

Why You Need to Provide the Topic First

Monitor your reaction to these sentences in which the topic comes first. Notice how finding out the topic first makes the information contained in the sentence much easier to process.

1. The attached checklist provides assistance in designing a system tailored to a customer's needs.
2. I'm concerned that my remarks may not be on target as I consider the discussion topics, the subject matter I am to address, and the divergent interests of the group.

What has happened now? Didn't your mind process the information as fast as you read it? Why? Because the topics appeared at the beginning of the sentences.

High-Impact Principle 5 is basic to effective, high-impact communication. It does not matter whether you are talking about a sentence, a paragraph, a memorandum, a report, or an entire book. It does not matter whether the communication is spoken or written. The receiver needs to know the subject or topic before any information can be processed.

SENTENCE VOICE

To be able to write high-impact sentences, you need to be familiar with one other structural aspect of a sentence, the **active voice.** You probably remember being told that there are two voices in English: **active** and **passive.** The following high-impact principle explains when to use each of these two voices.

HIGH-IMPACT PRINCIPLE 6:

For high-impact sentences:

a. Use the active voice as much as possible.
b. Minimize or avoid using the passive voice.

Active–Passive Differences

The traditional definition of the differences between the active and the passive voices provides a useful way for you to begin to understand these two voices. In this definition, an active sentence has the subject, which we will refer to from now on as the *true subject,* as the actor or doer in the sentence. The object in an active sentence is the receiver, or the thing or person that is acted upon.

A traditional active voice sentence, then, is

The secretary will cancel the meeting.

In this sentence, the *secretary* is the doer of the action, and the *meeting* receives the action—it is cancelled. In a passive sentence, the object gets moved to the subject position, and the true subject, that which does the action, gets moved to the object position. Thus, our traditional sentence becomes

The meeting was cancelled by the secretary.

In this passive structure, the *secretary* becomes the object of the sentence, and the *meeting* becomes the subject.

The following metaphor will help you to understand the difference between an active- and a passive-voice sentence even more clearly.

Funneling Information

Imagine three funnels by which information reaches the language-processing part of our minds: a subject funnel, a verb funnel, and an object funnel. Assume also that under the subject funnel is an ignition switch. When the subject goes through the subject funnel, the subject starts the mental language-processing "machinery." Once the subject starts the machinery, our minds can process the information presented in the verb, object, and other sentence parts.

If no subject is sent through the subject funnel to turn on the switch, words sent through the verb and object funnels merely stack up. No in-

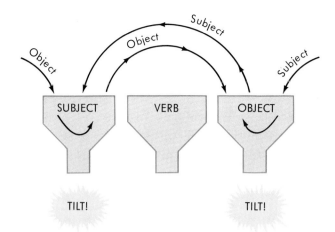

FIGURE 9.1
Passive confusion.

formation processing occurs. Your mind is busy, desperately trying to store the information until it is told the subject.

The funnel metaphor helps us to see why the active voice is so easy to understand and the passive voice so difficult. Here is a simple sentence written in the active voice:

Mr. Donnelly reviewed the operating plan.

Mr. Donnelly is the subject. *Reviewed* is the verb. *Operating plan* is the object. Now let's look at the same sentence expressed passively.

The operating plan was reviewed by Mr. Donnelly.

What takes place in your mind as you read this sentence? A momentary delay occurs because of your need to shift about the content in the funnels. The writer has played a trick on you by trying to put the object, *the operating plan,* down your subject funnel, and the subject, *Mr. Donnelly,* down the object funnel.

As Figure 9.1 depicts, your mind cries, "Tilt! Something's wrong!" The true object, *the operating plan,* doesn't fit in the subject funnel. As a result, the mind's language-processing machinery can't get to work— everything becomes stuck within its funnel. To solve this dilemma, the reader has to move the true subject, *Mr. Donnelly,* back to the subject funnel. Likewise, the reader has to move the true object, *the operating plan,* back to the object funnel. *Mr. Donnelly* can then pass through the subject funnel and trip the ignition switch that starts the language-processing machinery in motion.

> The active voice is easier to understand than the passive.

Passives Can Hide the True Subject

Reversal of funnel materials, that is, moving the true subject into the object position, is only part of the problem with the passive voice. Sentences in the passive voice often do not mention the true subject (the *doer* of the action). As a result, sentences in the passive voice can hide the true subject from the reader.

> The passive voice can hide the subject.

Let's examine another example. Here is an active version of a sentence:

Each manufacturing division should submit raw material inventory reports.

A passive version would take the subject, *each manufacturing division,* and make it the object of the preposition *by.* As a result, the sentence would read:

Raw material inventory reports should be submitted by each manufacturing division.

"Okay," you say, "this is a little confusing but not a major problem to my understanding of the sentence—at least not if I put a little effort into it." But watch what happens when we take the passive version one step further and cause the true subject, *each manufacturing division,* to disappear. Then the sentence becomes

Raw material inventory reports should be submitted.

Unless the reader is extremely familiar with the subject, it is impossible to determine *who* is supposed to make the submissions. That is why the passive voice and its penchant for secret subjects often causes confusion and ambiguity. It also can lead to lawsuits asking, "Who has contracted to do what?" Here are some other examples that illustrate this point:

Active	Passive	Passive, Missing Subject
The regional vice president makes requisitions through division manufacturing.	Requisitions are made through division manufacturing by the regional vice president.	Requisitions are made through division manufacturing. (Who makes the requisitions?)
HHS requested affirmative action plans.	Affirmative actions plans were requested by HHS.	Affirmative action plans were requested. (Who requests the plans?)
The personnel division handles interview training.	Interview training is handled by the personnel division.	Interview training is handled. (Who handles training?)
The public relations director writes news releases.	News releases are written by the public relations director.	News releases are written. (Who writes the releases?)

If you study these sentences carefully, you will notice that when the true subject is missing, it is very difficult for a reader to tell whether the sentence is active or passive. For that reason, it is helpful to have a second means of identifying the voice of a sentence. Fortunately, such a means is available.

How to Distinguish between the Active and Passive Voices

The grammatical trick for identifying whether a sentence is active or passive involves observing three related elements. First, every passive sentence has a form of the verb *to be* (that is, any of the words *am, are, is, was, were, be, being, been*). Second, every passive sentence has another verb in the past-participle form (for example, *given, written, seen*). And third, every passive sentence can have a *by*-phrase inserted after the past participle (for example, *by the sales force*).

Three signs of the passive voice.

Look at the sentences just shown. Notice that each time the sentence shifts from active to passive, a form of the verb *to be* and a past participle appear. Thus, the telltale verbs *are made, were requested, is handled,* and *are written* appear in both the middle and the right-hand column. Also notice that the sentences in the right-hand column are still passive even though the *by*-phrase does *not* appear in the sentence. In fact, these sentences are truly low impact because the true subject disappears completely from the sentence.

By remembering this passive shift, you will be able to identify whether a sentence is active or passive and be able to change it to achieve your desired impact. Remember that unless the subject of a sentence is at the beginning and the object is at the end, the reader will experience discomfort. And uncomfortable readers seldom read diligently.

One final note about active–passive differences concerns the appropriate usage of each. Active sentences are vital in high-impact, non-sensitive messages. Passive sentences also have a use, but that use is in sensitive situations. We will discuss the use of passive sentences in detail in Unit 6.

MEMO RESCUE ATTEMPT: STEP TWO

Let's apply our principles about simple, active-voice sentences that present the topic first to our Management Conference memo of page 147, and see what improvements result.

> Version B. Simple Active-Voice Sentences
> With Topic Presented First

TO: H. B. Smith

FROM: R. L. Greene

SUBJECT: Management Conference

DATE: August 3, 19——

We have had to cancel the August 29 Management Conference. This action was necessary because of many scheduling conflicts among the key people who were planning to attend. Immediate rescheduling of the conference was impossible because branch managers are under tremendous pressure to reach sales quotas. Although branch managers are aware of the conference's importance, they also realize that sales quotas are always of first importance. Furthermore, branch managers do not want to set a bad example for subordinates by leaving the branch at this very busy time.

The memo has improved greatly. Let's see what happens when, in the next chapter, we concern ourselves with high-impact appearance.

SUMMARY

The structure and voice of the sentences you use influence your message's impact. **Simple sentences** go quickly to the heart of the matter. As a result, simple sentences provide the best way for non-sensitive messages to transmit information as quickly and clearly as possible. **Complex sentences** also contribute to high-impact prose, especially when the sentence patterns need some variety. Thus, complex sentences should be added to non-sensitive messages whenever your writing risks sounding choppy.

In terms of sentence structure, you should always remember that the reader needs to know the topic first, in order to process information in the most efficient, orderly manner possible.

Finally, **sentence voice** also influences impact. The **active voice** presents information up-front, in a "true" subject–verb–object order. The result is that the sentence's subject appears at the beginning of the sentence and the reader can immediately process the sentence's information.

In a **passive-voice** sentence pattern, the true subject appears in the object's position and the true object appears in the subject's position. The result of such shifting is a low-impact sentence that is difficult to read because of the discomfort experienced by readers having to shift the true subjects and objects into their proper positions. To complicate matters further, passive structures also often contain a secret or missing subject, one that is dropped from the sentence as a result of the passive shift. These sentences are often extremely difficult to read because the readers may be unfamiliar with the true subject of the sentence.

REVIEW QUESTIONS

1. What basic advice should you follow to create high-impact sentences?

2. Why do simple sentences work well in business? *go to the heart of the matter*

3. What is the difference between a simple, a compound, and a complex sentence?

4. What is an independent clause? *Sentence cannot*

5. What is a dependent clause?

6. What does the type of sentences you use in your writing significantly affect? *readers ability to interpret the msg.*

7. What do readers need to know about a sentence before they can begin to understand its content? *Topic*

8. In what order do readers' minds most easily process language information?

9. What three elements are always present in a passive sentence?

DISCUSSION QUESTIONS

1. At the beginning of this chapter, the text notes:

   Some of what students are taught about sophisticated prose in creative writing classes is inappropriate in business writing. Likewise, some aspects of writing taught in business communication classes are inappropriate in creative writing classes.

   Explain this statement, giving examples.

2. Why do most businesspeople prefer simple, active sentences that present the topic first?

3. Editors and managers in technical and scientific professions sometimes encourage writers to use passive constructions. These people encourage this approach based on the premise that the passive voice provides an objective, authoritative tone to a piece of writing. How valid do you think this premise is? What are the risks and benefits of using the active voice for such publications?

5 Contain has subj & verb but cannot stand alone

by asking
8 ① What is the subj
 2. " action ↔ the subj taking –
 3. " is the object of the action

Chapter 10

HIGH-IMPACT APPEARANCE

OBJECTIVES

This chapter will help you to

●

Understand how the appearance and attractiveness of a letter, memo, or report affect its impact

●

Learn techniques by which you can dramatically increase the visual impact of your non-sensitive writing

●

Recognize the effectiveness of the system you have learned for handling non-sensitive business messages

A message can be written in clear, precise, conversational, Anglo-Saxon terminology. It can have a high percentage of short, simple sentences that present the topic first. It can be written entirely in the active voice. And, yet, the message can still have a low impact on the reader. How can this happen? The answer is simple. All a writer needs to do is to present a message in one huge paragraph covering the page from margin to margin.

This chapter will show you how to avoid this pitfall by keeping in mind the notion of **high-impact appearance**. Then, since appearance is the final element of the non-sensitive message system, the chapter will summarize and apply the system to a typical business memo.

THE IMPORTANCE OF VISUAL APPEAL

If high-impact writing is that which leaps off the page into the reader's mind, the appearance of each paragraph and of each page plays an important role in making writing high impact.

Paragraphing plays an important role in impact.

The final high-impact principle addresses the issue of appearance.

HIGH-IMPACT PRINCIPLE 7:

For high-impact appearance:

a. Vary the size of your paragraphs. Make most of them short—about three or four sentences per paragraph. People find short paragraphs easier to read than long ones.
b. Indent and itemize multiple ideas in paragraphs.
c. Allow plenty of white space on the page. Readers unconsciously react favorably to it.
d. Use headings wherever possible.

Visual Appeal through Lists

Why people like short paragraphs is obvious. But why they like itemized lists is less obvious. Consider the following two versions of the same one-sentence paragraph:

Readers like itemized lists.

Version A. Low Impact

The key point is that all too few companies possess a fully integrated scheme for breaking down corporate objectives into digestible chunks; establishing individual performance standards; establishing wage, salary, and employee benefit structures; appraising performance at regular intervals; and rewarding or taking remedial steps on the basis of performance.

Version B. High Impact

The key point is that all too few companies possess a fully integrated scheme for

1. Breaking down corporate objectives into digestible chunks;
2. Establishing individual performance standards;

3. Establishing wage, salary, and employee benefit structures;

4. Appraising performance at regular intervals;

5. Rewarding or taking remedial steps on the basis of performance.

White space helps present ideas in manageable bits.

Why is Version B so much easier to understand? The answer is that it lists items and uses **white space** to break up the ideas into bite-size pieces. Version A, by contrast, requires the reader to search for the semi-colons that indicate where a new item begins. White space, resulting from itemization, does a far better job of indicating the start of a new idea.

Applying High-Impact Principle 7

When writing is visually attractive to readers, they are much more likely to understand quickly what has been written. In the four examples that follow, we have chosen passages typical of business reports. These passages sometimes include long, passive sentences and Latinate words. See how the addition of white space dramatically improves the visual attractiveness and readability of even these hard-to-read passages.

I. Original

During the changeover from contract guards to security officers, the quality of the existing contract security service must be upgraded through the careful selection of vendors and implementation of acceptable contractual performance requirements. In those instances where guard services are provided by the landlord as part of the lease, appropriate negotiations must be conducted by Purchasing to terminate this service within the specified changeover time period.

I. High-Impact Version

During the changeover from contract guards to security officers, the quality of the existing contract security service must be upgraded through

1. The careful selection of vendors.

2. Implementation of acceptable contractual performance requirements.

In those instances where guard services are provided by the landlord as part of the lease, appropriate negotiations must be conducted by Purchasing to terminate this service within the specified changeover time period.

II. Original

To qualify for the achievement award, sales representatives must accomplish one of the following: They must sign twenty new accounts, accumulate 10,000 sales points, or sell 100 installed units within one year.

II. High-Impact Version

To qualify for the achievement award, a sales representative must accomplish one of the following within one year:

1. Sign twenty new accounts.
2. Accumulate 10,000 sales points.
3. Sell 100 installed units.

III. Original

The advent of reorganization and the migration of computer personnel to the Management Segment make it essential that we continue to provide transfer information to headquarters. Therefore, I am requesting authorization to conduct training sessions for these (approximately 2 percent) randomly selected personnel transferring to Management so that we may continue to provide the transfer information previously collected. I am also requesting that the personnel conducting these essential training activities be released temporarily from their customary assigned duties.

III. High-Impact Version

The advent of reorganization and the migration of computer personnel to the Management Segment make it essential that we continue to provide transfer information to headquarters. Because of this, I am requesting

1. Authorization to conduct training sessions for these (approximately 2 percent) randomly selected personnel transferring to Management so that we may continue to provide the transfer information previously collected.
2. That the personnel conducting these essential training activities be released temporarily from their customary assigned duties.

IV. Original

Based on our very good experience in Ohio, we are tentatively planning on two-and-a-half days for the meeting. I propose that one day be devoted to Time Management. Much will have happened since March, and we can profitably review and discuss (a) the status of State and Local programs—there are a lot of data, case studies and specific results; and (b) some proposed programs. The rest of the meeting should be devoted to general interest topics affecting all operations and timely reports and presentations. As in the past, I would ask each of you to send your recommendations for agenda items to Dorothy Barton well in advance of the meeting. Dorothy has prepared some topics we might cover, and these are attached.

IV. High-Impact Version

Based on our very good experience in Ohio, we are tentatively planning on two-and-a-half days for the meeting. Since much will have happened since March, I propose that we can profitably review and discuss the following:

a. The status of State and Local programs—there are a lot of data, case studies and specific results.

b. Some proposed programs.

c. Time management, timely reports, and presentations as well as topics affecting all operations.

As in the past, I would ask each of you to send your recommendations for agenda items to Dorothy Barton well in advance of the meeting. Dorothy has prepared some topics we might cover, and these are attached.

The Importance of White Space in College Writing

Although white space is probably the easiest of all impact strategies to implement, it is also the one students most frequently forget to use when they submit a written assignment for class. Yet, the ease of reading resulting from an effective use of white space can have a significant influence on the grade they will receive.

Think of what college professors face when they ask students to submit reports, term papers, or case analyses. They face grading as many as 100 papers ranging in length from 5 to 20 pages. Each paper needs to be evaluated and analyzed. Worse yet, most of the time, all papers deal with the same topic!

A paper with white space makes a better impression.

Which paper do you think will make a better first impression—one that is filled with large blocks of impenetrable print or one that has lots of indentations and short to medium-length paragraphs? The more visually attractive paper will make a better first impression and, in the end, probably receive a better final grade.

Overdoing a Good Thing

Do not make your lists too long.

We must offer one important warning. Just as eight glasses of water a day are good, and eighty are bad, allowing a list to go on and on makes a bad thing out of a good one. Likewise, several lists, one after the other with no prose interruptions, create a message as monotonous as one with long, bulky paragraphs. The key is always visual variety, using lists, paragraphs, indentions, or any other strategy that makes the message visually attractive to the reader.

Look at the following letter and decide for yourself the effectiveness of the long list of items.

CREDIT EVALUATORS, INC.
8024 Stinson Boulevard
Minneapolis, Minnesota 55432

September 30, 19——

Ms. Beverly Jamison
ABC Corporation
910 Parkdale Drive
Memphis, TN 38116

Dear Ms. Jamison:

Michael Davidson, owner of XYZ Office Furniture and Supplies, should be given limited credit. If Mr. Davidson proves to be a good customer, he should be considered for extended credit. Included below are the terms ABC should extend, background credit information supporting ABC's terms, and personal background information about Mr. Davidson.

1. $4,000 credit limit
2. Upon proof of asset-to-liabilities ratio improvement, credit extension to $25,000 should be considered
3. Basic rating: pay as agreed
4. Employees Credit Bureau personal rating: good
5. Personal home mortgage: paid in full as of this date
6. Nine months of operation of own business: 40% stock turnover
7. Graduate of DEF University with a degree in General Management
8. General Manager of large chain of retail office supply stores: five years
9. Past business association with LMN, Inc.: Mr. Davidson sometimes purchased $200,000 worth of merchandise from LMN
10. XYZ Office Furniture and Supplies located at 6290 Capri Street, Minneapolis, Minnesota 38118. Business is located in an area with large growth potential.

Sincerely,

Theodore Bambeneck

Theodore Bambeneck
Chief Credit Evaluator

No one wants to read all these listed items. In fact, few people would even be willing to read the list because of the way that the different items in the contract sentence are merged into one long list. Obviously, the passage would improve significantly if we (a) organized the ten items in the list into the three groups listed in the contract sentence and (b) changed some of the listed information into a prose format. Something like the following does the job much more effectively:

CREDIT EVALUATORS, INC.
8024 Stinson Boulevard
Minneapolis, Minnesota 55432

September 30, 19— —

Ms. Beverly Jamison
ABC Corporation
910 Parkdale Drive
Memphis, TN 38116

Dear Ms. Jamison:

Michael Davidson, owner of XYZ Office Furniture and Supplies, should be given limited credit. If Mr. Davidson proves to be a good customer, he should be considered for extended credit. Included below are

1. The terms ABC should extend,
2. Background credit information supporting ABC's terms, and
3. Personal background information about Mr. Davidson.

Credit Terms

ABC should extend Michael Davidson a $4,000 credit limit. When Mr. Davidson is able to provide proof of an improved asset-to-liabilities ratio, ABC should consider a credit extension—perhaps to as high as $25,000.

Background Credit Information

Some selected information we gathered about Mr. Davidson's credit background follows:

1. Basic credit rating: pay as agreed.
2. Employees Credit Bureau personal rating: good.
3. Personal home mortgage: paid in full as of this date.
4. Nine months of operation of own business: 40 percent stock turnover.

Personal Background Information

Michael Davidson is a graduate of DEF University with a degree in General Management. For five years he worked as General Manager of a large chain of retail office supply stores. He has past business association with LMN, Inc. and sometimes purchased $200,000 worth of merchandise from LMN.

XYZ Office Furniture and Supplies is located at
    6290 Capri Street
    Minneapolis, Minnesota 38118
His business is located in an area with large growth potential.

       Sincerely,

       Theodore Bambeneck

       Theodore Bambeneck
       Chief Credit Evaluator

MEMO RESCUE ATTEMPT: STEP THREE

Now let's apply the concept of white space to our Management Conference memo of page 147. Earlier, we made some improvements to it by changing its word choice and sentence structure. Let's see what white space will contribute.

    Version C. With White Space and Listed Items

TO: H. B. Smith

FROM: R. L. Greene

SUBJECT: Management Conference

DATE: August 3, 19——

The August 29 Management Conference has been canceled. Here is why:

1. Key people planning to attend had too many scheduling conflicts.
2. Immediate rescheduling of the conference was impossible because branch managers are under tremendous pressure to reach sales quotas. Although branch managers are aware of the importance of the conference, they realize that sales quotas are always of first importance.
3. Branch managers believe that if they left the branches early, they would set a bad example for their subordinates.

Notice how this final rescue attempt has used white space to list the three points given as reasons for canceling the conference. The information leaps into your mind far more easily. By applying the principles of high-impact writing, we have transformed an unreadable memo into one that gets the job done effectively.

PUTTING IT ALL TOGETHER:
ORGANIZATION AND IMPACT UNITED

You now have the tools to write clear non-sensitive messages.

Units 2 through 4 have focused on non-sensitive messages. Now you should understand how to organize messages through bottom-lining, how to use contract sentences and skeletal organization, and how and when to create high-impact prose. As a result, you now possess the tools necessary to write clear memos for the vast majority of situations you will encounter in business.

With this understanding, you can revise and rework even the poorest of written memos so that they are efficient and can get the job done effectively. To prove this statement, let's systematically clean up another difficult memo. We will apply the principles we have presented about organization and impact and see what improvements we can make in this seemingly impossible memo. Please notice that while we follow a sequence of steps to improve the memo, the actual order of the steps could be changed. Thus, for example, revisions for word choice could easily come before, rather than after, paragraph structure if a writer prefers such an order.

Original

TO: J. D. Gibbons

FROM: R. A. Turner

SUBJECT: Interoffice Systems

DATE: April 29, 19— —

While interoffice systems have been extant for approximately half a decade, still being generated are the definition, concept, and approach to be employed in moving these systems into external markets. Conceptions of how management might alter or alleviate matters on subsequent occasions are held by sources who have been involved with the project, and availability of interchange of experience from interoffice to external systems has to be improved. Fundamental to our product's success are contemplated to be installability, effortless utilization, and personal comfort of the user. For insurance of fruition, adaptation to the aforementioned thoughts could be considered.

It would be very difficult to revise a memo this terrible in one step. But if you break down the memo and approach it step by step using the principles you have learned, the task will not be as difficult. The first step is to figure out what the bottom line is and to insert a bottom-line sentence. Since the memo is relatively short, there is no need for a contract sentence and a skeletal framework.

Version A. Bottom-Line Sentence Added

TO: J. D. Gibbons

FROM: R. A. Turner

SUBJECT: Interoffice Systems

DATE: April 29, 19— —

A few thoughts could be interchanged on the subject of selling interoffice systems, for while the systems have been extant for approximately half a decade, still being generated are the definition, concept, and approach to be employed in moving these systems into external markets. Conceptions of how management might alter or alleviate matters on subsequent occasions are held by sources who have been involved with the project, and availability of interchange of experience from interoffice to external systems has to be improved. Fundamental to our product's success are contemplated to be installability, effortless utilization, and personal comfort of the user. For insurance of fruition, adaptation to the aforementioned thoughts could be considered.

Next, primarily for appearance, let's add white space by dividing the memo into paragraphs.

Version B. Divided into Paragraphs

TO: J. D. Gibbons

FROM: R. A. Turner

SUBJECT: Interoffice Systems

DATE: April 29, 19— —

A few thoughts could be interchanged on the subject of selling interoffice systems, for while the systems have been extant for approximately half a decade, still being generated are the definition, concept, and approach to be employed in moving these systems into external markets.

Conceptions of how management might alter or alleviate matters on subsequent occasions are held by sources who have been involved with the project, and availability of interchange of experience from interoffice to external systems has to be improved.

Fundamental to our product's success are contemplated to be installability, effortless utilization, and personal comfort of the user.

For insurance of fruition, adaptation to the aforementioned thoughts could be considered.

Now let's solve one of the major problems of this message by simplifying the words used.

Version C. Word Choice Simplified

TO: J. D. Gibbons

FROM: R. A. Turner

SUBJECT: Interoffice Systems

DATE: April 29, 19— —

A few thoughts could be exchanged on the subject of selling interoffice systems, for while the systems have been around for about five years, still being developed are the definition, concept, and approach to be employed in selling these systems to customers.

Ideas on how management might proceed differently (or better) in the future are held by people who have been working on the project, and the experience of those people who have used interoffice systems has to be made available to those planning to sell these systems.

Key to our product's success are thought to be ease of installation, simplicity of use, and careful attention to the personal comfort of the user.

For continued success to be ensured, these thoughts need to be kept constantly in mind.

This change helped a great deal. Now let's shorten the sentences and present the topics at the beginning of the sentences.

Version D. Sentences Shortened

TO: J. D. Gibbons

FROM: R. A. Turner

SUBJECT: Interoffice Systems

DATE: April 29, 19— —

A few thoughts could be exchanged on the subject of selling interoffice systems. The definition, concept, and approach to selling these systems to customers are still being developed, even though the systems have been around for about five years.

Ideas on how management might proceed differently (or better) in the future are held by people who have been working on the project. The experience of those people who have used interoffice systems has to be made available to those planning to sell these systems.

Keys to our product's success are thought to be installation, simplicity of use, and careful attention to the personal comfort of the user.

These thoughts need constantly to be kept in mind for continued success to be ensured.

Once we have shortened the sentences, we see that one of the major problems still remaining is that many of the sentences are passive. Let's make them active.

Version E. Sentences Made Active

TO: J. D. Gibbons

FROM: R. A. Turner

SUBJECT: Interoffice Systems

DATE: April 29, 19— —

I would like to exchange a few thoughts with you on the subject of selling interoffice systems. We still have not developed a well thought-out approach to selling these systems to customers, even though the systems have been around for about five years.

People who have been working on the project have ideas on how management might proceed differently (or better) in the future. Those people who have used interoffice systems must be able to share their experience with those planning to sell these systems.

The keys to our product's success are ease of operation, simplicity of use, and careful attention to the personal comfort of the user.

Keep these thoughts in mind, and we will ensure continued success.

Now let's increase white space through itemization and, in the process, eliminate a few other excess words.

TO: J. D. Gibbons

FROM: R. A. Turner

SUBJECT: Interoffice Systems

DATE: April 29, 19——

I would like to exchange a few thoughts with you on the subject of selling interoffice systems.

1. We still have not developed a well thought-out approach to selling these systems to customers, even though the systems have been around for about five years.

2. People who have been working on the project have ideas on how management might proceed differently (or better) in the future.

3. Those people who have used interoffice systems must be able to share their experience with those who are planning to sell these systems.

4. The keys to our product's success are ease of operation, simplicity of use, and careful attention to the personal comfort of the user.

Keep these thoughts in mind, and we will ensure continued success.

You have just witnessed how application of the principles of bottom-lining and high-impact writing can dramatically improve even the most poorly written non-sensitive message.

SUMMARY

Businesspeople who want to write high-impact messages must make sure that their messages have a **high-impact appearance** as well as content. Writers can select conversational words with Anglo-Saxon origins. They can insert simple, subject-verb-object sentences throughout the message. And they can check to see that most sentences are written in the active voice. But all their efforts prove useless if they forget to use the strategy of **white space.**

The best written message may lose its readers only because it lacks white space. Therefore, remember to make your high-impact message as visually attractive as you possibly can. Provide visual variety on the page through short paragraphs, headings, lists, and indentations. Without such techniques, you may find yourself wondering how your boss could possibly have overlooked or ignored the well-written message you recently sent.

REVIEW QUESTIONS

1. What effects on readers can the visual appearance of a document produce?

2. State four ways you can create high-impact paragraphs.

3. What is the concept of white space?

4. Why do businesspeople like short paragraphs and itemized lists?

5. Describe the steps you should use to edit your memos and reports.

DISCUSSION QUESTIONS

1. Discuss ways that white space can reinforce clear sentence structure, punctuation, and emphasis.

2. Employees of a major U.S. company often praise the company's unwritten rule that no internal memo can be longer than one page. What are the advantages and disadvantages of such a rule?

3. Some experts say word choice contributes most to high-impact messages. Other experts think sentence structure or white space has the most influence on impact. Which of these three techniques do you think has the greatest effect on impact? Why?

2. a) Vary the size, about 3-4 sentences
   b) indent + itemize multiple ideas
   c) allow plenty of white space on page
   d) use headings where possible

3. The concept of w.s. is to keep present ideas in manageable bits.

4. the message is easier to understand

5.

HIGH-IMPACT PRINCIPLES
REVIEW LIST

1

Words derived from Anglo-Saxon are high impact. Readers appreciate these words because they are readily understood, familiar, and clear.

2

When writing, use words you would use in normal business conversation.

3

Control wordiness by avoiding empty phrases and unnecessary words.

4

a. Use simple sentences for maximum impact.
b. Use compound sentences to lower a message's impact.
c. Use complex and simple sentences for variety and high impact.

5

Put the subject first as often as possible in sentences used in non-sensitive messages.

6

For high-impact sentences
a. Use the active voice as much as possible.
b. Minimize or avoid using the passive voice.

7

For high-impact appearance:
a. Vary the size of your paragraphs. Make most of them short—about three or four sentences per paragraph. People find short paragraphs easier to read than long ones.
b. Indent and itemize multiple ideas in paragraphs.
c. Allow plenty of white space on the page. Readers unconsciously react favorably to it.
d. Use headings wherever possible.

EXERCISES

Exercise 1
Word Choice

Which of the following examples demonstrate high-impact writing?

1. I consider Mr. Jones's attendance at Friday's meeting a <u>tertium quid.</u>

2. We need to take more than a maieutic approach to our training sessions.

3. Initial procurements will be handled by the home office purchasing department (in conjunction with legal, patent, and business practices functions) with the purpose of formulating acceptable procedures, terms and conditions as guidelines for subsequent procurements.

4. Your organization has a major interest in this process. And I see the expertise you have as a necessary basis for simplifying the procedures.

5. Jack, we recently spoke with Stan Jones relative to his comments on the management trainee program.

6. The director of finance disagrees with the strategy for three reasons.

7. Contemplating the current plethora of end-of-the-month workloads, we find it incumbent upon us to ensure that we spread the workload as evenly as possible across the entire month.

8. By cumulative habituation a bias of this character may come to have very substantial consequences for the range and scope of technological knowledge.

9. Only when a company's productivity effort encompasses the entire organization and all of its systems and procedures does it represent a genuinely strategic approach to productivity management.

10. Sound industrial policy could aid the performance of all the industrial countries.

Exercise 2
Word Choice

Rewrite the following sentences according to the High-Impact Principles discussed in Unit 4.

1. To most company executives, the prospect of sudden immersion in the insurance business via an insurance subsidiary is not an enticing one.

2. Our company happily furnishes documentation of our minority ownership to concerned parties.

3. There is another and better articulated reason why American businesspeople and industrialists eschew involvement in high-level social welfare planning.

4. Designing a suitable financial plan for compensating sales personnel is an important, difficult, and highly perplexing task.

5. Since some economic experts predict recurrent and increasingly severe recessions throughout the present decade, it appears that plant closings and large-scale layoffs and terminations will remain a recurring phenomenon.

6. Organizations suffering from varying degrees of vagueness and ambiguity would do well to follow the practices of successful organizations.

7. Sales are made because the customer needs the product and has systematically evaluated competing alternatives before making the selection.

8. The propensity for increased consumption is diminishing as a basic motive for consumer behavior.

9. Business educators need to employ a wide variety of pedagogical techniques to ensure that students develop the necessary interpersonal skills.

10. Critics often argue that executive compensation is excessive.

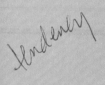

Exercise 3
Sentence Structure

In each of the following sets, choose the version that has a higher impact.

Set 1

a. In order to assure that the system will work smoothly, operators generally receive a certain amount of training from the equipment vendor and the center's supervisor should augment this training with information about the company's own procedures, formats, and media management system.

b. In order to assure that the system will work smoothly, operators generally receive a certain amount of training from the equipment vendor. The center's supervisor should augment this training with information about the company's own procedures, formats, and media management system.

Set 2

a. Getting a star performance out of any office automation system ultimately depends upon the quality—and selection—of the software that controls it, and choosing the appropriate programs can turn into a search for the proverbial needle in a haystack if you don't know what you want.

b. Getting a star performance out of any office automation system ultimately depends upon the quality—and selection—of the software that controls it. Choosing the appropriate programs can turn into a search for the proverbial needle in a haystack if you don't know what you want.

What factor influenced your choice in Sets 1 and 2?

Set 3

a. The client agreed to accept our apology after I visited him and discussed the problem.
b. After I visited the client and discussed the problem with him, he agreed to accept our apology.

Set 4

a. Because of problems with the phone system and with the electronic message board, I am concerned about communication in the office.
b. I am concerned about communication in the office, because of problems with the phone system and the electronic message board.

What factor influenced your choice in Sets 3 and 4?

Set 5

a. A visit was made to Mr. Johnson, and the project was approved.
b. Mr. Johnson was visited by me, and I approved the project.
c. I visited Mr. Johnson and approved the project.

Set 6

a. A reason to close the account was given.
b. A reason to close the account was given by the credit manager.
c. The credit manager gave a reason to close the account.

What factor influenced your choice in Sets 5 and 6?

Exercise 4
Sentence Structure

Decide whether each of the following sentences is active or passive.

1. The job enrichment project can be evaluated by Personnel from two perspectives.
2. I propose that one day be devoted by the directors to Quality Programs.
3. Note that the prioritized copies do not provide space for the Priority Ranking Space.
4. During April, Field Administration participated in a number of meetings and reviews pertinent to our productivity program efforts.
5. Serious attention to this review must be given.
6. This commitment has been met by XYZ.

7. The printout contains the latest sales figures.

8. A meeting of regional National Account/Special Systems Managers was conducted in Detroit from June 25 to June 26.

9. I am happy to announce the extension of this program to June 30 of this year.

10. Our marketing objective will be met through the advertising plan.

Exercise 5
Word Choice, Sentence Structure, and Appearance

Revise the following passages to make them higher impact.

1. Would you please get the plan of activity required to support this July 2 date document for me, outline our current view of the basis on which we will proceed with shipment in August, and for the rest of the year, see that appropriate work is underway within the division to support that shipment approach, and schedule necessary reviews both inside and outside of the division at the beginning of July.

2. It was noted that the first of July is a key date to review the overall status of the new system and to conclude our plans for moving this system to the field this year.

3. The new computer station provides working facilities for two operators simultaneously, and it has two desk-height work areas, each with a recessed keyboard and a display screen. The keyboard is situated at an angle with the desk, and the display screen is not far above the table surface, an arrangement that gives maximum convenience in operation and, with the source document in front of the display screen, allows the operator to check the data entry with a minimum of eye movement.

4. There are many companies that use computers for specialized purposes, that is, for activities other than processing business information, and often these groups have their own systems and programming staffs, and may operate their own computers as well, depending on the nature of the type of data and hardware requirements involved.

5. When a company initially acquires a computer, its primary need is for programming personnel to convert existing systems to the computer and to obtain systems analysts to improve the already converted systems and to develop new computer-based systems to improve the efficiency and profitability of company operations.

6. In most companies with field selling organizations, it is the compensation paid to salespeople that is the largest single element of selling cost and for this reason alone, it is important not to overpay salespeople, since to do so unnecessarily increases selling costs and reduces the company's profits.

7. There are times when managers are confronted with evidence that their subordinates hold a variety of attitudes toward them, toward the organization, and, especially, toward their own jobs, but what most managers are not sure of is how they should react to these attitudes.

8. Through electronic shopping, consumers will be in a position to acquire more knowledge about alternative offerings, knowledge concerning price, brand, retail outlet, and services, and armed with this knowledge, consumers may demand explanations of price differences, especially if the brands are identical or perceived to be close substitutes.

9. Developing a strong retail sales force is not a matter of luck; training is needed and adequate incentives must exist to motivate personnel to high levels of performance.

10. The importance of completely honest, open, and clear communication often is stressed in management literature and by managers themselves, but it is easy to find instances in which managers have counted on the fact that a message can be interpreted in more than one way.

CASES

The following Allgood Products cases provide an opportunity to practice the bottom-line organizational skills you learned in Units 2 and 3 and the impact strategies you learned in Unit 4. We have added additional questions to help you effectively control the impact in these cases.

Step 1: Plan

PLAN ORGANIZATION

What is the message's bottom line?

Is the message complex and/or long enough to need a contract sentence? Subcontract sentences? Skeletal organization? Graphics?

PLAN IMPACT

What types of words, sentences, and visual techniques will give the message its highest level of impact?

Step 2: Create

Compose a draft copy of the message.

Step 3: Review and Revise

ORGANIZATION

Is the bottom-line statement made clearly and promptly?

If needed:

- Is a contract sentence clearly presented? Are subcontract sentences used? Does the skeletal organization follow the order of the contract sentence?
- Are graphics used to present and clarify complex data? Are the graphics properly introduced, appropriate for the information conveyed, and free of bias and distortion?

IMPACT
Word Choice

Are the words conversational, that is, of Anglo-Saxon origin?

Are unnecessary or empty words and phrases eliminated?

SENTENCE STRUCTURE

Does the draft have an adequate mixture of simple and complex sentences?

Have compound sentences been used sparingly?

Do most sentences present the topic first?

Are most sentences in the active voice?

APPEARANCE

Is the message visually attractive?

Does the message use lists, indentations, headings, and so on, to increase white space?

Does the message avoid monotony (caused by overuse of white space techniques)?

Case 1
Flex-Time Proposal

You are working for Samuel Potnick, Treasurer and Vice President of Finance. Recently, Potnick commented to you that many of the people who work within his function seem tired and irritable. Furthermore, Potnick went on, his function has the highest yearly absentee rate in Allgood Products—an average of 12 missed days per employee.

When you show an interest in his problem, Potnick tells you that part of the problem is the life style typical of the people employed by his function. Thirty percent of his staff of thirty people live more than forty miles away and commute to work each day. The snarled rush-hour traffic inevitably leads to these employees being tired, nervous, and irritable. In addition, 40 percent of the employees who live nearby are young, married people with small children. When a child becomes ill, one of the parents has to miss work.

"What about turnover?" you ask.

"Minimal," Potnick replies. "These are young, two-career, professional families. Both spouses have planned to work all along."

"Anyway," he continues, "most of these young families are so deep in debt that they need two incomes."

The next day, Saturday, you are out playing tennis when a seemingly brilliant idea strikes you: Why not suggest flexible work hours for Samuel Potnick's function?

The more you think about this idea, the more you convince yourself that the idea just might work. The plan would permit employees to work for eight-hour segments any time between 7 A.M. and 10 P.M. The employees would sign up in advance for certain hours and would have to work during those hours unless other arrangements were made. Work quotas would have to be established to cover the eight-hour blocks. The first person to arrive in the morning would open the office, and the last person out would close it up. The employees would, of course, need keys to the office, but a multiple-lock system could be installed to control the areas employees have access to. After all, you realize, there is no reason why everyone has to be on the job between 9 and 5.

"Why," you ask yourself, "would this system be helpful? Is it worthwhile for me to propose such a program?" Well, for one thing, workers won't have to fight rush-hour traffic. This would certainly help the employees who drive from distant suburbs. Also, the freedom to choose their own schedule might lead to improvements in morale. Employees and their spouses may be able to coordinate their schedules and so reduce child-care expenses.

"Anything wrong with the plan?" you ask yourself. Well, for one thing, costs of heating, cooling, and lighting the office will increase. Also, with people coming and going at different times, the office will seem disorganized. And, not all people can handle the responsibility of working unsupervised.

Assignment

After weighing the pros and cons of flexible work hours, you decide that you have come up with an idea worth proposing. Write a memo to Samuel Potnick, asking him to authorize a preliminary study of such a plan. Be sure to describe your ideas in enough detail so that Potnick can make a preliminary judgment about your proposal.

Case 2
Annual Vacations

You are Mary Lou Higgins's assistant and have been assigned the task of analyzing an unusual problem: Allgood Products' policy urges but does not *demand* that all levels of management take their 30-days annual vacation. A surprising 38 percent of the company's management-level employees have already accrued more than 30 days of vacation time. Although the actual figures would be hard to determine quickly, Higgins's guess is that most of these employees have accrued 60 days or more.

Higgins has been advised by the company's medical department that such employees, by working constantly and taking little or no vacation, may develop stress reactions that will be damaging to their health over a period of time. If so, their overwork may actually be injurious not only to them but also to Allgood Products, which has to pay the premium on insurance benefits and fund a very generous sick-leave policy.

Higgins's instructions to you are, "This situation is really serious. I want you to look into it. Perhaps you ought to take a random sample of some of the individuals who are part of this 38 percent and conduct in-depth interviews with them. Then report your findings to me as soon as you can. We'll naturally cover all your travel expenses."

Acting upon her instructions, you had Mary Lou Higgins's staff randomly select from various locations 100 Allgood employees who have accrued over 50 days of vacation time. You then conducted in-depth interviews with them. Now, three weeks later, you feel that you can group the employees you interviewed into two main categories:

Category 1. Those who are motivated by fear
These fearful employees are of two types:
1a. Some of those interviewed perceive themselves to be—and may actually be—of marginal value to the company. Consequently, they fear that if they take a vacation, they may never be missed. Or they fear that in their absence somebody else may prove to be able to do their job better than they can.

1b. Some others clearly have the notion that their immediate superiors are "out to get them." Therefore, they claim they constantly work out of fear. Some of these employees may be overreacting, but you have no way of knowing from your interviews.

Category 2. Those who are obsessed with their work
These employees see themselves as hard "drivers" who are anxious to rise as rapidly in the company as possible. Consequently, taking vacation time just isn't in their plans. Work, not leisure activity, is what they worship.

Some are single, and constant work presents no serious social problems. Based on hints they gave during the interviews, some of the married managers seem to have unhappy home lives (possibly, of course, because of their excessive dedication to their jobs). They seem to enjoy life more on the job than they do at home. As they see it, a vacation that saddles them with having to spend time with families may be really no vacation at all.

ATTACHMENT A
AVERAGE NUMBER OF DAYS SICK LEAVE TAKEN BY 100 EMPLOYEES
IN TWO CATEGORIES (OVER A FIVE-YEAR PERIOD)

Category 1. Self-Styled "Fearful" Employees (N = 45)

Sick-Leave Days per Employee	Number of Employees	Yearly Average of Sick-Leave Days
26 and over	12	6.7
11–25	19	4.2
0–10	14	1.9

Category 2. Self-Styled "Hard-Driving" Employees (N = 55)

Sick-Leave Days per Employee	Number of Employees	Yearly Average of Sick-Leave Days
26 and over	1	17
11–25	7	2.5
0–10	47	0.6

On a hunch, you ask Higgins's staff to do a comparison of the days lost through sickness over the past five years by both groups. You want to determine whether the "hard drivers" have, as Allgood's medical department suggested, a poorer health record than do the "fearful" employees. Attachment A contains the information that the personnel records reveal. You note that the hard-driving group of employees (with the exception of one employee who has averaged 17 days of sick leave over the past five years) has a much better health record than does the fearful one. This makes it difficult for you to know what to recommend.

You are puzzled as to whether you should report your suspicions that psychological counseling for the fearful group might be better than forcing them to take vacations that will only put greater pressure on them to feel fearful. You are also not sure that forcing the hard-driving group to take vacations will be good for them either. After all, if hard work does not adversely affect their health (and increase Allgood's health insurance costs), then it should be the employees' business whether or not they take vacations.

You realize, of course, that the hard-drivers may be on the way to serious illnesses, but they do not seem to be developing stress reactions right now. All available evidence points out that they are healthier than are the fearful ones.

Because of your concern, you write a memo to Dr. Aaron Bernstein, Director of Allgood Products Medical Department, pointing out the results of your study and asking for advice. Dr. Bernstein's memo in response to yours states that there are "hundreds of studies in the medical literature supporting the idea that taking regular vacations is conducive to sound health and to the reduction of stress-related illness. The literature is so voluminous, and the conclusions so overwhelming, that all medical authorities and insurance companies urge employers to force employees, if necessary, to take annual vacations."

Assignment 1 — Progress Report

This morning you received the following note from Mary Lou Higgins:

What have you done so far about the vacation problem I asked you to look into? Have you made any progress? Let me know where you are on the project by the end of today.

Write a memo to Higgins telling her where you are in terms of this project. (Hint: You have collected all the information you intend to collect. Since you need to answer Higgins quickly, you should primarily emphasize what you have done, not your findings, conclusions, or recommendations.)

Assignment 2 — Report

Higgins has requested a copy of your final report by tomorrow morning. She says she was interested by your progress report and wants to know your conclusions before she attends the Executive Committee meeting (attended by all senior executives at Allgood). Write her a report stating your findings and drawing conclusions from them. Be sure to support all conclusions with the facts you have collected.

Assignment 3

Higgins has one more assignment for you. She says, "I am so impressed and intrigued by your study that I want you to do one more thing for me. Based on your findings, I would like you to prepare a report to the Executive Committee making recommendations about what Allgood should and should not do in terms of its Annual Vacation Policy. Should we allow employees to collect as much vacation leave as possible, or should we force them to use at least some portion of their leave?" Write this report for Mary Lou Higgins.

Case 3
Consulting Assignment

Carl Hilton, President of Allgood Products, calls you into his office. He tells you that he recently attended a presentation concerning the high costs of inefficiently written communications. The presentation was conducted by a large consulting company that was soliciting business.

Hilton says he was impressed by the presentation but does not want to spend a large amount of money finding out more about a problem he already knows exists. He does not doubt that Allgood's internal and external correspondence could be dramatically improved. But he wants to find out the steps that could be taken to improve writing at Allgood.

Hilton gives you the following assignment: "Gather up some samples of typical Allgood messages and study them. Then write a detailed memo telling me what you think about the way these messages are written. Be as clear and precise as you can about the messages and their problems."

Assignment 1

The attached letters, memos, and excerpts from reports are typical of those you collected. Notice that each sample is non-sensitive. Analyze these documents in terms of (a) the effectiveness of their organization and (b) the appropriateness of their impact. Write a memo reporting the results of your analysis to Carl Hilton.

An excerpt from a report on improving Allgood's collection procedures.

ATTACHMENT A

Establishing and maintaining effective management control over the collection function has become more important than ever in today's highly competitive credit environment. Intense competition for installment and revolving plan customers has created a situation where larger portfolios and increasing delinquency levels are taxing most collection functions to their limit. What is needed to assist with management of this vital function are additional tools allowing for significant automation of routine portions of collection activities. Statistical forecasting techniques have been employed for over 30 years in the assessment of the risk associated with new credit applicants. More recently, these same techniques have been applied successfully to forecasting the future behavior of existing customers based on past experience. Collection models have become well-accepted in the credit industry and presently are being used by banks, oil companies, department stores, other retailers, and finance companies to assist with the management of the collection function.

A typical memo sent by a busy executive. Names have been deleted for confidentiality.

TO:

FROM:

SUBJECT:

DATE:

Attached is a copy of the performance plan which we utilized in our last appraisal of managers in your department. I would like to have you take the next two or three weeks to go over this carefully and see whether or not it meets your expectations as to what your objectives are for 19— —. Please get a date on my calendar so we can spend an hour to discuss this in more detail sometime between March 3 and March 23. In addition to the normal performance criteria, I would like this year to establish some objectives which we may or may not wish to incorporate into the performance plan. Specifically, I would like you to set at least five things that you would like to have your department accomplish this year, that is, significant objectives that will have an impact on the personnel function. You are by no means limited to five; you can feel free to expand if you wish. These objectives should be discussed when we meet regarding the performance plan.

A typical letter to stockholders.

ATTACHMENT C

Dear Stockholder:

Allgood Products, Inc. offers a plan whereby holders of both classes of its common stock may automatically reinvest dividends toward purchase of additional shares of the company's Class A common stock without charge or brokerage fees. A prospectus explaining the plan in detail is available. Requests for the prospectus should be directed to the Corporate Secretary at the corporate office. As provided in the company's amended Certification of Incorporation, shares of the company's Class B common stock may be converted at any time into shares of Class A common stock on a one-for-one basis, with no payment or fee when sent to the company's transfer agent at the address shown below.

An excerpt from a typical market research report.

ATTACHMENT D

Hospitals today are developing new strategies to fill unoccupied beds. They are discounting charges, offering competitive per diem rates, or accepting pre-set amounts. In addition, hospitals are developing sophisticated marketing plans to attract specialized niche markets that feed their traditional referral networks. Recent trends suggest that finance is called upon more frequently to work with others in product pricing, revenue forecasting, and financial feasibility assessments of new programs and services, mergers, acquisitions, and joint ventures. The integration of finance and marketing is often times difficult, but the rewards are three-fold—realistic and effective strategic plans, growth in market share, and a healthier bottom line.

Assignment 2

Carl Hilton received and was pleased by your analysis of Allgood's messages. He now calls you in and gives you a new assignment. You are to write him a report suggesting ways Allgood can improve the efficiency of its letters, memos, and reports. Hilton tells you to base the report on the materials you used for your earlier analysis. He adds that in your report, you should include revisions of some of the documents you analyzed.

REFERENCES

Aldrich, P. G. (1987). Don't let your writing cost you clients. *National Public Accountants, 32,* 34–35.

Aldrich, P. G. (1985). Skirting Sexism. *Nation's Business, 73,* 34–36.

Antonoff, M. (1986). Getting them to read it. *Personal Computing, 10,* 96–105.

Bacon, M. S. (1983). What we should have said was. . . . *Association Management, 35,* 61–67.

Barr, L. (1986). How to take the stuffiness out of business writing. *Manage, 38,* 4–5.

Booher, D. (1984). Writing more but enjoying it less? *Training and Development Journal, 38,* 48–51.

Bureau of Business Practice, Inc. (1969). Action guide: How to write effective business reports.

Calkins, K. (1973). Cognate the averation fraught. *ABCA Bulletin, 36,* 14–19.

Cypert, S. A. (1985). Business writing that gets results. *Government Finance Review, 1,* 23–28.

Dulek, R. (1981). Six "sacrosanct" writing guidelines. *Personnel Journal, 60,* 932–933.

Ellsworth, J. (1981). Effective writing promotes goodwill. *Credit Union Executive, 21,* 38–39.

Ferrara, C. F. (1985). Business writing: Clearing up the muddle. *Systems/3X World, 13,* 31–35.

Five steps to better writing workshops. (1984). *Training, 21,* 14–73.

Genfan, H. (1976). Managerial communication. *Personnel Journal, 55,* 568–569, 579.

Hanft, P. and Roe, M. (1978). How to write well in business. *CA Magazine (Canada), 111,* 72–74.

Hennington, J. A. (1978). Memorandums—an effective communication tool for management. *ABCA Bulletin, 41,* 10–14.

Hoffer, M. (1980). Write it right. *Supervision, 42,* 12–13.

Joseph, A. M. (1984). The CLU who never learned how to write. *Journal of the American Society of CLU, 38,* 76–78.

Lariviere, E. A. (1986). Written communication tasks and competencies in insurance. *CPCU Journal, 39,* 174–179.

Lesikar, R. V. (1984). *Report writing for business.* Homewood, Illinois: Richard D. Irwin.

Lewis, P. V. (1972). Presenting the formal report to management. *Administrative Communication—A Survey.* Stillwater, OK: OSU Press, 301–304.

Macmillan, B. B. (1985). Seven ways to improve your writing skills. *Sales and Marketing Management, 134,* 75–76.

McCrum, R., Cran, W., and MacNeil, R. (1986). *The story of English.* New York: Viking.

Meyers, C. H. (1970). *Handbook of basic graphs: A modern approach.* Belmont, CA: Dickenson Publishing Co., Inc.

Mueller, D. (1980). Put clarity in your writing. IEEE *Transactions on Professional Communication, PC-23,* 173–178.

Pinsker, S. (1985). Business and communicating: Rework, revise, rewrite! *Business, 35,* 54–55.

Reimold, C. (1981). Business writing-clear and simple. IEEE *Transactions on Professional Communication, PC-24,* 184–185.

Reiter, M. J. (1967). Reports that communicate. *Management Services,* 27–30.

Robbins, H. Z., and Carriere, R. (1981). How to develop basic writing skills. *Massachusetts CPA Review, 55,* 17–20, 24–25.

Robinson, D. M. (1969). *Writing reports for management decisions.* Columbus, OH: Charles E. Merrill Co.

Shurter, R. L. (1971). *Written communication in business.* New York: McGraw-Hill Book Co.

Shurter, R. L., Williamson, P., and Broehl, W. G. (1965). *Business research and report writing.* New York: McGraw-Hill Book Co.

Sigband, N. B. (1976). *Communication for management and business.* Glenview, IL: Scott, Foresman and Co.

Spruell, G. (1986). Teaching people who already learned how to write, to write. *Training and Development Journal, 40,* 32–35.

Swift, M. H. (1973). Clear writing means clear thinking means. . . . *Harvard Business Review,* 59–62.

Tebeaux, E. (1981). Seven steps to effective business writing. *Texas Business Executive, 7,* 44–49, 53.

Wakin, E. (1986). The business of business writing. *Today's Office, 21,* 24–26.

Unit 5

ORGANIZING SENSITIVE MESSAGES

INTRA-TEXT MEMORANDUM

TO: Readers

FROM: Authors

SUBJECT: Unit 5

Unit 5 begins the discussion of how to handle sensitive messages. More specifically, Unit 5 explores the organizational options available for such messages. Thus, this unit examines the following highlighted sections of the Effective Communication Chart.

EFFECTIVE COMMUNICATION

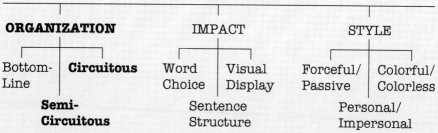

ORGANIZATION | IMPACT | STYLE

Bottom-Line | **Circuitous** | Word Choice | Visual Display | Forceful/Passive | Colorful/Colorless

Semi-Circuitous | Sentence Structure | Personal/Impersonal

Chapter 11 defines **sensitive messages** and then examines the complicating factors of these types of messages: the **direction** a message is sent, the **relationship** between writer and reader, and the **risk** involved in the situation.

Chapter 12 begins a discussion about the choices faced by the writer of a sensitive message. First, you will learn how to choose an organizational pattern. In sensitive messages, bottom-lining and stating your purpose directly may be dangerous or insulting. Chapter 12 explains other organizational strategies that could be used if bottom-lining seems dangerous or inappropriate. The names for these alternative strategies are **circuitous** and **semi-circuitous organizational patterns**.

Finally, Chapter 13 examines which organizational pattern fits best in each sensitive message situation.

By the time you have finished reading and studying Unit 5, you will have a complete understanding of the organizational options available to you.

These options—bottom-line, circuitous, or semi-circuitous organizational patterns—are the backbone of the sophisticated yet easy-to-use system for deciding how to organize even the most complex business message.

Chapter 11

SENSITIVE MESSAGES AND COMPLICATING BUSINESS FACTORS

OBJECTIVES

This chapter will help you to

•

Understand the different types of sensitive
business messages

•

Learn to identify two kinds of
persuasive situations

•

Identify three key situational factors that
influence the handling of sensitive
business messages

Units 2, 3, and 4, which dealt with non-sensitive messages, assumed you were always writing logical, non-emotional messages. In such cases, a writer's goal is to present information as directly and efficiently as possible. Writers in these situations do not have to worry about the reader's emotional reaction. They can safely assume that their readers want to be able to find, process, and act upon or dispose of information as quickly as possible.

Sending sensitive messages, however, is an entirely different matter. **Sensitive messages** elicit emotional reactions in readers. And it is the reader's probable reaction, not the writer's reaction to a message, that determines whether the message is sensitive or not.

Sensitive messages cause emotional reactions in readers.

Readers, moreover, respond not only to the message but also to other complicating factors, such as the writer's and reader's relative power positions, the writer's and reader's feelings toward each other, and their respective attitudes toward the topic being discussed. Thus, sensitive messages are much more difficult to cope with than are non-sensitive ones.

Readers' reactions determine if a message is sensitive.

The main reasons for these difficulties are that *real* people are on the other side of these messages, people with feelings, emotions, and power. These people may or may not like you, the message you are conveying, or the way you choose to say what you are saying. And in business, if someone does not like the way you have said something, that person may demote you, transfer you to a position with no opportunities for advancement, fire you, or refuse to do business with you.

Business readers have feelings, emotions, and power.

Of course, the opposite is also true. If someone likes the way you say something, or if someone likes the way you have handled a delicate situation, that person may praise you, give you the company's business, or offer you a promotion.

TYPES OF SENSITIVE MESSAGES

We must *always* remember when we categorize the message we are sending that it is the reader who determines the type of message we send. From this perspective, we can identify three types of sensitive messages— **positive**, **negative**, and **persuasive**. Here is how they are defined:

Readers respond to a sensitive message as positive, negative, or persuasive.

1. **Positive messages** convey good news. Such messages evoke feelings of gladness and pleasure in the reader.
2. **Negative messages** relay bad news, such as "No." These messages evoke feelings of dismay, anger, and disappointment.
3. **Persuasive messages** attempt to cause the reader to take an action desired by the writer. Such actions may range from paying money, to giving time, to accepting new ideas. The reader's reaction to such messages may, as you will see, be positive or negative.

It is easy to grasp immediately the effects that good-news and bad-news messages have on readers. But what about persuasive messages? It isn't quite so obvious how persuasive messages affect the reader's emotions. Let's experiment a bit and see if we can determine the effects persuasive messages have on readers.

Two Types of Persuasive Messages

Project yourself into the future. Assume you are a regional manager for a large government agency. In your region, there are one hundred employees. You are sitting at your desk trying to figure out how to organize two difficult persuasive messages that you must send out:

Situation 1
You have been asked by the director of your agency to try to get all of the hundred employees in your region to double their annual contributions to the United Way.

Situation 2
You have been advised by the agency's medical staff that a severe flu epidemic is predicted for the coming winter. You are asked to persuade each of your hundred employees to get a flu shot.

Naturally, since you can't *order* employees to double their charitable contributions or to get flu shots, the messages you must write must be persuasive. Now, ask yourself whether you would organize these two letters in the same way. Is there a difference between these two persuasive situations that might cause you to organize them differently?

Different persuasive messages elicit different reader responses.

Remember, focus on the *readers'* reaction. Thus, how these persuasive situations differ depends on how each message is likely to be perceived by the average employee. How average readers will react to a request to get a flu shot is different from how they will react to a request to double their contributions to the United Way. What specifically causes these different reactions?

Readers respond based on self-interest.

The answer lies in whether readers see anything good for *them* in the request or whether they see nothing whatsoever that will benefit them personally. We don't mean to imply that all readers are completely selfish. However, everyone naturally has a generous amount of self-interest.

Therefore, we have split our definition of persuasive messages into two categories that reflect the different feelings that can be experienced by readers:

Positive-persuasive messages are in the readers' best interests.

1. **Positive-persuasive situations**. Here, readers know deep inside that what is requested clearly benefits their ultimate interests. The situation is similar to when a parent urges a child to "wear your overshoes," "do your homework," or "go to bed early." We all recall grumbling about being nagged on such issues, but deep inside we knew we were being urged to do what was good for us. And when you can believe (even begrudgingly) that what is being requested benefits your interests, your emotional reaction to that message will differ decidedly from your reaction to a negative-persuasive message.

Negative-persuasive messages persuade readers to do something that does not seem beneficial to them.

2. **Negative-persuasive situations**. Here, the writer's task is to persuade readers to do something they don't want to do, something they perceive as harmful to their interests. For example, in the letter urging participation in the United Way campaign, each reader getting the message may feel, "Why should I? There's nothing in it for me personally."

This recognition of the dual nature of persuasive messages makes it necessary to reorganize the list of sensitive messages so that it doesn't just include negative and positive messages, but also positive-persuasive and negative-persuasive ones. Our list of sensitive messages now looks as follows:

- Positive
- Negative
- Positive-Persuasive
- Negative-Persuasive

SITUATIONAL FACTORS

Now that we have defined the various types of sensitive messages, we have to consider certain **situational factors** inherent in corporate communications. Sensitive messages do not exist in a vacuum. A wise writer takes into account certain factors that exist in a communication situation, factors over which we have no control. The first of these is the **direction** the message is sent. The second is the **relationship** that exists between writer and reader. The third is the **risk** involved in the situation.

The corporate environment influences messages.

Writers have no control over certain situational factors.

Situational Factor 1: Message Direction

Chapter 2 noted that everyone in an organization writes within a power hierarchy. Internally in the organization, everyone (except the CEO) is at a level subordinate to a higher level of authority (and even the CEO can be replaced by the Board of Directors). Consequently, the **direction** in which people within organizations must write—up, down, or across the hierarchy—is important. Also, when people write to others who are outside their organization, they have to consider whether their reader is in some sense their superior or their subordinate.

Businesspeople write within a power hierarchy.

Let us be specific about what we mean by the power hierarchy. Here are some simple definitions to use:

- Writers are in a lower power position when they are writing *upward* to the reader, such as when writing to superiors in their own organization, or to powerful external customers or government regulatory agencies.
- Writers are in a higher power position when they are writing *downward* to their reader, such as when writing to subordinates in their own organization, or to external readers who are dependent on the writer's good will (for example, suppliers deriving most of their business from the writer's company).
- Writers are in a lateral power position when they are writing to someone who is in an equal position, either internally or externally.

The Informal Organization   People with practical business experience know that power is ephemeral and shifting. Sometimes, the true power

In sensitive messages, you must take into account the hierarchical direction of the message. Here, a subordinate consults with a superior.

Wise writers adapt to formal and informal power structures.

sources of an organization today are not the ones reflected on the corporate chart. In most companies, a second, **informal organization** exists. Although it doesn't show up on the formal organization chart, this informal organization may more accurately reflect the power structure. Hence, smart writers pay attention to both the formal and the informal organization when they write.

Any number of examples can make obvious the importance of the secondary or informal organizational power structure. For example, suppose an elementary school teacher has a father who is the superintendent of the county's schools. Many people (perhaps even all the county principals) will view this teacher as potentially more powerful than they are in some situations—despite their higher location on the formal school organization chart.

Or take a case where a relatively new manager has obviously impressed a company president. Suppose, further, that this manager graduated from the same university as the president. Within the informal power hierarchy, this person may soon unofficially become one of the more influential people in the company.

Or, suppose, finally, that a vice president of a company is widely viewed as merely waiting for retirement. Assume, further, that while this vice president's replacement has not been formally approved, everyone knows who the new vice president is going to be. Experienced businesspeople working in such a situation will be sure the probable replacement is familiar with and approves all of their ongoing projects.

Whatever the case, you must always remember that writing up or down may involve more than merely looking at the corporate chart and viewing where your reader is. Wise writers know that both the formal and the informal organizations must be considered in sensitive communication situations.

Sensitive Message Directions   If we add to our list the direction that messages are sent in the formal (or informal) power hierarchy, our list of sensitive message types now looks like this:

- Positive Messages ↑
- Positive Messages ↓
- Negative Messages ↑
- Negative Messages ↓
- Positive-Persuasive Messages ↑
- Positive-Persuasive Messages ↓
- Negative-Persuasive Messages ↑
- Negative-Persuasive Messages ↓

Many of your internal communications will be sent laterally to co-workers and will be non-sensitive. However, you should treat sensitive lateral messages as though they were going up or down the organizational hierarchy.

Regard lateral messages as going either up or down.

Notice that the sensitive message directions identified deal only with messages going up or down, not laterally. In terms of organizational direction, sensitive lateral messages should be regarded as going either up or down, depending on such variables as your familiarity with the subject matter and your relationship with the reader.

An example will demonstrate this point. Suppose, for instance, you have worked on a number of affirmative action cases. Soon you will become known among your colleagues as an expert on this topic. If a coworker in a position similar to yours seeks advice from you about affirmative action, he or she will view you as a superior, at least on this topic. In other situations, when the coworker knows more about a topic than you do, then *you* will treat that coworker as a superior when dealing with this new topic.

Treat lateral readers as superiors when you are uncertain.

Finally, if you are unsure which direction to choose because you are unfamiliar with your reader or with the reader's knowledge about a particular topic, you should regard the message as being sent upward. The reasons for selecting an upward approach in an unknown situation are simple. If you do not know where someone stands on the informal power structure, it is safer to treat that reader as a superior. This approach also minimizes the possibilities that you will inadvertently insult or anger the otherwise unknown reader and protects you should this reader choose to show your message to other, higher-ranking individuals.

Situational Factor 2: Relationship between Writer and Reader

Large companies, and even many small companies, employ people from a variety of different backgrounds. These people have different interests, backgrounds, and often even different value systems. Engineers, statisticians, computer scientists, chemists, as well as people from finance, marketing, and accounting, often have different perceptions about their jobs, those of others, and how these jobs influence and affect the overall performance of the organization.

To complicate matters further, businesspeople often have to deal with external personnel who do business with or influence the organization in some way. Among the external personnel that businesspeople interact with are customers, suppliers of goods and services, and local, state, and federal officials. People in these positions add even greater variety to the types of interests, backgrounds, and values to which businesspeople must relate.

Businesspeople must interact with people of varying backgrounds and different interests.

Over time, businesspeople form varying types of **relationships** with people from all of these different backgrounds. They become close friends with some of their work associates; with others, they may maintain a professional or perhaps even a distant relationship. These relationships significantly influence communication and must be taken into account for all sensitive message situations. We, therefore, classify both internal and external relationships as being one of three types: *warm*, *neutral*, or *cold*.

To be effective, persuasive messages must meet the recipient's needs. Here, a team confers with an influential external business associate — the client.

Here is a definition of each type:

Relationships are defined as warm, neutral, or cold.

- A *warm* relationship is one in which the people are familiar with and feel comfortable with one another. They know and trust each other and are apt to accept one another's ideas with little or no suspicion or mistrust.

- A *neutral* relationship is one in which distance occurs, usually because the participants do not know each other personally. In this type of relationship, the participants perceive each other as faceless stereotypes. They feel neither hostility nor friendliness toward each other.

- A *cold* relationship is one in which distrust, dislike, or perhaps even hate, make the communication task especially difficult, almost impossible.

Situational Factor 3: Risk

The type of message you must write, the direction it is being sent, and the relationship you have with the reader all contribute to the sensitivity of your message. But one other factor also needs to be taken into account — the **risk** associated with the message.

Sensitive messages may be very dangerous or completely harmless.

The risk associated with a message can range from being completely harmless to highly dangerous. Positive and positive-persuasive messages are usually harmless and, therefore, pose little or no risk to the writer. Negative and negative-persuasive messages, on the other hand, can be highly dangerous and may result in an angered customer, an upset boss, or even the loss of your position. Let's examine some sensitive message situations that entail significant risk.

Negative messages are often high risk.

Suppose your boss asks you to review her newly created marketing plan. After you do so, you conclude that the plan is defective. What are the risks of writing the following letter?

```
TO:       "Boss"

FROM:     "You"

SUBJECT: Marketing Plan

DATE:     July 21, 19——
```

Your marketing plan is defective in three ways:

1. It overestimates potential demand for the product.
2. It assumes a decade of uninterrupted economic prosperity.
3. It does not sufficiently take into account the impact that new competition will have on sales.

Clearly, the effectiveness of this memo can't be judged solely in terms of the correctness of the prose, for the writing itself is fine. The sentences are short. The indented list provides plenty of white space. The memo is written in the active voice. It is an exemplary high-impact communication. But would most sensible businesspeople be likely to write a memo this blunt to their boss? No! The risks are simply too high. An experienced businessperson will soften the impact of this memo by writing in a more circuitous, diplomatic fashion. Something like the following might do:

A high-impact approach is sometimes too risky.

```
TO:       "Boss"

FROM:     "You"

SUBJECT: Marketing Plan

DATE:     July 21, 19——
```

The marketing plan being proposed is most interesting. There are, however, certain considerations that need to be taken into account. First, the potential demand for the product should perhaps be reevaluated from a broader perspective. There is a risk that the figures may need further clarification.

Second, additional forecasts about economic tendencies may need to be included. Assumptions about uninterrupted economic prosperity may need to be taken into account once these forecasts have been examined.

Finally, additional evaluation of the effects of new competition may need to be made. The addition of more competitors into the arena may cause sales to alter significantly from those projected.

Is this memo as bottom-lined as the first? No. Is it as high-impact? No, its sentences are long and in the passive voice. But is it a safer memo to send to a boss than the first? Definitely yes!

Let's examine a second situation where a negative message sent up actually caused trouble. This situation really occurred and resulted in the person who wrote the letter losing his job. The names of the company and of individuals involved in the case have, of course, been changed.

A man named George Smith retired from XYZ, Inc. Prior to retirement, he selected the retirement plan option that paid the highest amount monthly. This plan also meant, however, that in the event he died before his wife, his wife would receive no benefits from the company. Unfortunately, that is exactly what happened.

Mrs. Smith, distraught at learning the news that her husband's pension had stopped, wrote a series of letters to XYZ asking for clarification of the policy. She received a number of kind, circuitous, but clear replies from XYZ's personnel office that gently informed her about the choice her husband had made and XYZ's need to abide by her husband's decision.

Not satisfied, Mrs. Smith continued to press: "But I want the money. Can't we change my husband's decision?" Finally, an inexperienced assistant for XYZ got annoyed and sent the following letter to Mrs. Smith.

> Dear Mrs. Smith:
>
> The answer to your question is "No." Upon reaching the age of fifty-five, your deceased husband, George, elected retirement plan B. This plan called for him to receive a higher income upon reaching the age of sixty-five. This also meant, in the event of his death prior to yours, his pension would cease and you would receive no income whatsoever.

Apparently enjoying this merciless attack, the assistant also decided to tell her what would have happened had Mr. Smith elected a different plan:

> If Mr. Smith had elected plan A, he would have received, at the age of sixty-five, a lower pension. Under plan A, however, his death prior to yours would have meant that you would receive half pension until your own death.
>
> Yours is just one of the many complaints we receive about plan B. Unfortunately, there is nothing we can do about them.

When the boss learned about this letter, the assistant was fired on the spot. Why? Because the assistant had been cruel and inhumane to the wife of a former employee. Even worse, he had put his tactlessness in writing, thus embarrassing the whole company. The writer had not only risked his own position by sending this memo, but he had also risked the public image of XYZ, a company that took great care to appear concerned, even paternalistic.

Risk relates not only to an individual but to an entire company.

Endless numbers of examples of the risks involved in sensitive writing situations could be cited. All would serve to prove the same point, one that bears repetition thoughout your life: Be careful when you write, especially when you are involved in an emotionally charged situation. And by "be careful," we mean more than just "be careful to write *clearly*." We mean "be careful of people's feelings and their possible reactions to what you say, when you say it, and how you state your message."

Exercise caution when writing in sensitive situations.

SUMMARY

This chapter has dealt with the factors you must take into account when you need to write sensitive messages, as summarized in this chart:

Type of Message to Be Sent	Direction Message Sent	Relationship between Writer and Reader	Resultant Risk
Negative	Up?	Warm?	Dangerous?
Positive		Neutral?	
Negative-Persuasive			
Positive-Persuasive	Down?	Cold?	Safe?

We have referred to these as situational factors. There is little you can usually do to change them. You cannot realistically change a negative letter into a positive one. Nor can you change the direction a message must be sent or, at least in the short run, the type of relationship you have with your reader. But there are factors involved in the successful handling of sensitive messages that you *can* control. The next chapter deals with the first *choice* you can make—how to organize your sensitive message.

REVIEW QUESTIONS

1. Define a sensitive message.
2. Name three complicating factors readers respond to in a message.
3. Why are sensitive messages so difficult to write?
4. What determines whether a message is sensitive or not?
5. Name the three types of sensitive messages and define them in terms of their effects on readers.
6. What is a positive-persuasive message?
7. What is a negative-persuasive message?
8. What are the three situational factors in a communication situation?
9. Name the three types of internal and external relationships involving people who must communicate.
10. What is an important point to remember when you are involved in an emotionally charged situation?

DISCUSSION QUESTIONS

1. Which do you think will have a greater influence upon the success of your business career, the sensitive or the non-sensitive messages you write? Why?
2. Chapter 11 develops the following list of message types and message directions:

- Positive Messages ↑
- Positive Messages ↓
- Negative Messages ↑
- Negative Messages ↓
- Positive-Persuasive Messages ↑
- Positive-Persuasive Messages ↓
- Negative-Persuasive Messages ↑
- Negative-Persuasive Messages ↓

Which type do you think is the most difficult to write? Which type do you think is the simplest to write? Explain the reasons for your selections.

3. A favorite saying about business is "Who you know is more important than what you know." Apply this adage to the situational factors developed in this chapter. In what ways does the message of the adage agree with the situational factors? In what ways do the situational factors not agree with the adage?

Chapter 12

TWO ORGANIZATIONAL ALTERNATIVES

OBJECTIVES

This chapter will help you to

●

Recognize differences between a bottom-line, a circuitous, and a semi-circuitous organizational pattern

●

Organize messages in a circuitous and a semi-circuitous organizational pattern

In many situations, bottom-lining a sensitive message may simply be out of the question. This chapter introduces you to two alternative organizational patterns that can be used in situations where a bottom-line approach seems too blunt, insulting, or tactless. These two alternatives we call **circuitous** and **semi-circuitous organizational patterns.**

In Chapter 3, we asked you to think of the term *organizational pattern* as meaning a writer's choice of *when* to state the purpose of the message. Once you define organization as *when* something is said, you will be able to make a simple choice. That choice is either (a) to state your purpose immediately and directly—that is, to bottom-line the message, or (b) to withhold your purpose temporarily. This second alternative leads either to a circuitous or to a semi-circuitous approach. Let's examine each approach.

Circuitous and semi-circuitous patterns are alternatives to a bottom-line approach.

CIRCUITOUS ORGANIZATIONAL PATTERN

In a **circuitous organizational pattern,** you withhold the bottom line, or the purpose of your message, until you have had a chance to prepare your reader to accept that message. This alternative is used most often in negative messages. Generally, people seem to agree that negative messages sent upward should roughly follow four steps. The writer

A circuitous organizational pattern delays the statement of purpose.

- Step 1: Begins on a pleasant or at least a neutral note.
- Step 2: Gives the reasons for the negative first, before the negative message is revealed.
- Step 3: States the message's purpose only after the reader has been prepared for the negative.
- Step 4: Offers alternative proposals, compromises, future hopes, or, if none of these is appropriate, some sort of pleasant, off-the-subject ending.

These steps, while time-honored, are not, of course, unchangeable, and should be modified depending upon a variety of circumstances that will be discussed in this and the next chapter. Let's begin our discussion by studying an example of the circuitous pattern.

Suppose the Occupational Safety and Health Association (OSHA) has inspected the XYZ Manufacturing Company and has discovered a number of violations of federal safety regulations. OSHA then orders corrections of the violations and, two months later, performs a reinspection. The reinspection reveals that company officials have made a "good-faith" effort to comply with the government's regulations. However, a few additional corrections are still necessary.

Assume also that OSHA officials know that the President of XYZ Company, James Blasko, is a close personal friend of Senator Charles Becker, Chairperson of the Senate Advisory Board that oversees OSHA's activities and that recommends allocations for OSHA's budget. No one within OSHA knows if Blasko and Senator Becker have discussed this matter, but any OSHA official writing to the President of XYZ would certainly want to be careful of inadvertently insulting a senator's good friend. At the same time, XYZ needs to be in full compliance with OSHA's standards. Which of the following two letters would handle this sensitive situation more effectively?

Letter A

Mr. James Blasko
President
XYZ Manufacturing Company
24 Nunnaly Street
Des Moines, IA 50322

Dear Mr. Blasko:

We have examined the corrective actions you took based on our hazard report and are sorry to report that you are still not in compliance with OSHA standards.

In particular, you are still in violation in the following areas:

1. Seed cleaning
2. Storage
3. Grain drying
4. Pump operations

All of your other corrective actions met OSHA standards.

A detailed report with explanations follows.

Letter B

Mr. James Blasko
President
XYZ Manufacturing Company
24 Nunnaly Street
Des Moines, IA 50322

Dear Mr. Blasko:

We have examined the corrective actions you took based on our hazard report and are pleased to note that you are now in compliance in more than 90 percent of the areas previously cited.

> Additional work is required in a few more areas. In particular, seed cleaning, storage, grain drying, and pump operations still need further work. The attached report contains a detailed explanation of what still must be done to be in full compliance with OSHA standards.
>
> You are to be congratulated for the corrective actions you have already taken. Let us know if you need any advice on the corrections that still need to be made.

Letter A is bottom-lined and high impact. Its message is clear and to the point. Letter B is also clear, but it is not bottom-lined, nor is it as high impact. Letter B begins and ends with praise for the reader's company, and it tactfully combines an offer of additional assistance with a reminder that further corrections still are needed. But the two most important questions about the difference between these two letters are the following:

A non-bottom-lined approach sometimes gets the job done better than a bottom-lined approach.

1. If you were an OSHA official, which of the two letters would you rather have the company president see?
2. If you were an OSHA official, which of the two letters would you rather have Senator Becker see?

The answer to both questions is Letter B.

Minimize Negative Reactions

Some readers doubtless will think that we are contradicting ourselves when we admit that the circuitous pattern has some utility in business writing. For many pages, we have extolled the virtues of bottom-line communications like Letter A. But remember, prior to this unit, we were discussing only non-sensitive messages. Furthermore, our definition of effective business writing is writing that gets a job done with minimal negative reaction on the reader's part. Getting a reader angry is unlikely to be the best way to get a job done effectively. Although being circuitous in organization may initially be more time-consuming for both the writer and the reader, it may save time, in the long run, for highly sensitive situations.

Effective business writing gets the job done with minimal negative reaction.

A circuitous approach can sometimes save time.

For example, suppose a very important customer writes to describe a problem concerning allegedly defective drive shafts in a product made by your company. You study the problem and learn that your company, XYZ, Inc., is in no way responsible for the problem. Therefore, you dictate the following bottom-lined explanation. Remember that the reader, as a customer, is in a superior position to yours.

XYZ, INCORPORATED
2520 Penn Plaza
New York, NY 10039

May 26, 19— —

Mr. Kenneth Mogren
853 W. 95th Street
New York, NY 10025

Dear Mr. Mogren:

We are not responsible for the cracking problems you encountered with our drive shafts. The fault lies with the way the casing was installed. Our contract states that installation is your responsibility.

We appreciate your business and look forward to future dealings with you. Let us know if we can help you in any way.

Sincerely,

Douglas Emanual
Customer Service
Representative

A bottom-line approach is not always risk free.

A bottom-line approach is not always the most efficient approach.

Is the letter efficient? Does it get the job done? The answer to both questions can be "yes" only if you assume that brevity is the *only* important aspect of writing. What risks are incurred by this letter's bottom-line organization? At worst, Mogren will be so angered by the letter's bluntness that he will stop doing business with Emanual's company. That certainly would not be getting the real job done.

At best, the letter may cause the angry customer to write or call a high-level executive in Emanual's company, attacking his letter and stating how he was hurt and angered by it. What may happen then? Besides upsetting his boss, Emanual will probably be sent to visit the customer with orders to apologize for his behavior and to offer a detailed explanation of why the drive shafts are undergoing the difficulties mentioned. How efficient would the brief letter seem then?

Now let's see how a circuitous organizational pattern works in the following letter to Mogren. How do you think Mogren would react to this circuitous, but still brief, version?

XYZ, INCORPORATED
2520 Penn Plaza
New York, NY 10039

May 26, 19— —

Mr. Kenneth Mogren
853 W. 95th St.
New York, NY 10025

Dear Mr. Mogren:

Thank you for your letter reporting the cracking problems you have encountered with our drive shafts.

Since many of the industries we supply have experienced similar problems, we have conducted a great deal of research into this situation. Our studies show that the fault usually lies with the way a customer or some outside contractor has installed the casing.

I hope this answer leads to a solution for you. Let me know if I can help in any other way.

Sincerely,

Douglas Emanual

Douglas Emanual
Customer Service
Representative

The circuitous pattern obviously dulls the letter somewhat. But does the overall letter work? Does it get the job done while minimizing the chance of a bad reaction from the reader? The answer is "not really." In essence, the letter says

1. Thanks for writing.
2. The problem is not ours.
3. Good luck in solving your problem.

This version technically may not be organized in a bottom-line fashion, but its brevity makes the negative message appear in the third sentence. And that message is clear: "It's your problem, not ours!"

Therefore, let's see how lengthening the letter prepares the reader for the negative message. Neither Version A nor B gives the company credit

A circuitous approach does not involve brevity.

for all the work that it did. Why not tell Mogren all that was done on his behalf? In doing so, writers must remember that the principle messages being sent are that (a) Mogren is a good customer, (b) we want to retain his good will and his business, but (c) we still do not want to accept responsibility for the problem. Let's construct a third, less risky, circuitous version and see if it accomplishes this task.

Version C

XYZ, INCORPORATED
2520 Penn Plaza
New York, NY 10039

May 26, 19——

Mr. Kenneth Mogren
853 W. 95th St.
New York, NY 10025

Dear Mr. Mogren:

Thank you for your letter expressing concern about the drive shaft casings we supplied. Since everyone at XYZ, Inc. appreciates the significant amount of business you do with us, I immediately began a search to see if we could find some ways of resolving the issue for you.

What I have done for you.

After receiving your letter, I first met with John Davis, Head of Product Design, and members of our structural engineering staff. We reexamined all of the design components and checked to make sure that the drive shaft we supplied met your requested specifications. Since it did, we decided to look elsewhere for answers.

Problems other companies had.

About two years ago, ABC, Inc. had a similar experience with a casing we had provided. I, therefore, called Mary Church at ABC and inquired about what ABC's engineers had found. Mary told me that after an extensive analysis, ABC's design engineers found that the installation procedure used at ABC was causing the cracks. ABC utilized a drive torque approach when installing the drive shaft. This approach applied too much tension to the casing and caused some hairline cracks in it. Eventually, these cracks widened, with final results similar to yours.

Personalized solution.

Mary said that after ABC made the discovery, it shifted to a drive centimeter installation system and has had no problem since this change. I know that you use a drive torque approach.

You may, therefore, want to give some consideration to the possibility that it is causing hairline cracks.

I also checked with some structural engineering consultants at a local university. The consultants said that they had heard of situations similar to yours in a variety of industries that use casings with the dimensions you requested. They said that many of these problems were solved by rechecking the design and by shortening the steel mold used on the front end. Apparently, the mold sometimes catches onto the train shaft, applying pressure. This pressure eventually causes cracks.

The mold also seems to allow some moisture into the casing, which, of course, also results in increased wear. I am sure you will want to have your engineers look into this as a possible reason for the cracking.

Mr. Mogren, we will be more than happy to work with you on redesigning the casing dimensions if this latter situation proves to be a contributing cause.

Again, everyone at XYZ appreciates your business. I hope this letter provides detailed answers for the situation you described. Please let us know whenever we can be of assistance to you.

Sincerely,

Douglas Emanual

Douglas Emanual
Customer Service
Representative

For you, I went beyond the realm of normal assistance.

Here's what to do.

We'll help all we can.

This draft seems to work, especially by the way it does the following:

1. Shifts between being personal when concentrating on what the writer did for the reader, and being impersonal when dealing specifically with Mogren's problems.
2. Offers conclusions in a circuitous, diplomatic fashion. The suggested corrections come after, not before, the analysis and are not lumped together in a high-impact, punchy fashion. Obviously, the writer thought that a high-impact approach, though clear, might prove dangerous.
3. Goes into extreme detail about everything, and sacrifices brevity for tactful full disclosure.

Why are we extolling the virtues of a non-bottom-lined, long-winded letter like this? The answer is that in this situation we are looking for a writing strategy that gets a job done and that spends the least amount of words, time, and total effort in doing so. Although Version C is obviously longer and, therefore, took more time to write, it is still probably the most efficient. If the first two versions had seriously offended Mogren, how much additional correspondence and/or how many apologetic personal

Though longer, a circuitous approach is sometimes more efficient.

visits might have been required to retain him as a customer? How much time and energy would these have consumed? And if we had lost his future business, would we be getting the real job done?

Risks of a Circuitous Approach

In a number of internal communications, especially when people have to write something negative up to superiors, the circuitous organizational pattern carries some unwanted and often unnecessary risks. The superiors may conclude that the writers are so inept that they simply don't know how to come to the point, and that they are long-winded. Or, superiors may be so confused by a circuitously organized memo that they do not understand the writer's message and take actions entirely different from those desired. Or, worst of all, the superiors may see right through the writer's circuitousness, may regard it as sheer manipulation, and will brand such a writer as a tricky con artist.

Hence, the circuitous pattern should be used with extreme caution inside your own organization and only with a distinct awareness of the risks being taken. The last thing you want to do is to get a bad reputation with people you must work with day after day.

Yet, it is normal for all of us to want to be circuitous when we have to convey information that will irritate a reader or that will make us look bad. When we have to report that we failed to do what we should have, we, naturally, want to have a chance to offer all our excuses before we confess the bad news. Regardless of how understandable such a tendency is, we must always remember that people in higher positions in organizations become irritated when subordinates deliver bad news in a roundabout way. And we want to avoid, at all costs, having our superiors see us as tricky or long-winded.

You may find yourself, however, in an internal situation where bottom-lining is simply too blunt, and a circuitous pattern is too full of risks. In such cases, we strongly suggest that you consider using the semi-circuitous organizational pattern.

The circuitous approach carries risks when used internally.

Don't use a circuitous approach if it makes you appear tricky.

A semi-circuitous pattern avoids bluntness and the appearance of being manipulative.

SEMI-CIRCUITOUS ORGANIZATIONAL PATTERN

A **semi-circuitous organizational pattern** does not actually present the bottom line first. Instead, it uses a contract sentence at the beginning of the message to tell the reader where the bottom line can be found. In doing so, it also implicitly suggests that the reader wait before turning to that bottom line. In essence, the contract sentence tells the reader, "This, in general, is my topic, but before I tell you my conclusions, I'm going to ask you to consider A, next B, and finally C. Then I will present my conclusions (and/or recommendations)."

A primary advantage to the semi-circuitous approach is that it minimizes the possibility of your readers concluding that you are trying to manipulate them. The contract sentence admits that you are not going to bottom-line the message. It states that, for reasons you hope to make clear

A semi-circuitous approach uses a contract sentence but delays the bottom line.

later in the memo, you have chosen to reserve the bottom-line message for last. The reader may still prefer a bottom-lined memo, but the reader cannot charge you with being sneaky. After all, if readers so desire, they can turn immediately to the bottom line. But if they don't, you at least have a chance to prepare them before you tell them something you have reason to believe will upset them.

Readers don't feel manipulated by a semi-circuitous approach.

Applying a Semi-Circuitous Approach

Let's look at an example of a semi-circuitous approach. Suppose your boss, the Director of Management Services, has developed a strategy for automating the office. She has developed this strategy into a written plan that she asks you to evaluate. You do so but have some recommendations to offer that run counter to those in your boss's plan. Rather than presenting opposing views bluntly, you decide that you need to set the stage first. However, you fear that if you are circuitous, you will appear less than forthright. Therefore, you use the semi-circuitous pattern and create a contract sentence telling the reader that the bottom line (that is, the contradictory recommendations) is delayed until the end of the report.

TO: Ann Harris

FROM: "You"

SUBJECT: Office Automation Evaluation

DATE: October 14, 19——

This memo deals with your request for an evaluation of the office automation strategy you propose implementing. In the following analysis, four aspects of the strategy are considered:

1. productivity potential

2. staff and location investment

3. paperwork investment

4. future networking options

Recommendations derived from my analysis of these four factors will then be presented.

A semi-circuitous approach is a useful compromise in situations where (a) bottom-lining will seem blunt or rude and (b) circuitousness will seem manipulative. It is, therefore, a useful strategy for a number of sensitive situations.

Use a semi-circuitous approach in various kinds of sensitive situations.

Here is a typical example of a semi-circuitous approach being used very effectively. A very large company ran an employee suggestion program called "If I Were President of ABCD Company, I Would Do the Following. . . . " The purpose was not only to solicit good ideas, but was also intended to improve public relations with employees. Even though ABCD's president strongly preferred to bottom-line all his messages, he recognized that if he sent out blunt letters rejecting some of the ideas submitted, the recipients would be demoralized instead of encouraged by the program. The president chose to have the responses sent as letters rather than as internal memos so as to lend an air of formality to the program and to distance the program from the ongoing internal operations of the company.

Notice in the following letter the care with which the corporate president rejected a suggestion made by one of the company's employees. Notice also how a contract sentence is used so as to enable the president *to appear* to bottom-line (as is expected of top executives) the message while at the same time he also appears tactful and sensitive to the employee's feelings.

Version A

ABCD CORPORATION
6300 Wesley Terrace
Des Plaines, IL 60018

March 15, 19—

Ms. Frances Arnold
1940 Algonquin Street
Des Plaines, IL 60016

Dear Frances:

Thank you for your February 28 submission to our "If I Were President of ABCD" program. Your recommendations relative to improving the Planning function were very much appreciated. Planning is an increasingly important area, not only in the division but throughout the corporation.

Your ideas for improving the process are very good, and I want to comment on the specifics. Therefore, permit me first to address your suggestions about the Centralized Planning Staff. Then, let me discuss your ideas about changes with reference to Management Plans and Practices.

Centralized Planning Staff

As for your first suggestion, let me concede that this function is indeed understaffed. However, a plan has already been established to increase the department headcount.

The second part of your suggestion included merging several departments: Market Research, Forecasting, Corporate Planning, and Planning Control.

As you know, all but Planning Control are currently part of the same organization. Within this organization, Market Research and Forecasting are part of the same department. Planning Control has not been included because we feel it should not be an integral part of a department whose major responsibilities deal with the mechanics of producing the plan.

Planning Control was originally conceived as a management system whose primary mission was to control changes to the established plan, and this has been extremely effective. There have been several recommendations that Planning Control should be expanded to include the development of plans. We are currently investigating not only the question of expanding its function, but also its reporting structure under a new mission.

Management Plans and Practices

Your recommendation is sound. But the approach to planning that you recommend has previously been implemented.

For the reasons outlined above, your two specific recommendations will not be implemented, and this letter will also conclude their consideration under the "If I Were President of ABCD" program. Nevertheless, I commend the thoughtful manner in which your ideas were presented, and I do appreciate your having brought them to my attention.

Sincerely,

Oliver Littleton

Oliver Littleton
President

Let's dissect this letter which, incidentally, pleased the woman who received it very much. What do we notice?

1. It begins on a neutral note. The first paragraph doesn't say no right away—but neither does it say yes. Yet while not saying yes, it still manages to say some positive things about Frances Arnold's ideas.

2. The first paragraph ends with a contract statement, "permit me first to. . . . Then, . . . " However, the contract statement tactfully omits the final part of the letter, the rejection. Such an approach would in most business circles be regarded as discreet, not dishonest. The letter could certainly not be labeled tactful if the contract statement had said the following:

    Permit me first to address the Centralized Planning Staff, then Management Practices. Finally, at the end of my letter, I will reject your suggestion.

3. The letter then proceeds to educate the reader by commenting on the specifics of her suggestions. In other words, it gives the reasons for the "no" before the "no" is actually stated in the last paragraph.

4. The president does not allow the letter to end on this negative (and potentially discouraging) note. Instead, he quickly turns to sincere praise of the "thoughtful manner" in which Frances Arnold presented her ideas.

To accomplish his purposes—and to meet the reader's needs—the president recognized that this type of "no" letter must be fairly long. A brief "no" letter in this situation would be regarded by most readers as curt, brusque, insensitive, or insulting. If you doubt these reactions, consider what Arnold's probable reaction would have been had she received the following letter, instead of the one she actually did receive:

Version B

ABCD CORPORATION
6300 Wesley Terrace
Des Plaines, IL 60018

March 15, 19— —

Ms. Frances Arnold
1940 Algonquin Street
Des Plaines, IL 60016

Dear Frances:

Both of the suggestions you submitted to the "If I Were President of ABCD" program have been rejected and will not be implemented. Better luck next time!

Sincerely,

Oliver Littleton

Oliver Littleton
President

SUMMARY

You can choose from three organizational patterns:

1. The **bottom-line organizational pattern,** which states the bottom line (purpose) at the beginning. The reader immediately learns the message's purpose and, therefore, knows what the rest of the message will clarify, document, and/or justify.

2. The **circuitous organizational pattern,** which withholds the bottom line by beginning in a cordial, pleasant way. Then, the message makes the

reader sift his or her way through explanatory material to find the bottom line. After the bottom line appears, it is followed by additional cordial or compromise offerings.

3. The **semi-circuitous organizational pattern,** which does not disclose the bottom line at the beginning of the memo or report, but uses a contract statement to tell the reader where to find the message's bottom line. Implied is the suggestion that the reader is asked to wait before reading the bottom line.

The only organizational issue that remains to be examined is when to use each approach. That is the topic of Chapter 13.

REVIEW QUESTIONS

1. What are two alternative organizational patterns to bottom-lining?

2. Describe the circuitous organizational pattern.

3. What four steps do circuitous messages generally follow?

4. Define effective business writing.

5. How does a circuitous approach make business writing effective?

6. What are some of the risks of a circuitous approach?

7. What are we usually trying to do when we organize a message circuitously?

8. What is a semi-circuitous organizational pattern?

9. In what types of situations is a semi-circuitous approach useful?

DISCUSSION QUESTIONS

1. Examine the following statement: "Effective business writers walk a thin line between being tactful and diplomatic and being honest and open." Discuss ways that bottom-line, circuitous, and semi-circuitous organizational patterns can help businesspeople "walk" such a line.

2. Some people equate the circuitous and the semi-circuitous organizational patterns with being dishonest. Do you think such an equation is legitimate? Explain your answer.

3. Identify some of the times that you have noticed others using a bottom line, a circuitous, or a semi-circuitous organizational pattern when talking or writing to you. How did you feel about the pattern these people chose to use? Was the pattern effective? Did you ever feel manipulated or distrustful of a person because of the organizational pattern that person used? If so, when did you have such feelings and did these feelings ultimately affect the way you reacted to that person?

Chapter 13

HOW TO SELECT ORGANIZATIONAL PATTERNS OF SENSITIVE MESSAGES

Objectives

This chapter will help you to

•

Select the most effective organizational pattern for positive messages sent up and down

•

Select the most effective organizational pattern for internal and external negative messages sent up and down

•

Select the most effective organizational pattern for internal and external negative-persuasive messages sent up and down

Chapter 12 defined three organizational patterns to choose from: bottom-line, circuitous, and semi-circuitous. The question that now remains is this: Which organizational pattern is most likely to succeed in positive, negative, and persuasive messages? Further, how does whether the message is being sent up or down and internally or externally affect its organizational pattern? This chapter will answer these questions.

This chapter shows when each organizational pattern works best.

As you examine this chapter, you will notice that we have developed a message chart to help you keep track of the advice offered. Because you will be studying a variety of messages in this chapter, this chart will provide a handy way for you to keep track of the organizational advice that you will receive. The chart will suggest whether a message should be organized directly, that is, in a bottom-line fashion, or whether the message should be organized circuitously or semi-circuitously.

The message chart helps you keep track of the advice.

POSITIVE MESSAGES—UP OR DOWN

Message Chart

Message Type	Positive ↑↓	Internal Negative ↑	External Negative ↑	Negative ↓	Positive-Persuasive ↑↓	Internal Negative-Persuasive ↓	Internal Negative-Persuasive ↑	External Negative-Persuasive ↑
Organizational Pattern	Bottom-Line	Semi-Circuitous	Circuitous	Bottom-Line	Bottom-Line	Semi-Circuitous	Semi-Circuitous	Circuitous

Since a positive message creates pleasant feelings in the reader, it usually makes little difference whether a good news message is sent up or down the power hierarchy. Furthermore, it makes little difference whether the good news is sent internally or externally. Regardless of where or to whom the message is going, you should always consider bottom-lining a positive message. Why be circuitous when writing something positive such as, "I'm happy to tell you that you got the raise"? Unfortunately, some business writers tend to bury their purpose and write good news memos that actually read like bad news because of their organizational pattern. Effective business writers adhere to Bottom-Line Principle 10:

Bottom-line positive messages.

BOTTOM-LINE PRINCIPLE 10:
Always bottom-line good news. There is no conflict between bottom-lining and writing positive messages.

To illustrate the wisdom of this advice, let's analyze two versions of a common situation. Imagine that you have bought a very expensive cashmere sweater, but you don't like it. You return the sweater to the exclusive clothing store where you bought it. Which do you prefer, the manager's approach in Scenario I or in Scenario II?

Scenario I
You walk into the store and say you want to return the sweater. The manager says, "Have you worn it? Have you washed it? Has it been

dry-cleaned? What's wrong with it? Why don't you like it? Is this a spot I see?" When he gets through questioning you, he says, "Oh, by the way, our store always stands behind its merchandise. You can either get your money back or make an exchange."

Scenario II

You walk into the store and say you want to return the sweater. The manager says, "Of course our store always stands behind its merchandise. You can either have your money back or make an exchange. By the way, I need to ask some questions for our buyer's benefit. Have you worn it? Have you washed it? etc. . . . "

Positive messages are sometimes accidentally organized circuitously.

When people are asked which scenario they prefer, they invariably vote strongly in favor of Scenario II. Yet, when they need to write a positive business communication, many will organize their letters according to Scenario I. The reason? Probably because they want to "set the stage" before they give the customer the money back. In essence, as they write they want to conduct one last mental review before they actually give the money back. These writers thereby create a historical record of their thoughts and inadvertently organize their "yes" letter exactly as they would a circuitous "no" letter.

Good News in Disguise

Below is an actual, though disguised, situation that shows how foolish it is not to use a direct approach with good news. Employees at a company's headquarters came to work one morning and found the following memo on their desks. Because of new building construction at that location, parking had already become a troublesome problem and employees were highly sensitive about the subject. If you were one of these already irritated employees, how would this memo have struck you?

TO: All Employees at Pebble Brook Location

FROM: R. T. Thomasino

SUBJECT: Pebble Brook Construction

DATE: April 5, 19——

As you know, construction of the new building at Pebble Brook temporarily eliminated a number of parking spaces. In order for XYZ Construction Company to begin construction of its fifth building, the parking presently utilized in this area will be eliminated on Wednesday, May 2.

XYZ Construction has converted several of the landscaped areas around the parking lots to temporary parking until parking under construction is completed. These temporary areas provide 43 spaces as a net addition to those lost to construction of both new buildings.

The first phase of 100 spaces in the new parking area is scheduled for partial completion by October 1, with total completion by December 1.

The first paragraph infuriated everyone: "What? You mean ALL parking is going to be eliminated!!" In their agitation, many read only the first paragraph and never got to the good news—which was where? Buried at the end of the second paragraph! The fact that the message actually conveyed good news was completely masked by the circuitous organizational pattern that reserved the good news for the end of the memo.

Be careful not to accidentally hide good news.

In a positive but highly sensitive situation like this, bottom-lining will significantly improve the emotional reaction of your reader. A bottom-lined message like the following would have done a much better job.

TO: All Employees at Pebble Brook Location

FROM: R. T. Thomasino

SUBJECT: Pebble Brook Construction

DATE: April 5, 19——

You will be pleased to learn that soon we will have 43 additional parking spaces. These result from a conversion of several landscaped areas into a temporary parking lot....

The second example also demonstrates why positive messages are classified as sensitive. Positive messages, if not handled properly, can, and often do, cause strong negative emotions in a reader. Hence, a mishandled positive message can cause writers problems that could easily have been avoided.

Don't let positive messages cause unnecessary problems.

INTERNAL NEGATIVE MESSAGES—UP

Message Chart

Message Type	Positive ↑↓	Internal Negative ↑	External Negative ↑	Negative ↓	Positive-Persuasive ↑↓	Internal Negative-Persuasive ↓	Internal Negative-Persuasive ↑	External Negative-Persuasive ↑
Organizational Pattern	Bottom-Line	Semi-Circuitous	Circuitous	Bottom-Line	Bottom-Line	Semi-Circuitous	Semi-Circuitous	Circuitous

Although it makes no difference whether a positive message is sent up or down, it often makes a tremendous difference in the case of negative messages. Having to send a negative message at all presents a sensitive writing situation. And having to send that negative message up makes the job far, far more sensitive and difficult to handle.

Negative messages are highly sensitive.

When you have to convey any kind of bad news to a superior, you are obviously at risk because the reader is in a higher power position than you are. If you are forced to report some failure on your part, you are certainly faced with the most dangerous of all negative situations.

Power positions are important in negative messages.

Naturally, businesspeople have to send negative messages up internally as well as externally. Since a difference exists in the way negative messages sent up are handled internally and externally, we are going to deal with each type separately. First, we will examine negative messages that are sent up internally. Item **a** of Bottom-Line Principle 11 gives sound advice about how you should handle such messages:

BOTTOM-LINE PRINCIPLE 11:
Think twice before bottom-lining negative messages upward.

a. If the message is being sent internally, a semi-circuitous approach is probably best.

Note that we say, "Think twice." We don't say, "*Never* bottom-line" such a message. The decision is yours, but always remember the inherent dangers in bottom-lining negative messages upward:

1. Bosses (despite any claims that they like direct messages) may well resent a directly stated negative message from a subordinate.
2. Even if bosses really *are* able to handle direct messages, an internal memo is actually quite public. The word processing center staff see it, as will the bosses' secretaries, as may any person who has access to the files. (And in the modern electronic office, almost all files are available to everybody!) Anytime there is an audience involved, it is usually wise to be especially tactful.

Suppose, for example, that you are *required* to give your opinion of a marketing plan that your boss has just spent weeks developing. Suppose further that your analysis of the plan reveals some major flaws with it. You see that those flaws could cause the plan to fail, cost the company money, and severely embarrass your boss in the eyes of his or her superiors.

Despite the drawbacks of the marketing plan, would it be wise to bottom-line such a memo like this?

Version A. Bottom-Line

TO: "Boss"

FROM: "You"

SUBJECT: Marketing Plan

DATE: June 1, 19——

The marketing plan being proposed has major flaws. These flaws may embarrass you and cost the agency significant sums of money. These flaws are:

1. ....
2. ....
3. ....

Most superiors would not appreciate such blunt candor. Even if your relationship with your boss were so warm and close that he or she could accept this direct criticism from you personally, your boss will still be fearful of the potential audience such a memo might have. In a business, a memo like this would remain in the files to document the apparently crude way you dealt with a superior, a fact that might eventually haunt you. Thus, neither you nor your boss should want such a document in the files.

Bottom-lining negative messages to superiors is high-risk.

A circuitous approach might prove much safer and more diplomatic in a delicate situation like this. Let's study such a memo:

Version B. Circuitous

TO: "Boss"

FROM: "You"

SUBJECT: Marketing Plan

DATE: June 1, 19——

At your request, a careful analysis of the marketing plan has been conducted. The analysis reveals many good points about the plan. Specifically, it will:

1. ....
2. ....
3. ....

But, while the plan will accomplish much, evidence also indicates that further consideration should be given to some factors that might conceivably produce less-than-hoped-for consequences. These are mentioned only for the purpose of enabling the addition of possible refinements to an already valuable plan of action.

Here are the areas in which the analysis indicates additional consideration may be needed.

1. ....
2. ....
3. ....

As we noted earlier, this circuitous approach is risky. Many bosses might find this circuitous memo much to their liking. Others, depending on their personality and your relationship with them, may resent your rather obvious attempt to flatter them before coming out with your criticisms. They may resent your fairly obvious attempt to "con" them.

Being circuitous in negative messages to superiors is high-risk.

Does this mean that no matter whether we are direct or circuitous we are wrong? No, it means that both choices are dangerous in many negative message up situations and that you should think carefully before you use either organizational pattern. As always, your choice of organizational pattern should be influenced by the relative warmth of your relationship with your superior and by your perceptions of the boss's feelings about a topic. These perceptions can come from a variety of different sources, including past conversations with your superior.

Fortunately, the semi-circuitous approach can also be considered. Let's see how this memo would begin if we used a semi-circuitous pattern:

Version C. Semi-Circuitous

TO: "Boss"

FROM: "You"

SUBJECT: Marketing Plan

DATE: June 1, 19— —

At your request, a complete analysis of the marketing plan has been conducted.

This report will present the results of that analysis in the following order:

1. The plan's strengths.
2. Areas needing additional consideration and possible refinement.

Following an examination of these two points, recommendations for possible changes in the plan will be offered for your consideration.

This semi-circuitous memo begins diplomatically and avoids the risks of the bottom-line's bluntness and the circuitous pattern's seeming manipulative. Most superiors would appreciate both the efficiency and the tactfulness of this approach.

The semi-circuitous organizational pattern will find its greatest use in situations where writers conclude that (a) if they bottom-line their message, they will seem blunt and insensitive and (b) if they are circuitous, they will appear either manipulative or extremely wordy. The semi-circuitous organizational pattern, hence, will be used most frequently in messages sent *within* an organization. It is most applicable in situations where writer and reader have to work together over a long period of time. Internally, it is important, over the long run, to avoid seeming either abrasive or evasive. This is essential between writers and readers who must retain each other's good will and respect.

Let's take up another case of a negative message to be sent up within an organization:

The Layoff Case

At a recent staff meeting, Ben Jackson, the President of XYZ Company, told you that he expects industry sales to continue to be depressed for at least another year. He wants you and other staff as-

A semi-circuitous approach works best in negative messages to superiors.

sistants to look into ways to cut costs. Your specific assignment is to explore the possibility of laying off 20 percent of the work force. "That's the last possible step I want to take," he says about your assignment, "especially since so many of our employees are sole supporters of their families."

Your research into the work force quickly reveals that XYZ employs far too many workers. You are certain that 25 percent of these employees could be released without having any negative effect upon the company's operations. In fact, such a release would probably lead to smoother operations and to a more efficient use of other workers.

Other staff assistants tell you that they are finding few, if any, ways of cutting expenditures. You therefore know that layoffs will be the only way XYZ can bring its operating expenses into line. You also know that this course of action is not one that Jackson wants to take. The other staff assistants have asked you to prepare the report for Jackson.

Should you bottom-line this message? The factors involved in your communication are as follows:

1. *What is the bottom line?* It is "XYZ can reduce its work force by 25 percent."
2. *What is your relationship to the reader?* The reader is your superior.
3. *What is the type of message?* It is negative, because it tells Jackson information he would rather not hear.
4. *What is the reader's likely response to the message?* Probably negative.

With this information in mind, we apply Bottom-Line Principle 11 and decide to think twice about whether to bottom-line or be circuitous. First, we try a well-written, bottom-line approach.

Version A. Bottom-Line

TO: Ben Jackson

FROM: "You, Director of Personnel"

SUBJECT: Cost Reductions

DATE: January 15, 19——

XYZ can reduce the work force by 25 percent while having no noticeable effect on the company's operational effectiveness.

What do you think of this version? It is bottom-lined, but is the risk of being direct in this negative message to your superior too great? Does it seem as if you are being blunt and uncaring? Undoubtedly it does, in this instance. Therefore, let's see how a circuitous organizational pattern would look.

Bottom-lining negatives to superiors can sound like upward delegation.

TO: Ben Jackson

FROM: "You, Director of Personnel"

SUBJECT: Cost Reductions

DATE: January 15, 19— —

I endorse the goal of holding costs down that you set forth at Friday's meeting. Such moves are of use not only in a recession, but also in times of prosperity. As I examined the findings of the study you asked me to do, a number of considerations came to mind. I will share these with you.

[Paragraphs 2, 3, and so on, would offer these findings.]

I hope you will agree with me that these are serious considerations. Many of them are unexpected. Whatever the case, however, the findings seem to indicate that XYZ can reduce the work force by 25 percent while showing no appreciable change in the company's organizational effectiveness.

We have taken preliminary steps to begin a more detailed study of these findings. . . .

A circuitous approach in negative messages sent up can sound evasive.

The circuitous pattern runs its usual risk of appearing evasive, manipulative, or wordy.

The question still remains whether a semi-circuitous organizational pattern might not be far better than either a bottom-line or a circuitous pattern. Let's see how such a memo might begin:

Version C. Semi-Circuitous

TO: Ben Jackson

FROM: "You, Director of Personnel"

SUBJECT: Cost Reductions

DATE: January 15, 19— —

I have completed the cost-reduction study you requested at last Friday's staff meeting. This report will first provide a brief explanation of each staff member's findings. It will then provide a detailed analysis of the possibilities for staff reduction through work force layoffs. Finally, it will draw conclusions about such a possibility.

[Report follows.]

Semi-circuitous again works best in negative messages to superiors.

At least in this semi-circuitous version, the writer is not running the risk of being thought manipulative. Furthermore, the reader may well read the report as it is presented, and not turn first to the conclusions. If this happens, the memo has achieved the desired result of the circuitously organized message.

What if Jackson denies your request to consider your analysis and turns immediately to the conclusions? No harm is done. The reader has, by his actions, turned your tactful, semi-circuitous memo into a bottom-lined one. But since the reader did this by choice, how could he or she blame you for being tactless? Moreover, this semi-circuitous memo will cause fewer problems if people see it in the files.

EXTERNAL NEGATIVE MESSAGES—UP

Message Chart

Message Type	Positive ↑↓	Internal Negative ↑	External Negative ↑	Negative ↓	Positive-Persuasive ↑↓	Internal Negative-Persuasive ↓	Internal Negative-Persuasive ↑	External Negative-Persuasive ↑
Organizational Pattern	Bottom-Line	Semi-Circuitous	Circuitous	Bottom-Line	Bottom-Line	Semi-Circuitous	Semi-Circuitous	Circuitous

Earlier, we mentioned that a circuitous organization pattern finds its best use in situations where negative messages must be sent up to important persons outside of the company. That's why we have added a second item to Bottom-Line Principle 11:

BOTTOM-LINE PRINCIPLE 11:
Think twice before bottom-lining negative messages upward.

a. If the message is being sent internally, a semi-circuitous approach is probably best.
b. If the message is being sent externally, consider a circuitous approach.

Let's look at a negative message that was sent externally. A large corporation had to write to a very famous inventor, a man the company wanted to keep happy because of his scientific standing and his potential future value to the industry. Yet the company had to say no to the inventor's latest idea.

External negative messages have different needs from internal ones.

In this situation, the inventor had offered an idea he had patented to the corporation for its consideration and possible use in its products. Several months went by before the inventor received a letter telling him that the corporation had no interest in licensing the use of his invention.

The inventor wrote an angry response to the corporation's management, reproaching it for taking such a long time just to say no. Since the company had not intended to offend the inventor by its delay, a sensitive letter, similar to the one that follows, was written, intending to soothe the angry inventor's upset feelings. Remember that this is still a negative message being sent up—up because of the inventor's potential future importance—and so does not emphasize the "bad news."

ABC COMPANY
5522 W. Kennedy Blvd.
Tampa, FL 33609

January 12, 19— —

Dr. Alvin Cadek
10850 Tradeport Drive
Orlando, FL 32827

Dear Dr. Cadek:

Thank you for your letter of January 5. I appreciate your candid expression of your concerns, and because you took the time
to write, I believe that you are giving me the opportunity to
clarify the conditions that caused delay.

COMMENTARY

**Notice the pleasant beginning. Also, notice that the letter "an-
nounces" the topic but does not reveal the writer's answer to
Dr. Cadek.**

The review of ideas and inventions received from outside the
company is one of the areas it has not been possible to automate. Every submission must be handled on an individual basis
and reviewed by the appropriate people, who may be scattered
throughout the organization. As is to be expected, because of
other responsibilities, these engineers and marketing representatives are often away on field trips of several weeks' dura-
tion and cannot always immediately respond to a request for
an evaluation of a submitted idea.

COMMENTARY

The writer tactfully implies a major reason for the delay.

I first sent your proposal to marketing requirements people in
New York. They advised me that they are already aware of the
basic idea. However, because of work being done in our Georgia
laboratory, they suggested that your material be forwarded
there for consideration with the hope that there was something
in your material that could be applied to a potential project under consideration. These people agreed that your idea has potential but found nothing in the proposal of which they were
not already aware.

COMMENTARY
The writer explains the extra steps that were taken and the reasons for the answer he previously gave.

The delay was unfortunate, and I can understand your concern. However, in cases like this, when one group within the company suggests that another consider the material, I always feel that it is best to take a little more time and be sure that we have considered every aspect of a proposal. I assure you that the delay was caused only by our desire to find anything that could be mutually beneficial.

COMMENTARY
The writer again stresses the steps taken and the seriousness with which the reader's proposal was treated.

Please keep XYZ in mind for any future ideas you are considering. As I have tried to stress, we are most favorably impressed by your creativity.

COMMENTARY
The writer ends pleasantly and courteously.

At first, the length of this letter seems extreme, but remember that it does not matter how it seems to *us*. It is how it seems to Dr. Cadek that is of importance. The goal was to make an angry, hurt inventor feel better about the company and its rejection of his invention. Notice also that the writer frequently chose an extremely personal approach in an attempt to reassure the inventor that the "big" company was personally interested in him and his ideas.

If you are still unsure about whether this letter is too long, ask yourself how you think Dr. Cadek would have reacted to this bottom-lined response:

ABC COMPANY
5522 W. Kennedy Blvd.
Tampa, FL 33609

January 12, 19——

Dr. Alvin Cadek
10850 Tradeport Drive
Orlando, FL 32827

Dear Dr. Cadek:

Regardless of the amount of time it took us to conclude that we have no interest in your idea, the fact remains that we don't.

Negative messages generally
need to be longer than
positive messages.

Readers want explanations to
accompany bad news.

Longer negative letters give
an impression of a writer's
concern.

Even though nobody likes to be rejected, people still react better to longer rejection letters than they do to short ones. A long letter appears as if the person doing the rejecting at least had the courtesy to explain the reasons fully. Remember when you were a child. What was the first thing you'd say after your mother or father told you no? Wasn't it "Why, Mommy?" or "Why, Daddy?" As we grow older, we don't change too much in this regard. We still like (as Dr. Cadek did) to be told the reasons *why* behind a negative decision on the part of a superior, rather than just to be told no.

A long letter in negative situations like this suggests also that management regarded the reader as a fellow human being and took his request seriously. Management did not simply give a blanket refusal without any consideration of the legitimacy of the case being considered.

You will notice that the circuitous approach to this negative message sent up allowed the letter to accomplish four important aspects of such a letter. The approach includes

1. a pleasant, cordial—or, at least, neutral—beginning
2. an explanation of the reasons for the negative message
3. a statement of the negative message in flat, low-impact terms
4. a pleasant, cordial, positive ending.

One final question remains about the Cadek letter: Would a semi-circuitous approach have worked just as well? Our feeling is that it would have worked, but not so effectively as did the circuitous approach. Here is how the semi-circuitous approach to the Cadek letter would have begun:

ABC COMPANY
5522 W. Kennedy Blvd.
Tampa, FL 33609

January 12, 19——

Dr. Alvin Cadek
10850 Tradeport Drive
Orlando, FL 32837

Dear Dr. Cadek:

Thank you for your letter of January 5, concerning the delay in advising you that we already knew about the basic ideas presented in your suggestion. I appreciate your candid expression of dissatisfaction, and because you took the time to write, I believe that you are giving me the opportunity to clarify the conditions that caused delay. Therefore, let me first explain the procedures we follow when a new patent idea is presented. Then, let me explain why our decision took the shape it did.

In an external message, frankness is less valuable than in messages to people you work with daily. You do not have to reveal your strategy to the reader. In this external case, the beginning paragraph of the semi-circuitous letter admits, essentially, that "We're going to give a long, detailed, somewhat boring explanation of what we did. And, of course, we're not going to change our mind."

The circuitous approach, in a negative external message like this one, works better because it doesn't reveal its strategy to the reader. Yes, frankly, it *does* manipulate the reader by allowing him or her to hold onto the hope, however slight, that the writer might have a change of heart and end up saying yes. But by delaying the answer, the circuitous approach gives the writer a chance to justify thoroughly the reasons for the "no" before finally dashing the reader's hopes. Hence, it actually is more sensitive to the reader's feelings than is either the bottom-line approach or the semi-circuitous approach.

Circuitous works better than semi-circuitous in external negative messages.

NEGATIVE MESSAGES—DOWN

Message Chart

Message Type	Positive ↑↓	Internal Negative ↑	External Negative ↑	Negative ↓	Positive-Persuasive ↑↓	Internal Negative-Persuasive ↓	Internal Negative-Persuasive ↑	External Negative-Persuasive ↑
Organizational Pattern	Bottom-Line	Semi-Circuitous	Circuitous	Bottom-Line	Bottom-Line	Semi-Circuitous	Semi-Circuitous	Circuitous

How should negative messages sent downward be organized? If you are the boss and are writing down, you are not in much risk. On the other hand, there are times when bosses are fearful of appearing overbearing or downright nasty in their communications to subordinates.

In reality, most bosses can organize downwardly sent messages any way they like. Usually, they choose to be direct. Experience indicates, moreover, that subordinates expect leaders to give orders and to communicate their wishes directly and forcefully. The vast majority of businesspeople regard it as sheer artifice for a superior to hedge and not bottom-line bad news sent to subordinates. Bottom-Line Principle 12, therefore, states:

Negative messages sent downward can often be direct.

BOTTOM-LINE PRINCIPLE 12:
Bottom-line downward messages unless extenuating circumstances are involved.

Subordinates' Expectations

Subordinates prefer a bottom-line approach in negative messages to them.

Why do subordinates expect a superior to bottom-line messages? Business-people report that in business your personal success depends upon the skills and power of your superior. People want leaders who exemplify in their communications that they are in charge, that they can lead, and that they can protect common interests as necessary. That is why, we have found, subordinates prefer a bottom-line approach in negative messages coming down to them. Such an approach not only demonstrates that the leader has power but also that he or she is going to be direct about using it.

Using a bottom-line pattern does not mean that bosses have a license to be overbearing or rude. Far from it. Most veteran superiors have learned how to bottom-line tactfully even negative messages and to include statements that make the negative appear less objectionable to the subordinate. Here is some advice for you to remember when you are the boss and have to give bad news to a subordinate:

Negative messages sent down must still be diplomatic and tactful.

Emphasize that you know the reader expects you to be straightforward and honest (you are, so you might as well receive credit for it). For example, you might begin like this:

> Jim, I'm going to be honest with you about the Simmons Account. I know that you have put a terrific effort into bringing the account into line with our expectation. But despite all your work, outside factors have kept you from achieving this goal. Therefore, I have decided that, starting now, Mary Brown will be the account executive for Simmons.

Stress or imply that you are being straightforward because you would never attempt to deceive someone you respect as much as you do your reader. For instance, you might say:

> Sarah, you and I have always enjoyed a straightforward relationship. So let me tell you right off that there are three probable reasons why your plans won't work.

Temper your bottom-line approach with praise for the reader.

> If anyone could have salvaged this project from the wastebasket, it was you. In fact, the project only survived as long as it did thanks to your untiring devotion.

Whenever possible, include explanations for a negative decision along with the decision. Few people will take no for an answer and not ask for an explanation. That is the problem with bottom-line letters that state, "The answer to your request is 'no.'" The fault is not in the bottom-line organizational pattern used; it lies in the lack of explanation for the negative.

The following negative message down is bottom-lined, but its effect is softened by the application of the advice we just gave. Most readers would react favorably to this next memo.

```
TO:         Greg Ramos

FROM:       "Boss"

SUBJECT:    XYZ Campaign

DATE:       August 18, 19——
```

You have worked so hard on the XYZ campaign that I owe it to you not to keep you in suspense. At present, the proposed XYZ advertising campaign cannot be implemented.

Because you know of my respect for your creative abilities, I know you will want me to be forthright about the reasons behind this decision. Specifically:

1. ....

2. ....

3. ....

Greg, you have done an excellent job developing the concept on which to base this campaign. I fully recognize and appreciate the work you put into it. Once the problems mentioned above are solved satisfactorily, it may well be possible to resume work on the campaign.

Once again, thanks for a job well done.

PERSUASIVE MESSAGES

Persuasive messages involve an effort to induce a reader to take a particular action. This action may or may not be in the reader's best interest. That is why, as we noted earlier, persuasive messages fall into two categories: positive-persuasive and negative-persuasive. Before examining the organizational patterns appropriate to persuasive messages, you must keep two things in mind.

Persuasive messages try to make readers take actions.

First, the goal of persuasion is not to fool or seduce your readers. As we noted earlier, at your job you will have to live among the people with whom you work and do business. In the long run in business, the most effective way of being really persuasive is to have earned a reputation for honesty and sincerity. In business, not only is honesty the best policy, but honesty is probably the *only* policy. Within the organization you work for, or in written dealings between organizations, you had better not mislead, vaguely misrepresent, or seduce.

Persuasive messages must be honest, not tricky.

Second, remember that the content of a memo or letter plays a crucial role in the success you can expect in a persuasive situation. Regardless of what organizational pattern you choose and what style you use, your efforts may fail *unless you complement these strategies with meaningful and honest evidence in support of your case.*[1]

Content influences the effectiveness of persuasion.

[1]For a detailed discussion of logical analysis and use of evidence, read Unit C, "How To Analyze Cases," p. 577.

With these two qualifications in mind, let's examine persuasive situations to determine which organizational pattern works most effectively in positive-persuasive and negative-persuasive messages.

Positive-Persuasive Messages — Up And Down

Message Chart

Message Type	Positive ↑↓	Internal Negative ↑	External Negative ↑	Negative ↓	Positive-Persuasive ↑↓	Internal Negative-Persuasive ↓	Internal Negative-Persuasive ↑	External Negative-Persuasive ↑
Organizational Pattern	Bottom-Line	Semi-Circuitous	Circuitous	Bottom-Line	Bottom-Line	Semi-Circuitous	Semi-Circuitous	Circuitous

Bottom-Line Principle 13 gives advice on how to organize positive-persuasive messages:

BOTTOM-LINE PRINCIPLE 13:
In positive-persuasive situations, up or down, bottom-line your request.

Positive-persuasive messages can be bottom-lined.

When your task is to persuade readers to do something for their own good and when those readers know (even if only deep down in their awareness) that your request is for their own good, you should bottom-line the message and use a direct organizational pattern. It doesn't matter much whether you are writing up or down. If you are trying to persuade your boss (or your best customer) to do what is good for him or her, you should bottom-line your suggestion.

Here's another real, but disguised, memo that went to all employees of a large company, urging them to use a new shuttle-bus service between office locations.

> TO: All Employees
>
> FROM: Director of Transportation
>
> SUBJECT: Shuttle-Bus Service
>
> DATE: May 7, 19——
>
> As you are aware, we are having a number of traffic problems between our Pebble Brook and Valleyview buildings. Employees are taking their vehicles from one building to the other and are parking in slots not assigned to them. Naturally, when an employee's slot is taken, he or she parks elsewhere—usually in another employee's slot—and complicates matters further. The result of all this is hurt feelings and damaged employee morale.
>
> To combat this problem, a parking and traffic committee was formed to suggest solutions. After studying a number of alternatives, the committee recommended a shuttle-bus service between the buildings. We urge you to use this service.

> In ninety days the service will be monitored and evaluated for usage, energy savings, and other benefits. It will be continued or terminated based on this evaluation.
>
> Details of the service are....

You cannot fail to notice that the writer has used a circuitous organizational pattern better suited to a negative message. The memo does not get to the purpose until the middle of the second paragraph, where the committee's recommendation of a shuttle service has been carefully buried.

What is so negative about this shuttle service? Won't it solve or at least alleviate a problem that has been bothering all personnel? This message really attempts to persuade people to do something that is positive to their interests. Therefore, it should be bottom-lined, like this:

Positive-persuasive messages persuade people to act in their best interests.

> TO: All Employees
>
> FROM: Director of Transportation
>
> SUBJECT: Shuttle-Bus Service
>
> DATE: May 7, 19——
>
> We are pleased to announce a new shuttle-bus service between our Pebble Brook and Valleyview buildings. This service will begin on June 4 and will allow you to go from building to building without using your own vehicles.

Businesspeople are busy. Everybody is after them—not just you – wanting them to do something. Therefore, if you have something you want the reader to do and that something is in the reader's best interest, the best way to gain the reader's interest and attention is to explain clearly just what you want. If you make it easy for the reader to do what you want—"Just initial a copy of this request and return it to me, and I'll begin the project immediately"—you increase your probability of success.

Positive-persuasive messages should explain clearly what the reader should do.

Internal Negative-Persuasive Messages—Down

Message Chart

Message Type	Positive ↑↓	Internal Negative ↑	External Negative ↑	Negative ↓	Positive-Persuasive ↑↓	Internal Negative-Persuasive ↓	Internal Negative-Persuasive ↑	External Negative-Persuasive ↑
Organizational Pattern	Bottom-Line	Semi-Circuitous	Circuitous	Bottom-Line	Bottom-Line	Semi-Circuitous	Semi-Circuitous	Circuitous

Wise writers approach negative-persuasive situations much more gingerly than they do positive-persuasive situations. This is necessary because negative-persuasive messages present writers with the difficult task of persuading readers to do something they do not want to do. When such messages are sent internally, the situation becomes especially delicate be-

Negative-persuasive messages are difficult and risky.

cause you do not want to offend or be caught manipulating your superior or your subordinate.

A bottom-line approach to a negative-persuasive down situation is very risky. Think, for instance, of the human-relations consequences of the following memo sent to a subordinate:

TO: "Subordinate"

FROM: "Boss"

SUBJECT: Postponing Vacation

DATE: September 26, 19— —

I am writing to request that you delay the start of your vacation for ten days. Here are three reasons for my request:

1. ....

2. ....

3. ....

Bottom-lining negative-persuasive messages downward hurts superior—subordinate relations.

Can the boss use such a direct approach if he or she wants? Certainly. Because of his or her superior power position, the boss can organize the message in a direct, bottom-line fashion. Will such an approach enhance relations between management and employees? It is doubtful. In fact, the bottom-line approach here may cause a significant rift between the superior and the subordinate, one that may eventually not only damage goodwill but also productivity.

Remember, in Chapter 11 we posed the situation that required you, as a branch manager, to write a letter to one hundred employees in your branch, urging them to double their contributions to the United Way. This type of internal negative-persuasive situation presents difficulties because you simply cannot order people to contribute to a charity.

A bottom-line organization pattern, then, is too risky, since employees will resent superiors using their authority to coerce them into taking an action that should be completely voluntary. On the other hand, a circuitous approach is also highly risky because of the fear of seeming manipulative to people with whom one works daily. This is just as true when a superior writes downward as it is when a subordinate writes upward. In neither case does one want to run the risk of looking like a con artist in action.

Semi-Circuitous to the Rescue

Since a bottom-line and a circuitous approach are both too risky, the logical alternative is a semi-circuitous organizational pattern. Let's try this pattern on the United Way contributions situation.

As we plan for this memo, we recognize that our purpose is to get employees to increase their contributions by a significant amount. To accomplish this task, we will have to prepare readers thoroughly for the predominant message—the need for them to double their contributions. We will have to inform readers about the various services that the United

Way provides for the community, remind them of their civic and moral responsibilities, and explain the United Way's need for additional funding. All of this will have to be done before the request for doubling contributions is made.

Here is how the memo might read if the writer were to follow this advice:

TO: All Branch Employees

FROM: "Branch Manager"

SUBJECT: United Way

DATE: February 16, 19——

As we all realize, the time to consider our support for the United Way has again arrived. Allow me to refresh your memories both about the vital services that the United Way provides our community and our needs to help with such services. I'll also explain some special circumstances that United Way is facing and then make a special request of you for this year.

Few of us need reminding that the United Way supports such activities as....

[The memo then examines, in a high-impact manner, the well-known community functions United Way performs.]

But the United Way also deals with other support services such as these which are not commonly known.

[The memo continues a high-impact approach and explores less commonly known United Way services.]

We all recognize also that we are in an era when the private sector is being urged to carry a far greater share of the burden for social services formerly carried by the federal government. Never in recent years has the need been greater for us, as members of the private sector, to do more of a charitable nature.

For this reason, our company, and hence our branch, has been asked by United Way officials to assume our fair share of this burden. Because of our prominence in the community and in the business world, we have been asked to set a high standard for the giving of others. The actual goal is that we double the amount of contributions we raised last year.

No one knows more than I how formidable a task this is. But I'm sure that all of us will rise to this occasion, as we have to so many occasions in the past. We must show once again that our company has as great a motivation to achieve civic and moral goals as it does to achieve financial ones.

The memo ends by offering details about how employees should go about making their contributions.

Obviously a negative-persuasive memo such as this one is only part of the process that determines whether a company doubles its contribution to United Way. Other personal and economic factors also influence the outcome. However, if success is measured by raising the most money possible while encountering the fewest personnel problems from potential givers, then the semi-circuitous approach here could prove to be a rousing success. For from this latter perspective, a semi-circuitous organizational pattern does its job more effectively than any other possible approach.

Internal Negative-Persuasive Messages—Up

Message Chart

Message Type	Positive ⇅	Internal Negative ↑	External Negative ↑	Negative ↓	Positive-Persuasive ⇅	Internal Negative-Persuasive ↓	Internal Negative-Persuasive ↑	External Negative-Persuasive ↑
Organizational Pattern	Bottom-Line	Semi-Circuitous	Circuitous	Bottom-Line	Bottom-Line	Semi-Circuitous	Semi-Circuitous	Circuitous

An internal negative-persuasive situation sent up presents another difficult situation to handle. Here is a case where a boss was in favor of immediately implementing a voluntary education program for the corporation. The writer, a subordinate, attempted to persuade the boss to delay taking action.

TO: "Boss"

FROM: "Subordinate"

SUBJECT: Voluntary Education Program

DATE: February 4, 19——

Bill Blaze has completed the study of a voluntary education program for headquarters staff. Bill reviewed his findings with me on January 14.

In summary, Bill found that the recent history of voluntary education programs at other sites indicates diminishing employee interest. Additionally, support expense increases both in terms of equipment costs and instructor-student ratio.

The report also notes that local schools and colleges provide a wide variety of programs at minimal cost. Headquarters personnel can communicate related information about these external programs to management and employees. This avenue means that although consideration of a formal program might

---

need to be postponed, a survey is needed on employee interest and participation in such programs. Additionally, further investigation of self-study courses should provide helpful data for future alternatives.

A copy of the Voluntary Education Report is attached.

Needless to say, it takes a great deal of effort even to guess at the action being requested.

What would have made the Voluntary Education memo more effective? Since a bottom-line approach would obviously be too blunt and a circuitous approach has proven too vague, the only other organizational approach to try is semi-circuitous. Notice how the following memo minimizes the risks of appearing too pushy or too manipulative.

Being circuitous in negative-persuasive messages sent upward results in a vague message.

Semi-circuitous works best for most internal negative-persuasive messages.

TO.   "Boss"

FROM: "Subordinate"

SUBJECT: Voluntary Education Program

DATE: February 4, 19— —

Bill Blaze has completed the study of a voluntary education program for headquarters staff. Bill reviewed his findings with me on January 14. In this memo, I will first present a summary of Bill's findings and then offer my recommendations.

Summary of Findings

Bill found that the recent history of in-house training at other sites indicates diminishing employee interest. Additionally, support expense increases both in terms of equipment costs and instructor-student ratio.

The report also notes that local schools and colleges provide a wide variety of programs at minimal cost. Headquarters personnel can communicate information about these external programs to management and employees.

Recommendation

Bill's findings lead me to recommend that we postpone implementing such a program at the present time. Instead, for now, we should:

1. Gather a reading on employee interest and participation in such programs.
2. Study the possibility of further use of guided learning centers.

A copy of the Voluntary Education Report is attached.

The semi-circuitous approach, combined with the higher impact created by white space, significantly decreases the risk associated with this memo and significantly increases the probability that the boss will follow Bill's recommendation.

Semi-Circuitous to the Rescue—Again

Let's consider one other instance where a semi-circuitous organization would work in a negative-persuasive message. In this situation, Ted Piland, Vice President of Human Resource Management, asked a subordinate, Dale Spadoni, to look into a dispute that occurred between secretaries in the word processing center and Mary Burke, their supervisor. Spadoni was told to focus most of his attention on Mary Burke and to make appropriate suggestions for dealing with her situation.

Spadoni, however, felt insecure about the task. Burke's performance clearly was open to questions, but the writer knew that Burke had been with the company for a long time and had been a former private secretary to Piland himself. For that reason, he decided to use a semi-circuitous approach in his report to Piland, one that even went so far as to tell him where the bottom line occurred if he desired to go to it immediately.

TO: Ted Piland

FROM: Dale Spadoni

SUBJECT: Incident concerning Mary Burke

DATE: October 14, 19——

I have, as you requested, looked into the incident concerning Mary Burke. In this report I will cover the following topics: the background of Mary Burke; the employees' opinion of Ms. Burke; the results of an interview with Nancy Fisher, Director of Personnel; and suggestions for a solution to this incident.

Background of Mary Burke

Ms. Burke has worked very hard for our agency. She is an accurate stenographer and counselor. She will talk with employees at length to improve their productivity. However, sometimes her counseling is not effective, and employees will continue to overlook their responsibilities. When asked to reprimand an employee, Ms. Burke becomes very upset at the thought of "throwing someone out in the street." In such cases, Ms. Burke asks Nancy Fisher or Ted Piland to help handle the task.

Employees' Opinions of Mary Burke

Although most employees find Ms. Burke very likeable, her office staff sometimes complains that she gives unfair workloads. One associate even went as far as saying that Ms. Burke is a "patsy": she'll believe any excuses for absenteeism or sloppy work, and not only excuse the employee, but cover for him or her as well. I find this fact to be very disturbing.

Interview with Director of Personnel

I spoke with Nancy Fisher after lunch today. Since one of Ms. Fisher's first duties was appointing Ms. Burke as supervisor of the word processing center, I feel that Ms. Fisher's opinion is very important to this issue. Ms. Fisher agreed that Ms. Burke is a diligent worker. Ms. Fisher commented that she receives many compliments about the fast, accurate work done at the Center.

However, Ms. Fisher is very upset that Ms. Burke is not properly disciplining her employees. Ms. Fisher also said Ms. Burke has the highest turnover rate in the company (over 25 percent), except for the foundry. Ms. Fisher's biggest complaint is that Ms. Burke refuses to discharge employees. Furthermore, Ms. Fisher has had to discharge six of Ms. Burke's employees in the past two years.

In conclusion, Ms. Fisher stated that she wished she had a "real supervisor there," and that Ms. Burke "can either take on all the disciplining and firing of her people or take an early retirement."

Suggestions

Inadequate supervision seems to be the main issue in the word processing center. Someone needs to have a meeting (at length, if necessary) with Ms. Burke and explain in detail her job's specific duties (including disciplining and firing her employees).

After Ms. Burke's duties are made perfectly clear and Ms. Burke begins performing them, it is hoped that her employees will stop complaining and the Word Processing Center will run smoothly.

If you need any further information concerning the findings on this issue, please call me.

This letter is truly a classic example of the semi-circuitous approach. Notice how the contract sentence not only reveals the organization of the entire report but also how each subsection begins by praising Mary Burke and then proceeds to explain in detail the areas in which she needs to improve.

This approach not only removed the subordinate from a very uncomfortable situation, but it also proved to anyone who read this report that he could perform effectively, even in the most delicate of situations. Bottom-Line Principle 14, then, deals with internal negative-persuasive situations that are sent both up and down:

Use a semi-circuitous organizational pattern for most internal negative-persuasive situations.

External Negative-Persuasive Messages — Up

Message Chart

Message Type	Positive $\uparrow\downarrow$	Internal Negative $\uparrow$	External Negative $\uparrow$	Negative $\downarrow$	Positive-Persuasive $\uparrow\downarrow$	Internal Negative-Persuasive $\downarrow$	Internal Negative-Persuasive $\uparrow$	External Negative-Persuasive $\uparrow$
Organizational Pattern	Bottom-Line	Semi-Circuitous	Circuitous	Bottom-Line	Bottom-Line	Semi-Circuitous	Semi-Circuitous	Circuitous

An external negative-persuasive message sent up tries to persuade a customer or someone outside of your organization to take a particular action that the person does not initially want to take. Here are some examples of situations in which negative messages frequently have to be sent outside of the organization. The messages are directed to people who, for one reason or another, are in a higher power position than the writer:

1. A letter to a stockholder explaining why the company has had to cut its dividend.

2. A letter to an important customer demanding prompt payment of an overdue bill.

3. A letter to the Environmental Protection Commission reporting that your company has failed to make the required changes in its waste disposal methods.

Bottom-Line Principle 15 offers advice for organizing upwardly sent external negative-persuasive messages.

Use a circuitous pattern for most external negative-persuasive situations.

Writers are usually more distant from external than from internal readers.

The organizational difference between an internal and an external negative-persuasive message — that is, semi-circuitous versus circuitous — develops from the different types of relationships readers have. The relationship between you and an external reader is usually not so close as it is between you and your boss. The same demands for bottom-lining are, therefore, not present. Also, the fear of seeming manipulative and the risk associated with this perception are much less important. As a result, a circuitous approach works quite effectively in such highly sensitive situations.

The Sales Letter as an External Negative-Persuasive Letter

The most familiar type of external negative-persuasive letter sent up is the sales letter. Though sometimes organized as a positive-persuasive letter, sales letters are usually handled as external negative-persuasive messages that are sent up. Here is a typical example of such a letter. This example encourages the reader to subscribe to a magazine:

Sales letters are external negative-persuasive messages.

XYZ MAGAZINE
540 E. Madison Street
Chicago, IL 60602

March 13, 19——

Ms. Kimberly Barnum
100 Vine Street
Cincinn~~ati~~ ~~OH~~

0·C

#45·36

45·36 ×
1·0825 =
49·10 *

49·10 *

~~0,000? You have a chance to do~~ ...ving a raffle to provide you with ... the bucks."

... a winner. And the best way for ... bscribe to XYZ Magazine!

[T .... nt detail about how subscribers
cai .... so on, by subscribing to XYZ
Ma

"Wl ... ask. Simple. Just fill out
the ...wait for the raffle. And while
you' ...ing, you will be receiving weekly issues of XYZ Magazine, a leading self-improvement magazine for winners like you.

Start today. Fill out the card, drop it in the mail, and before you can shout "I want to be a winner!" XYZ Magazine will be coming to your door. Join today! Before it's too late!

Sincerely,

Hazel Odewahn

Hazel Odewahn

Unit 6 will examine the stylistic aspects of such a letter. In terms of organization, however, notice how essential the circuitous pattern is to the letter. Readers are virtually lured into reading it—with cash rewards being promised or implied before the statement of purpose occurs.

Sales letters are circuitous.

We're sure you're familiar with a number of these types of persuasive letters. You have probably even noticed that often the circuitousness begins before you even open the letter. The envelope has messages promising you fame and fortune; sometimes it states that you are already a winner if you open the envelope. In short, the writers do everything possible just to persuade you to begin reading the message.

External negative-persuasive messages are rarely, if ever, sent downward.

One final note about externally sent negative-persuasive messages. You have probably noticed that we deal with these messages only as going up, not up and down as we did with internal negative-persuasive messages. The reason for this approach is that such messages rarely, if ever, are sent downward. If one is writing down externally, the situation would most likely involve someone in a corporation writing to one of its suppliers or to someone in a smaller company dependent upon the larger company's business. In reality, if the more powerful company tried to persuade the less powerful company to take a particular action, the persuasion would come less from the letter than through the purchasing power that the larger company exerted over the lesser company. Consequently, the power factor here is so important that it outweighs and nullifies any organizational decision made.

SUMMARY

An understanding of the three basic organizational patterns—bottom-line, circuitous, and semi-circuitous—presents you with powerful weapons to use in controlling various communication situations. Yet, deciding when to use each weapon is difficult. In some situations, such as those that are positive, a bottom-line approach works well regardless of whether the message is going up or down. Other messages require other organizational patterns.

Message Type	Positive $\uparrow\downarrow$	Internal Negative $\uparrow$	External Negative $\uparrow$	Negative $\downarrow$	Positive-Persuasive $\uparrow\downarrow$	Internal Negative-Persuasive $\downarrow$	Internal Negative-Persuasive $\uparrow$	External Negative-Persuasive $\uparrow$
Organizational Pattern	Bottom-Line	Semi-Circuitous	Circuitous	Bottom-Line	Bottom-Line	Semi-Circuitous	Semi-Circuitous	Circuitous

In negative and negative-persuasive messages sent up, you will want to be more cautious with your organizational selections. As a general principle, in such situations the circuitous or the semi-circuitous approaches have the greatest likelihood of achieving the desired result.

A negative message sent downward, on the other hand, will probably have its greatest likelihood for success if it is bottom-lined.

A negative-persuasive message sent down is probably best served by the semi-circuitous approach, which avoids the appearance of being manipulative but at the same time gives the writer a chance to condition the reader's mind.

Remember that extenuating circumstances may be present on the job. These factors may contradict the generally appropriate advice of this chapter. When such circumstances are present, use your common sense and be tactful in choosing an appropriate organizational pattern.

REVIEW QUESTIONS

1. What can happen when you do not use a direct approach when writing a good-news letter?

2. What organizational pattern should you use when writing a negative message upward internally? *Semi circular*

3. What influences your choice of organizational pattern? *message type and direction*

4. What advice should you remember when you are the boss and have to give bad news to a subordinate? *be tactful*

5. In the long run, what is the most effective way of being really persuasive in business?

6. What organizational pattern should you use when writing a positive-persuasive message upward or downward? *bottom-line*

7. Why are internal negative-persuasive messages that are sent upward especially delicate? *high risk of appear of manipulative n too pushy*

DISCUSSION QUESTIONS

1. This chapter notes that people prefer more detailed explanations when receiving negative messages than they do when receiving positive messages. Why do you suppose this situation exists? How do your observations of this tendency affect the way you organize each of these messages?

2. Suppose you have to write an external negative-persuasive message to a customer you know very well. In fact, suppose this customer is one of your best friends. Would this relationship influence the organizational pattern you choose to use? Why or why not?

3. Discuss some common persuasive strategies you see daily—either in the mail, in magazine advertisements, or on television. What organizational patterns do you observe being used in these situations? How effective are the patterns?

1. many ppl will read only the first paragraph; get angry → stop reading

BOTTOM-LINE PRINCIPLES 10–15
REVIEW LIST

10

Always bottom-line good news. There is no conflict between bottom-lining and writing positive messages.

11

Think twice before bottom-lining negative messages upward.
a. If the message is being sent internally, a semi-circuitous approach is probably best.
b. If the message is being sent externally, consider a circuitous approach.

12

Bottom-line downward messages unless extenuating circumstances are involved.

13

In positive-persuasive situations, up or down, bottom-line your request.

14

Use a semi-circuitous organizational pattern for most internal negative-persuasive situations.

15

Use a circuitous pattern for most external negative-persuasive situations.

EXERCISES

The following two sets of exercises provide mini-cases for you to think about and upon which you can practice different organizational strategies. Set 1 involves fun, mostly personal exercises for you to discuss and/or try to write. Some of these situations could, of course, be handled with a phone call, though the same organizational principles would apply.

Set 2 involves some realistic business cases you may someday face. You should gain valuable insights about different organizational strategies by discussing and trying to write messages for these situations.

Exercise Set 1

1. Your cousin writes that he is coming to the town where you are attending college. He writes that he is very much looking forward to visiting you and spending time with you. He asks if it would be okay for him to stay with you in your apartment for the Friday and Saturday nights he will be in town.

   You have a very small efficiency apartment that you share with a roommate. You also had plans for the entire weekend your cousin is planning to visit. You have no desire to include him in your plans, especially because from the time you were a small child, you never liked your cousin. You must write a letter to him, telling him that it would not be possible for him to stay at your apartment and suggesting that the two of you shouldn't even bother visiting one another.
   a. What kind of message are you being asked to send?
   b. How do you think your cousin will view this message?
   c. Which organizational pattern would probably prove more effective? Why?

2. Your mother writes from home to tell you that your younger brother has very much neglected his work in the first semester of his senior year of high school. Your mother asks you to write to convince your brother that high school grades are important credentials, especially if he hopes to go to college.
   a. What kind of message is it that you are being asked to send?
   b. Do you think your mother and your brother will see the message in the same light?
   c. Should you organize the message according to how your mother will regard the message or how your brother will?
   d. Which organizational pattern would probably prove more effective? Why?

3. You have been asked to spend the summer with friends in Hawaii. This is a chance of a lifetime for you, since you have always wanted to go to Hawaii. You had planned to spend the summer vacationing with your family in Florida. This has been a family tradition for years and your parents always look forward to it. You have to write a letter to

your parents, telling them that you will not be able to join them in Florida.

    a. What kind of message is it that you are being asked to write?

    b. Do you think your family will see the message in the same light as you do?

    c. Should you organize the letter according to how your parents will regard the message?

    d. Which organizational pattern would probably prove more effective? Why?

4. You have to write a letter to a family member, telling her you can't attend a big birthday celebration. Your family thinks birthdays are very important and always celebrates them. The celebration is planned for the weekend before you have two major finals on Monday. The finals are in your most difficult classes, and you must spend the weekend studying.

    a. What kind of message are you being asked to write?

    b. Do you think the family member will see the message in the same light as you do?

    c. Should you organize the letter according to how the family member will regard the message?

    d. Which organizational pattern would probably prove more effective? Why?

Exercise Set 2

1. Your boss has asked you to complete a report by Friday. She needs the report to prepare for a Monday morning meeting. You have been constantly interrupted while working on the report. Some of the interruptions have involved business; others have been personal. You now recognize that you will not be able to finish the report until Saturday evening.

    Your boss is working out of town and won't return until Friday morning. You decide to send her a message through the company's electronic mail system, telling her that you will finish the report Saturday evening and will deliver it to her home as soon as the report is finished.

    a. What organizational response seems called for in this case? Why?

    b. Write a rough draft of the message, adding whatever details you find necessary.

2. You have been appointed chairperson of your department's blood drive. You must write to ten of your departmental associates, persuading them to donate blood within the next week. If these associates make a contribution before the drive ends, your department will have 100 percent participation. No other department in the company has achieved this status.

    a. What organizational response seems called for in this case? Why?

    b. Write a rough draft of the message, adding whatever details you find necessary.

3. You work as a sales representative for a large paper company. You have an assigned territory and a large customer base that involves

mostly repeat business. You have just learned that effective the first day of next month your company will raise the price of its products by 20 percent. Similar products sold by competing firms will now be priced on average about 10 percent below those sold by your company. However, your company still provides better service, faster delivery, and other positive features. You must now write a letter to all of your customers, announcing the price increase.

   a. What organizational response seems called for in this case? Why?

   b. Write a rough draft of the message, adding whatever details you find necessary.

4. You work as a marketing representative for a large computer company. Six months ago, you sold an X100 computer system to a very large customer, ABC, Inc. The X100 system cost ABC $4.5 million dollars and was installed last month. Also last month, your company announced its newest large computer line, the X200. The X200 is 48 percent more powerful than the X100, but would cost ABC only $4.2 million dollars to install.

   The President of ABC writes and makes a request of you. ABC would like you to install an X200 for *no cost* whatsoever! The President maintains you knew that the X200 was forthcoming but that you chose to sell his company the X100 to unload the old system and to get the higher price.

   The President's assertion is not true. Marketing representatives never know about a new product until it is announced publicly. You cannot, therefore, effectively give him an X200 for free. You can, however, give him a special price on the X200. For only $1.8 million dollars, you can have the company's X100 replaced by the newer, more powerful X200. You must now write to the President to tell him that you cannot grant his request but that you can offer a compromise.

   a. What organizational response seems called for in this case? Why?

   b. Write a rough draft of the message, adding whatever details you find necessary.

5. Your company has received a complaint from a valued customer who insists that the personal computer he purchased has destroyed several diskettes. The customer is demanding that your company replace these diskettes and send him another personal computer. You sent a technician to investigate this claim and found out that it was the diskettes that were defective and not the computer. You must write a letter to this customer explaining the situation.

   a. What organizational response seems called for in this case? Why?

   b. Write a rough draft of the message, adding whatever details you find necessary.

CASES

The following two cases describe sensitive situations in which you become involved. As you examine these cases and complete the assignments that follow them, be sure to consider these organizational choices and the related factors that influence them:

Type of Message to Be Sent	Direction Message Sent	Relationship between Writer and Reader	Resultant Risk
Negative	Up?	Warm?	Dangerous?
Positive		Neutral?	
Negative-Persuasive			
Positive-Persuasive	Down?	Cold?	Safe?

Case 1
Management Training Program

Every year, Allgood Products, Inc., the company you work for, hires about five management trainees from colleges. The new employees are always two MBA's and three people who have recently completed an undergraduate degree in various business school majors. The management training program (known as MTP) was designed and implemented in Allgood by Carl Hilton, President of the company.

The focus of the first year of the MTP is to give the new recruit an overview of all the various functions of the corporation. In the second year, trainees are assigned to work as staff assistants to higher-level managers. The training program is estimated to cost the company approximately twice the salary paid out to the trainee during the two years of training.

In the first year, new recruits spend approximately an equal amount of time in each of the management functions. Time, therefore, is spent in sales, purchasing, manufacturing, product design, human resources, and finance. The first year ends with two weeks devoted to the study of corporate long-range planning. In this part of the program, Hilton gives the now-no-longer-new recruits an idea of where the company has been and where it plans to go.

Because you are close to the age of many of the young men and women who are currently in the first year of the MTP, you have become friendly with some of them. You learn from them that they regard the first year of the training program as a joke. This is not surprising to you, because you felt the same way about the MTP when you were in it.

The MBA's are resentful because the program treats them the same way it treats those who have not spent an extra year obtaining advanced business education. They feel that an MBA could, and should, be indoctrinated in a matter of a few weeks, rather than a whole year. They regard the first year as a waste of money, a waste of time, and an insult to their educational background. They feel ready to enter directly into the second year of the MTP.

The BS and BA holders in the program also have strong negative feelings about the first year, but for different reasons. They say that they spend so little time at each of the functional areas that they really don't get much out of the experience. They jokingly call the type of experience the program gives them a "Whitman's Sampler" because it gives them a lot of variety, but no depth.

The jobs they are assigned to do, in their opinion, are largely trivial. They claim they know that many of the reports they write end up in the company's wastebaskets. According to them, nobody pays any attention to what they say or do. To a degree, they feel guilty about taking the company's money while they waste their time. The BS and BA recruits say that what they hunger for is a meaningful assignment and a chance to learn directly "on the job." They want to learn a specialty, not a little bit of everything. Most disturbingly, the new recruits this year told you that they are shopping around for jobs with different companies.

You report the grumblings about the MTP to your boss, Mary Lou Higgins, Vice President of Personnel. She tells you, "The quality of the MTP is very important to the future success of Allgood Products. If there are improvements that need to be made in the program, Mr. Hilton would be the first to implement them. Don't forget, it was he who designed and implemented the program at Allgood Products. Remember, also, that Mr. Hilton goes by facts, and that's all, not hearsay evidence and secondhand opinions. Even your own feelings are nothing more than an uninformed opinion. If you handed him your unsupported opinions as facts, he'd probably be very upset with you.

"So," Higgins continues, why don't you investigate this situation more thoroughly and put together a report on your findings? Try to get some objectivity into this matter. As far as I know, the MTP has never been evaluated in the six years it has been in operation."

Although you really don't much relish the assignment and regret having voiced your opinions to Mary Lou Higgins, she is your boss and she has spoken. After more than three weeks of part-time investigation and interviews, here is what you learn:

1. When you go back to the recruits who had been grumbling and tell them that you are working on a formal report to Carl Hilton on trainee attitudes toward the first year of the MTP, you get very disappointing results. The grumblers suddenly are not at all interested in cooperating. Their impression is that you are simply going to get them (and yourself) into big trouble. They claim that the MTP is Hilton's pet, and that the last person who criticized it "got his head bitten off!"

   Consequently, when you ask for permission to quote them, you discover that they regard this request with horror. When you ask for specifics about precisely those areas of the first year that they perceive to be least valuable, you find suddenly that the opinions offered now by the trainees become much more guarded and noncommittal than they were when you were informally chatting with them.

2. You take a trip to a nearby university library and look up some articles about management training programs. The conclusions of these articles are highly contradictory. Furthermore, you have no way of knowing whether the programs written about are sufficiently similar to Allgood's to be comparable.

3. You seek and receive permission from Mary Lou Higgins to request that all middle managers in Allgood Products query their subordinates about how they valued the first year of the training program when they went through it. The managers agree to do so, but to date they have reported nothing to you.

4. It occurs to you that people who left Allgood after going though the training program might feel freer to express their opinions about the training program. Furthermore, you want to find out whether these former trainees left Allgood Products because the training program had actually alienated them from the company.

   Therefore, you obtain from Mary Lou Higgins a list of ten former trainees who left the company in the six years since Carl Hilton instituted the training program. You write to all ten, seeking their opinions. You receive four answers almost immediately. Three say the training program, especially its first year, is indeed of very dubious merit. One says the training program, overall, is very fine indeed. Two more weeks go by, and you receive no further answers. Consequently, you assume that you are not going to receive answers from the other six former trainees. You note that the opinions of the three respondents who did not like the training program coincide exactly with the unguarded criticisms of the current trainees.

   You learn from Mary Lou Higgins that thirty people (including ten MBA's) have gone through the program since its inception. Of the ten who have left, four were MBA's.

5. You visit with the director of training of a large neighboring manufacturing company and get details about its management training program. You find that, with minor exceptions, both Allgood Products and this company have identical training programs.

   You ask the director of that program whether it is common for trainees to be critical of a training program while they are in it. The answer you get is: "These young men and women have spent so much of their lives in school that they regard a training program as a continuation of schooling. They find it unnecessary. They want to get on with the job and to start advancing up the corporate ladder. What they don't recognize is that we lose money on training them and that without training, these young people wander aimlessly around a company before they really understand what the total corporate activity entails."

You go to Mary Lou Higgins and tell her about the inadequacy of the information you have gathered. "Too bad," she responds. "I've already mentioned your study to Mr. Hilton. He's anxious to see what you've found out. In fact, he just sent me the following note through the electronic mail system." Higgins hands you the following note:

Mary Lou,

Whatever happened to that person you mentioned who was evaluating the MTP program? Please have that person send the MTP report directly to me. You know, I was the one who originated the program and I still think it's a program that forms the backbone of Allgood's management philosophy. I will be interested in seeing if your assistant agrees with me.

Carl
Carl

Assignment 1

Write Carl Hilton a report detailing your findings and drawing conclusions about the effectiveness of the present program.

Assignment 2

Carl Hilton calls you into his office and tells you he was impressed by your report (see Assignment 1). "But I still don't know what I should do," he adds. He, therefore, asks you to write a second report, one that makes recommendations for improving the MTP program. "Make the recommendations based on your findings," he adds, "and be sure to support all of your suggestions." Write this report.

Case 2
Applicant Rejection Letters

Mary Lou Higgins, Vice President of Personnel for Allgood Products, Inc., has just returned from a national Personnel Administrator (PA) meeting at which she heard a speaker say, "The dumbest thing you can do is to tell a person you've rejected that he or she is 'qualified.'" This doesn't make sense to you until she explains that, in an effort to let rejected applicants down "easy," many interviewers will overly praise them. That is, they will write something to the effect that "You certainly are well-qualified for the job, but unfortunately we can't use you." Another favorite phrase is "With the excellent qualifications you have, you will surely have no trouble getting a job."

The PA speaker's point was that "kindness" of this type can embroil you and your company in a legal mess. A rejected applicant (and his or her attorney) might take you literally and argue that since "*you* say I'm qualified, you *must* hire me." There is a chance that a judge might agree with the applicant.

The speaker claimed that these kinds of statements are especially dangerous because they imply that the candidate who was selected was chosen for reasons other than competence. Such reasons might, it could be argued, include illegal considerations such as race, age, and sex. The danger is especially acute (according to the PA speaker) when you put these positive statements about qualifications in the rejection letter. The applicant then has a written, signed document to show the court. As a lawyer once said, "One bad thing about putting things in writing is that it is exceedingly difficult to deny that you said them."

You are currently working as the administrative assistant to Mary Lou Higgins. She directs you to look over the file of rejection form letters that Allgood's personnel department has used over the past years. These form letters are used because there are so many applicants for jobs at Allgood that it became an onerous task to compose individual letters to every applicant. Gradually the wording of these form letters has become regarded as "sacred" and has never been questioned. As you examine the letters, you see that some of them do tell the rejected applicants that they were qualified for the jobs they sought. Some of the letters specifically state that the applicant possessed the very skills that were advertised as requisite for the position.

Higgins tells you that she has just consulted with Milton Berg, Allgood Products' Corporate Counsel, who expressed the belief that the company should write only to a person who is actually being offered a job. "Forget the unsuccessful applicant. Just because someone applies for a job doesn't give him or her a legal right to an explanation as to why he or she is not acceptable. It is too dangerous." But, Higgins says, she knows that Maxwell Allgood's personal code of politeness will demand that the company show the courtesy of responding to applicants and letting them know that they are not going to be offered a job.

She tells you that Milton Berg said, "It would be safer if the company said something on the order of 'I'm sorry, but we can't offer you the job.' but not give any kind of legally arguable reasons as to why we are not hiring them."

Higgins is upset by Berg's advice, especially since it is supported by some of the things the PA national meeting speaker said. "It just seems rude," she says, "even cruel to me. No one likes to be rejected. People want to know why they weren't hired. Couldn't we mention that the applicant is qualified but is just not what we need right now? After all, Allgood doesn't want to make enemies of those who unsuccessfully apply for jobs with us. We at Allgood are a fine bunch of caring people; we don't want to give rejected applicants the impression that we don't care about their feelings. If a hundred people apply for a single job, we don't want ninety-nine of them bad-mouthing us because of the crude manner in which we rejected them."

She concludes by telling you that Maxwell Allgood and his father and grandfather before him built the company with a commitment to loyalty to employees and sympathetic, humane treatment to everyone in the community. Allgood also has stated that he fully realizes that anyone can sue the company at any time and that there can never be a guarantee that any action (or inaction) will insure freedom from litigation or avoid complaints about discrimination. But he will not willingly sacrifice courtesy for legal security.

Higgins concludes by saying, "Look, I don't expect you to go through all the form rejection letters we have stored in our computer. There must be fifty or sixty of them. Some of them I know are out of date. So I've selected just eight of them for you to consider." She hands you the eight form letters, and asks you to complete two assignments.

Assignment 1

"Here is what I want you to do," Mary Lou Higgins says. "I want you to put yourself in the position of a person who might receive each of these letters. Evaluate that letter from the recipient's point of view. Naturally, you are going to have to keep in mind some of the legal cautions that apply, but, for the most part, I want you to focus on the person's feelings and show common courtesy. I want you to write a report to me, summarizing how you think people will react to *each* of these letters. Concentrate both on how these letters are organized and on the potential effect or impact these letters will have based on their word choice, sentence structure, and appearance.

Assignment 2

Higgins asks you to change each of these letters so that (a) it is not offensive to the reader, (b) it gets the negative message across, and (c) it avoids legal complications of the type Higgins, Berg, and the PA speaker are concerned about.

1—Potential College Recruit for Management Training Program: Rejection After Campus Interview

_____ J. J. Jones
123 Main Street
Anytown, USA XXXXX

*too brief & negative
— insulting.*

Dear _____ Jones:

Thank you for taking the time to interview with our Allgood Products, Inc. recruiter on the _____ campus.

We have processed your application. Unfortunately, we regret to inform you that your qualifications were not equal to those of other applicants.

Therefore, we can offer no encouragement to you about possible employment with Allgood Products.

Thank you again for your interest in Allgood Products.

Sincerely,

2—College Recruit for Managment Training Program: Rejection After Second Interview on Company Premises

_____ J. J. Jones
123 Main Street
Anytown, USA XXXXX

Dear _____ Jones:

Many of the managers with whom you discussed employment during your recent visit were greatly impressed with your academic qualifications, which are excellent indeed and fully meet our requirements.

After all aspects were evaluated, however, it was concluded that an offer of employment should not be made.

We assure you that we did enjoy and appreciate the opportunity to get to know you and to learn of your career interests. We wish you luck in finding suitable employment.

Sincerely,

3—Unsolicited Walk-in or Write-in: Unqualified

not encouraging

_____ J. J. Jones
123 Main Street
Anytown, USA XXXXX

Dear _____ Jones:

We have processed your application for employment with Allgood Products, Inc.

We regret that we cannot be encouraging, as there are many applicants whose qualifications are superior to yours.

Thanks for seeking employment with us.

Sincerely,

4—Applicant: Overqualified for Work Available

_____ J. J. Jones
123 Main Street
Anytown, USA XXXXX

Dear _____ Jones:

Thank you for applying for employment with Allgood Products, Inc. We have processed your application and have determined that you are over-qualified for any positions we have available.

Please accept our best wishes toward finding employment consistent with your education and experience.

Sincerely,

5—Applicant, Summer Work: Rejection

_____ J. J. Jones
123 Main Street
Anytown, USA XXXXX

Dear _____ Jones:

All summer employment openings have been filled. Thank you for applying.

Sincerely,

6—Write-in; Retain for Future Consideration

_____ J. J. Jones
123 Main Street
Anytown, USA XXXXX

Dear _____ Jones:

Thank you for your interest in employment at Allgood Products, Inc.

Unfortunately, we have many more applicants than we can place, so competition for our employment opportunities is intense. At the time your inquiry was received, other candidates had already been identified to fill our available openings. However, in the event our situation should change, we would like to maintain your file for twelve months to be considered on a competitive basis with others. During this time, there is no need to reapply. If you wish to update your application, simply write our office, and we will add any new information to your file.

We can assure you that our files are reviewed, and your qualifications will be given every consideration as openings develop.

Sincerely,

7—Looking for Management Position: Rejection

_____ J. J. Jones
123 Main Street
Anytown, USA XXXXX

Dear _____ Jones:

Thank you for your interest in a management position with Allgood Products, Inc. Your experience and accomplishments are impressive and would fully meet our requirements.

However, Allgood traditionally promotes people to management and to senior staff positions from within the company. In this way, the company guarantees that its management possesses a wide variety of practical, prior experience with Allgood. For this reason, positions that are suitable to your interests are not available.

We do appreciate your interest in Allgood and we wish you success in locating a challenging new career opportunity.

Sincerely,

8—Applicant for Personnel Position: Rejection

_____ J. J. Jones
123 Main Street
Anytown, USA XXXXX

Dear _____ Jones:

Thank you for your interest in a personnel position with Allgood Products, Inc. You certainly have all the experience and training necessary for personnel work.

In general, our personnel staff is made up of employees who have a wide variety of prior experiences with Allgood. By staffing the area with experienced employees, we are sure that the people in personnel have practical knowledge of Allgood policies. For this reason, applicants are seldom hired directly into personnel.

Again, we thank you for your interest in Allgood Products. We wish you success in locating a rewarding career.

Sincerely,

REFERENCES

Brent D. (1985). Indirect structure and reader response. *The Journal of Business Communication, 22,* 5–8.

Butenhoff, C. (1977). Bad writing can be good business. *ABCA Bulletin, 40,* 12–13.

Crowell, B. M. (1984). Writing for readers: Three perspectives on audience. *College Composition and Communication, 30,* 172–185.

Ede, L. and Lunsford, A. (1984). Audience addressed/audience invoked: The role of audience in composition theory and pedagogy. *College Composition and Communication, 30,* 155–171.

Flower, L. (1981). *Problem-solving strategies for writing.* New York: Harcourt Brace Jovanovich.

Gibb, J. R. (1961). Defensive communication. *Journal of Communication, 2,* 141–148.

Gordon, R. (1988). The difference between feeling defensive and feeling understood. *The Journal of Business Communication, 25,* 53–64.

Gordon, R. D. (1985). Empathy: State of the art and science. *Journal of Communication Studies, 4,* 16–21.

Hunter, B. (1985). The softening of business communication. *Communication World, 2,* 27–29.

Lahiff, J. M. and Hatfield, J. D. (1978). The winds of change and managerial communication practices. *The Journal of Business Communication, 15,* 19–28.

McCallister, L. (1983). Predicted employee compliance to downward communication styles. *The Journal of Business Communication, 20,* 67–79.

Mendelson, M. (1988). Teaching arrangement inductively. *The Journal of Business Communication, 25,* 67–84.

Minto, B. (1978). *The pyramid principle: Logic in writing.* London: Minto International.

O'Keefe, D. J. and Sypher, H. E. (1981). Cognitive complexity measures and the relationship of cognitive complexity to communication. *Human Communication Research, 8,* 72–92.

Ong, W. (1975). The writer's audience is always a fiction. *PMLA, 90,* 247–257.

Read, W. H. (1962). Upward communication in industrial hierarchies. *Human Relations, 15,* 3–15.

Roberts, K. and O'Reilly, C. (1974). Failures in upward communication: Three possible culprits. *Academy of Management Journal, 17,* 205–215.

Roundy, N. and Thralls, C. (1983). Modeling the communication context: A procedure for revision and evaluation in business writing. *The Journal of Business Communication, 20,* 27–46.

Salerno, D. (1988). An interpersonal approach to writing negative messages. *The Journal of Business Communication, 25,* 41–52.

Unit 6

CONTROLLING STYLE IN NON-SENSITIVE AND SENSITIVE MESSAGES

TO: Readers

FROM: Authors

SUBJECT: Unit 6

Unit 6 completes the Effective Communication chart by covering the topic of **style.**

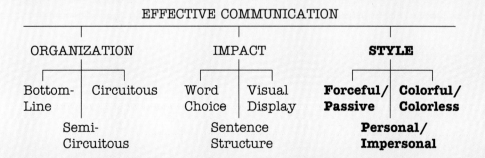

EFFECTIVE COMMUNICATION

ORGANIZATION	IMPACT	**STYLE**
Bottom-Line | Circuitous	Word Choice | Visual Display	**Forceful/ Passive** | **Colorful/ Colorless**
Semi-Circuitous	Sentence Structure	**Personal/ Impersonal**

Your ability to vary your style of writing is critically important in all business messages, but especially so in sensitive messages.

Chapter 14 defines two critical terms used throughout this unit: **style** and **tone.** Chapter 15 follows with precise definitions of the six basic types of styles available to you. It also contains explanations of how to write in these styles.

Finally, Chapters 16 and 17 deal with the vital question of which style works best in which writing situation. Chapter 16 deals with style in positive and negative messages and Chapter 17 with style in persuasive situations.

At this stage of the book, you have learned so much about organization and impact that when we now ask you to focus on style, it will be difficult for you not to consider organization and impact. That is quite natural; literary critics have long held that writing is an "organic whole." That means that it is like a living organism. If you take a written work apart to study its parts, it dies; it is no longer the same as it was before dissection. To teach writing, we must take writing specimens apart, just as scientists dissect formerly living creatures so that students can study how each part separately contributes to the whole being.

Now we ask you to focus solely on the writing styles of the examples we use. Don't let yourself start thinking about the organization of a writing specimen, or its impact. Just respond to its style, the way it is expressed in words. Please know that we will soon put everything back together for you so that when we have finished separately describing the parts of the system, you can once again consider a piece of writing as a totality to which every part contributes its individual effect.

Chapter 14

INTRODUCTION TO STYLE AND TONE

OBJECTIVES

This chapter will help you to

•

Understand what style in business writing is

•

Appreciate how style influences how a communication is received

•

Distinguish between style and tone in business writing

•

Realize how styles must vary to meet the needs of different situations and readers

Style is the *way* something is said or written, as distinguished from the substance of what is conveyed. In writing, your style results from (a) the particular words you select to express your ideas and (b) the types of sentences you use to deliver those ideas. What else can writing style result from? In writing, there is no tone of voice or body gesture to impart additional meaning, as there is in spoken presentations.

The main cause of difference between literary writing styles and business writing styles lies in their respective *audience* and *purpose*. Business writers address themselves mainly to a particular person, in a particular situation, to accomplish a particular purpose. Literary writers use a unique style to express themselves to a more general audience; they are not writing to accomplish a particular transaction or to get a certain job done, as businesspeople are. Therefore, the use of writing style in business writing differs from its use in literature. In business, a writer's style cannot be divorced from the content of the message(s) being conveyed, nor from the circumstances under which the communication takes place, nor from the personal likes, dislikes, position, and power held by the reader.

Style is the way something is said or written, not its content.

In business writing, the purpose of style is to help get a job done.

WHAT GIVES YOUR MESSAGES THEIR TONE?

How does **tone** differ from **style?** In written business communication, tone comes from what a reader "reads into" the words and sentences used.

Tone is a word that is frequently applied to written communications. You frequently hear statements such as, "I don't like the tone of this letter. I don't like it at all." You hear people refer to a communication's nasty tone, its whining tone, its mocking tone, its pleasant tone, its flat tone, its tone of high seriousness, or its tone of self-importance. We know what all of these adjectives mean. But what does the word *tone* itself mean?

The concept of tone in written communication is borrowed from oral communication, where it mostly refers to a person's tone of voice—the pitch or inflection employed by the speaker to add meaning beyond that carried by the actual words used. That is why we often hear terms like "sarcastic," "caustic," "sincere," and "soothing" associated with tone. Each is a feeling derived beyond the content being communicated.

But can a piece of writing have a good or bad tone? Obviously, a writer's tone of voice cannot actually be heard by a reader, but many readers think it can. That is why they say things such as, "I don't like this letter's tone!" They are reading into the message some additional—usually emotional—meaning beyond that denoted specifically by the words themselves.

Distinguishing Tone from Style

How, then, does tone differ from style, from the way something is said? Aren't style and tone the same thing? The answer is yes and no. Style and tone can be considered as opposite sides of a single coin. A writer uses a given style and organizational pattern to convey a message. The reader may or may not react emotionally to what the writer has said and the way it has been said. Tone, therefore, is inferred by readers through their emotional reactions to the writer's style of expression. That is why tone is defined as the capacity a given document's style, organizational pattern, and visual display have for producing an emotional reaction in the reader.

Difficulty of Controlling Tone

One of the reasons why business writing is so complex is that the reader's reaction may actually be independent of both the content of the message and the style in which it is delivered. You simply cannot always predict the mood or frame of mind that the reader will be in at the time of reading your communication. Hence, it is difficult for a writer to control tone—or the reader's reaction to what you have written.

For example, there may be circumstances quite apart from the communication that have recently affected the life of the reader at home or at work. Perhaps the reader had an argument with his or her spouse the previous evening. Maybe the reader experienced a disappointment in his or her own performance at a recent staff conference. Such circumstances may cause the reader to react negatively at that moment to any kind of communication delivered in any kind of style.

Everyone has probably, at one time or another, received an unanticipated reaction to a communication, a reaction that the message was not meant to elicit. Suppose, for instance, that Sam Gordon, a man you work with, has just been privately but severely criticized by his boss for his handling of a complaint by Acme, Inc., a very important customer. Just yesterday, Gordon had boasted to you how his letter to Acme was going to calm Acme down and prevent further trouble. In fact, the reverse had occurred, but neither of you knew it.

So, when you next see Sam Gordon you say, "That was really a first-rate job you did on the Acme situation." What reaction might Gordon have to your compliment? Most likely, "Oh, sure. Thanks for the sarcasm!"

Face-to-face, of course, it is far easier to deal with a situation such as this than it is when writing. Once you notice that your innocent comment has upset Gordon, you can immediately begin to say and do things to reassure him that you were not trying to be sarcastic.

However, the situation is not so simple in writing. Anticipating a reader's exact reaction is seldom easy, because it is impossible to predict events that occur between the time you send a message and the time a reader reads it.

When the reader's reaction is largely independent of either the content of your message or your style, there is nothing you can do in advance to head off an unpredictable situation. The kind of situation that *can* be improved occurs when the reader's reaction *is* largely dependent on both the content of the message and the style in which it is presented. For example, we all know that people do not like to be told no in any situation where they want a positive response. In such a case, the reader's reaction stems mainly from the negative content of the message. The more negative the message, the more sensitive the reader is likely to be to the way in which the ''no'' has been presented. The effect of a negative message can be reduced if the writer uses (a) an appropriate style of delivery and (b) an appropriate organizational pattern.

Tone problems often occur in sensitive messages, especially negative ones.

Positive Messages Are Sensitive Too

Style is also important in positive messages. Although it is much easier to become upset when being told no than when being told yes, it is still possible to be told yes in such a begrudging, condescending, or nasty way that we react negatively to the style in spite of the positive content of the message. Thus, writers must be sensitive to style in both positive and negative message situations. Of course, they must be especially sensitive when the communcation conveys an unpleasant message.

In summary, tone problems usually occur in sensitive messages. Tone is what the reader infers from what the writer says (the message), how the writer says it (the style), and when the writer chooses to present the sensitive message (the organizational pattern). The type of message is usually not within the writer's control (bad news, after all, is bad news), but the style and organizational pattern are.

Seven Simple Ways to Make Readers Angry

In addition to being sensitive to the reaction you may evoke in readers by message, organization, and style, you must consider that readers may be especially sensitive in certain areas. At times, readers may read in accusations or insults that the writer never intended, at least not consciously.

We have all received letters in which we feel the tone is so negative that we suspect it must have been intentional. Perhaps the writer's deeper feelings have crept in without his or her being conscious of them and have affected a word choice or a turn of phrase.

Sometimes it takes only a short phrase—or even a single word—to cause a reader to feel that there is a negative tone in a message. For example:

Avoid using words that run high risks of causing tone problems.

1. Some readers react quite negatively to words and phrases that may subtly imply they are liars:
   - ''You claim that . . .''
   - ''You state that . . .''
   - ''According to you, . . .''

2. Others become incensed at real or imaginary implications that they are stupid:
   - ''As I've told you many times, . . .''
   - ''Even a child could understand . . .''

3. Many react negatively to perceived implications that they are merely gripers:
   - ''We have received your complaint . . .'' (''What?'' says the reader. ''I *never* complain. Everybody else does, not me!'')

4. Readers are particularly sensitive about letter openings:
   - "I was sorry to hear about your troubles with our product." ("Oh?" says the prickly reader. "You weren't sorry I had trouble; you were just sorry to *hear* about it.")

5. Letter closings contain sensitive elements, too, especially when they bring up problems that the letter has already resolved:
   - "I sincerely hope that these actions will compensate you adequately for all the problems you experienced with our product."

6. Some people are especially sensitive about errors in their names, titles, and personal status:
   - *Mr.* to a woman
   - *Miss* or *Mrs.* to a woman who does not wish to be categorized by her marital status
   - *Mrs.* to a single woman
   - *Mr., Ms.,* or *Mrs.* to a *Dr.*
   - *Dear Helen* or *Dear Bob* from a stranger

7. Many readers are very sensitive about certain words associated with gender, age, race, and other personal attributes:
   - girl
   - boy
   - *his* instead of *his or her*
   - identifying a person as *black* or *female* when others are not identified as *white* or *male*

Remember that the writer implies something with every word and phrase, and the reader may infer something entirely different from what the writer has in mind. As writers, all we can do is be aware of the fact that certain areas can be trouble spots for some readers. Therefore, we should avoid using words and phrases that have even a slight possibility of evoking a negative reaction.

KEYS TO DETERMINING STYLES AND THEIR TONE IMPLICATIONS

Since style is the way something is said, and tone is the reader's response to the way the message is said, it is possible to identify the different styles available to the business writer and to consider the tone implications of each.

Let's use a case[1] to begin such an examination. Assume that you are a manager in a very large information processing company. You receive the following letter:

[1]Adapted from John S. Fielden, "What Do You Mean You Don't Like My Style?" *Harvard Business Review*, May–June 1982. Copyright © 1982 by the President and Fellows of Harvard College; all rights reserved.

COMMUNITY GENERAL HOSPITAL
Anytown, USA 12345

January 23, 19— —

Ms./Mr. _____
XYZ Corporation
Anytown, USA 12345

Dear _____:

As you know, I respect your professional opinion highly. The advice your people have given us at ABCD Corporation, as we have moved into a comprehensive information system over the past three years, has been very helpful.

I'm writing to you now, however, in my role as Chairman of the Executive Committee of the Trustees of Community General Hospital. The Executive Committee has decided to establish a skilled (volunteer) data processing evaluation team to assess proposals to automate our hospital's information flow.

I have suggested your name to my committee as a member of that evaluation team. I know you can get real satisfaction by helping your community in this way. Please say "yes." I look forward to being able to count on your advice.

Let me hear from you soon.

Sincerely,

Frank J. Scalpel

Frank J. Scalpel
Chairman, Executive Committee

As a manager with XYZ, Inc. you would have a conflict of interest if you accepted this appointment. You know that XYZ will be submitting a proposal to install the proposed comprehensive information system for Community General Hospital. However, Frank Scalpel is the Vice President of Finance of ABCD Corporation, a very good customer of your company. You know Scalpel well, having worked with him on community programs as well as in business situations.

Read the following four versions of a letter to Scalpel. Each version delivers the same message, but each is written in a different (but typical) business style. These are, of course, not the only possible styles in which the letter could be written, but they are typical and lend themselves to profitable discussion. As you read each version, think about its style and answer this question:

Does the style of each version (that is, the way the message is communicated) seem

- forceful or passive?
- personal or impersonal?
- colorful or colorless?

Then answer these questions:

	A	B	C	D
- Which version's style do I like best?	___	___	___	___
- Which version's style most resembles the style I customarily use?	___	✓	___	___

In answering each of these questions, you will, of course, be discovering aspects of the tone implications of each style.

Version A

Dear Mr. Scalpel:

As you realize, this litigious age makes it necessary for large companies often to take stringent measures not only to avoid conflicts of interest on the part of their employees, but also to preclude even the very suggestion of conflict. And, since my company intends to submit a proposal with reference to automating the hospital's information flow, it would not appear seemly for me to be part of an evaluation team assessing competitors' proposals. Even if I were to excuse myself from consideration of the XYZ proposal, I still would be vulnerable to charges that I gave short shrift to competitors' offerings.

If there is any other way that I can serve the committee that will not raise this specter of conflict of interest, you know that I would find it pleasurable to be of service as always.

Sincerely,

Version B

Passive

Dear Frank,

Your comments relative to your respect for my professional opinion are most appreciated. Moreover, your invitation to serve on the hospital's data processing evaluation team is received with gratitude, albeit with some concern.

The evaluation team must be composed of persons free of alliances with any of the vendors submitting proposals. A proposal surely will be submitted by XYZ, Inc., my company. For that reason, it is felt that my services on the team could be construed as a conflict of interest.

Perhaps help can be given in some other way. Again, please be assured that your invitation has been appreciated.

Sincerely,

Version C *forceful*

Dear Frank,

Thanks for suggesting my name as a possible member of your data processing evaluation team. I wish I could serve, but I cannot.

XYZ intends, naturally, to submit a proposal to automate the hospital's information flow. You can see the position of conflict I would be in if I were on the evaluation team.

Just let me know of any other way I can be of help. You know I would be more than willing. Thanks again for the invitation.

Sincerely,

Version D

Dear Frank, *colorful*

Thanks for the kind words and the invitation. Sure wish I could say yes. Can't, though.

XYZ intends to submit a sure-fire proposal on automating the hospital's information. Shouldn't be judge and advocate at the same time!

Any other way I can help ... just give me a buzz. Thanks again.

Cordially,

Let's Compare Reactions

In evaluating these letters, you have begun to explore your reactions to each style's tone. Compare your notes with the following observations.

Version A is **impersonal.** In many situations, most people react some-what negatively to this style of prose because it seems to push them away from the writer. The choice of words reveals a cerebral quality on the part of the writer that, while flattering to the reader's intelligence, also seems to parade the vocabulary of the writer.

Version B has a non-aggressive, **passive** style. Readers' reactions will probably be neither strongly positive nor strongly negative. The reason is that it makes heavy use of the passive voice and Latinate words. Instead of saying, "I appreciate your comments," it says, "Your comments are most appreciated," "Your invitation is received," and "It is felt that my services could be construed . . ." This use of the passive voice enables the writer to be subordinated modestly to the back of sentences or to disappear completely: I appreciated your comments. $\longrightarrow$ Your comments were appreciated by me. $\longrightarrow$ Your comments were appreciated.

The passive style of writing is one many persons with engineering, mathematics, or scientific backgrounds find familiar. It is sometimes appropriate to those fields, but it is certainly not colorful; nor is it forceful. Many persons will recognize it as being their own style.

Version C is as **forceful** as a firm handshake. Almost everybody in business will like this style, although lower level managers often find themselves afraid to write so forthrightly to superiors (and, as a result, often find themselves retreating into the style of Versions A and B: Version A to make themselves look intelligent and impersonal, or Version B so as to appear more passive and, hence, less bossy). Persons who find Version B congenial may doubt the appropriateness of Version C. Persons in higher-level positions find Version C more appealing than do lower-level persons.

Version D goes beyond being forceful; it is so breezy and **colorful** that many businesspeople would reject it out-of-hand, even if they were very close acquaintances of Frank Scalpel's. "Sounds like an advertisement," some will say. "The extremely informal style does not convey to Mr. Scalpel the seriousness with which you took his invitation," others will say. The persons who like this style (and think Scalpel will also) will say, "It is sprightly and pleasant, so why shouldn't it have a positive effect on Mr. Scalpel?"

Key: Effect on Reader

As you considered your responses, you may have found yourself objecting to some of the questions asked. You might have thought, "What difference does it make which version *I* like? Or which version most resembles *my* customary style? What really matters is which version Mr. Scalpel will like best!"

Circumstances not only alter cases; they alter the "you" that it is wise for your style to project. Sometimes it's wise for "you" to be forceful; at other times your forcefulness would be very risky. Sometimes being sprightly and colorful is appropriate; at other times it would be ludicrous. There are times to be personal in style and times to be highly impersonal.

Here is a specific instance. Suppose you write a paper for an economics professor and receive great praise and a good grade for the way the paper is written. The professor especially liked the fact that you wrote in formal prose—that is, in an impersonal, passive, colorless style. (After all, this is the way articles are written in the best journals in economics.)

Taking this praise to heart, you next write a paper for a creative writing class you are taking as an elective. You use the same "learned journal" prose that you used in economics. What happens? Most likely, you receive a poor grade for your efforts and an accompanying note telling you your style is boring. It is "too impersonal, too passive, and completely lacking in color."

Each professor approached the papers from a different professional background and with different expectations. Their reactions to style were different. The economics professor is a social scientist. The professional

Styles must vary to fit the circumstances and the reader.

prose he or she prefers, and is used to reading, is usually impersonal, passive, and completely colorless. The creative writing professor likes and expects an entirely different style of writing from you. In business, too, it does not matter what style the *writer* likes. It matters far more what the reader likes and what style will get the job done most effectively.

That is why we say that in business writing, style cannot be considered alone, apart from the situation or from what you know and expect about a reader. You just can't write to please yourself. Expert writers select the style that best fits a given situation and a particular reader's probable tastes.

SUMMARY

Style is a very important concept to a business writer: It is made up of the words and sentences that a writer chooses in order to produce a desired reaction in a given reader or readers.

Tone, in turn, is the reader's response to the way a message is written. It is the reader's reaction to the words, sentences, and paragraphs that the writer chooses to use. Although this reaction can be controlled somewhat by how writers word the message (that is, by the message's style), readers also bring along a number of external factors (mood, financial circumstances, random events) that influence their reactions to a given style. Tone can be somewhat controlled by choosing style carefully.

Finally, you have seen different styles elicit different reactions from readers. The same message written in different styles elicits totally different responses from the reader. What is most important, however, is not the writer's ability to shift styles but the writer's ability to write in whatever style best elicits a desired response from a reader. To accomplish this goal, writers need (a) a more detailed understanding of the styles available to them and (b) a knowledge of which style works best in which situation. Those are the topics of the following chapters.

REVIEW QUESTIONS

1. What is the definition of style?
2. How do the purposes of literary style and business style differ?
3. What is tone?
4. Explain what is meant by "style and tone are opposite sides of the same coin."

5. Why is it difficult, and sometimes impossible, to control the tone of a written message?
6. In what type of messages do tone problems most occur?
7. What are some of the words that cause negative reactions in readers?

DISCUSSION QUESTIONS

1. What question is missing from those asked about the four versions of the letter to Frank Scalpel? What factor is more important than the style you like and the style you customarily use?

2. Does style communicate in non-verbal ways, such as one's hair style or style of dress?

Chapter 15

SIX KEY STYLES THAT CREATE YOUR MESSAGE'S TONE

OBJECTIVES

This chapter will help you to

Learn the six basic styles of business writing

Learn how to change writing from one style to another

Appreciate that different messages in the same document may require different styles

Realize that the message expressing the bottom line is the predominant message for which a strategy must be developed

In order to show how choice of style influences a sensitive message, we need to define six basic business styles:

There are six basic business styles.

Forceful   versus   Passive
Personal   versus   Impersonal
Colorful   versus   Colorless

SIX STYLES TO SUIT YOUR GOALS

For a Forceful Style

A **forceful** style conveys strength and a sense of responsibility for what is being said. Used in the right situation, it is highly effective. Used at the wrong time, it can prove exceedingly harmful. Your style will be forceful if you do the following:

A forceful style conveys strength.

- Use the active voice; avoid the passive.
  Say, "I have decided not to recommend you for promotion," instead of, "Your promotion has not been recommended."

- Give orders—use the imperative!
  Say, "Correct this error immediately" ("you" is understood as the subject) instead of, "A correction should be made" (which leaves the reader wondering who should make it).

- Bottom-line your sentences. Put important points first.
  If your point is that your company has won a contract, say, "ABCD won the contract, although the bidding was intense and highly competitive," not "Although the bidding was intense and highly competitive, ABCD won the contract."

- Adopt a tone of confidence and assurance about what you say by avoiding qualifiers such as
  possibly
  maybe
  perhaps
  It could be concluded that . . .
  Some might conclude that . . .

Here is a forceful memo reminding employees about rules governing coffee breaks.

TO: All Office Staff

FROM: "Boss"

SUBJECT: Coffee Breaks

DATE: September 26, 19——

NOTICE: Each employee must observe the rules about coffee breaks:

1. Take no more than one fifteen-minute break per half day.

2. Coordinate your break with coworkers so that there is adequate telephone coverage.

3. Do not engage in loud conversations that distract the attention of those still working.

For a Passive Style

A passive style lacks harshness.

Except in technical and scientific prose where its use is often conventional, a **passive** style lacks vigor, but it also lacks blunt abrasiveness. Appropriately used, it can prove to be a valuable ally. Your style will be passive if you do the following:

- Avoid the imperative—never give an order.
  Say, "A more effective and time-saving presentation of ideas should be achieved before our next meeting," as opposed to, "Do a better job of presenting your ideas at our next meeting. Respect my time and get right to the point!"
- Use the passive voice often because the passive moves what was the subject to the end of the sentence or omits it entirely.
  Say, "Resources are being wasted," instead of, "Resources are being wasted by your company" or the even more forceful, "You are wasting resources."
- Use some Latinate words to weaken the impact.
  Say, "Eliminate ornate terms that obscure interpretation," instead of, "Avoid big words that cloud your meaning."
- Use qualifiers ("possibly," "maybe," "could be"), especially if the reader will not like what you are saying.

Here is the same memo written in a passive style.

TO: All Office Staff

FROM: "Boss"

SUBJECT: Coffee Breaks

DATE: September 26, 19——

NOTICE: It would be appreciated if the following rules relative to coffee breaks could be observed:

1. If possible, no more than one fifteen-minute break should be taken per half day.

2. So that adequate telephone coverage is assured, every attempt should be made to coordinate your break with those of coworkers.

3. In order not to distract attention of those still working, loud conversations need to be avoided.

For a Personal Style

A **personal** style sounds like a normal business conversation, like one businessperson talking with another. It does not sound like a policy manual. Perhaps this style should really be called a "personable" style, because it exudes charm and warmth. Your style will be personal if you do the following:

A personal style makes readers feel as if someone is talking with them.

- Use personal pronouns—especially "you" and "I."
  Say, "I so much appreciate the work you've done," instead of, "What has been accomplished is appreciated."

- Use people's names (first names, when appropriate) instead of referring to them by title.
  Say, "Bill James attended the merger meeting," instead of "ABCD's director attended the merger meeting."

- Use short sentences that capture the staccato quality of ordinary conversation.
  Say, "I discussed your proposal with Frank. He's all for it!" as opposed to, "This is to inform you that your proposal was taken up at Friday's meeting and it was regarded with favor."

- Use contractions ("can't," "won't," "shouldn't") to sound informal and conversational.

- Direct questions at the reader just as you do in conversations.
  Say, "How would your company like to save $10 thousand per year?"

Here is our sample memo written in a personal style.

TO: Joe, Mary, Bill, Bob

FROM: "Boss"

SUBJECT: Coffee Breaks

DATE: September 26, 19— —

Don't you think we all need an occasional reminder about coffee break rules? If we do, here it is:

1. We should never take more than one fifteen-minute break per half day.

2. All of us should coordinate our breaks so that we provide adequate telephone coverage.

3. Let's not talk too loud on breaks. We don't want to disturb those who are still working.

For an Impersonal Style

An **impersonal** style sounds like a journal or a government policy manual rather than a person conversing. It avoids the implication of seeming close to people; often it seems quite cerebral and distant. Your style will be impersonal if you do the following:

An impersonal style sounds more like a learned journal article than a person talking.

- Avoid using people's names, especially first names. Refer to people (if at all) by title or job description.

- Avoid using personal pronouns, especially "I" and "you."

- Avoid the brisk, direct, "chatty" style of conversation.

- Use the passive voice to make yourself conveniently disappear when desirable.
  Say, "A possible conclusion is that an error has been made in the calculations," instead of, "I think your calculations are wrong."

- Avoid taking responsibility for negative statements by attributing them to faceless, impersonal "others."
  Say, "It is more than possible that several objections to your proposed plans might be raised by some observers," or, "Several objections might be raised by those opposed to your plans," instead of, "I have several objections to your plans."

Here is an impersonal version of the coffee break memo.

TO: All Office Staff

FROM: "Boss"

SUBJECT: Coffee Breaks

DATE: September 26, 19——

Since some employees have complained of laxity on the part of too many employees, a reminder as to coffee break rules is in order. Specifically:

1. Breaks amount to fifteen minutes per half day.

2. Breaks must be coordinated and adequate phone coverage assured.

3. Loud conversations should be avoided.

For a Colorful Style

A colorful style is vivid, like most advertisements.

A **colorful** style usually has a literary quality, seen in poetry or even in advertisements. Colorful writing such as "Where emerald seas kiss the golden sands" can be found in travel brochures and in advertisements in general. If well used, a colorful style will increase the impact of your prose. Inappropriately used, say, in a typical business report, a colorful style may startle readers, possibly even causing them to laugh. Your style will be colorful if you do the following:

- Insert some adjectives and adverbs.
  Instead of, "This proposal will save corporate resources," say, "This [choose one] hard-hitting/productivity-building/money-saving proposal will easily/surely/quickly/immediately save hard-earned/increasingly scarce/carefully guarded corporate resources."

- Use (if appropriate) metaphors (A is B), similes (A is like B), or other figures of speech to make a point.
  Say, "This machine is truly a miracle of design" or "This program is like magic in its ability to . . . "

Here is how the coffee break memo would look if it were written in a colorful style.

TO: All Office Staff

FROM: "Boss"

SUBJECT: Coffee Breaks

DATE: September 26, 19——

The good old American coffee break is truly "the pause that refreshes." But let's play the game according to the rules. Remember:

1. We're entitled to 15 minutes of cups, coffee, and camaraderie once every morning and afternoon.
2. Let's not all dash to the coffee pot at once. Some of us ought to cover the phones.
3. Help keep the chatter down to a loud roar! Let's not make it hard for our coworkers to hear themselves think.

For a Colorless Style

A **colorless** style results from a blending of the passive and the impersonal styles and, hence, produces little emotional reaction in the reader. Your style will be colorless if, in addition to blending the passive and impersonal styles, you do the following:

A colorless style is not poetic or witty and usually also is passive and impersonal.

- Avoid using adjectives, adverbs, metaphors, similes, and other figures of speech.
- Use only formal words and expressions that best serve to freeze out any semblance of wit, liveliness, and vigor from the writing.

Since a colorless example would look very much like a combination of the passive and the impersonal examples we have given above, there is no need for an additional illustration.

PUTTING IT ALL TOGETHER: USING STYLE

If you are like most readers, you are probably surprised to see the different effects that various styles produce on readers. You probably never realized—at least not consciously—that the same message could be expressed in so many different ways and have so many different effects. Naturally, some of the sample memos written in one style appealed to you more than ones written in other style combinations. Appropriate match of style and message type will be the subject of Chapters 16 and 17.

Let's examine some typical business situations where you might find it helpful to be able to shift easily from one style to another.

Management Development Case

Assume you are Jo Jacobs, Manager of Management Development Training. You have been assigned the job of reminding all headquarters managers that they must, this year as in prior years, work up a plan for each of their subordinates to receive thirty hours of training annually. You write the following draft and show it to your manager for approval:

Version A. Forceful

TO: All Headquarters Managers

FROM: Jo Jacobs

SUBJECT: Annual Training Plan

DATE: January 6, 19— —

Education is just as important this year as any. Between now and the end of the month, make up a sound education plan for all members of your group. Remember, all staff must receive thirty hours of management training annually.

Feel free to come in and talk about your plans at any time. Turn in your plan by the end of the month; keep a copy handy and use it monthly to check your progress and modify it.

Give me any such modifications.

Check your education plans against your vacation plans to make sure there are no conflicts.

After reading Version A, Jacobs's manager, the Personnel Director, tells her to make it less forceful. The tone seems to the Personnel Director, rightly or wrongly, to be too "pushy." After all, these headquarters managers are a pretty powerful group. Therefore, he wants Jo to be less forceful in the way she delivers this message to them. She must revise according to the instructions given.

Applying what you have learned about various styles, you see clearly why Jacobs's manager felt this memo's tone was too forceful. Look at the stream of imperatives, or orders, she has used:

- "Make up a sound education plan"
- "Remember, all staff must"
- "Feel free to come in"
- "Turn in your plan"
- "Keep a copy handy"

- "Use it monthly"
- "Give me your modifications"
- "Check your education plans"

If you were Jo Jacobs, you would want to shift to a style that does not appear to give so many orders. But you would not want the style to be completely passive, because you are trying to persuade readers to take the actions desired. So, you decide to move your style toward the personal, instead of toward the passive. Perhaps, in this way, you can create a draft that sounds as if you are talking with the staff, not bossing them around:

Version B. Personal

TO: All Headquarters Staff

FROM: Jo Jacobs

SUBJECT: Annual Training Plan

DATE: January 6, 19——

Don't you agree that education is at least as important this year as any? So it's time for me to remind you to make up this year's education plans for all members of your group.

I will be available at any time to discuss your plans with you. And I'd find it especially helpful if your plan could be turned in to me by the end of the month. Does that deadline present any serious problem? If so, let me know.

Remember, it's always advisable to keep a copy of your plan handy so that you can refer to it monthly to check progress and make modifications. Remember also that these modifications should be shared with our office.

One final reminder: Check vacation plans against education plans to make sure there are no conflicts. May I have the plans for your people as soon as possible?

The Personnel Director compares Version B with Version A and agrees that the revision is clearly less forceful. The number of imperatives has been reduced, yet none of the content has been changed. Everything asked of the readers in the first draft is asked of them here, but the styles and the resultant tones of the two versions are very different.

Jo Jacobs now agrees with her manager; she sees that the style of the first version was inappropriately forceful. The style of the second version seems far warmer and more personal because it is more conversational. By changing her style, she has engineered a memo that has a better chance of pleasing both her readers and her manager. The term *engineered* is important because, thanks to her understanding of how to shift styles, she made stylistic improvements scientifically, not accidentally.

Let's apply style considerations to another case.

Conference Invitation Case

Assume you are Al Drake, who needs to write a memo encouraging his company's branch sales force to invite manufacturing executives from customer companies to a conference on current manufacturing problems. This conference, which you are in charge of this year, is sponsored annually by Drake's company. As Al Drake, you write the following draft:

Version A. Passive and Impersonal

TO: All Branch Sales Personnel

FROM: Al Drake

SUBJECT: Annual Executive Conference on Manufacturing

DATE: October 2, 19——

A presentation will be made by Dr. J. R. Adleson of the London Institute of Technology at this year's Manufacturing Executive Conference to be held on October 27.

Efforts should be made to support this conference by encouraging attendance by appropriate customer personnel.

Brochures and enrollment instructions have been made available from Sales Headquarters and are obtainable from this office.

Your boss does not find the draft satisfactory. She does not think it is sufficiently forceful, personal, or colorful.

Let's see what you can do with this memo. As is shown below, you now notice certain shortcomings in the original draft and quickly decide on the appropriate revisions:

Original	Revision
The memo is expressed completely in the passive voice ("will be made," "should be made," "have been made").	To make the memo forceful, you will use the active voice and include some imperatives.
The memo is completely impersonal; there are no personal pronouns and only one name (Dr. Adleson).	You will make it personal by adding personal pronouns. And you will make it sound like a conversation with the readers, perhaps by adding a question that should evoke a response.
It is flat and colorless.	To make it colorful, you will add adjectives and adverbs.

Here is what results from your efforts:

Version B. Forceful and Personal

TO: All Branch Sales Personnel

FROM: Al Drake

SUBJECT: Annual Executive Conference on Manufacturing

DATE: October 2, 19— —

Are you going to let your valued customers miss this year's exciting and innovative Manufacturing Executive Conference on October 27? Make sure you don't!

Tell them that the highlight of this important conference will be a stimulating presentation by the highly respected Dr. J. R. Adleson of London's renowned Institute of Technology.

Do everything you can to make this year's conference the biggest and best attended ever.

Attractive, informative brochures, available from my office, contain the simple enrollment instructions. Request as many brochures as you need. We will send them immediately for you to share with your customers.

You pause and analyze your revision.

1. Is it forceful? Yes. Four of the six sentences are imperatives ("Make sure," "Tell," "Do," and "Request").

2. Is it personal? Yes. It begins with a question. It contains plenty of personal pronouns ("your," "them," "you," "my," "you," and "you"). The imperatives also contain an "understood you"; so these four sentences also are addressed personally to the "understood you," the reader.

3. Is it colorful? Yes. (Note all the adjectives: "valued," "exciting," "innovative," "stimulating," "highly respected," "renowned," "biggest and best," "attractive," "informative," "simple," and an adverb, "immediately".)

Perhaps this version seems too manipulative, too clever, and too much like an advertisement. If you think this draft's style will not be effective, you will have no choice but to take up the problem with your boss. You have done exactly what she told you to do. If, after reading this draft, she asks you to make it somewhat less forceful, personal, and colorful, you will be able to do so.

TWO CAUTIONS ABOUT STYLE

Some styles are mutually exclusive: forceful and passive, personal and impersonal, colorful and colorless.

Before we leave this chapter, you must keep in mind two very important cautions about these six styles. First, some of the styles are mutually exclusive and some are not. Those that are mutually exclusive because they are polar opposites are forceful and passive, personal and impersonal, and colorful and colorless. You cannot write forcefully and passively at the same time. And you cannot write personally and impersonally simultaneously. Nor can you write colorfully and colorlessly in the same sentence.

Those styles that are not polar opposites do overlap to a degree. A passive style has some qualities in common with the impersonal style. Moreover, both the passive and impersonal styles are colorless. A forceful style is more likely to contain some qualities of the personal style, but not those of the impersonal style. And the colorful style can easily be added to any other style except, by definition, to the colorless style. You can write forcefully and colorfully, or personally and colorfully. It is even possible to combine the colorful style with the passive and the impersonal styles. But while such a combination is possible, it is rarely if ever found in practice.

Some styles often occur together: passive and impersonal, forceful and personal.

Despite these qualifications, there is a sufficient and clear distinction among these style definitions to enable us to put them to good purpose. By using these definitions, you can quickly identify a piece of writing as exhibiting one particular style, or a combination of styles that in practice frequently seem to occur together (such as passive and impersonal or forceful and personal). In fact, these combinations are so frequently found that you may soon find yourself referring to a piece of writing as being written in the passive/impersonal style or the forceful/personal style. (The following summary clarifies this discussion.)

A document often contains more than one message, but one is usually predominant.

There is a second caution. It is very important for you to appreciate that since a document (especially ones longer than one or two paragraphs) usually will contain more than one message, each message may require being expressed in a different style (or style combination) from the other messages. For example, the first paragraph of a letter may be written in a personal style (just to say ''hello,'' so to speak), but the rest of the letter may need to be written in a completely impersonal style. However, except in very long documents, one message is usually predominant because it contains the bottom line (such as ''no''). A wise writer, therefore, will often strategically use different styles for different parts of a sensitive document.

SUMMARY OF EXCLUSIVE VERSUS SIMULTANEOUS WRITING STYLES

A. Business Writing Styles That Are Mutually Exclusive Because They Are Polar Opposites

Forceful _____	Passive
Personal _____	Impersonal
Colorful _____	Colorless

B. Business Writing Styles That Contain Some Elements in Common and That Frequently Occur Simultaneously

- **Passive** often contains some elements of **impersonal**, especially when a passive sentence such as "The program was carefully designed by Amanda Dover" is changed to "The program was carefully designed." Hence, **passive** and **impersonal** are frequently found occurring in combination.

- **Forceful** and **personal** contain some elements in common. For example, an imperative such as "Do your work," involves the invisible but "understood" personal pronoun "you," representing the **personal** style. Yet, who could argue that "Do your work" is not forceful? Therefore, **forceful** and **personal** also frequently occur together.

- **Colorless** exhibits essentially the same characteristics as the **passive** and the **impersonal** styles, neither of which usually require much editing to be made **colorless**.

C. Colorful, the One Style Easily Added to Others

- A **colorful** style can result from the addition of adjectives, adverbs, and figures of speech to any of the other styles—except, of course, **colorless**. (For example, take a sentence that is both **passive** and **impersonal**, such as "This job was finished." To make it **colorful**, we can simply rewrite it like this: "This terrifically difficult, almost impossible job was, after a Herculean effort, finally finished.")

SUMMARY

Business messages can be written in six basic styles—**forceful, passive, personal, impersonal, colorful, or colorless**. Forceful and passive are mutually exclusive, as are personal and impersonal. However, passive and impersonal can and often do occur in combination. The same is true about forceful and personal.

Business documents, except very short ones, usually contain more than one message, although usually only one is predominant. Each message may or may not be written in the same style. This chapter has defined these styles and has urged you to practice learning how to write each one. Proficiency in using the various business styles will enable you to use the style that best suits a given message. Knowing which style is best is the topic of the chapters that follow.

REVIEW QUESTIONS

1. What are the characteristics of the following styles?
   - a. forceful
   - b. passive
   - c. personal
   - d. impersonal
   - e. colorful
   - f. colorless

2. Which styles are mutually exclusive because they are polar opposites?

3. Which styles often overlap in day-to-day business writing? *Passive + impersonal*

4. Can a colorful style be used in conjunction with any other style or styles? *Yes except colorless*

5. Can a document contain more than one message?

6. What is meant by a predominant message? *one that contains a bottom line*

DISCUSSION QUESTIONS

1. Do you think you could reasonably use our six prose style definitions to describe different management styles? If so, how?

2. Some of these styles do not produce what many people would call "good writing." Why is this an irrelevant issue in business writing? Is there a "good" writing style in general?

Chapter 16

STYLE IN POSITIVE AND NEGATIVE MESSAGES

OBJECTIVES

This chapter will help you to

•

Compare your reactions to various style choices to those of businesspeople

•

Contribute to the development of style principles for positive and negative messages sent up or down internally, within the power hierarchy

Now that styles have been classified and defined, the next and very important question to answer is this: Which style, or styles, are most appropriate for which message situations? That is, when should a business writer be forceful or passive? Or personal or impersonal? Under what communication situations is a colorful style effective?

The choice of style depends, as do other choices, on the type of message you are sending and on whether you are sending it up or down in the power hierarchy.

Our discussion in Chapters 16, 17, and 18 deals only with internal communication, those going up or down the power hierarchy of any business organization. Later, in Chapter 19, we will deal with two message types (negative sent upward and negative-persuasive sent upward) that must be handled differently from those sent internally. In this chapter, we begin by considering internal positive and negative messages sent upward and downward. In the next chapter, we will consider style in relation to internally sent persuasive messages.

BACKGROUND OF SAMPLE MEMOS

To assess your reactions to various styles in specific message situations, we will ask you to react to a series of memos written in response to a series of mini-cases. These memos are written in the various styles we have defined. You will be asked to decide which style best suits each case. Before you do so, however, you need to know four things about the sample memos that will follow:

The following sample memos are all in a bottom-line organizational pattern to force focus on style.

1. *Each memo is bottom-lined.* Because we want you to focus on, and react to, style alone, every sample memo is written in a direct, bottom-lined organizational pattern. *This pattern is used regardless of whether or not this pattern makes sense in that message situation.*

This means that even a negative message written to be sent upward will be bottom-lined. We are forced to do this simply for consistency. By keeping strictly to one organizational pattern, we force you to react to style alone. If we shifted organizational patterns from case to case or from memo to memo, you would not know whether your reaction was caused by style or by a changed organizational pattern. Since all sample memos are bottom-lined, you can be assured that you *must* be reacting to style alone. Moreover, we have also eliminated subject and date lines from these sample memos as another way to keep your focus solely on the prose style and on who is writing to whom.

Some styles used in sample memos obviously do not fit situations and, hence, are jarring.

2. *The memo styles are not caricatures.* The exclusive use of a particular style in a few of these memos will undoubtedly, on occasion, seem exaggerated. However, you should know that none of these memos is intended to be a caricature of normal business prose. When a sample memo's style seems overdone, it is usually because the style under consideration does not fit a case situation. This is the very point we are studying. It is not enough to say that not every style is appropriate in every situation. What we want to know is which style, or styles, *are* appropriate in given message situations and which are not.

Obviously, some styles will jar in some situations. A colorful way of writing is found regularly, for example, in advertising and public relations writing. Yet some of the colorful versions of memos you will read will sound very odd in a non-advertising context. That oddity, we ask you to recognize, is not inherent in the colorful style. The apparent oddity results from a colorful style being used in the wrong situation.

In summary, all sample memos are written in the way some real business people actually write in *some* situations (even if not necessarily in the situation under consideration).

3. *Much business writing is highly informal.* Some of our sample memos reflect a trend toward informality. Some businesspeople today intentionally write colloquially. They are also prone to use "shop talk" or the unique jargon of their trade or profession.

The sample memos are written in normal, colloquial business prose.

Furthermore, some of the sample memos use clichés. These are used to be consistent with the phrasing of many businesspeople. If a cliché such as "caught like a rat in a trap" clearly describes a situation, these are the very words many businesspeople will use. They don't have time to try to create original metaphors. (If you think this is easy to do, try it. Only creative writers have the facility to create original figures of speech, and then not easily.) Remember, businesspeople write to get jobs done, not to win prizes.

4. *The advice on style is based on field work.* The final factor we need to explain is that after each sample memo, we report on the styles that businesspeople preferred. We are able to do this because over several years we showed the identical sample memos used in this book to business groups and sought their opinions. We forced them, as we will you, to make choices between styles that were polar opposites—that is, to choose between forceful and passive, personal and impersonal, and colorful and colorless. From their responses we developed the style principles of the following chapters. Naturally, we make no claims that non-business groups will react the same way as businesspeople. But then, in your business career, you will be writing to people with backgrounds and tastes in prose very similar to those held by the businesspeople who helped us develop these style principles.

Reactions of businesspeople to sample memos helped form the style principles that follow.

POSITIVE MESSAGES UP OR DOWN

We begin by discussing the style choices that are most likely to be successful for positive messages. In our discussion about organizing positive messages (Chapter 13), we said that no matter whether you were sending positive messages up or down you should always use a direct, bottom-line organization. This bottom-line pattern maximizes the positive effect of the favorable message. We showed that by not bottom-lining you may lead the reader to expect bad news.

The same type of thinking applies to your choice of style in positive messages written either up or down. Regardless of their direction, you should choose the writing style (or combination of styles) that best complements the good news, for it is stylistically possible to express good news

The style chosen should complement a positive message.

in such a way as to blunt the positive effect on the reader that such good news deserves. We will develop the first of our style principles after considering the responses to the following case.

Household Products, Inc. Case 1

Assume you are Director of Public Relations for Household Products, Inc., a very large company. The President of the company asks you to draft a letter to stockholders to be included in the company's annual report. This letter will be signed by the President and will be read by every stockholder who receives the report. You work diligently on the letter, preparing several drafts before finally selecting the one that you submit for the President's reaction. Fortunately, the President likes your letter. He sends a good-news memo back to you.

Now ask yourself which of the following two memos you would rather have received from the President if you were the Director of Public Relations.

Version A. Forceful

TO: "Public Relations Director"

FROM: "Corporation President"

Congratulations on the stockholders' letter. It is one of the best ever.

The letter has punch and vitality. It will certainly please the stockholders.

Do not change a word; it is perfect!

Version B. Passive

TO: "Public Relations Director"

FROM: "Corporation President"

The stockholders' letter has been judged favorably; no prior letter has been valued so highly.

Characteristic of the letter are vitality and punch. Stockholders should be pleased by it.

Changes are not called for, as perfection was achieved.

Doubtless, you, like virtually all businesspeople, would strongly prefer to receive Version A. The passive Version B sounds so halfhearted that it blunts much of the good-news message's effectiveness.

You are now ready to understand our first style principle:

Now assess whether you think a personal or an impersonal style works better in this positive message. Which of these two versions of the memo from the President would you prefer receiving?

Version C. Personal

TO: "Public Relations Director"

FROM: "Corporation President"

Congratulations on your stockholders' letter, J. J. It's one of the best I've ever seen!

The letter has punch and vitality. You have truly created a message that will please our stockholders.

Could a word be changed? No, it's perfect!

Version D. Impersonal

TO: "Public Relations Director"

FROM: "Corporation President"

Congratulations on the stockholders' letter, which is one of the best.

The letter has punch and vitality and presents a message that should truly please the stockholders.

No words need changing, as the letter is perfect.

The difference between these two versions may not be as blatant as was the case between the forceful and the passive styles. Yet it is still quite obvious that the personal style works more effectively here.

Some people worry about using a personal style even in the most positive of situations. They worry about such concerns as: "I always thought you shouldn't begin a sentence with *I*" Or, "Doesn't the use of *I* make the writer seem egocentric?" People with scientific or engineering backgrounds may wonder, "I never was allowed to use *I* or any other personal pronoun in a technical report. So I always thought you should never use *I* or *you* in a business letter." Experienced businesspeople, however, believe that a personal style enhances the effect of a positive message. Hence, our style principle now reads like this:

STYLE PRINCIPLE 1:
Maximize the effect of positive messages by using

a. A forceful rather than a passive style.
b. A personal rather than an impersonal style.

What about the choice of a colorful or colorless style? In most business situations, as you will soon see, it is wise to minimize or avoid the use of a colorful style. But in positive messages, especially in positive messages sent downward, a colorful style can be effective.

See whether you respond favorably to the following colorful version of the President's letter to the Director of Public Relations. (There's no need to show you colorless versions of memos used in this and future cases; you will either like the colorful version or you won't.

Version E. Colorful

> TO: "Public Relations Director"
>
> FROM: "Corporation President"
>
> Congratulations on the great stockholders' letter you wrote, J. J. What a wordsmith you are!
>
> The letter's punch and vitality makes dreary economic facts sound like music to the stockholders' ears. It'll have the stockholders dancing in the aisles.
>
> Don't change a word. It's a work of art!

If you were the person receiving this memo from the company President, you might well find this colorful style very suitable to such a positive message. In fact, the overly exuberant, colorful figures of speech might be quite acceptable in this positive message situation. Therefore, our style principle can be finalized as follows:

STYLE PRINCIPLE 1:

Maximize the effect of positive messages by using

a. A forceful rather than a passive style.
b. A personal rather than an impersonal style.
c. A colorful style, if a touch of humor, lightheartedness, or poetic imagery is appropriate.

Arguments can easily be made in favor of either the forceful, the personal, or even the colorful versions we have considered. Therefore, the most effective test of the accuracy of Style Principle 1 might be to create a version that does just the opposite. In other words, show how this memo would read if it were written in a passive, impersonal, colorless style. Here is that memo:

Version F. Passive, Impersonal, and Colorless

> TO: "Public Relations Director"
>
> FROM: "Corporation President"
>
> Comments about the proposed stockholders' letter are the following:

1. A favorable reaction by stockholders probably will be produced by this approach.

2. It is also likely that no negative employee reaction will occur.

NEGATIVE MESSAGES

In a positive message, the choice of appropriate style serves to maximize the positive qualities of the message. In negative messages, however, writers want to determine which style best *minimizes* the negative qualities of the message. They want to reduce as much as possible the risk frequently implicit when someone has to be told "No!" Therefore, we will begin with negative messages sent up, since these are the most risky.

For negative messages, the style chosen should lessen the effect of the bad news on readers.

Negative Messages Up

Negative messages written upward are the ones most likely to cause bad reader reactions. These are the messages for which an inappropriate style has the greatest potential to cause trouble. Now we will alter our case to help us develop a style principle for negative messages sent up.

Style choices are most critical in negative messages sent up.

Household Products, Inc. Case 2

The President of the corporation has written a draft of a letter to stockholders to be included in the company's annual report. To obtain typical reader feedback, the President has selected a few rank-and-file employees in the Finance Department to review the letter. Suppose you were one of those employees chosen. Your analysis of the letter reveals some faults. You decide to share your criticisms frankly with the President.

What style is best to use? Let's begin by comparing versions of your response written in forceful and passive styles. Version A illustrates a forceful style.

Version A. Forceful

TO: "Corporation President"

FROM: "Finance Employee"

Here are my comments about the proposed letter to stockholders you circulated for employee reaction:

1. Don't come so close to a guarantee of increased profits in the fourth quarter. This is risky.

2. Stop being defensive about the company's performance this year. This insults those of us who worked as hard as we could.

You easily see why Version A is forceful. It gives commands. Its imperative sentences are short and full of punch. In fact, the memo is so forceful that it seems brave, perhaps to the point of being foolhardy in a negative situation sent up. Businesspeople feel strongly, as you probably do also, that most prudent lower level employees would not write in this style to the Presidents of their corporations. Now consider passive Version B.

Version B. Passive

> TO: "Corporation President"
>
> FROM: "Finance Employee"
>
> In reference to your request for employee comments about the proposed stockholder letter, the following observations could be made.
>
> A guarantee of increased profits in the fourth quarter seems to be implied and, as a result, a possibly unnecessary risk may be incurred.
>
> Also, a less defensive posture could be taken about the company's performance this year. Such a posture would be appreciated by most employees.

Where Version A's sentence structure uses the direct, subject-verb-object order of the active voice, Version B's sentences are passive and, hence, indirect. These are some of its passive expressions:

- "observations could be made."
- "guarantee . . . seems to be implied."
- "risk may be incurred."
- "posture could be taken."
- "posture would be appreciated."

How do you think a powerful reader would react to each of these versions? Most businesspeople feel that although the passive style may well be regarded as undesirable, in the abstract, as a style of writing, it is clearly safer in a negative up situation than is the forceful style of Version A.

Therefore, when you have to write up to someone who is powerful (and with whom you have not established a warm personal relationship), you are safer if you use a style of writing that is decidedly less forceful than is Version A. In fact, based on common sense, you could wisely conclude that the lower the position writers hold when writing negative messages upward, the less forceful their style probably should be. Consequently, the second style principle begins as follows:

For a negative message sent upward, use

a. A passive rather than a forceful style

Now let's determine whether a personal or an impersonal style works best in this negative up situation. Here are personal and impersonal versions of the letter to the President.

Version C. Personal

TO: "Corporation President"

FROM: "Finance Employee"

I would like to give you my comments about your proposed letter to stockholders which you circulated for our reaction:

1. If I were you, I don't think I would want to appear to be making a personal guarantee of increased profits in the fourth quarter. None of us would like to see you run the risk of building false expectations among stockholders.

2. I think you should also ask yourself this question: "How do you think your own employees will react to this letter, not just how do you think stockholders will react?" If you do, I think you will come to the conclusion that this draft of the letter makes you sound very defensive about all of our performances this year. I know that I personally worked as hard as I could, and I am sure that goes for the rest of the employees.

I hope these comments prove helpful to you as you decide upon the final draft of the stockholder letter.

Version D. Impersonal

TO: "Corporation President"

FROM: "Finance Employee"

Here are the requested comments about the proposed stockholder letter:

1. Some stockholders might feel that there is an implied guarantee of fourth-quarter profits. This could inadvertently build unfounded stockholder expectations.

2. There appears to be a note of defensiveness about this year's corporate performance which could adversely affect the morale of some employees.

Version C, while frank, is about as warm and personal a communication as it is possible to write in this situation. It is tactful and constructive. But it raises other questions:

- Is the intensely personal nature of this letter likely to cause a negative reaction on the part of the reader?

- Is it appropriate for someone at a lower level in a corporation to write so personally, even familiarly, to the President of a company?

- And, even more important, is it wise to be so very personal, warm, and friendly when writing something that is negative to the expectations of the reader—especially when the reader is so very much the writer's superior?

Version D seems to handle the situation better. Its impersonal style gives the memo an all-business attitude. It uses no personal pronouns or names, nor is it conversational. It does not pose questions to the reader. It simply and straightforwardly conveys the same negative message as Version C, but does it impersonally.

Why is an impersonal style preferable in situations where negative messages are sent up? A personal style of writing tends, by its very nature, to bring the writer more directly into the picture. As a result, the negative message becomes more clearly identified as coming from the writer *personally*. The more personal writers become in the upward communication of negative messages, the more those writers may tend to worsen the situation for themselves. Version D wisely attributes negatives not personally to the writer but to faceless others at hypothetical arms' reach—it does so through such words as "some stockholders," "some employees."

Now let's consider the final style choice in this negative communication written up—a colorful versus a colorless way of saying things. Here is a colorful version of the letter to the President.

Version E. Colorful

> TO: "Corporation President"
>
> FROM: "Finance Employee"
>
> Here is my frank feedback about the letter to stockholders you passed around for comment:
>
> 1. Some hungry lawyer will surely pounce—like a cat on a mouse—on your seeming guarantee of increased fourth-quarter profits!
>
> 2. Why publicly cry the blues about this year's performance? Most of us feel like sticking our heads in the oven as it is!

Most likely you strongly rejected the extremely colorful style of this negative message sent upward. It is highly unlikely that a corporation president would like to receive, from a subordinate, a memo written in such a breezy, colloquial style. The use of figures of speech such as "cat on a mouse" and "sticking our heads in the oven," despite their being clichés, increases the effect this memo has on the reader. And since this message is negative, it is foolish to use a style that increases its effect. It would, we feel sure, be the rare subordinate who would even think of sending such a memo. Therefore, the additions to Style Principle 2 are:

STYLE PRINCIPLE 2:

For a negative message sent upward, use

a. A passive rather than a forceful style.
b. An impersonal rather than a personal style.
c. A colorless style.

Let's follow the advice of Style Principle 2 and rewrite this letter in the passive, impersonal, colorless styles recommended. See how you like the result.

> TO: "Corporation President"
>
> FROM: "Finance Employee"
>
> This memo responds to your request for opinions relative to the proposed stockholders' letter.
>
> 1. It is possible that some stockholders might draw the conclusion that a guarantee of fourth-quarter profits is being made. Perhaps some greater qualification of this statement might be considered.
>
> 2. It is also possible that some employees might feel that this draft places the company in the position of sounding defensive about our performance this year. A revision that reassures the stockholders of the dedication of all employees to a more profitable future might be more suitable to both internal and external audiences.

There it is. It is certainly far more passive than forceful. You will notice that this version uses the impersonal style to allow the writer to avoid taking personal responsibility for the negatives. All negative thoughts are attributed to the way "some stockholders" and "some employees" *might* react. The memo consistently qualifies its statements very nicely by making everything conditional. It does this through such expressions as, "It is possible that. . . ."

This version is safe and it does get the job done. Moreover, since it tactfully tells the truth, it should prove helpful to the President. If, on the other hand, the President violently disagrees with the content of the message, this style of writing has not put the writer in a vulnerable position.

Negative Messages Down

Next we will discuss the style choices that are most appropriate in situations where negative information has to be conveyed downward from a writer who has power over the reader. To determine the answer, we will change the case situation to read as follows.

Household Products, Inc. Case 3

This time, it is the President of the corporation who does not like the draft of a proposed letter to stockholders that he is supposed to sign for inclusion in the annual report. Consequently, the President must convey his negative feedback to his subordinate, the Director of Public Relations, who is responsible for the draft.

As before, we begin by examining two versions of the letter from the President to the Public Relations Director. Version A is forceful in style; Version B is passive. Which would you choose if you were the President?

Version A. Forceful

TO: "Public Relations Director"

FROM: "Corporation President"

Here are my comments on the proposed letter to stockholders:

1. Don't make me sound as if I am almost guaranteeing increased profits in the fourth quarter. Too risky.
2. Don't make me sound so defensive about our performance this year. People in the company did the best they could and they expect me to stand up for them with shareholders.

Version B. Passive

TO: "Public Relations Director"

FROM: "Corporation President"

After the draft of the proposed letter to stockholders was read by me, and after careful consideration was given to the letter's potential effect on investors as well as employees, certain observations can be made.

A guarantee of profits in the fourth quarter could be inferred by some readers, and an unnecessary risk therefore run by us.

Similarly, a posture of defensiveness about the company's performance this year could be construed as casting negative aspersions on the efforts of all employees.

In Version A, the style is forceful because it uses the active voice instead of the passive. It also contains the imperative (giving orders), and direct sentences and itemized paragraphs. By contrast, Version B uses a passive, object-verb-subject sentence structure.

Writers in as powerful a position as this corporate president can, of course, be as forceful as they want to be. But for reasons of human relations, high-level executives want to avoid appearing overbearing. They have nothing to prove through the use of too forceful a style; their position speaks for itself. But neither do they want to appear ineffectual as in the passive version.

Therefore, Style Principle 3 begins with this advice:

STYLE PRINCIPLE 3:
For a negative message sent downward, use

a. A semi-forceful style.

Notice that the advice is to be **semi-forceful,** not forceful, for although superiors should write downward forcefully, they usually do not want to sound as though they were barking commands.

Next, we must make a choice between a personal and an impersonal style in a negative message sent downward. Which of the following two versions would you select if you were the President?

Version C. Personal

TO: "Public Relations Director"

FROM: "Corporation President"

You asked for my comments on a letter to stockholders you drafted:

1. Why do you make me sound as if I'm guaranteeing increased fourth-quarter profits? You must know that this is risky.

2. And why make me appear so defensive about our performance this year? You make it look as if I'm not standing up for all those people who work so hard in the company. Just ask yourself how Mary Jones in data processing or Harry Arnold in the mail room would react to this letter.

Version D. Impersonal

TO: "Public Relations Director"

FROM: "Corporation President"

Comments on the proposed letter to stockholders are as follows:

1. It is risky to sound as if a guarantee of fourth-quarter profits is being made.

2. A less defensive posture about corporate performance this year seem advisable from the viewpoint of employee morale.

Powerful writers writing down avoid using too forceful a style.

Version C is quite personal in style. Notice the frequent use of the pronoun "you." Notice also how the use of individual names—"Mary Jones" and "Harry Arnold"—really personalizes the memo. Note how the use of questions makes it appear as if one person is actually conversing with another. But these qualities of highly personal writing, however desirable they may be in many situations, do not seem so desirable in a negative letter, even one written downward in an organization.

A personal style's use of questions seems to scold the reader in negative situations.

Most top executives did not get to the top by being insensitive to the feelings of those with whom they work. To write a highly personal but negative message downward in an organization is to run a certain risk. Just think of the times you've heard people say, "Now let's not get personal about this" or, "He took it personally and got angry." A personal style, almost by definition, increases the probability of something negative being taken personally. For example, the very questions that make the memo sound conversational, serve in this negative situation to make the Public Relations Director feel as if the President is scolding him personally.

By contrast, Version D seems to be "all business." It states the facts coldly and impersonally. Yet, this coldness and impersonality seem to be received better than does the personal style of Version C. Therefore, Style Principle 3 suggests the following:

STYLE PRINCIPLE 3:
For a negative message sent downward, use

a. A semi-forceful style.
b. An impersonal rather than a personal style.

Finally, imagine now that the President wondered if the memo to the Public Relations Director would benefit from being made more colorful, as in this version:

Version E. Colorful

TO: "Public Relations Director"

FROM: "Corporation President"

You asked for my comments on the letter to stockholders you whipped up:

1. I'm not Santa Claus, you know. Maybe *he* can guarantee increased fourth-quarter profits, but I sure can't!

2. And then you make me stop being Kris Kringle and turn me into Poor Nelle, crying about how miserably we have done this year.

A colorful style makes a negative situation more negative.

Of course, you realize that negative situations are *not* occasions in which to be colorful. A colorful style increases the effect on the reader through its use of stimulating adjectives, adverbs, and colloquial figures of speech. As a result, it tends to worsen negative situations, and this holds true whether the writer is in a position of low or high power. A colorful style is, therefore, again inadvisable, as the now-finished style principle shows.

For a negative message sent downward, use

a. A semi-forceful style.
b. An impersonal rather than a personal style.
c. A colorless style.

Let's see how a letter written by the Corporation President to the Public Relations Director might look if it had followed the guidelines of Style Principle 3 and had been written in a semi-forceful, impersonal, and colorless style.

Version F. Semi-Forceful, Impersonal, and Colorless

TO: "Public Relations Director"

FROM: "Corporation President"

Please make the following changes in the draft of the proposed stockholder letter:

1. Eliminate the implied guarantee of profits in the fourth quarter. Too risky.
2. Revise the fourth paragraph where the tone seems defensive about our performance this year. Instead, reassure stockholders about the dedication of all employees to a more profitable future.

Note that this version captures much of what is desirable in an impersonal style; yet it is sufficiently forceful because of its use of the imperative ("eliminate this"; "revise that"). These sentences give orders without using the word *you*. However, these orders are preceded by an all-important word—*please*—that softens the forcefulness of the style. This memo should get the job done without seeming offensive or insulting to the Public Relations Director.

SUMMARY

Three general principles emerge from the study of style in positive and negative messages. The first is that, when writing downward, a forceful or a semi-forceful style is appropriate, no matter whether the message is positive or negative.

The second is that colorful writing, while regarded with some amusement by the average businessperson, can sometimes be acceptable in positive messages.

The third generalization is that negative messages and an impersonal style go together. Whether the negative message goes upward or downward, impersonal proves to be a favorable style.

Chapter 16   Style in Positive and Negative Messages   307

In the next chapter, we will see that these generalizations are also applicable in determining the styles most appropriate to use in persuasive situations.

REVIEW QUESTIONS

1. What does the choice of style depend on?
2. How can you maximize the favorable effect of a positive message?
3. What is the risk of using an inappropriate style in a positive message?
4. What type of message is most likely to cause bad reactions in readers?
5. What style should you use when writing a negative message upward?
6. What style should you use when writing a negative message downward?
7. What are the risks of using an inappropriate style in a negative message?
8. What three general principles emerge from the study of style in positive and negative messages?

DISCUSSION QUESTIONS

1. In any organization, which flows upward more quickly, a positive or a negative message? Why?
2. Which message, positive or negative, is most likely to use style to lessen the effect on readers?
3. At what point does the use of style for purposes of influencing your reader cross over the line and become unethical?
4. What can bosses do to make it easier for subordinates to give them honest but tactful feedback on negative information?
5. Consider how certain styles interact in negative messages. What effect does, say, personal have upon forceful? Colorful upon personal? Passive upon impersonal? What do you think explains these interactions?

1. on type of message whether

Chapter 17

STYLE CHOICES IN PERSUASIVE SITUATIONS

OBJECTIVES

This chapter will help you to

●

Appreciate why persuasive situations should be divided according to whether they are positive or negative to a reader's interests

●

Learn which styles will have the greatest chance of increasing or decreasing the persuasiveness of each type of persuasive message sent internally

In our discussion of style, it has been important to consider whether the writer is writing from a higher or a lower power position. Nowhere is this distinction more necessary than in the area of persuasive situations, where you need to talk readers into doing what you want them to do, whether they want to do so or not. In cases where writers have total power over readers, writers do not need to persuade. They can simply *order* something done. Really powerful people can merely hint at what they desire, and it will be instantly done by subordinates. Consequently, it is much, much easier to write successful persuasive messages downward than it is to write them upward.

However, seldom in business do people enjoy total power over those to whom they write. They certainly never have this power during their early years. Furthermore, even if you have power over subordinates, persuasion is a less threatening approach to take than giving orders is. Persuasion is also often more effective in the long run. Therefore, whether you are the boss or an employee, you must learn how to persuade readers to take the action, or to form the opinions you want them to.

In Chapter 11, we discussed the two basic types of persuasive messages:

1. **Positive-Persuasive.** In this type, readers know (even if they need persuading to admit it) that what is requested is actually positive to their interests.

2. **Negative-Persuasive.** Here readers are asked to do something they don't want to do, something that (even if they think deeply about it) is clearly negative to a good portion of their interests.

We will examine each type separately, since the styles appropriate to each are necessarily quite different. Remember, we are dealing with persuasive messages sent internally. Chapter 19 will deal with those externally sent messages that require different handling.

POSITIVE-PERSUASIVE MESSAGES

Choosing the style best suited to positive-persuasive messages is not fraught with much danger. In trying to persuade people to do what they know is for their own good, you would have to be overbearingly tactless in order to make them angry. At the same time, some style choices are, as you will see, far preferable to others.

Forceful versus Passive Style

Let's examine a simple case to see which styles best fit its circumstances.

Ling Laboratories, Inc. Case

As Personnel Director of Ling Laboratories, Inc., you have to compose a memo to be sent to all eligible employees reminding them to sign

Since we seldom have total power over others, we need to learn to persuade.

Persuasive messages sent down are obviously easier to write than ones sent up.

What's in it for the reader determines whether a persuasive message is positive or negative.

Positive-persuasive messages urge readers to do what is basically good for them.

up for their vacations by April 30. The rule is this: if they do not select a vacation time by April 30, they will have a time arbitrarily assigned to them.

Here are forceful and passive versions of such a memo.

Version A. Forceful

TO: Employees

FROM: "Personnel Director"

Reminder: Sign up for vacations before the April 30 deadline. Select the vacation time you want by this date or accept a time assigned to you arbitrarily.

Version B. Passive

TO: Employees

FROM: "Personnel Director"

It is necessary to remind you that vacation times must be selected by you before the April 30 deadline After that date, vacation times will be assigned arbitrarily.

Obviously, a reminder to sign up for a vacation time period is not insulting. In fact, either version of this reminder is apt to be appreciated. However, the forceful version is the choice of most businesspeople. Accordingly, our next Style Principle begins as follows:

STYLE PRINCIPLE 4:

For a positive-persuasive message (up or down), use

a. A forceful style.

Personal versus Impersonal Style

Here are a personal and an impersonal approach to this case. Which seems preferable to you?

Version C. Personal

TO: Employees

FROM: "Personnel Director"

Do you want to choose the time for your vacation? If so, I want you to sign up for your vacation before the April 30 deadline. I urge you to remember that after this deadline, you will have to be arbitrarily assigned a vacation time.

> TO: Employees
>
> FROM: "Personnel Director"
>
> This memo is to remind all eligible employees that vacation times must be selected by the April 30 deadline. If vacation times are not selected by this date, it will be necessary to assign them to those who failed to state a preference.

Again, since the situation is positive rather than negative, a personal approach seems to carry little risk and conveys the message in an appropriate manner. In fact, readers might even view the personal approach as better demonstrating a superior's care and concern for his or her subordinates. This advice is now captured in our next Style Principle.

STYLE PRINCIPLE 4:
For a positive-persuasive message (up or down), use

a. A forceful style.
b. A personal style.

Colorful versus Colorless

Finally, examine this colorful example and consider its appropriateness.

Version E. Colorful

> TO: Employees
>
> FROM: "Personnel Director"
>
> Planning on vacationing in Tucson? How would you like doing so in July? Or how about Minneapolis in November? Or Yellowstone in December?
>
> These may be one of the vacation times assigned to your if you fail to sign up for your vacation.
>
> The April 30 deadline is sneaking up. So open up that calendar, peruse a few dates, and hustle over to Room 201 to lock up the times most convenient for you.

In a limited number of situations, a colorful style might prove appropriate, and this situation may be one of them. Depending on the writer's management style and on his or her relationshp with coworkers, a colorful, lighthearted approach might prove an effective way of handling a slightly sensitive, positive situation. After all, the colorful imagery and comical questions are occurring within the context of a positive message. Readers would have to be particularly sour and humorless to take offense at this colorful memo since it is urging them to do what is clearly in their best interests.

In the case of positive-persuasive messages, it does not matter whether the message is being sent up or down. Style Principle 4, therefore, summarizes style advice for both upward and downward situations.

STYLE PRINCIPLE 4:

For a positive-persuasive message (up or down), use

a. A forceful style.
b. A personal style.
c. A colorful style if appropriate.

Let's apply this principle to a final version of a memo.

Version F. Forceful and Personal

TO: Employees

FROM: "Personnel Director"

Please sign up for your vacation time before the April 30 dead-line. This is the only way you can assure getting the dates you want and not ones assigned arbitrarily. Talk things over, think things through, but please act now or as soon as possible!

NEGATIVE-PERSUASIVE MESSAGES

Negative-persuasive messages are naturally more fraught with prob-lems than are positive messages. Therefore, the direction the message is sent significantly influences the style selections in negative-persuasive messages.

Negative-persuasive messages urge readers to do what they basically see no personal profit in doing.

Negative-Persuasive Messages Down

Here is a sample case to use to test your reactions to various styles in a negative-persuasive message sent downward.

Pan-National Corporation Case 1

The Executive Vice President of Pan-National Corporation writes to all headquarters department managers urging them to set a good ex-ample for other employees by being more punctual about their times of reporting to work and quitting. However, since this is a first re-minder, and since some readers may, in fact, be innocent, the Vice President does not choose to issue a general "Now here this!" type of order. Instead, he wants to persuade them to set a good example.

The message sent here is clearly negative, and it is persuasive because the boss has not issued an order. The readers are asked to be more punc-tual, a request that implies a criticism of their behavior. The communication is from a person in a higher power position to a person in a lower power position; therefore, it is sent downward.

Forceful versus Passive Style

Compare these two versions of the letter written by the Executive Vice President. The first is forceful and the second is passive in style.

Version A. Forceful

TO: All Headquarters Department Managers

FROM: "Executive Vice President"

I strongly urge each of you to set a good example for your subordinates by:

1. Reporting to work on time each day, and
2. Not quitting until 5:00 P.M. or later.

I request your complete cooperation.

Version B. Passive

TO: All Headquarters Department Managers

FROM: "Executive Vice President"

A good example will be set for subordinates if superiors report to work on time and leave not before 5:00 P.M. Full cooperation is requested.

How advisable do you think it is to be forceful, as opposed to passive, in this situation?

The passive style of Version B has some appeal because the case stated that the Executive Vice President did not want to make it a "Now hear this" type of communication. On the other hand, Version B makes the Executive Vice President seem to lack force. He seems reluctant to lead. As you studied this version, you probably wondered if a top executive would really sign such a passive message.

The forceful version, by contrast, sounds more like what we would expect from a person in charge. The businesspeople we asked feared that it seemed too forceful in this first reminder memo. Their advice was the same as seen earlier in our discussion of negative messages sent downward. The position held by a high-level writer in itself lends force to the message. For that reason, the advice advanced by Style Principle 5 is that a semi-forceful style is most appropriate for negative-persuasive messages sent downward.

Managers want to project an image of polite forcefulness and not appear overbearing in their downward writing.

STYLE PRINCIPLE 5:
For a negative-persuasive message sent downward, use

a. A semi-forceful style to avoid sounding overbearing.

Personal versus Impersonal Style

Now let's see whether you prefer a personal or impersonal style in a negative-persuasive message written downwards.

Version C. Personal

TO: All Headquarters Managers

FROM: "Executive Vice President"

How do you think you would feel if your boss consistently reported to work later than you? Then made matters worse by leaving early? Not very good, I suspect.

Therefore, I know you will do all you can to set a good example for the people who report to you. In this tight economy, you and your fellow workers will want to make your contributions to our company's efficiency and productivity.

Version D. Impersonal

TO: All Headquarters Managers

FROM: "Executive Vice President"

The punctuality with which management reports to work in the morning and leaves at night sets an example for subordinates. Therfore, the announced beginning and ending times of work should be closely observed so as to make clear to subordinates that punctuality is basic to a well-run organization.

How did you react to each version? Most likely, you found that the addition of personal, conversational qualities served to weaken the effectiveness of Version C.

Why did you probably prefer Version D? Perhaps because you felt that the impersonality of the style decreased the likelihood of readers feeling that they are being scolded personally. The personal style of Version C makes the memo sound more like a person actually lecturing the reader. You can almost see the writer shaking a finger at the reader. Style Principle 5 reflects this finding:

A personal style seems to scold readers in negative situations.

STYLE PRINCIPLE 5:
For a negative-persuasive message sent downward, use

a. A semi-forceful style to avoid sounding overbearing.
b. An impersonal style.

Colorful versus Colorless Style

What about being colorful? Does a colorful style suit this negative-persuasive situation? See what you think.

TO: All Headquarters Managers

FROM: "Executive Vice President"

Chaucer put it well: "If gold will rust, what then will iron do?"

Are we having that extra cup of coffee in the mornings? And showing up late as a result? Are we thinking so much about an afternoon nine holes that we are leaving early?

These are tough economic times and unless we lead by example, we are not going to encourage the high productivity and efficiency that have made our company great.

You might admire the writing here. Its cleverness may make you think that this colorful version might have some possibilities of being effective. The draft displays a certain amount of tact. Its constant use of figures of speech imparts an almost literary tone that makes the negative aspects of the message seem more abstract and less of a personal criticism. Unfortunately, however, the memo's message is still negative.

In this situation, the negative message clashes with the lighthearted nature of the colorful style. As a result, you, like most businesspeople, probably rejected the use of this colorful style because you perceived that it runs a risk of appearing phony, exaggerated, or pretentious. Most businesspeople felt that it would be the rare top executive who would sign such a colorful letter, no matter how much its literary style might be admirable. In fact, it is the very literary qualities that make this well-written version seem unbusinesslike. Style Principle 5 reflects this in its final addition:

Businesspeople reject colorful style in negative messages.

STYLE PRINCIPLE 5:
For a negative-persuasive message sent downward, use

a. A semi-forceful style to avoid sounding overbearing.
b. An impersonal style.
c. A colorless style.

Here is a memo that follows the advice of Style Principle 5.

Version F. Semi-Forceful, Impersonal, and Colorless

TO: All Headquarters Managers

FROM: "Executive Vice President"

It is necessary that management set a good example for subordinates by:

1. Reporting to work on time each day.
2. Not quitting before 5:00 P.M.

By doing so, managers make clear to others that punctuality is basic to a well-run organization. Please assist in this effort.

This letter would probably prove to be quite effective. Notice how the forceful style has been softened by the device of saying "It is necessary" instead of "You must." Also effective is the addition of the magic word "please." This somewhat forceful style lessens the risk of the memo's appearing to be overbearing. Yet, the sentence structure is active rather than passive, and the memo even ends with an imperative—"Please assist in this effort," no matter how politely it has been delivered. An interesting feature of the imperative is this: Despite its implied "you," the use of the imperative is still vastly more impersonal than is true of expressions like "You must assist in this effort," or "You must assist us in this effort," or "We expect your complete cooperation." All of the latter, as you see, add some of the personal pronouns found in the personal style.

Next, we will consider the styles that work best in a negative-persuasie message sent upward.

Politely worded imperatives are the stock-in-trade of the effective downward communicator.

Negative-Persuasive Messages Up

Trying to get bosses to do something they do not want to do is perhaps the most difficult—and risky—of all writing situations. Approach these situations with extreme caution, paying special attention to the style you select.

To determine which style has the highest probability of success, let's change the last scenario slightly. Here is a situation involving a negative-persuasive message sent upward.

Pan-National Corporation Case 2

A lower-level employee writes to the Vice President to request that he force headquarters office managers to obey the rules about starting and quitting times.

This task, obviously, is a most challenging one. But let's add two other pieces of information to make it even more interesting. First, let's assume that the writer has a genuine concern about this problem. The writer is not just someone trying to make trouble—or to get fired. Second, let's assume also that the Vice President will not read anonymous, unsigned memos or letters. Hence, the writer must sign his or her name. With this in mind, let's examine which styles cope with this situation most effectively.

Forceful versus Passive Style

Does a forceful or a passive style work better when a lower level employee tries to persuade a Vice President to do what the employee wants, especially when the Vice President doesn't want to do it?

Version A. Forceful

TO: "Vice President"

FROM: "Lower-Level Employee"

You owe it to all of us who report to work on time to make sure that our managers do so also. Take it from me, they don't!

Many regularly arrive an hour or two late. Also some simply drift off an hour or more before the announced quitting time.

And don't let them tell you it's because they worked late the nights before. They didn't!

I'm sorry to be so blunt about this, but I'm sure I'm not the only one who thinks you should take strong and immediate action.

Version B. Passive

TO: "Vice President"

FROM: "Lower-Level Employee"

This is a request that a study be made of the punctuality of our management—when they report to work and when they leave. There is the perception that many managers report late and leave early. There is also the feeling that late work hours the night before should not be accepted as a valid excuse.

If that study indicates that some reminders should be issued, such appropriate steps will be appreciated by many.

How persuasive did you feel the forceful style of Version A would be? By being so forceful in style, this memo clearly runs the risk of making the Vice President wonder, "Who does this person think is boss around here?" The forceful style definitely makes the superior feel chastised. It, therefore, seems obvious that such a forceful style is not only highly inappropriate in this situation, but that it also exposes the writer to considerable risk.

As weak and passive as Version B is in style, it is far more likely to prove effective with a Vice President than would the forceful version. The softness and lack of force in the passive version imparts a tone of tactfulness and respectfulness. It certainly does not raise the issue of "Who's the boss?" The superior would feel far less defensive and less under attack by the style of Version B.

A tactful but honest upward communication of the truth is the stock-in-trade of the effective subordinate.

As with the previous negative-persuasive situation, however, in this situation a great deal depends on your relationship with a superior and on the environment in which you are working. Some bosses really *do* like to be told things directly. But many bosses *say* they like to be told things directly but actually take offense at undiplomatic approaches such as that in Version A. It is highly doubtful that *any* Vice President would like Version A.

That is why Style Principle 6 begins by recommending a passive style in negative-persuasive messages written upward:

STYLE PRINCIPLE 6:

For a negative-persuasive message sent upward, use

a. A passive rather than a forceful style.

Personal versus Impersonal Style

What happens if the lower-level person writes to the Vice President in a personal style, as in Version C, or in an impersonal style, as in Version D?

Version C. Personal

> TO: "Vice President"
>
> FROM: "Lower-Level Employee"
>
> I want to make a serious request of you. And I believe that there may be many other rank and file employees who feel just as strongly as I do.
>
> Please pay personal attention to when our managers report to work and when they leave. Then ask yourself this: Do these managers need a reminder of what our starting and quitting times actually are?
>
> And please don't assume that these managers arrive late because they work late. No, some are coming in late and leaving early day after day.
>
> I ask you to please look into this situation.

Version D. Impersonal

> TO: "Vice President"
>
> FROM: "Lower-Level Employee"
>
> The purpose of this memo is to request that a study be made of the punctuality of management, both in terms of their reporting time and their time of leaving for the day.
>
> Late arrival can be justified for some on the basis of having worked late the night before. However, for others the norm has become late arrival and early departure on the same day.
>
> If this study indicates, as is possible, that action should be taken, such action will be appreciated.

Which style did you find more effective? Most business people feel strongly that the impersonal style proves far more effective than the personal style in negative-persuasive situations sent upward. Why? The answer seems to be evolving with some consistency: negative messages and a personal style simply do not seem to mix.

Honest upward communication of negative information is made more acceptable by an impersonal style.

Remember that every time a negative situation has been examined, the preferred style has been the impersonal style. Thus, while it is brave and forthright to tell a superior "I don't like your pet marketing plan," it is far more diplomatic and tactful to say, "It is possible that certain changes might make the marketing plan even more effective." That is why Style Principle 6 makes the following recommendation:

STYLE PRINCIPLE 6:

For a negative-persuasive message sent upward, use

a. A passive rather than a forceful style.
b. An impersonal style.

Colorful versus Colorless Style

Finally, let's decide whether an upward negative-persuasive letter should be written in a colorful style.

Version E. Colorful

TO: "Vice President"

FROM: "Lower-Level Employee"

Why should managers get away scot free coming to work late and leaving early? Rules are made for everybody.

Some of our bosses are keeping banker's hours in the morning and golfer's hours in the afternoon.

And the old excuse of having to work late the night before is just hogwash in many cases!

The rest of us second-class citizens have gotten upset enough to ask me to blow the whistle.

Once again, being colorful in a negative business situation is not effective. In this situation, the superior is being asked essentially to start doing his or her job. The best course is to couch that rather insulting request in the style that enhances the chances of the request to be granted and minimizes the chance of offending this powerful reader. Being colorful imparts a frivolous and breezy tone that businesspeople feel will consciously or subconsciously annoy superiors. Style Principle 6 summarizes these conclusions:

STYLE PRINCIPLE 6:

For a negative-persuasive message sent upward, use

a. A passive rather than a forceful style.
b. An impersonal style.
c. A colorless style.

Here is the memo that results from following the advice offered in Style Principle 6:

Version F. Passive, Impersonal, and Colorless

TO: "Vice President"

FROM: "Lower-Level Employee"

Morale considerations indicate that a study of management's punctuality should be seriously considered. In particular, such a study should focus on the reporting to work and leaving times of managers.

Having worked late the night before does, of course, justify late arrivals on some occasions. However, it is a commonly held perception that late arrival and early departure on the same day have become the norm in many instances for many managers.

For these reasons, a study of managerial punctuality might well conclude that there is indeed a need for remedial action. Such a study in itself would be widely appreciated.

SUMMARY

Persuasive situations are perhaps the most challenging of business writing situations. Yet, the generalizations made at the conclusion of the last chapter remain consistent—a forceful style is generally appropriate in any message sent downward and an impersonal style is appropriate in any negative message sent upward or downward.

Positive-persuasive messages require for best chance of success a forceful, personal and, if appropriate, colorful style. **Negative-persuasive** messages sent downward need a semi-forceful, impersonal, and colorless style, and negative-persuasive messages sent upward require a passive, impersonal, colorless style.

It is important to note again and again that all of this advice needs to be tempered by common sense and has to be tailored to the needs of a particular situation. But in the vast majority of situations, the style advice given here will prove to be correct.

REVIEW QUESTIONS

1. What is a positive-persuasive situation?
2. What is a negative-persuasive situation?

3. What style should you use in a positive-persuasive message sent upward or downward?

4. What style should you use in a negative-persuasive message sent downward?

5. What style should you use in a negative-persuasive message sent upward?

6. What are perhaps the most challenging of business writing situations? Why are they challenging?

7. What generalizations can you make about negative-persuasive messages and the personal style?

8. What generalizations are you able to make about the risks and benefits of a colorful style?

DISCUSSION QUESTIONS

1. In our sample memos, we have used only the direct, bottom-lined organizational pattern. Which of our three organizational patterns—bottom-lined, circuitous, or semi-circuitous—do you feel would be most appropriate in each persuasive situation?

2. Do you at this point believe that style is more or less important than organization in making persuasive messages more effective? Why do you think so?

STYLE PRINCIPLES
REVIEW LIST

1

Maximize the effect of positive messages by using
a. A forceful rather than a passive style.
b. A personal rather than an impersonal style.
c. A colorful style, if a touch of humor, lighthearted-ness, or poetic imagery is appropriate.

2

For a negative message sent upward, use
a. A passive rather than a forceful style.
b. An impersonal rather than a personal style.
c. A colorless style.

3

For a negative message sent downward, use
a. A semi-forceful style.
b. An impersonal rather than a personal style.
c. A colorless style.

4

For a positive-persuasive message (up or down), use
a. A forceful style.
b. A personal style.
c. A colorful style, if appropriate.

5

For a negative-persuasive message sent downward, use
a. A semi-forceful style to avoid sounding overbearing.
b. An impersonal style.
c. A colorless style.

6

For a negative-persuasive message sent upward, use
a. A passive rather than a forceful style.
b. An impersonal style.
c. A colorless style.

EXERCISES

Exercise 1

Assignment 1

Change the voice of the following sentences—from active to passive or vice versa. And revise each sentence you make active so that it is also forceful. For example, consider this passive voice sentence: "Proxies are solicited by management." Turned into the active voice, it would read, "Management solicits proxies." To make it forceful in style, we would write "Managers, solicit proxies."

1. Such announcements should be made by the Board of Directors.
2. The legal department should first be consulted by any insider so as to keep within restrictions on insider trading.
3. No such deductions are permitted taxpayers by the IRS.
4. The board of Atlantic Research, Inc. told stockholders that it had earned a profit of $1,463,000 in the past fiscal year.
5. Blue Cross and Blue Shield policies cover all our employees.
6. ACME, Inc. has just increased its dividend from $1.00 to $1.25 per share.
7. The market expected the dividend to be the same as last year's, or even lower.
8. Interest rates should be explained in detail by bankers making loans to car buyers.
9. The speaker should be introduced by the past president of the club.
10. An entirely independent sales force ought to be developed by top management.

Assignment 2

Revise each sentence in Assignment 1 so that it is written in a personal style. For example, consider, "Proxies are solicited by management." Written in a personal style, it might read like this: "As management, don't you think it's our right to solicit proxies?"

Assignment 3

Revise each sentence in Assignment 1 so that it is written in a colorful style. For example, take "Proxies are solicited by management." Made more colorful, it might read like this: "All-important proxies are vigorously solicited by aggressive management."

Exercise 2 *hw*

Write memos conveying the following facts in these five styles: forceful, passive, personal, impersonal, and colorful.
Here are the facts:

1. A meeting is scheduled for 1:30 P.M. on September 16, 19——.
2. All staff must attend, with the exception of one person from each department who will cover that department's phone.
3. The speaker will be Eloise O'Reilly.
4. The topic is "New Market Research Techniques."
5. The meeting will last two hours.

Bottom-line this non-sensitive memo and make it as high impact as possible. After you have written these memos, decide which style seems most effective and why.

Write one memo — give direction ∧ style.

Exercise 3 *hw*

Your boss tells you to rewrite the following letter to customers. Each year, your company markets new products. Since some of these new products are technologically complex, your company conducts a training program for customers' sales personnel to acquaint them fully with the workings of the new lines. The draft of the letter you have written needs, your boss feels, to be made more forceful and personal in style. Also, she cannot understand why you don't bottom-line this positive-persuasive message more than you have. Revise this draft according to her suggestions.

Dear _____:

The enclosed questionnaire was designed to give us information so that we can make this year's sales training program most useful to you and your sales force.

Your opinions about past programs and our tentative plans for this year will help us to serve your needs. If you will fill out and return the questionnaire as soon as possible, we can let you and our other dealers know promptly about the changes recommended.

We will greatly appreciate your assistance in this important phase of our training program.

Exercise 4

As B. F. Lopez, you have written the following draft of a memo inviting the office staff, plus the field salespeople, to the annual office Christmas party.

TO: All ABC'ers

FROM: B. F. "Santa" Lopez

SUBJECT: Annual Christmas Party

DATE: December 15, 19——

How can you "Ho! Ho! Ho!" if you forget our annual Christmas party? It's Friday, the 23rd, as soon as the office closes—and it can't close soon enough for me, and, a hundred to one, for you, too!

Come by sled or ski; doesn't matter so long as you come with bells on. We've got a partridge (but no pear tree, some fruit freak ate all the pears!), but we still need you. If you don't want onions and coal in your sock, you better be here!

You show the memo to your boss, Hazel Armstrong, the Office Manager. She chuckles but then worries whether the memo is too colorful. She asks you to revise this positive-persuasive message so as to make it far less colorful. Write this new draft.

Exercise 5

Henry Wadsworth is retiring from your company after forty years of service as a top salesman. Tom Chen, your boss, who is presiding over Wadsworth's retirement dinner, asks you, his assistant, to draft a letter to Henry that Chen can read aloud at Wadsworth's retirement ceremony. He reminds you that Wadsworth has been a top salesman; so the boss wants the letter to have, as he puts it, "punch and zing!" Here is the draft you have written following Tom Chen's instructions:

Dear Henry,

Congratulating you on your well-earned retirement is as completely inadequate as congratulating Jack Nicklaus for his decades of championship-level golf.

Like Nicklaus to duffers, you have been a positive inspiration to all of us in sales. You've shown that championship-level selling can continue year after year—if we'd only try as hard as you.

You have been an absolute inspiration to all of us who go out to the sales wars shoulder to shoulder with you. No one will ever take your place in our sincere devotion, our deepest respect, and our eternal memories.

Everyone in the company joins me in wishing you the ultimate in joy and happiness for many years ahead.

Actually, you think the draft is, in some ways, quite good. But you think it is too colorful to be appropriate; in fact, you'd personally feel embarrassed to read it in public. But you can't be sure whether or not Tom Chen would. So, to play it safe, you do a second version of the letter to

Wadsworth, in which you make it somewhat less colorful but still keep it warm and personal in style.

Assignment 1

Write that revised memo.

Assignment 2

Write a brief memo to your boss critiquing each letter, but leaving the choice of which to use up to him.

CASES

Each of the assignments following Case 1 ("Fine's New Sales Bonus System") in this unit tells you how to handle a situation. Your job is to put into practice what you have learned about writing in various styles. You are also called on to apply what you learned in Unit 5 about effective use of the semi-circuitous organizational pattern.

The second assignment to Case 2, "Alexander Compton's Son," asks you to write a negative message that at first glance seems to be directed external to the company, but actually is not since Compton, Sr. is a retired Allgood employee.

Case 1
Fine's New Sales Bonus System

Part 1

You are assistant to Stephanie Archer, Allgood Products' Sales Manager for Bakery Products, whose division has failed this year to meet its sales quota by 10 percent. Archer believes that her division's failure to meet its quota was not caused by any shortcomings on her part. Nor does she think it a reflection on the true sales abilities of her sales force. Rather, she blames the implementation of a changed bonus system that Cyrus Fine, Vice President of Marketing, introduced at the beginning of the current fiscal year. Fine's system bases its bonus on a salesperson's performance over the immediate past year. If, for example, salespeople exceed their quota by 10 percent in year A, the next year's quota would be set at 110 percent of the prior year's.

Stephanie Archer feels that this is a foolish system, because clever salespeople can play games with it. For example, they could sell only 90 percent of the quota set for them in year A, and as a result receive a reduced quota for the following year which they could then exceed by 25 percent. In this way, they can guarantee themselves a very sizeable bonus every other year. Moreover, on every "off" year they could, in effect, take a mini-vacation.

Fine has asked her to explain in writing why her division has failed to meet its quota. She, of course, must tell Fine the truth as she sees it, but she knows how sensitive he is.

Assignment 1

Write a draft of a memo to Cyrus Fine for Stephanie Archer to sign if she approves of it. Since Fine will not like the predominant message, you have to write a negative-persuasive memo upward, attempting to explain how his system may well have led Archer's salespeople to produce a 10 percent lower sales volume so that their next year's quota would be set lower. Your memo should be semi-circuitous in organization, somewhat neutral in impact, and written in a passive, impersonal, and colorless style. This advice seems in keeping with Fine's probable emotional reaction to your message.

Assignment 2

Cyrus Fine has rejected the argument that Stephanie Archer advances in Assignment 1. Archer feels very strongly that she would like to take her concern about Cyrus Fine's bonus plan all the way to the Executive Committee (composed of all senior executives in Allgood Products, Inc.), if necessary. She asks you to draft a memo to Cyrus Fine that will state frankly, but tactfully, that she still challenges his bonus system and, because of his rejection of her argument, she wants his permission to appeal that rejection to the Executive Committee. Write a draft of a memo from Archer to Fine, asking permission to take her case to the Executive Committee. (Her request is only for the record as Fine actually cannot refuse to allow an appeal to higher authority.)

Naturally, even though Fine will have to give approval to Archer's request, he will not like taking this action. If the Executive Committee also rejects Archer, Fine will resent her "escalation" of a matter that was clearly in his jurisdiction. And, if the Committee agrees with Archer, Fine will suffer serious professional embarrassment. Therefore, your boss, Stephanie Archer, stands to lose either way in terms of her standing with Cyrus Fine. Here is what you decide to do:

1. Write a draft of Archer's memo to Fine as requested, asking for permission to present her case to the Executive Committee. This is even more of a negative-persuasive message up than was the memo in Assignment 1; however, the same advice applies to organization, impact, and style.

2. Write a covering memo to Archer, trying to argue her out of attempting to seek permission to go over her boss' head. Since Archer is angry and will not want to listen to your advice, you once again have a negative-persuasive memo to write and send up. You should build your argument around the fact that Archer has no proof that Fine's bonus system is the villain. The problem may simply be her salespeople's poor performance. You can also argue that one year is not a sufficient amount of time for a proper judging of Fine's system. Your relationship with Archer is good, but you know that she is sensitive about this point.

Fine's New Sales Bonus System

Part 2

You are Carlos Lopez's assistant. Lopez, Sales Manager for Frozen Food Products, has exceeded his quota by over 11 percent. Nevertheless, he, like Stephanie Archer, does not like the bonus system that Cyrus Fine has instituted. He feels strongly that his people could have far exceeded their quota this year if it hadn't been for Fine's system. Lopez has no intentions of asking Fine to take his concerns to the Executive Committee, but he does want to express in writing to Fine similar concerns to those felt by Stephanie Archer. Like Archer, Lopez feels that it is very tempting for salespeople to alternate "vacation" years with years in which they produce far in excess of their quota.

Assignment 1

Lopez asks you to write a draft of a memo to Fine, expressing honestly Lopez's negative opinion of the new bonus plan. You realize that this clearly is a negative message sent upward, since Fine will not at all like to hear that Lopez does not like his plan. The advice you have been given in this text for an internal negative message sent upward is that it should be semi-circuitous in organization, somewhat low in impact, and should use a passive, impersonal, and colorless style. Since Lopez is not requesting anything of Fine, the message is not persuasive in any way. Lopez just wants to put his concerns on the record, politely and not aggressively. Write that memo draft.

Assignment 2

Carlos Lopez decides to write a memo to Stephanie Archer, telling her that he also finds fault with Cyrus Fine's bonus plan, and to try to persuade her not to take her concerns to the Executive Committee. He wants to point out how damaging this could be, especially in a year where her division has not met its quota.

At first, Lopez thought he should not put his opinions in writing but should merely talk with Stephanie Archer. However, he was concerned that his position might be distorted by the emotion of the situation or that he might even be quoted out of context. Therefore, he decided that putting his opinion in writing was actually safer. (Since in Assignment 1, Lopez had already communicated honestly to Fine his concerns about the bonus plan, he need not worry about sharing these concerns with Archer.)

You are asked by Lopez to draft this memo to Archer. You realize that the two messages in this memo are both positive. The message that Lopez agrees with Archer about how the bonus system may be misused by salespeople is positive. The argument that it is not in Archer's best interests to attempt to "escalate" the argument over Fine's head to the Executive Committee is positive-persuasive. For both messages, the text has recommended a direct, bottom-lined organization, as well as a very forceful, personal style displayed in a high-impact fashion. (In this sensitive case a colorful style is probably not appropriate.) Write this draft memo.

Fine's New Sales Bonus System

Part 3

Cyrus Fine is really upset with Stephanie Archer. He believes that she is trying to blame his system for what was the fault of her people. He was especially annoyed, after learning through the grapevine, that Archer had seriously considered asking to go over his head to take her case to the Executive Committee. He learned (not from Carlos Lopez) that Lopez had talked her out of doing so. Fine has decided that it is necessary to reprimand Archer in writing for the record.

Assignment

As Cyrus Fine's assistant, you are asked to write a memo for Fine's signature, to be sent to Archer, pointing out that her division has done the poorest of all three divisions and that all three have operated under the new bonus system. Specifically, Frozen Foods, under Carlos Lopez, exceeded its quota by more than 11 percent. Instant Foods, under Linda McNally, came in just at quota. Therefore, he wants Archer to be told to face up to her responsibility and to urge her salespeople on to a better performance rather than continuing to use his new bonus system as a convenient scapegoat for her group's poor performance.

You realize that this is a negative message sent downward. The text has advised that it be bottom-lined in organization, of average impact, and written in a somewhat forceful, impersonal, and colorless style. Write that draft memo.

Fine's New Sales Bonus System

Part 4

Cyrus Fine receives Carlos Lopez's memo and decides to put his response to Lopez in writing. His memo will state that he refuses to change the bonus system, but that he wants the memo to reflect the fact that Fine is very pleased with Lopez's efforts and wants him and his people to keep up the good work.

Assignment

You realize that this memo contains two quite different messages. One—refusing to change the new bonus system—will be negative to Lopez. The second, complimenting Lopez's efforts, will be positively received. You must decide which message should come first, and then follow the text's advice about how to write each.

Naturally, you decide to put the positive message first. You bottom-line the good news in a high-impact, forceful, personal fashion. When you begin to deliver the negative message, you also bottom-line the paragraph, but you shift to a somewhat forceful, impersonal, and colorless style. For the ending, you should hark back to the positive message, once again thanking Lopez.

Write that draft memo.

Case 2
Alexander Compton's Son

Read

Alexander Compton, a retired Allgood executive who worked for the company for more than thirty years, wrote the letter on page 333 to Maxwell Allgood, who sent it down to Mary Lou Higgins with a note saying, "Check this out for me, will you, Mary Lou? Alex Compton, we both know, is an old friend and deserves a sensitive reply. By the way, did his boy get fair treatment?"

You are currently functioning as staff assistant to Mary Lou Higgins. "What's your first impression about this situation?" Higgins asks you.

"Well," you respond, "Mr. Compton did work for Allgood for over thirty years. He deserves respect. Why shouldn't the son of a retired Allgood employee get some sort of special consideration?"

"What makes you think he didn't?"

"Well, the son, Carl, has a 3.6 average from State University, and he was an industrial management major. I don't know why he wouldn't qualify for the training program."

"Well," says Higgins, "you've got a lot to learn about the recruitment process. In the old days, we did have a system of giving preferential hiring to the sons of former employees. But you notice, I said *sons*. In the old days at Allgood, you wouldn't have seen a woman in a Vice Presidential position. I might have been working as a secretary, but you wouldn't have seen me here in this executive office.

"Also, as you well know, the laws in the U.S. make it illegal to give preferential treatment to any one group of citizens, even sons—or daughters—of old employees.

"So, one of the prices we pay for this social progress is that nice old men like Mr. Compton get their feelings hurt when their children simply don't stack up against the general competition.

"When I was younger, I used to get angry about letters like this. I wanted someone to write back some sort of 'How *dare* you demand special treatment for your son! This is America! This is a land of equal opportunity, and we are truly an equal opportunity employer!' But that's no good. Mr. Compton deserves better. I remember him well, a nice kindly old man, and I am sure he is hurt because his son was turned down.

"Anyway," Higgins concludes, "go check this out for me, will you?"

You first go to the Central Employment Office, which is located outside the chain-link fence surrounding the factory area and ask to see Emily Roswell, the Employment Manager. She is glad to help. She gets out Carl Compton's file and expresses willingness to go over it with you. She tells you that Compton does indeed appear on the surface to be a viable candidate. His grades and extracurricular activities are fine. In fact, he was brought in for an interview with regular recruiters for Allgood Products and eventually was even interviewed by both Cyrus Fine and Frank Finnegan.

She shows you their written evaluations of Carl. Both agreed that something about Carl's manner affected them negatively. He seemed to both of them to be "cocky," to be assuming that he already had the job simply because his father had worked for Allgood for so long. During the interview, Carl Compton had intimated that his father would be writing to Maxwell Allgood sometime in the near future. In short, both agreed that he looked like a potential source of trouble and both recommended against hiring him into the management training program.

1812 Oak Lane
Lancaster, PA 17601

January 26, 19——

Mr. Maxwell Allgood
Chairman and Chief Executive Officer
Allgood Products, Inc.
1 Communications Circle
Kansas City, MO 64142

Dear Max:

Can you help me? My son Carl will be graduating next month from
State University where he obtained a 3.6 average (out of 4.0) while completing work for a degree in business administration. Because of our
family's long association with Allgood Products, Carl specifically set out
to do most of his class work in courses related to industrial management. He not only handled his scholastic work in a highly satisfactory
manner, but he also distinguished himself in a variety of important
campus activities. We were especially proud that in several of those extracurricular activities Carl held elective office—which certainly attests
to his peers' respect for him.

In my own view, he is well qualified to be considered for Allgood's management training program. Not only has he taken the appropriate college courses, in addition he has taken the initiative to become familiar
with the current product lines of Allgood and your major competitors.
Further, he has visited many of the retail stores carrying Allgood products in our part of the state and talked with them about customer acceptance of the product.

Today, he received a letter from your Central Employment Office stating
that because of the limited number of openings and the intense competition for those that do exist, he is not a likely candidate for your management training program.

I still remember with considerable pride your generous comments concerning my own contributions to Allgood when you were the speaker at
my retirement banquet.

Your help in this matter will certainly be appreciated.

Sincerely,

Alexander Compton

Alexander Compton

Assignment 1

Mary Lou Higgins asks you to write a report of your findings to Maxwell Allgood, for her signature. Remember, Allgood is very busy and will want your findings to be presented in a bottom-lined, high-impact fashion.

Assignment 2

Higgins asks that you write a draft of a letter politely denying Alexander Compton's request. The letter is to be signed by Maxwell Allgood.

"How much of the true facts do you think Mr. Allgood would want to tell Mr. Compton?" you ask.

"Well," answers Higgins, "I know that Mr. Allgood would want to tell the truth, but I imagine that he would want only to tell Mr. Compton anything that would be beneficial to getting the young man a job somewhere else. Carl Compton might behave quite differently when applying for a job in a company where his father had worked. I do know that Mr. Allgood certainly would not want to point out Mr. Fine and Mr. Finnegan to Compton as the ones who actually rejected Carl. Nor would he want to insult Carl in a letter to his father. Tell as many of the facts as are helpful. Be polite, but make it clear that this decision is final. Don't open the door for a second interview."

Write that draft letter.

REFERENCES

Bracher, P. (1987). Process, pedagogy, and business writing. *The Journal of Business Communication, 24,* 43–50.

Ewing, D. W. (1974). The protean communicator. *Management Review, 63,* 13–23.

Fielden, J. S. (1982). "What do you mean you don't like my style?" *Harvard Business Review, 60,* 128–138.

Gilsdorf, J. W. (1986). Executives' and academics' perceptions of the need for instruction in written persuasion. *The Journal of Business Communication, 23,* 55–68.

Harris, J. A. (1986). MBA: What ever happened to the class of '76. *Successful Executive* (Canada), *1,* 34–40.

Kallendorf, C. and Kallendorf, C. (1985). The figures of speech, ethos, and Aristotle: Notes toward a rhetoric of business communication. *The Journal of Business Communication, 22,* 35–50.

Ley, P. S. (1974). Style in analytical writing. *Journal of Commercial Bank Lending, 56,* 61–66.

Limaye, M. (1983). The syntax of persuasion: Two business letters of request. *The Journal of Business Communication, 20,* 17–30.

Locker, K. (1982). Theoretical justifications for using reader benefits. *The Journal of Business Communication, 19,* 51–65.

Matthews, D. (1985). Write for results, not style. *Communication World, 2,* 26–27.

Mendelson, M. (1987). Business prose and the nature of the plain style. *The Journal of Business Communication, 24,* 3–18.

Mendleson, J., Golen, S., and Adams, P. (1986). Humor in managerial communication. *Industrial Management and Data Systems* (UK), 5–8.

Mintz, H. K. (1972). Business writing styles for the 70s. *Business Horizons, 15,* 83–87.

Motes, W. H., Fielden, J. S., and Dulek, R. E. (1987). Survey cover letter works if you write it right. *Marketing News, 21,* 26–27.

Murphy, G. D. and Cherry, C. L. (1984). Solve business writing problems—one, two, three. *Training and Development Journal, 38,* 100–101.

Ozaki, S. (1975). Business English from a human point of view. *The Journal of Business Communication, 12,* 27–31.

Perelman, C. (1982). *The realm of rhetoric,* trans. Kluback, W., Notre Dame: University of Notre Dame Press.

Richards, P. (1979). The material fallacy . . . pitfall to persuasion. *Manage, 31,* 18–21.

Selzer, J. (1983). Teaching rhetorical principles in business writing, in *Teaching business writing,* ed. Halpern, J. Urbana, IL: American Business Communication Association, 6–21.

Smeltzer, L. R. (1981). The relationship between writing style and leadership style. *The Journal of Business Communication, 18,* 23–32.

Smeltzer, L. R. and Werbel, J. D. (1986). Gender differences in managerial communication: Fact or folk-linguistics? *The Journal of Business Communication, 23,* 41–50.

Suchan, J. and Dulek, R. E. (1986). An empirical assessment of style. *The Journal of Business Communication, 23,* 57–66.

Whitburn, M. (1976). Personality in scientific and technical writing. *The Journal of Technical Writing, 6,* 299–306.

Williams, J. (1981). *Style: Ten lessons in clarity and grace.* Glenview, IL: Scott Foresman.

Wimsatt, W. (1967). Style as meaning, in *Essays on the language of literature,* eds. Chatman, S. and Levine, S. Boston: Houghton Mifflin.

Wisdom, J. C. (1987). Some suggestions for preparing successful loan proposals. *Practical Accountant, 20,* 42–43.

Unit 7

STYLE, ORGANIZATION, IMPACT, AND THE STRATEGY WHEEL

INTRA-TEXT MEMORANDUM

TO: Readers

FROM: Authors

SUBJECT: Unit 7

This unit brings together the multiple elements of the communication system that we have discussed separately. It shows how **organization, impact,** and **style** interact to influence how a reader will react to various messages in different situations.

You may remember that in Unit 1 we stated our intention of temporarily treating organization, impact, and style as if they were separate entities, even though they actually interrelate in reality. Now we can abandon the unreal notion that organization, impact, and style operate independently and study how they influence and affect one another.

Chapter 18 provides insights into the remarkable ways organization and impact influence each other. The chapter demonstrates how certain styles operate so as to increase or decrease the effect of certain organizational patterns on readers.

Chapter 19 focuses on the Strategy Wheel and describes how it has been put together and how best to use it. The Strategy Wheel gives advice about the appropriate organizational patterns, styles, and levels of impact suitable to various messages. The Strategy Wheel serves as a highly useful memory tool by summarizing the advice about which types of organizational pattern, style, and impact suit which message type. It will help you make intelligent and informed decisions about how best to handle even the most difficult of communication situations.

Chapter 18

THE INTERACTION OF STYLE AND ORGANIZATION

OBJECTIVES

This chapter will help you to

•

Understand better how style and organization interact synergistically

•

Learn how to increase or decrease a message's effect on a reader by the careful "engineering" of style and organization

Style and organization do not exist independently of each other. Just the reverse is true. They interact extensively. In business situations, you have to not only take this interaction into account, but you must be able to use it to achieve your goals.

STYLE AND ORGANIZATION

In our discussion of the interaction of organization and style, we will deal only with the two basic organizational patterns—**bottom-line** and **circuitous.** Since the semi-circuitous and circuitous patterns are affected the same way by style, there is no need to discuss them separately.

Style and a Bottom-Line Organization

As Figure 18.1 shows, the three basic style choices— between **forceful** and **passive,** between **personal** and **impersonal,** and between **colorful** and **colorless**—can be used either to increase or to decrease the effect an organizational pattern exerts on a reader.

In Figure 18.1, the small style arrows pointing in the same direction as the large organization arrow show that a direct, bottom-lined organization plus a forceful, personal, or even a colorful style will work together to produce an effect greater than that produced by the sum of the effects

Style can increase or decrease the effect of organization on a reader.

Forceful, personal, and colorful styles increase the effect of bottom-line organization.

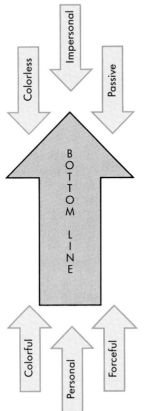

Using a passive, impersonal, or colorless style with a bottom-lined, direct organizational pattern softens the impact that pattern has on a reader.

Styles that decrease the effect of a bottom-lined message.

Using a forceful, personal, or colorful style with a bottom-lined, direct organizational pattern increases the impact that pattern has on a reader.

Styles that increase the effect of a bottom-lined message.

FIGURE 18.1
How style and organizational pattern interact to increase or decrease a bottom-lined message's effect on a reader.

of each. (The word for this interaction is *synergism;* organization and style are working synergistically in their combined effects on a reader because the effect of the whole is greater than the sum of its parts.) Figure 18.1 also shows the reverse effect when the passive, impersonal, and colorless styles are used to counteract the effect of a bottom-line organization.

Demonstration of Interaction

Here is a demonstration of what we have just stated. Suppose you have the pleasant task of informing a subordinate named Joan Myers that she is about to be promoted to Assistant Personnel Manager for a division. Since this message is positive, it should follow a bottom-line organization and have a forceful, personal style, as the following memo does:

Version A. Bottom-Lined, Forceful, and Personal

TO: Joan Myers

FROM: "Boss"

DATE: February 1, 19——

Congratulations! You are to be promoted to Assistant Personnel Manager for Division One effective February 15.

Keep up the good work!

Clearly, the forceful, personal style and the direct organizational pattern complement each other and give this positive message great strength, clarity, and personal warmth. The way the promotion is announced could not possibly seem begrudging or halfhearted to the reader.

Figure 18.1 also demonstrates that organization and style can be used to counteract, or blunt, each other's effects on the reader. It shows that a passive, impersonal style can be used to counteract and decrease the effect of a directly organized message. Version B of our memo to Myers demonstrates what happens when an impersonal, passive style is used in conjunction with a bottom-lined or direct organizational pattern:

Version B. Bottom-Lined, Passive, and Impersonal

TO: Joan Myers

FROM: "Boss"

DATE: February 1, 19——

A promotion to Assistant Personnel Manager, effective February 15, has been approved.

It is anticipated that past good work will be continued.

If you were Joan Myers, how would you react to this second version? Wouldn't you be hurt by the seeming halfheartedness, even coldness, of this memo? It is not at all clear that the writer is personally happy about Joan's promotion. The use of the passive has buried the subject and may even suggest that the writer wishes someone else had received Myers's promotion.

Style and a Circuitous Organization

Figure 18.2 illustrates what happens when various styles interrelate with a circuitous organizational pattern. It also shows that use of a forceful, personal, or colorful style will work toward counteracting the effect of a circuitous organizational pattern. Version C of the memo demonstrates this interaction by presenting the same good news to Joan Myers in a circuitous organizational pattern, but using the same forceful, personal style found in Version A:

Forceful, personal, and colorful styles will offset the blandness of circuitous organization.

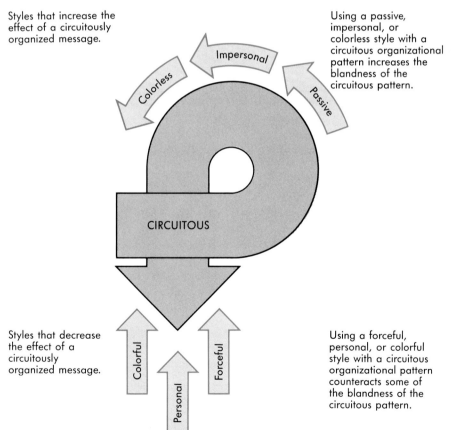

Styles that increase the effect of a circuitously organized message.

Using a passive, impersonal, or colorless style with a circuitous organizational pattern increases the blandness of the circuitous pattern.

Styles that decrease the effect of a circuitously organized message.

Using a forceful, personal, or colorful style with a circuitous organizational pattern counteracts some of the blandness of the circuitous pattern.

FIGURE 18.2

How style and organizational pattern interact to increase or decrease a circuitously organized message's effect on a reader.

Version C. Circuitous, Forceful, and Personal

TO: Joan Myers

FROM: "Boss"

DATE: February 1, 19— —

We have thoroughly screened all internal personnel whose qualifications and experience serve to make them candidates for the position of Assistant Personnel Manager. There were many outstanding candidates.

Your qualifications are excellent and your experience more than sufficient. I assure you that every factor in your favor was considered.

For these reasons, I am delighted to inform you that you are to be promoted to Assistant Personnel Manager for Division One, effective February 15. Congratulations!

Passive, impersonal, and colorless styles will add to the blandness of circuitous organization.

What do you think Myers's reaction would be to this version? Won't the delay in telling the good news negatively affect the way she will react? As you see, the circuitous organizational pattern counteracts, and even overwhelms, the forceful, personal style and leads Myers to anticipate that bad news instead of good will be presented in the third paragraph.

Finally, as Figure 18.2 also demonstrates, a circuitous organizational pattern plus a passive, impersonal style can be used to create a message that is difficult to read and utterly unsuited to a positive message. Version D of the memo demonstrates what happens when a circuitous pattern and a passive, impersonal style are at work together:

Version D. Circuitous, Passive, and Impersonal

TO: Joan Myers

FROM: "Boss"

DATE: February 1, 19— —

All internal personnel whose qualifications and experience serve to make them candidates for the position of Assistant Personnel Manager have been thoroughly screened. Many outstanding candidates were evaluated.

It is necessary to report that the qualifications and experience presented by you were more than sufficient. Every factor that could be deemed favorable was considered.

For these reasons, your promotion to Assistant Personnel Manager for Division One, effective February 15, has been approved.

This example clearly offers another demonstration of the interaction of organizational pattern and style. In such a positive situation, the use of a circuitous organizational pattern—combined with a passive, impersonal style—produces a communication that is either ludicrous, insulting, or both.

Style, Organization, and Job Rejection Letters

Let's consider another situation illustrating that style and organization have an effect on tone—that is, on the reader's reaction to what is written. This time, a circuitous organizational pattern and a passive, impersonal style work together to provide a useful, rather than a ludicrous, example. Here is a form letter typical of those used by large companies to reject college graduates who interviewed for jobs. As you will see, this form letter is not sufficiently sensitive to the feelings of the rejected applicant.

> Ms. Rebecca Davis
> 123 Main Street
> Anytown, USA 12345
>
>
> Dear Ms. Davis:
>
> Thank you for taking the time to interview with our recruiter on your campus.
>
> We have processed your application. Your qualifications, unfortunately, were not equal to those of other applicants.
>
> Therefore, we can offer you no encouragement about possible employment with ABCD.
>
> Thank you again for considering our company.
>
> > Sincerely,

Despite the brevity of this negative message sent downward, we can see that the writer has combined a circuitous organization with a forceful, personal style. We could analyze this letter as follows:

- The first sentence-paragraph says something nice but does not contain the predominant idea of the communication, which is the candidate's rejection.
- The brevity of the first paragraph does not adequately buffer the twin blows to the reader's ego that follow immediately.
- "We have *processed* your application" imparts a poor tone. Davis may picture her application going through a machine, like a sausage. Then she is told that her qualifications were not equal to those of others. This is gratuitously insulting. The woman asked for a job, not for a disparagement of her qualifications.
- The third paragraph tells her no.

- The last paragraph is a feeble attempt to be civil, but amounts only to a rubber-stamp expression meaning nothing.

Why might Davis react unfavorably to this letter? Why wouldn't she like its tone? The letter follows the time-honored "bury the negative," circuitous organizational pattern, but it fails because the forceful style of writing, with its high-impact, active voice sentences, deals powerful psychological blows to the reader. Also, the personal style imparts, as is common in negative messages, a personal rejection by "us" of "you."

A better letter would have resulted if a passive style more suited to the letter's negative content had been used. This way, the predominant negative message would have been delivered in as impersonal a style as possible. The letter would also have been improved if the circuitous organizational pattern had been made even more circuitous—by lengthening the letter so as to give Davis the impression that time had been spent considering her application. See what you think of this longer version:

Ms. Rebecca Davis
123 Main Street
Anytown, U.S.A. 12345

Dear Ms. Davis:

The time you spent interviewing with us was much appreciated. Through such an in-depth interview, an opportunity to learn more about your career goals and interests was obtained.

The application you submitted has been reviewed with great interest, as were, of course, the applications of the many other fine graduates who, like you, interviewed with ABCD.

As was communicated during the interview, few openings are available at this time. And for each of these openings, there are an overwhelming number of applicants. Therefore, many strong candidates such as yourself cannot be encouraged.

We thank you, however, for giving us the chance to talk with you. And we wish you success in your future career.

Sincerely,

Notice how this letter uses a passive, but not completely impersonal style through the first two buffering paragraphs. When it gets to the actual rejection (which is expressed in a mildly flattering way), it becomes even more impersonal in style. Notice, then, how the style shifts immediately to a very personal style for the last paragraph. Naturally, nothing the company tells Davis (other than "yes") will please her. But the second version should (a) hurt her less than the first version and (b) represent the company better if Davis shows the letter to her friends or family (as she well might).

SUMMARY

Although up to this chapter we had treated **organization** and **style** as if they were self-contained entities independent of each other, we have now shown how each message element exerts influence on the other. Certain styles reinforce and increase the effect of certain organizational patterns. Likewise, certain styles counteract and lower the effect of certain organizational patterns.

An awareness of how these factors influence each other enables you to engineer the effect of any business message you choose to send. All of these interactions are summarized in the Strategy Wheel, which is taken up in Chapter 19.

REVIEW QUESTIONS

1. What effect does a forceful, personal, colorful style have on a bottom-lined message?

2. What effect does a passive, impersonal, colorless style have on a bottom-lined message?

3. What effect does a forceful, personal, colorful style have on a circuitously organized message?

4. What effect does a passive, impersonal, colorless style have on a circuitously organized message?

DISCUSSION QUESTIONS

1. Where does the predominant message have to appear when a bottom-line organization is used? How can style be used to alleviate the effect of that message if it is negative?

2. In a circuitously organized message, a negative message is expressed late in the document and may be written in a passive, impersonal, colorless style. Does this mean that other probably more positive messages earlier in the letter must be organized the same way and written in the same style as that recommended for the predominant message? Why or why not?

Chapter 19

THE STRATEGY WHEEL

OBJECTIVES

This chapter will help you to

•

Learn how the Strategy Wheel should
be used

•

Focus on the different strategies required for
external negative and negative-persuasive
messages sent upward

•

Make writing tasks easier and safer through
upgrading of messages

•

Realize why the Strategy Wheel's advice will
seem inappropriate if you have not changed
the setting after upgrading

This text has covered in depth the individual choices that you as a successful business writer must make in order to produce a communication that meets the goal of all business writing—that of getting a job done with minimal negative results.

To help you remember all these choices, we have developed the Strategy Wheel (found at the back of the text) to help you answer the following questions:

1. What message have I decided to send? Is it sensitive or not?
2. Is the message being sent internally or externally?
3. What is the recipient's power position relative to mine?
4. Which organizational pattern is most appropriate to the message I am sending?
5. What style best suits the message (or messages) contained in my communication?
6. What level of impact is appropriate for that message (or messages)?

The Strategy Wheel does not include answers to all of the questions shown (on the following pages) in Figure 19.1, the Flow Chart of our system. It was a practical impossibility to have the Wheel cover these two additional questions:

1. What is my relationship with the reader?
2. How risky is it to send this proposed message?

Answers to these questions are so subjective, and, hence, so varied situation by situation, that any attempt to offer specific answers proved impossible.

Nevertheless, the Strategy Wheel will help you decide upon the most *probably* successful choice of style, organization, and impact for each message type. Please notice that we say "probably," for there are few, if any, guarantees that can be made about a subject as complex as communication. This is especially true of sensitive situations where you don't know your reader, or where that reader's emotions are unpredictable.

The Strategy Wheel summarizes advice.

CORRECT MESSAGE SELECTION IS THE KEY

We will begin our discussion of effective use of the Strategy Wheel with our choice of message type. This is, of course, the key decision you must make. There is a saying about computers: "Put garbage in and you get garbage out." The same is true about the Strategy Wheel. You have to identify the message type correctly—determining whether the **predominant message** is negative, positive, persuasive (negative or positive), or non-sensitive. You also have to know the direction in which the message is going—up or down. Only then will the open windows beneath the message category you have chosen give sensible advice about organization, style, and impact.

You must dial the right message choice. The Strategy Wheel cannot think for you.

If you decide it is too dangerous to send the proposed message, you must return to START and go through the process again to determine what message can be sent.

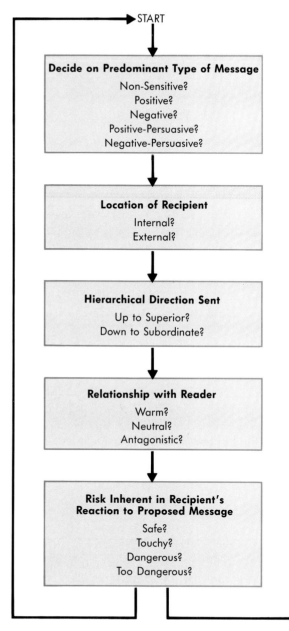

START

Decide on Predominant Type of Message
Non-Sensitive?
Positive?
Negative?
Positive-Persuasive?
Negative-Persuasive?

Location of Recipient
Internal?
External?

Hierarchical Direction Sent
Up to Superior?
Down to Subordinate?

Relationship with Reader
Warm?
Neutral?
Antagonistic?

Risk Inherent in Recipient's Reaction to Proposed Message
Safe?
Touchy?
Dangerous?
Too Dangerous?

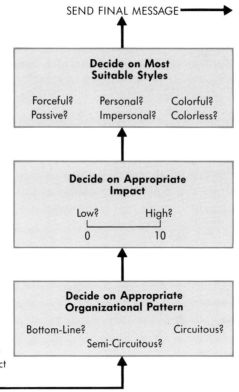

SEND FINAL MESSAGE ⟶

**Decide on Most
Suitable Styles**

Forceful?   Personal?   Colorful?
Passive?   Impersonal?   Colorless?

**Decide on Appropriate
Impact**

Low?   High?
├──────────────┤
0   10

**Decide on Appropriate
Organizational Pattern**

Bottom-Line?   Circuitous?
              Semi-Circuitous?

Once you have decided on the appropriate message, you can proceed to make choices of organization, impact, and style best suited to producing the desired effect on the recipient.

This caution is clearly depicted in the Flow Chart. If a predominant message seems, upon reflection, to be too risky, or just too foolish, to send, then you must double back and rethink your message choice.

A specific example proves this point most effectively. Suppose you must refuse a request made by an important customer. Obviously, the bottom-line message is "no," but you are not foolish enough to make that negative message the sole message you would send. You have learned to keep in mind always that a letter, memo, or report—especially a long one—will probably contain several messages. But only one is the predominant message, the message that conveys the bottom line of the communication. So, because the bottom-line message here is negative and the message is to be sent externally, the Strategy Wheel tells you to be circuitous. This method allows you to begin and end your letter with some neutral, or, if possible, pleasant messages, such as, "We really appreciated hearing from you about . . . ," or, "Please know that we would be most happy to meet with you and to discuss ways that we could be of service to you."

Thus, the predominant message, the "no," can be sandwiched between two or more positive messages. Naturally, these pleasant messages should be written in the style recommended for positive, or at least non-sensitive messages, and not in the style recommended for negative messages. The recommendation of the Strategy Wheel applies to the *predominant* message. It doesn't matter whether it takes you a single sentence or several paragraphs to present that predominant message. But following the Wheel's advice while writing that sentence, or those paragraphs, will greatly increase your chances of stating the negative predominant message in the most palatable fashion to the reader.

A predominant negative message can be buffered by surrounding it with more positive messages.

The predominant message sometimes is only one sentence long.

Range of Impact

Chapter 18 dealt with the interaction of style and organization. But, as we learned earlier in Unit 4, impact also affects how a reader will react to a message. Moreover, impact also interacts with style and organization to produce a further synergistic effect.

As a convenient way to make recommendations about impact on the Strategy Wheel, we have used numbers on a scale of 1 to 10 to signify the level of impact that is recommended. Level 1 refers to extremely low impact, an almost unreadable combination of Latinate words, passive, convoluted sentences, and a complete absence of white space. Level 10 refers to highly readable prose that uses familiar words, short, active voice sentences, merciful paragraphing, and appropriate itemization to afford white space.

Impact is rated 1 to 10 on the Strategy Wheel.

APPLYING THE STRATEGY WHEEL IN DIFFICULT SITUATIONS

To test the effectiveness of the Strategy Wheel's advice, let's first examine its advice in the context of one of the more difficult writing situations we described—negative messages sent up. And let's examine the Wheel's advice about how to handle these messages when they are sent internally and externally. Here is the hypothetical case situation we will use.

Hunter-Creek, Inc. Case

Your firm, the ABCD Corporation, has been doing extensive business with a local supplier, Hunter-Creek, Inc. As a staff assistant to Harold Allen, the Vice President for Management Information Services, you have been given the assignment of investigating whether Hunter-Creek has been living up to its contractual arrangements with your company. What Harold Allen is concerned about is a report received last May that Hunter-Creek, Inc. was licensing software at lower rates to other firms. Allen had these rumors substantiated through the efforts of a study team that reported to him in July. The report revealed that one of ABCD's primary competitors, the XYZ Company, and some others were receiving these lower software rates.

In reading the contract, you find that Hunter-Creek has indeed been living up to the contract. Therefore, the conclusion you reach is that Allen simply negotiated an uneconomical contract with Hunter-Creek.

What complicates matters is that you learn that Harold Allen will be especially embarrassed by your findings because it was he who negotiated the contract originally, and also because he and Chris Miller, the President of Hunter-Creek, are old friends.

In this situation, you clearly have to write an internal negative message up to Harold Allen, a Vice President and your boss. The bad news is that he has negotiated a very poor contract. This message is made even more negative by the fact that Allen may well have been taken advantage of by Miller, an old friend, a severe embarrassment in itself.

The Strategy Wheel's advice about internal negative messages up is that they should be organized semi-circuitously. This clearly is better than hitting Allen with a blunt announcement saying, "The purpose of this memo is to report that ABCD's contract with Hunter-Creek, which you negotiated, is on terms unfavorable to our interests."

The Strategy Wheel also recommends that the styles used should be passive, impersonal, and colorless. This style advice seems sound, because there is always a risk in being too forceful with one's superior. And an impersonal style seems appropriate in a situation like this, where the superior probably won't like at all the fact that you know that he personally is at fault. As far as impact goes, the Strategy Wheel recommends a level of 4. It is set at 4, rather than lower, because you are writing to your boss, someone you work with daily. Writing him a memo with an impact lower than 4 would indicate that you were deliberately making the memo very hard to read. Here is the memo that might result from the advice we have just given.

TO: Harold Allen

FROM: "You, Staff Assistant"

SUBJECT: Hunter-Creek, Inc. Contract Provisions

DATE: August 6, 19———

A detailed examination of the Hunter-Creek, Inc. contract was recently completed. This memo outlines, in chronological order, the steps taken in our analysis. Then, this memo presents the conclusion arrived at after analysis.

Last May, it was learned that Hunter-Creek, Inc. might be licensing software at varying rates to different firms. Furthermore, it was rumored that ABCD's most recent contract with Hunter-Creek might not be at one of these more favorable rates. To substantiate this possibility, a study team was formed and proceeded to look into this situation. On July 14, it was documented that a primary competitor, XYZ, Inc. (among others) was receiving advantageous discounts.

A close examination of the wording of our contract, however, revealed that Hunter-Creek is not in violation. Our contract does not provide for receipt of discounts similar to those being received by our competition.

You will notice that this memo is organized semi-circuitously. The first paragraph has a contract sentence that states where the conclusion is, but the negative conclusion itself has not been put in the first paragraph.

You will also notice that stylistically the entire memo, even the first two paragraphs that merely convey the facts of the situation, is written in a passive, impersonal style. The reason for this choice is that these paragraphs are not just conveying information; they are really conveying sensitive, soon to be disclosed as negative, information to Allen. Therefore, these styles are used to soften the effect of the presentation of this information. As far as impact is concerned, the memo would rate at about the level of 4 recommended by the Strategy Wheel. The sentences are not overly long, and the memo is divided into three paragraphs. However, white space is kept to a minimum, and there is no listing of unpleasant facts to leap off the page and negatively effect the reader. Moreover, the avoidance of headings serves to help keep Allen's eyes from leaping to the conclusion immediately.

External Messages Are Different

Now let's consider a strategy for an external negative message sent up. Assume that in the Hunter-Creek case, Harold Allen, the Vice President of Management Information Systems for your company, ABCD Corporation, has read your memo that gave him the unpleasant facts about the bad contract he negotiated. Now he has asked you to prepare a draft of a letter to Hunter-Creek's President, arguing persuasively for the renegotiation of the contract based on the facts that you have uncovered.

If he likes the draft of the letter, Allen will send it out over his signature. You turn to the Strategy Wheel for advice. You decide that you are going to write an external negative-persuasive message sent up. (The direction is up because Hunter-Creek has a *bona fide* contract; therefore, ABCD is in the begging position.)

The organizational pattern recommended (as Chapter 13 explained) is circuitous. This makes sense in this instance, since there is every reason for Miller, the President of Hunter-Creek, to expect Allen to live up to the contract. A great deal of persuasion will have to be undertaken before the request for contract renegotiation can be made. Obviously, then, a circuitous organization must be used. A semi-circuitous organizational pattern in this case would not be useful because the reader might very well go directly to the bottom-line request. And remember, this request asks him to do what he does not want to, nor is legally required to do. A semi-circuitous organization would, therefore, give the reader too much of a chance to raise defenses before you have had the opportunity of presenting your argument.

The Strategy Wheel recognizes that the circuitous pattern will in itself significantly lower the effect on the reader. Thus, for the letter to have any chance whatsoever of convincing, it will have to be made more persuasive through a careful selection of style and impact. The Wheel recommends that you write forcefully, personally, and, if appropriate in a given situation, even colorfully. It also recommends that you present the letter in as high a level of impact as appropriate to this situation. Here is how the letter might appear if you followed the Wheel's advice.

ABCD CORPORATION
6300 Wesley Terrace, Des Plaines, IL 60018

An example of an external negative-persuasive message sent up.

August 27, 19— —

Mr. Chris Miller
President
Hunter-Creek Incorporated
7214 Central Avenue
Nashville, TN 37205

Dear Chris:

As you know, our companies have enjoyed doing business with each other for the past eight years. During that time, we have been pleased with the software products you have supplied us with. We have also been satisfied with their price and with the service you have offered. We hope that our companies will continue doing business for many years in the future.

There is, however, a matter that I need to discuss with you. As long ago as last May, we learned of the possibility that Hunter-Creek, Inc. might be licensing software at varying rates to different firms. We were disturbed by the possibility that ABCD's most recent contract with Hunter-Creek may not be at one of the more favorable rates. Naturally, we found this hard to believe; hence, a study team was formed to look into the situation.

It was documented on July 14, that one of our primary competitors, XYZ, Inc., as well as others, were receiving advantageous discounts. We feel sure that this has occurred without your knowledge. We also feel sure that you will want to consider the matter of a renegotiation of our contract.

I look forward to hearing from you as soon as you have verified the facts of this situation.

Sincerely,

Harold Allen

Harold Allen
Vice President
Management Information
Services

External Negative Messages Up

The other message that is treated differently externally than internally is the negative message sent up.

The advice given by the Strategy Wheel for an external negative message sent up differs from its internal counterpart in that it contains the advice given in Chapter 13, and tells you to be circuitous, rather than semi-circuitous. In an external letter, there is not the same fear of appearing manipulative or evasive as there is when you are writing to a superior you work with daily over a long period.

Suppose you now are Chris Miller, the President of Hunter-Creek, Inc., and an old friend of Harold Allen. You have received his letter asking for a renegotiation of the contract. You decide to tell Allen "no." Since ABCD is an important customer of Hunter-Creek's, the negative message is being sent up. Here is how Miller's letter to Allen might appear.

HUNTER-CREEK, INCORPORATED
7214 Central Avenue, Nashville, TN 37205

January 10, 19— —

Mr. Harold Allen
Vice President
Management Information Services
ABCD Corporation
6300 Wesley Terrace
Des Plaines, IL 60018

Dear Harold:

Your letter requesting renegotiation of our contract has been given most serious consideration by our legal department. Special attention was paid to determining the process by which other companies, including some of your competitors, received contracts entitling them to favorable discounts.

Here is what has been determined. Shortly after the contractual relationship between our companies was signed, economic pressures by our competitors forced us to offer special incentives to induce potential customers to deal with us rather than with our competition. It is unfortunate, in retrospect, that the timing of your contract preceded the period when such discounts were available. It is also unfortunate that because of legal constraints it will be impossible to enter into renegotiations of contracts, not only with ABCD Corporation but with all other companies who signed contracts prior to the period when special discounts were being offered.

Please know that I sincerely regret that this accident of timing puts your company at a temporary disadvantage. Know also that everything possible will be done to offer the best possible service to ABCD and to further our mutually advantageous relationship.

Sincerely,

Chris Miller

Chris Miller

As you see, Miller's letter is indeed circuitously organized and has employed a passive, impersonal, colorless style and a very low level of impact.

A PRACTICAL WARNING ABOUT THE STRATEGY WHEEL

You must remember that the Strategy Wheel is a primitive computer. Like all computers, it cannot think. If you misjudge the type of message that you think best fits a situation, and consequently dial the Wheel to that wrong message type, the advice given will not be appropriate to the actual message situation at hand. Let's illustrate this warning by taking up a difficult persuasive message case.

Hallberg Associates, Inc. Case

Shirley Hallberg, managing partner of Hallberg Associates, the most successful advertising company in town, and an important customer, complains bitterly about the fact that charges for servicing her electronic office equipment keep going up. But here is the reason. Her machines are quite out of date, and few other customers still use such antiquated equipment. Hence, the costs to your company of carrying parts, training repair people in how to repair the obsolete equipment, and the like, have to be passed on to an ever-smaller pool of customers. Hallberg demands an explanation for the steadily rising service and repair costs.

When writers first consider the response they have to make to this customer, some diagnose the message as being a negative message sent up. After all, don't we have to explain to the customer that her service charges have steadily gone up because she insists on repairing outmoded equipment? Surely, this message will be received as a negative one, perhaps even as insulting. However, our telling her about the problems in servicing her obsolete equipment is not going to bring tears of sympathy to her eyes.

For an external negative message sent up, the Strategy Wheel suggests the use of a circuitous organizational pattern, and a passive, impersonal, and colorless style with an impact level of 2 to 4. But when writers try to follow this advice, the resulting letter seems bland, weak, and extremely ineffectual. Such a letter is certainly not going to satisfy the customer.

As writers think about this case more deeply, they begin to see that writing a letter trying to justify these rising charges by blaming the client is not only extremely difficult, but it is also probably foolish. Further reflection often leads writers to decide that it is wiser—and far easier—to try to persuade the customer to buy new equipment that, in the long run, will be cheaper because it can be serviced far less frequently and expensively.

Hence, what writers do in this process of reconsideration is to rediagnose the predominant message as being *positive-persuasive*, rather than negative. But, unfortunately, they sometimes fail to change the Strategy Wheel's dial setting because they have failed to take into consideration the fact that they have so dramatically changed their diagnosis! Therefore, they continue to follow the Wheel's advice about negative messages written upward. As a result, the draft of the letter they put together is circuitous, passive, impersonal, colorless, and very low in impact. Hence, their message is completely ineffectual.

If you change your message choice, don't forget to redial the Wheel!

Since the message they now want to write is actually positive-persuasive, the Strategy Wheel must be dialed to indicate a positive-persuasive message sent up. Now the Wheel tells them that the letter they write should follow a bottom-line organization, and be forceful and personal in style (and possibly even a bit colorful). Moreover, it should be very high in impact. Following this advice will make the letter more closely resemble what they hope for, and far more likely to prove persuasive to the reader.

Heed this warning yourself, especially when diagnosing negative-persuasive and negative messages that are sent up. You will have an almost irresistible—and highly *sensible*—tendency to try always to move from a negative diagnosis toward a more positive one. *If you make such a change, make sure that you change your dialing on the Strategy Wheel.* If you have moved mentally toward preferring sending a positive-persuasive message, then make sure you physically dial that type of message on the Wheel.

Final Questions

Ask yourself this critical question after you have made what you think is your best diagnosis of the type of predominant message you need to send:

- If I follow the advice given by the Strategy Wheel, does it seem probable that the resultant letter will get the desired job done?

If your answer to this question is no, or significantly shaky, ask yourself one further question:

- Have I failed to choose the right message, the one that has the best chance of getting the job done in this situation?

Upgrading Your Message

As you seek to determine which predominant message will best get the job done with minimal risk, you should always seek to **upgrade** the message, moving it away from the negative and risky, and toward the positive and safe.

Negative letters that are sent up are obviously the hardest letters to write, because they are the riskiest. But if you have to tell an important customer no, how can you possibly make that predominant message more positive? The answer, of course, is: If you can't, you can't. And, if you

Upgrading messages avoids
negativity and consequent
risk.

can't, then follow the Strategy Wheel's advice about negative messages sent up, and hope to minimize damage to your interests.

But you should always *try* to upgrade a message. You should ask yourself one final question:

- Can I upgrade the message, moving it away from the negative and risky, and toward the positive and safe.

For example, in our discussion of the Hallberg Associates case, the writer upgraded the message to the irate customer by moving the message away from a negative one to a positive-persuasive message. Hence, the writer was able to focus on a positive solution to the customer's problems—suggesting new equipment that would prove not only more efficient but actually cheaper in the long run.

But suppose the writer felt that such a step was too pushy, that Shirley Hallberg would only be angered further if such an overt sales pitch were made. Does that mean there are no upgrading possibilities left? Not at all. The writer could have redefined the message from negative to non-sensitive. The writer could have calmly and dispassionately informed the reader why costs have risen and will continue to rise. The writer could perhaps hint that there is a possible solution to her problems, if she is interested. This hint, if successful, might open the door to a positive-persuasive approach being taken in a second letter, or a personal visit.

SUMMARY

The Strategy Wheel is a handy device that makes quickly available the essentials of the system you have learned. The Wheel suggests an appropriate organizational pattern, style, and level of impact for each basic message situation.

As with any aid, you should use the Wheel intelligently. The advice it offers can be applied to any difficult or puzzling communication situation. However, the advice should also be accompanied by common sense and business acumen. Any number of tangential, business, or personal factors may influence the way you should handle a situation. The Wheel has no way of factoring in two critical considerations that are part of our system as described in the Flow Chart of Figure 19.1. These critical factors are the quality of the relationship existing between you and your reader and the amount of risk that is inherent in a communication situation. You have to assess these yourself.

Finally, it is important to use the Wheel correctly. If the Wheel's advice seems inconsistent or inappropriate for a given situation, it is probable that you have dialed the wrong type of **predominant message** on it. Before redialing the Wheel, decide whether there is a chance of upgrading the message, moving it away from the negative and toward the positive or the non-sensitive. A change in message type dialed on the Wheel should bring sound advice about how best to handle even the most vexing of situations.

advice

REVIEW QUESTIONS

1. What does the Strategy Wheel do? What does it not do? *Gives a summary of*

2. When you double back on the Flow Chart to rediagnose the message you want to send, what must you do with the Strategy Wheel?

3. Define and give examples of upgrading a message.

4. Is the Strategy Wheel's advice infallible?

5. What elements of the Flow Chart have to be factored in by the writer? *attitudes + risks*

DISCUSSION QUESTIONS

1. Why are externally sent negative and negative-persuasive messages sent up treated differently from their internal counterparts?

2. Why can a single sentence often contain the predominant message? Give some examples.

EXERCISES

NOTE: The following exercises are intended to give you practice in using the Strategy Wheel to help you answer the following questions about business messages:

1. What message or messages should be included in the memo or letter?
2. If there is more than one message, which message is the predominant, or the bottom-line one?
3. In what order do you wish to place these messages?
4. Is it possible, if you are not satisfied with this predominant message, to upgrade it?
5. What organizational pattern is appropriate for each message you finally decide to include?
6. What style is appropriate for each message?
7. What impact is appropriate for each message?
8. If you are forced by the demands of the reader to use a bottom-line, direct organization in a sensitive message, can you use passive, impersonal, colorless styles (as shown in Figure 18.1) to blunt the effect of the direct organization?
9. If a situation calls for you to be circuitous, should you heighten the effect on a reader by using a more forceful, personal style, plus a higher level of impact?

For each of the following exercises, make sound decisions with the help of the Strategy Wheel. Do *not* actually write the memos or letters. Simply make notes of the decisions you make in response to the nine questions just presented.

 Exercise 1

Yesterday you were to meet Pat Jones for lunch at a classy downtown restaurant. Pat is an important employee of one of your firm's major customers. The two of you were to discuss a new business venture between your two companies.

Both you and Pat had to travel more than ten miles to your luncheon. You had to travel from a western suburb to downtown, and Pat had to travel from an eastern suburb to downtown. Unfortunately, yesterday an unexpected but severe ice storm hit town. Special news bulletins on radio and television urged everyone to stay off the highways except in severe emergencies.

You decided that the travel risk was too great and called Pat's office to reschedule the meeting. No one answered the phones—an obvious indication that the office was closed due to the storm. You also tried to call Pat at home, but again no one answered. You decided that Pat was probably stuck somewhere and went home for the day since your office too was closing.

The next morning you return to work and are greeted by a very angry superior. The superior states, "Pat Jones called me at home yesterday afternoon. Jones risked 'life and limb' to meet you downtown for lunch and you never showed up! How dare you stand up an important customer?"

"I want you," your superior continues, "to set up that meeting with Jones immediately!

"And we better not lose any business out of this," your boss adds while leaving the room.

You promptly call Pat to apologize and reschedule the meeting. However, Jones's secretary refuses to let your call go through, claiming that Jones is on another line with an *important* call. Your later efforts to call Jones again prove futile, since the secretary now claims Jones is out.

You visit Jones's office, and Jones refuses to see you. Consequently, your only recourse is to write a letter apologizing for the mishap and proposing a future meeting.

What is the best strategy to use in this sensitive letter situation? (Remember—to guide your thinking, answer the nine questions posed in the introduction to these exercises.)

Exercise 2

You are assigned to work in the internal auditing section of your organization. Here are some situations you confront.

Situation A

You have been auditing some travel expense accounts submitted by Samuel Mayer, the President of your company. For some of his car rentals and hotel bills and meals, Mayer has not submitted receipts. Company policy states that you cannot approve payment of these bills unless he either supplies the receipts or writes a personal letter explaining that they are lost and offers some willingness to have the amounts verified. Your boss tells you that it is part of your job to write the appropriate memo to the President. What is the best strategy in this situation?

Situation B

Molly Ferguson, a new recruit in your company's management training program, has also lost or forgotten to enclose some receipts from a trip she was authorized to make. What strategy would you use in this memo to Ferguson?

Situation C

Harold Barnes, the Chairman of the Board of your company, forgets, from time to time, to keep accurate travel records. Because of his unique position in the company, in the past you have asked Beverly Marchetti, his secretary, to write letters to you explaining Barnes's lack of receipts and justifying the accuracy of the amounts he has claimed. However, since this procedure is not in accord with your company's policy (which requires letters of explanation from the *person* who has lost his or her receipts), you have become increasingly concerned about getting into trouble, now that audit time is approaching. You need to make absolutely sure that neither you nor Marchetti is going to get into trouble because of your covering up for Barnes's lapses.

You decide that something had better be on record about this. Therefore, you decide to put the matter in writing before Steve Jensen, the Vice President of Finance, to make sure that your arrangement with Barnes's secretary is all right. What strategy would you use?

Situation D

Steve Jensen tells you that company policies must be implemented in exactly the same way for all, and that no favoritism can be shown to anyone, not even to Barnes. Given this instruction, what strategy would you use in a memo to the chairman?

Situation E

After you write your memo to Harold Barnes, you realize that you owe an explanation to Beverly Marchetti, Barnes's secretary. What strategy is best in this memo?

Exercise 3

Numerous complaints have come to the attention of your boss, Katherine Muller, that employees are abusing the coffee break hours. The work rules state that employees have one fifteen-minute break at 10:30 A.M. and one again at 2:30 P.M. Muller, who is the office manager, has asked you to look into the situation.

You wander around the office observing the behavior of your co-workers. You notice that people seem to operate on different internal "clocks." Some seem to need a break immediately after coming in, then again immediately after lunch. Others seem to abide by the rules and take their breaks at the suggested times. After talking with several of the employees, you find that the general work rule is not really being flouted in spirit, but is instead revised according to the personal needs of individuals. There is no evidence that people are taking more than the allowed two fifteen-minute breaks each day, but there is great evidence that most people prefer more flexibility in setting the times for those coffee breaks.

In addition, you have been told that there are employees with various health problems who need flexibility with regard to restroom breaks; others need sugar intake at certain times. Still others are of a nervous or restless disposition that requires them to leave their desks from time to time.

You immediately report these facts to Katherine Muller. She rebuts with strong arguments for having regularly scheduled coffee breaks. If people simply wander away from their desks at times of their own choosing, she says, then others cannot be sure exactly when they can and cannot be reached by phone. Also, when calls come in from outside the company, as many do, a very bad impression of the office is given if the phone call is not answered promptly. Muller points out that by having a regularly scheduled coffee break time, certain persons, on a rotating basis, can be assigned the responsibility of answering the phones of their coworkers at times when those coworkers are on coffee break.

Muller feels it necessary to send a memo to all, reminding them of their work responsibilities and of the work rules. She cautions, however, that most of the complaints are coming from a minority (but still a sizable number) of the employees who resent their coworkers taking coffee breaks whenever they feel like it.

Given these facts, what strategy is best for this first memo? If this memo were to prove ineffectual, what strategy would you use in subsequent memos?

CASES

The exercises in this unit should have prepared you well to handle the following cases on your own. Use the Flow Chart on pp. 350–351, the Strategy Wheel, and the nine questions asked in the introduction to the exercises of this unit to help you develop the best strategy for accomplishing the communication task posed by each case.

Case 1
Instant Microwaveable Products

Part 1

Linda McNally, Sales Manager for Instant Foods of Allgood Products, Inc., believes that modern technology, plus the popularity of microwave ovens, indicates a continuing, profitable future for instant foods to be cooked in a microwave oven. Such foods would include cake mixes, snacks, and the like.

McNally also believes that the continued popularity of the microwave may adversely affect some of the frozen food products that Allgood and other manufacturers sell. She feels that modern working couples already do not even like to boil water in which to cook frozen vegetables. They want instant products, frozen or otherwise, that can be popped in the microwave and served a few minutes later.

She knows that Cyrus Fine, Vice President of Marketing, will not readily agree with her projections, especially since Carlos Lopez's Frozen Foods division has outsold all food divisions this year. Yet, she wants forthrightly to argue that more money should be invested by Allgood Products, Inc. in development of a constant stream of new instant foods for microwave use, as well as the development of "me-too" products that mimic other companies' best sellers.

She asks you, her assistant, to spend several days canvassing supermarkets and asking about new instant food products for microwave use that have appeared in the past year or two. She tells you that there is no easy way to know what products competitors have in research and development. Therefore, in her report she will have to base her case on information you gather about actual products that have already reached the market.

Assignment

You are to go to local supermarkets to collect available evidence about new microwaveable instant food products; use the data you have collected in a report to McNally.

Linda McNally has conveyed to Cyrus Fine the facts you uncovered about new microwaveable products that are now on grocery store shelves. Fine says he agrees with her opinion that there is a tremendous growth market in such instant foods. He compliments her on the research her assistant has done in supermarkets, but points out that he is not the only one who has to be convinced.

The actual physical creation of new products for manufacture is, of course, under the direction of Frank Finnegan, Vice President of Production. Therefore, Fine feels that McNally's ideas must also be considered by Finnegan. However, he warns her that he knows that Finnegan takes a dim view of salespeople who, it appears to him, are always coming up with supposedly "hot" new products. He points out that it will take much more than visits to relatively local supermarkets and a cataloging of products on the shelf to convince Finnegan.

Cyrus Fine asks Linda McNally to revise her report and send it to Frank Finnegan. He states that she should use the local supermarket information only as an attention-getter. The report must recognize that such an important decision cannot be based on a few supermarket visits by an assistant. Consequently, the report should make every attempt to get Finnegan to take leadership himself; Finnegan should ask his research and development people to find out what they can about the products other companies may have under development. Also, the report should try to persuade Finnegan to ask his R & D people to focus greater efforts on developing new instant foods for microwaves. Cyrus Fine tells McNally that she may state that he has asked her to write to Finnegan and that her request has his endorsement.

Assignment

As McNally's assistant, you are asked to draft this report. You should feel free to use any information contained in your earlier report that was sent to Cyrus Fine. You consider the message you are sending, and recognize that it contains both positive and negative elements. The negatives could result from Finnegan's inference that you are criticizing his people for not having devoted more time and money to researching and developing microwaveable instant products.

Follow the Flow Chart's steps. Use the Strategy Wheel to decide on appropriate organization, style, and impact for each message in this report. You know from the Master Case that Finnegan demands that everything sent to him be bottom-lined. Yet you know that the Strategy Wheel's advice to use a semi-circuitous pattern is probably sound in this situation.

You are working as an administrative assistant to Maxwell Allgood. He motions for you to come into his office and shows you a letter he has just received from Alvin Bigelow. Bigelow is the owner of Big & Best, a very large chain of Midwestern grocery stores that carry the Allgood line. Big & Best is one of Allgood Products' largest customers. Here is Bigelow's letter:

BIG & BEST
609 McKinley Street Kansas City MO 64142

July 12, 19——

Mr. Maxwell Allgood
Chairman, Chief Executive Officer
Allgood Products, Inc.
1 Communications Circle
Kansas City, MO 64142

Dear Max:

I was really shocked and disappointed to learn that Harry Schwartz, Big & Best's Manager of Inventory Control, has been recruited and hired away by Allgood Products. Schwartz's loss, coming as unexpectedly as it has, has caused severe disruptions in our operations.

I can't imagine why you would allow your Mr. Frank Finnegan to meet his needs for managerial talent at the expense of my company, one of your oldest and largest customers. It is so stupid that I can only conclude that you knew nothing about it.

When I notified Carl Hilton of this event, he deplored Schwartz's hiring and supported my belief that Schwartz should not have been hired by Allgood. Hilton said he would speak with Finnegan and make arrangements for Schwartz's return.

And now, Hilton tells me he can do nothing! Can you imagine? Well, certainly you can do something to remedy this unconscionable pirating of one of my most valuable managers!

I will expect to hear from you promptly. Please inform your Mr. Finnegan that he is gambling with very high stakes.

Sincerely,

Alvin Bigelow

Alvin Bigelow

"What I want you to do first," Allgood says to you, "is to gather the facts about this situation. Then I want you to draft some sort of written reply to Bigelow. I know I'm going to have to talk with him right away by phone, but I also know he is going to want something in writing. Besides, I want what I say to be in writing. I really can't trust him not to distort whatever I've said to him over the telephone. It will be far safer for me to have things in black and white."

You decide to start with Frank Finnegan, Vice President of Manufacturing. After explaining that Allgood has sent you to get the facts, you show Finnegan a copy of the letter Maxwell Allgood received from Bigelow.

Upon reading it, Finnegan explodes. "This is a lot of nonsense!" exclaims Finnegan. "I didn't recruit Schwartz. I never even heard of him until he came around to see me about a month ago and said he was definitely going to make a move. He said he was fed up with Bigelow. I'm sure that if we hadn't hired Schwartz, somebody else would have."

You thank Finnegan for the information and next head for the office of Carl Hilton, President of Allgood Products. After a brief wait, Hilton's secretary tells you he will see you.

"I'm here," you explain, "because Mr. Allgood asked me to find out the facts about the hiring of Harry Schwartz. Mr. Bigelow is really mad. Here's a copy of the letter he wrote Mr. Allgood."

"Oh, for heaven's sakes," sputters Hilton, after reading the letter. "He's making a mountain out of a mole hill. Last week I must have spent 10 to 15 percent of my time over at Big & Best smoothing down Bigelow's ruffled feathers."

"I'm sorry to ask this, Mr. Hilton," you venture, "but I'm just trying to get the facts for Mr. Allgood. Why does Mr. Bigelow believe that you said you could get Schwartz to be 'un-hired' by Allgood?"

"Listen, kid, you don't *say* anything to Bigelow. He doesn't ever listen to anyone. You just go sit in his office and listen to him sound off. He told me that I *had* to get Schwartz unhired and sent back to Big & Best. This, of course, was ridiculous. But he was so mad, I thought there was no sense in even trying to reason with him. So, I just turned around and left. I waited a day or so until I thought he had cooled off some, and then I went back and told him that there was really nothing we could do. I explained that if we were to terminate Schwartz just because keeping him might cost us some business, I think Schwartz would have a justifiable case against us. As a matter of fact, I checked this out with Milton Berg, our counsel, and he assured me I was right. There is no way we can fire Schwartz and force him to go back to Big & Best. Bigelow is just going to have to face facts."

You return to your desk prepared to fulfill your assignment. You know your first job is to write a bottom-lined report of your findings to Maxwell Allgood.

Your second job is to draft a response to Alvin Bigelow that Allgood can consider signing. This letter should make it clear that Allgood is certainly more than willing to sit down and discuss matters with Bigelow, but the letter should make clear the legal impossibility of firing Schwartz and in some magical way making him return to Big & Best. Naturally, since Bigelow is such an important customer to Allgood Products, this letter must exercise the utmost tact.

Assignment

Write that report to Maxwell Allgood, as well as a draft of the letter to Bigelow for Allgood to consider signing. Use the Flow Chart and the Strategy Wheel to help devise the best strategy for each communication you must write.

REFERENCES

Bednar, D. A. (1982). Relationships between communicator style and managerial performance in complex organizations: A field study. *The Journal of Business Communication, 19*, 51–76.

Bialaszewski, D. and Giallourakis, M. (1985). Perceived communication skills and resultant trust perceptions within the channel of distribution. *The Journal of the Academy of Marketing Science, 13*, 206–217.

Casson, J. J. (1987). How to respond when unemployed managers call. *Advanced Management Journal, 52*, 30–32.

DeGise, R. (1979). A systems approach to business writing. *Supervisory Management, 24*, 24–28.

Denton, L. W. (1985). The etiquette of American business correspondence, in *Studies in the history of business writing*, eds., Douglas, G. H. and Hildebrandt, H. W. Urbana, IL: The Association for Business Communication.

Doheny-Faring, S. (1986). Writing in an emerging organization: An ethnographic study. *Written Communications, 3*, 158–185.

Fielden, J. S. (1982). What do you mean you don't like my style? *Harvard Business Review, 60*, 128–138.

Fielden, J. S. and Dulek, R. E. (1987). What is effective business writing? *Business Horizons, 30*, 62–66.

Flatley, M. E. (1982). A comparative analysis of the written communication of managers at various organizational levels in the private business sector. *The Journal of Business Communication, 19*, 35–50.

Foy, F. C. (1973). Annual reports don't have to be dull. *Harvard Business Review, 51*, 49–50.

Golen, S. and Titkemeyer, M. A. (1982). Educating for excellence. *Management World, 11*, 26–27.

Grayson, A. (1986). Do your automated reports report on you? *Computerworld, 20*, 62–63.

Hildebrandt, H. W. (1982). Executive choice: Business communication. *Journal of Communication Management, 11*, 8–11.

Kimes, J. D. (1979). The need for clarity in business writing. *Financial Executive, 47*, 16–23.

Kinneavy, J. (1971). *A theory of discourse.* New York: Norton.

Lanham, R. (1974). *Style: An anti-textbook.* New Haven: Yale University Press.

Lundborg, L. (1980). The voice of business, in *The state of the language*, eds. Michaels, L. and Ricks, C. Berkeley: University of California Press.

Luthans, F. and Larsen, J. K. (1986). How managers really communicate. *Human Relations, 39*, 161–178.

Mason, R. (1979). Better business writing for banks. *Banker's Magazine, 162*, 56–60.

Max, R. R. (1977). Better business writing—what's your communications 'IQ.' *Supervisory Management, 22*, 12–15.

McCallister, L. (1983). Predicted employee compliance to downward communication styles. *The Journal of Business Communication, 20,* 67–79.

Osgood, C. (1960). Some effects of motivation on style of encoding, in *Style in language,* ed. Sebeak, T. New York: John Wiley and Sons.

Shapiro, I. S. (1984). Managerial communication: The view from inside. *California Management Review, 27,* 157–172.

Weiss, A. (1977). Better business writing—the audience comes first. *Supervisory Management, 22,* 2–11.

Weiss, A. (1977). Follow the rules—most of the time. *Supervisory Management, 22,* 22–29.

Photo Essay 2

COMPUTER GRAPHICS

Exciting developments have taken place in the burgeoning field of computer graphics. The widespread availability of personal computers along with the development of advanced, easy-to-use software packages have provided businesses with graphics capabilities unavailable less than five years ago. Managers or their staff assistants can now design and produce colorful, clear, attractive visuals for use in letters, memos, and reports. Or they can create slides and transparencies directly from the computer screen for use in meetings or presentations. Or, if they prefer, they can project visuals on the computer screen directly onto large screens.

Here are some typical computer-generated graphics. Specially designed software packages help businesspeople develop high-quality versions of traditional visuals such as bar, pie, and line charts. These packages also permit the

development of tables of contents, maps, and even scattered plot diagrams, a type of graphic used in research to describe the relationship between two variables with a large number of data points.

A wide range of graphics software packages is available for both personal and business use. Costs for such packages range from a few dollars to hundreds and thousands of dollars. The businessperson's needs, the type of computer equipment available, and the operator's level of expertise guide the selection of the appropriate software.

One of the most common ways to create computer graphics is to select lines, angles, and curves from a menu. Then, with the help of a mouse—a table-top device that sends messages to the computer according to the operator's instructions—you can adjust the length and/or the curve of the line and, if you wish, fill in and color the spaces.

Graphics can also be created through software programs that generate visuals from raw data or columns of numbers. You simply record the necessary information and then select the appropriate chart. This color bar chart was created in such a way.

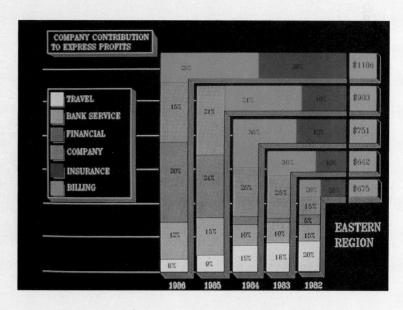

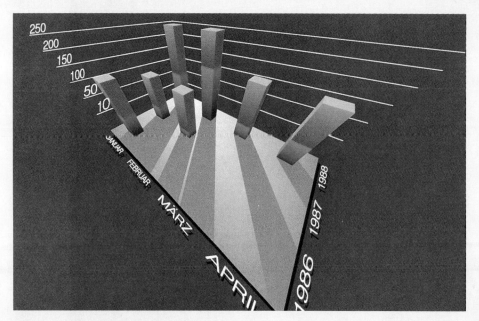

These two complex computer-generated graphics were made into
slides. Notice how striking the three dimensional effect makes the bar
chart. Notice also the sweeping, almost mobile feeling presented in the
graphic map. A few years ago, because of equipment costs in the
range of $125,000 to $200,000, companies had to order such slides
from production companies. Today, with equipment costs below
$12,000, companies can make these slides in-house.

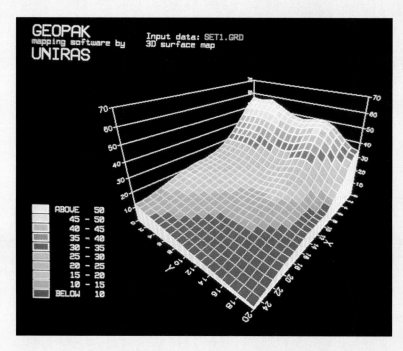

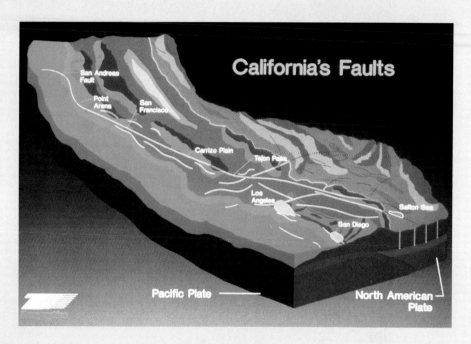

Color has proven a tremendous addition to graphics packages. Shown here are some of the various color options now available. Various graphics packages offer up to 256 colors for use in any given graph or table, with over 256,000 colors to choose from if shading is included. One system even advertizes having available 64 shades of gray!

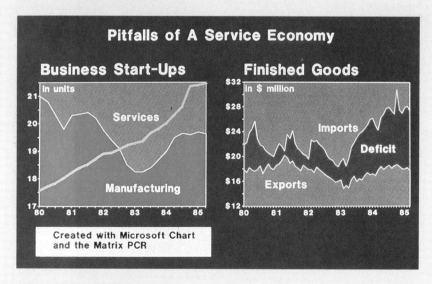

Graphics packages even allow people to create and alter designs on the computer screen. This capability is highly useful to businesses involved in engineering and design applications. These pictures show people examining a three-dimensional globe and a highly detailed mechanical drawing. Using an advanced graphics package, you can examine the objects on the screen in a variety of different ways. For instance, you can

- *pan* the object, looking at one screen at a time from one end of the object to the other;
- *scale* the object, changing the size of the whole or of any individual part;
- *rotate* the object, spinning the entire image around a chosen axis; or you can
- *clip* or *window* the image, viewing it from different angles simultaneously in boxes on the screen.

Plotters, such as the one shown here, allow businesspeople to make paper copies of the drawings on the computer's screen. Pen plotters commonly use from one to eight pens to draw these designs line-by-line onto various media. Electrostatic plotters, a newer addition to the plotter market, maintain the same high-quality output as pen plotters but operate faster since they print images all at once, much as laser printers do.

With the use of a scanner, businesspeople can now even have existing drawings or photos "read" onto the computer screen and then altered in any of a number of different ways. This is a picture of the New York skyline that was read onto a computer screen. Once onto the screen, this picture can be shaded differently, retouched for imperfections, or even altered significantly, such as having the Twin Towers reduced to half their size.

IBM's Storyboard Plus software has enabled businesses to have self-contained computer presentations. Such presentations occur on the computer screen rather than on slides or transparencies. An operator uses a storyboard to select and sequence appropriate graphs, charts, text, and illustrations. The computer then conducts the presentation by itself. Once programmed, the presentation can fade and dissolve images into other images, enlarge and reduce backgrounds or other parts of the image, and can even include spoken and musical soundtracks. Though unlikely to ever replace presenters, such programs can enliven even the dullest or most technical of presentations.

Unit 8

ORAL BUSINESS PRESENTATIONS

INTRA-TEXT MEMORANDUM

TO: Readers

FROM: Authors

SUBJECT: Unit 8

Unit 1 noted that the business communication system presented in this text had applications that went beyond written presentations. This unit applies the system to two additional communication situations: oral business presentations and listening.

Chapter 20 explains how to apply the communication system you have learned to oral business presentations. Such presentations may occur in front of an audience of hundreds or in front of a single person sitting on the other side of a desk. These presentations occur at department meetings, in board rooms, or in front of customers. No matter where they occur, however, you always want to be prepared and to do your best to convey a positive message about your abilities as a presenter. Such a message could have a very positive effect upon your career.

Chapter 21 examines how to apply the communication system you have learned to listening and other non-verbal situations. Listening is an activity we engage in on a daily basis. Unfortunately, although we do it a lot, we seldom do it well. This chapter will provide you with information on how to listen effectively. We include reminders on listening for a true bottom line and for using your knowledge about style to separate emotional from analytical listening.

Chapter 21 also explores a vital but often overlooked area of listening: non-verbal communication. Truly effective business listeners listen with both their eyes and their ears. This chapter will provide you with tips on how to do just that.

Chapter 20

PRINCIPLES OF EFFECTIVE ORAL BUSINESS PRESENTATIONS

OBJECTIVES

This chapter will help you to

•

Understand how the communication system you have learned applies to oral as well as to written business presentations

•

Learn to plan, organize, and prepare effective oral business presentations

•

Understand and apply key presentation principles to the delivery of your presentation

Effective oral business presentations are someday going to be vital to your career. Your ability to convey information, inspire confidence, and be persuasive are qualities leaders look for when they select people for promotion. And these abilities are displayed every time you go before a group to speak. Picture yourself in the following situations. See how comfortable you would feel.

Your ability to present information orally will influence your business career.

- *Situation 1:* As the recipient of an award, you are seated at the head table at your company's annual awards banquet. You are scheduled to address more than 250 managers and their spouses. You listen intently as the President of your corporation describes your accomplishments. Then, as you expected, you are called to the podium to give what is probably the most important speech you will ever give. You walk to the podium, pause, look at your audience and . . .

- *Situation 2:* You check the lighting in the small conference room. You count the handouts to make certain an adequate number are available. You count the number of blank pages on the flip chart and check to see that a spare bulb is available for the overhead projector. In a few moments, you will be presenting a sales proposal to five vice presidents from five different firms. If two of the five accept your proposal, you will set a new record for yearly sales. You draw a deep breath as the door opens and . . .

- *Situation 3:* You are a Branch Manager for a large international corporation. You enter the Corporate Training Headquarters' conference room to explain your branch's training needs to Thomas Sardelli, the Manager of Training and Development, and to two of Sardelli's top trainers. You enter the office empty handed, sit in the middle of the conference table, and begin to address the group . . .

Each situation depicts a typical oral business presentation. Such presentations range from formal speeches to small group discussions. But no matter where they occur or who is in attendance, such presentations will always be important to you and your career. Through business presentations you will present proposals, share your research results, describe your company's activities, and try to convince others that your company's product is the best on the market. And your success or failure at each of these activities will depend upon your ability to present your information effectively. This chapter will help you perform this task.

Business presentations may be formal or informal and may occur before large or small groups.

Many aspects of the communication system you have already learned are as applicable to business presentations as they are to written business messages. Once you recognize how to plan and apply these aspects to a presentation, you have the tools necessary to conduct effective business presentations.

The communication system applies to oral as well as written presentations.

STRATEGIC PLANNING

A well thought-out strategy is critical for a good presentation. All successful presenters, even those whose delivery and coherent flow of ideas seem effortless, have worked diligently beforehand planning a strategy for

Effective presentations require advance planning.

Many important presentations take place in informal settings.

their presentation. Presentation Principle 1 explains the essentials of this planning process:

PRESENTATION PRINCIPLE 1:
Plan your presentation by

a. Analyzing your audience and your message.
b. Deciding on the outline, content, and impact desired and the memory and visual aids needed.
c. Controlling seating arrangements.
d. Planning for and controlling nervousness.

Analyzing Audience and Message

Audience and **message analysis** are vital first steps to an effective oral presentation. Smart presenters examine the audience and the effect that their message will have on the audience before making any decisions about the organization, style, or level of impact to use in their presentations. Here are some specific audience- and message-analysis questions that effective presenters answer first when constructing their presentations.

What kind of relationship will you have with the audience?

Will the audience be hostile, friendly, or neutral toward you? Will it be inclined to agree with you? Will you be regarded as an expert on your topic or merely as someone voicing uninformed opinions? Does the audience have reason to trust what you are saying? Or, do you have to prove your expertise in some way—either overt or subtle?

Are you in power over the audience? Or are they in power over you?

As with written messages, if you are in power, you run far less risk in making any presentation, and strategic choices are of lesser importance. But if you are not in power, your choices become critical. If the audience is your company's biggest customer (and your boss is listening to see how persuasive you can be), you are obviously at great risk if you fail to devise a persuasive and effective strategy.

Given the message you must deliver, what kind of response from your listeners is the best you can possibly achieve?

Your answer to this question cannot be vague. You must focus your efforts on exactly what you want to accomplish. If you want to persuade your listeners to take a certain course of action, you must figure out—just as you learned to do before beginning to write—what organizational pattern, style of delivery, and level of impact will most likely bring about the desired audience response.

If your message is good news to your listeners, you should by all means bottom-line your message! And deliver it in terms as personal, forceful, and colorful as seem appropriate.

If your message is negative to your audience, you probably should consider a circuitous (or at least a semi-circuitous) organizational pattern, plus a passive, impersonal, colorless style. This strategy should make you appear more serious, more concerned, and more caring about the bad news than would a more directly organized, forceful, high-impact delivery. Of course, no matter how you deliver really bad news, the audience is not going to stand up and cheer. But with the proper delivery, you will gain their acceptance and avoid their hostility.

What is the most positive message you can, in all honesty, deliver in this situation?

Just as writers plan a strategy for their messages, speakers must develop a strategy that allows them to put the best face possible on their message and still remain honest. Don't seek to trick the audience. Instead, look at your message from the audience's point of view and present what you say in terms that are as positive as is honestly possible.

Deciding on Outline, Content, Impact, and Memory and Visual Aids

Outline   An outline is merely a notation of how you have decided to organize the content of your presentation. The outline you develop should resemble the skeletal outline of a report. For example, if your presentation is non-sensitive, you should present the bottom line first and follow it with a statement of where your talk is going. Many speakers will use such an

Margin notes:

Audiences judge both your message and your credibility.

Your position in the power hierarchy affects your presentation.

Adapt your organizational pattern and style to your message.

Make your message as positive as possible.

A non-sensitive presentation can use a bottom-line, contract sentence type of outline.

outline as their first visual aid to show how they will fulfill their contract statement through sub-headings and sub-contract statements, if such are necessary.

Content   The content of a presentation is the actual message you are sending—or, in terms used earlier in the text, WHAT you have to say. And, of course, the content of a business presentation breaks down into the same categories used for written messages: non-sensitive and sensitive, with positive, negative, and persuasive messages as categories of sensitive messages.

Impact   It is the rare situation that would lead a presenter to plan on a low-impact presentation. Therefore, we will concentrate on how to create a high-impact presentation. In an oral presentation, impact refers to maintaining the listener's attention and interest in the content of the presentation. As when writing, you will want to have your words leap into the listener's mind. Here are some ways to help achieve high impact.

Control the length of a presentation. Presentations, unlike written messages, force listeners to surrender control over their time. Readers can look at a long report and choose to read it carefully, casually, or not at all, but listeners at a lengthy presentation are essentially trapped by the process. Only extremely brave, busy, or powerful listeners can interrupt a presenter and ask for the bottom line.

To complicate matters further, most presenters find themselves and their topics interesting and enjoyable. Audiences, however, don't always agree. Therefore, do your best to control the length of your presentation. A general rule of thumb is that any presentation longer than ten minutes runs the risk of losing listeners' attention. The more important your listeners are, the more they will demand that you bottom-line a presentation. So, keep your presentation short—if possible, less than ten minutes long.

Admittedly, some subjects require a longer presentation. In such cases, you must provide regular breaks in the presentation. For example, you can try the following:

- Find ways to involve your audience, or at least certain members of your audience, in the discussion. This gives your audience an opportunity to shift from the passive role of listener to the active role of participant.
- Ask questions or give exercises, anything reasonable and professional that will serve to get the audience personally involved. This may range from creation of discussion groups who will report on a topic, to questions and answers going back and forth between the audience and the speaker.

In short, the more people participate in a presentation, the more apt they are to enjoy and remember it.

Make your presentation both useful and entertaining. Every effective presentation mixes useful, practical information with entertainment. The proportions of each depends upon the situation. A five-minute presentation given before the board of directors of a major corporation should be highly useful and relevant, with little emphasis on entertainment. But a

High-impact business presentations keep the listeners' attention.

Do not assume that audiences always want to listen to your presentation.

Try to involve your audience in longer presentations.

Involve the audience with relevant and useful exercises.

Select an appropriate balance of useful and entertaining information.

ten-minute after-dinner speech at a corporate Christmas party should be highly entertaining, perhaps with some useful information slipped in.

Most businesspeople feel quite confident about the usefulness of the information they are presenting, but they often worry about how to be entertaining. Does this mean that they should tell jokes at the beginning and end of their presentation? No. Entertainment in business presentations is not expected to be derived from jokes. In fact, jokes are usually regarded as inappropriate in a formal business presentation. Furthermore, joke telling detracts from the seriousness of the situation and often interrupts the flow or coherent development of the presentation.

Entertainment does not mean telling jokes.

On the other hand, relevant anecdotes and stories present a quite appropriate way of providing entertainment without interrupting the flow of the presentation. If possible, anecdotes or stories should be lighthearted and interesting, but more importantly, they should be used to reinforce, clarify, or support a point the speaker is making. In this way, the anecdote or story not only entertains and renews interest, but it also clarifies the points being made.

Relevant anecdotes and stories reinforce the content of a presentation.

Memory Aids and Visual Aids Notecards and notepads are the two most frequently used memory aids. Both can provide effective support to a presenter so long as the presenter remembers that these are tools to use, not crutches to lean on. Also, as we will note again later, these supporting tools should not become supporting toys; that is, they should not become objects that presenters tinker and play with during their presentations.

Use notecards or notepads as reminders of your main points.

When using notecards or notepads, be sure to use them only to remind you of key facts or figures. Do not write your entire presentation on them. Make sure that you glance at them only occasionally during the presentation. Above all, do not read from them. Notepads and notecards

Visual aids help bottom-line your presentation's message.

do not excuse you from thoroughly preparing and practicing your presentation. Nor does their presence mean you should not be totally familiar with the content of your presentation. You should be. Notecards and notepads are merely insurance policies to make certain that you remember where you are going and the key points you planned to make.

Audio-visual aids are a useful supplement to most presentations. As we discussed in Chapter 7, an effective graph can often clarify, simplify, or convey a message better than any words can. Moreover, visuals lend authority to the message and show that the presenter has prepared carefully.

Visual aids can serve a purpose similar to that of notecards.

Visuals can also serve as cue cards to remind presenters what to say. Just a few key words on the screen can help the presenter to avoid relying on notepads and notecards. What seems like a key-word summary to the audience really is a key-idea reminder to the presenter. With such visuals, speakers need never pause to look down at their notes.

There are four basic ways to present audio-visuals:

- flipcharts and blackboards
- transparencies
- 35mm slides
- film and videotapes

The major advantages and disadvantages of each are summarized in Table 20.1.

Besides preparing your visual aids, you must, of course, make sure that the room where you will make your presentation contains the necessary equipment—projectors, cameras, dimmer switches, window shades, and the like.

Controlling Seating Arrangements

The seating arrangement for a presentation significantly affects the amount and type of audience participation you can expect. For example, a common bargaining technique used by negotiators desirous of forcing a quick settlement by the opposition is to put hard, uncomfortable chairs in a poorly ventilated room.

Seating arrangements can make an audience feel psychologically close to or distant from the speaker and the speaker's message. Seating arrangements also determine the ease or difficulty of using certain audio-visual aids. Some seating arrangements better enable audiences to see slides, rather than transparencies. Some are just the opposite. Figures 20.1, 20.2, and 20.3 demonstrate the most common seating arrangements used in presentations, along with the major advantages and disadvantages of each arrangement. In some instances, you can control these features. In others, you simply have to work with the room setting assigned to you.

The seating arrangement influences how you present and how your audience responds to you.

Planning for and Controlling Nervousness

No matter how much you tell yourself in advance that you will not be nervous during a business presentation, the odds are that you will be. Fortunately, some degree of nervousness is good, not bad. Experienced

TABLE 20.1
Visual Aids

Flipcharts and Blackboards

Advantages

Adaptable. Presenter can modify the content of the presentation as needs dictate.

Minimal equipment needed.

Easy to use.

Disadvantages

Presenter needs good graphic skills.

Can look messy.

Writing on blackboards may slow pace of presentation.

Use limited to small groups.

Transparencies

Advantages

Easy to see if well prepared.

Adaptable—presenters can choose to skip portions by removing charts; or presenters can have extra charts available if additional information is needed.

Flexible—presenters can mark on visuals.

Minimal equipment needs—overhead projector, screen, electrical source.

Disadvantages

Takes time to prepare effective transparencies.

Transparencies can be dropped or misplaced during a presentation.

Limits mobility of a presenter—must remain close to overhead projector.

35 mm Slides

Advantages

Easy to use if well made.

Can be used with large audiences.

Minimal equipment required—projector, screen, electrical source.

Shows advance planning.

Provide a professional "feel" to the presentation.

Disadvantages

Usually require a darkened room.

Nicely done slides can be expensive—though costs are dropping.

Limited flexibility.

Order of presentation is difficult to change unless order of slides is also changed.

Sometimes cause mechanical problems (i.e., slides stick in projector).

Film and Videotape

Advantages

Easy to see.

Minimize effort of presenter.

Disadvantages

Can be expensive to make or purchase.

Require expensive equipment, monitors, receiver, recorders, and so on.

Limited flexibility.

Presentation must follow the content of the tape or film.

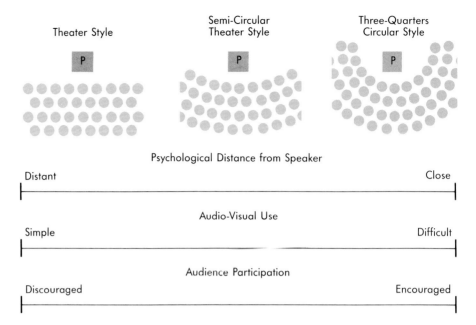

FIGURE 20.1
Arrangements suitable for large groups (75 or more people).

Theater Style

Semi-Circular
Theater Style

Three-Quarters
Circular Style

Psychological Distance from Speaker

Distant   Close

Audio-Visual Use

Simple   Difficult

Audience Participation

Discouraged   Encouraged

presenters plan for nervousness and put it to work for them as controlled energy. Controlled energy enables you to take your nervousness and translate it into positive actions that augment and supplement your presentation.

Rather than wringing your hands nervously or letting them shake noticeably in front of a group, plan to translate that nervousness into

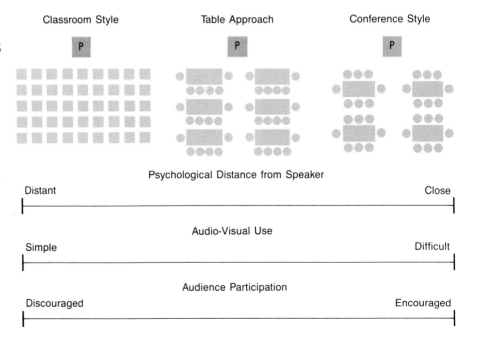

FIGURE 20.2
Arrangements suitable for medium-sized groups (30–75 people).

Classroom Style

Table Approach

Conference Style

Psychological Distance from Speaker

Distant   Close

Audio-Visual Use

Simple   Difficult

Audience Participation

Discouraged   Encouraged

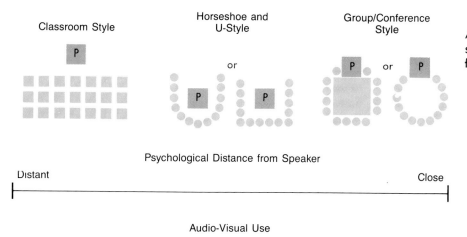

FIGURE 20.3

Arrangements suitable for small-sized groups (30 and fewer).

Classroom Style

Horseshoe and U-Style

Group/Conference Style

Psychological Distance from Speaker

Distant   Close

Audio-Visual Use

Simple   Difficult

Audience Participation

Discouraged   Encouraged

energetic but controlled gestures. Move your arms, dissipating your nervous energy in arm and hand movements that punctuate your points.

Translate nervousness into controlled hand and arm gestures.

Translate other parts of your nervousness into facial energy. Smile, raise or lower your eyebrows, laugh—in short, abandon that nervous deadpan look. The audience wants you to seem animated and will like it.

If the room allows, you can even translate some of your nervous energy into physical movement. Move around, walking from one side of the podium to the other or toward the audience as appropriate. Such movements seem dynamic to an audience. They will never suspect the speaker of coping with presentation anxiety.

If appropriate, walk about while presenting.

Suppose that you are still worried about displaying your nervousness. If so, there is one very simple thing you can do to cover your nervousness: *Get the audience busy at once.* Plan an exercise for the audience to do at the beginning of your presentation. Let this exercise be one that requires them to focus their attention on something other than you.

Plan exercises for the audience to do at the beginning of a presentation.

The reason for this advice is simple: The most difficult part of a presentation is its beginning. It is when the audience will pay its closest attention to the presenter. Unfortunately, the beginning is also the presenter's most tense time. Therefore, by forcing the audience immediately to get busy on some task—answering a questionnaire, taking a pretest, or even introducing themselves—you move attention away from you to something else. While the audience is performing the task assigned, you have an opportunity to walk around, to review what you will say first, and to become accustomed to being in front of the group. Then, when you begin your actual presentation, you will find yourself to be more relaxed in the knowledge that the audience has become a group working with you rather than sitting in critical judgment over you.

The delivery of a presentation is usually not very difficult if you have completed all the planning steps described in Presentation Principle 1. The next four presentation principles will help you deliver your presentations effectively.

PRESENTATION PRINCIPLE 2:
Be natural. Remember that a presentation is a controlled conversation, not an oration.

Talk with your listeners, not at them.

The most important aspect of a presentation is your ability to make it appear that you are talking *with* your listeners, not talking *at* them. An important part of your delivery, then, comes from within; it comes from your ability to be yourself, to be natural. Too often, discussions about effective oral presentations stress the superficialities of a presentation, such as how you should stand or how you must control your hand movements. Although such advice is indeed important (and we ourselves will offer some such advice later), it tends to put far too much emphasis on the purely mechanical elements of a presentation. To do so means to overlook the most important part of your presentation: your willingness to be yourself, to be natural, not phony and stylized.

By advising you to be yourself, we are not implying that if you are in a bad mood, you have the right to shout at or insult your listeners. All we are saying is that you have to assess yourself, know your particular abilities and weaknesses, and use and control them to achieve your goals.

Use your strengths and control your weaknesses in a presentation.

For instance, if you are not good at telling humorous stories, you would be ill-advised to pin your hopes for the success of your presentation on being humorous. Some people can tell funny stories; others cannot. Go with your strengths and package them as effectively as possible.

Assess your personality and adapt it to the needs of your particular situation and audience. You should realize that there is more than one facet to your personality. For instance, you most likely act differently in class than you do with your friends, with your family, or on the job. Presentations often call for speakers to draw upon more than one facet of their personalities. You may have occasion to be serious in some parts of your presentation and lighthearted in other parts.

Adjust your personality to the situation and the audience.

Regardless of which personality traits you draw upon, they *must* be facets of your real personality. Don't attempt to act like someone else (unless you are a great actor, which most of us are not). Audiences who perceive that speakers are pretentious (that is, pretending to be more than they are) immediately turn hostile and unreceptive. Even professional actors, who should have the greatest ability to portray different personalities, point out that they too draw on various facets of their own personalities to make their characters seem natural.

Even when adjusting your personality, always be natural.

Body Language and Gestures

Another important aspect of a presenter's delivery involves body language and gestures. Thus, Presentation Principle 3 states:

PRESENTATION PRINCIPLE 3:

Remember that your body language and your gestures are communicating also. So,

a. Use eye contact effectively.
b. Make your head movements add to, not detract from, your presentation.
c. Control your hand gestures.

Eye Contact   You must look at your audience. Whether you are talking to five or to five hundred people, you must establish eye contact with your listeners. If you look above the heads of your listeners, you give them the feeling that you do not care about them and are aloof.

When seeking eye contact with an audience, don't move from one person to another in an organized pattern. Don't establish eye contact with the first person in a row, then move to the second person, the third person, and so on. Listeners quickly recognize that such movements are artificial and mechanical, rather than sincere. Instead, establish eye contact with a person at one place in the room; then move to another person in a different part of the room. Continue moving back and forth in a random pattern.

Eye contact doesn't mean just a quick glance; it means a long look. As a general rule of thumb, hold your eye contact a minimum of three seconds. Holding it for five seconds is even better. The longer you establish such eye contact, the higher your probability is of keeping your audience attentive and involved.

One of the amazing aspects of effective eye contact is that once you have established it with one individual in the audience, you can then establish eye contact with others in the audience and for quite a while keep the attention of those you first looked at. Of course, after a period of time has elapsed, you should reestablish eye contact and so maintain rapport with those you looked at earlier.

Another characteristic of eye contact is that, depending on the size of the room, you can often establish a rapport with a number of individuals at the same time. If you are presenting to a sizable number of people, you can establish eye contact with one person in a particular area of the room and have ten, fifteen, perhaps even twenty people think you are looking at them. This makes it possible for effective public speakers to deliver seemingly personalized presentations to very large, relatively impersonal groups.

Eye contact doesn't *really* have to be "eye-to-eye" contact. With large audiences, especially, the appearance of eye contact is more important than the reality. If for some personal reason you find it distracting to look someone directly in the eye, simply select some other part of that person's face and concentrate on that. Oddly enough, people will believe you are looking them directly in the eye.

Head Movements   Head movements can either detract from or support your presentation, depending on the movement you use.

Positive head gestures can significantly improve and support a presentation. A positive gesture is that of nodding your head in an up-and-

Always establish eye contact with your listeners.

Once you establish eye contact, hold it for three to five seconds.

In large rooms, you can establish eye contact with groups as well as with individuals.

Eye contact and hand gestures play an important role in oral presentations.

down, "yes" type of movement. The movement should not be so pronounced as to be obvious; nor should it be constant. A positive nodding of the head helps gain agreement from listeners.

Positive head gestures reinforce presentations.

Speakers who fail to pay attention to their head movements often unconsciously move their heads in one of two distracting ways. The most common is a movement from side to side, from one shoulder to the other. Usually, the shoulders and much of the presenter's upper body also end up swaying from side to side. Even the most interested listener eventually becomes distracted and disturbed by the spectacle of a speaker twisting back and forth.

Avoid head gestures that detract from or contradict the message you are sending.

Perhaps in an attempt to address both the left and right sides of an audience, other presenters twist their heads from left to right and back, giving the impression that they are shaking their heads "no." The effect is a subconscious physical denial of whatever it is they are saying. Such gestures can obviously undercut even the most positive of presentations. Think how you would feel if a superior, while orally praising your performance, shook her head as if she were saying something negative. Would you not suspect that the subconscious gesture spoke louder than the words?

Hand Gestures   Inexperienced presenters often regard hands as being useless or, worse, "in the way" during a presentation. As a result, they either try to hide their hands behind their back, resulting in a formal military "at-ease" stance, or they clasp them together in front, resulting in a prayerful, submissive stance. A good rule to follow is not to let your hands touch each other or any part of your body. By keeping your hands away from other parts of your body, you can avoid tugging nervously at your collar, wringing your hands piteously, embarrassingly scratching yourself, or running your fingers nervously through your hair. Once your hands are forced to stay away from your body, they have a chance to do what hands are supposed to do in presentations—make appropriate gestures.

Your hands and arms should support and reinforce what you are saying. When they do this, the effectiveness of your presentation should increase significantly. As your hands become active, you must pay attention to the kind of gestures they are making. Hands speak loudly; so you want to make sure they are saying what you want them to say.

Specifically, remember that the friendliest gesture, one that even animals respond to, is one in which the palms are presented up, with your fingers extended. Such a response serves to elicit from an audience support for and agreement with a message. A pointed finger, however, especially one accompanied by an extended arm, has just the opposite effect. It seems to accuse listeners; hence, it appears threatening to them.

Use your hands to make controlled gestures.

Voice and Tone

We tend to think of our voice as something over which we have little or no control. But, in truth, many aspects of voice can and should be controlled in a presentation. Thus, Presentation Principle 4 states:

PRESENTATION PRINCIPLE 4:
Control your voice and the tone of your presentation.

In Chapter 13, we discussed style and tone in writing. We stated that although writers can control the style in which they write, they cannot control the tone. As people read a message, they can read into it a tone of voice that can distort what the writer intended. But in oral presentations, we do have—or should have—some degree of control over tone. For, after all, it is the speaker's voice, not a reader's, that delivers the message. Surely the speaker's tone of voice plays an important part in how listeners perceive a message. And because speakers can to some degree control their voice, they have more influence than a writer does upon tone.

You can control both style and tone in oral presentations.

It is, therefore, necessary to modify and add to the terminology we used to describe the various writing styles. Such additions will make these terms more applicable to oral presentations.

Forceful Style   A forceful speaking style uses imperatives and high-impact sentences to suggest confidence, security, and authority. Speakers use this style when they want to be in command and in control of the audience and the topic. The body language accompanying a forceful style of oral presentation involves shoulders thrown back, chin thrust forward, and hand gestures that are pronounced, sharp, and that move toward the audience.

Forceful styles show command and control.

Passive Style   A passive speaking style uses language similar to that used in the passive style of writing. But to this definition should be added a tone of voice that is the opposite of forceful. It should be relaxed, almost a monotone, and will appear to be presenting information in as non-threatening, non-demanding a style as possible. A passive presentation style, like a passive style in writing, should be used to achieve low-impact presentations for highly sensitive, usually negative, situations.

Passive styles are non-threatening and non-demanding.

Personal Style   All of the elements described in a personal writing style should be used in a personal speaking style. Accompanying these elements should be the insertion of personal anecdotes and stories that make the topic seem a part of the speaker's life and experiences. Questions asked of the audience can elicit personal give-and-take. Open-palmed, hands-up gestures should be used frequently. Eye contact should be used to increase the personal interrelationship between speaker and members of the audience. The volume of the voice should be controlled and the tone conversational. Speakers use a personal style to draw the audience closer to them.

Personal styles involve the audience in the presentation.

Impersonal Style   Here, the presentation lacks personal references, personal anecdotes, and use of people's names. Gestures are subdued and, if possible, completely eliminated. The voice level is a monotone. Eye contact is minimized. The effect sought is that of an expert delivering an impersonal statement of facts. And as with the passive style, the impersonal style should be used only when speakers want to distance themselves from the message being delivered.

Impersonal styles create distance between the presenter and the audience.

Colorful Style   Here, in addition to using metaphors, similes, and many adjectives and adverbs, the speaker adds flamboyance to the delivery. Gestures are broad and all-encompassing. The speaker's voice is often loud, and the speaking rate varies greatly at times—approaching break-neck speeds at times and being tortoise-paced at others. The speaker's expressions and the general tenor of the presentation become excited and emotional. A colorful style is used to convey information and to exert obvious and gripping emotional pull on the audience. This emotional pull can be entertaining at times.

Colorful styles elicit excitement and emotion.

Colorless Style   Here, the speaker combines the elements of passive and impersonal writing styles with those of passive and impersonal presentation skills. The result is a relatively dry, lifeless, straight-to-the-point form of presentation.

Colorless styles are straight to the point and unemotional.

New Presentation Terms

Some new terms apply solely to oral presentations. You should familiarize yourself with them.

Pitch   **Pitch** is the frequency level of the voice, which can range from high to low. To keep an audience's interest, you should change your pitch in accordance with your message.

Adjust pitch to the message being sent.

A higher pitch range will demonstrate excitement and anticipation. But if the pitch is too high, it will imply anxiety and nervousness. A lower pitch seems to convey a feeling of seriousness. But again, be careful, for a consistently lower pitch can also lead to monotony of presentation and probable loss of audience attention.

Projection   **Projection** refers to how you throw your voice toward the audience. Projection more accurately describes voice control than does volume (volume refers to loudness and softness, which, of course, should vary in your presentation).

Projection involves throwing your voice toward the audience.

Enunciation   **Enunciation** refers to the clarity and accuracy with which you pronounce your words. Avoid words you may stumble over. Pay attention to word endings, particularly words with *ing* endings, and make sure you pronounce these as clearly and as accurately as possible. If you have a regional accent (and most of us do), try to minimize it in presentations before audiences from another region.

Enunciate your words as clearly as possible.

Speed   This term refers to the rate at which you speak. As a general rule, you should slow your speed when discussing complex ideas. But when talking about ideas that are easy to understand, increase your speed accordingly. However, even at your fastest rate, the number of words spoken per minute should not exceed 175.

Adjust your speed to the complexity of the topic and the size of the room.

The size of the room in which you are speaking, as well as the presence of a microphone, also influences the speed at which you speak. If you are speaking in a large room and/or into a microphone, slow down your speech dramatically—to a snail's pace—to avoid an echo effect. What seems so slow to you will probably sound just fine to people in your audience.

Pauses   Beginning presenters often fail to recognize the importance of **pausing.** Yet pausing can be one of the most important presentation skills. First, it is an effective means of building suspense and anticipation and of drawing attention to your topic and yourself. You have probably seen many popular speakers on television who have learned to seize the attention of their audiences through a well-placed pause.

In addition to being a way of gaining attention, pauses are also a means of demonstrating confidence in front of a group of people. It takes great courage to permit silence to take over a room. The speaker who is a master of the dramatic pause demonstrates courage and usually gains respect from the entire audience.

Pauses demonstrate confidence.

Finally, pauses are an effective way of beginning a presentation. They allow you to gain control of an audience even before you say a word. Experienced speakers who need not worry about being nervous develop the habit of beginning every presentation in basically the same manner. They do the following:

- Walk confidently (surely and slowly) to the front of the room.
- Face the audience and establish eye contact.
- Pause for two or three seconds before beginning to speak.

Such a beginning not only allows them to gain their composure, but it also firmly informs their listeners that these speakers are in control.

PRESENTATION PRINCIPLE 5:
Practice, practice, practice.

After you have chosen a strategy and put together your audio-visuals, you must practice your delivery. Practice and repetition are the only ways to become an effective presenter. Practicing helps you become familiar with your material. It also helps you to try out different styles of presentation and gives you an opportunity to analyze and determine the approaches that work best both for you and for your material.

Practice under different conditions and for different groups.

Practice alone in your room in front of a mirror. Practice in front of friends or acquaintances who are willing to give you a bit of their time. Practice with a tape recorder; then, play back the tape and listen to and analyze your projection, pauses, and so on. But, by all means, practice before you give your presentation.

Effective presentations are in many ways similar to dramatic sporting events. The audience sees only the end product of the presentation: the gymnast scoring a perfect ten in the Olympics, the tight end catching the winning pass in the Rose Bowl, the diver descending gracefully from the ten-meter diving board—and the presenter achieving all of his or her goals in a presentation while figuratively holding the audience in the palm of his or her hand. Each of these events is the result of hours and hours of practice that presenters have needed to perform to perfect their skills. Good presenters, like good athletes, always devote ample time to practicing.

SUMMARY

Most of the communication strategies we have discussed throughout this text apply as much to oral business presentations as they do to written messages. Decisions about organization, impact, and style are equally appropriate for many oral and written assignments. In both situations, the issue of **audience and message analysis**—that is, concern with whether you are sending the message to a superior or a subordinate, your relationship with the receiver of the message, and that receiver's feelings toward you and toward your message—is vital to the successful transmission of information.

Business presentations, however, have numerous additional factors that need to be taken into consideration. The setting in which the message is being delivered, the visuals the presenter chooses, and the presenter's delivery (including gestures, voice, and tone) all have significant influence on how the audience responds to the message. Fortunately, once a presenter understands these factors, he or she can take them into consideration. The result is an effective business presentation.

REVIEW QUESTIONS

1. What aspects of your relationship with an audience are important when you make an oral presentation?

2. How can you prepare your presentation with the comfort and full attention of your audience in mind?

3. How long should your presentation be? Why?

4. If your subject requires a long presentation, what can you do to introduce regular breaks in the presentation?

5. Your presentation should be informative. What else should it be?

6. What are four ways in which visuals can be presented?

7. How does the seating arrangement affect the presentation?

8. How should you establish eye contact with your audience?

9. Why is it important to establish eye contact with your audience?

10. How can positive head gestures improve and support a presentation?

11. How can negative head gestures undercut a presentation?

12. What should you do with your hands in a presentation?

13. What does a forceful speaking tone in a presentation mean?

14. What five aspects of voice control help you impart a given style in oral presentations?

15. Why are pauses important in an oral presentation?

DISCUSSION QUESTIONS

1. In what ways will business presentations be vital to your career? Do you think the importance of presentations will increase or decrease as your career progresses? Explain the reasons for your answers.

2. "If it is good to be nervous before and during a presentation, then logic would dictate that it is bad not to be nervous before and during a presentation." Discuss the validity of this statement. Include in your discussion an analysis of the benefits and risks of not being nervous and of being nervous during a presentation.

3. As a general rule, which do you think is more difficult for you to be as a presenter—informative or entertaining? Explain the reasons for your answer.

Chapter 21

LISTENING AND NON-VERBAL COMMUNICATION

OBJECTIVES

This chapter will help you to

•

Understand the important part listening plays in the communication process

•

Appreciate how aspects of the communication system you have learned can, when applied to listening, make you a more effective listener

•

Recognize that effective receipt of information involves receipt of non-verbal as well as verbal messages

Business communication can be understood as a three-part process involving writing, speaking, and listening. This chapter completes discussion of the process. But effective business communicators do not listen just with their ears; they also use their eyes. That is why this chapter explores two related topics, listening and non-verbal communication. Fortunately, both topics can be understood within the framework of our communication system, and that is the approach we will use throughout this chapter.

LISTENING

The physical process of hearing should not be confused with listening. When we hear something, our ears receive sound waves and transmit them to the brain. But listening also involves the process by which the brain translates those sound waves into verbal, as well as into non-verbal, meanings. The squealing of brakes, the crying of a baby, and the beauties of music all communicate a variety of sound waves that are sometimes heard and other times listened to.

Hearing and listening are two different skills.

We are so surrounded by sound throughout the day that, in self-defense, we tune much of it out. But when we choose to listen, really to *listen*, we are making a conscious decision to focus all our mental energy on a specific source of potentially meaningful sound.

Listening involves a conscious decision to focus mental energy.

Listening is a complex process that involves a variety of related but different skills. An understanding of the listening process will help you understand and put to work the specific skills involved in the listening process. Most descriptions of the listening process point out five different aspects of listening.

The listening process involves five different aspects.

1. *Hearing.* The act of receiving the sound waves being sent and transmitting these sound waves to the brain.
2. *Understanding.* The act of comprehending the meaning of the different sound waves.
3. *Remembering.* The act of storing the information that is being processed.
4. *Interpreting.* The act of assigning significance and meaning to the information being processed.
5. *Evaluating.* Making judgments about the validity, objectivity, value, usefulness, and other facets of a piece of information.

These aspects do not, of course, occur in a discrete sequence. They often occur simultaneously, with the listener interpreting, remembering, and evaluating information all in one mental action.

Barriers to Listening

Before we can present specific principles to help you become a better listener, you must first recognize the two most significant barriers to effective listening. These are the following:

1. Taking listening for granted.
2. Failing to concentrate.

Taking Listening for Granted   The main problem with listening is that we do it so much we tend to forget we are doing it. As a result, most of us have become sloppy listeners, taking for granted that we will automatically digest, understand, interpret, and even remember what we have heard. We pay much more conscious attention to other communication activities, such as reading and speaking, than we do to listening.

People often forget they are listening.

Think, for instance, of the distinctions we make among talking, reading, and listening. If you are at your desk going through your electronic mail and someone asks, "What are you doing?" you'd answer, "I'm reading my mail." But if you and a co-worker are in deep discussion, and someone asks, "What are you doing?" you'd answer, "I'm talking with Joe." Few people would say, "I'm listening to Joe." In some strange way, stating that you are "listening to," instead of "talking with" Joe may actually be taken as insulting by Joe.

Listening is an important business activity.

In spite of the fact that the only thing we usually admit listening to is music, listening is actually one of our main business activities. Managers spend up to 70 percent of their time communicating, with 45 percent of that time spent listening (Crittendon and Crittendon, 3–4). Furthermore, approximately 60 percent of the misunderstandings that occur in business result from poor listening habits (Franco, 33). Obviously, good managers know how to listen effectively.

Concentration is essential to good listening.

Failing to Concentrate   Lack of concentration about what is being said is the second impediment to effective listening. Concentration is especially critical because we can listen much more rapidly than others can speak. Listeners can receive and comprehend information at a rate of 250 words per minute, whereas people talk at a rate of about 125 words per minute (Rainer, 88). Some people contend that while speakers talk at a rate of 125–150 words per minute, the brain can listen to and process 600–800 words per minute (Lewis and Graham, 25). Whichever number is more accurate, it is obvious that in listening, the brain has a significant amount of "down time." Therefore, it is important for us as listeners to put that down time to work by using it to repeat the speaker's main points to ourselves, categorizing them, evaluating them, and storing them, at least in our short-term memory.

PRINCIPLES OF EFFECTIVE BUSINESS LISTENING

The following principles will help you become an effective listener in a business context. These principles will apply the communication system you have learned to help you become a good listener.

Listening for the Bottom Line

Bottom-line listeners are perceptive. They listen for the real bottom line of a message, regardless of how that message may be hidden among other trivial or intentionally misleading messages. In a sense, they listen with what psychologists call the "third ear" to get at the bottom line of what someone is *really* saying. Listening Principle 1 addresses this issue.

LISTENING PRINCIPLE 1:

Always listen for the real bottom line of what someone is saying. Sometimes this calls for listening with a "third ear."

An employee hinting that he or she is thinking about taking early retirement may actually be saying something like "Tell me you think I'm still productive, even though I'm fifty-seven." Managers who are good listeners "hear" such hidden bottom lines and take steps to deal with the real, not the apparent situation.

Listen for what people are really trying to say.

Naturally, bottom-line listeners do not always have to respond kindly to hidden bottom-line messages. These people can serve as aggressive listeners who force speakers to come to the point and deal with the real issues. The following case is a disguised account of an experience that actually took place. It provides a clear example of the need we sometimes have to demand that the true bottom line be expressed frankly.

Some situations require aggressive listening.

The Bored Board of Directors Case

The Board of Directors of Zenith Mutual Fund Group were in attendance at their monthly meeting. One hour of their crowded agenda was devoted to hearing a presentation by John Cahill, Vice President of Eagle Bank of New York. Cahill was scheduled to explain why his bank was asking for a 25 percent increase in fees charged the various Zenith Funds for custodial and shareholder accounting services.

John Cahill faced the assembled directors, all of whom were busy, hard-driving executives in their own right. He passed out a twenty-page, spiral-bound, expensively embossed brochure describing the various and extensive services offered by Eagle Bank. In a soft voice that barely could be heard, Cahill began to read each of the bulleted points listed on page one of the brochure, and to make comments about each. Ten minutes later, he was on point four of page one.

In the meantime, the directors thumbed through the brochure; not a word in it addressed the issue of why the asked-for 25 percent increase in charges was justified. Most of the board members dozed and daydreamed during Cahill's presentation; one member actually read the *Wall Street Journal* under the table.

Undaunted, John Cahill continued his presentation. After he had spent twenty-five minutes of his allotted hour, and had only gotten as far as page five of the brochure, one board member raised his hand and said, "Pardon me, Mr. Cahill. But this detail doesn't really mean too much to us. Is it germane to the point at hand?"

"Oh, yes," replied Cahill. "These details are critical to an understanding of the services we render."

After fifty-five minutes had passed, John Cahill had finally reached page thirteen of the brochure. At this point, another board member spoke up, saying, "I really don't wish to be rude, Mr. Cahill. But not only is just about everything you are telling us absolutely meaningless, but speaking for myself, none of what you have said seems pertinent whatsoever to the issue of whether a 25 percent raise in your fees is justified." Glancing at his watch, he said, "You've got less than five minutes left. How about getting to the point of this meeting?"

Cahill responded blandly, "Certainly. Now that you've got most of the background, I guess it is appropriate to address the issue of the proposed fee increase. I have worked out a profit-and-loss statement for each of the six Waterman funds that we manage."

He then pulled a wrinkled scrap of paper from his pocket (copies of which he shared with no one) and stated that for last year, the bank had lost money on servicing each fund. The amounts of the losses ranged from $116,000 on the largest fund to $25,000 on the smallest. He ended by pointing out that the bank had not raised its charges for the past three years.

One of the board members asked a member of the fund's technical staff present, "Have you verified the profit-and-loss figures that Mr. Cahill has presented?" The staff person nodded.

At this point, the Chairman of the Board said, "Well, I'm satisfied. I think if Mr. Cahill would be kind enough to leave the board room at this point, we can bring the issue immediately to a vote."

Mr. Cahill thanked the group, and left the meeting. After he had left, one of the board members said, "I think that we've just sat through the worst presentation in the history of man. I think someone should tell Cahill just that." Another said, "Why in the world couldn't he have shared the cost figures with us in the beginning and saved us fifty-five minutes listening to a bunch of details about some system that we have absolutely no interest in?"

Another said, "I certainly agree with you, but let's get it over with. I move we accept the fee increase." It was so voted.

Informed of the board's decision, John Cahill returned to his bank and reported to the President. "How did your presentation go?" asked the President. "It went just great," responded Cahill. "I got the fee raised to $8 a share, as we wanted."

"Good presentation!" said the President.

And indeed it was a good presentation, because it got the job done. Cahill accomplished his objective. He knew he was presenting the bad news of a request for a fee increase. Consequently, he organized his presentation in a manner recommended for negative-persuasive messages, delaying giving the bottom line until it was too late for the board to cross-examine him thoroughly. In the process, he bored his audience practically witless, so much so that in their desire to get the intolerable meeting over with they gave him what he wanted. If he had presented the bottom-line request for a fee increase first, the board could have spent the bulk of the hour cross-examining him.

The facts of the matter are these: Cahill had made a brilliant presentation. It was the board that had failed in its listening function.

How should the board have responded? Since they were in a power position over Cahill, they should have met their responsibility to the fund's shareholders by responding with aggressive listening. They should have insisted that Cahill cease his filibustering and specify the bottom line. In essence, they should have applied the "So-what?" test to the first fifty-five minutes of Cahill's presentation.

Aggressive listening involves demanding to learn the bottom line.

In summary, effective listeners always listen for the true bottom line. They use their "third ear" for kindly purposes, recognizing when someone is fishing for a compliment. On other occasions, bottom-line listeners can become aggressive, and ask probing questions that prevent a circuitous speaker from trying to lead them away from the real bottom-line.

Listening, Style, and Impact

We saw in the bored Board of Directors case how a clever speaker used a circuitous organization, a passive, impersonal, and colorless style, and low impact to lull his audience into inattention. If the directors had heeded Listening Principle 2 they would not have been taken in.

LISTENING PRINCIPLE 2:
Be aware of how the style and the level of impact the speaker uses affect you emotionally. To defend yourself, try to listen logically.

Other speakers make conscious efforts to involve listeners personally. A highly personal style involving words such as "my friends," "you and me," and references to political icons such as Franklin D. Roosevelt, John F. Kennedy, or Martin Luther King, are often sprinkled throughout their talk. Their presentations may be reinforced by friendly, non-verbal gestures, such as upturned palms, or outstretched arms that seem to embrace the audience. They will also use colorful, even poetic language to play on the emotions of their audience.

A personal style can be used to influence a listener's emotions.

In other instances, speakers will use a highly forceful style to threaten listeners with, say, damnation if they do not mend their ways. Or they will attempt to make an audience angry with a common foe; political speakers usually denounce the opposing party and its disservice to the voters.

Regardless of what style a speaker uses, effective, bottom-line listeners will be wary of becoming so taken in that they lose objectivity to the extent that they make an emotional rather than an analytical decision. Business listeners who are prone to make judgments based more on emotion than on logic are seldom, if ever, effective business leaders.

Effective business listeners make judgments based on analysis rather than on emotion.

NON-VERBAL COMMUNICATION

What people see influences them even more than what they hear.

Even though this book has concentrated on verbal communication, this focus does not mean that all or even most communication takes place in a verbal mode.

The message people receive is often based more on what they see than on what they hear. One study, for example, noted that people's attitudes and feelings are communicated more by the body (55 percent) than by either the voice (38 percent) or by spoken words (7 percent) (Trimby, 12). Moreover, listeners judge the accuracy of information they hear more by their perception of non-verbal cues than by verbal ones. When people verbalize one message while at the same time non-verbally conveying a different message, listeners are far more likely to believe the non-verbal rather than the verbal message (Sheppard, 31–32). Therefore, Listening Principle 3 suggests that business people must refine and hone their ability to "listen" by observing the behavior of speakers.

Listen with your eyes as well as your ears to pick up non-verbal messages.

There are, of course, a variety of non-verbal cues that we respond to automatically, without even realizing we are doing so. Studies indicate that some non-verbal communication takes place below our level of consciousness. For example, the pupils of our eyes dilate when we are physically attracted to someone. When this occurs, the other person subconsciously notices this change in behavior and responds either favorably or negatively. But reflex behavior such as this occurs at a subconscious level; hence, we have little or no control over the sending and receiving of basic behavioral signals.

Some non-verbal communication takes place at a subconscious level.

An Intelligent Approach To Non-Verbal Communication

A number of popular books covering the topic of non-verbal communication have recently appeared on the market. Most of these books acknowledge the importance of non-verbal communication and then go on to offer specific interpretations for certain non-verbal actions. How men cross their legs, how women sit in a chair, how hard someone squeezes your hand when shaking it: Each action is assigned a very specific and precise meaning.

Although these interpretations of certain non-verbal actions may be correct in some, and perhaps even in the majority of instances, intelligent observers recognize that the assignment of narrow interpretations to particular actions is a highly questionable activity. Any number of circumstances could arise that would prove the information false.

Be wary of interpretations of non-verbal communication that are too specific.

Suppose while walking in a mall you see two women sitting side by side in a restaurant. Between the two women is a cane. One of the women is elderly and frail looking. The other looks young and vital. Which of the two do you assume, based on non-verbal appearance, is the one who needs the cane? The elderly woman, of course. But everyone would agree that the younger woman could be the one who needs the cane. In fact, the cane may not belong to either woman—someone else may have asked them to watch it while he or she tried walking about without its help.

The point is obvious but well worth remembering. You want to be observant of non-verbal behavior in a business setting. But you also want to be an intelligent observer. Thus, you should identify the interpretations you are making about a certain situation and always check to make sure that other facets of the message, either the verbal part of the message or other non-verbal components, bear out the interpretations you have derived.

Make certain that the verbal and the non-verbal message you interpret are similar to each other.

With this warning in mind, we encourage you to pay attention to three specific non-verbal components in most business settings. These three components are facial gestures, body movements, and surroundings. Let us briefly point out highlights to watch for in each area.

The way we use our eyes affects the message we communicate.

Facial Expressions

The face sends many non-verbal signals.

The eyes send the most non-verbal signals from the face.

The face is the most important area to watch for non-verbal messages. Smiles, frowns, furrowed brows, and pursed lips all provide insight into a speaker's feelings, motives, and ideas. The most important area to watch within the face are the eyes. Effective non-verbal listeners listen to the eyes of others.

Many studies have been conducted regarding the meaning and significance of different types of visual responses. Remembering our earlier warning about the dangers of limited interpretations of non-verbal gestures, we offer you a brief summary of generalizations about the meaning of eye gestures.[1]

- "Looking someone in the eye" is generally regarded with favor, although excessive eye contact may be regarded as staring, and, hence, as being rude.
- Focusing eyes straight ahead is regarded generally as evidence of non-involved listening.
- Looking up to the right indicates that someone is correlating the information with some relevant facts.
- Looking up to the left implies that someone is remembering a past experience.
- Focusing eyes on the ceiling suggests that someone is analyzing the topic under discussion.

[1]Reprinted with permission from *SUCCESSFUL MEETINGS Magazine*, copyright © 1987, BILL COMMUNICATIONS, INC.

- Casting eyes downward indicates emotional involvement with the message being sent.
- Looking away for an extended period of time shows disengagement and withdrawal from the topic.

Even if these generalizations are true only in certain instances, they still point out the importance of eye contact in non-verbal situations. Further, they suggest that intelligent non-verbal observers always watch the eyes of others to gain additional perspective on the message being sent.

Body Movements

Intelligent non-verbal watchers always pay attention to the non-verbal movements others make when talking, especially those related to one's hands. Nervous habits such as rolling a pen between your hands, jiggling coins in your pockets, or playing with and taking apart paper clips can provide a variety of different clues about different people. These actions may indicate that a person is uncomfortable about a topic under discussion, or they may indicate that a person is hurried and concerned about being on time for a different appointment. Of course, these gestures might also mean the speaker is merely a nervous sort of person who likes to fiddle with things when he or she talks. Whatever the meaning, experienced businesspeople watch for such tendencies and subtly attach meaning to the gestures based on their familiarity with the speaker's mannerisms.

Pay attention to body movements and gestures.

Surroundings

Experienced non-verbal watchers are also adept at interpreting the surroundings in which a message is sent. Office size and location are particularly important features of most business settings. Most businesses assign larger offices to more important and more established people, with corner offices often going to even higher-ranked individuals. The number of windows in an office is also important, with more windows being given to more important individuals. (That is why corner offices are often the most sought after by the most powerful individuals.)

Even the arrangement of furniture in an office sends vital non-verbal signals to people who pay attention. Some managers set up desks so as to provide a barrier between themselves and anyone who enters. Others place a desk against a wall so that the officeholder can turn and sit side by side with visitors. Some managers will place comfortable leather chairs beside their desks; others will place firm wooden chairs in the same location. These and a variety of other factors, even including how bright or dim the office lighting is, provide valuable insights into how the office holders see themselves in relationship to others.

Pay attention to business surroundings, especially the location, size, and arrangement of business offices.

In terms of Listening Principle 3, then, we need to remember that effective business communicators go beyond evaluating words to interpret what is really being communicated. They listen both to what is being said verbally and to what is being said non-verbally. And by comparing the two messages, these listeners derive important clues about the accuracy and legitimacy of the messages being sent.

SUMMARY

From a business perspective, listening is a complex activity that involves more than the mere passive reception of a message. Intelligent businesspeople engage actively in the listening process, always striving to determine a speaker's true bottom line. These listeners pay attention to the style and level of impact that the speaker selects, and they are careful to minimize the emotional effect that a speaker's message has upon them.

Finally, effective business listeners listen with their eyes as well as their ears. They are aware of the non-verbal contexts that surround business messages, and they make an effort to ensure that the verbal and the non-verbal signals send the same message.

REVIEW QUESTIONS

1. In addition to hearing, what other process does listening demand?
2. What are five different aspects of listening?
3. What are the two most significant barriers to effective listening?
4. What does listening with a "third ear" mean?
5. As a listener, what may have an emotional effect on you?
6. What is the most important part of the body to watch for non-verbal messages?
7. What may the eye gesture of looking up to the right indicate?
8. What may the eye gesture of looking away for an extended period indicate?
9. What may nervous habits such as rolling a pen between your hands or jiggling coins in your pockets indicate?
10. What vital non-verbal signals can the arrangement of an office send?

DISCUSSION QUESTIONS

1. Identify some day-to-day situations in which aggressive listening would be appropriate. Explain the advantages and disadvantages of aggressive listening in such situations.
2. The text warns against "the assignment of narrow interpretations to particular actions." Is such a warning important? Why? Also, why do people seem to like or approve of such narrow interpretations?
3. Is it possible for a speaker to deceive someone by intentionally sending false non-verbal signals? Explain the reason for your answer.

PRESENTATION PRINCPLES
REVIEW LIST

1

Plan your presentation by
a. Analyzing your audience and your message.
b. Deciding on the outline, content, and impact desired and the memory and visual aids needed.
c. Controlling seating arrangements.
d. Planning for and controlling nervousness.

2

Be natural. Remember that a presentation is a controlled conversation, not an oration.

3

Remember that your body language and your gestures are communicating also. So,
a Use eye contact effectively.
b. Make your head movements add to, not detract from, your presentation.
c. Control your hand gestures.

4

Control your voice and the tone of your presentation.

5

Practice, practice, practice.

LISTENING PRINCIPLES
REVIEW LIST

1

Always listen for the real bottom line of what someone is saying. Sometimes this calls for listening with a "third ear."

2

Be aware of how the style and the level of impact the speaker uses affect you emotionally. To defend yourself, try to listen logically.

3

Listen with your eyes as well as with your ears.

EXERCISES

Exercise 1

Prepare and practice telling two humorous anecdotes, stories, or even jokes. Tell one of these stories in front of your class. Have class members and your instructor comment upon and critique your presentation. Immediately following this evaluation, tell the second anecdote or story. Have class members and your instructor comment upon improvements in your presentation.

Exercise 2

Prepare a five-minute informational presentation on a topic that you know more about than most of your class members. This topic may range from hobbies to special interests, such as snorkeling, lobster-catching, descriptions of places you have visited, or any other topic you choose. Present your information to the class.

Have class members and your instructor comment on the effectiveness of your presentation. Have them concentrate on (1) how well they understood your presentation, (2) how effectively you kept their interest in the topic, and (3) how the non-verbal gestures you used or should have used made your presentation effective.

Exercise 3

Prepare a presentation on a sensitive or highly emotional topic. This topic may relate to a local or campus issue, or to a national issue such as women's rights, immigration laws, or criminal justice. Choose a viewpoint for your presentation, such as being against capital punishment.

Before giving your presentation in front of the class, tell the class members that they must listen as though they were members of some group opposed to your side of the issue. For example, if you are doing a presentation in favor of gun control, the class could be told to listen as though they were members of the National Rifle Association. Give a three-minute presentation before the class; then answer questions from the class. Note: Class members must ask questions from the perspective you have assigned to them.

After completing the presentation and answering the questions, have the class members and your instructor evaluate your performance. Have them concentrate on (1) the style choices you made, such as forceful versus passive and personal versus impersonal; (2) the accuracy with which you listened to and answered the questions you were asked; and (3) the non-verbal mannerisms you used during the presentation and the question-and-answer period.

Exercise 4

Watch a local and a national newscast. Pay special attention to the way reporters present information. Make a two-minute presentation of your observations to the class.

Exercise 5

Watch an interview show, preferably one that concentrates on controversial topics. Study the ways the interviewer and the guests ask, listen to, and respond to questions. Also pay attention to the non-verbal communication behaviors of the participants. Make a two-minute presentation of your observations to the class.

Exercise 6

Watch a talk or variety show that concentrates on entertainment. Study the ways the interviewer and the guests ask, listen, and respond to questions. Also pay attention to the nonverbal communication of the participants. Make a two-minute presentation of your observations to the class.

Exercise 7

Watch an interview show that concentrates on controversial topics and a talk or variety show that concentrates on entertainment. Study the ways that interviewers use similar and different techniques, including different non-verbal gestures and different ways of listening to their guests. Make a three-minute presentation to the class comparing and contrasting the oral, listening, and non-verbal strategies used in these shows.

CASES

Case 1
Presenting to the Executive Committee

Read Unit 4's "Annual Vacation" case. Assume that you had written the report to the Executive Committee.

Assignment

Mary Lou Higgins agrees that your written report is fine, but she knows that the Executive Committee will expect her to present not just this detailed written report but also an oral report giving the bottom line of your findings. She has arranged for you to attend the Executive Committee meeting and has asked that you spend no more than five minutes in presenting your findings. Make that oral report; feel free to make transparencies of any graphics that would support your presentation.

Case 2
An Upward
Negative-Persuasive Presentation

Read Unit 6's "Fine's New Sales Bonus System" case, Part 1. Then complete the following assignment.

Assignment

Stephanie Archer has decided that a persuasive presentation is the best way to convince Cyrus Fine that the bonus system is faulty. Because she is going to be out of town for two weeks, and because you were actively involved in this issue, she has assigned you to deliver the presentation to Fine and two of his staff assistants.

Organize, prepare, and deliver this presentation. Be sure to include whatever graphics are appropriate.

Case 3
Selecting a Bottom-Line Presentation

Review and select an appropriate case from the cases at the end of Units 2, 3, or 4. Suppose you have been told to present your response orally in a five-minute presentation. Prepare and deliver such a presentation.

Case 4
Selecting a Sensitive Presentation

Review and select an appropriate case from the cases at the end of Units 5, 6, or 7. Suppose you have been told to present your answer orally in a five-minute presentation. Prepare and deliver such a presentation.

REFERENCES

Bartram, P. (1985). The communication of results: The neglected art in market research? *Marketing Intelligence and Planning, 3,* 3–13.

Bowman, J. P. and Branchaw, B. (1980). *Successful communication in business.* San Francisco: Harper & Row.

Bowen, C. P., Jr. (1973). Let's put realism into management development. *Harvard Business Review, 5,* 86–87.

Bruce, L. (1987). Mirror behavior lends wings to better understanding. *International Management, 42,* 35–36.

Chaney, L. H. and Simon, J. C. (1983). Managing your image: How non-verbal images can spur your success. *Management World, 12,* 36–37.

Crittenden, W. F. and Crittenden, V. L. (1985). Listening—a skill necessary for supervisory success. *Supervision, 47,* 3–5.

DeMeuse, K. P. (1987). A review of the effects of non-verbal cues on the performance appraisal process. *The Journal of Occupational Psychology, 60,* 207–226.

Ewald, H. R. and Stine, D. (1983). Speech act theory and business communication conventions. *The Journal of Business Communication, 20,* 13–25.

Fast, J. (1970). *Body language.* New York: M. Evans and Company.

Fielden, J. S. (1989). "Why can't managers communicate?" *Business, 39,* 41.

Franco, John J. (1986). Teaching customer service staff to listen. *Credit World, 75,* 32–35.

Gibson, G. M. and Glenn, E. C. (1982). Oral communication in business textbooks: A twenty-four year survey. *The Journal of Business Communication, 19,* 39–50.

Halpern, J. (1984). Differences between speaking and writing and their implications for teaching. *College Composition and Communication, 35,* 345–357.

Hamilton, C. and Kleiner, B. H. (1987). Steps to better listening. *Personnel Journal, 66,* 20–21.

Kallendorf, C. and Kallendorf, C. (1984). A new topical system for corporate speech writing. *The Journal of Business Communication, 21,* 3–14.

Kallendorf, C. and Kallendorf, C. (1985). The figures of speech, ethos, and Aristotle: Notes toward a rhetoric of business communication. *The Journal of Business Communication, 22,* 35–50.

Karger, T. (1988). Proactive listening can expand the role of researchers. *Marketing News, 22,* 14.

Konopacki, A. (1987). Eye language: Clues to your prospects' thoughts. *Medical Marketing and Media, 22,* 66–72.

Konopacki, A. (1987). Making eye contact. *Successful Meetings, 36,* 57–58.

Lewis, M. H. and Reinsch, N. L., Jr. (1988). Listening in organizational environments. *The Journal of Business Communication, 25,* 49–67.

Lewis, T. D. and Graham, G. H. (1988). Six ways to improve your communication skills. *Internal Auditor, 45,* 24–27.

Liggett, S. (1985). Speaking/writing relationships and business communication. *The Journal of Business Communication, 22*, 47–56.

McClelland, V. A. (1988). Upward communication: Is anyone listening? *Personnel Journal, 57*, 124–131.

McCroskey, J. C. (1972). *An introduction to rhetorical communication.* Englewood Cliffs, NJ: Prentice-Hall, Inc.

Meuse, L. (1980). *Making business and technical presentations.* Boston: CBI Publishers.

Micheli, L., Cespedes, F., Byker, D., and Raymond, T. (1984). *Managerial communication.* Glenview, IL: Scott, Foresman & Co.

Molloy, J. T. (1975). *Dress for success.* New York: Peter H. Wyden.

Montague, A. (1971). *Touching: The human significance of the skin.* New York: Perennial Library.

Moutoux, D. and Porte, M. (1980). Small talk in industry. *The Journal of Business Communication, 17*, 3–12.

Munter, M. (1987). *Business communication: Strategy and skill.* Englewood Cliffs, NJ: Prentice-Hall, Inc.

Newman, J. B. and Horowitz, M. (1965). Writing and speaking. *College Composition and Communication, 16*, 160–164.

Nierenberg, G. and Calero, H. H. (1975). *How to read a person like a book.* New York: Pocketbooks.

O'Donnell, R. C. (1974). Syntactic differences between speaking and writing. *American Speech, 49*, 102–110.

Page, W. T. (1985). Helping the nervous presenter: Research and prescriptions. *The Journal of Business Communication, 22*, 9–20.

Powell, J. T. (1986). Stress listening: Coping with angry confrontations. *Personnel Journal, 65*, 27–30.

Preston, P. (1979). *Communication for managers.* Englewood Cliffs, NJ: Prentice-Hall, Inc.

Rainer, J. P. (1988). Mastering the art of listening. *Healthcare Financial Management, 42*, 88.

Rasberry, R. and Lemoine, L. (1986). *Effective managerial communication.* Boston: Kent Publishing Co.

Rosenfeld, L. and Civikly, J. (1976). *With words unspoken: The non-verbal experience.* New York: Holt, Rinehart and Winston.

Sheppard, Thomas (1986). Silent Signals. *Supervisory Management, 31*, 31–33.

Smeltzer, L. R. and Watson, K. W. (1985). A test of instructional strategies for listening improvement in a simulated business setting. *The Journal of Business Communication, 22*, 33–42.

Townsend, J. (1985). Paralinguistics: How the non-verbal aspects of speech affect our ability to communicate. *The Journal of European Industrial Training, 9*, 27–31.

Trimby, M. J. (1988). What do you really mean? *Management World, 17*, 12–13.

Woodcock, B. E. (1979). Characteristic oral and written business communication problems of selected managerial trainees. *The Journal of Business Communication, 16*, 33–42.

Unit 9

PRINCIPLES OF INTERNATIONAL COMMUNICATION

INTRA-TEXT MEMORANDUM

TO: Readers

FROM: Authors

SUBJECT: Unit 9

Unit 9 will help you learn how to communicate effectively in international business settings. Effective communication becomes especially difficult in the international arena. When conducting business in an international context, you have to communicate with people who often hold vastly different cultural values. Understanding these cultural values is critical because they underlie and dramatically affect communication.

Fortunately, the problems in communicating effectively in international settings are not entirely unmanageable. Chapter 22, the first chapter in this unit, demonstrates that effective communication is possible in international settings only if we

1. Understand and adapt to certain key **cultural sensitivities** before engaging in written and oral exchanges with people from other cultures.

2. Are aware of the concept of **cultural context,** a highly useful way of classifying and categorizing different cultural perspectives toward communication.

Chapter 23, the second chapter in this unit, offers specific principles for effective written and oral presentations in international situations. Most of the principles are based on the previous chapter's discussion of cultural sensitivies and cultural context.

By the time you finish studying these two chapters, you will have a broader understanding of how to communicate in international situations. And you will also see that the communication system you have learned has wider-ranging applications than you probably imagined.

Chapter 22

CULTURAL SENSITIVITIES AND CULTURAL CONTEXTS

OBJECTIVES

This chapter will help you to

•

Learn what is meant by
international communication

•

Understand that you must adapt your
communication strategies to another
culture's sensitivities

•

Realize that other cultures' attitudes toward
material wealth, work, time, and acceptable
behavior vary widely from our own

•

Learn something about how another culture
thinks by knowing its cultural context

Written and oral business communication takes place in every developed and developing country in the world. Each country has its own form of business communication, which it conducts either in its own language or in that of another country. An understanding of written and oral communication from this broad and challenging perspective—a perspective generally labeled **international communication**—will be important to your survival in modern business in an increasingly multi-national world.

What exactly do people mean by *international communication?* The answer is that international communication refers to any communication taking place between two people of different countries. Hence, international communication occurs whenever an international business transaction occurs, whether that transaction is conducted orally or in writing.

International communication refers to oral or written exchanges between people from different nations.

THE IMPORTANCE OF INTERNATIONAL COMMUNICATION

Why do you need to know anything about international communication? The answer is that international communication will not only someday be important to you, but it is important already. The rapid growth of multi-national corporations makes effectiveness in international communication ever more critical. If trends continue, it is more than possible that at the end of the decade multinational corporations will control approximately half of the world's assets. Thus, even if you are not now working for one of these companies, the odds are high that you will be interacting with other people who do work for them.

Increasingly, international corporations are working towards greater collaboration and communication among their subsidiaries that are spread throughout the world. International marketing and production strategies must be agreed upon; common management policies and practicies must

Many American business-people do business with or work for international companies.

This is the Bank of America building in Taipei, Taiwan.

be developed. As a result, the amount of international communication increases greatly every year.

It is, of course, impossible for specific advice to be offered about how to communicate effectively with *every* culture and subculture of the world. But it is possible to offer some general understanding of the broad cultural groups that exist in the world of trade. Moreover, we can help you adapt the communication system you have already learned so that it can be applied to various cultures. If you understand cultural sensitivities and the cultural context in which people communicate, you can make more informed decisions about (a) how to organize a written or oral presentation for people from a given culture and (b) what style of writing or oral presentation will probably be most effective.

Cultural Sensitivities

Throughout this text, we have stressed the complex nature of effective communication. We analyzed situational factors, risks, and an awareness of the important differences between messages being sent up or down internal and external power hierarchies. The intent of this analysis was to provide concrete ways for you to adapt the organization, impact and style of a given message to the demands of a particular situation and a particular audience.

The same demands are made on communication in the international arena. However, in international communication, the demands are made vastly more complex because different cultural factors are added to the mix. The first new factor is that you and your reader or listener may very well hold significantly different cultural values. It is crucial in international communications that businesspeople be aware of a foreign country's **cultural sensitivities.**

Cultural sensitivities result from standards of behavior that a reader or listener from a different culture expects you to know and in most instances conform to. These standards seldom exist in written form because everyone in a given culture knows them so well. There is, therefore, no reason for them to be put in writing. In fact, these sensitivities, or rules of behavior, are so deeply ingrained that a member of that culture may become irritated or even insulted should you violate one or more of them. Even more discouraging is the fact that you may be unable to identify the source of their irritation because you do not understand the importance of that culturally sensitive issue.

Of course, any violation of a cultural standard, even one that does not directly relate to communication, can have an adverse effect upon a communication. Consider, for example, someone who has all the qualifications necessary for a managerial job but who shows up for an interview wearing a jogging suit. No matter how much you had previously decided not to judge that person by exterior appearance, it is inevitable that you will and that this violation of a cultural norm will negatively affect your decision to hire the person.

It is important for you to become acquainted with the major areas of cultural sensitivity, especially those that pertain to communication. You must always keep in mind that the way you interpret data, process infor-

Adapting a message's organization, impact, and style to another culture's sensitivities is a complicated process.

mation, and assign meanings to words and gestures will in all probability be different from the way a reader or listener from another culture will do so. It is also wise to learn to adapt the organizational pattern, impact, and style of your communications to take into account any cultural sensitivities.

The cultural sensitives we are concerned with relate to differences in attitudes about material goods, time, social expectations, and language. We will explore each of these in detail.

Differing Material Values

INTERNATIONAL COMMUNICATION PRINCIPLE 1:
Be aware that different cultures may hold differing material values. Hence, materialistic arguments that motivate and persuade people in one culture may not serve the same ends in another culture.

People from every culture work hard to achieve whatever their culture feels is most worth attaining. The goals may vary from culture to culture. In one culture a goal may be acquisition of material wealth; in another, this aim may not have much value. Therefore, your task becomes that of finding out what people in the culture you are dealing with most value.

Not all cultures value material wealth.

In the Hindu culture, for example, the practices of business and trade rank low as a way of spending one's life, even if wealth results. Hence, it would be difficult to motivate persons in such a culture by holding out promises of increased business success and/or personal wealth. In fact, such promises might actually be insulting.

It is especially important to note the differing views toward materialism in socialist countries. Here, a stress on individual gain, personal wealth, or material acquisitions might offend people's social and political values as well as their cultural beliefs.

Differing Views of Time

INTERNATIONAL COMMUNICATION PRINCIPLE 2:
Remember that time has different meanings and different connotations in various cultures.

In the American culture, it is rude to be five minutes late to a business meeting. But in Latin American cultures, it is unusual if everyone arrives at the announced time—or even an hour later. American business culture is replete with stories about business leaders who are proud to start meetings always on time, no matter who is late. Such people are astounded to realize that businesspeople in other cultures are equally proud of their culture's relaxed attitude toward time and fixed schedules.

Many cultures do not worship time and punctuality.

In some cultures, time is not measured in fixed units. To people in these cultures, time is what transpires naturally, as seeds mature into crops, or as a lamb grows into a sheep. Time is a natural thing, not an artificial business construct. These attitudes continue even though the country in which these people live may be well on the road to industrialization. Whether the country is industrialized or not, persuading factory

Many Americans are now working in places such as Abu Dhabi and, hence, must be aware of cultural sensitivities.

workers to keep factory production schedules in such cultures is a major task.

Differing concepts about time become important in written and oral communication because they extend beyond casual social conversation to permeate the workplace. In some instances, a simple listing of beginning, break, and quitting times may seem so strange and unimportant to foreign workers that the schedule is simply ignored. In other instances, employees may refuse to adhere to an assigned completion date for a particular project. Scheduling production dates based on the arrival of supplies from certain international concerns at a specified time may be difficult. Such dates may be of little or no concern to the supplier, even if the dates have been agreed upon orally or have been put in writing.

Differing Social Expectations

INTERNATIONAL COMMUNICATION PRINCIPLE 3:
Learn about the social expectations of the people with whom you deal.

a. Avoid non-verbal gestures and actions that might inadvertently insult your reader or listener.
b. Recognize the surprising importance of non-business small talk to members of some cultures.

c. Be especially aware of the different cultural meanings assigned to positive and negative responses.

d. Be able to cope with silence.

Accidental Non-Verbal Insults   Often a seemingly meaningless gesture on the part of a person from one country may inadvertently be a grievous insult to a person from another culture. It is, therefore, wise for you to learn about these gestures, especially if you have to make a presentation to listeners from another culture.

There are many such gestures. For example, it is a deep insult within Arab cultures to show someone the bottom of one's shoe or foot, for this is the part that touches the base earth. Thus, the seemingly meaningless gesture of crossing your legs may inadvertently be insulting to someone not aware that the gesture signifies nothing in North American culture. In strict Muslim cultures, it is also an insult to touch the ground, to shake hands, or to touch anyone or anything with the left hand, to look someone directly in the eye, to wear shoes in someone's house, or to speak before being formally introduced.

Each culture has its behavioral taboos.

It is thus wise for you to learn about the sensitivities of people in the culture you will be dealing with before you begin to interact with them. You can begin to learn about such sensitivities from books, but you will learn more from people who have worked in and/or lived within such cultures.

Non-Business Small Talk   People from many other cultures do not have the same reverence for efficient, "all-business" communication as Americans do. Indulging in what we may think is irrelevant small talk can endear you to listeners or readers from such cultures. For example, in many European and South American countries, it is polite for visitors to show great interest in their host's academic and intellectual abilities. To listen intently while potential customers recite their latest poem creates a favorable impression. In these countries, businesspeople are not ashamed to be poets or playwrights or artists and will spend great amounts of time discussing the arts. If, when they read their latest poem or show their most recent painting, a visitor shows irritation or even a lack of appreciation, or through body language reveals a desire to get on with business, there probably will be no deal.

Non-business small talk is a critical element in international dealings.

In France, favorable impressions are made by the visitor who can speak French correctly. If that is impossible (and it *is* almost impossible for a non-native speaker), the visitor should at least be able to discuss French culture, history, and France's economic and industrial advances. Germans also expect visitors to know something about their music, their theater, and their vast literature. The same is true about Russians and about people from most other cultures.

Positive and Negative Responses   Attitudes toward the expression of positive and negative responses significantly differ among peoples of the world. Whereas some cultures, including the American, value candidness, honesty, and "telling it like it is," other cultures find such behavior rude, mean-spirited, and insulting to the listeners. Many cultures place a very high priority on not hurting someone's feelings; hence, saying "no" is a real problem. Perhaps this is the basis for the old saying in the field of diplomacy: a "yes" answer means "maybe"; a "maybe" answer means "no"; and a "no" answer means that the person saying "no" is not a diplomat. We may laugh at this, but it expresses exactly the way people from many cultures feel.

The Japanese, for example, are very reluctant to say "no." Therefore, an apparent "yes" answer can mean, "Yes, I understand what you are saying," or "Yes, you certainly have made a point." But it doesn't necessarily mean, "Yes, I will do exactly what you ask me to." The same holds true for many other Asian cultures. The last way someone from such a culture would ever respond to someone else is to state a blunt "no." Instead, that person would do everything possible to avoid saying something negative. To do so would be impolite and would bring discredit to the person who behaved so crudely. Hence, in such cultures, "maybe" usually means "no."

Politeness, in many cultures, replaces frankness and can mislead a person from another culture.

Silence   In the American culture, silence is regarded as bad because it is regarded as a waste of time, and efficiency is valued. To sit silently and not respond promptly to someone is impolite, even insulting. Therefore, Americans become very uneasy when faced with someone who doesn't promptly respond and who instead simply sits and stares into space.

People from Asian cultures, on the other hand, have a deep respect for silence. They become upset if their silence is interrupted, especially if the other person gets impatient and answers his or her own questions with some statement like "And, of course, you agree." In such cultures, silence is not impolite, but the act of putting words in another's mouth is. To them, silence in response to a question is in *itself* a communication. The silence usually implies that something negative has entered their mind and that they are too polite to contradict or disagree. At such times, you should either wait out the silence or change topics by asking a different, less sensitive question.

Some cultures respect silence; some fear and dislike it.

The Importance of Language

INTERNATIONAL COMMUNICATION PRINCIPLE 4:
English is the language of international business today, but you should learn at least one other language.

Language has always presented a sensitive issue between different groups of people. A person's language is not only a matter of nationalistic pride, but it also in some measure determines what we know, who we are, and what we believe.

Fortunately for American businesspeople who do not speak a foreign language, English is the commercial language of the world. Here are some statistics to document this claim (Pei, 300–301):

- Over 300 million people use English as their primary language.
- 650 million more use English as a second language.

- English is accepted as the official language in twenty-nine countries.
- About three fourths of the world's mail is written in English.
- English is the language used in 60 percent of the world's radio stations.
- English is the most widely studied language in the countries in which it is not native.

There is yet additional evidence about how prevalent English is today:

- English is by far the primary foreign language studied by German students.
- In Scandinavian countries, English is the leading foreign language spoken and studied.
- In Asia and Africa, English is often the official language of meetings and gatherings.
- Foreign-based multinational corporations, such as SKF of Sweden and Philips of the Netherlands, use English as the official company language.

Although English presently dominates the international business scene, it is *not* the only language used. Furthermore, it would be narrow-minded to assume that English will dominate forever. Seeds of change are already being planted because an ever-increasing number of countries are beginning to demand that contracts be drawn and that negotiations be conducted only in the language of the area. Belgium, Spain, Thailand, and West Germany are cases in point, and India, Pakistan, and Sri Lanka are also heading that way. It can, therefore, be argued that over time English will become less of an international language than it is now. Consequently, you would be wise to prepare for this shift by gaining some knowledge of at least one other language.

English is today's international commercial language, but this is changing.

Furthermore, you should recognize that if all the people in a particular culture were represented by a pyramid, only the very apex of that pyramid would signify the number of people who really can speak and read English well enough for an American who knows nothing about that culture's language to do business with them successfully. The rest of the people represented by the bulk of the pyramid speak little if any English. The people at the top are probably so directly engaged in international business that they have, through education and experience, developed a working knowledge of English. If you get a job that requires you to communicate not just with top executives but with factory workers, for example, the chances of their understanding English are remote. Also, although some people in foreign countries are able to understand written English, many have real difficulty with spoken English. This is especially true when someone speaks with a regional accent unfamiliar to the foreign listener or when someone speaks too fast.

In international business, knowing another language demonstrates to others your sophistication, your lack of provincialism. It demonstrates your awareness that even though English is your native language, and even though English is the language of international business, you are broad-minded and intelligent enough to recognize that other languages

Knowing even one other language broadens you internationally.

are important to your work. Furthermore, it shows that you are serious enough to have made the effort to learn another language. Even if the language you learn is not one you eventually do business in, your knowledge of another language will increase the respect your business associates have for you.

What language should you learn? The answer depends on many factors, largely related to the type of business you are, or will be, engaged in, and where your organization does business. For example, a knowledge of Arabic could prove valuable to many businesspeople largely because of the capital and buying power oil-rich Arabic-speaking nations have acquired. The Soviet Union's bloc of East European countries are using both German and Russian as commercial languages. The rise of Japan to a primary world economic power makes knowledge of Japanese a very valuable asset for any businessperson.

The language you prefer to learn is up to you. However, one point is clear—if you decide to work in international business, you should not narrow-mindedly and naively assume that eventually everyone in the world will and must learn English. That assumption is wrong.

CULTURAL CONTEXT

You must do your homework on a foreign culture before you do business.

This discussion of cultural sensitivities has demonstrated how complex international communication can be. You need to do your homework before you begin to communicate in a given international setting. You must gain as much information as is reasonably possible regarding the cultural values, beliefs, and expectations of the group or groups with which you are dealing.

Although such information is necessary, another important aspect of international communication that you need to be familiar with is the **cultural context** in which communications take place. The concept of cultural context is essential to understand since it provides a useful way for you to realize that it is not just words that communicate in certain cultures; it is in the entire context of a culture that communication takes place.

Cultures may be categorized as high- or low-context.

Edward T. Hall's concept of cultural context provides a practical system for classifying cultural differences toward language. This system, which will be explained on the next pages, divides cultures into a continuum that ranges from those that are **high context** in their use of language to those that are very **low context.** Knowing the difference between high- and low-context cultures and the different ways people in these cultures view language is vital for us to be able to understand even the most basic aspects of international communication. Figure 22.1 shows where different cultures fit on the continuum as developed by Hall.

High-Context Cultures

High-context cultures are essentially oral cultures based on personal trust. In such cultures, what you say in writing is much less important than what your general reputation is. Hence, the social context in which an agreement is made counts, in many instances, more than what has been

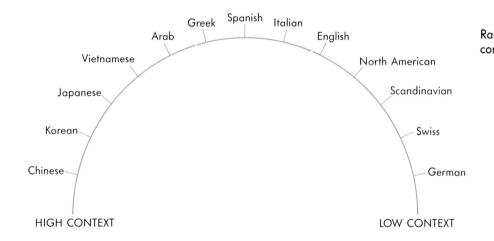

FIGURE 22.1
Range of high- and low-context cultures.

put in writing. In other words, the social and personal context in which an agreement is forged is just as important, if not more important, than the actual written statement of the deal. A large part of this context, therefore, involves both parties knowing much about each other and each other's record of integrity. People from such cultures place significant weight both on their assessment of you as an individual and on their opinion of the organization you work for.

In high-context cultures, people care most about *who* they are dealing with.

Members of high-context cultures place much more emphasis on oral agreements than on written documentation. Your commitment to take a particular action or deliver a piece of goods is bound not by law or by a written agreement but by your desire to protect your own, your family's, and your company's good name. Should you fail to meet such a commit-

Oral agreement outweighs written agreement in high-context cultures.

Americans doing business internationally must understand the nature of high-context cultures.

Chapter 22 Cultural Sensitivities and Cultural Contexts 423

ment, you will damage not only your own reputation but also that of your company, of your family, and even of your ancestors. And the damage is often irreparable.

With so much at stake in a communication, it is easy to see why people from high-context cultures such as the Japanese and the Korean often want to go slowly before arriving at any kind of agreement. As a result, communications in those countries involve a far more elaborate process, a ritual that allows the participants from both sides to become thoroughly acquainted before a business transaction takes place.

Negotiations are slow and ritualistic in high-context cultures.

Businesspeople in the Middle East or Far East also will want you first to sit and talk with them in a leisurely way. They will want to get to know the way you think, what you are like, what your company is like. Their aim is to answer one critical question: Is your company made up of people of integrity? Is it safe or even wise to deal with people like you and your company? People from high-context cultures need to have such questions answered before they will consider doing business with you.

When in such a high-context culture, it is important for you to put aside your desire for efficiency in communications. Business meetings must be allowed to unfold and to include many topics that may initially seem completely irrelevant to the particular business transaction. Thus, it is not uncommon to have half-day or even full-day meetings spent mainly on discussions about family, friends, interests, hobbies, and the like.

What is really going on at such meetings is not merely small talk. It is an examination of the kind of person you and your colleagues are, and the kind of organization that is represented. The judgments made about you and your company will largely determine whether a business transaction will ever take place.

In high-context cultures, a deal is not based solely on hard facts.

In a high-context culture, a deal is not just the result of an analysis of cold, hard business facts. Transactions result from a building up of relationships. Those relationships cannot be developed through talk that focuses solely on the details of a deal. Thus, when communicating in high-context cultures, you should carefully follow the advice of International Communication Principles 5 and 6:

INTERNATIONAL COMMUNICATION PRINCIPLE 5:
In high-context cultures, place little or no emphasis on

a. Efficiency.
b Written agreements (except, of course, when such agreements become mandatory).
c. Spelling out all specific aspects of a negotiation.

INTERNATIONAL COMMUNICATION PRINCIPLE 6:
In high-context cultures, place great emphasis on demonstrating

a. Your character.
b. Your company's character.
c. Your and your company's trustworthiness.

Low-Context Cultures

Low-context cultures—such as the German, Swiss, Scandinavian, American, and Canadian—exhibit many characteristics completely contradicting those of high-context cultures. Consequently, International Communication Principle 7 presents the reverse of International Communication Principle 5:

INTERNATIONAL COMMUNICATION PRINCIPLE 7:
In low-context cultures, place great emphasis on

a. Efficiency.
b. Written documentation.
c. Spelling out all specific aspects of a negotiation.

Low-context cultures are highly competitive. People who are involved daily in aggressive, dog-eat-dog competition with each other are naturally highly defensive. In such cultures, business deals, with very rare exception, are not concluded by a handshake or a word orally given, but by a specific written legal agreement between the parties. In low-context cultures, what counts in most business transactions is only what has been actually written down in contractual form and approved by lawyers on both sides.

Low-context cultures are legalistic and respect iron-clad contracts.

In low-context cultures, the environment in which the communication takes place plays little, if any, part in the understanding between parties to an agreement. It is not uncommon in some low-context cultures for parties to shout at each other all night long and later think nothing of the insults when the final details of an agreement have been negotiated and put in writing. The loud, aggressive behavior of the parties in the negotiation will exert no influence whatsoever on the way that the terms of the contract must be carried out.

Differences between High- and Low-Context Business Practices

A vivid example of the differences between two completely opposite cultural contexts is indicated by the difference in the number of practicing attorneys in a high-context country such as Japan and a low-context country such as the United States. Recent estimates indicate that there are approximately 16,900 lawyers (including public prosecutors and judges) in Japan and over 710,000 in the United States. This means that the United States, with approximately twice the population of Japan, has more than forty-two times the number of lawyers.

However, even though low-context cultures demonstrate low tolerance for trust, these cultures are highly forgiving. In a low-context culture, someone who violates the law is punished according to that law; but then, after fulfilling the demands of the punishment, he or she often goes right back into business. Low-context cultures are also much more permissive toward failure and toward letting a person or a company try again. Bank-

TABLE 22.1	Factors/Dimensions	High-Context	Low-Context
Summary of High- and Low-Context Culture	Lawyers	Less important	More important
	Speaking in close distance	Comfortable	Uncomfortable
	Superior's responsibility	Responsible for subordinate's mistake	Less responsible for subordinate's mistake
	Competitive bidding	Not effective method	Effective method
	Hard work as success	Belief in weaker	Belief in stronger
	Industry	Busy not healthy	Busy natural
	Future improvement	Less confidence	High confidence
	Countries	Hong Kong, Taiwan	U.S.A.

Warren J. Keegan, GLOBAL MARKETING MANAGEMENT, 4/E, ©1989, p. 117. Adapted by permission of Prentice-Hall, Inc., Englewood Cliffs, NJ.

ruptcies and liquidations are legitimate avenues by which people can avoid responsibility for debts.

High-context cultures, by contrast, are most unforgiving. In such cultures, people who cheat or break their word receive a punishment far more severe than any legal punishment a low-context culture could impose. If persons in a low-context culture violate a contract, they are fined but remain in business. If persons in a high-context culture violate an agreement, they suffer a loss of reputation (or "face") that may well put their organization permanently out of business. People who break their word in a high-context culture may not be criminally prosecuted, but they are socially ostracized and are never forgiven.

Low-context cultures punish and forgive. High-context cultures ostracize wrong-doers.

The code of honor of organizations in high-context cultures demands that the head of the organization take full and personal responsibility. Often, heads of companies feel an obligation to resign to preserve their honor, as well as that of their families. Thus, when a Japanese airliner crashed into the sea, it was normal and expected that the airline president would publicly apologize, accept full responsibility, and offer to resign. Even when a famous Japanese golfer was accused of merely associating with underworld figures, he withdrew from the tour and issued a public apology to all his fans and sponsors. The thought of a drawn-out legal battle to clear his name and to argue that he had a right to associate with whomever he pleased (a likely response in a low-context culture) would never occur to a person raised in a high-context setting.

Table 22-1 provides an interesting synopsis of basic beliefs and factors that influence responses in high- and low-context cultures.

SUMMARY

We have provided a theoretical framework that will enable you to analyze how best to communicate in various international situations. This framework should help you to make reasonably intelligent generalizations about other cultures you may encounter in your business career.

If you have to communicate with someone from a culture different from your own, your communication is headed for failure unless you take time to learn about the **cultural sensitivities** of the country. If you go one step further and supplement your knowledge of a culture's sensitivities with a knowledge of whether that country has **high-** or **low-context** attitudes toward communication, you should be capable of making informed decisions about how to organize your messages. You will even be able to determine which styles to use. But the issues of choosing organizational patterns and styles in international situations deserve even more detailed attention. These topics will be taken up in the next chapter.

REVIEW QUESTIONS

1. What is international communication?

2. Why is international communication steadily becoming more important to American businesspeople?

3. What is meant by *cultural sensitivities?*

4. Do people in different cultures share the same attitudes toward time? Explain your answer.

5. Why can the gesture of crossing one's legs while talking be insulting in an Arab culture?

6. To be polite, what should a visitor to many European and South American countries show an interest in?

7. How can a visitor make a favorable impression in France?

8. What do Germans expect visitors to know?

9. In Japan, what may an apparent "yes" answer mean?

10. How is silence regarded in different cultures?

11. Which language is the business language of the world today?

12. How is the concept of cultural context of use to you in international communication?

13. What are some of the characteristics of a high-context culture?

14. What are some of the characteristics of a low-context culture?

15. Name some countries that have low-context cultures.

DISCUSSION QUESTIONS

1. Think of some groups and organizations to which you belong—your immediate family, your church, your clubs, fraternities, and sororities. Would you classify them as high context or low context?

2. Do you think the number of lawyers practicing in the U.S. has caused us to be a low-context culture? Or is it because we are and always were historically a low-context culture that causes our society to need so many lawyers?

Canada - low context.

Chapter 23

WRITING AND PRESENTING IN INTERNATIONAL SITUATIONS

OBJECTIVES

This chapter will help you to

●

Understand how the categorization of cultures into high context and low context will help you to adapt our communication system to international use

●

Appreciate how foreign power hierarchies affect the style and organization of messages

●

Realize that different cultures have differing style preferences

●

Adapt written and oral presentations to the needs and cultural sensitivities of foreign cultures

Understanding a culture's sensitivities and knowing where that culture falls in the high- and low-context spectrum are both essential to effective international communication. An awareness of these concepts undergirds the specific advice we can give in this chapter about effective written and oral presentations in various international situations.

PRINCIPLES OF EFFECTIVE WRITING IN INTERNATIONAL SETTINGS

INTERNATIONAL WRITING PRINCIPLE 1:
In communication with people from a high-context culture, delay bottom-lining non-sensitive messages until you have established a mutual trust.

The higher the context of a culture, the more we should question the wisdom of bottom-lining any *early* communications sent to people in that culture. In cultures where language is used not so much to document as to reveal the personal qualities of the individuals and their companies, preliminary written communications may need to be longer, more elaborate, and seemingly less focused on the business being handled.

In high-context cultures, bottom-line concepts apply only after mutual trust is established.

Such written communications would occur during the sounding-out or getting-acquainted period. Then, once mutual trust has been attained, communications may become more bottom-lined. In fact, written business contracts that are drawn up after this initial period may be very short and bottom-lined, as they are written largely for the record. The reason is that the parties to the agreement probably have spent long hours, or even days, slowly hammering out the details orally.

INTERNATIONAL WRITING PRINCIPLE 2:
Pay special attention to the differences in power between you and your reader.

We have already shown how, in American culture, the direction a message is sent up or down the power hierarchy exerts a significant influence on how that message should be organized. In many international businesses, such power distinctions are far more important than they are in the United States.

In Malaysia, for example, government bureaucrats feel free to bottom-line everything they write down to ordinary citizens. But businesspeople writing up to the government asking for permission to do something are expected to be circuitous to the greatest possible extent. The longer the letter, the more respect it shows. Moreover, businesspeople are expected to include many long paragraphs praising the bureaucrat and the administration in the most lavish terms.

Hierarchical power distinctions, which are very strong in some cultures, greatly influence appropriateness of organizational pattern.

In the Japanese culture, too, the rank a communicator holds in the power structure significantly influences how the message is organized. In a sales transaction, for example, the party higher in power, the buyer, is referred to by the word *onsha* (your great company) while the seller is referred to as *otaku* (your company). This word difference suggests clearly that when writing to *onsha*, you do *not* bottom-line.

Remember, not all cultures are high context. Low-context cultures such as the German, Canadian, American, Swiss, and Scandinavian prefer business messages to be very directly organized, even to the point of being extremely terse.

INTERNATIONAL WRITING PRINCIPLE 3:
Adapt your style of writing to the preferences of the culture to which your readers belong.

Different cultures have markedly different style preferences.

Culture clearly affects the style in which messages are expected to be written. If a culture places a high priority on politeness, even communications sent downward in an organization will be phrased in ways that seem polite and respectful and, hence, will be less forceful in style than an American might expect. Writing to those they work closely with, people in a high-context culture will tend to phrase requests so as to give the appearance that the reader has the (actually quite fictional) option of refusing to do what is asked. As a result, forceful imperatives such as "Do this!" or "Do that!" are not needed and, in fact, are avoided. Hence, a passive style of writing is often used.

What about the use of a personal style? In high-context cultures, more informal written communication takes place than in low-context cultures. Much information is exchanged through informal personal notes written at the bottom of documents. A personal style works effectively in such cultures because a writer has less need to write defensively and hence, he or she does not need to use a passive, impersonal style. Why is this so? In a culture that concerns itself more with the context surrounding a document, rather than with the document itself, written messages do not loom so large. Nor are they as likely to be the basis of litigation. In such cultures, there is group accountability. Lower-level and middle-level employees do not have to document everything so formally because they do not have the same need to defend themselves on the record. Workers in cultures such as the Japanese feel themselves to be part of a team, rather than individuals on whom superiors may dump responsibility for a mistake. The team to which they belong will absorb some of the responsibility should something go wrong. Hence, they feel much freer to rely on informal, personal notes rather than on formal memos to document that they did everything according to the "book."

Group responsibility in some cultures minimizes the need for defensive formal memos for the record.

As far as use of a colorful style of writing is concerned, we must recognize that each language has its own implicit style. Sometimes that cultural style is colorful. For example, Arabic is a poetic language filled with exaggerations, adjectives, and metaphors. Compared to English, it is highly colorful. But Arabs do not react to this colorful writing in the same way as Americans would; it is just their normal way of expressing ideas. Romance languages also delight in colorful verbal turns of phrase. Double meanings, metaphors—all the things English-speakers refer to as colorful—abound.

Stylistic color in various languages differs widely.

Other cultures prefer just the reverse. Germans, for example, avoid colorful exaggeration and hyperbole in their writing, believing that people from other cultural contexts exaggerate, abuse superlatives such as *most, best,* and *newest,* and demonstrate egocentrism by overusing the personal pronouns *I* and *my*. A passive, impersonal style would therefore be best in communications with persons from that culture.

Incidentally, it is interesting to note that the French, too, prefer a passive, impersonal style. Despite the stereotypes of the impassioned French speaker, politician, or lover, most French idioms are passive or impersonal—far more than even English idioms.

Some cultures reject a personal style in business writing.

INTERNATIONAL WRITING PRINCIPLE 4:
Avoid jargon, slang, clichés, and idiomatic expressions as much as possible.

To improve chances that your writing will be understood, you should avoid jargon and slang. Even simple expressions such as "I hope things are going well with you" may cause confusion. "What specific 'things' is the writer referring to?" the reader might wonder. Common expressions, such as "We finally got the show on the road," and "Let's get rolling," can be perplexing if a foreigner tries to translate them literally. Clever terms such as "first among equals" or "last but not least" should be avoided because such statements often cannot be literally translated.

Some idioms defy translation.

INTERNATIONAL WRITING PRINCIPLE 5:
Be precise. Depend on a word's denotative meaning rather than its connotative meaning.

Be specific and absolutely clear as to what you want the reader to do. (Of course, still be polite.) It is so easy to be unintentionally vague. Here is a true example.

Politely state precisely what you want of a foreign reader.

An American came down for breakfast in Acapulco and said cheerily to the waiter, "How's the coffee today?" The waiter responded, "Fine, Señor. Very fine." The American sat down and waited. Nothing happened. So he turned to the waiter again and said, "I asked you about the coffee." The waiter looked at him a little perplexed and said, "Yes, you did, Señor; yes, you did." It was only then that the American recognized that what he had said had no literal meaning to a non-native English-speaker. This time he said, politely, "Bring me coffee now, *por favor.*" The waiter said, *"Sí, Señor!"* and promptly brought the coffee.

Remember this anecdote when you write to a foreign reader. Make sure you state explicitly what you want.

Sometimes even with the best of intentions, gross misunderstandings occur. There is a story of an American writing instrument being sold in Latin American markets. The advertisement told potential purchasers that they could "avoid embarrassment" by using the particular product. The writers *thought* they were telling readers that the pen would not leak ink in their pocket. The only trouble was that the Spanish word *embarazada* means "pregnant." So, the implication was that women who wanted to avoid becoming pregnant should carry this pen in their pocket.

Be careful that translation of your words doesn't cause misunderstanding.

INTERNATIONAL WRITING PRINCIPLE 6:
Do not assume that foreigners understand English in all its subtleties and technicalities. Whenever possible, enclose a translation in the reader's language.

If you are not sure about the foreign reader's ability to understand English, you should write as simply as possible, keeping idiomatic expressions to a minimum. If there is still a question about the foreigner's ability to read your message, a translation by your own translator, if one is available, will not be in any way insulting to the recipient. In fact, it will be appreciated and regarded as smart business.

Moreover, the availability of a translation makes it less tempting for some foreign readers to file your letters away instead of responding. Such a lack of response does occur occasionally because readers are either too polite to admit that they could not understand what you wrote or because they do not want to go to the trouble and expense of getting your letter translated.

Don't hesitate to enclose a translation in the reader's language.

PRINCIPLES OF EFFECTIVE ORAL PRESENTATION IN INTERNATIONAL SETTINGS

Because many cultures do not put as much emphasis as we do on transacting business in written form, you must be able to tailor oral presentations to specific cultures. Here are eight principles that should prove valuable.

INTERNATIONAL PRESENTATION PRINCIPLE 1:
Respect the desire of many foreign audiences for greater formality of presentation.

Different cultures hold different standards about what constitutes an effective oral presentation. Americans, for example, prize presentations that sound natural, not rehearsed. People in some other cultures consider a less formal, conversational presentation to be unprofessional. It appears to them that the speaker has not respected them sufficiently to make much of an effort in rehearsing beforehand. To them, speakers who write on blackboards or on overhead projector transparencies give the impression that they have not bothered to develop finished visual aids prior to the actual presentation.

Many cultures consider informal presentations unprofessional.

INTERNATIONAL PRESENTATION PRINCIPLE 2:
Speak slowly, clearly, and simply. Try to refer to things that are applicable across cultures.

Oral presentations to cross-cultural audiences must not only be expressed in simple language with few idiomatic expressions, they should also not contain references to purely national or regional activities that do

Akio Morita, Chairman and CEO of Sony Corporation, addresses a group of American businesspeople. People from other cultures doing business in the U.S. must also make cultural adaptations.

not have meaning across cultures. In one presentation before an international audience, the speaker referred to Monday Night Football only to see in the glazed eyes of his audience that they had no idea what he was talking about.

In another instance, an American businessman was making a presentation to a group of international executives. During the course of his presentation, he presented the "So-what?" test we discussed in Chapter 4. It soon became obvious that the Japanese members of the audience were absolutely baffled by "So what?" as a concept. To try to offer a simple, clarifying illustration, the speaker said to the Japanese businesspeople, "Imagine that someone walked into your office and told you 'It is raining outside.' What would you say to that?" The Japanese members around the table sat silently. After several minutes of silence, one of them replied, "I'd say, 'Thank you.' "

References in a presentation must be to events and concepts familiar to listeners.

Later, during a recess in the program, another Japanese manager, who was more Westernized, explained to the surprised speaker that the basis for this answer lay in the Japanese concept of teamwork. If somebody were to come into a Japanese manager's office to tell him or her that it was raining outside, the answer clearly would be "Thank you." Why? Because the manager would be absolutely certain that the information was given for a purpose and that the purpose would be revealed in good time. Hence, it would never occur to Japanese managers to ask "So what?"

INTERNATIONAL PRESENTATION PRINCIPLE 3:
Sprinkle your presentation with some words and phrases from the language of your listeners.

Make an effort to learn at least something about the audience's language and culture.

It is regarded as good manners for you at least to make an attempt to learn a few phrases of your host's language. This knowledge shows that you have attempted to learn something about the other person's language and, by implication, his or her culture and background.

All of us have seen how politicians regularly make use of a partial knowledge of another country's language when they visit that country. If the president of the United States visits Mexico and says in Spanish, *"Buenos días. Me gusta estar aquí"* ("Hello. I'm pleased to be here"), the audience cheers wildly. Various popes, as well, have taken care to deliver at least part of their sermons in the native language of the country visited. All readers and listeners will appreciate any effort you make to learn even a few words of their language.

INTERNATIONAL PRESENTATION PRINCIPLE 4:
Allow for differences in behavior of foreign audiences.

Foreign audiences may behave differently from American audiences.

What is accepted as normal audience behavior during an oral presentation varies from culture to culture. Members of a Japanese audience may sit and nod their heads and say nothing, or they may start talking among themselves in Japanese. They may even get up and leave the room, or may simply pretend they are asleep. These actions mean that something you have said is disturbing to them. Take heed; get off that topic until you can figure out what is so bothersome to them.

In some African cultures and in Asia, people will not normally make eye contact when talking, especially in superior–subordinate conversations. They have been raised to believe that subordinates would be acting in a brash and insulting way if they looked their superiors directly in the eye. Therefore, presenters should recognize that if African or Asian audiences do not seem to pay attention to what is being said and instead stare at the floor, it does not necessarily mean they are not paying attention; nor does it necessarily mean that they are rejecting you. It may only be their way of showing respect.

INTERNATIONAL PRESENTATION PRINCIPLE 5:
Have patience; design your presentation's length, completeness, and "interruptability" with the culture of the audience in mind.

In all presentations to foreign audiences, you should be patient. You should invite people to let you know if you are not making yourself clear. To be polite, speakers should also apologize for not being able to give the presentation in the other person's language. Members of the audience who ask questions in English will welcome being complimented on their ability to speak English. You should also be patient in allowing those who ask questions time to search for the precise English word they need.

You must be especially careful in high-context cultures not to indulge in the hard, fast sales pitch that efficiently drives toward selling a product. You must learn to take more time; you must realize that you cannot simply fly in, make a pitch, and leave.

In all foreign countries, you must adjust the pace of your presentation to local expectations. This is especially true when presenting to Arabs. In fact, for such audiences it is often necessary to design a presentation so that it forms short, separate segments that allow time for questions and for digestion of what has been presented. Why? Because Arabs communicate in what is referred to as "loops." They will mix circuitous, even irrelevant, conversation with talk that goes directly to the bottom line.

Adapt your presentation to the expected behavior of a foreign audience.

Arabs require a presentation to have frequent breaks so that they can talk about various topics unrelated to the business situation. Then they will be ready to loop back and listen intently to further presentation of the business topic. But soon they will again need a break to talk about something unrelated to the business at hand. If the presenter becomes impatient and insists on focusing solely on the subject, the Arab audience will become irritated. Thus, the presenter must take these behavioral expectations into account in the design of the presentation.

Arabs are not the only people with different behavioral expectations from ours. The French and some other Europeans find it very impolite, for example, to talk about business during a meal; the same is true in Hispanic cultures. Hence, where dealing with businesspeople from certain cultures, Americans must not build a presentation around a business lunch or dinner. To do so would be considered improper.

INTERNATIONAL PRESENTATION PRINCIPLE 6:
When making presentations in a high-context culture, provide information about your company prior to the presentation.

Following this principle shows that you fully understand that your company is under scrutiny, just as you are. It shows that you are sophisticated enough to know that the members of the audience are in the process of determining whether you and your company are entities in whom they can put their trust. In presentations, therefore, you should supply a great amount of detail about your company's history and about the people who hold the important positions in your organization. Often it is wise to offer their resumes for scrutiny and even to tell about their personal interests outside of business, especially when these interests are related to civic and charitable activities.

Send facts about your company and its management to some audiences long before your presentation.

It is also important to mention your company's longevity in a field. In many cultures, being in business for some time indicates that a company is effective in the marketplace. However, be careful with dates. People from ancient cultures may be amused to see how Americans will boast about their company having been in business since, for example, 1955. In many cultures, 1955 is like the day before yesterday.

INTERNATIONAL PRESENTATION PRINCIPLE 7:
Match rank and age of the presenter to rank and age of important members of foreign audiences.

Some cultures revere age and experience more than Americans do.

When picking a person to be a presenter, make sure that person is as close as possible in age and rank to the members of the audience. In many cultures, if the presenter is not approximately the same age as the members of the audience, credibility and protocol problems result.

In some American companies, people rise rapidly to high positions at early ages. But it may be an absolute disaster to send them as presenters into a culture such as Japan's, where age is revered and a person does not assume a high position until later in life. The young, supposedly dynamic presenter may actually, by his or her very age, be communicating a corporate message that is demeaning and insulting to the more seasoned listeners. Many foreign corporations avoid doing business with someone who in their culture would be considered almost a child.

It is also important to recognize that the role of women in business and society differs greatly from culture to culture. It is unthinkable, for example, in fundamentalist Muslim cultures, for a woman to be involved in a commercial endeavor. For an American company to send a female executive abroad to negotiate with businessmen from such cultures would be a monumentally poor decision.

INTERNATIONAL PRESENTATION PRINCIPLE 8:
Be careful about what your body language and your tone of voice communicate.

When audiences are not fluent in the speaker's language, the speaker's gestures, body language, and tone of voice take over the communicating.

Sometimes people from differing cultures read (or misread) a presenter's body language. This body language may accidentally communicate something quite different from what the speaker's words state. Some experts claim that more than half of what we communicate does not involve words. Even if this is an overstatement, it would certainly not be an exaggeration to state that body language must obviously play a very important role when you are making presentations to people who do not fully understand what you say. It is natural for them to judge your meaning and attitudes from the physical way you communicate rather than from the words you utter. Exercise control over the gestures you make with your hands, the expressions your face conveys, and even over what your stance may communicate.

Although listeners may not fully understand what you are saying, they will react to your tone of voice. Notice, for example, how softly people from most Asian cultures speak. Australians, Americans, and even the British often seem to Asians to be loud and aggressive. This is not true of other cultures. Business discourse in Latin American, Greek, Italian, and Central European countries will often include loud, seemingly heated exchanges of opinion that mean nothing personal nor anything truly aggressive. But oral presentation in such tones of voice to a culture shocked by such loudness would doubtless spell disaster.

SUMMARY

Communicating in an international setting is obviously complex, confusing, and difficult, but success is not impossible. You should be able to communicate as effectively and efficiently as possible, no matter what culture or group you must deal with, if

- You keep in mind what you know about organization and style.
- You do your homework and learn about a culture's sensitivities and its cultural context.
- You follow the principles offered in this chapter.

REVIEW QUESTIONS

1. In which cultural context is it wise to bottom-line non-sensitive communications?

2. In high-context cultures, why does more informal written communication take place than in low-context cultures?

3. To improve the chances that your writing to a foreigner is understood, what should you avoid? *Jargon + slang*

4. What should you do if you are not sure about a foreign reader's ability to understand English? *Write simple + enclose a translation*

5. Americans prefer an oral presentation to sound natural and unrehearsed. Do other cultures admire natural-sounding oral presentations? How do they regard such presentations?

6. In some cultures, what impression does a speaker who writes on a blackboard or on an overhead projector transparency give listeners?

7. What are some things you can do to show good manners when you make a presentation to an international audience?

8. How would you design a presentation's length, completeness, and "interruptability" if it were aimed at an audience from an Arab culture?

9. Why is building a presentation around a business lunch a mistake in many foreign cultures?

10. In a high-context culture, what should you provide well in advance of your presentation? Why?

11. Why is the age of a presenter often important in an oral presentation to foreign audiences?

12. Why does body language play a large part when you are presenting to a foreign audience?

DISCUSSION QUESTIONS

1. We have been warned that the reverence of American business for youth (resulting in early retirement for people above the age of fifty-five) may cause problems when we send young but high-ranking businesspeople abroad to make presentations and hold negotiations. Do you think that this suggests a more serious problem for American business? Do you think we lose strength by supporting or imposing such early retirement practices?

2. Some cultures frown on female business executives. What do you think can be done to protect the rights of American businesswomen to do business in all foreign cultures?

INTERNATIONAL COMMUNICATION PRINCIPLES
REVIEW LIST

1

Be aware that different cultures may hold differing material values. Hence, materialistic arguments that motivate and persuade people in one culture may not serve the same ends in another culture.

2

Remember that time has different meanings and different connotations in various cultures.

3

Learn about the social expectations of the people with whom you deal.
a. Avoid non-verbal gestures and actions that might inadvertently insult your reader or listener.
b. Recognize the surprising importance of non-business small talk to members of some cultures.
c. Be especially aware of the different cultural meanings assigned to positive and negative responses.
d. Be able to cope with silence.

4

English is the language of international business today, but you should learn at least one other language.

5

In high-context cultures, place little or no emphasis on
a. Efficiency.
b. Written agreements (except, of course, when such agreements become mandatory).
c. Spelling out all specific aspects of a negotiation.

6

In high-context cultures, place great emphasis on demonstrating
a. Your character.
b. Your company's character.
c. Your and your company's trustworthiness.

7

In low-context cultures, place great emphasis on
a. Efficiency.
b. Written documentation.
c. Spelling out all specific aspects of a negotiation.

INTERNATIONAL WRITING PRINCIPLES
REVIEW LIST

1

In communication with people from a high-context culture, delay bottom-lining non-sensitive messages until you have established a mutual trust.

— image

2

Pay special attention to the differences in power between you and your reader.

3

Adapt your style of writing to the preferences of the culture to which your readers belong. *avoid slang*

4

Avoid jargon, slang, clichés, and idiomatic expressions as much as possible.

5

Be precise. Depend on a word's denotative meaning rather than its connotative meaning.

figuratively

6

Do not assume that foreigners understand English in all its subtleties and technicalities. Whenever possible, enclose a translation in the reader's language.

439

INTERNATIONAL PRESENTATION PRINCIPLES
REVIEW LIST

1

Respect the desire of many foreign audiences for greater formality of presentation.

2

Speak slowly, clearly, and simply. Try to refer to things that are applicable across cultures.

3

Sprinkle your presentation with some words and phrases from the language of your listeners.

4

Allow for differences in behavior of foreign audiences.

5

Have patience; design your presentation's length, completeness, and "interruptability" with the culture of the audience in mind.

6

When making presentations in a high-context culture, provide information about your company prior to the presentation.

7

Match rank and age of the presenter to rank and age of important members of foreign audiences.

8

Be careful about what your body language and your tone of voice communicate.

EXERCISES

Exercise 1

Select one of the following important trading nations: Japan, Saudi Arabia, France, or Brazil. Research that nation's cultural attitudes toward:

1. time.
2. material gain and the profit motive.
3. women, especially in business.
4. written versus oral agreements.
5. acceptable places and times of doing business.
6. conducting business in English.

Exercise 2

Decide whether a high- or a low-context culture would value the following:

1. One's word, orally given.
2. The notion that time is money.
3. Length of time allowed for negotiations.
4. Doing business with friends and relatives.
5. Social change.
6. Bonds between people.
7. Lawyers.
8. The idea that hard work is the main requirement for success.

Exercise 3

 Rephrase the following colloquial statements so that they are expressed in simple terms understandable to (and translatable by) foreigners.

1. Let's get the ball rolling.
2. We'll kick off the meeting with a pip of a video promo.
3. Please let me know your feelings. I'm all ears.
4. Will the members of the audience please take their seats.
5. Acme, Inc., as I get it, is simply dragging its heels on making a decision.
6. We'd better get busy and pull our chestnuts out of the fire.
7. My feeling is that the judge should throw the book at him.
8. She'd better throw cold water on that idea.

9. Make no bones about it; we are vulnerable.
10. You've hit the nail on the head; let's bury the hatchet and get back to business as usual.
11. We've got plenty of other fish to fry.
12. When all is said and done, we're all in the same boat.
13. We simply have too many irons in the fire for our own good.
14. If we don't watch out, we'll get the short end of the stick.
15. Let's not go off the deep end, and above all, let's not cut off our nose to spite our face.

CASES

The following cases will allow you to put to practical use the knowledge you have gained about effective communication with members of other trading cultures. These cases can serve as discussion exercises, or they can be the basis for written or oral presentations.

For each case, identify the various messages that are to be sent on the basis of how each will be received by the reader(s). Then consider the advice given throughout the text about the best organization, style, and impact to use.

Case 1
New Foods from Asia

Because of the ever-increasing diversity of ethnic groups living in the United States, Cyrus Fine, Vice President of Marketing, believes that All-good Products, Inc. would do well to institute a wider range of frozen foods and instant foods. These new food products would be intended not just to be sold to various ethnic groups, but also to popularize foods of different cultures for possible acceptance by other cultural groups within the United States. He points out the fact that Italian, Chinese, and Mexican foods, once introduced, have become as American as the proverbial apple pie. "Would," he wonders, "seemingly odd Japanese foods such as sushi [raw fish] have even a chance of becoming popular with most Americans? If so, sushi could certainly be sold frozen. And what about Korean food? Kimchi [spicy, pickled cabbage] is already sold; there may be other dishes that need introducing. Thai food also is being introduced in some big city restaurants.

"I want us to visit these countries, try their foods, see what's on the shelves, and see if we can't bring back ideas for some sure-fire products that Allgood can produce and help popularize."

"Carlos," Fine says to Carlos Lopez, Sales Manager of Frozen Foods, "I want you to spend two weeks visiting Japan, Korea, and Thailand. The Grocery Retailer's Association will be glad to help you make arrangements to visit some of the large manufacturers and wholesalers of various frozen foods. Of course, you won't be able to spend too much time in any one place. I suggest that you set up luncheon meetings where you can make a quick presentation and find out about what they have to offer that might prove appealing in U.S. markets. I'm going to ask the GMA to make sure that these Asian producers and wholesalers send their top people to meet with you. I only wish that I could go with you, but I think this is a great opportunity for you to expand your horizons and mature internationally."

Assignment

You are Carlos Lopez's assistant. He is, naturally, very excited about his forthcoming trip to the three Asian countries. He tells you all that Cyrus Fine has told him. However, from what you have learned (from the chapters in this unit) Lopez's trip as planned by Fine seems headed for trouble. Lopez says to you, "I know you've been studying international communications. Could you put together a brief report giving me advice about (a) what I should do in preparation for the trip, (b) how I should conduct myself when meeting Asian businesspeople, and (c) what topics you think I need to cover in my presentation to these important businesspeople at the luncheon meetings."

You are pleased to have this opportunity to share with Lopez some constructive suggestions. Assume that neither Fine nor Lopez really understands much about cultural sensitivities and that Lopez will be grateful for any constructive advice. Write your thoughts in a memo to Lopez so that he can consider them and perhaps present them to Cyrus Fine.

International Case 2
New Dried Foods from the Arabs

Cyrus Fine, Vice President of Marketing, continues to be excited about opportunities for Allgood Products, Inc. to bring new ethnic foods to the American table. Therefore, Fine repeats much of what he said to Carlos Lopez (see Case 1) to Linda McNally, Sales Manager of Instant Foods. Fine wants McNally to investigate a different geographical area and a quite different culture, that of the Arabs.

"The United States," Fine says, "already has plenty of dried foods from Asia—everything from noodles to rice to dry soups. But I wonder what our Arab neighbors have to offer in the way of dried foods? Surely their cuisine must be far different from anything Americans are used to."

He tells Linda that he wants her to visit not only Arab markets in Saudi Arabia, Jordan, and South Yemen, but also to consult with leading businesspeople involved in manufacturing and selling dried Arab foods. He tells Linda that he wants her to complete her investigation and all meetings in a week to ten days. As he did with Lopez, Fine again suggests that business be conducted in these countries through presentations made around luncheons.

Assignment

As Linda McNally's assistant, you realize that she is the wrong person to send as a representative of Allgood Products to an Arab culture. You also know that the plan for quick business meetings is culturally wrong. Accordingly, you decide to put your thoughts in order to present them in writing to McNally so that she can consider them and perhaps present them to Cyrus Fine.

Write that memo documenting why you think McNally is the wrong person to send and why the way the business trip is planned around quick luncheon meetings is a mistake. Assume that neither Fine nor McNally really understands much about the cultural sensitivities that you have mastered in this unit.

International Case 3
An International Introduction
to Allgood Products, Inc.

Cyrus Fine has learned from the feedback that Lopez and McNally have given him (thanks to your memos in Cases 1 and 2) that both Arab and Asian cultures desire to know a great deal about a company and its people before deciding to do business.

Assignment

Fine asks you, as his assistant, to draft a description of Allgood Products and its people. The description should not be more than two double-spaced, typewritten pages in length, and should use only words that are simple, common, and as free as possible of idiomatic expressions. Using the Master Case as your guide, write that description.

International Case 4
Adapting Time Schedules
to Cultural Realities

Frank Finnegan, Vice President of Production at Allgood Products, Inc., has appointed Bryan Dillman to be Production Manager for the frozen foods branch of the production department. For many years, the food processing operations in Salinas, California have been buying fresh fruits and vegetables from Mexico, especially during the winter months. Fresh produce is trucked in to Salinas for processing.

Bryan Dillman has had twenty years of production experience with Arthur and Sons, a manufacturer of frozen french fries, potato puffs, and other items, based in Iowa. Consequently, Dillman has not had much experience in dealing with people from other cultures. All of the products that he purchased for Arthur and Sons were grown in the potato-growing areas of Iowa and the northern Midwest.

When Dillman took over as Production Manager for Frozen Foods, he noted that the production schedules in the Salinas plant were frequently behind schedule, especially in the winter. Dillman, therefore, wrote a stern memo to James Wood, in charge of processing in Salinas, California, expressing his displeasure with the erratic adherence to schedules in the plant. Dillman made it clear that he expected immediate improvement.

Assume you are James Wood. The reason that your production schedules are so erratic is strictly because the produce arriving from Mexico seldom, if ever, arrives on the date scheduled. Since Mexico is the most economical source of fresh fruits and vegetables in the winter, you long ago gave up attempting to change the Mexican suppliers' mode of doing business. Instead, you have simply accommodated your own winter production schedule to their seemingly unchangeable cultural standards.

Assignment

As James Wood, write a memo to Bryan Dillman explaining the futility of attempting to change the cultural behavior of another ethnic group and justifying the fact that the way you are handling production is the only way possible given these sources of supply.

REFERENCES

Borgeois III, L. J. and Boltvinik, M. (1981). OD in cross cultural setting: Latin America. *California Management Review, 23*(3), 75–81.

Campbell, D. T. (1964). Distinguishing differences in perception form failures of communication in cross cultural studies. In *Cross cultural understanding: Epistemology in anthropology,* Northrop, P. S. C. and Livingston, H. H. New York: Harper & Row.

Choe, S. T. (1984). An empirical study of cultural differences: High- and low-context cultures. *Marketing Comes of Age,* Proceedings of the Annual Meeting of the Southern Marketing Association.

Copeland, L. and Griggs, L. (1985). *Going international.* New York: Random House.

Dymsza, W. A. and Negandhi, A. R. (1983). Introduction to cross cultural management issues. *Journal of International Business Studies, 14,* 15–16.

Everett, J. E., Stening, B. W., and Longton, P. A. (1982). Some evidence for an international managerial culture. *Journal of Management Studies, 19,* 153–162.

Gould, J. W., McGuire, P. T., and Sing, C. T. (1983). Adequacy of Hong Kong-California business communication methods. *The Journal of Business Communication, 20,* 33–40.

Hall, E. T. (1959). *The silent language.* Greenwich, CT: Fawcett.

Hall, E. T. (1960). The silent language in overseas business. *Harvard Business Review, 38,* 87–95.

Hall, E. T. (1976). *Beyond culture.* Garden City, NY: Anchor Press/Doubleday.

Hall, E. T. (1976). How cultures collide. *Psychology Today, 10,* 66–97.

Halpern, J. W. (1983). Business communication in China: A second perspective. *The Journal of Business Communication, 20,* 43–55.

Hayes, R. D. (1972). The executive abroad: Minimizing behavioral problems. *Business Horizons, 15,* 87–93.

Haywood, R. (1987). You can't just shout louder to be heard in Europe. *Communication World, 4,* 29–31, 35.

Hubbard, B. (1986). Business communications: The race to communicate. *Director, 39,* 67–84.

Johnston, J. (1980). Business communication in Japan. *The Journal of Business Communication, 17,* 65–70.

Keegan, W. J. (1989). *Global marketing management,* fourth edition. Englewood Cliffs, NJ: Prentice-Hall, Inc.

Keegan, W. J. (1980). *Multinational marketing management,* second edition. Englewood Cliffs, NJ: Prentice-Hall, Inc.

Kilpatrick, R. H. (1984). International business communication practices. *The Journal of Business Communication, 21,* 33–44.

Lathan, M. G. (1982). Internationalizing business communication. *Mid-South Business Journal, 2,* 16–18.

McConnell, J. E. (1977). Promoting U.S. exports through more effective communication between government and business. *The Journal of Business Communication, 15,* 3–18.

Pei, M. (1965). *The story of language.* Philadelphia: J. B. Lippincott Co., 300–301.

Price, N. N. (1982). TAS bureaus are being reborn as multicommunication centers. *Telephony, 203,* 28–29, 98.

Ricks, D. (1983). *Big business blunders: Mistakes in multinational marketing.* Homewood, IL: Dow Jones-Irwin.

Ronen, S. (1986). *Comparative and multinational management.* New York: John Wiley & Sons.

Shipping's just ship-shape at northern telecom (1983). *Modern Office Procedures, 28,* 120–122.

Stull, J. B. (1986). Demonstrating empathy for foreign-born employees through openness and acceptance: A quasi-experimental field study. *The Journal of Business Communication, 23,* 31–40.

Sullivan, J. J. and Kameda, N. (1982). The concept of profit and Japanese-American business communication problems. *The Journal of Business Communication, 19,* 33–39.

Tanaka, I. (1983). Developing electronic conference systems for business communication. *OEP Office Equipment and Products, 12,* 66–68, 95.

Terpstra, V. and David, K. (1985). *The cultural environment of international business,* second edition. Cincinnati: South-Western Publishing, 32–35.

Watanabe, Y. (1987). Foreign affiliates in Japan: The search for professional manpower/The report by the study group on manpower for foreign affiliates in Japan (part 1). *Business Japan, 32,* 24–29.

Williams, E. D., Hayflich, P. F., and Gaston, J. (1986). Training: The challenges of a multi-cultural work force. *Personnel Journal, 65,* 148–151.

Unit 10

CONCLUSION

Chapter 24

The Ethics of Effective Communication

TO: Readers

FROM: Authors

SUBJECT: Unit 10

Unit 10 contains only one chapter. Its aim is to show the importance of ethical considerations in the communication process. The chapter shows that honesty is not just the _best_ policy; it is the _only_ policy possible in long-run work situations where colleagues who cannot be trusted are shunned—or fired. Rather than lecture you, this chapter reminds you that _you_ are responsible for your actions; you are responsible for your motives.

The chapter also serves as a fitting conclusion to, and summary of, the effective communication system you have learned as it applies ethical considerations to organization, style, and impact.

THE ETHICS
OF EFFECTIVE
COMMUNICATION

OBJECTIVES

This chapter will help you to

•

Review the communication system covered
in all preceding chapters

•

Understand that for any business
organization to function effectively, the
highest of ethical standards of
communication must be rigidly adhered to

•

Realize that what you have learned can
enable you to handle highly negative
situations in an honest, ethical, but tactfully
effective fashion

Efficient, effective, get-the-job done, tactful, diplomatic—these are some of the terms we have used throughout this text to describe what we want your business communications to be. But that is not enough. What you write must be honest. What you write must convince others you work with that you are an ethical, moral person.

THE WRITER'S MOTIVES

The first and only principle presented in this chapter asks you to examine your true purpose in communicating.

ETHICS PRINCIPLE:
The writer's motives determine whether a communication is ethical or unethical. Therefore, always consider your underlying motives when communicating.

A misstatement that is accidental is not dishonest. A misstatement that is deliberate, with intention to mislead or defraud, is unethical. Notice that this ethics principle does not focus on the organization of a communication, its style, or its impact. It focuses on the writer's motives. Here is why. Business messages in themselves are neither ethical nor unethical. They simply exist. What determines whether a message is ethical or not stems from what the writer intends that message to accomplish. The most perfectly written sales proposal, for example, will be unethical if the writer has included in it many promises that he or she has no intention of keeping.

Writers' motives make messages either ethical or dishonest.

Corporations and Cultural Context

In the terms of **cultural context** used in Chapter 22, *internally* the context of most large, successful corporations is very high. What you are, how much you can be believed, and how much you can be trusted to do what you say you will do, all play just as important a role in determining your future success in a large corporation as they would play in a high-context culture such as Japan's.

Internally, large corporate cultures are necessarily high context.

While popular movies often depict American businesspeople as greedy and manipulative, it is incorrect to assume that this is true. Most readers of this text are, or soon will be, businesspeople. Will you inevitably become unethical as soon as you begin working in business? Of course not. Will you want to work with or for people whose words—spoken or written—mean little or nothing? Naturally not. In the internal workings of an organization, honesty is not only the best policy, it is the *only* policy.

Organization and Ethics

We have consistently tried to stress ethical behavior in this text. In our discussion of the **bottom-line** organizational pattern, for instance, we told you that businesspeople respect someone who communicates straight out, without equivocation, evasion, or manipulation. Not only is such forthright communication efficient, but it also gives evidence of mutual trust between sender and receiver and shows that subordinates are not afraid to tell the truth to their superiors.

Being **circuitous** was recommended only for very limited, difficult situations. Its use lies in external negative and external negative-persuasive messages sent upward.

However, if an upwardly sent, external negative message is bottom-lined, it runs a high risk of being perceived by the reader as insulting. Hence, it is rude to bottom-line an external negative message up. And it would be equally foolish to bottom-line an external negative-persuasive message sent upward. Because in this situation the reader does not want to do what we, the writer, are asking, we need to prepare the reader carefully before presenting the request. This forces us to be circuitous. We are not being unethical; the message still appears. We are applying common sense.

For internal situations in which a bottom-line organizational pattern risks seeming to be blunt or rude but where a circuitous organizational pattern risks seeming manipulative or dishonest, we suggested you use a **semi-circuitous** organizational pattern. This organizational pattern allows us honestly to tell readers exactly where in the document they can find the bottom line. At the same time, this pattern requests the reader's indulgence to refrain from reading the bottom line until we have had the opportunity to set the stage and justify some possibly disturbing conclusions or recommendations.

Impact and Ethics

With regard to **impact,** you learned how to control word choice, sentence selection, and appearance to achieve a desired effect upon a reader receiving a negative message. This desired effect should not stem from a wish to deceive. It should stem from your sense of what is appropriate, much as your tone of voice, or its volume, would vary depending upon what seems suitable for the situation and your audience.

Style and Ethics

Similarly, with regard to **style,** you learned how to adapt the style combinations available to you to different situations and to different readers. We have stressed that no one style is perfect for all situations, or for all readers. The reader's feelings and emotions are always an integral part of

Being circuitous is permissible in external messages.

Semi-circuitous organization is the only internal alternative to bottom-lining.

Adaptations in style and impact can soften negative messages.

every communication, especially when that communication involves a negative or a highly charged emotional message.

It is our hope that when you yourself become a manager, you will never stifle honest feedback from your subordinates, and you will teach subordinates how to report negative messages in ways that do not hurt your feelings or those of other people. We have tried to assist you by giving you the skills to handle sensitive situations with honesty but also with tact and diplomacy. We hope that as a skillful manager and communicator, you will be able to contribute to the creation of an organization in which there are no significant barriers to open and honest communication, even in the communication of negative information upward.

CASE ILLUSTRATION

Throughout this text, we have used cases to illustrate and teach many of the more complex communication principles. Since ethics is such a highly complex area, one final case will summarize what we have discussed about handling sensitive situations. The case will also demonstrate the importance of honesty and forthrightness in a close working relationship.[1]

> The "Boss" arrives at the office, flushed with excitement and waving a sheaf of handwritten papers. "This is it!" she cries. "I've worked all weekend on it, and I've got it! Here's a marketing plan that can't fail. I'm going to get it copied; then I want each of you," she exclaims, looking at Mary, Bill, and Harry, her subordinates, "to critique it and give me your comments. I'll expect them in writing by tomorrow morning."

By noon the next day, the boss sits at her desk to read the three critiques she has received. The first she picks up is from Harry.

> TO: "Boss"
>
> FROM: Harry
>
> SUBJECT: Proposed Marketing Plan
>
> DATE: March 15, 19——
>
> I think there are three things wrong with your proposed marketing plan. Specifically:
>
> 1. You base all sales projections on the unsupportable assumption of a three-year continuation of low-interest rates.
>
> 2. You state, without proof, that Manufacturing will be able to overcome, within <u>six months</u>, its present inability to produce the product in the quantities assumed by your sales projections.

[1]Material in this chapter is adapted from "Clear Writing Is Not Enough." Reprinted, by permission of publisher, from MANAGEMENT REVIEW, April 1989, © 1989, American Management Association, New York. All rights reserved.

3. You do not even consider the possibility, let alone the probability, that forcing high-quantity production may lead to quality deterioration, resulting in returns, servicing requirements, and potential loss of future sales.

As the boss reads Harry's memo, her face first falls and then becomes tense with resentment. She struggles with herself to keep from being defensive, but loses the struggle. "Harry may be right," she thinks. "And I guess he's honest but, gosh, he's abrasive!"

COMMENTARY

This impression of Harry's abrasiveness, once in the Boss's mind, is never going to change. Harry's reputation thereafter is that he is too insensitive to people's feelings to be an effective manager and motivator of people. As years go by, Harry never is given an assignment involving the smooth handling of people; hence, he never goes far in the company.

What have we learned? Should we conclude that blunt honesty is the worst policy? Let's defer our answer until we have considered Mary's and then Bill's responses.

TO: "Boss"

FROM: Mary

SUBJECT: Proposed Marketing Plan

DATE: March 15, 19——

Thank you for giving me the opportunity to comment on your proposed marketing plan. It shows every evidence of the care and thought you put into it.

It is indeed encouraging that you feel so strongly that interest rates will continue to be low over the next three years. Many economists share your view, and we all hope such will be the case.

Your confidence in Manufacturing's ability to rise above its current difficulties with the product is also inspiring. I found it especially encouraging when you point out in your proposal...

COMMENTARY

Here Mary quotes liberally from two long paragraphs contained in the boss's draft.

Equally reassuring is your confidence in Manufacturing's ability to produce quality as well as quantity. We need such reassurance, since sales projections could be severely damaged by any lowering in the quality of the product our company is justly respected for.

COMMENTARY

Mary fills another half-page with equally innocuous statements.

It is only right that some downside risks be mentioned. Isn't it possible, for example, that interest rates may not stay low for the entire three-year period? Shouldn't other less favorable scenarios be considered and planned for?

What might happen if Manufacturing cannot meet the quantity goals postulated by your plan? And what might result if such quantity goals were met at the expense of product quality?

After the boss's trying experience with Harry's memo, Mary's memo at first seems far more tactful. But when the boss gets to the fourth and final page of the memo, only to find the same criticisms of her marketing plan that Harry had so bluntly presented, she mutters to herself, "I sure didn't like Harry's blunt, almost insulting approach to offering his criticism. But at least he wasn't as manipulative as Mary is. Obviously, Mary thinks just as poorly of my plan as Harry does, but she has tried to con me for three and a half pages before coming to the point."

COMMENTARY

The boss mentally marks Mary down as being not only evasive and manipulative, but also as someone who thinks that she, the boss, is stupid enough to fall for so transparent a ploy. Mary, therefore, also suffers permanent damage in the boss's eyes.

Then the boss picks up Bill's memo:

TO: "Boss"

FROM: Bill

SUBJECT: Proposed Marketing Plan

DATE: March 15, 19— —

Thank you for giving me the privilege of reading your proposed marketing plan. It is a fine reflection on how hard you have worked on it.

Frankly, I can find nothing in it to find fault with. I have every confidence in your ability to project accurately and realistically the sales of this new product over the next three years.

You may count on my every effort to do my small part in making the plan a profitable reality.

The boss immediately concludes that Bill's memo makes Harry's and Mary's look good by comparison. For Bill is either an out-and-out liar, or he is intellectually far inferior to both Mary and Harry in his ability to identify flaws in the marketing plan.

This conclusion, incidentally, forces the boss to recall certain other suspicions she had as to Bill's integrity and to set in motion processes that eventually lead to the loss of Bill's job.

Being Ethical Makes Good Business Sense

The case we just illustrated shows why we state that a corporate culture functions internally much as does a high-context national culture. Within an organization's hierarchy, we are writing, for the most part, to people who are higher in power than we are. What they think of us, and what conclusions they reach about our integrity, our intelligence, and our sensitivity clearly will affect the progress we make in that company.

Conflicting Demands of Tact and Honesty

We have constantly dealt with the ever-present tension between two opposing demands placed on subordinates—(a) that they must be tactful, but not manipulative, and (b) that they must tell the truth but not tactlessly. To achieve both ends, we have to make sensible choices among (a) how we organize a message, (b) how we "say" that message (that is, the style in which we write the message), and (c) how we format, or visually present, the message.

Let us see how we can use organization, style, and impact to extricate ourselves from the dilemma faced by Harry, Mary, and Bill. Let us tell the boss the negative truth about her flawed marketing plan without looking either manipulative or insultingly blunt. (Lying, as Bill did, is so unethical and ineffectual as to be out of the question.)

First, we must decide how to organize our negative message. We have seen from the boss's reaction to Harry's memo that bottom-lining the criticism did not work. But we have also seen that being as circuitous as Mary will likely trigger the suspicion in the boss's mind that we are being manipulative and insincere.

Does this mean that no matter what organizational pattern we choose in this negative message sent up, we are faced with a problem? No. It is true that Harry was too blunt. He should have realized that he had to communicate the negative message tactfully, not only because the boss is Harry's superior, but because she had worked hard over the weekend and was very proud of her draft of the proposed marketing plan.

But wasn't Mary's approach tactful? Yes, it was, but it failed the critical test of being honest. Clearly then, our task is to be tactful, but we must do it in a way that is honest and not manipulative. As we know, this calls for a semi-circuitous organizational pattern with a low-impact appearance, and when we reach the part of the memo where the predominant negative message is delivered, the tactful use of a passive, impersonal style is required. We start by using a personal style as we present our contract statement.

TO: "Boss"

FROM: "You"

SUBJECT: Proposed Marketing Plan

DATE: March 15, 19——

Here is the report you asked for on the proposed marketing plan. My report will cover (a) an analysis of interest-rate projections, (b) production quantity goals, and (c) matters concerning continued quality of product. Following these discussions, I will offer suggestions as to possible alterations in the plan for your consideration. I ask you to read my discussion first before turning to the section on suggestions for changes to the plan. In this way, I will have an opportunity to justify these suggestions by describing the logical analysis on which I have based them.

As you can see in the beginning of this memo, we have not been manipulative. A semi-circuitous organizational pattern enables us to tell the boss honestly that "suggestions for changes" to the plan are going to be presented. But we have forthrightly asked her to give us the opportunity to prepare her for these criticisms by showing the logic on which they rest. The boss may not like the criticisms when she gets to them, but she cannot feel that we have been either blunt and abrasive or evasive and manipulative.

Now consider defensive weapon number two—the style in which we might write the letter. There is no need to be defensive until the point where we give the boss negative criticism about her plan. Ethically, we must give her these criticisms; otherwise, we are not worth having as subordinates. Yet, we are concerned about looking as if we are scolding the boss for having overlooked certain things. We are also concerned about the boss's feelings—and there is nothing unethical whatsoever about being concerned with the feelings of others. Consequently, we decide to use a passive, impersonal style because it enables us to make negative statements honestly but not personally. It avoids personal finger-shaking. Look at the difference between Harry's statement to the boss:

I think there are three things wrong with your proposed marketing plan.

and the following passive, impersonal version:

There are certain suggestions for improvements to the plan that may be worthy of consideration.

In response to anyone who might feel that changing Harry's statement is unethical, here is our answer. Our experience has led us to the firm conclusion that only when people learn how to present unpleasant truths to superiors in a safe, palatable fashion can they have the courage to send honest but highly negative messages upward.

Tactful use of organization, style, and impact helps us tell the truth safely.

Admittedly, if this were an ideal world, where bosses do not have insecurities, or where their subordinates did not chuckle over how Mary or Harry "told the boss off," such use of stylistic devices might be unnecessary. In the modern business world, however, it is good and ethical to use any honest method to tell the truth in an organization and, at the same time, not offend the important person who receives the bad news.

But, as we have learned, control over the impact a communication exerts on a reader gives us another tool that can help us present truths to a boss in a way that gets them across in a more palatable fashion. In the case of the memo under discussion, the section that conveys the criticism of the boss's plan should be written in longer sentences and bulkier paragraphs. Furthermore, the negativity of the criticism can and should be offset by positive suggestions. Upgrading a message from negative to positive, if this is at all possible, is not unethical.

Notice how the following version of the critical part of the report combines a low-impact presentation with a passive, impersonal style, and then adds positive suggestions for action that should be appreciated by the boss.

Suggestions for Consideration

There are certain suggestions for improvements to the plan which may be worthy of consideration. First, because of the potential volatility of interest rates over the three-year period covered by the plan, perhaps it would be wise to consider presenting sales projections based on various interest rates. Of course, that rate or range of rates that are thought to be most likely to occur should be pointed out. Offering projections based on other rates might reduce the plan's vulnerability to charges that other rates have not been taken into account.

It might also be worthwhile to consider requesting from Manufacturing written estimates of their ability to produce the product in projected quantities within six months. If Manufacturing argues, as they well might, that high quantity production will surely lead to deterioration in product quality (resulting in returns, servicing requirements, and the like), the burden will be on Manufacturing to explain why. If such explanations are not acceptable to top management, your marketing plan, at least under one of the interest rate assumptions offered, should have every chance of being approved.

Notice first how these negative thoughts are expressed in long sentences and paragraphs. Notice how the passive, impersonal style makes it seem less like a subordinate personally reprimanding and lecturing the boss. Notice, finally, how qualifiers increase the tact and deference with which the ideas are presented—"perhaps it would be wise to consider" and the constant use of the words "might" and "may."

Necessary defensive writing is not in itself dishonest.

But are these last crucial paragraphs written as clearly as we possibly could write them? Of course not. These criticisms were expressed far more clearly and vigorously in Harry's memo. But Harry hurt the boss's feelings and damaged himself by so doing. We have not lied, but we have told the truth in a way that is deferential to the boss's feelings and her position of superiority. In the real world, we must realize that there are many times when we must write defensively, and to do so honestly but very tactfully is not unethical.

Unconscious Distortion

Our ethics principle focuses properly on your motives when communicating. But none of us can be completely in touch with, or in full control over, our occasional inclinations to confuse facts and opinions, nor our subconscious desire to favor what we like best. Therefore, to protect your reputation for both meticulous honesty and diligence, make sure that you double- and triple-check your communications to make certain that you are not guilty of unintentional distortion of the truth. Specifically, you should concentrate on the following:

> Triple-check to make sure that you have not been less than honest because of confusion of opinion with fact or subconscious bias.

1. Make sure that all opinions are clearly labeled as such, and that the source of each opinion is stated. If it is Bill Jones's opinion that new car sales will fall next year by 10 percent, state that this is Bill Jones's opinion. Furthermore, make every attempt to discover Jones's track record as a forecaster, and communicate that, too.

2. If facts are reported, recognize that they are not facts just because you say they are. You must offer any necessary supporting verification for any facts that are not obviously true. For example, if you state that the population of New Orleans in 1990 was a certain figure, you can easily support this by stating "according to the latest U.S. Census figures." But if you claim that the population of any city in an undeveloped nation is a specific number, you would find it most difficult to offer support.

3. Be certain to be honest (not only with your reader, but with yourself as well) about recognizing and overtly stating a personal bias. Suppose you are asked to evaluate whether your company has afforded women employees equal opportunities for advancement into higher paying management positions. Suppose you are passionately convinced, even before doing the study, that your company has either done far too much or far too little for women. If such is the case, you should announce your bias to your boss before taking on the assignment. And if the boss still asks you to do the study, you should admit early in that report the possibility of your bias distorting your perception and analysis of the facts since persons other than your boss probably will see what you have written.

4. Make absolutely certain that you have presented those graphics that best summarize data fairly and without distortion. Also, be sure that prose introductions of graphics do not seduce the reader into interpreting a graphic in the way you subconsciously desire.

5. Recognize and fight against the normal tendency to commit errors of omission, rather than commission, in communication. It is so easy for all of us to seize on and report facts that support our viewpoint, and to ignore, or belittle, those that are contrary to our interests.

SUMMARY

You alone are responsible for your motives and your communication behavior.

Earlier in this chapter we observed that honesty is not only the best policy in business—it is the only policy. We have tried to stress this point in a variety of ways throughout this text. We have shown you how to tell the truth in ways that are effective as well as safe. People usually lie when they are afraid to tell the truth. Although we have encouraged you to be honest and to have integrity in all of your communication endeavors, we recognize that this advice would be hollow unless we followed it up by showing you how best to express that truth. We think you now know that finding that best way results from the right choices of organization, style, and impact.

In the final outcome, of course, you alone will have to determine whether what you are doing in any communication situation is or is not ethical. You will have to be honest with yourself about your motives. No list of principles, rules, or ancient adages will ultimately make a difference. Ethics is a matter of right and wrong, and most people know when they are considering doing something that is right or wrong. The communication principles that we have developed for this book should in no way be taken as substitutes for your ethical principles or as tools by which to mislead, fool, or seduce readers and audiences. We encourage you to use these communication tools for the right ends, and we are sure you will.

REVIEW QUESTIONS

1. What should you always consider when communicating?

2. What determines whether or not a communication is ethical?

3. Complete this sentence: In business, honesty is not only the best policy, it is _____.

4. In the final outcome, who will have to determine whether what you are doing in any communication situation is or is not ethical?

DISCUSSION QUESTIONS

1. A famous critic of business once wrote that the practice of business is amoral, that the pursuit of profits is all. Do you agree? What arguments can be used against this position?

2. If you got a job that involved writing advertising copy for a product that you do not believe in, should you resign? If not, how would you justify writing such persuasive messages?

Ace

high   low

valuable   not

1.

2.
Negotiations are
3.   slow   ritualistic

4.

5.

6.

7.   less important   move up

8.

EX 3 441 - 42

12/9

Case 445

CASES

Ethics is a subject best studied through cases that are based on actual situations. Therefore, this unit contains no exercises, but instead asks you to deal ethically with the following fascinating but difficult cases involving both ethics and effective communication. As always, the Flow Chart and the Strategy Wheel will help you decide on the probably most honest, yet safest way of communicating the messages required by each assigned task (see Chapter 19).

Case 1
Human Rights and
Corporate Responsibility

Part 1

In this part of the case, assume you are R. L. Greenspan, a member of a group of employees working in Allgood Products' corporate office. You are very concerned because the company has considerable investment in a Latin American country that we will call San Sebastian. San Sebastian is controlled by a military junta that is not the slightest bit hesitant about violating human rights. Escapees from San Sebastian have been on the news in recent weeks pointing out the fact that the colonels in charge of the country have imprisoned and allegedly tortured literally thousands of dissidents on the slightest pretext.

Some of the escaped dissidents have named Allgood Products as a company that supports the military regime simply because it is good business for Allgood. Many tropical fruits, coffees, and the like, are purchased from San Sebastian wholesalers. Furthermore, it has been disclosed that Allgood has invested heavily in the stocks of many of the wholesalers from whom products are bought. It is alleged that these companies are highly supportive of the military regime and that they pay their workers next to nothing. If workers even think of forming a union, the military is called in to break up any public meetings.

Assignment

You have been asked by your coworkers to draft a memo to Samuel Potnick, who heads Allgood Products' investment committee, for the signature of the other employees who feel strongly that (a) Allgood Products should divest itself of all interests in companies based in San Sebastian and (b) Allgood Products should vigorously denounce the military regime for its inhuman treatment of people. Your coworkers have asked that you make this letter as effective as you possibly can to convince Potnick to take these actions.

You realize that Potnick is not likely to be easily convinced. However, you agree to do as your associates requested. Write the appropriate memo to Samuel Potnick from R. L. Greenspan.

Case 1
Human Rights and
Corporate Responsibility

Part 2

In this part of the case, you are to assume you are A. C. Bickley, Samuel Potnick's assistant. Potnick has received the letter from the disgruntled employees asking for divestiture of interests in companies based in San Sebastian. Reacting rather emotionally, he tells you, as his assistant, to write a memo for his signature informing the dissident employees that he must deny their request because his function is to maximize income to stockholders, not to further any political goals. He asks you to remind them that not all stockholders in Allgood Products are rich, and that many are the proverbial widows and orphans dependent on dividends paid out of profits. Furthermore, Potnick argues, not all stockholders will hold political beliefs similar to those of the disgruntled employees and might resent deeply any actions taken against San Sebastian, a nation with faults, but still a friend of the United States.

His final suggestion is that those who have complained should spend their time on work that will benefit Allgood, rather than wasting time on international politics.

Assignment

Write a draft of a memo to R. L. Greenspan that follows your boss's instructions, yet pays heed to the Strategy Wheel's advice in communication situations like this.

Case 1
Human Rights and
Corporate Responsibility

Part 3

Assume now that you are once again R. L. Greenspan, the spokesperson for the employees who want Allgood Products to stop investing in San Sebastian. After receiving Samuel Potnick's letter refusing your request, you meet with your coworkers. You decide once again to attempt to convince Potnick that Allgood Products, by furthering human rights anywhere in the world, creates the image of the kind of company that people want to work for and that customers will want to do business with. The argument the group suggests you make is this: By withdrawing all investments in, and by stopping doing business with San Sebastian, Allgood Products will be taking actions that will be good for the company and its profits in the long run.

Assignment

Write that memo to Samuel Potnick.

Case 1
Human Rights and
Corporate Responsibility

Part 4

Samuel Potnick responds to the second letter he has just received from the unhappy employees by telling you, his assistant A. C. Bickley, that you should draft a memo for him to sign once again denying the employees' request. Tell them, he says, that they could do more good for the people of San Sebastian if they were to petition political figures, not him, because his primary concern is financial, not political, as his first letter to them said. He continues to hold the position that his job is that of maximizing profits for shareholders, not getting involved in political concerns that he feels are actually none of his or the company's business.

Assignment

Write the memo that Potnick has requested.

Case 1
Human Rights and
Corporate Responsibility

Part 5

Samuel Potnick is concerned because his letters to the protesting employees have done no good. Now the employees seem to have gotten the attention of Maxwell Allgood himself and have him questioning whether the company is indeed behaving responsibly toward the people of San Sebastian.

Maxwell Allgood urges Samuel Potnick to get the unhappy employees busy on some activity that may more directly benefit the people of San Sebastian. He believes such activities will be more productive than the expenditure of time in a futile attempt to persuade Potnick to do what he believes he or the company morally cannot do—that is, put political interests above those of the stockholders who depend on dividends.

Consequently, Potnick tells you, his assistant A. C. Bickley, to see if you can't this time write a positive-persuasive message that will persuade the employees that Allgood Products is willing to work together with appropriate political figures *if* those political figures will take the leadership. Potnick tells you that Allgood really believes that it is improper for the company to interfere in what is essentially State Department business. However, Potnick wants the employees to know that both he and Maxwell Allgood are very concerned about the situation, just as they are.

Potnick tells you to suggest that the employees pick a leading political figure, such as a senator who has expressed concerns about San Sebastian, and to write to him or her stating that Allgood Products, and Maxwell Allgood himself, are concerned about the situation in San Sebastian. Further, you should express the company's desire to work closely with this political figure, and with the appropriate State Department authorities, to attempt to ease tensions in San Sebastian.

Assignment

Write that memo to R. L. Greenspan, spokesperson for the concerned employees.

Case 1
Human Rights and
Corporate Responsibility

Part 6

Maxwell Allgood has been informed that a group of stockholders, deeply concerned about publicity in the media about Allgood Products, Inc.'s investments in San Sebastian, plans to disrupt the annual stockholders' meeting. The meeting is to be held in the ballroom of the Regal Towers in San Francisco in just two weeks.

Allgood meets with Samuel Potnick and Carl Hilton, Allgood's President, to discuss what actions should be taken.

"You know, Max," states Potnick, "I have just as much of a moral dilemma about our investments in San Sebastian companies as has anyone. But things just aren't as simple as people who only see one side of a situation would like to make them. Each of us in this room has a moral, fiduciary responsibility to all our stockholders, not just to ourselves. You know better than anyone, Max, that many of the people who have bought stock in Allgood Products are not rich. Many elderly people depend on our dividends, and our dividends depend on our profits."

"Sure, Sam," Carl Hilton says. "Max knows that, but many of our employees don't, and now, apparently, some of our stockholders don't believe that maximization of profits is a real obligation. They argue that corporations have a higher moral responsibility than that of making money."

"You know what this reminds me of?" Maxwell Allgood reminisces. "One time, years ago, I got a call from the Captain of one of the maritime vessels we had hired to transport bananas up from Central America. He said that he was faced with hundreds of thousands of dollars worth of bananas about to rot on a loading dock because the inspectors in charge of agricultural shipments were demanding a bribe of $10,000 before they would allow the bananas to be loaded. Since I had given strict orders to all people working for Allgood that under no circumstances should we get involved in bribery, regardless of how customary such practices might be in another country, he asked me what he should do.

"Well, I'll tell you, Sam, it wasn't easy for me either. If I didn't authorize him to pay the bribe, our stockholders were going to take a tremendous beating. After all, it was not entirely my personal money that was likely to rot on the docks with the bananas. It was also the money of many other investors. And I had a real responsibility for looking out for their economic well-being, as well as my own. I told him to pay the bribe and be done with it. But now, as you know, no one can do that. We would all be subject to penalties if we did offer a bribe."

Hilton responds, "You know, if we let this group of stockholders dictate to us at the meeting, we may end up being forced to take actions that would run completely counter to the best interests of the majority of shareholders. These few unhappy stockholders and those disgruntled employees have no authority to speak for the majority of stockholders."

"Right," says Allgood, "and we've only got two weeks to decide what to do." He looks at Samuel Potnick. "Sam, did you have any luck in persuading those concerned employees to find some prominent political figure who would lead the charge, with us being willing to go along?"

"I don't know," Potnick answers. "I heard they wrote a letter to Senator Butler, but whether they received a reply or not I don't know."

"I'll tell you what," Carl Hilton intersperses. "I'm not as deeply involved in this case as are you, Max, and you, Sam. Let me sit down and do some thinking and then put some thoughts in the form of a statement that you could read at the shareholders' meeting. One thing I think is absolutely certain. Max, you have to strike first and very hard to get your point across. You cannot let the meeting be disrupted or be put in a defensive position where you may seem to be on the run, or be made to appear opposed to some very lofty ideals. You tell me essentially what position you want to take, and I'll put together a brief but hard-hitting statement for you to read at the very beginning of the meeting."

Assignment

If you were Maxwell Allgood, what position would you take in this situation? Do you agree with Carl Hilton's statement that his speech should be hard-hitting and directly to the point? Formulate for yourself the statement you want Allgood to make.

Case 2
Bill Roper's Forced Retirement

Maxwell Allgood is meeting with Mary Lou Higgins. The topic is: What to do about Bill Roper. Here are the facts of the situation.

Bill Roper is fifty-six years old. He has been with the company for thirty-one years. In his early years, he was the star salesman in the Instant Foods Division. Roper would long ago have been promoted to the rank of vice president if he had not been beset by serious family and personal problems.

At the time of his greatest productivity, when his promotion to vice president was hanging in the balance, Roper's wife had to be hospitalized for mental illness in an expensive sanitarium where she still is under treatment. That was ten years ago. Almost concurrent with the breakdown of his wife, one of Roper's sons dropped out of college, joined a commune, and has refused to speak to his father since. Roper's other son became deeply involved with drugs, and has himself been hospitalized off and on for the past six or seven years. Struggling against such odds, it is understandable that Roper himself should have cracked under the strain. He began to drink heavily and, as he did so, began to suffer failures to meet his sales quotas in each of the last five years.

Higgins and Allgood are meeting today to deal with the fact that Roper has been repeatedly found wandering in a drunken stupor in the factory in Minneapolis where some of his old friends still work. There are, of course, strict rules about drinking in the factory and Roper has been removed forcibly twice and taken home to sleep it off. Just this morning, the third such event took place. Higgins received a call from none other than Frank Finnegan, Vice President of Production, stating that something must be done about Roper. Finnegan simply cannot allow Roper to ignore the safety rules in the factory. Higgins has come to discuss taking action with Maxwell Allgood.

The reason for Higgins's concern is that Bill Roper has been over the years a close, personal friend of Maxwell Allgood's. Allgood is on record as saying that if it hadn't been for Bill Roper, the company would not have prospered as much as it did twenty to twenty-five years ago. "He was the best salesman I ever saw and a wonderful person," Maxwell Allgood said. "It's just that tragic family he has had to cope with that has brought him to this state of affairs."

Higgins says, "Max, something simply has to be done about Bill and done right now. You know it as well as I do. I know he is a friend of yours. But what I want to do is to take responsibility for writing Roper a letter attempting to persuade him to recognize his alcoholism, enter into a rehabilitation treatment center, and see if he can't lick his problems. I'd like your permission to put him on a six-month leave of absence with full pay, pay all costs of rehabilitation, and guarantee him his present job back at the end of six months if—and only if—he has straightened out. But the price of all this is that he will have to agree in writing, right now, to accept early retirement if he ever breaks down again. The Legal Department tells us that if he refuses to agree to this in writing, we will have to bring him before the disciplinary board on charges of having chronically violated our safety rules and proceed against him on that basis, rather than on the basis of his decreased sales performance."

Maxwell Allgood responds, "Mary Lou, I know you're right. I hate to see it done, but I guess it has to be. But here is what I want you to do. Please remember that Bill Roper is more sinned against than sinning. I care for him very deeply, so when you write the letter, show real concern. Try to persuade him that what you are asking is for his own good as well as for the good of all of us. Show compassion and understanding. I hope you won't mind if I ask you to let me see a draft of the letter before it goes out to Bill."

Assignment

Assume you are Mary Lou Higgins. Write that letter to Bill Roper. NOTE: *If* you decide that you think it best that the letter you write to Roper be signed by Maxwell Allgood, write it that way and simply make this clear to Allgood.

REFERENCES

Bragg, A. (1987). On the firing line. *Sales and Marketing Management, 138,* 42–45.

Broussard, R. D. and Brannen, D. E. (1986). Credential distortions: Personnel practitioners give their views. *Personnel Administrator, 31,* 129–146.

Ely, E. S. (1985). How to unmask bogus job seekers. *Computer Decisions, 17,* 100–107.

Falconer, T. (1987). How to be the perfect victim. *Canadian Business, 60,* 52–55.

Golen, S., Powers, C., and Titkemeyer, M. A. (1985). How to teach ethics in a basic business communication class—committee report of the 1983 teaching methodology and concepts committee, subcommittee I. *The Journal of Business Communication, 22,* 75–83.

Krohn, F. B. (1985). A general semantics approach to teaching business ethics. *The Journal of Business Communication, 22,* 59–66.

Nilsen, T. R. (1974). *Ethics of speech communication.* New York, NY: Bobbs Merrill.

Proctor, M. L. (1982). Don't forget to debrief. *Security Management, 26,* 28–29.

Rentz, K. C. and Debs, M. B. (1987). Language and corporate values: Teaching ethics in business writing courses. *The Journal of Business Communication, 24,* 37–48.

Schwartz, S. J. (1980). How to dehire: A guide for the manager. *Human Resource Management, 19,* 22–25.

Schweitzer, J. A. (1982). Effectively securing business communications. *Security Management, 26,* 157–160.

Varner, I. I. (1979). Business ethics—intuition or logic? *The Journal of Business Communication, 16,* 27–32.

SPECIAL
FEATURES

INTRA-TEXT MEMORANDUM

TO: Readers

FROM: Authors

SUBJECT: Special Features Section

This Special Features section covers topics that are not a direct part of the communication system developed in the text. Unit A provides information for those involved in searching for employment. Unit B presents detailed information about grammar, punctuation, and format—information that you may already know but need to review. And Unit C helps those students enrolled in a class requiring analysis of long, complex cases.

We have distinguished these units from the others in the text by labeling them A, B, and C, and the chapters in the units as A-1, A-2, B-1, and so on. This labeling system merely shows that the material covered in the Special Features section does not fit directly into the communication system. It is not intended to diminish the importance of the material presented here. In fact, depending on the needs and skills you bring to this class, you may find some, and perhaps all, of the Special Features section vital to your development.

Unit A, "The Application Package," offers practical advice on how to begin a search for a new job. Chapter A-1, "The Application Letter," provides helpful hints about how to (a) begin a search for employment and (b) construct application letters that provide you with the highest probability of being chosen for an interview or a job offer.

The second chapter in Unit A, "The Resume," informs you about the two traditional types of resumes used by most applicants: the **chronological** and **functional resume**. This chapter shows you how to construct both types of resumes and offers you advice about when each type works most effectively. In addition, this chapter is filled with practical tips on how to write your resume so that your skills and other favorable qualities have the greatest likelihood of being recognized by potential employers.

The final chapter in Unit A, "The Interview," offers advice about how to prepare for an interview, how to conduct yourself at the interview, and how to analyze your performance after you have completed the interview.

Unit B, "Reviewing The Basics," provides a practical review of the fundamentals of effective written business communication. Chapter B-1, "A Businessperson's Guide to Grammar" and Chapter B-2, "A Businessperson's Guide to Punctuation," present what is essential for you to know in business about grammar and punctuation. These chapters cover topics that our experience indicates are necessary for you to know.

The final chapter in Unit B is "Formatting Letters, Memos, and Formal Reports." Format refers to the placement of parts of a letter or memo and also involves attachments or other materials that accompany formal reports. A variety of conventions or rules exists about formatting different types of documents. This chapter will show you a few of the most common formats.

Unit C, "How To Analyze Cases," is the final unit in the Special Features section. Chapter C-1, "Case Analysis," provides an in-depth look at rules to follow in analyzing cases. In addition, this chapter provides detailed advice about solving business problems in a rigorous and logical fashion.

Chapter C-2, "Applying Analysis to a Case," combines the material learned in "Case Analysis" with other information developed throughout the text. This chapter shows you how to analyze a complex case and to write a report on that case in an effective and efficient manner. Thus, while the first chapter in this text promises to provide you with information about how to communicate to "get a job done," the last chapter ends by showing you how to get a job done in a case-oriented class.

In summary, this section offers a wealth of information for you to study and use. Whatever your skills or needs, we know you will find some of the Special Features material beneficial.

Unit A

THE APPLICATION PACKAGE

THE APPLICATION LETTER

OBJECTIVES

This chapter will help you to

●

Be aware of places you can learn about job openings

●

Understand the benefits of an application letter

●

Write effective application letters

If you are presently looking for work or if you plan to start your search in the near future, application letters and resumes are very important to you. If you presently have a good job, the information in this chapter, although not immediately relevant to you, may soon be. Most people shift jobs frequently in their first five years of work. People get married and may change cities. Others seek happiness by moving closer to (or farther away from) their roots. For many reasons, people shift jobs several times before settling down.

A number of management experts believe that competitive pressures in the 1990s may force those companies that have implied lifetime employment guarantees to abandon this approach. These experts predict that, on the average, a professional employee can expect an average of only five years with a given company. Therefore, the odds are high that you will need information about how to put together effective job-seeking letters and resumes.

WHERE TO LOOK FOR EMPLOYMENT

Where should you begin your search for employment? The answer, of course, is in different places. The most logical place to begin is your college or university's placement office. Most large companies that send recruiters to college campuses to interview prospective employees prefer to use placement offices rather than going to the trouble of scheduling interviews themselves. Because of their experience with and knowledge of recruiters' preferences, personnel in placement offices can offer valuable advice about how to prepare a resume and how to conduct yourself in an interview. Many of these placement offices also provide background information about the companies that have scheduled interviews.

Look beyond Your College Placement Office

Although college placement offices are a good place to start, they should not be the only place to look. Why? Because such facilities have built-in limitations. First, these offices must serve the needs of all students on campus. Placement office personnel cannot act as your personal agents. Furthermore, when you use your college's placement office, you are competing with all your peers on campus. Unless you stand out as the best student on campus or at least in your major, or unless you have some special characteristics that distinguish you from all other students, you are just one of the many students that recruiters will interview on the various campuses they visit.

In addition, as a result of staff shortages and large numbers of students, college placement offices can offer only generic advice. Each student is told the same information about how to prepare a resume and how to behave at an interview. This makes it difficult for you to create that special something to differentiate you from all other students interviewed by a recruiter.

Finally, a placement office provides interviews with only a limited number of companies. A school cannot invite to its campus all the companies hiring capable employees at any one time. Furthermore, smaller firms often cannot afford to send professional recruiters to a number of different schools. The firms that do choose to interview at your college often have been attracted by your institution's particular strengths. For instance, if your university has a strong engineering program, firms with engineering openings will most likely recruit on your campus. Such firms may have no great interest in interviewing people in your major, be it marketing or personnel or accounting. Conversely, if your school has a strong accounting program, you can be sure that a number of the big accounting firms will interview on your campus—a fact that may not be favorable for marketing and finance majors.

Other Places to Find Employment Opportunities

If your college is not noted for its excellence in your major (and a visit to the placement office will soon tell you the hard facts about this), you will have to work harder and on your own to obtain interviews. You should still begin your search at the placement office, but here are some other sources that you should consider examining for employment openings.

- *Libraries.* Both public and college libraries, especially business libraries, can give you information about thousands of companies that may have positions available. Ask to see where the library stores its annual reports. These will provide useful information about companies and the directions they are going in. The reports may even give some hints about these companies' future employment needs.

- *Professional associations.* Learn about the professional associations that relate to your major. Often these associations retain listings of jobs available in particular specialties. You can also pick up leads and learn about employment trends by reading the publications that these associations produce or by attending the meetings of these associations. You may make valuable employment contacts at such meetings.

- *Newspapers.* The classified sections in local newspapers do, on relatively rare occasions, provide help for job seekers. But larger papers, such as the *Wall Street Journal*, the *New York Times*, and the *Washington Post*, provide a ready, daily source of companies advertising for employees throughout the country.

- *Alumni associations.* If your school or college has an active alumni association, see if you can obtain names of association members who work in job areas of interest to you. Try to find out their job titles, where they work, their mailing addresses, and their work phone numbers. Then begin to call and/or write to them, actively seeking their support and assistance. Do not be shy about seeking their help. Most older alumni are pleased to be able to help a younger graduate of their school.

In this process, focus special attention on alumni who hold prestigious or powerful positions. If you can get them to offer advice—or even better, to give you specific leads—you can then follow up the leads and mention the attention-getting fact that this important person suggested that you write and ask about employment.

Fraternities and sororities also usually have alumni associations. If you are a member of one of these organizations, obtain a list of its alumni and take steps to make these persons aware of your interest in employment.

- *Friends and associates.* People you have known in the past—or perhaps some your parents have known—often provide a ready source of information about job openings. Contact these people. Let them know the kind of job you are seeking and tell them your qualifications. Try to include a resume with this letter—and then wait to see what happens. People are often surprised at the positive results such contacts can produce.

- *Telephone directories.* Directories provide a handy list of potential employers. A detailed look at such directories provides you with the names of many different firms you never even knew existed. Often you can simply call the firms and learn much about their needs, interests, and goals. If there are possibilities, be sure to ask for the name and title of the person in charge of hiring.

Phone directories may seem an unusual source for job prospecting, but they can work effectively. One accounting major decided that his grades were not good enough to allow him to be hired by a major accounting firm. This fact did not particularly disturb him because all along he had wanted to work for a smaller CPA firm. However, much to his dismay, he discovered that such firms seldom interviewed on his college campus.

Rather than lamenting his fate, he planned a week-long, statewide tour of the cities in which he wanted to work. He drove to each city, found a phone directory, and called each local accounting firm to inquire about positions. In some instances, he gained interviews; in other instances, he learned about other firms that had positions available; on some occasions, he was told to call back later.

This resourceful student did not even let rejections go unnoticed. He sent letters to each of the firms he had contacted and included a recent resume. The letters thanked the firms for taking time to talk to him (even if the only contact had been through a phone conversation), briefly explained his qualifications, and included a resume for them to consider should a job become available. Amazingly, it was this last step, revealing his polite unwillingness to be rejected, that eventually led to his finding employment. A firm that at first had no openings suddenly had one and contacted the young man for an interview.

Pursue Jobs Actively

One final word of advice concerns the need to pursue positions actively. The myth of the Hollywood starlet discovered at a soda fountain is largely that—a myth. Most Hollywood actors end up being "discovered" only after they trudge from studio to studio, usually for years, actively seeking any kind of role. In all probability, the same will hold true for you. You too have to show initiative, find leads, write letters, make phone calls, and constantly ask for interviews. The worst thing that can happen is that you will get rejected.

As a general rule, businesspeople do admire controlled assertiveness. They are seldom offended by requests as to whether their firms have positions available. In fact, more often than not, such requests subtly flatter them. Wouldn't you like working with a firm that others want to work for? Be aggressive in selling yourself. If you act shy and reluctant, you signal the potential buyer that you have doubts about your own worth.

THE APPLICATION LETTER

People often comment, "Why bother sending an application letter? The readers have my resume; isn't that all that they really care about?" The answer to these questions lies not just in what the application letter says but also in what it implies.

Implications of the Application Letter

A complete, thorough application letter implies that the applicant is not just checking this company off a list of companies he or she is applying to. It suggests that the applicant is interested in working for this particular company and has taken time to prove that interest by writing a letter specifically tailored to that company's needs and interests.

Think, for instance, what the following letter implies about the applicant's genuine interest in working for XYZ, Inc.

> Dear Employment Office:
>
> Please consider the enclosed resume for the marketing position you have available. I appreciate your interest in my qualifications and look forward to hearing from you soon.

Needless to say, such a letter may actually harm even an impressive resume. It is obviously a form letter. No employer will be delighted to be approached so casually. Writing an individually tailored application letter shows your specific interest in a particular company. And that interest surely cannot hurt.

Although this expression of interest is perhaps the most important reason for writing an application letter, it is certainly not the only one.

Here are some other reasons to write a detailed, thorough application letter. It gives you an opportunity to

- Highlight and emphasize key points contained in your resume.
- Interpret, adapt, and tailor the information in your resume to the needs of this particular company.
- Convey, through organizational and stylistic options available to you, key personality traits that match those desired by the organization.
- Demonstrate the writing skills that many companies are seeking.

Tailoring your letter so that it clearly refers to work in a particular company is not especially hard to do today. Thanks to the various word processing packages, you can compose and store one or two generic application letters and then add appropriate details and information to make the letter seem aimed at a particular company. Thus, you can easily write individual letters to many different companies.

Remember, however, that being thorough and complete does not mean being long-winded and dull. Only in the most extraordinary circumstances should a letter exceed one page in length. As a general rule of thumb, letters should range from three quarters of a page to a full page in length.

Strategy in Application Letters

Is it possible to develop an exact strategy that is best for you to use in your application letter? Yes, but as always, you have to begin by considering the situational factors.

- *Are you writing up or down?* Up, of course. You are the one asking for an interview and a job.
- *What is your relationship with your reader?* In most instances, the relationship is neutral rather than warm or antagonistic because neither you nor your reader know each other personally.
- *What is the risk involved?* Not much, if any. The worst that can happen is that the potential employer will refuse to answer your letter, or tell you no. Even if such a refusal occurs, you are no worse off than you would have been had you not inquired about employment.

Next, after you have considered the situational factors, ask yourself what type of message are you sending. Here are some possible answers.

If you are an absolutely sensational student, with much desirable work experience, you are in the position of being able to write a positive-persuasive letter. It is fairly easy to persuade employers that, by hiring you, they would be doing a very good thing for their company. If you are fortunate enough to be able to write a positive-persuasive message, that message should have a direct organizational pattern, be high-impact, and use a personal, but probably not (in this case) very forceful, style. You do not want to look pushy or conceited. Finally, the message should be rather colorless since you don't know all the people who will read the letter.

What if you have limited work experience and your grade point average (GPA) places you in the bottom half of your graduating class? You have a much harder letter to write. Should you write a negative-persuasive message that tries to convince the recruiter that you do possess skills and knowledge that are not apparent on the surface?

No, this approach would be too transparent. Recruiters would easily see what you are trying to do. A far better strategy is to upgrade your message to positive-persuasive and try to build a positive case based on some other aspects of your work and experience.

Identification of the overall strategy to be used in application letters enables us to develop our first principle for these letters:

APPLICATION PRINCIPLE 1:

As a general rule, view an application letter as a positive-persuasive message that should

a. Have a bottom-line organization.
b. Contain a contract sentence, if appropriate.

Because Application Principle 1 applies only to the beginning of an application letter, let's focus on how to get started.

The Beginning

The opening paragraph of an application letter is especially important because, first, it tells the reader what you are seeking (that is, the bottom line of your letter), and second, it serves to create an image in the reader's mind as to the type of businessperson you are.

What is the bottom line of an application letter? You can have two closely related purposes. You write either

1. To let the potential employer know that you are interested in and available to fill a position. The implication is that you hope the employer will take the next step and invite you to provide more information and/or write you to come for an interview; or
2. To ask directly for that interview.

Hence, your letter might begin like this:

Dear Mr. Cargile:

Please consider me as an applicant for the accounting position you advertised in the Wall Street Journal.

or, like this

Dear Mr. Samson:

I am writing to request an interview for the accounting position you advertised in the New York Times.

Since recruiters are busy people, most appreciate the efficiency of either of these initial statements.

The first paragraph of an application letter makes a very loud statement about yourself. By bottom-lining your letter and by including a contract sentence that organizes your thoughts for the reader, you provide some rather obvious hints about the kind of businessperson you are. What you want is to have words like "efficient" and "forthright" arise in your reader's mind.

At the beginning, tell the reader where you learned about the job opening (for example, through an advertisement in the *New York Times* or through your university's placement office). If someone told you about the position, particularly if that person has connections with or is respected by the company, ask him or her for permission to use his or her name in the opening. Your first two sentences might then begin:

Dear Ms. Edwards:

Walt Smith recently informed me that you have a position available for a financial analyst. I am therefore applying for the position.

You should also address your application letter to a specific person. A letter mailed to a named individual is received much more favorably than is one that is addressed to "To Whom It May Concern." For this reason, direct mailing companies spend considerable amounts of time and money creating and purchasing mailing lists containing specific names and addresses. These companies put a great deal of effort into making their mailing seem as personal as possible. That is also the reason we advised you earlier in this chapter to search out names of people to write to and names to "drop" into your opening sentences.

What style should you use? Application Principle 2 gives the answer:

APPLICATION PRINCIPLE 2:
Adapt the style of your letter to the type of work applied for and to the public image of the reader's organization.

A highly forceful, highly personal style might prove effective if you are applying for a position in sales or advertising. But that style would surely backfire if used in an application for an accounting or engineering position. Imagine how an accountant might react upon receipt of an application letter that began as follows:

Dear Ms. Ingram:

Roses are red,
Violets are blue;
I'd like to do
Accounting for you!

Admittedly, I'm no poet, but I think you'll agree that I have the academic qualifications and experience you can use to make your firm "Numero Uno" in the Tucson area!

You have to use common sense. If you are an accounting major, ask yourself, "What style of writing would my accounting professor probably like?" It is a reasonable gamble that he or she will not be far different in acquired tastes from other accountants practicing in the field.

However, the style that might please an accountant might not please a sales manager. For example, how would most salespeople react to the style used in this letter's beginning?

Dear Mr. Mayer:

The position of assistant sales manager is being sought. Many years have been spent preparing for such a career. It is, therefore, respectfully requested that full consideration for the position be given to this application.

Certain jobs attract certain kinds of people. But equally important, certain companies attract certain kinds of employees. If, for example, you are applying for a position as a financial analyst with a large, New York investment banking firm, you might not be too wise to begin as follows:

Dear Mr. Strickland:

As the son of two farmers, I learned the value of hard work at an early age. And those rural lessons I learned have stayed with me. Could they be of use to you?

The Middle

Now let's consider the middle portion—the body—of an application letter. In this section you must deliver your positive-persuasive message and do your best to justify why you are a person who should be seriously considered for the job. Application Principles 3 and 4 offer sensible advice on how to accomplish this task:

APPLICATION PRINCIPLE 3:
Emphasize your strengths.

APPLICATION PRINCIPLE 4:
Adapt the body of your letter to the company's needs, not yours.

Let's briefly examine the significance of these two principles.

Assessing Your Strengths and Weaknesses   At the beginning of your job search, you need to make an honest assessment of your strengths and weaknesses. Most of your efforts should concentrate on your strengths. It is imperative that you be honest with yourself about those strengths and separate fact from fiction. Only refer to those strengths you can prove and document. Recruiters are not going to be taken in easily, for they are professional judges of people. They know that you may claim to be a leader, but unless you have past experiences that document such claims, your claims are worthless. How about strengths such as integrity, intelligence, and a willingness to work hard? Each is worth emphasizing, but only *if* you can substantiate your case.

Once you have analyzed yourself and your experiences, you have to decide how you can make them relate to the company's particular needs. But how can you know what most companies want? Or how can you know what is important to them in their search for qualified applicants? Every company—and many different positions within each company—places different demands on job applicants. Yet certain general characteristics are desired by most companies. Among these characteristics are the following:

1. The ability to get things done.
2. Honesty and integrity.
3. Dependability.
4. Initiative.
5. Communication ability.

Students often have difficulty deciding whether or not to include their GPA in their resume or application letter. Most placement offices recommend this procedure:

- If your grades place you *in* the lower 50th percentile of your class, don't include them.
- If your grades place you in the top 25th percentile, include them.
- If you are between the 50th and 75th percentile, it's up to you.

Probably the most sensible rule of thumb is to do whatever makes you look the best. If your grades during your junior and senior years are decidedly higher than those you received during your freshman and sophomore years, then report your grades for the last sixty hours. If you are a finance major and your grades in this field are higher than your other grades, and you are applying for a finance job, by all means mention them. But again, be sure to add that the grade point average you are mentioning refers only to grades in your major field, not to your overall average. Recruiters will carefully check all claims you make about yourself.

Adapting to the Company's Needs   Through a little research and through common sense, you often can adapt your skills precisely to what a company wants.[1] Following are some examples of how to tailor application letters effectively.

One applicant was aware that the bank he was applying to was active in community affairs. He, therefore, used part of the application letter to stress his own involvement in such affairs. Here is what the paragraph said:

> I have been actively involved in a variety of community service organizations. My fund-raising work with the United Way,

[1]Material in this section is adapted from Ronald Dulek and James Suchan, "Application Letters: A Neglected Area in the Job Search," *Business Horizons* 31, Nov.–Dec. 1988, 20–75.

YMCA, Chamber of Commerce, and the Kiwanis Club reflects my belief that bank officers need to be directly involved with and contribute their talents to the community.

Unlike a resume, where the style is often limited to verb and noun phrases and the third-person point of view, the application letter gives you more stylistic options. Therefore, the application letter provides you with an opportunity to convey key personality traits that match those desired by the organization.

For example, a young, aggressive salesperson wanted to work for a new, entrepreneurial computer company. In addition to providing a well-crafted, visually appealing resume, she included the following information in her application letter:

As you can tell, I want to sell for XYZ. And I'm certain I'd be good at it. My computer knowledge:

- Lotus 1-2-3,
- dBase III, and
- various word processing packages,

my previous sales experience:

- leading the Northeast Territory three years in a row for my present employer,

and my educational background:

- an MBA from the University of Washington,

make me confident I can do the job! To whet your appetite, I've provided in my resume some important details about my qualifications and accomplishments.

The two brief, active-voice sentences at the beginning of the paragraph, along with the personal, forceful style and the documentation of her qualifications, work together to create a confident, aggressive image for the job applicant.

Although some readers might feel that this writer sounds arrogant and overbearing, the company's marketing director was looking for sales representatives who had the energy and confidence necessary to battle the competition. And the job applicant, *who had done her homework and knew the type of people the marketing department was looking for,* realized the best way to convey this image was in an individualized letter of application.

Different images or personalities are appropriate for different jobs and different companies. An auditor working for a medium-sized company in the South wanted, for a variety of personal and professional reasons, to relocate to a large urban area in the Midwest. What he wrote was deliberately low-keyed, but personal.

As the enclosed resume demonstrates, I have three years of auditing experience with a traditional Big Eight accounting firm. During this time I conducted audits, reviewed tax cases, and testified for the company in various litigations. I even gained experience in the takeover arena, serving twice on teams analyzing the financial health of prospective takeover targets. In one of these cases, I was credited with uncovering financial data that could have led our client company into a disastrous investment.

The medium-length sentences and the personal style create an image of the writer that is appropriate to an accounting job. The forcefulness of the prior letter from the person seeking a sales job, (or its brashness, depending on how the reader reacts) would probably have seemed unprofessional to a CPA.

It is important to add that you must be sure to convey a personality consistent with your own. You must not merely write fiction designed to impress a reader. If a fake or phony letter leads to an interview during which you exhibit a personality far different from the one you projected in your application letter, the interviewer may have good reason to question your integrity, not to mention your common sense.

The Ending

Remember that you are the seller. The reader, you hope, is the buyer. You must do everything possible to make compliance with what you want as easy as possible. Giving both your phone number and your address encourages the recruiter to take the initiative. Furthermore, businesspeople, as we pointed out earlier, respect people who know what they want and go after it. This advice is reflected in the next principle.

APPLICATION PRINCIPLE 5:
Be assertive in seeking an interview. Try to make the interview date; don't force the interviewer to chase you.

Here are some pointers on how to end your letter:

- Avoid limp, weak, or apologetic endings.
- Sound confident and assertive. Use positive, forceful endings, such as "I look forward to hearing from you."
- Say when you will be in town and that you want to have an interview during that period.
- Be reasonably forceful. Tell the reader you will be phoning to set up a definite time for an interview.

Observe how the following ending profits from these suggestions:

Our spring break is from March 9 to 14. I will be in Des Moines during that period, and I would very much appreciate an opportunity to talk with you. To respect demands on your time, I will call two weeks before March 9 to see if an appointment can be made. In the meantime, thank you for your consideration.

PUTTING IT ALL TOGETHER: A SAMPLE APPLICATION LETTER

Let's create a sample application letter that encompasses all the advice you have learned about application letters. Study this letter and the marginal comments that explain the strategies being used. However, we strongly warn you not to copy it. The risks of doing so are far too great.

850 Voltair Terrace, SE
Gainesville, FL 34984
February 14, 19——

Mr. Kevin Stuart
Personnel Director
Douglas Kelly Enterprises
95 Landmark Court
Tampa, FL 33609

Dear Mr. Stuart:

Please consider me as an applicant for the Management Training position you advertised in the Wall Street Journal. A resume offering a detailed description of my education and experience is enclosed. Let me briefly highlight key points on the resume and explain how they could be beneficial to Douglas Kelly Enterprises.

Bottom-line statement.

Contract sentence adapted to reader.

Education

The undergraduate degree I will receive next June will be a Bachelor of Science in Business Administration, with a major in General Management. I selected this major to gain the broad perspective of business functions that you listed as a requirement in your advertisement.

Educational experience adapted to reader.

In addition to having taken more than 35 hours in management-focused courses, I have also completed more than 18 hours in each of the following business functions: Accounting, Finance, and Marketing. Throughout these courses I have maintained a grade point average of 3.5 out of a possible 4.0, an average that ranks me in the top 10 percent of my graduating

Specific evidence of educational accomplishments.

class. Recently, I was nominated for Beta Gamma Sigma, a national business school honorary society.

Experience

To supplement my academic training, and to help finance my education, I have worked part-time throughout my college career. Most recently, for the past two years, I have been employed as a broker's assistant at the Gainesville office of J. C. Bradford Investment Company. My duties here range from posting books for brokers to conducting preliminary research for clients.

The financial research skills I have developed at J. C. Bradford could certainly prove beneficial to some of the acquisition activities in which Douglas Kelly Enterprises engages. Incidentally, these part-time jobs have helped me pay more than 80% of the costs for my degree.

Mr. Stuart, I am interested in becoming a productive employee for Douglas Kelly Enterprises. I will call you next week to establish a time convenient for you to discuss this possibility in more detail.

Sincerely,

Mark McLean

Mark McLean

Left margin annotations:

Specific work experience mentioned.

Work experience adapted to reader.

Confident ending.

SUMMARY

Your search for employment, or for better employment, should be a wide-ranging search that explores a number of different sources. College and university placement offices provide a useful starting point for such a search. However, these should serve only as a beginning source for learning about openings. Other areas to consult include libraries, professional associations, newspapers, alumni associations, friends, and telephone directories. Each of these references may unveil to you positions of which others are unaware and for which you are perfectly suited.

Once you identify the position or positions you want, you need to develop one or more versions of an effective application letter. The letter can be organized in a bottom-line fashion, and may even include, if appropriate, a contract sentence. The style of the letter should be adopted to the image of the company to which you are applying. Most often, this means the style should be somewhat forceful and personal, with little or no colorfulness.

This application letter should highlight the key points on your resume. It should also point out your strengths and should show readers how these strengths can be beneficial to their company.

Finally, the application letter should end on a positive, forceful, forward-looking note. At the very least, the letter should convey your confidence that the reader will respond positively. Whenever possible, the letter should explain the next action that the writer intends to take, such as calling the reader to set up a time for an interview.

REVIEW QUESTIONS

1. Where is the most logical place to begin your search for employment?

2. Name some other sources you should consult for employment openings.

3. Why do you need to send an application letter?

4. Cite three reasons for writing a detailed application letter.

5. How long should an application letter be?

6. What are the situational factors you must consider before writing an application letter?

7. If you are an excellent student, what type of message should your application letter be?

8. If you have no work experience and your grade point average places you in the bottom half of your graduating class, what type of message should your application letter be?

9. As a general rule, how should an application letter be organized and what should it contain?

10. What is the *real* bottom line of an application letter?

11. In your application letter, when should you tell your reader where you learned about the job opening?

12. Why is it important to know the name of the person to whom you should address your application letter?

13. What does the choice of style for your application letter depend on?

14. What are the rules of thumb most placement offices recommend regarding the inclusion of a GPA in application letters?

15. How should you end your application letter?

THE RESUME

OBJECTIVES

This chapter will help you to

●

Construct an effective chronological resume

●

Put together an effective functional resume

●

Understand the advantages and disadvantages of chronological and functional resumes

Preparation of a resume can be a difficult, often frustrating, experience. No matter how old you are, you will have a difficult time capturing all your education, your accomplishments, and your personal qualities on one or two blank pages. The task seems mind-boggling.

Despite the difficulty of the task, however, you can construct a high-impact resume, one that has an excellent chance of separating you from your competition. You can accomplish this task following either a **chronological** or a **functional** format.

MANY WAYS TO WRITE A RESUME

At the beginning we need to acknowledge a most important factor about writing resumes: *There is no one way to construct a resume that will guarantee success in your hunt for a position.*

Often students and even some experienced employees talk about resumes as though only one format, one way of creating resumes, is acceptable. This is wrong; no such format exists.

Just as with your application letters, you will have to tailor your resume to the demands and values of the readers and companies you plan to send it to. If you are applying for a job as a copywriter with an advertising firm, for example, you will want your resume to show originality, creativity, and dash. You may use colored paper, or bold lettering, or a cartoon, or a plastic gimmick—anything to show that you are the kind of creative, daring, clever person such a firm might be looking for. Just the reverse strategy would be appropriate if you are applying for most other business positions.

Our only principle regarding resumes examines the need to adapt your resume to the job you are seeking and to your own qualifications.

RESUME PRINCIPLE:

Tailor your resume to

a. The position you are seeking, and
b. The qualifications you want to emphasize.

TYPES OF RESUMES

Although styles of writing and presentation in resumes may vary, resumes fall basically into one of two types: chronological or functional.

The Chronological Resume

A chronological resume is the most traditional of the two resume forms. Its focus is on the writer's education and experience. Some insertions about how to interpret this education and experience can be included.

A chronological resume gains its name from the fact that most of the information presented is organized by dates under a set of predetermined headings. Items grouped under each heading are organized in reverse time order, listing the most recent experiences first and most distant last. For example, under the heading of *Education*, if your most recent college degree is your bachelor of science, you would list it before the associate of arts degree you earned at a community college.

The following information may be presented in a chronological resume. Some of it is optional, as you will see later in this chapter.

- *Identification*. Include your name, address, and telephone number.
- *Objective*. Include a statement defining the position you are looking for and/or your career goals.
- *Education*. Include colleges attended, degrees, majors, minors, and special training.
- *Work Experience*. Include names of firms, brief descriptions of positions and duties, and supervisors' names, if appropriate.
- *Special Qualifications*. Include organizational memberships, including offices held, honors, and special accomplishments.
- *Special Interests*. Include hobbies and interests.
- *References*. Include names of people who have agreed to comment on your character, experience, and/or education. You may also offer to provide such a list.

The best way to learn about resumes is to go through the process of constructing one. Let's put together two chronological resumes that include each of the seven pieces of information just given.

Putting Together a Chronological Resume

Identification   Vital identifying pieces of information to include are (1) your name, centered and in bold print, (2) a present as well as a permanent address, if applicable, and (3) phone numbers where you can be reached.

AMY SMITH

Present Address: Permanent Address:
5632 High Street South   23 Perrin Avenue
Columbus, OH 43207   Lafayette, IN 47901
Phone: (414) 555-2317   Phone: (217) 555-8132

PATRICK JONES

Present Address: Home Address:
25 Lakeview Estates   141 Monroe Avenue
Tuscaloosa, AL 35486   San Diego, CA 92116
(205) 555-8930   (619) 555-1924

Present and permanent addresses are important to include. Personnel directors may not have a position immediately available, but they will place your application in a file for future reference. By having your permanent address on file, they will be able to locate you at a later date should a suitable job turn up.

The permanent address does not have to be yours. It can be that of parents, grandparents, brothers or sisters, friends, or anyone who can forward communications to you.

Job or Career Objective   Most resumes, but not all, contain a statement defining the type of job you seek; some contain a statement of your career goals. Here are two samples:

Amy Smith

JOB OBJECTIVE: A sales position that will provide opportunities to use administrative, organizational, and human relations skills.

Patrick Jones

CAREER OBJECTIVE: An entry-level training position in a health care profession with possibilities for advancement into mid- and upper-level administrative positions.

A surprisingly strong difference of opinion exists about whether a job objective or career objective should be included.

Those who argue in favor of including an objective believe that it provides a definition of your job interests and shows that you have planned your career path. In addition, proponents argue, such a statement portrays you as a goal-oriented person who is realistic about your expectations.

Since the issue is questionable, if you do include an objective, be careful not to inflate your career aspirations. If you allude to any special traits you possess, do not make them sound far greater than they reasonably could be. For instance, avoid such boasting as in the following objective:

Example of a Boastful Objective

JOB OBJECTIVE: A challenging and rewarding sales position that will give me an opportunity to capitalize on my unique personality, my superior analytical mind, and my ability to work harder and longer than any of my contemporaries.

If you choose to mention long-term goals in your objective, then change the title of this section from *Job* to *Career Objective*. But be careful. Even if you are extremely optimistic about your future progress, don't fall into the trap of sounding like someone who wants (and expects) to get to the top too quickly and easily. Businesspeople want ambitious people, certainly, but not overly ambitious ones who are likely to chafe about having to wait to earn promotions. Here is a career objective that immediately ruined the applicant's chances:

Example of an Overly Ambitious Objective

CAREER OBJECTIVE: A sales position that will enable me to move quickly through the corporate ranks, advancing to the vice presidential level within five years.

Several arguments can be advanced against stating objectives. Some people argue that such objectives are meaningless because everyone has the same basic ambition—to find a position and to do as well as possible within that position. Others feel that applicants frequently are tempted into making unsupported boasts about their special traits (e.g., "To use my proven sales ability to rise to Vice President-Marketing in ten years").

Education   Here, you should first mention your most recent degree and the school you most recently attended. Mention previous degrees later. Below are two examples of ways to handle this section:

Amy Smith

EDUCATION: The Ohio State University, Columbus, OH
Candidate for Bachelor of Science in Business Administration, May 1992
Major: Marketing; Minor: Finance
Average in Major: 3.8/4.0
Overall Average: 3.2/4.0

Dayton Community College, Dayton, OH
Associate of Arts Degree, May 1990

Have also completed courses at the University of California at Berkeley, and Purdue University

Patrick Jones

EDUCATION: The University of Alabama, University, AL 35486
Degree: Bachelor of Science (expected) May, 1992
Major: Health Care Management
Minor: Political Science
Grade Point Average: 3.25 out of a possible 4.0

Selected relevant courses:

Major Field Courses	Other Professional Courses
• Analysis of Health Care Systems	• Intermediate Financial Management
• Health Care Management Internship	• Management Communications
• Introduction to Health Systems	• Management of Group Behavior
• Legal Aspects of Health Care	• Regional Economics

Notice that all of the schools attended are listed, including those the candidate attended briefly. Does that mean that you have to list *every* school you have attended? The answer is that you should be honest but also use common sense. If, for instance, you took one summer school course purely for enrichment purposes at a local college, it is certainly permissible not to list that course. But at the same time, don't lie or withhold vital information. If you attended a college for two years but failed to graduate, you still have to account for that time period in your life. You should, therefore, list this experience, although it is certainly not necessary for you to highlight the fact that you didn't graduate.

So, be honest, but use common sense. List what is relevant to you and what is important for the employer to know, but don't give too detailed a breakdown of your education.

You probably also noticed that both of the sample Education sections have grade point averages listed. In fact, Amy Smith's resume lists grade point average twice: once by overall average and once by major field average. Should you list your average? Again, it depends. Many interviewers admit that, all else being equal (though it seldom is), grade point average can be a determining factor in selecting a candidate to be interviewed.

You may wish to consider some strategies in listing your grade point average. We say "strategies" because job-seeking is a selling process. Therefore, you are expected to put your best foot forward. Recruiters know that. So, with advice similar to that given in Chapter A-1, we urge you to do the following:

- List your grade point average in your major if this average is significantly higher than your overall average.
- List your grade point average for the last 45 to 60 hours of your college work if this average is significantly higher than your cumulative average.
- List your grade point average *and* add an interpretative clause telling where that grade point average ranks you in your major, school, or college. This strategy is particularly useful if you are enrolled in a rigorous program known for its low grade point average.

These strategies are not dishonest as long as you tell the reader what you are reporting. Furthermore, many employers are actually most interested in the grades in your major field or in your last sixty hours. Many of these people, having attended college themselves, remember that the first two years of college are often a difficult adjustment period, a period in which they, like you, had to make a transition to new surroundings, to being on their own, or to adapt to any number of other complicating and distracting factors.

Telling where your grade point average ranks you within your major, school, or college is particularly useful if you are in a rigorous academic setting. Some colleges grade more rigorously than others do. In some schools, a 3.5 out of a possible 4.0 grade point average might rank you in the top 25 percent of your class. In other schools, the same grade point average might rank you in the top 3 percent of your class. If you are in the latter group, interpret your grade point average for the reader by revealing where that grade point average ranks you. By doing so, you can make your case even more impressive. You could include a statement like the following:

Grade Point Average: 3.1 out of possible 4.0. This average ranks in the top 20 percent of the senior class.

One final note about grade point average. If you choose to list it, be sure also to list the overall point system being used. In other words, if your school has a four-point system (A = 4.0), be sure to list your average either with a brief explanation (GPA: 3.4 out of a possible 4.0) or with a slash (GPA 3.4/4.0).

Listing courses, as in the second Education section example, is optional. Listing courses serves its purpose best when you want to emphasize some specialized, technical, or recognizably difficult courses you have taken. This procedure also works well when you wish to document breadth as well as specialization in your curriculum. In other words, a list of courses dealing with history, literature, and philosophy can counteract possible objections that your education has been too narrowly focused on business subjects.

If necessary, you can use this course list to improve the look of your resume. If your resume already looks too long, do not list your courses. On the other hand, if your resume looks unbalanced (for example, if the second and final page of your resume has only one or two items on it and is less than one-fourth full), this insertion can be useful both for informational and aesthetic reasons.

Work Experience   Work experience, like education, is listed in reverse chronological order, with the most recent job listed first.

Amy Smith

WORK EXPERIENCE:	1988 and 1991 (summers) Holiday Inn Corporation, Lafayette, IN Assistant Night Manager • Coordinated night-shift activities • Managed front desk operations • Conducted night audits
	1989–90 (part-time) Rosie O'Grady's, Columbus, OH Hostess • Supervised cash register • Oversaw waiter/waitress duties
	1988–89 (part-time) L. S. Ayres Department Store, Dayton, OH Salesperson • Sold jewelry, outerwear, and men's clothing • Won June 1989 Sales Award
	Other positions held: Embers Restaurant, Lafayette City Library, Burger King. All in Lafayette, IN.
	NOTE: These jobs in combination with student loans covered 100 percent of my educational expenses.

Patrick Jones

WORK
EXPERIENCE: Administrative Assistant, Health Care Nursing Facility,
Birmingham, AL
1989–91 (summers)
Supervised maintenance personnel and delivery system for this
50-bed facility. Also responsible for some supervisory and
support services.

Department Supervisor, USA Oil, Personnel Department,
Houston, TX
1987–89
Responsible for obtaining, scheduling, and overseeing field
assignments for 15 on-the-well laborers.

Young Men's Christian Association, Mobile, AL
1985–87 (part-time job)
Responsible for supervision and daily operation of this
recreational facility. Supervised a staff of part-time employees
and directed four on-site camping trips.

Notice also that repeat jobs (such as summer jobs held for successive summers) are listed once but with separate dates. In some instances, people return for another summer with the same firm but are assigned to a completely different type of work. Even in these instances, you are wise to handle such changes within one job description, although it is permissible to list these jobs more than once if the experiences were extremely different.

Notice also that the most recent and/or the most relevant jobs are highlighted with a brief description of the duties performed. The inclusion of this information offers resume writers an opportunity to demonstrate some qualities (such as initiative, responsibility, maturity, or leadership), depending on what areas they choose to emphasize.

Not all the jobs listed have to include a description of duties. People who have held more than three or four jobs must be careful not to let too many descriptions start to bore and/or become meaningless to the reader. In such cases, try to highlight only the specific duties of your most relevant or most impressive positions. Don't try to explain everything you have ever done in every job you have ever had!

Often students express concern that their part-time, summer or temporary jobs bear little or no relevance to the professional type of work they are applying for. Our general advice is "Don't worry about it." Few employers expect new applicants to have had vast, relevant experience. The fact that you have had work experience is in itself impressive enough.

You should seldom worry about any type of work experience you have had. Even lower-level jobs can be very impressive. We often meet people who earned much of their college tuition by delivering pizzas or waiting on tables. Amazingly, they are frequently embarrassed about having done such work and are reluctant to list it on a resume. Admiration for people who work and pay their own bills is still alive and well in American business. Notice how, in the first example, Amy Smith has noted that she paid her college tuition through loans and part-time work.

If you have had such experiences—and no other important jobs—by all means list them.

What do you do in the worst-case scenario, one in which you have had no job experience? You have to make the best out of what you have done. You may have to present some of your non-profit jobs as if they were past employment. For instance, if you were a member of a social organization, such as a fraternity or a sorority, you should mention some of the work you performed here. Or, if you were a member of certain campus organizations, you may want to explain work you did there. But don't count on fooling anyone. It is best that you list such experiences under the generic heading of "Experience" rather than under the more specific heading of "Work Experience."

Special Qualifications   This section can be an important addition to your qualifications, especially if you have had little work experience. By listing college activities or community involvement, you can show valuable experience and initiative that employers regard favorably. Here are two examples:

Amy Smith

ACTIVITIES:	International Marketing Association • President, 1991 • Treasurer, 1990 Dean's Student Council Student Advisory Committee University Ad Club YWCA Young Adult Club
HONORS:	Dean's List—four semesters Omicron Delta Kappa—approximately 5 percent of all graduating seniors are elected to this honorary society Presidential Scholarship (1990 and 1991)

Patrick Jones

EXTRACURRICULAR ACTIVITIES AND HONORS:	Beta Gamma Sigma (National Business Honorary Society) Dean's List (two semesters) Health Care Management Society J. H. Menning Award for Excellence in Written Communication Student Executive Council Student Government Association

Again, use common sense in listing such activities. Think twice before you list organizations that have negative reputations with significant portions of the public or those that suggest exclusivity or "high society." Furthermore, recognize that businesspeople are not always familiar with some very impressive academic awards, or with the Greek initials of honorary societies. To prevent some of your most important honors from being overlooked, simply insert parenthetical definitions of the award's significance. (Notice how Amy Smith used this strategy to define the importance of Omicron Delta Kappa.)

Listing college activities is also important to those who have very high grade point averages, 3.75 and above. Activities for such people demonstrate that they are not just "grinds" or "bookworms" but that they are well-rounded. Good grades are impressive, but they are even more impressive if the interviewer knows that the job candidate has the ability to interact successfully with people.

Finally, if you, like most of us, find yourself with few honors, it is acceptable to list activities, awards, and honors together.

Special Interests   Special interests should be listed alphabetically.

Amy Smith

INTERESTS: Horseback riding, running, snow skiing

Patrick Jones

INTERESTS: Chess, golf, jogging, snow skiing, water skiing.

Let's briefly discuss the content you should consider listing under "Interests." As a general rule, you should include at least three different interests so that you do not appear narrow or lacking in interests. On the other hand, you should not list more than six hobbies or interests so that you do not give the appearance of being too involved in activities other than your professional career.

Although the Interests section is not the most important one in the resume, it can prove useful to you. When organizations look for someone to hire, they are looking for the most competent professional person available. But often they are also looking for someone who fits in with their group. An honest listing of your interests will often provide a preliminary indication of your prospects for such a fit.

We doubt that anyone has ever been refused an interview because he or she lacked the proper interests. Employers are willing to talk to the applicant to see if a fit is available. But we do know of a number of instances where applicants who listed interests seemed to feel that one or more of their interests helped them get an interview.

Be careful, however, not to overstate or fictionalize your interests. You may get caught in the interview. Personal interests sometimes are so unimportant that writers regard them as nothing more than blanks to be filled in. For example, an applicant may list photography as an interest, meaning that he or she likes to admire photographs. Unfortunately, people who overstate their interests overlook the fact that this resume may be sent to a number of different individuals within an organization. If you visit an organization, you will often interview with, or at least meet, many different people who have examined your resume. Some will quite naturally attempt to put you at ease by asking you about the interests you have listed. There is every chance that some interviewer will be an amateur photographer. And if you are not prepared to talk with some intelligence about photography, you have severely damaged your case by being phony.

A worst-case demonstration of the dangers of overstating interests occurred when a job candidate listed jogging as a hobby even though he had never run more than one block in his life. The candidate was interviewed on campus and, when questioned about this hobby, responded that he jogged approximately five miles a day, five times a week. The applicant was trying to impress the interviewer—or at least was trying to avoid the fact that he had lied on his resume. Three weeks later, the applicant was invited to an on-site interview at this company. He was also told to bring running equipment with him since some of his interviewers belonged to a noon-time jogging group. The group members thought it might be fun and relaxing for him to join them for a quick five-mile workout! Needless to say, the applicant refused the invitation to the interview.

References   You can select among three options: (1) you can omit this section entirely, (2) you can dispose of it by stating "References will be furnished upon request," or (3) you can list names of references, including both mailing addresses and phone numbers where these people can be reached. The following are examples of Options 2 and 3.

Amy Smith

References are available upon request.

Patrick Jones

REFERENCES: Dr. Chadwick Hilton
Dean, College of Management
The University of Alabama in Birmingham
Birmingham, AL 35248
(205) 555-1298

Dr. Michael Hesse
Professor of Health Care Management
The University of Alabama in Birmingham
Birmingham, AL 35248
(205) 555-1389

Ms. Martha Williams
Vice President, Humana Health Services
Louisville, KY 40206
(414) 555-1242

Most people opt either to omit references entirely or to state that they can be furnished on request. Option 3, however, has some utility, especially if you can present an impressive list of references. If you have had the opportunity to work for or perhaps take courses from people who are highly respected in your chosen profession, or by the prospective employer, by all means list them. Other applicants choose Option 3 because they hope that, even though their references are not famous people, the interviewer may know one of the references and perhaps phone him or her about their qualifications. But be careful: don't list people who do not know you well; and don't list people without first asking their permission! Moreover, don't list someone unless you are certain that he or she will give you a favorable recommendation. A weak recommendation from an important person can do more damage to job prospects than would no recommendation at all.

Asking people if you can list them as a reference is both courteous and wise. If people agree to be listed as references, give them an updated copy of your resume. This copy will not only remind them that you have listed them, but it will also serve as a source of information about you should a prospective employer call. References can quickly pull out a copy of the resume, refresh their memory about you, and speak specifically about your abilities.

One other piece of practical advice applies if you still have some part of your college career left to complete. It is likely that some professors in your school or college are prominent in their field. Find out who they are and enroll in their courses. Try to earn their respect by doing very well in their classes. Then, when the time comes to list references, you will have access to an impressive name to put at the top of your list.

Information Not to Include in the Resume

Some information should *not* be listed anywhere in your resume. Specifically, do not include information about race or religion, as it is illegal for such factors to enter into the hiring decision. It is also illegal for recruiters to require a photograph of the applicant. Marital status and age also cannot legally enter into the hiring decision.

It may also be foolish for you to include information on your financial status or requirements. That is, you may not want to limit yourself by including information about the lowest salary that will attract you. You may also limit your opportunities by specifying that you prefer certain locations. Who knows? If a company made the right offer, you might decide to move anywhere.

Putting It All Together: Sample Chronological Resumes

Here are the complete chronological resumes we have discussed, section by section. Again, we remind you that no one format is preferable. The resume's appearance and its appropriateness for the position you are seeking are the best guides as to which format works best. Notice, however, that each resume is neatly organized and that each presents a logical and consistent system of indentation and spacing.

AMY SMITH

Present Address:	Permanent Address:
5632 High Street South	23 Perrin Avenue
Columbus, OH 43207	Lafayette, IN 47901
Phone: (414) 555-2317	Phone: (217) 555-8132

JOB OBJECTIVE: A sales position that will provide opportunities to use administrative, organizational, and human relations skills.

EDUCATION: The Ohio State University, Columbus, OH
Candidate for Bachelor of Science in Business Administration, May 1992
Major: Marketing; Minor: Finance
Average in Major: 3.8/4.0
Overall Average: 3.2/4.0

Dayton Community College, Dayton, OH
Associate of Arts Degree, May 1990

Have also completed courses at the University of California at Berkeley, and Purdue University

WORK EXPERIENCE: 1988 and 1991 (summers)
Holiday Inn Corporation, Lafayette, IN
Assistant Night Manager
• Coordinated night-shift activities
• Managed front desk operations
• Conducted night audits

1989–90 (part-time)
Rosie O'Grady's, Columbus, OH
Hostess
• Supervised cash register
• Oversaw waiter/waitress duties

1988–89 (part-time)
L. S. Ayres Department Store, Dayton, OH
Salesperson
• Sold jewelry, outerwear, and men's clothing
• Won June 1989 Sales Award

Other positions held: Embers Restaurant, Lafayette City Library, Burger King. All in Lafayette, IN.

NOTE: These jobs in combination with student loans covered 100 percent of my educational expenses.

ACTIVITIES: International Marketing Association
• President, 1991
• Treasurer, 1990
Dean's Student Council
Student Advisory Committee
University Ad Club
YWCA Young Adult Club

HONORS: Dean's List—four semesters
Omicron Delta Kappa—approximately 5 percent of all graduating seniors are elected to this honorary society
Presidential Scholarship (1990 and 1991)

INTERESTS: Horseback riding, running, snow skiing

References are available upon request.

PATRICK JONES

Present Address:	Home Address:
25 Lakeview Estates	141 Monroe Avenue
Tuscaloosa, AL 35486	San Diego, CA 92116
Phone: (205) 555-8930	Phone: (619) 555-1924

CAREER OBJECTIVE: An entry-level training position in a health care profession with possibilities for advancement into mid- and upper-level administrative positions.

EDUCATION: The University of Alabama, University, AL 35486
Degree: Bachelor of Science (Expected) May, 1992
Major: Health Care Management
Minor: Political Science
Grade Point Average: 3.25 out of a possible 4.0

Selected relevant courses:

Major Field Courses	Other Professional Courses
• Analysis of Health Care Systems	• Intermediate Financial Management
• Health Care Management Internship	• Management Communications
• Introduction to Health Systems	• Management of Group Behavior
• Legal Aspects of Health Care	• Regional Economics

WORK EXPERIENCE: Administrative Assistant, Health Care Nursing Facility, Birmingham, AL
1989–91 (summers)
Supervised maintenance personnel and delivery system for this 50-bed facility. Also responsible for some supervisory and support services.

Department Supervisor, USA Oil, Personnel Department, Houston, TX
1987–89
Responsible for obtaining, scheduling, and overseeing field assignments for 15 on-the-well laborers.

Young Men's Christian Association, Mobile, AL
1985–87 (part-time job)
Responsible for supervision and daily operation of this recreational facility. Supervised a staff of part-time employees and directed four on-site camping trips.

EXTRA-CURRICULAR ACTIVITIES AND HONORS: Beta Gamma Sigma (National Business Honorary Society)
Dean's List (two semesters)
Health Care Management Society
J. H. Menning Award for Excellence in Written Communication
Student Executive Council
Student Government Association

INTERESTS: Chess, golf, jogging, snow skiing, water skiing.

REFERENCES: Dr. Chadwick Hilton
Dean, College of Management
The University of Alabama in Birmingham
Birmingham, AL 35248
(205) 555-1298

Dr. Michael Hesse
Professor of Health Care Management
The University of Alabama in Birmingham
Birmingham, AL 35248
(205) 555-1389

Ms. Martha Williams
Vice President, Humana Health Services
Louisville, KY 40206
(414) 555-1242

Functional Resumes

A functional resume places emphasis on accomplishments rather than time. Dates may be used within such a resume, but they are subordinated to accomplishments and are not allowed to influence the overall arrangement of the resume.

A functional resume gives you an opportunity to tie together somewhat varied experiences and to tailor them to the needs of the company to which you are applying. In essence, you demonstrate that your skills are transferable, that what you practiced and learned in one situation can be easily applied to another situation.

It is, of course, impossible to create a sample resume that highlights all the different functions you could choose to stress. The following list provides some of the many possible headings you can use in such a resume.

FUNCTIONS

Accounting	Financing
Administering	Fund Raising
Analyzing	Guiding
Budgeting	Initiating
Calculating	Managing
Communicating	Motivating
Coordinating	Negotiating
Counselling	Organizing
Creating	Persuading
Deciding	Planning
Delegating	Researching
Designing	Selling
Evaluating	Supervising

These are only some of the headings possible within a functional resume. You can probably think of many more.

Let's put together a sample functional resume. But remember that we are selecting only a few of the many possible topics you could choose to emphasize. The opening sections of a functional resume are handled much the same way as in the chronological resume.

WILLIAM STOKES

Present Address:	Permanent Address:
104 Broadway	15-A Westchester Avenue
State College, PA 16802	White Plains, NY 10601
(215) 555-4914	(914) 555-1701

OBJECTIVE: A challenging sales position that requires a responsible leader who communicates effectively and has strong organizational and interpersonal skills.

The same strengths and weaknesses that apply to a career or job objective in a chronological resume also apply here. One different element deserves mention in this resume, however. It is possible to use the Objective section of a functional resume to create a very subtle contract sentence for the remainder of your resume. In other words, as our sample demonstrates, the remainder of this resume will concentrate on the following three topics:

- Responsibility
- Communication
- Organizational Skills

Functional resumes differ from chronological resumes in terms of points of emphasis. A chronological resume will stress specifically the jobs an applicant held and will subordinate information about how that job applies to the applicant's qualifications. A functional resume, by contrast, places greater emphasis on the skills developed or the experiences accumulated through a past job and subordinates what the job actually was. The following example demonstrates the experience-based focus of a functional resume:

RECORD OF RESPONSIBILITY: Have a proven record of being able to handle important tasks effectively and efficiently.

Assisted in sales and analysis of stock offerings for a major New York brokerage firm.

Arranged and administered a tax-planning seminar for the above program.

Handled sales and financial situations in a variety of different settings.

> Interacted successfully with the public while working
> part-time as a waiter.
>
> Served two terms as Treasurer of ABC fraternity.

One key to an effective functional resume is that, as much as possible, the candidate support his or her broad generalizations with some specific proof. Thus, mention of previous jobs provides valid and important support for the broad, generalized category of Responsibility.

This stress on interpreting experiences and accomplishments should continue throughout the body of a functional resume. The following sections demonstrate how this stress should continue:

COMMUNICATION SKILLS: Completed six hours of English Composition.

Completed a total of nine hours of courses specializing in written and oral business communication.

Served as campaign coordinator and public relations director for candidate for President of Student Government Association.

ORGANIZATIONAL SKILLS: Served two terms as Student President of the American Marketing Association. During this time
- memberships increased 15 percent.
- organization was voted best AMA division in state.
- established key subcommittees to continue organizational development.

Again, specific facts are used to substantiate the broad claims being made. Of course, a functional resume can also be used to make broader claims that are a bit more difficult to prove. Here is an example of unsupported claims about a candidate's interpersonal skills that would serve only to weaken a resume.

INTERPERSONAL SKILLS: Attentive listener, willing to lend a sympathetic ear when appropriate and needed.

Able to attain trust and rapport with various types of individuals.

Concerned and empathetic, willing to help out those in need.

The disadvantage to such claims is that they are so general that it is difficult, if not impossible, to substantiate them accurately. The advantage to such claims is that by mentioning them, you prove your awareness and concern with such topics, even though you may not be able to document your concern. In general, although the functional resume invites and permits such broad claims, we urge you to limit your use of these types of statements. One or two categories are acceptable, but if the entire resume stays at this general level, the lack of substantiating evidence will make a negative impression on readers.

Finally, regardless of what topics you choose to insert into the functional resume, you also have to include a few specific pieces of information. You should, therefore, at least briefly list, with limited or no explanation, some of your past employers, a synopsis of your educational training, a brief description of your personal interests, and, if appropriate, a list of references. The following example shows the information that can be used.

EMPLOYERS AND POSITIONS:	Salomon Brothers Stock Analyst Supervisor: J. P. Barto 1 New York Plaza New York, NY 10004 (212) 555-8810 Summers 1990–91
	Bloomingdale's Department Store Sales Representative Men's Sportswear Supervisor: Ann Higgins 1000 Third Avenue New York, NY 10022 (212) 555-9186 Summers 1988–89
	The Fish House Waiter Supervisor: Harvey Killian 2881 Broadway New York, NY 10027 (212) 555-1234 September–May 1988–89
EDUCATION:	The Pennsylvania State University, State College, PA Bachelor of Science; Major: Marketing; Minor: Political Science Graduation Date: May 1992—planned September 1990–present
	The State University of New York, Albany Campus September 1989–May 1990
	Columbia University, New York September 1988–May 1989
PERSONAL INTERESTS:	Basketball Karate Snow and water skiing Theater

Putting It All Together: A Sample Functional Resume

Below is the entire sample functional resume. As with the chronological resume, you could format the information in many different ways. The important point to remember is that the format should be pleasing to the eye and be appropriate to the job for which you are applying.

WILLIAM STOKES

Present Address:
104 Broadway
State College, PA 16802
(215) 555-4914

Permanent Address:
15-A Westchester Avenue
White Plains, NY 10601
(914) 555-1701

OBJECTIVE:

A challenging sales position that requires a responsible leader who communicates effectively and has strong organizational and interpersonal skills.

RECORD OF RESPONSIBILITY:

Have a proven record of being able to handle important tasks effectively and efficiently.

Assisted in sales and analysis of stock offerings for a major New York brokerage firm.

Arranged and administered a tax-planning seminar for the above program.

Handled sales and financial situations in a variety of different settings.

Interacted successfully with the public while working part-time as a waiter.

Served two terms as Treasurer of ABC fraternity.

COMMUNICATION SKILLS:

Completed six hours of English Composition.

Completed a total of nine hours of courses specializing in written and oral business communication.

Served as campaign coordinator and public relations director for candidate for President of Student Government Association.

ORGANIZATIONAL SKILLS:

Served two terms as Student President of the American Marketing Association. During this time
• memberships increased 15 percent.
• organization was voted best AMA division in state.
• established key subcommittees to continue organizational development.

EMPLOYERS AND POSITIONS:

Salomon Brothers
Stock Analyst
Supervisor: J. P. Barto
1 New York Plaza
New York, NY 10004
(212) 555-8810
Summers 1990–91

Bloomingdale's Department Store
Sales Representative
Men's Sportswear
Supervisor: Ann Higgins
1000 Third Avenue
New York, NY 10022
(212) 555-9186
Summers 1988–89

The Fish House
Waiter
Supervisor: Harvey Killian
2881 Broadway
New York, NY 10027
(212) 555-1234
September–May 1988–89

EDUCATION:

The Pennsylvania State University, State College, PA
Bachelor of Science; Major: Marketing; Minor: Political Science
Graduation Date: May 1992—planned
September 1990–present

The State University of New York, Albany Campus
September 1989–May 1990

Columbia University, New York
September 1988–May 1989

PERSONAL INTERESTS:

Basketball
Karate
Snow and water skiing
Theater

SUMMARY

The **chronological** and the **functional resumes** are the two types you can choose between when constructing your resume. You should use the one that most fits your qualifications and that is most suitable for the type of job you are seeking.

The chronological resume is organized by time, with the most recent experiences listed first. A functional resume places more emphasis on accomplishments and provides opportunities for you to demonstrate how your skills and training can be applied to other situations.

Remember, though, that neither type is unchangeable. You should vary and adjust the format of your resume to meet the demands of your particular needs or those of the company to which you are applying.

REVIEW QUESTIONS

1. Is there one specific way to construct a resume that will guarantee success in your hunt for a job?

2. What is a chronological resume?

3. What information is presented in a chronological resume?

4. What is the best way to learn about writing a resume?

5. Why do you put a permanent and a present address on a resume?

6. Give reasons for and against stating a job or career objective in your resume.

7. Should you list *every* school you have attended on your resume? Why or why not?

8. Name two strategies you can use in listing your grade point average on your resume.

9. What can you show by listing college activities and community involvement?

10. Under "Interests" on your resume, you should list at least _____ but not more than _____ . Why?

11. What might happen if you overstate your interests?

12. Name two pieces of information you should not list on your resume.

13. Should you include a photograph with your resume?

14. What are the three options you have regarding references?

15. What is a functional resume and why is it used?

16. How can you use the "Objective" section of a resume to your advantage?

THE INTERVIEW

OBJECTIVES:

This chapter will help you to

•

Discover the importance of advance
preparation for interviews

•

Determine how to conduct yourself
at an interview

•

Learn to analyze your performance
after the interview ends

The best possible reward for having written an effective application letter and resume occurs when you receive a phone call or a letter inviting you to interview for a position. Few events are more exciting, and few are more nerve-wracking, than to interview for a job you would really like. This chapter provides advice on how best to present yourself in such an interview.

INTERVIEW FORMATS

Job interviews can take place in a number of different formats. Specifically:

- Most colleges and universities have placement offices where students sign up for and receive interviews with recruiters who are visiting the campus. These interviews are usually of a preliminary nature and, if successful, result in a follow-up interview in which the applicant is invited to visit the company.
- Other organizations avoid conducting campus interviews. They simply examine application letters and resumes to determine who they will invite to visit their company.

THREE STEPS IN THE INTERVIEW PROCESS

No matter which type of interview you attend, however, you will want to be certain to follow three distinct steps in the process. These steps can be summarized under the headings Prepare, Execute, and Evaluate. Let's examine what each step involves.

Step 1: Prepare

Preparing for the interview involves three distinct but equally important steps. Interview Principle 1 examines these steps.

INTERVIEW PRINCIPLE 1:
Prepare for your interview by

a. Assessing your career goals.
b. Anticipating difficult questions and preparing appropriate answers.
c. Studying and learning about your prospective employer.

Assessing Career Goals You must conduct an honest evaluation of yourself and of what you want to accomplish before you attend any interview. In fact, you would be well-advised to conduct such an assessment even before you send out application letters and resumes.

You must set some general career goals for yourself. Decide what industry or industries are of interest to you. Identify (a) jobs that you would enjoy doing and (b) jobs in which you know you would perform well. Recognize that (a) and (b) are not always identical. Analyze and determine how dedicated you are to a career and decide on a prospective career path that suits your abilities, interests, and commitment.

You are not, of course, obligated to follow exactly what you decide in this analysis. Experience and other factors will make you modify your objectives as time passes. But you are well-advised to have such objectives in mind before you begin your career. And you should certainly have such objectives in mind before you attend an interview.

While developing your career goals, you should always keep in mind that, in general, the past is the best predictor of the future. Everyone enjoys hearing stories of the person who flunked out of college and then went on to become a multimillionaire. But such stories are the exception rather than the rule. The vast majority of successful business people have a past that foretold their success. These people were successful in college and were even more successful in early jobs and in other assignments they undertook.

You must consider the importance of past accomplishments while you set your career goals. If you have not done well, say, in accounting and finance, it is probably foolish to set as your objective becoming a partner in a prestigious accounting firm. If your personality is naturally shy and withdrawn, do not plan to become a super-salesperson.

Instead, realistically look at your strengths and interests and adapt to them. Select career objectives that fit your goals and interests. And most importantly, set objectives that are realistically based on past performance.

Anticipating Questions and Preparing Answers Much of an interview consists of questions and answers. You should, therefore, prepare answers to those questions you can expect to be asked. Here are ten frequently asked questions:

1. What are your long- and short-range goals?
2. What do you want to accomplish in life?
3. What can you tell me about yourself?
4. What are your greatest strengths?
5. What are your greatest weaknesses?
6. Why should we hire you?
7. What special contributions can you make to our organization?
8. What are your two most important accomplishments?
9. How has your college education prepared you for this job?
10. Why are you interested in working for us?

In addition to being prepared to answer traditional questions such as these, you should also prepare for questions that might apply to you alone. Carefully examine your resume and see if you can determine what these questions might be. Three items of particular importance that interviewers often ask about are these:

1. *Time gaps.* You may have long periods of time that are unaccounted for on your resume.

2. *Frequent job changing.* This item is of more importance for full-time than for part-time jobs. Most employers expect students enrolled full time in college to change jobs frequently, especially between summers.

3. *Overqualification.* You must be able to explain why you would spend time and effort gaining a level of education or experience far beyond that needed for the position you are applying for.

Learning about Your Potential Employer   Preparing for an interview is an information-gathering process. As we have just seen, one step of the process involves gathering information about yourself and what you want to accomplish. A second step, one that frequently exerts a significant influence on whether the interview will go well or poorly, involves gathering information about the company interviewing you.

Intelligent job applicants do their homework in advance; they study the firm and the industry or industries in which that firm competes. At the minimum, you should obtain a copy of the company's annual report and study it thoroughly.

A visit to a local or campus library often enables applicants to learn about a company and the product or service it markets. If you can find some intelligent questions to ask about the company, you will show a level of interest above the average. Such questions can demonstrate your interest in the firm and the fact that you did some advance homework.

Potential employers will often send interviewees information about the company. This information may include company bulletins, copies of its house organ, or the company's annual report. Not only is such information useful in telling about the recruiter's company, it is also a subtle way for the company to determine your level of interest in working for them. Failure to look at these materials sends an important and often dangerous signal not only about your level of interest, but also about your common sense.

Therefore, thoroughly study any information the company sends you. If you have questions based on this information, write them down and ask them at the appropriate time. But be careful to avoid questions that are already answered by the materials provided to you.

Furthermore, going beyond studying what has been sent you is often wise. Nothing is wrong with gathering additional specific information about the company, the job you are applying for, or even about specific individuals who work for the company. The annual report provides names of the president, vice president, and other high-ranking individuals. Your familiarity with these names and appropriate questions about these individuals may demonstrate a willingness on your part to know more about the company.

If you can gather advance information about the requirements, demands, or needs of the specific job you are seeking, by all means do so. Often, past or present employees of the company can help you with such information. The more you know in advance, the more you can demonstrate your desire to work for that organization.

Step 2: Execute

We use the term *execute* to mean you must perform effectively at your interview. To help you execute, perhaps the best advice we can offer is for you to reread Chapter 20, "Principles of Effective Oral Business Presentation," and Chapter 21, "Listening and Non-Verbal Communication." The relevance of this advice derives from the fact that much of the interview process involves others (a) observing your ability to present information effectively and (b) noting your willingness to listen to what is being said.

If you keep in mind the importance of presenting and listening well, and combine that realization with the advice offered in the following four principles, you will be able to perform effectively in even the most challenging interview.

INTERVIEW PRINCIPLE 2:
Show a sense of purpose; know where you want to be in the future.

In general, recruiters want to hire people who reveal a sense of purpose, a knowledge of where they are going. Revealing a sense of purpose is possible only if you have done your career planning homework. Your previous decisions about a career path and future accomplishments enable you to demonstrate that you are a person who knows what you want to do. The tone of the entire interview can be set by your having thoroughly thought through your career objectives.

Suddenly, instead of being an applicant for a job, you are a person trying to determine whether or not the job fits your career objectives. You now are in the position of determining whether your objectives match the company's needs. You have gained a healthy perspective for any interviewee. An important benefit to this is that it causes you to show an appropriate level of confidence. You no longer appear desperate for a job— *any* job. Instead, you come across as looking for the *right* job. As we will point out in Interview Principle 3, conveying this impression, within reason, can be a strong point in your favor.

INTERVIEW PRINCIPLE 3:
Focus on how you can benefit the company, rather than focusing on how the company can benefit you.

By its very nature, an interview focuses on the candidate. Candidates for a position are always trying to prove their qualifications. Unfortunately, this approach can sometimes lead job candidates to talk too much about their qualifications. Or they may begin to inquire too much about how a particular company can benefit them.

By definition, employers are looking for people who can do a good job for them. Personal development and satisfaction are important benefits in this process, but they are mainly important in terms of how they can benefit the company.

Therefore, you should frame most of your answers in terms of how you can benefit the company. It might be appropriate to state your desire to be Vice President of Manufacturing in ten years if you explain that your reason for having this desire is based not on self-conceit but on your belief that this is the position that would enable you to accomplish many ends that would benefit the company. Think of how different that answer is from one that says:

> I want to be Vice President of Manufacturing in ten years so that I can make more than $150,000 a year, buy a Jaguar, and have a condo in the Bahamas.

Both answers show highly motivated individuals, but the purposes behind the motivation—self-fulfillment through company growth, versus self-fulfillment through personal gratification—are significantly different.

INTERVIEW PRINCIPLE 4:
Apply the communication system of this text.

Throughout this text, we have reminded you that the ability to communicate is a valuable skill to have. This fact is no secret to experienced businesspeople. One of the main skills interviewers will be watching for will be your ability to express yourself clearly and appropriately.

Remember the bottom-line principles and apply them whenever you are answering non-sensitive questions. If you have to provide a long answer to a question, try to give the bottom line first. If you have to answer some non-sensitive questions in writing, then you should not only bottom-line your responses, but also use a contract sentence if your topic is complex. Go over your rough draft the next morning to make sure your writing is high impact.

Almost every interview involves at least one highly sensitive question. Watch for such a question and adjust your response accordingly. Because of the risks associated with a circuitous approach, you should use a semi-circuitous pattern to organize answers to sensitive questions. Tell the interviewer that you need to explain a few things before you present the bottom line of your answer. And, of course, a passive, impersonal style is often highly useful when responding to sensitive questions.

INTERVIEW PRINCIPLE 5:
Maintain your personal integrity.

The stress associated with an interview, combined with the desire to obtain the best job possible, can tempt even the most honest interviewees to pretend to be someone they are not or to possess talents they do not have. Perhaps your career goal doesn't seem to fit what the company wants. Or maybe it becomes clear that your personality makes you unsuitable for jobs the company has available.

Be careful at such times. It is only natural to try to adapt yourself to the demands of the interviewer and the company. But there is a point where adaptation crosses over into deception. And if you cross over that point, you are in serious trouble. For, if you start to pose as something other than what you are, of if you claim to have goals you don't really

The moment of truth: In an interview you must live up to the claims of your resume.

have, the results could be disastrous. Suppose your deception works and you are offered the job. What do you do then? Not much. Unless you are a great actor or actress, and are brilliantly able to do a job you are temperamentally unsuited for, you will soon be unmasked.

Therefore, we find ourselves once again offering the advice we have so frequently offered: be tactful and diplomatic, but most importantly, *be honest*. Never lie when answering a question. Do not pretend to know things you do not really know. Do not pretend to have done things you have not really done. Jobs are lost everyday when applicants, in trying to make the best impression possible, cross over the line between honest persuasion and dishonesty. Once you have crossed that line, you can usually never step back. And if an interviewer ever finds that you crossed that line, you will not get the job offer.

Step 3: Evaluate

The final step in the job hunting process is to evaluate your performance after the interview. Assess honestly how you handled yourself. What do you think you did well? What areas will you strive to improve in your next interview?

Also, assess the company and the people you met at the interview. How easy would they be to work with? Do they possess the qualities you are looking for in the people with whom you hope to work? Will you be provided with appropriate opportunities for growth and advancement? Did you meet any important people who might be willing to serve as mentors to you? These and any number of other questions should be considered after every interview.

One final note: remember to send thank you notes to the people who interviewed you. Any number of employers have told us that when they have to decide between two equally qualified applicants, they very often choose the one who sent a thank you note.

The thank you note is, of course, a positive-persuasive letter. It thanks the reader for the interview and for any friendly activities he or she has performed. The letter may express your interest in particular facets of a job, or may mention some items of information that the interviewer told the interviewee. Regardless of the content, the letter should be pleasant, friendly, and should demonstrate the good manners of the writer. Such manners often receive a most pleasant reward.

SUMMARY

Interviewing is a stressful but necessary step in the job-hunting process. Advance preparation is one way to minimize the stress and to perform more effectively at the interview. Advance preparation means doing a thorough self-analysis before the interview, including a determination of your career goals and objectives. It also means gathering information about the job, the people, and the company with which you are interviewing.

At the interview, be sure to communicate that you have career goals and be certain to express these goals in terms of how they can benefit the company. And, as we have mentioned so often, remember to apply the communication system you have learned throughout this text, but apply it with integrity. For in interviews as in all communication situations, honesty is not just the best policy; it is the only policy.

When the interview concludes, do a thorough self-analysis of your performance. Determine areas you handled well and areas you will improve at your next opportunity. And, finally, remember good manners and courtesy by sending thank you notes to all of the appropriate people. Such manners may have long-term positive results.

REVIEW QUESTIONS

1. What are three important ways to prepare for your interview?

2. What are three important items interviewers often ask about?

3. What does asking intelligent questions about a company during an interview show to the interviewer?

4. What does much of an interview consist of?

5. Whose benefit should the interview focus on—yours or the company's?

6. What is one of the main skills interviewers will be watching for?

7. What should you do after you return from an interview?

APPLICATION PRINCIPLES
REVIEW LIST

1

As a general rule, view an application letter as a positive-persuasive message that should
a. Have a bottom-line organization.
b. Contain a contract sentence, if appropriate.

2

Adapt the style of your letter to the type of work applied for and to the public image of the reader's organization.

3

Emphasize your strengths.

4

Adapt the body of your letter to the company's needs, not yours.

5

Be assertive in seeking an interview. Try to make the interview date; don't force the interviewer to chase you.

RESUME PRINCIPLE

Tailor your resume to
a. The position you are seeking, and
b. The qualifications you want to emphasize.

INTERVIEW PRINCIPLES
REVIEW LIST

1

Prepare for your interview by
a. Assessing your career goals.
b. Anticipating difficult questions and preparing appropriate answers.
c. Studying and learning about your prospective employer.

2

Show a sense of purpose; know where you want to be in the future.

3

Focus on how you can benefit the company, rather than focusing on how the company can benefit you.

4

Apply the communication system of this text.

5

Maintain your personal integrity.

EXERCISES

Exercise 1

Change the following resume into (a) a chronological resume and (b) a functional resume. Pay special attention to the order and format of items and the material that should and should not be included.

THE LIFE, TIMES, AND ACCOMPLISHMENTS OF THOMAS SANDERS

PROFESSIONAL AFFILIATIONS AND AWARDS:	IEEE Computer Society Awarded National Merit Scholarship Member, Engineering Management Society Member, Professional Communication Society
TRAINING PROGRAMS ATTENDED:	Selling By Objectives—A two-part course held by Sales International, February 1988 Instrument Product Training at Power Computers—Part II, Athens, Georgia, June 1989 Instrument Product Training at Power Computers—Part I, Athens, Georgia, June 1988 Personal Computational and Instrument Training at Power Computers, Los Angeles, California, June 1985
OBJECTIVE:	After working for six years in the marketing and sales departments of Power Computers, Inc., I returned to college to obtain an MBA. I'm now seeking employment with a company where I can apply my skills and experience in information management and analysis.
PLACES WHERE I CAN BE REACHED AT PRESENT:	Florida State University, P.O. Box 9408, Tallahassee, FL 32798, 904-555-9807
PERMANENT ADDRESS:	4111 Colonial Drive, 404-555-9889, Atlanta, GA 30303
EXPERIENCE:	February 1980 to December 1985. Greene Star Limited, Greely, Colorado (distributors of Power Computer Products). Sales engineer responsible for sales and marketing activities of instrument products for the western region of the United States. Developing customer contacts; introduction of new products; coordinating seminars and symposiums, etc., were carried out successfully. December 1985 to July 1990. Power Computer Company, Senior Sales Engineer who was responsible for sales and related activities of personal

computation and instrument products of Power Computers. This included conducting technical visits and technical seminars and product demonstrations, as well as arranging customer visits and installing and integrating automated test systems at customer sites. I also carried out project feasibility studies and have successfully coordinated with the establishment of an electronic calibration laboratory with traceability to international standards.

EDUCATION: Master of Business Administration with a concentration in marketing. Florida State University, Tallahassee, FL. Bachelor of Science in Electronics and Communication Engineering, The University of Colorado, Boulder, CO.

ADDITIONAL EXPERIENCE: Familiar with IBM PC and compatible computers. Broad knowledge of various word processing and data gathering packages. Graduate Teaching Assistant with full teaching responsibility in the Department of Mathematics at Florida State University for two semesters.

Exercise 2

Thomas Sanders has decided to apply for a variety of different jobs. He has hired you to write letters for him. Write application letters for Mr. Sanders for the following positions. Be sure to adapt each letter to the demands of the particular position.

Position: Marketing Manager
Address: Gregory Mills
Vice President of Sales
ABC Construction Inc.
108 Stoneleigh Road
Holden, MA 01520

Position: Design Engineer
Address: Judith Bachler
Head, Engineering Department
ABC Systems, Inc.
4929 Bridlepath
Macungie, PA 18062

Position: Personnel Director
Address: Joe Albrecht
Vice President of Personnel
Rochester Community Hospital
Rochester, MN 55904

Exercise 3

Call local firms in your area. Arrange a fifteen- or thirty-minute meeting with one or more of the firm's interviewers. Ask these interviewers questions about what they look for in application letters, resumes, and interviews. Report your findings to the class.

Exercise 4

Prepare an application letter and resume for the job you would like to hold when you graduate.

Unit B

REVIEWING THE BASICS

A BUSINESSPERSON'S GUIDE TO GRAMMAR

OBJECTIVES

This chapter will help you to

•

Realize that grammatical mistakes reflect poorly on your education and background

•

Understand the importance of correct grammar in contracts and other business documents

•

Appreciate that grammatically vague or incorrect writing frequently becomes the basis for lawsuits

•

Master all the grammatical knowledge you will probably ever need in your business career

Knowledge of grammar is important to your business career. You simply cannot write effectively unless what you write shows that you have mastered basic grammar. More importantly, you will be unable to achieve success in an organization made up of educated people unless you write and speak correctly. For example, if you are working as staff assistant to a manager, you do not want to run the risk of submitting for your manager's signature a letter that contains grammatical mistakes. Nor should you count on secretarial support or the word processing center to correct your spelling and grammar mistakes. To expect this is to delegate to others your own responsibility for presenting the image you want and need for advancement.

Correct grammar contributes to the clarity of what you write. It also contributes to the image your messages convey. Make no mistake about it: the image you project in what you write and say is important. Think, for instance, of the prejudgment you would make about a writer who would allow the following sentence to appear in a corporate document:

There are only one way to handle the problem.

In our reactions to incorrect grammar, we make judgments not only about people's education, but also about their social standing, even their intelligence. The nicest business clothing, the most fashionable hairstyling, and the most tasteful of blouses or ties cannot make up for ignorance of the basics of grammar.

Social pressures, as important as they are, do not constitute the main reason businesspeople must use correct grammar in what they write. Ours is an age of seemingly endless lawsuits. Vaguely written agreements, understandings, and contracts are very frequently the basis of litigation. Lawsuits often concern the proper interpretation of written statements that are so vague that they are subject to differing interpretations.

Suppose the following sentence appeared in a contract:

John Smith and Richard Roe agree to release each other from all damages claimed by each in this litigation. He will, however, be paid the sum of $1,000 per month for the period of two years.

Who is "he"—Smith or Roe? Surely there is more at stake here than losing five points on a test for making a grammar mistake about a vague pronoun. This mistake could cost either Smith or Roe $24,000!

HOW WELL DO YOU KNOW GRAMMAR?

Some readers may feel that grammar is easy, that they mastered it in junior high school. If you think you fall into this category, take a very simple pretest to see where you stand and to evaluate whether you really need the review of grammar that follows.

Grammar Pretest

Assume that you are now a manager. The following ten passages appear in memos written by your assistants for you to sign. Can you identify and name the grammatical errors in these ten examples so that you can tell your assistants what they did wrong? (No, you can't merely rewrite these passages. You're the boss. As the manager, you have to be able to tell your assistants what is wrong and how to correct it themselves.)

Tell your subordinates the name of each of the grammatical errors they made in the following examples. Can you do it? Try the following:

1. A few offices have consistently processed more than 40 percent of the month's activity in the last three work days. Attached for your information and appropriate action are a list of those offices that fall into this category.

2. An inventor may qualify for one or more award points for an Invention Award only if they are regular employees.

3. The capabilities and resources of each functional area is defined below.

4. After considering the current productivity requirements in the field, it is incumbent upon us to insure that we spread the workload as evenly as possible across the entire month.

5. We have decided to hold a national managers' meeting June 4–7. We have also decided to continue holding regional meetings yearly. This should please most in-state managers.

6. Neither the warehouse in Cleveland nor the Dallas transportation department have responsibility for delivering equipment to the exhibit site.

7. Originally designed for use in the personal computing and research environment, the sales of this product have proved wider than planned.

8. After setting the headcount requirement, it will be necessary to move ahead to make our New York group responsible for developing an effective regional sales force.

9. The ability to develop hard-hitting audio-visual presentations and to deliver them effectively is the mark of a real professional. Customers expect these from top salespeople.

10. After analyzing the data, a decision was made to go ahead with production of the 6362 Model C1 Printer attachment.

(The answers can be found at the end of Exercise 1 on pages 572–3.)

If you missed none or only one of these examples, you have a good grasp of basic grammar and need read no further. If you missed two or three, you are not in bad shape, but you need improvement and should profit from reading this chapter. After all, you cannot go through life with 20 to 30 percent of your memos and letters marred by grammatical mistakes. In business, 70 or 80 percent correct is not good enough! If you missed most of these examples, you need to read this special feature on grammar very carefully.

UNDERSTANDING GRAMMAR THROUGH TWO COMMON-SENSE PRINCIPLES

Many students claim they have a mental block about grammar. If you fall into this category, let's get to work on overcoming any block you may have.

The rules of grammar are actually not very complex. Most of them are derived from two concepts that are so logical that you already know them. The following two questions (which you can answer easily) contain these two basic concepts:

1. Do you believe that a word or an idea *cannot* be singular and plural at the same time?

Yes	No
[ ]	[ ]

2. Do you believe that words that relate to or influence the meaning of other words should be placed as close as possible to the word or words they influence?

Yes	No
[ ]	[ ]

Of course you answered "yes" to these two questions. But perhaps you don't realize that by doing so you have shown that you should be able to correctly identify two basic types of grammatical mistakes, those involving **number disagreement** and those involving **lack of coherence.**

These two types of mistakes constitute most of the grammatical mistakes we make. You, as the manager of your own and others' writing, should be able to identify these mistakes when they appear in letters or memos for which you are responsible.

Let's turn the two simple questions we asked about number and coherence into the first two grammar principles:

GRAMMAR PRINCIPLE 1:
Do not write sentences in which words change from singular to plural, or vice versa.

GRAMMAR PRINCIPLE 2:
Put words that influence the meaning of other words as close as possible to the words they influence.

As we said before, number and coherence mistakes resulting from the violation of these two principles account for a very high percentage of the grammar errors found in business writing. So if you learn to avoid making these types of mistakes, you will have made a great step forward. We will take up number mistakes first.

NUMBER MISTAKES

A number mistake is a violation of the first grammar principle. You must not write sentences in which words change from singular to plural, or vice versa. There are two types of such number mistakes:

1. Lack of number agreement between pronoun and antecedent (the word the pronoun refers to).
2. Lack of number agreement between subject and verb.

A pronoun is a word that takes the place of a noun, a noun being the name of a person, place, or thing. The noun that the pronoun stands for is called the **antecedent.** The antecedent is the word from which the pronoun gets its meaning. For example, the word *it* means nothing unless you know what *it* refers to. The word *she* means nothing unless you know who *she* is.

Avoiding Pronoun-Antecedent Mistakes

The full grammar rule is this: "A pronoun must agree with its antecedent in gender, number, and person." This statement is correct, but it can be greatly simplified for our practical purposes.

Consider gender. No native English-speaking person makes mistakes in pronoun gender. One of the very good things about English is that it (unlike many other languages) uses natural gender. In many foreign languages, gender is far from natural. In German, for example, the word *girl* is neuter *(das Mädchen)*. In French, the word for *desk* is masculine *(le bureau)*. But in English, the gender of a word is the same as the natural gender of the thing described. A girl is a *she*. A boy is a *he*. A desk is an *it*. No one in a U.S. corporation is going to write, "We need another desk. Order him by Friday." Or, "Mary Smith asked me to contact you about the secretarial work. It thought you could give me specific information about what you need."

Person mistakes are actually part of number mistakes. If you say "They does," *they* is the wrong person for the verb *does*. You must use the third-person singular (*he* or *she*) instead of the third-person plural (*they*). The verb *does* is singular and, hence, requires a singular subject.

When we speak, we commonly ignore number mistakes. We all say such things as "Everyone should take their seats." Or we say "Notre Dame has a fine football tradition. They always hope to win all their games each year." But *everyone* is singular, and *their* is plural. *Notre Dame* is singular, and *their* is plural. Even if we argue that *Notre Dame* can be a collective noun and hence be regarded as plural, we still have to contend with the fact that by saying "Notre Dame *has*," we have made *Notre Dame* singular. Therefore, the writer cannot magically make the school plural and say *their*. Such mistakes in spoken communication may not be serious. But what about such mistakes in an important business document? Consider the following:

> Our executive committee is to meet with their counterparts from U.S. Amalgamated Industries to discuss the disagreement over financial terms. They are authorized to reduce terms by up to 10 percent.

Because of a shift in number, the reader is confused about who *they* are. Just who is authorized to reduce terms by up to 10 percent? *Our executive committee* is singular. *Their counterparts* is plural. *They* is plural. Who are *they? Our committee?* Or *their counterparts* from U.S. Amalgamated? Grammatically, *they* would have to mean U.S. Amalgamated's executives (because *their counterparts* is plural and, hence, agrees in number with *they*). But we suspect the writer meant *they* to refer to *our committee.* If readers had to base an important decision on the information reported, they would be severely handicapped.

Practice in Pronoun-Antecedent Number Agreement

Here are a few sentences that will give you a chance to practice your new knowledge.

> 1. A senior may qualify for the Dean's List only if they are a full-time student.

This one is easy. Since *a senior* obviously implies just one person, the writer cannot refer to that one person as *they.*

> 2. ABC, Inc. has requested that their order be sent before March 15.

The question immediately arises: Is *ABC, Inc.* a collective noun that can be referred to in the plural by the word *their*? The British, for instance, will regard a word such as *the public* or the name of a company as plural because it is collective. A British headline might read, "The public are up in arms!" In American usage, however, we tend to think of collective nouns such as *the company* as singular. Here, *ABC, Inc.* is singular, and so the writer uses the singular word *has* instead of *have.* The correct American version, of course, is "ABC, Inc. has requested that *its* order be sent before March 15." We have become so accustomed to hearing companies referred to as *their, them,* and *they* that we must take particular care to avoid this error.

> 3. Ask the office in San Francisco to initiate this order and make sure that they follow up on it.

At first glance, this sentence seems simple because the error is similar to the one in sentence 2. A closer look, however, reveals that the correction is not so simple. If the writer changes *they* to *it*—so as to make *the office* singular—then the sentence ends with the rather nonsensical statement:

"Make sure that it follows up on it." This sentence, although grammatically correct, sounds silly.

To correct this sentence, we have to look more carefully at what causes a pronoun-antecedent mistake. Often when people are writing, they forget what the real referent is for the pronoun. In other words, while they write *office*, they have in mind the *people* in the office. This shift sometimes causes the writer later to use a plural pronoun such as *they*. The writer needs to put in the real referent for *they*, whether it is *the staff, people*, or *John and Mary*. Thus, a correction for this sentence would be: "Ask John and Mary in the San Francisco office to initiate this order and make sure that they follow up on it." *They* is all right here, because *John and Mary* are plural.

Avoiding Subject-Verb Number Mistakes

Most subject and verb number disagreements found in business messages result more from carelessness than from real ignorance. However, a few tricky subject-verb number disagreements are worthy of special attention. Let's look briefly at some of these.

1. The capabilities and resources of each functional area is defined below.

The writer here mistakenly assumes that the phrase closest to the verb (*each functional area*) is the subject. It is not. The subject, *capabilities and resources*, is plural and therefore demands the plural verb *are*, not the singular *is*.

2. Attached for your information and appropriate action are a list of those offices that fall into this category.

Here, the writer is again confused about what the subject is and whether it is singular or plural. The word *are* indicates that the writer thinks that the subject is *information and action*. Neither of them is the right subject. The subject is *list*, which is singular; hence, the verb should be *is*, not *are*.

3. Neither Hertz nor National bill our company for drop-off charges on any one-way rental.

This is a tricky one, but there is a rule to follow. When two subjects are separated by *nor* or *or*, the verb should agree with the subject that follows the *nor* or the *or*. Since in this sentence *National* follows *nor*, and *National* is singular, the verb should be *bills*, not *bill*.

If the subject following the *or* or *nor* is plural, the verb should be plural:

Neither Hertz nor the other rental companies bill our company for drop-off charges on any one-way rental.

Other rental companies are plural, so the plural form of the verb, *bill*, is correct.

COHERENCE MISTAKES

Coherence mistakes are violations of the second grammar principle: words relating to or influencing the meaning of other words should be placed as close as possible to the words they influence. When people fail to follow this principle, they write incoherently. Incoherence is the most serious and yet the most common problem in all types of writing, not just in business writing. It is the most serious because, as you will see, incoherent writing is almost impossible to understand unless the reader mentally rewrites it coherently.

Two types of grammatical errors involve faulty coherence—**misplaced modifiers** and **dangling modifiers.**

Most people think the concept of misplaced and dangling modifiers is very difficult. Actually, it is very simple.

Remember the Brick Metaphor When Correcting Coherence Mistakes

In business, you are not expected to be a great prose stylist; you are expected to be what we call a good verbal bricklayer. Coherent writing results from putting all the verbal bricks we use in a logical order.

Since we are going to use this brick metaphor a lot, we need to explain our use of the word *brick*. For our purposes, a brick is a unit of thought that must be positioned in a logical relationship to all of the other units of thought in a piece of writing. A brick can be any of the following:

- a word, phrase, or clause within a sentence
- a sentence within a paragraph
- a paragraph within a letter or report
- a section within a report

The concept of bricks and the writer's role as bricklayer is important. All of us have in our minds a brickyard full of stock words and phrases. If we are good writers, we select the bricks we want and put them on the page in a coherent fashion, as in Figure B-1.1. Brick 1 obviously goes first. Brick 2 goes next. Brick 3 follows brick 2. Then we must deal with bricks 3a and 3b, which modify brick 3. Therefore, bricks 3a and 3b must be placed either before or after brick 3. We decide to put them after brick 3. Bricks 4 and 5 conclude the sentence.

If you put your verbal bricks on the page in a logical sequence like this, your reader will have no trouble following and understanding what you have written—unless, of course, you have chosen particularly obscure

FIGURE B1.1
Coherent sentences lead logically from one thought to the next, like well-laid bricks.

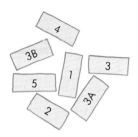

FIGURE B1.2

Incoherent sentences are jumbles of thoughts, like piles of bricks.

words. But that would not be a mistake in coherence; it would be a mistake of word choice.

Figure B-1.2 shows how bad writers perform. They take their bricks and simply dump them onto the page, in a heap. In effect, they say to their readers, "*You* sort them out. *You* figure out what we mean." That's what the writer has done in the following jumble of bricks masquerading as a communication.

> TO: Branch Managers
>
> FROM: Director of Management Training
>
> SUBJECT: Management Effectiveness Conference
>
> DATE: September 17, 19——
>
> We have, unless circumstances preclude, scheduled the next Management Effectiveness Conference to be attended by all management personnel not otherwise burdened by administrative necessities for the night of January 11 and all day January 12; therefore, you should expect to be advised provided you signify your intended participation before November 30 by Bill Swanson of hotel, dinner, and theater reservations for the first night of the Conference, January 11. The Management Effectiveness Conference is part of our managerial recognition program, the agenda of which is attached—meeting to be held in the Twelfth Floor Conference Room—and will be attended by an outstanding manager and GM from each Region/District. Giving people attending an overview of your area, wedding, where permissible, status report on current problems and the outlook for next year would be an excellent use of your time on the agenda. Coordinating the area if you have any questions is Jim Shapely.

Your Mental Compiler: What It Is and How It Works

An amazing fact about the Management Effectiveness Conference memo you have just read is that, if you work hard enough at it, you can indeed understand it, despite its terrible incoherence. All of us have become so used to bad writing that we have developed a sort of *mental compiler* in our minds. A *compiler* is a term we borrowed from computer terminology. It is a device that translates one computer language into another. Our mental compiler translates incoherent prose into some semblance of coherent prose and allows us to receive and process (that is, understand) the information presented. Or, put simply, our mental compiler moves words into their proper places so that we can make some sense out of incoherent writing.

To see how your compiler works, look at this very simple but incoherent sentence.

Advertising will never save the company, if kept at a minimum.

Let's do what is very difficult: turn off our compilers so that we read the bricks of this sentence as they *actually* are written—not as our compiler would rearrange them logically. Now we see the following:

Advertising	will never save	the company,	if kept at a minimum.
(subject brick)	(verbal brick)	(object brick)	(modifying phrase)

As you attempt to understand this sentence, remember that words related to or influencing the meaning of other words should be placed as close as possible to the words they influence. Note that the phrase *if kept at a minimum* is placed next to the word *company*. Therefore, the only way you can logically process the sentence as it is actually written is to view the *company* as that which is being kept at a minimum. But if you do this, you immediately see that this interpretation does not make sense. So, subconsciously you immediately turn on your compiler, which promptly moves the phrase *if kept at a minimum* next to *advertising*, where it belongs. Now you can process the revised sentence.

Advertising, if kept at a minimum, will never save the company.

The sentence's words have been arranged coherently by your compiler. All of this compiler activity happens unconsciously—and in a flash.

Now let's look at a more bizarre example of incoherence to see how your compiler responds.

I'm happy to sign your petition protesting pollution of our city's lake, which I am enclosing in this envelope.

This type of incoherence is the source of much humor. (It was Groucho Marx's stock in trade. "I once shot an elephant in my pajamas," said Groucho. "How he got in my pajamas, I'll never know!") In our sample sentence, you, trying your best to be logical, look at the brick *which I am enclosing in this envelope* and note that it is next to and apparently modifies *lake*. Naturally, you think this juxtaposition of ideas is ridiculous. You reject such illogical, incoherently presented data, and turn your compiler on. With the aid of your compiler, you seek the answer to what is being enclosed in the envelope. The *petition*, of course, is the answer, not *the lake*. So you mentally rewrite and "read" this sentence as follows:

I am happy to sign your petition protesting pollution of our city's lake. The signed petition is enclosed.

Up to this point, you may be thinking how amazing and useful a mental machine this compiler is. It can save you hours of work, you may be tempted to decide; it makes any effort to write coherent prose unnecessary. You can simply throw the bricks on the page and let the reader determine where they belong. Unfortunately, this assumption has a flaw. When readers have to use their compilers, they become irritated, short-tempered, and sometimes hostile. Let's see what causes readers to react in this way. Recall our sample sentence:

Advertising will never save the company, if kept at a minimum.

If a sentence like this, awkward and incoherent though it may be, occurs infrequently, it causes readers minimal discomfort. The compiler cuts in and—whisk!—the bricks are rearranged in a coherent fashion so that the brain can process the information rapidly. This all happens so quickly that readers are seldom bothered by the effort.

But what happens if another sentence with misplaced bricks soon appears? Then another? Then another? Soon your compiler begins to wear down. Your compiler is like a sprinter, not a long-distance runner. It can operate only for short periods of time without causing you psychological discomfort. Ask yourself how much you suffered when trying to read the Managment Effectiveness Conference memo.

Suppose we were to ask you to rewrite that memo. How long would it take you to rewrite it so that it would be completely coherent? We think that even the best of editors would take a few minutes just to figure out what the writer was talking about. The editor then might spend perhaps fifteen minutes or so rewriting the memo to make it perfectly coherent. But ask yourself how long it took you to read the original memo and to battle your way through to some semblance of understanding. Just a very few minutes.

Did you really appreciate what a fantastic mental exercise your brain performed? In a matter of seconds, it edited a piece of incoherent writing and made it coherent. And it did all this in mid-air, so to speak, without benefit of pencil and paper. This was a phenomenal and exhausting mental exercise. Can you imagine how exhausting it would be if you forced your compiler to wade through a ten-page report written by such a writer? Bad writers put their readers through this task every time they try to communicate.

Self-Editing

Writers also have compilers, but their compilers are naturally biased in favor of whatever they have written. Unlike readers, writers know what they meant to say, as opposed to what they actually wrote. We have all had the experience of pointing out incoherence in something a friend has written. But even after you've pointed them out, your friend may have difficulty seeing what is wrong. Why is this so? Because your friend's compiler knows what he or she meant to say, even though the words did not actually come out that way.

So, if a friend tells you there is something incoherent about what you have written, recognize that he or she will be able to identify your coherence mistakes a lot more readily than you will. If there is no friend to tell you whether what you have written makes sense, you must learn to turn off your own compiler and look honestly and objectively at what you have *actually* written, not at what you *think* you have written.

Only with your compiler turned off can you examine your own sentence bricks with ruthless detachment. That is why even good writers like to "sleep on" what they have written. In what is called (for good reason) the "cold light of morning," what they have written may not look so good and may need a great deal of editing. So don't be upset if, with your compiler turned off, something you wrote earlier may look very poor indeed. Don't worry if you find that you have not written a perfectly coherent first draft. Few of us do so. Let that draft get "cold" overnight (or longer); then turn off your compiler, find the misplaced bricks, rearrange them coherently, and strive to construct a message that clearly and logically expresses your thoughts.

The Compiler and Self-Editing

Mental editing is your compiler's function. The only problem is that the editing does not take place in print. You need to be able to compose on paper what your compiler does mentally. We will try to help you do just that. Take the following simple sentence.

> All fruits have been removed from the shelves that have even a chance of contamination.

You feel immediately that your compiler is having difficulty processing this sentence. Something is incoherent about it. Your compiler then will reduce this sentence to its component units of thought and seek to rearrange them logically. We will imitate the compiler and separate the sentence into its component bricks and number each in the order in which the writer has presented them:

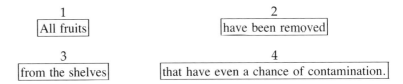

We see that brick 4, obviously, does not modify brick 3; yet, it is placed next to brick 3. How does your compiler proceed? Let's imagine (as Figure B-1.3 shows) that the compiler is a sort of derrick that has a hook hanging from its boom. When the compiler wants to move a brick, it lowers the hook, picks up the offending brick, and moves it to the location in the sentence where it belongs.

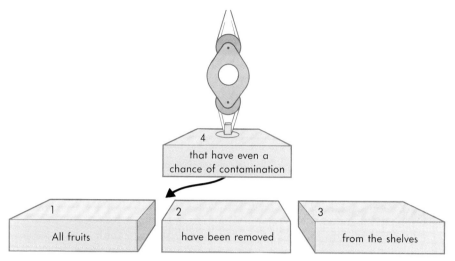

FIGURE B1.3
Your compiler in action.

In this case, your compiler has difficulty processing the brick *that have even a chance of contamination* because it does not modify *from the shelves.* The compiler asks, "What does brick 4, *that have even a chance of contamination,* relate to?" The answer is, as Figure B-1.3 shows, brick 1. Therefore, your compiler will drop brick 4 between bricks 1 and 2. The sentence now reads coherently, "All fruits that have even a chance of contamination have been removed from the shelves."

Correcting Misplaced Modifiers

What you and your compiler have been correcting are, of course, misplaced modifiers (which are nothing more than misplaced bricks). Let's correct a few more sentences:

> Our Canadian division has provided us with a statement of the current requirements under the Canadian Immigration Act for temporary entry into Canada, which is attached.

This sentence makes it sound as if Canada *is attached.* Your compiler has to figure out what really is *attached* and then move the bricks around. Obviously, the *statement of the current requirements* is what is attached. But why should a sloppy writer force the reader to figure out what the writer means? The way a good writer would present these thoughts is

> Our Canadian division has provided us with the attached statement of current requirements under the Canadian Immigration Act for temporary entry into Canada.

Now let's look at two of the sentences used in the pretest.

> After considering the current productivity requirements in the field, it is incumbent upon us to insure that we spread the workload as evenly as possible across the entire month.

This sentence presents an interesting example of how your compiler works unconsciously. Only when you turn your compiler off and force yourself to read what the writer actually wrote (not the instant revision your compiler presents), will you see that the word *it* is what is *considering the current productivity requirements.* Remember, words that relate to each other should be placed as close as possible in a piece of writing. Obviously, it is *us* that can be *considering* . . . , but *it* is closer to the *considering* brick than *us* is.

The misplaced brick can be corrected by moving the brick beginning *after considering* next to *us,* like this:

> It is incumbent upon us, after considering the current productivity requirements in the field, to insure that we spread the workload as evenly as possible across the entire month.

Our next sentence is a type of incorrect statement your compiler handles so easily that you may not even have been aware that anything was mentally edited.

> Originally designed for use in the personal computing and research environment, the sales of this product have proved wider than planned.

With your compiler firmly turned off, you will see that the sentence says that the *sales* were *originally designed for use.* . . . This is because *sales* is the closest noun to the *originally designed* brick. But how can *sales* be *originally designed for use? This product,* not *the sales,* was. Hence, what your compiler actually presents to your brain for processing is the following:

> This product, which was originally designed for use in the personal computing and research environment, has proved to have wider sales than planned.

Dangling Modifiers

What happens if your compiler lifts a brick up, but then discovers no word in the sentence it can modify? What can your compiler do when there is no logical place to place a brick?

The answer is *nothing.* The brick continues to dangle on the hook! Naturally, this is called a **dangling modifier.** Consider this example:

> After deciding on a course of action, the best strategy seemed to be to buy, not make, the components.

After you divide the sentence into its component bricks, your compiler asks, "Who is deciding on a course of action?" The compiler then finds itself facing the choices illustrated in Figure B-1.4.

Which brick is capable of *deciding on a course of action?* The compiler is perplexed. The brick modifies nothing. Or, more accurately, it modifies a word that the writer has not put into the sentence. Hence it dangles. In effect, such dangling modifiers actually modify what we call "secret sub-

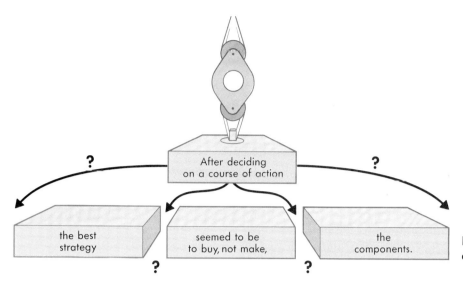

jects." A writer may have a subject in mind, but if he or she has neglected to put that subject into the written sentence, we can only guess who or what it is. The subject capable of *deciding*, is needed as follows:

> After deciding on a course of action, <u>management</u> believed that the best strategy seemed to be to buy, not make, the components.

Dangling modifiers can be an extremely dangerous type of mistake for business writers to make. Why? Because dangling modifiers allow readers to invent a subject the writer has failed to specify. Readers may very well invent a subject that suits *their* convenience, not the writer's.

Let's look at a few instances in which a dangling modifier allows readers to do just that.

> After setting the terms for payment for the machinery, it will be necessary to take up the matter of quality assurance.

Who is setting the terms for payment? Your company? The customer's company? Sentences like this often end up in court. Now consider this sentence:

> Using the given figures, it is clear that my department bears no responsibility for the contractual failure.

Who is using the given figures? Who is deciding that the writer's department bears no responsibility? Certainly, *it* can't use figures. There is no word in the sentence that can use figures. Hence, the *using the given figures* brick dangles.

Avoiding Dangling Modifiers

You can avoid dangling modifiers. Dangling modifiers have a penchant for following introductory phrases that are introduced by present participles. A present participle is a verb ending in *ing*—for example, *ordering, operating, analyzing,* or *deciding.*[1] The cure is to avoid writing introductory phrases that contain present participles.

Why do introductory phrases beginning with participles cause trouble? Take a look at the following participial phrase:

> After analyzing the pension plan, . . .

What do you think will follow this phrase? You expect the next subject to be the person or thing doing the action described by the participle, that is, *analyzing the pension plan.* Note that we said next subject, not the next noun. In the example, the next noun is *plan,* that which is being *analyzed,* not the person who is doing the analyzing. The person who is doing the analyzing must follow as the subject of the sentence. If that subject of the action is missing, the participial phrase will dangle.

Consider another example:

> Developing the Retirement Benefit Plan, . . .

Who is *developing* the plan? You expect the next subject to be the person doing the developing.

In case you have any doubts about the way you react to participial phrases, some comical examples will prove our point.

> After swimming three laps around the pool, soft drinks were served.

Didn't you laugh at the thought of soft drinks swimming three laps in the pool?

> Walking down the street, the stone lion in front of the library came into view.

How can a stone lion walk down the street? You laugh because you expect the first subject following a participial phrase to be the thing that is doing the action expressed by the participle.

Now let's turn to some business examples:

> Analyzing in detail the individual answers collected and comparing them with the group responses, information about the effectiveness of this learning experience can be obtained.

Ask yourself, "Who is analyzing and comparing?" Certainly not the word *information.* A secret subject is doing the analysis and comparison. The only way to correct this sentence is to rewrite it so that its subject is the person or persons doing the analysis and comparison. Something like this will do:

---

[1] There is another kind of word ending in *ing*—a gerund. A gerund is a present participle used as a noun (e.g., "Swimming is fun."). Don't worry about gerunds; they can't dangle.

The researchers, analyzing in detail the individual answers collected and comparing them with the group responses, obtained information about the effectiveness of this learning experience.

Avoiding Vague Pronoun Reference

Many communication problems in business result from vague pronoun reference. Undoubtedly, that is why lawyers long ago coined such phrases as "party of the first part" and "party of the second part" in order to avoid the use of potentially vague pronouns such as "he," "she," and "they."

One principle that all readers need to remember is this:

GRAMMAR PRINCIPLE 3:
Avoid using pronouns as much as possible in important documents. Use nouns.

You must always worry about whether a pronoun will be subject to an interpretation different from that which you intended. The cure is to use nouns instead of pronouns in important documents, even though nouns may seem repetitive. The following memo is a disguised version of an actual memo that caused great confusion in a company. The memo almost was the basis of a lawsuit.

After thorough investigation of the recent conflict between ABC, Inc., and XYZ Corp., it was concluded that the branch offices had responsibility for transmitting to the customers all relevant costs to be expected in installing the 3730 Distributed Office Support System. They had no authority to the contrary, and they should have understood that incidental costs would be charged to them. They were instead vague.

They certainly were vague. But who are *they*? *They* can refer both to the customers and to the branch offices. Readers, not being told clearly which party *they* is, can freely substitute whatever meaning suits their convenience. Such vague pronoun references invite lawsuits.

Vague pronoun reference is simply another violation of Grammar Principle 2—words relating to or influencing the meaning of other words should be placed as close as possible to the words they influence. In fact, a pronoun has little meaning until the reader infers that meaning from the pronoun's location relative to the nouns in the sentence. Thus, coherence in the use and placement of pronouns becomes doubly important, as Grammar Principle 4 shows:

GRAMMAR PRINCIPLE 4:
A reader expects the noun closest to a pronoun and agreeing with it in gender and number to be the noun that pronoun refers to.

Here is a comical example, just to convince you of the truth of this principle:

If raw milk does not agree with the baby, boil it.

The cure for such a vague pronoun is to apply Grammar Principle 3 and to replace the pronoun *it* with a noun.

If raw milk does not agree with the baby, boil the milk.

Now let's apply Grammar Principle 4 to the following sentence:

They finished their assignments, but they were too late.

The second *they* can refer either to *assignments* or to the first *they*. You think the reference is to *assignments,* but you are not sure. Your compiler is helpless when faced with such a vague pronoun. If you had to make a choice, you would assume that the *assignments* were too late, because *assignments* is the nearest plural, neuter noun to *they*. Only the author knows what was late—the *assignments* or the persons referred to as *they*. If we assume, say, that "students" were *they*, we could rewrite the sentence correctly like this:

Although they finished their assignments, the students were late in submitting these assignments.

In making this correction, we have applied both Grammar Principles 3 and 4.

Consider this next passage:

All sophisticated corporations should insure themselves against disaster and the consequent loss of vital records. It provides for the resumption of corporate activity in as short a period of time as possible.

Your compiler simply cannot handle vagueness like this. What does *it* refer to? The nearest singular, neuter noun is *loss*; the next is *disaster*. There is no noun in the sentence that can be the antecedent of *it*. We guess that *it* refers to the act of "insuring the corporation," a phrase that is not in the sentence. The writer should have written the second sentence as follows:

Such corporate disaster insurance would provide the capability for the company to resume normal activity as soon as possible.

Try this sentence:

The manager told the director he was wrong.

Again, the compiler is perplexed. According to the rule, *he* should refer to *director*. But does it? Since only the writer can possibly know who was wrong, we cannot logically correct this sentence. In the next example, however, we can make a correction.

Arrange either desks or chairs for seating so that they will be able to take notes if they so desire.

What does *they* refer to? *Desks* or *chairs,* the nearest nouns, make no sense. Desks and chairs cannot take notes. Obviously, *they* refers to people of some sort—members of the audience, trainees, participants, students, or so on. Therefore, the correction would merely involve substituting one of these for *they*—". . . so that trainees will be able to take notes . . ."

How can you process the following sentence?

He offered to resign, but it was refused.

Here is a classic example of how your compiler will quickly invent a referent for a vague pronoun. The *it* here does not refer to any noun in the sentence (*to resign* is a verb, not a noun). Your compiler performs its usual magic and turns *to resign* into *resignation,* thus creating the noun that is needed. Now you "read" what you know the writer meant to write:

He offered his resignation, but it was refused.

The final grammar principle deals with pronoun placement.

GRAMMAR PRINCIPLE 5:
Because a pronoun means little until a reader knows what noun it refers to, put the noun first and follow with the pronoun.

Let's look at an example:

Perhaps it was not made clear, but it had been discussed over several months, so surely all managers have had a chance to discuss this change in policy.

Until the reader gets to the end of this sentence, he or she does not know what *it* refers to. The sentence would have been easily read if it had been written this way:

Perhaps this change of policy was not made clear, but it had been discussed over several months; so surely all managers have had a chance to discuss it.

Poor writers really misuse pronouns when they write a puzzler like this:

Perhaps it was not made clear, but the criteria have been defined in several ways.

This is difficult to understand. *It* is singular. *Criteria* is plural. But does the writer intend *it* to refer to *criteria*? Has the writer simply made a number mistake or does *it* refer to a noun that is not in the sentence? The application of Grammar Principle 5 would begin the sentence with the noun and follow with the pronoun.

Perhaps the criteria was not made clear, but it was defined in several ways.

This sentence is, of course, still wrong, because the writer has committed a number mistake. The writer apparently thinks *criteria* is singular (*criterion* is, of course, the singular). Your compiler now can fix the mistake quickly, like this:

Perhaps the criterion was not made clear, but it. . . .

OR

Perhaps the criteria were not made clear, but they. . . .

CASE ERRORS

There is one final problem area that needs to be discussed—case errors. The **case** of a noun or pronoun marks its function in the sentence. Pronouns, for example, may be in either the subjective or objective case and, as Table B-1.1 shows, may have different forms for each case.

Case is a complicated grammatical subject, so we will deal here only with the two most common case errors made by businesspeople. These are:

- The failure to recognize when a pronoun is the object of a preposition, and, hence, is in the objective case.
- The failure to realize that words in apposition must be in the same case as the word they refer to.

Object of a Preposition

In daily conversation, we hear people saying "between you and I." *Between* is a preposition; therefore, *I* must be in the objective case. It should be "between you and *me*."

Note: Be sure to recognize when words like *before, after,* and *until* are used as adverbs rather than prepositions. For example:

Before you and I decide on what to say, let us consider our options.

Here, *before* is used as an adverb. The subjects of the sentence are *you* and *I*; therefore, both should be in the nominative case. The same would be true if this sentence began with "After you and I decide . . ." or "Until you and I decide . . . ."

Sometimes it is difficult to determine when a preposition like *before* is used as an adverb. Consider this sentence:

Mary will present before John and [<u>me</u> or <u>I</u>?]

TABLE B-1.1 Two Cases of Pronouns	Subjective Objective	I me	we us	you	he him	she her	it	they them	who who(m)

The answer depends on whether you mean "before John and I speak" or "Mary will speak before (i.e., physically in front of) John and me."

Apposition

Words are in **apposition** when they are placed next to each other and the second one explains the first. They must be in the same case. For example:

> We, John, Mary, and I, will be the next presenters.

To write, "John, Mary, and *me*" is wrong because all these words— *we, John, Mary,* and *I*—are the subjects of this sentence.

The same holds true if these words are direct objects of a verb or objects of a preposition:

> Bill will attempt to please us, John, Mary, and <u>me</u>.

Here, *us* and *me* are both objects of the verb *to please.*

> Give the trophy to any one of <u>us, John, Mary,</u> or <u>me.</u>

Here, *us* and *me* are objects of the preposition *to.*

SUMMARY

Let's first summarize what you have learned about grammar in business messages. Basically, to be grammatically correct in business, you need to pay special attention to two categories of mistakes: **number** and **coherence**. Within the number category, you need to check for two types of mistakes: subject-verb agreement and pronoun-antecedent agreement. Within the coherence category, you need to check for errors in modification (dangling and misplaced modifiers) and in vague pronoun reference.

Once you have conquered these five points—subject-verb agreement, pronoun-antecedent agreement, misplaced modifiers, dangling modifiers, and vague pronoun reference—you will have removed the major stumbling blocks that bother most business writers.

(Grammar exercises appear at the end of Unit B.)

A BUSINESSPERSON'S GUIDE TO PUNCTUATION

OBJECTIVES

This chapter will help you to

•

Master the most important punctuation rules
and conventions

•

Realize that incorrect punctuation, like
incorrect grammar, can make business
documents the basis of lawsuits

Some punctuation rules you *need* to know. Other punctuation rules you *might want* to know. But to function effectively in a business context, you need to concentrate only on those rules you need to know. Therefore, we will take a practical, down-to-earth approach to punctuation. We will explain important punctuation rules in detail and omit coverage of rules that are of little or no importance to the average businessperson.

One of the difficult aspects of punctuation is that it is not always based on logic, at least not the kind of logic businesspeople are familiar with. Instead, punctuation is partly logical, partly conventional. **Conventions** are nothing more than rules people agree upon for certain things. For example, it is conventional that a football field is one hundred yards long. There is no logical reason why; people have simply agreed that this size is the conventional and accepted length of a football field. Yet, there are no set dimensions for golf courses. So too with some aspects of punctuation. There really is not much logic behind some rules; they are just rules and all you need do is to remember them.

A PRAGMATIC APPROACH TO PUNCTUATION RULES

Punctuation can be confusing; much of it is optional. Sometimes you put in a comma; sometimes you don't. Busy people often needlessly spend time deciding whether they should or shouldn't use a comma.

To spare you from memorizing all the optional punctuation situations, this chapter is going to take a simplified approach. Rather than explore all of the options for certain situations, we will make the choice and tell you one way to punctuate something correctly. There will, of course, be other ways to punctuate some of these situations. Someone may one day say to you, about something you have written, "You didn't *have* to put a comma there." If that happens, all you have to do is ask, "Is what I've done wrong?" If you have followed our advice, the answer will be, "No, it's not wrong." And knowing one correct way to punctuate each situation is good enough for most businesspeople.

Avoiding Unnecessary Punctuation Problems

Most of the punctuation problems you will have to deal with will occur in the sentences *you* write. How much of a problem you cause yourself is up to you. If you write complicated sentences, you probably will have problems punctuating them. In fact, most sentences that are hard to punctuate really need rewriting rather than better punctuation. Look, for instance, at the following passage:

> Under the new rules set forth in this legislation situations occasional as they may be may arise that do not conform to the new rules as is the case for example with some retailers who pre-list catalogue items for sale at a specified price but then re-

serve the right to raise prices if proven costs go up on products listed in the catalogue.

In its present state, this passage would be extremely difficult to punctuate. But if you divide the passage into shorter sentences, as you were advised to do in Chapter 9, it becomes easier to punctuate. It also becomes a far better piece of writing. Revised, the passage might look like this:

Under the new rules set forth in this legislation, situations may occasionally arise that do not conform to the new rules. For example, some retailers may pre-list catalogue items for sale at a specified price. However, they may reserve the right to raise prices on products listed in the catalogue. They can do so only if they can prove that their costs went up.

Understanding Sentence Structure

As our last example illustrates, "correct" punctuation is made easy if you really understand sentence structure. And as Chapter 9 demonstrates, there are only three types of sentences a business writer needs to compose—simple, compound, and complex. Once you are aware of how each of these sentences is constructed, you should have little trouble with punctuation.

Before we go further, let's review some grammatical terms. A **sentence**, for our purpose, is

1. One or more independent clauses, or
2. A combination of one or more independent and one or more dependent clauses.

A **clause** is a group of words containing a **subject** (the person or thing that acts) and a **predicate** (the word or group of words that tells what the subject is or does). Clauses that can stand alone are **independent**; those that cannot stand alone are **dependent**. Here is an example of an independent clause:

I bought the stock.

This sentence is complete and self-sufficient; it can stand by itself. But watch what happens with the addition of a few simple words:

1. Although I bought the stock,
2. Before I bought the stock,
3. Since I bought the stock,
4. After I bought the stock,

With the insertion of words such as *although, before, since,* and *after,* the clause is made unable to stand alone. Even though, as a clause, it has a subject and a predicate, it seems to hang in mid-air, so to speak. It needs to be completed, for example, like this:

Although I bought the stock, I later regretted it.

I later regretted it is an independent clause. The dependent clause has now been joined to an independent clause, thus making a complete sentence.

With these definitions in mind, we can now begin to apply the rules of punctuation to each of the three types of sentences.

Punctuating Simple Sentences

It is easy to punctuate a simple sentence. Put a capital letter at the beginning and the appropriate punctuation mark at the end of the sentence. The end punctuation mark will be either a period, a question mark, or an exclamation mark. For most sentences, the period is the mark of final punctuation.

Punctuating Joined-Together Sentences

You can join two related sentences by inserting a semi-colon between them.

I bought the stock; I will take the consequences.

The use of the semi-colon here is similar to the use of the period in that it indicates that there are two separate sentences. However, a semi-colon indicates a degree of separation *less* than that marked by the period.

A *compound sentence* results from the joining of two independent clauses by a **coordinating conjunction**—*and, or, but,* or *nor.* The question that arises is whether a comma must precede coordinating conjunctions. You can correctly write

I bought the stock, and I will take the consequences.

However, the use of a comma *plus* a coordinating conjunction is optional in certain situations.

Some people argue that you do not need to put a comma before a coordinating conjunction like *and* when the two independent sentences joined together are short. That may be true, but we argue that it's much easier to remember a single, simple rule rather than debating how short is short. Since you must use a comma before a coordinating conjunction when the two clauses are long or not closely related to each other, you might as well put the comma before *and, but, or,* and *nor* when joining all compound sentences.

A word of warning is necessary here. Modern usage is now permitting the words *however, then, yet, therefore, so,* and *thus* to be treated as coordinating conjunctions when they separate two independent clauses. However, in formal business writing, we urge you not to do so. Such words are *not* coordinating conjunctions; they are adverbs. So when writers put a comma before them, thinking they are joining two independent clauses, these writers are incorrect in the eyes of most businesspeople. Any punctuation practice that is subject to argument (and litigation) is avoided by most businesspeople. Therefore, the punctuation of the following sentence is to be avoided.

Incorrect
I bought the stock, therefore I will take the consequences.

If you use *however, therefore,* or any of those types of adverbs between two sentences, you should place a semi-colon before the adverb and a comma after, like this:

Correct
I bought the stock; therefore, I will take the consequences.[1]

Punctuating Sentences with Compound Predicates

You should also learn to punctuate a related type of sentence, one with a compound predicate or, in other words, two independent clauses with the same grammatical subject. Here is an example:

I attended the meeting and paid my own expenses.

Because this sentence is not a compound sentence, no comma should be placed in front of the coordinating conjunction *and*.
Here are three more examples:

1. Our noise abatement program is workable and should be implemented immediately.
2. We have contacted Pace, Inc. but now plan to wait until we hear from Frederickson & Co.
3. The committee approved the report and forwarded it to all supervisory personnel.

Each of these sentences has a compound predicate. Each consists of one subject and two predicates joined by a conjunction (*and, but, or,* or *nor*). Hence, in none of these sentences should a comma be placed before the conjunction.

---

[1]Be sure to notice that the rule we are discussing here applies to using *however, therefore,* and other such words, to connect two independent clauses. When these words are used as interjections (that is, words tossed into the middle of sentences, and not used to join clauses), they should have commas before and after them. For example, it is correct to write

I bought the stock based on my broker's recommendation. I will, however, have to accept the consequences of the decision.

Perhaps the easiest way to remember the comma–conjunction relationship is to visualize it as follows:

COMMA? YES!

Subject—Verb . . . $\begin{cases} , \text{and} \\ , \text{but} \\ , \text{or} \\ , \text{nor} \end{cases}$ . . . Subject—Verb

COMMA? NO!

Subject—Verb . . . $\begin{cases} \text{and} \\ \text{but} \\ \text{or} \\ \text{nor} \end{cases}$ . . . Verb

In summary, a comma is placed in front of a coordinating conjunction when a subject and verb are found on both sides of that conjunction. When a subject appears only on one side, that is, when verbs on both sides of the conjunction refer to the same subject, *no comma should be used.*

Punctuating Complex Sentences

Here are two rules that can help you to punctuate complex sentences correctly.

PUNCTUATION PRINCIPLE 1:
Words or groups of words that are presented out of subject–predicate order in a sentence are set off by commas.

PUNCTUATION PRINCIPLE 2:
Modifiers that are parenthetical and, hence, *not necessary* to the meaning of the sentence are set off by commas.

Let's apply these two principles to complex sentences, which, as you remember, are composed of one or more independent clauses joined to one or more dependent clauses. Here are our simplified rules for punctuating such sentences:

1. *If a dependent clause comes first, set it off from the independent clause by a comma.*

For example, "Before I bought the stock, I thoroughly analyzed the company." *Before I bought the stock* is a dependent clause and cannot stand alone. So, as the rule states, when a dependent clause comes first, join it to the independent clause and use a comma.

2. *When the dependent clause follows the independent clause, apply Punctuation Principle 2 to determine whether a comma between the clauses is necessary.*

For example, consider this sentence: "I sold my stock because I needed cash." First, we determine that *because I needed cash* is necessary to the sentence. Then, we apply Punctuation Principle 2 (modifiers that are parenthetical and not necessary to the meaning of the sentence are set off by commas) and find that no comma is needed before *because*. This sounds difficult but is really quite simple. Look at the following sentence:

> I always make a negative decision whenever I do not have enough facts.

I always make a negative decision is an independent clause, and *whenever I do not have enough facts* is a dependent clause. Now apply Principle 2. Is the meaning of the independent clause *I always make a negative decision* changed by the addition of the dependent clause *whenever I do not have enough facts*? The answer is yes. *I always make a negative decision* has quite a different meaning from *I always make a negative decision whenever I do not have enough facts*. Therefore, as the rule states, the independent and the necessary dependent clause should not be separated by a comma.

Consider another example:

> ABC Company won the contract although competition was intense.

Should there be a comma before the word *although*? The answer is yes. The dependent clause *although competition was intense* is parenthetical; the clause is not necessary to the meaning of the basic independent sentence, *ABC Company won the contract.*

But the following sentence presents an entirely different situation:

> ABC Company won the contract because its lobbyists exerted political influence.

Does the dependent clause, *because its lobbyists exerted political influence,* significantly influence the meaning of the independent clause, *ABC Company won the contract*? The answer is yes; therefore, the dependent clause should *not* be set off by a comma. If a comma were put before the word *because,* it would imply to the reader that the dependent clause is not necessary to the essential meaning of the main independent clause. Since the dependent clause is essential, the correct way of conveying this information to the reader is to write the sentence without a comma.

What if a dependent clause falls in the middle of a sentence? Fortunately, Principle 2 applies again. A dependent clause falling in the middle of a sentence *is set off by commas* if it is *not* necessary to the meaning of the sentence. But the clause is not set off by commas if it *is* necessary to the meaning of the sentence.

How do these rules work in practice? Consider these two ways of punctuating this common proverb.

1. People <u>who live in glass houses</u> should not throw stones.
2. People, <u>who live in glass houses,</u> should not throw stones.

Commas around a dependent clause essentially serve the same function as parentheses. These surrounding commas tell the reader that the clause encased in commas is parenthetical and not necessary to the meaning of the sentence. Therefore, in sentence 2, the commas around the underlined dependent clause tell the reader that the clause *who live in glass houses* is unnecessary and that the real meaning is this:

People should not throw stones.

Obviously, this interpretation completely destroys the real meaning of the proverb, that a particular type of people, those who live in glass houses, should not throw stones.

Let's try another example:

1. All of my money which was invested in XYZ stock was lost.
2. All of my money, which was invested in XYZ stock, was lost.

Do you see the difference between 1 and 2? In 1, the only money that was lost was that which was invested in XYZ stock. In 2, the reader is told that *all* of the writer's money was lost, not just that invested in XYZ stock. (Also note that in sentence 1, you can replace *which* with *that*. In sentence 2, you cannot.)

Almost all business sentences fall within the four types mentioned in this chapter—simple, compound, complex, and compound-predicate. Since you now know how each of these should be punctuated, you should have very little difficulty punctuating *most* of what you write. We say "most" because there are some aspects of punctuation left that should be covered. One of these is phrases.

Punctuating Phrases

A **phrase** is a group of words not containing a subject and a predicate. If that group of words contained a subject and a predicate, it would be a clause. If it contained a subject, a predicate, and could stand alone, it would be an independent clause (or a sentence). Since phrases are groups of words that do not contain a subject and a predicate, they cannot stand alone.

How do you punctuate phrases? Again, apply Punctuation Principles 1 and 2, repeated here:

PUNCTUATION PRINCIPLE 1:
Words or groups of words that are presented out of subject–predicate order in a sentence are set off by commas.

PUNCTUATION PRINCIPLE 2:
Modifiers that are parenthetical and, hence, *not necessary* to the meaning of the sentence are set off by commas.

Let's first see how Principle 1 applies to phrases. Consider this sentence:

I made that decision early in January.

The statement is written in subject–predicate order; hence, it requires no internal punctuation. But if part of the predicate is moved so that the sentence reads: "Early in January, I made that decision," you are correct to insert a comma after the introductory phrase, *early in January.* (Again, this is an instance where it is actually optional to use a comma after a short introductory phrase. However, you are correct if you do place commas after such phrases, and the comma does make the sentence easier to read.)

Now let's see how Principle 2 applies to phrases. Principle 2, remember, says that modifiers that are not absolutely necessary to a sentence's meaning are to be set off by commas. Here is a series of such sentences:

Business, <u>alas</u>, is terrible.

<u>Alas</u>, business is terrible.

<u>To tell the truth</u>, I'm busy.

Nothing, <u>on the other hand</u>, will prevent me from trying to make the sale.

<u>Nevertheless</u>, I shall try.

Each of the underlined words or phrases, *alas, to tell the truth, on the other hand, nevertheless,* is unnecessary to the meaning of the sentence. Therefore, it is correct to set off each by commas.

Commas in a Series

There is a use of the comma that does not fall under Principles 1 and 2— the use of commas in punctuating items in a series. Principle 3 will help us in this situation.

PUNCTUATION PRINCIPLE 3:
In a series with three or more items, separate the items by commas. In a series with only two items, do not separate the items with a comma.

Look at the following sentence:

John wrote his report and then went home.

This sentence has one subject and two predicates. The two predicates are *wrote his report* and *then went home.* Since there are only two items in the list, they are not separated by a comma.

Now look at the following sentence:

John wrote his report, proofread it thoroughly, and then went home.

Since there are more than two items in this sentence, the individual items are separated by commas.

The same rule applies to the next sentence:

John and Bill wrote their reports on Tuesday night.

John and Bill are only two items in the series; therefore, no comma is needed between them. Compare that with:

John, Bill, and Jim wrote their reports on Tuesday night.

Here, commas are used to separate each of the items in the series.

Many people view as optional the last comma in the series. That is, they would view "John, Bill and Jim wrote their reports on Tuesday night" as correct. But please remember that our advice deals solely with business writing, writing that must be accurate because it is the stuff of contracts and agreements, and always subject to potential litigation. The so-called serial comma helps make writing more accurate.

The colors of the flags were red, yellow, white and blue.

How many flags were there? Three or four? Was the last flag *blue,* or was it *white and blue?* In a sentence like this, the lack of a comma before the last item in a series larger than two can cause confusion.

Suppose the sentence stating that John, Bill, and Jim wrote reports had been written like this:

John, Bill and Jim wrote their reports on Tuesday night.

Did Bill and Jim work together on one report? Who knows. But by putting a comma before *and Jim,* the writer made the meaning clear.

Look at another business instance where the lack of a comma in a series could easily lead to a legal argument over what was meant:

Lone Eagle Truck Lines, Inc., has the sole and exclusive right to transport the following products from Tijuana, Mexico, to Los Angeles, California: produce, textiles, light electronic parts and machinery.

The issue here is whether Lone Eagle Truck Lines has the sole right to transport only *light electronic* machinery or machinery of all sorts. If this sentence as written went to court, the absence of a comma before the last *and* would lead the judge to rule that the right referred only to *light electronic machinery.*

The Apostrophe

Let's review another frequently used punctuation mark, the **apostrophe**. Some linguists speculate its usage will die out within the next thirty to forty years, but until that happens, businesspeople should know the basic principles of apostrophes.

Apostrophes are used to show possession or to signify contractions. Here are a few simple rules to follow:

1. Apostrophe *s* is added to possessive words that do not end in *s*.
2. An apostrophe but no *s* is added to possessive words that end in *s*. However, apostrophe *s* is added to proper names that end in *s*.
3. An apostrophe but no *s* is added to plural words that show possession.
4. An apostrophe is placed in contracted words to show that letters are missing.

Look at the difference between the correct and incorrect usage of apostrophes in the following sentences.

Incorrect	*Correct*
John Smiths report should arrive by Friday.	John Smith's report should arrive by Friday.
AVIS business discounts need to be used by all of our managers.	AVIS's business discounts need to be used by all of our managers.
Its too late.	It's too late.
The office lost it's lights.	The office lost its lights.

In sentence 1, it is clear that Smith owns the report; it is Smith's report. Therefore, the apostrophe is needed to show possession. In sentence 2, the proper name AVIS ends in *s*. Therefore, apostrophe *s* is added. In the third example, *it's too late* is a contraction of the words *it is*. Therefore, *its* needs to be *it's*.

Finally, in sentence 4, the apostrophe is *not* necessary because the word *its* is *not* a contraction in this sentence. This last example can be especially confusing. The possessive *its* does not contain an apostrophe. *It's* equals *it is*, but *its* equals possession. The best way to remember this difference is to remember that *it* apostrophe *s* stands for *it is*, and then test whether *it is* fits in the sentence.

The office lost its lights.

To determine whether or not the apostrophe belongs, the writer can simply substitute *it is* for *its*. If an apostrophe were needed, the sentence would read:

The office lost it is lights.

Since that does not make sense, it is obvious that *its* here is a possessive, not a contraction, and does not need an apostrophe.

An old saying might also help you remember the difference:

When is its, it's?
When it is it is.

SECONDARY RULES OF PUNCTUATION

There are other punctuation marks that you may be called on to know from time to time. All of these are conventions; they depend on memory, not logic. Among the most important of these secondary marks are ellipses, dashes, parentheses, quotation marks, and brackets. Here is a summary of when to use each.

Ellipsis

Occasionally, you will come across three dots in the middle of a sentence. This means that words have been omitted from a statement that is being quoted. This omission is called **ellipsis**, and the dots that indicate the omission are called ellipsis points or ellipses. (A fourth dot at the end of a sentence merely stands for the period.)

1. Original
At any specific point in time, especially the time at which its management confronts a management problem, a business has a number of strategic goals that may be threatened.

2. With omission
At any specific point ... a business has a number of strategic goals that may be threatened.

The Dash

The **dash** is used to indicate a sudden or unexpected shift in the flow of a statement or to heighten surprise. Dashes are also used to take the place of parentheses.

1. Movies are better than ever—or so the press agents say!
2. Lyndon Johnson—our former president—was born in Texas.
3. Patriots—and I trust we are all patriots at a time like this— will not hesitate to act.

Parentheses

Parentheses are used (1) to enclose examples or parenthetical material, (2) to enclose material that is only loosely connected with the main thought of the sentence, and (3) to set off itemized numbers or letters—as in this sentence.

The book quoted (Fried's Pedagogical Methods) contains much useful information.

Brackets

Brackets are used (1) to mark an interpolation added by writers to material they are quoting and (2) to enclose a parenthetical expression in a part of a sentence that is already enclosed by parentheses. For example:

1. The book quoted from (Fried's Pedagogical Methods [3rd Edition]) contains much useful information.

2. The book quoted from contained much useful information (or so the author [Fried, Pedagogical Methods, 3rd Edition] claims).

Quotation Marks

All marks of punctuation (except the semi-colon, colon, and, in special cases, the question mark and the exclamation point) should be placed within quotation marks. Consider these examples:

1. Words like "patriotism," "democracy," and "free enterprise" are often employed for their effect.

2. "What?" said the Controller, "I will not do it!"; then she strode from the conference room.

3. Is there such a word as "phooey"? (To put the question mark inside the quotation mark would signal that the mark refers to the word *phooey* and not to the entire sentence.)

SUMMARY

Punctuation is not the *most* important aspect of writing, but it is important, especially when it helps to clarify meanings and intentions. For this reason, punctuation can have very important legal ramifications, with interpretations and meanings depending on the insertion of certain marks of punctuation.

We, therefore, encourage you to exercise care and common sense when punctuating. As much as possible, avoid simple, obvious errors in punctuation. But be careful not to waste too much valuable time worrying about whether to use or not use an optional comma. Let good judgment be your guide, and you should have no problems.

(Punctuation exercises appear at the end of Unit B.)

FORMATTING LETTERS, MEMOS, AND FORMAL REPORTS

OBJECTIVES

This chapter will help you to

●

Identify the parts of business letters, memos, and formal reports

●

Understand the placement of the different parts within business messages

●

Determine what information should and should not be included within each part of a business letter or memo

●

Be aware of the types of attachments that often accompany formal reports

The format of a business document refers to the way its parts are put together. In other words, format involves placement, for example, deciding where to place basic sections of a letter, such as the inside address, the return address, and the typed signature.

The best advice about format is that it should not draw attention to itself—unless, as in certain persuasive situations, you want it to. At all other times, you should construct your business documents in such a way that the reader seldom, if ever, even notices the format.

The company you work for will most likely have its own designated format for letters, memos, reports, and internal electronic correspondence. If you follow that format, you will accomplish the task of not letting format draw attention to itself.

Business documents are of three main types: the letter, which is used primarily for messages sent outside the organization; the memo (and memo report), which is sent inside the organization; and the formal report, which is sent either inside or outside the organization. This chapter will provide advice for formatting each of these documents.

THE BUSINESS LETTER

Basic Parts of a Business Letter

The six basic parts of a business letter are these:

1. the printed letterhead, typed heading, and date,
2. the inside address,
3. the salutation,
4. the body of the letter,
5. the complimentary close,
6. the typed signature.

Each part fits within an overall framework that runs from the letterhead at the top of the page to the signature at the end.

Placement of the Parts

Figures B-3.1 and B-3.2 show how the six parts of the letter fit within the letter's framework. Think of each part as a block. In the format called a full block format, all of the blocks begin at the left-hand margin. Thus, the blocks appear as in Figure B-3.1.

In the modified block format, three of the blocks—the heading and/or date box, the complimentary closing box, and the typed signature box begin at the center of the page. Thus, the format shifts and looks as in Figure B-3.2.

Incidentally, this description in terms of blocks is not only useful for overall placement of the parts, but it is also useful for internal spacing. If you remember the block format, you can also remember that you single-

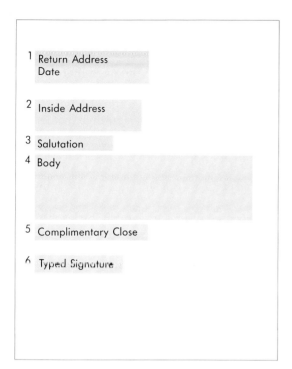

FIGURE B3.1
Full block format.

space *within* each block and, in most instances, you double-space *between* them.

The exceptions to the double-spacing rule are in the distance between the heading and the inside address and in the distance between the com-

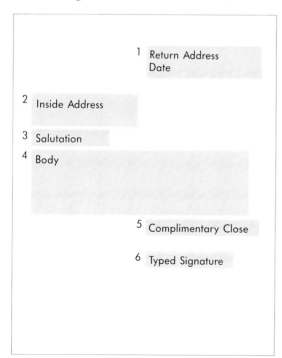

FIGURE B3.2
Modified block format.

plimentary closing and the typed signature. The distance between the heading and the inside address varies, based on how the letter centers on the page. The goal is to have the finished letter look as if slightly more of the printing and typing appear on the upper half of the page than on the lower half.

The distance between the complimentary closing and the typed signature also varies, so as to leave room for writers to sign their name. As a general rule, the distance between the complimentary closing and the typed signature block is four spaces.

Content of the Basic Parts of a Business Letter

Once you are aware of how the different sections fit within the letter, you can begin to pay attention to what goes into each part. The following information is generally included in each part.

Heading   The heading consists of the writer's full address and the date. Most often, all of this information, except for the date, is contained in the company's letterhead. If you are not using company letterhead, give the writer's full address, including the writer's street, city, state, and ZIP code.

The heading should be typed twelve to thirteen lines from the top of the page, with the date typed directly below the last line of the address. If you are using company letterhead, type the date two spaces below the last line of the letterhead.

Be sure to spell out words such as "street," "avenue," or "north," instead of using abbreviations. Never abbreviate the month or year in the date line. Following is an example of a non-company heading:

187 Market Place
Baltimore, MD 21222
March 8, 19——

Inside Address   The inside address consists of the full name, title, company, and address of the recipient. Normally, you would begin the inside address two to four spaces below the date. But, as we mentioned earlier, the spacing can be adjusted if the letter is unusually long or short. The inside address should always be aligned with the left margin and should always begin with "Mr.," "Ms.," "Miss," "Mrs.," or a professional title before the recipient's name. Titles such as "Captain" or "Professor" should never be abbreviated, but "Dr." is the preferred form. Unless you know that a woman prefers "Miss" or "Mrs.," address women without a professional title as "Ms.," whether they are married or unmarried.

Here is an example of an inside address:

Mr. James Harris
Vice President
Acme Industries
18 Bayshore Boulevard
Tampa, FL 33606

Notice that the recipient's business title, Vice President, is fully typed, not abbreviated. Abbreviations should not be used for such titles.

Salutation   In most business letters, the salutation consists of the recipient's title and last name, followed by a colon. The salutation is always typed at the left margin, two lines below the inside address. If you do not know the gender of the person you are writing to, you may use a title appropriate to the context of the letter, such as:

Dear Customer: *(From a department store)*
Dear Homeowner: *(From an insurance agent)*
Dear Parts Manager: *(From an auto-parts dealer)*

Another approach to use when you do not know the person's gender is to use the person's full name (Dear Chris Stone).

Often, you have to write letters to large companies or organizations without knowing the name of the person you are writing to. In such cases, you can address the letter to the company, identify the subject in an attention line or a subject line, and omit a salutation. Here are two examples:

Acme Business Systems
98 Gaston Street
Raleigh, NC 27603

Attention: Personnel Department

Acme Business Systems
98 Gaston Street
Raleigh, NC 27603

Subject: Hiring of New Employees

Body of a Letter   You should begin the body of the letter two lines below the salutation or the subject line, if no salutation is used. You should single-space within paragraphs and double-space between them. If a letter is exceptionally short, you can double-space within paragraphs. But if you double-space within paragraphs, you should indent the first line of each paragraph five spaces. The right margin should be about as wide as the left margin. The margins can be adjusted to accommodate the length of the letter.

If a letter is longer than one page, do not use letterhead for the second page. You should always carry over at least two lines of the letter if you must use a second page. The second page should have a heading that includes the name of the recipient, the date, and the page number. This heading may be typed across the page or in the upper left corner. Here is an example of each approach:

Mr. John Sparks   2   March 30, 19——

Mr. John Sparks
Page 2
March 30, 19——

Complimentary Closing   The complimentary closing should be typed two lines below the last line of the body of the letter. You should capitalize only the first letter of the first word in the complimentary closing and follow the expression with a comma. The two most common complimentary closings used in business letters are "Sincerely" and "Cordially." Either can be used at any time.

Signature Line   As we noted earlier, the writer's name is typed four spaces below the complimentary closing. The letter is signed between the complimentary closing and the typed name of the writer. Since the signature line is helpful for addressing a return letter, it should include the writer's full name, business, title, and department (if appropriate). The writer's business title should never be abbreviated. If the writer's title is given in the letterhead, it is not necessary to include it in the signature line.

Additional Parts of a Business Letter

Additional parts are sometimes included within a business letter.

Typist's Initials   The typist's initials should be typed two lines below the typed name of the writer and are preceded by the writer's initials. The typist's initials should always start at the left margin and should be typed in one of two following manners:

NGB/bp

NGB:bp

The first three letters are the writer's initials, typed all in capital letters. The last two letters are the typist's initials, typed in lower case. Typist's initials are not needed if the writer of the letter is also the typist.

Enclosure Notation   An enclosure notation should be typed directly below the typist's initials or two lines below the typed name of the writer if no typist's initials are used. An enclosure notation should be used if enclosed items may not be obvious to the reader. The enclosed items should also be mentioned in the body of the letter.

Enclosures may be noted in several different ways. The following are a few ways to note enclosures:

Enclosure: Financial Report

Enclosures (3)

Enc.

Copy Notation   A copy notation should be typed directly below the enclosure notation or two spaces below the typed name of the writer. A copy notation is used to let the recipient of a letter know that a copy is being sent to someone else. Here is an example of a copy notation:

cc: Mrs. Betty Cord

Putting Together a Business Letter

Let's put together our parts and the content of our blocks to see how the letters appear.

Full Block Format   A business letter presented in full block style has all of the typing beginning at the left-hand margin. This format is the most preferred because it is the easiest to type. It requires no tab sets or indented margins.

Here is an example of a business letter typed in the full block format:

187 Market Place
Baltimore, MD 21222
March 8, 19——

Mr. James Harris
Vice President
ACME Industries
18 Bayshore Boulevard
Tampa, FL 33606

Dear Mr. Harris:

_____
_____
_____

_____
_____

Sincerely,

Lawrence B. Steele

Lawrence B. Steele
Vice President

LBS/bp
Enc.

Modified Block Format   As we noted earlier, in a letter typed in a modified block format, the heading and complimentary closing begin at the center line. The first line of paragraphs may be indented or typed at the left-hand margin. Everything else is typed at the left-hand margin.

Here is an example of a business letter typed in the modified block format:

187 Market Place
Baltimore, MD 21222
March 8, 19——

Mr. James Harris
Vice President
ACME Industries
18 Bayshore Boulevard
Tampa, FL 33606

Dear Mr. Harris:

_____
_____
_____

_____
_____

Sincerely,

Lawrence B. Steele

Lawrence B. Steele
Vice President

LBS/bp
cc: H. M. Jacobs

Again, we remind you that a number of other letter formats also exist. But these two formats will suffice for most business situations.

The Memo

The memo format is perhaps the simplest of all correspondence formats. Usually a company will have paper already printed with the approved format. Basically, the format consists of a label—usually MEMORANDUM,

MEMO, or INTEROFFICE CORRESPONDENCE—and a listing of four other topics:

DATE:
TO:
FROM:
SUBJECT:

The first three headings are, of course, self-explanatory. The fourth heading, the subject line, briefly introduces readers to the subject of the memo. The subject line is used as a guide for filing memos.

Some business writers include a reference line below the subject line; other business writers find the line redundant. When used, the reference line refers readers to other relevant documents, such as "Your memo of 5/15/90." Also note that:

- The body of the memo is usually single-spaced, with double-spacing between paragraphs.
- If a memo goes to a second page, a heading similar to that in a letter is used.
- Elements such as typist's initials, enclosures, and copy notations are included in the same location as on a letter.

Finally, and most importantly, a memo does *not* have a complimentary closing. Instead, the writer merely signs his or her initials beside the name section in the heading. A writer seldom formally signs a memo—only if there is some legal reason for having to do so. In most instances that a signature is necessary, the writer shifts the memo to a letter format.

Following is a typical memo format.

M E M O R A N D U M

DATE: March 30, 19——

TO: James Harris

FROM: Larry Steele

SUBJECT: Employee Overtime

_____

_____

_____

_____

_____

_____

LS/bp
Enc.

The Formal Report

In Chapter 7, we mentioned that you may occasionally have jobs that require you to write formal business reports. In that chapter, we discussed the body of the report. However, such reports sometimes contain certain special elements. Here are the main parts that sometimes accompany formal reports:

Letter of Transmittal   If you are sending your report to someone at another location, you should consider including a letter of transmittal. This letter mentions the attached report and usually explains the report's purpose. Some businesspeople put this letter to special use by including a summary of the report's findings. Others use this letter to acknowledge assistance, to highlight points of significance, or to direct the reader's attention toward special features or findings in the report.

Abstracts or Executive Summaries   Abstracts or executive summaries are the ultimate bottom line. These synopses are either attached to or placed at the beginning of the report. Abstracts and summaries can save readers immense amounts of time by revealing the report's findings, conclusions, and/or recommendations. Contract sentences can be included in these summaries to do an even better job of guiding the reader through the report.

The length of the summary depends on the complexity of the report and the needs of the reader. It may range in length from one paragraph to two or more pages. Here is an actual, though disguised, example of a summary attached to the front of a 105-page sales proposal. Notice how it bottom-lines the entire report and includes a contract sentence to guide the reader's progress:

SUMMARY

The attached report recommends that ABC purchase the XYZ telecommunications system. This sytem, designed for office complexes such as ABC's, can handle internal and external calls through different lines and uses micro-switch settings to distinguish between the relay sources. The report explains the following three aspects of the system in detail:

1. The XYZ telecommunications design.
2. The way XYZ design meets the needs of ABC's office complex.
3. The necessary design modifications and costs of the system.

Footnotes and Bibliography   Business reports that use outside sources need to footnote these sources. In most instances, these reports need bibliographies either to list all the sources consulted or to provide places where readers can seek additional information.

The proper form for footnotes and bibliographies changes based on the source used. The four most commonly used guides for constructing bibliographies and footnotes are these:

- *A Manual for Writers* by Kate Turabian, 5th Edition.
- *The Chicago Manual of Style,* 13th Edition.
- *MLA Handbook for Writers of Research Papers,* 3rd Edition.
- *Publication Manual of the American Psychological Association,* 3rd Edition.

Find out which guide, if any, is generally used in your industry and use that one.

Additional Parts of a Formal Report   A number of other elements are sometimes also attached to formal business reports. Among these elements are a table of contents, a list of illustrations, a glossary, a list of symbols, and appendices. If you choose to use any of these supplements, we suggest you consult any of the handbooks we have just listed. Each provides ample information about employing these supplemental features.

SUMMARY

Format is most effective when it does not draw attention to itself. You can accomplish the task of formatting most easily by using your company's standard methods for letters, memos, and reports.

Business letters have six basic parts: (1) the letterhead and date, (2) the inside address, (3) the salutation, (4) the body, (5) the complimentary closing, and (6) the typed signature. These parts appear in the order we have just given.

Business memos contain four pieces of information that appear at the very beginning of the memo. This information consists of (1) the date the memo is sent, (2) the person to whom the memo is sent, (3) the writer of the memo, and (4) the subject of the memo. Unlike a letter, a memo does not have a complimentary closing.

Finally, formal reports may have attachments or supplementary information. This information consists of letters of transmittal that accompany the report, abstracts, or executive summaries that synopsize the report, and footnotes and bibliographies that provide information about sources for the report.

REVIEW QUESTIONS

1. What are the six basic parts of a business letter?

2. What are the two most common formats of a business letter?

3. What five topics are listed in the label of a memo?

4. Does a memo have a complimentary closing?

5. What is a letter of transmittal?

6. What is an abstract?

7. What are the four most commonly used guides for constructing bibliographies and footnotes?

GRAMMAR PRINCIPLES
REVIEW LIST

1

Do not write sentences in which words change from singular to plural, or vice versa.

2

Put words that influence the meaning of other words as close as possible to the words they influence.

3

Avoid using pronouns as much as possible in important documents. Use nouns.

4

A reader expects the noun closest to a pronoun and agreeing with it in gender and number to be the noun that pronoun refers to.

5

Because a pronoun means little until a reader knows what noun it refers to, you are usually wise to put the noun first and follow with the pronoun.

PUNCTUATION PRINCIPLES
REVIEW LIST

1

Words or groups of words that are presented out of subject-predicate order in a sentence are set off by commas.

2

Modifiers that are parenthetical and, hence, *not necessary* to the meaning of the sentence are set off by commas.

3

In a series with three or more items, separate the items with commas. In a series with only two items, do not separate the items by a comma.

EXERCISES

Exercise 1

Listed below are the ten sentences with grammar mistakes that made up the pretest you took at the beginning of Chapter B-1. Take this test to see how much you have learned. Some of these have been discussed in the chapter, so there should be no reason for your not being able to identify and name each error.

1. A few offices have consistently processed more than 40 percent of the month's activity in the last three work days. Attached for your information and appropriate action are a list of those offices that fall into this category.

2. An inventor may qualify for one or more award points for an Invention Award only if they are regular employees.

3. The capabilities and resources of each functional area is defined below.

4. After considering the current productivity requirements in the field, it is incumbent upon us to insure that we spread the workload as evenly as possible across the entire month.

5. We have decided to hold a national managers' meeting June 4-7. We have also decided to continue holding regional meetings yearly. This should please most in-state managers.

6. Neither the warehouse in Cleveland nor the Dallas transportation department have responsibility for delivering equipment to the exhibit site.

7. Originally designed for use in the personal computing and research environment, the sales of this product have proved wider than planned.

8. After setting the headcount requirement, it will be necessary to move ahead to make our New York group responsible for developing an effective regional sales force.

9. The ability to develop hard-hitting audio-visual presentations and to deliver them effectively is the mark of a real professional. Customers expect these from top salespeople.

10. After analyzing the data, a decision was made to go ahead with production of the 6362 Model C1 Printer attachment.

Answers to the Pretest and to Exercise 1.

1. Lack of number agreement between subject and verb. (*List* is singular. *Are* is plural. Correct verb would be *is*.)

2. Lack of number agreement between pronoun *they* and its antecedent

noun, *inventor*. (Correct pronoun should be *he* or *she*. Changing *they* to *he* or *she* requires changing *are* to *is*.)

3. Lack of number agreement between subject and verb. (The subject is *capabilities and resources*; therefore, the verb should be *are*, not *is*.)

4. Misplaced modifier. (*It* cannot *consider*. The *considering* phrase needs to be placed near the word in the sentence that does the considering; that is, *we*.)

5. Vague pronoun. (What does *this* refer to?)

6. Lack of number agreement between subject and verb. (*The Dallas transportation department*, the subject following *nor* and hence the word that determines the number of the verb, is singular and thus requires a singular verb, *has*, not *have*.)

7. Misplaced modifier. (*This product* was *designed*. The *sales* were not designed.)

8. Dangling modifier. (No subject in this sentence can be *setting the head-count requirements*; *it* certainly can't. Therefore, the phrase beginning with the participle *setting* dangles.)

9. Vague pronoun. (What does *these* refer to?)

10. Dangling modifier. (No subject in this sentence can be *analyzing the data*; therefore, again, a participle phrase dangles.)

Exercise 2

Correct the format of the following letter.

ACME Corporation
Jan. 19, 19——
98 West Park Street
Raleigh, NC 27609

556 19th St.
Johanna Barnes
San Francisco, CA 38201

Dear Miss Barnes;

_____
_____
_____

_____
_____
_____

John S. Jones
Vice Pres.

jsjlf

Exercise 3

Correct the format of the following memorandum.

SUBJECT: Inter-Office Correspondence

DATE; March 21, 199—

FROM: Sheay McFall

TO: Penny Piland

_____
_____
_____

_____
_____
_____

Sincerely,

Sheay McFall

rewrite correctly

Exercise 4

Place a capital letter *C* beside each correct sentence. Place *one* of the following symbols beside sentences that are grammatically incorrect:

- S-V—Subject-Verb Agreement
- P-A—Pronoun-Antecedent Agreement
- DM—Dangling Modifier
- MM—Misplaced Modifier
- VR—Vague Pronoun Reference

Correct the sentences that are grammatically incorrect.

1. The branch has received the extra staff they requested. *it* *S-V*
2. Having agreed to the proposal, Ms. Jones's next move is to make the necessary provisions for its implementation.
3. Everybody who participates are eligible for promotion.
4. A report will be in your office tomorrow morning showing the facility's projected needs.
5. The branch maintains that their facilities meet inspection requirements.
6. The air conditioner has been repaired about six times during the last two years by maintenance engineering.
7. The faculty of this institution is well known. They should soon help our university to be ranked as one of the nation's top research institutions. *P-A* *The faculty members*

8. The sales goal and personnel requirements of each corporate division is defined below.

9. Using this software package, it is possible for a printer to produce three-color graphics.

10. The result from the pilot sessions indicate that a six-day training session sets too rapid a pace for some students. Therefore, the class length will remain at seven days.

11. I look forward in implementing your new system to working with you.

12. The ADF development group deserves thanks for their assistance in developing the seminar.

13. We run the training sessions described in the brochures, but to insure relevance we orient them to the different needs of each client group.

14. Thank you for the opportunity to present our proposal in Monday's conference with you and your staff as a solution to problem management.

15. If you have any questions regarding this study, please let me know.

16. We actively solicit your responses to these proposals. They are important because we want to incorporate corrections and additions before sending them out.

17. After identifying the problems, the managers hired a consultant to attack them. (the problems)

18. English Composition was my favorite course. It was filled with students who are grammatically proficient.

19. After examining the proposal, it was sent to the legal department.

20. The associate director, and the director, was involved in negotiations.

21. Before investing in any company, financial statements must be first approved by our financial analyst.

22. By changing policy procedures, breakage should be eliminated.

23. I intend to give you an unfit rating on this year's performance appraisal owing to your failure in an on-time manner to submit all required reports.

24. I can appreciate your concern regarding hazards associated with storing this chemical and suggest that due to the small amounts you have in storage, you make arrangements with the Denver facility to maintain and eliminate this facility's having to deal with it.

Exercise 5

Punctuate the following sentences correctly.

1. Although XYZ, Inc. competed hard for the contract ABC Company won out.

2. ABC Company won the contract, because it used insider information illegally.
3. ABC Company won the contract even though XYZ, Inc. competed vigorously.
4. ABC Company won the contract XYZ, Inc. competed vigorously.
5. XYZ, Inc. competed vigorously, yet ABC Company won the contract.
6. XYZ, Inc. competed vigorously but ABC Company won the contract.
7. XYZ, Inc. competed vigorously, and did everything possible to win the contract.
8. All XYZ, Inc.s' hopes which were the one's based on winning the contract were dashed.
9. XYZ, Inc. always decides negatively on whether or not to bid on a contract whenever facts are obscure.
10. Whenever facts are obscure XYZ, Inc. always decides negatively on whether to bid on a contract.
11. Nothing nothing at all will stop our company from succeeding.
12. We first prepared our bid then proofread it and finally submitted it.
13. We prepared our report I'm sorry to admit with less care than usual.
14. Its far to early to know the outcome.
15. Jones business records have been audited.

Exercise 6

Explain how different punctuation causes different interpretations to be made of these sentences:

Set 1

a. All of our resources which were invested in this project were lost.
b. All of our resources, which were invested in this project, were lost.

Set 2

a. The colors of this year's line of appliances are white, oyster, lime, yellow and bronze.
b. The colors of this year's line of appliances are white, oyster, lime, yellow, and bronze.

Set 3

a. Companies which skirt closely along the edges of the law should avoid attracting the attention of the IRS.
b. Companies, which skirt closely along the edge of the law, should avoid attracting the attention of the IRS.

Unit C

HOW TO ANALYZE CASES

CASE ANALYSIS

OBJECTIVES

This chapter will help you to

•

Understand how the case "game" is played to give students experience in making decisions in business situations that are as close as possible to real life

•

Learn how to solve business problems in a rigorous and logical fashion

In this Special Features chapter, we focus on how to determine just what messages we want to send in response to complex case situations. Therefore, this chapter deals with the analysis that must be undertaken *before* you begin following the steps outlined in the Flow Chart we discussed in Chapter 19.

If, for example, you conclude, after your analysis of a complex case, that you must tell superiors highly negative information, then you know that you are dealing with either a negative or a negative-persuasive message sent up. If you decide that sending such information is too risky you should (as the Flow Chart suggests) rethink your message selection. Can it be upgraded to a less risky message? If it cannot, then the Strategy Wheel will advise you what the best way to communicate your negative message probably is.

Fortunately, businesspeople tell us that many, if not most, situations requiring analysis are not particularly sensitive. And this is probably also true about most long complex cases you will be assigned in college.

PLAYING THE CASE GAME

In many colleges, business students have to write realistic, businesslike reports based on complex case situations. In order for you to write such analytical reports, you need to know how case instruction works—or, in other words, how you play the game.

A case may consist of fifty or more pages of voluminous detail about a company, the industry in which it operates, the company's personnel, its financial statements, and the like. Or, a case can be merely one or two pages long. If instructors want students to analyze and manipulate great amounts of data, they will assign lengthy, detailed cases.

Making decisions in the world of the case is not very different from making actual decisions. It is true that in the business world, things constantly change and that in cases they do not. But at the very instant that executives make decisions in real life, they do not know with certainty any more about what is going to happen in the future than students do when they are analyzing a case. Frequently, students contend that in actual situations, they would be able to find out certain bits of information that are not given them in the case. That is often quite true, but just the reverse is also true. When executives sit down to make a decision, they very seldom have available to them as much information as students are given in a lengthy, well-written case. In actual situations or in case analysis, we all have to make decisions on the basis of the best information available to us at a given point in time.

Staying in Bounds

The "game" of case analysis has certain rules. You are asked to make your decisions based on the evidence you have before you. You cannot invent information that is not included in the case. Furthermore, you should not attempt to discover more evidence than is given in the case. For example, if a company is identified by name, you should not telephone that company (or research its annual reports) to find out more information about the situation depicted in the case. To do so is to go out of bounds.

This is a very difficult concept for most students to comprehend, especially the good students. All their lives, they have been rewarded for diligence, for digging out facts from libraries, and for presenting as factually up-to-date a report as possible. It comes as a great shock to many students who have been rewarded all their academic lives for a certain type of behavior, to find that this type of behavior is frowned upon.

This does not mean that you are prevented from using any *commonly* known information. If a case, for example, involves a retailing decision to be made by K-Mart executives, it is unreasonable to expect that you would not know that Zayre and Wal-Mart offer stiff competition to K-Mart in many areas of the country. It would not matter whether or not the case specifically mentioned this obvious fact or not. Therefore, there is no reason why you could not bring this knowledge into your analysis of the case.

As another example, you could bring into your analysis commonly known historical population growth trends for a geographical area—whether or not the case data included these. But you would have to restrict yourself to any such figures that would be readily available to anyone in the case situation *at the time of the case.* If the case takes place in 1979, for instance, characters in the case could not know details about geographical trends that actually took place in the late 1980s.

Let's take another example. Assume that a case is set in the early part of 1983. A company president, Henry Jones, is undecided about whether he should buy new machinery and go into production of a new product immediately or to wait and see how the economy acts over the latter part of the year. If you, as a student, rush to the library, discover that the economy did indeed improve in the latter part of 1983, and write a report stating that Jones should quickly buy the machinery and get into production as fast as possible because the economy is going to improve dramatically, you would be running out of bounds. Knowledge of improvement in the economy could not have been commonly available information at the time of the case situation.

Case analysis is a *logical game,* and as a student you must play according to its rules. You are given a certain fixed batch of information. You must analyze this information as best you can and proceed logically to make decisions or to make recommendations that are supported by case evidence, common sense, and common knowledge at the time.

Original Thinking

Teachers who are advocates of case instruction argue that conventional teaching by lecture and textbook gives an advantage to students with good memories. Case instruction, by contrast, does not *tell*; it does not lecture. It puts less of a premium on sheer memory, forcing students to think analytically, logically, and independently, perhaps for the first time in their academic experience. Students are forced to make decisions and put themselves in situations where, in real life, there could well be serious repercussions resulting from the decisions they make. Through case analysis, students develop skills that, later on the job, they can use to tackle nebulous business situations, analyze them, and develop plans of action based on logic.

No Single Right Answer

One final rule to the case game is this: *There is no single right answer*. It is possible that two students can both write excellent analyses of a case and yet present diametrically opposite recommendations for action. Since this is often true in real life, it is also true in case analysis. Should the advertising budget be cut or should it be increased? Should the training program be cut back or should it be expanded? A person with a conservative financial orientation would probably look at the evidence of a case and argue that both the advertising budget and the training program should be cut back immediately. Someone with a marketing or personnel orientation would quite possibly come to the strong conclusion that both operations should be dramatically increased. Who is correct? In real life, only the passage of time will tell, and not always even then.

But while there is no single right answer, there is an almost infinite range of wrong answers. Any answer is wrong, in case analysis, when it is based on faulty logic, jumping to conclusions, and failure to consider all the available, pertinent facts.

Experiential Learning

The benefit of case education is that it is experiential. After students have experienced analyzing many cases and have learned to make decisions in a world of chaos and uncertainty, they will have become more mature and rational.

The true test of the effectiveness of a student's analysis of a case rests on the thoroughness and logic of the reasoning upon which recommendations are based. Case instruction is not a guessing game where, if you guess the right solution, you receive praise. It is a logical game. You will receive praise only when your solution derives logically from your analysis of the data and from the inferences you have drawn.

THE NATURE OF CASE EVIDENCE

When students begin to play the case game, they frequently become confused about what is factual and what is not. Some general rules will help you identify facts.

Stated Facts

Take as truth whatever a case states to be a fact. If a case states that the company is experiencing a poor cash-flow situation, you can safely assume that the company is indeed having cash problems. If it states that sales of a given product during the past year amounted to $428,615.92, you can be sure that sales were, to the penny, exactly as given. You do not have to worry about being given false information. To do so would make a mockery out of case instruction.

Fact versus Opinion

Assess the credibility of those who offer opinions. If the case states that Joanne Greenman, the Sales Manager of Consolidated Corporation, believes that "sales are going to double next year," all you can be sure of is that Greenman believes this to be true. But does that in itself make Greenman's belief factual? What you need to do is test the probable accuracy of her belief.

Evidence may be included in the case that will enable you to evaluate Greenman's track record as a prognosticator. If there is evidence that her predictions have been largely correct over the past ten years, you could hardly be criticized for assuming that her present prediction is probably correct—that is, if no other case data argue against Greenman's opinion. But you should never lose sight of the fact that, regardless of the probability of a prediction being correct, you are still dealing with an *opinion,* not a *fact.*

Therefore, you should look for evidence in the case that may give an indication of the likelihood of sales sharply increasing or decreasing. For example, industry sales trends may be included somewhere in the case. Or perhaps the case contains the opinions of other industry experts that support or refute Greenman's opinion. Perhaps the case mentions market research done by the company that indicates high future customer acceptance of the company's products.

Verifying Opinions

Bear in mind that some opinions are verifiable and some are not. Greenman's opinion that sales are going to double next year can only *really* be verified by waiting and seeing what happens next year. However, you could see whether her opinion is strengthened or weakened by the trend of sales of the company's products over the past ten years, if such figures were included in the case data.

Do's and Don't's of Dealing with Opinions

When dealing with opinions, you should always take great pains to observe the following do's and don't's:

1. Do *not* confuse opinions with facts.
2. *Do* try to determine how informed or uninformed the person offering an opinion seems to be.
3. *Do* try to determine whether the opinion can be verified and made far more "factual" than it seems at first.

The burden rests on you to marshal evidence to back up your statements. If, for example, after studying a case you conclude that sales will probably go up next year, you owe your reader an explanation of how you arrived at that conclusion. Rather than say, "Sales will probably go up next year" and stop there, you must support your position with case data, like this:

> Sales will probably rise next year. An extrapolation of sales growth over the past ten years indicates a probable 10 percent increase, assuming business conditions remain largely unchanged. Back orders have never been higher in the company's history. Finally, the company's own market research department forecasts strong and continued consumer acceptance of new products.

Do Not Merely Restate Case Facts

Another warning that many students should heed about case analysis is this: Do not merely restate the facts of the case. Do not spend time presenting a pointless summary of the general picture of the case. No one wants you to rewrite the case and present a list of its facts to the instructor.

HOW TO ANALYZE A CASE

In our discussions of bottom-lining, we have urged writers to present the bottom line of their analysis at the very beginning of a report. In a *non-sensitive* report, we still strongly recommend that you bottom-line the results. If your readers will regard your recommendations as being *negative* to their interest, your report is a *sensitive* one. In such a situation, this text has recommended that you use a semi-circuitous organization.

Remember our warning that bottom-lining is not synonymous with being superficial. Disciplined analysts do not merely read a case, jump to conclusions, and quit. The solution and the recommendations you may want to bottom-line later can only be developed after you have rigorously gone through seven steps:

1. Making a preliminary definition of the problem posed by the case.
2. Identifying the restrictions on your freedom to arrive at certain types of solutions.
3. Determining your objective. That is, asking yourself, "What is the best solution to the problem that is possible under the restrictions posed by the situation?"
4. Establishing criteria by which to evaluate (or "yardsticks" by which to measure) alternative courses of action that are feasible under the given restrictions on your freedom to act.
5. Developing reasonable alternative courses of action.
6. Applying your evaluation criteria to each alternative to determine how well it meets your objective.
7. Drawing conclusions and/or making recommendations.

Preliminary Definition of the Problem

Effective business cases are designed to be solved. When you read a particular case, you learn about the company, the appropriate personnel in the company, and the company's history and products. But as you read along, you begin to see that the principal character in the case faces a dilemma, a problem or obstacle that stands in the way of his or her company's achieving a particular goal.

In many courses that students take in college, the object might be to study the causes of how the company ever got itself in such a state. Other courses might discuss the sociology of the situation in which the people find themselves, or the psychological elements of the situation. But in managerial courses, the emphasis is invariably on *action*.

How the company got into such a situation is usually beside the point. How it can get out of the mess and stay out of it in the future—that is what business decision making is all about.

But your job, as you read a case, is to attempt to identify the problem or problems that must be addressed by the management in order to deliver their company from its particular dilemma. Problem-solving, of course, begins with this identification or definition of the problem. Are there undesirable conditions that are presently disturbing company operations? Or is there a high expectation that undesirable conditions will arise in the future, making action necessary today?

It is important that you be able to prove *by using case evidence* that the problem you pose is really the problem that should be addressed. Offering recommendations to cure a production problem, for example, when the real problem is financial, is worthless.

In some cases, especially those in introductory courses, you will find the problem overtly stated by the case writer. The case may begin:

> Richard Serrano, President of Argus Manufacturing Company, has a problem. He does not know whether to purchase a new machine or to have the old one repaired. On the one hand, cash is short; on the other, the company can no longer meet its production schedule because of the constant breakdowns of the present machinery.

The problem here is whether to buy a new machine or have the old one repaired. The statement of the problem even rules out the possibility of doing nothing, because it states that "the company can no longer meet its production schedule because of the constant breakdowns of the present machinery." Therefore, what you have to do is to sift through the evidence given in the case and determine which course of action (purchasing new machinery or having the old machinery repaired) is the one to recommend to Serrano.

In more advanced courses, you will probably be given cases that do not spell out the problem so clearly. In many instances, a great deal of the effort you spend on analysis will be related to identifying precisely what the *basic* problem is. What is at the root of the many distresses the company is suffering? Do the symptoms of distress have a common denominator?

In this important first part of your analysis, you should ask these questions:

1. What troubles, or symptoms of troubles, are afflicting the company at present?
2. What problems, obstacles, or unresolved dilemmas stand in the way of the company eliminating or minimizing these symptoms of distress?
3. Do these symptoms have a common cause? If so, what is it?
4. What proof is there that what you perceive to be the basic problem is indeed the problem that should be addressed?

Then there is one final but highly practical question you must ask yourself: "Have I posed a problem (or problems) for which there is not enough case evidence given to support a logical solution?" For example, if you read a case that contains eighteen pages of detailed information about the company's marketing activities, it would be foolish of you to decide that the problem is really that the company is having difficulties in quality control on the production line. You must recognize that case analysis is a logical exercise. Do not raise issues or pose problems that cannot be solved because the case has presented no evidence on which a solution can be based.

As you attempt to define a problem, you may find it helpful to think in general terms about the various categories of problems that exist in cases. Here are just a few:

Significant versus Trivial Problems   Some problems faced by companies are earth-shattering; others are trivial to the point of being unworthy of concern. You may be given a case where the problem is essentially trivial and all the characters in the case are making much ado about nothing.

Your greatest contribution to the situation may be to say, in effect:

> The Vice President of Finance and the Vice President of Marketing are overreacting to a problem whose effect is quite probably only temporary. If nothing is done, the problem will probably go away by itself. Certainly, it is causing no significant difficulties at present. Therefore, I suspect that the solution to this case is to help these two vice presidents discover that the basic problem is their own emotional reaction, rather than a serious economic situation facing the company.

In fact, some problems may be so trivial that they are more imaginary than real. Although few cases pose purely imaginary problems, real life does. Much of what we spend time worrying about is imaginary; many of our fears turn out to be unfounded. Therefore, it is wise in case analysis to determine whether at least some of the fears expressed by case characters may be unwarranted when checked against available case data.

Solvable versus Unsolvable Problems   Sometimes a case poses an unsolvable problem. For example, a company that insists on manufacturing only buggy whips will face a constantly declining market, and unless the shortage of petroleum becomes far more acute than is likely, this company's problem of how to reverse a declining market is essentially unsolvable. In a situation like this, the case analysis may pose a much more sensible problem to consider—that of determining what new products the company might manufacture, given its existing plant, equipment, expertise, and finances.

Urgent versus Deferrable Problems   In some cases, the need to solve a problem is urgent because the company is failing financially. Unless the outflow of cash can be staunched, the company will soon be bankrupt. In such a situation, you would be foolish to state the problem as one requiring a great deal of study and consideration before action should be taken. In fact, the very urgency of the situation becomes an essential factor in the problem definition. For example, the problem might be stated in this way:

> The company needs to stem the outflow of cash immediately— or, if that is impossible, to set in motion a plan for an orderly entrance into bankruptcy proceedings.

Such a problem cannot be deferred.

Urgent problems are short-run—unless the urgent situation will not go away. Then the problems are both short- and long-run problems. In many cases, a company will face both kinds of problems. For example, a company may wonder what to do about a rash of industrial accidents in the factory caused by some employees being under the influence of alcohol or drugs. Is the problem the immediate one about whether or not to fire the guilty employees without causing union unrest, or is it the long-run one about how to educate all employees as to the dangers of addiction? Should the company place its emphasis on establishing a rehabilitation program?

Identifying the Restrictions on Your Freedom to Act

After you have read the case and have preliminarily defined the problem to your satisfaction, you have to think about what factors are present that restrict your freedom to seek an ideal solution. In light of the constraints that exist on your freedom of action, is the solution you are seeking feasible? Or is it too impractical? Let's look at some of the constraints that affect whether you can seek an ideal solution or whether you must be willing to settle for some stop-gap course of action. Some of the most common restrictions are those of time, dollars, personnel, and public opinion.

Time Restrictions   You have to determine from the case if, for example, you have the time to consider further research into a problem. Or must you act *now* because the urgency of the problem requires immediate action?

Dollar Restrictions   Novice case analysts will recommend extensive investigation, surveying, or detailed analysis of evidence that may not only take up possibly limited time, but also could cost many thousands of dollars that the company may not, in fact, want to spend to solve this type of problem. Always keep in mind that, in business, almost any course of action costs money. You should evaluate the solution in terms of the dollars available to fund it.

Personnel Restrictions   Sometimes the kind of investigation you would like to make would require the services of a certain expert or specialist who may not be available to you. Or that investigation might tie up, say, ten employees for six months and, hence, not be feasible.

Legal Restrictions   Many otherwise appealing solutions to problems are out of the question because of some legal consideration. Businesses are under constant pressures from state and federal regulations covering affirmative action, civil rights, safety and health, product safety, and the like.

Public Opinion   Public opinion also frequently serves as a constraint on action. Most companies will consider public opinion when addressing a problem such as closing down a plant or cutting back on numbers of employees.

Determining the Best Solution Possible Under the Circumstances

Think through the restrictions on your ability to solve the problem in the case. Then decide on the best solution possible under the various constraints on your ability to seek an ideal solution.

Consider the case situation we mentioned earlier in this chapter, where the question was whether Richard Serrano, President of Argus Manufacturing Company, should repair the old machinery or buy new machinery. As you think through the ramifications of the problem, you realize the time restriction—something must be done immediately, since the company is currently unable to meet its production schedule because of the constant breakdowns of the old machinery. But consideration of time constraints leads you to recognize that shutting down the factory while you install the new machinery will also make the company unable to meet its production schedule, at least in the short run. You also discover that there are financial constraints. The company is short on cash, and with current interest rates so high, borrowing the money to buy the new machinery will put a considerable financial burden on the company. You see no particular personnel restrictions on your freedom to make the decision, although the Vice President of Manufacturing would clearly like the new machinery, and the Vice President of Finance would clearly prefer a solution that did not put the company into financial difficulty. Therefore, an astute writer of a case analysis might state the problem and the best solution possible like this:

> Argus Manufacturing Company is unable to tolerate constant breakdowns in its machinery any longer. Argus must determine a way of
>
> 1. Replacing its old machinery in such a way as to minimize disruption to the production schedule.
> 2. Financing the new machinery in such a way as to minimize the risk of later financial collapse of the company.
> 3. Taking action immediately, as all parties agree that further delay is intolerable.

As you can see, a sophisticated case analysis may divide the problem into several statements, each reflecting the influence of a restriction that is placed upon a solution. In this instance, we have recognized that the company faces problems that have both short-run and long-run implications. We have defined the problem faced by Argus Manufacturing Company in such a way that it has both production implications and financial implications.

Above all, do not define your problem in such a way that it cannot realistically be solved. This could occur when

1. The type of problem you have defined is basically unsolvable by any one company (such as the problem of inflation);
2. The solution requires millions of dollars that the company does not have;
3. The company is "bleeding to death" financially and at least a year would be needed to conduct the investigation necessary to solve the problem;
4. The way you have defined the problem is so insensitive that you will be fired, or a personnel uproar will result as soon as your report is read;
5. You have defined a problem for which no case evidence exists on which to base a solution.

Establishing Evaluation Criteria

Step five in our problem-solving process involves evaluating alternative solutions to the problem you have defined. But first, how do you compare, weigh, or assess these alternatives? What do you use as a yardstick or scale?

You have to establish criteria by which to compare and evaluate possible alternative solutions. You then must determine how close each proposed alternative solution comes to meeting the objectives you have established. Sensible decisions require that goals be set. For example, suppose you meet a man walking down your main street. He asks you, "Am I going in the right direction?" How can you answer? It all depends on where he wants to go. If he then states his goal, "I want to get to the courthouse," an answer to his question is possible. So too in business; in order to decide the worth of a particular alternative, you need to know what you are seeking to achieve.

Imagine a case where two factory workers get drunk and injure each other. Their supervisor fires the two workers on the spot. But the supervisor fails to obtain statements from witnesses or to arrange for a sobriety test to be administered. What criteria would you set by which to evaluate various alternatives for action in this case? Wouldn't the criteria look something like this?

> A course of action that will accomplish the following should be selected:
>
> 1. Keep us out of a legal quarrel over the lack of documentation.
> 2. Head off union involvement that might lead to a grievance—or even a possible strike.
> 3. If possible, not publicly undercut the supervisor who failed to obtain necessary supporting evidence.
> 4. Not give a signal to all employees that drinking and carousing on the job can go unpunished.

Each alternative solution you propose should be evaluated in terms of how close it comes to meeting as many of the criteria as possible.

Developing Reasonable Alternative Courses of Action

In case-oriented courses, you will find great emphasis being placed on taking action—on doing things. Business school professors like to teach aspiring managers to be decisive, to make decisions, to take action. But the actions you take must be reasonable and responsible, not farfetched or foolhardy. As you consider a given alternative, you must learn to identify potential unfortunate consequences of taking that action.

For example, in the case where the decision has to be made on how to install new machinery in Argus Manufacturing Company without bankrupting the company, we must recognize that a consequence of solving the problem by purchasing new machinery is that the action may lock the company for a long time into the manufacture of the particular product made by that machinery. If so, the decision to purchase new machinery should take second place to the question of whether the company is wise or is not wise to continue producing that product.

Maybe there is another alternative that should be considered, such as getting rid of the old machinery and getting out of the manufacture of that particular product. This alternative course of action could be considered if it turns out to be very difficult to get the machinery installed quickly without great disruption, or that it would be extremely dangerous to the company to invest so much money in the new machinery.

Applying Your Evaluation Criteria
to Each Alternative

At this point in your analysis, you must evaluate each of the alternative actions against the criteria you have defined to determine to what extent it accomplishes your objectives.

For example, in the prior case of the two factory workers who were fired by their supervisor for carousing on the job, we set certain goals. Now we need to see how close various alternative actions can come to meeting these goals.

1. One possible alternative is to do nothing. But will this meet our goals?

   Although it would publicly support the actions of our supervisor, and give a strong signal to other employees that they must behave, it is too risky. Because of the lack of documentation by the supervisor, this alternative will not preclude legal or union difficulties.

   Hence, this alternative fails to meet these criteria.

2. A second alternative is that the fired workers could be contacted and quietly rehired. However,

   a. This action would publicly undercut the authority of the supervisor.
   b. It would also give the wrong signal to other employees about expected behavior on the job.
   c. But it would meet the goals of heading off union or legal difficulties.

   Thus, this alternative meets exactly half of our goals. Is a better alternative available?

3. Suppose the employees were placed on suspension instead of being fired, pending proper investigation of the situation?

   a. This would head off legal problems (such as having to defend the firing in the absence of any documented evidence of wrongful behavior). Furthermore, if the union were brought in to make sure that evidence was collected fairly, grievances could be headed off. (Surely the union would not publicly condone drunken behavior in the factory.)
   b. This alternative would not seriously undermine the authority of the supervisor. (Actually, it represents an attempt to save the supervisor from the consequences of impulsively firing the workers without solid evidence.)
   c. It would give a proper signal to other employees.

   Therefore, in our conclusions, we would recommend alternative three as best meeting our objective decision criteria.

As you have just seen, you must anticipate to the best of your ability the probable results of taking each alternative course of action. You must consider judiciously the advantages and disadvantages of each alternative. You must include in your report an objective analysis of both sides, taking into consideration the benefits and liabilities, of each of the alternatives.

Students are often tempted not to include in their report an analysis of alternatives that have failed to meet the evaluation criteria. This is clearly a mistake. Should the reader be left to conclude that you only considered one alternative and have recommended it? How is the reader to know, unless you include discussion in your report, that you have considered all feasible alternatives before settling on the one recommended?

Your thought processes should resemble a court trial aimed at determining which course of action best meets your goals. The various alternatives march in, each with its own lawyer (you must play this part for each of the alternatives and play it objectively and fairly). The lawyer argues the alternative's case before the judge. Naturally, the lawyer will tell what is right with the alternative and will point out most vigorously the faults of all the other alternatives.

However, by the time the lawyers have had their say, the judge has a fairly complete picture of all the assets and liabilities of each of the alternatives. Now the judge must apply the evaluation criteria to all the evidence and decide which of the alternatives seems to offer the maximum benefits and the minimum liabilities.

This decision is precisely what you, now as the judge, must make, and you must present the reader with a record of *how* you have made this final judgment. You must explain fully those bits of evidence you feel are most significant, and why you feel they are so significant. You must recommend a course of action that, in your best judgment, is the one that will maximize the benefits and minimize the liabilities.

Drawing Conclusions

In most cases, you must come to a conclusion and/or offer a recommendation. You must expect to feel often that the case has simply not given you enough information on which to base your conclusion. But, as we pointed out earlier, in most long cases you will actually have been given far more evidence and facts than would be available to you at the point of decision in real life. Therefore, most instructors will not allow you to conclude, "There is not enough evidence here. I can recommend nothing!" What you must do if you truly believe you need more evidence is to

- Itemize those steps that should be taken (and by whom) in order to obtain needed information.
- Assess the probable cost of information gathering and take into consideration whether or not time pressures for a decision allow you the luxury of waiting to get further information.
- Show how you would use this additional information to arrive at a firm decision at a later time.

When you have logically worked your way through to your final conclusion, or your recommendation, then—and only then—do you apply the principles of bottom-lining. It is here that you must again pay attention to the warning we raised earlier in our discussion of bottom-lining: *Bottom-lining is not a synonym for superficiality.* You cannot merely bottom-line a conclusion or recommendation and simply walk away, expecting praise from your boss. You must back up that bottom-lined recommendation with a detailed statement of exactly how you arrived at that recommendation. Doing so will require you to take the boss step-by-step through your reasoning process.

You must, of course, decide whether all the details of your analysis belong in the main body of the report or whether they belong in appendices. But wherever they are placed, they must be presented. Above all, your recommendations must be thoroughly justified and supported by a logical marshaling of evidence available to you (through the case) at the moment of decision.

SUMMARY

Cases force students to analyze situations and exercise independent thinking. In this process, cases broaden students' educational experiences by showing them that success in business depends more on their ability to identify, handle, and solve problems than it does on rote memorization.

People who are effective at playing the "case game" usually follow similar steps or procedures while seeking the solution to a problem. First, they define the basic problem of the situation, including restrictions involved in the case. Next, they determine their objectives, establish evaluation criteria, and develop reasonable courses of action. Finally, effective case analyzers compare possible courses of action against their evaluation criteria and draw conclusions or make recommendations about the case.

APPLYING ANALYSIS TO A CASE

OBJECTIVES

This chapter will help you to

•

Analyze a case

•

Realize the importance of outlining
your analysis

•

Learn how to develop a sample report
from an outline

Let us put into practice what we have learned about analyzing a case. In what follows, we will first present the case; next, an outline analysis of that case; and finally, a sample written report based on that analysis of the case.

INEQUITABLE SALARIES CASE

Early in October 1987, Samuel Potnick, Vice President of Finance of Allgood Products, Inc., phoned Carl Hilton, President and COO of Allgood, to ask for advice on a problem that had arisen in his department.

"It started off as a seemingly minor matter, a response to necessity," Potnick said, "but it's loaded with dynamite now. I don't really know what we should do."

A few hours later, Potnick visited Hilton's office to see if they could work out a course of action that would solve Potnick's problem. In response to Hilton's request, Potnick related the facts of the situation.

A week before, Potnick had received a request for a conference from John Thornton, an extremely promising young man in the financial control section. Thornton has an MBA from a prominent West Coast business school and has done excellent work during his two years of employment with Allgood Products. Essentially, Thornton had come in to register a complaint about the way he felt he was being treated by the company. "When I joined Allgood Products, I started at $28,000 and spent two years being raised to the princely sum of $31,000. Furthermore, I had to spend eighteen months in a training program. Now you're bringing people into the company—right out of graduate school—and paying them $32,000 to start without making them go through the training program. I don't think it's fair. I like Allgood Products and my work fine, but I'm going to be forced to start looking elsewhere unless you can give me some assurance that my salary is going to go up fast enough to put me at a comparatively higher position than the new MBA's just being hired. And I think that a fair salary for me would be $36,000!"

Potnick had replied, "Have you talked with Al Johnson?" (Al Johnson was Thornton's immediate superior in the control section.)

"Yes," Thornton replied, "and that's why I had to see you. Al's position is that his hands are tied. Salary scales are set for the company as a whole, not by individual sections. He tells me that I am already getting the maximum possible for my length of service and that these new people were hired at higher than scale as a result of a special exception that Mr. Hilton made."

This was true, Hilton reflected. The college market this year had been remarkably tight. Competition for top new MBA's was keen. Since Allgood Products had badly needed new, high-caliber management trainees, he had authorized the company recruiters to go as high as necessary to get the right junior people. Five new MBA's had been hired, two of whom had been assigned directly to the financial control section. Moreover, the training program had been waived for these recruits as a result of their claim that they had not heard good reports of Allgood's program and wanted to side-step it.

Hilton was aware that Thornton was just one of many junior managers in the company whose salaries were low in comparison with those of the new recruits. In their conversation, Hilton shared the following thoughts with Potnick. Hilton said that he estimated that at least 50 junior people among the company's 275 managers could easily feel as Thornton did. As Thornton expressed it, a salary of at least $36,000, starting next March, would be what it would take to make his compensation seem equitable in relation to the new people's pay. In fact, Hilton estimated that the cost to equalize pay scales would be about $5,000 per person among the 50 low-level managers directly concerned.

"But then what?" Hilton continued. The gap between the pay of lower-level and higher-level managers at Allgood Products had already been narrowed in recent years as a result of ever-increasing starting salaries necessitated by conditions in the college personnel market. Raising lower-level salaries approximately $5,000 across the board above and beyond normal raises based on present salary policy, would almost eliminate the existing salary gap. The cost of no better than maintaining the present salary gap was, of course, a $5,000 across-the-board raise to the senior group as well.

It was true, of course, that some of the 50 junior managers and many of the 225 more senior managers could be retained without salary adjustment. Some were not worth more and could not get better salaries by leaving. Some, if they left, would not be sorely missed. Others were committed by family and personal interests to the locale in which Allgood Products operated. But Hilton estimated that 40 percent of the senior managers were highly mobile and could easily obtain positions elsewhere and that 90 percent of the junior personnel could move profitably. Furthermore, Thornton was not the first in the company to complain about uncompetitive salaries. Many of the senior managers had let him know that their salaries were not keeping pace with those paid by other companies. There was, he knew, considerable unrest.

Hilton said that no one knew better than Potnick that Allgood's profits during the past three years had amounted to $6,250,000 on sales of $250,000,000. The company's cash position was only fair, with cost demands for new capital outlays expected to be heavy in the next few years for production modernization. The company's debt position lent little encouragement to the prospect of heavy borrowing. Furthermore, money was currently tight, and interest rates were almost prohibitive and were expected to remain so until government restrictions on money were relaxed at some indefinite future date. Finally, Hilton knew, top management would not consider raising money through the sale of stock because the market was currently severely depressed and likely to remain low for many months, once again as a result of the money shortage in the economy.

Hilton knew that he would have to recommend action to Maxwell Allgood himself and that Allgood probably would put that recommendation before the Board of Directors if the amount involved was high, as it seemed sure to be.

Hilton pointed this out to Potnick and said, "Sam, not only is this matter of urgent concern to you, but you are in the best position to estimate the financial impact of any alternative courses of action we might consider. Would you have your people work up a report on this so that I can take it to Max and to the Board for approval?" Potnick said he would do so and left Hilton's office to work on it.

OUTLINE ANALYSIS

As Samuel Potnick's assistant, you would begin by outlining your analysis of the situation. The following outline analysis, however, should not be confused with what is expected in a written analysis. This outline is merely the skeleton from which the final report could be written.

Sample Outline

I. Problems Facing Allgood
   A. How to achieve an equitable, yet competitive salary structure at an affordable cost.
   B. How to keep the services of valuable junior managers like Thornton.

II. Restrictions on Decision
   A. Personnel
      1. Action taken must not reward marginal performers at all ranks.
      2. Action must address salary inequities that exist at present.
      3. Action must not worsen the shortage of high-caliber junior people at Allgood Products.
   B. Time
      1. Must act quickly. Thornton is threatening to quit soon.
      2. If solution to the problem is deferred, Allgood risks losing not only Thornton but also other mobile young managers who may follow his lead.
   C. Dollar
      Money is short because:
      1. Profits as a percent of sales have not been high.
      2. Demands for capital outlays are expected to be great.

III. Objective(s)
   A. Long-Run
      Achieve salary harmony and equity within Allgood Products without jeopardizing the company's profitability and cash position.
   B. Short-Run
      Retain Thornton and other mobile junior and senior managers, but not reward marginal performers.

IV. Criteria for Evaluation of Alternatives

A. Any salary changes must reward deserving personnel, avoid perpetuation of any existing inequities, and lay the foundation for future hiring and retention of good personnel.

B. The situation seems to Hilton to be urgent; so proposals should remedy the difficulties as soon as possible.

C. Recommended courses of action must be financially feasible in times of tight funds.

V. Possible Alternatives for Action

A. Defer action completely.

B. Raise Thornton's salary and delay action on others.

C. Raise salaries $5,000 for all or selected groups of managers.

1. All junior managers.

2. Selected junior managers (90 percent).

3. All senior managers.

4. Selected senior managers (40 percent).

5. All junior and senior managers.

6. All senior and selected junior managers.

7. All junior and selected senior managers.

8. Selected junior and selected senior managers.

D. Raise salaries gradually for the above groups, stepping up to the $5,000 level over a period of time.

VI. Evaluation of Alternatives

A. Defer Action
Advantages

▪ Takes pressure off cash situation.

▪ Avoids "panic" solution.

Disadvantages

▪ Problem will not go away.

▪ May lose good junior managers like Thornton.

▪ May cost the company more in the long run in terms of expenses to recruit replacements for those who quit.

Summary: Does not satisfactorily meet criteria for decision.

B. Raise Thornton's Salary Only
Advantages

▪ Satisfies Thornton.

Disadvantages

▪ All the disadvantages of Alternative A above, plus creates one more instance of salary inequity. Not fair to others in Thornton's situation.

Summary: Does not satisfy enough criteria.

C. Raise Salaries $5,000 for all or Selected Groups of Managers

   1. For all junior managers

    Advantages

- Retains supply of future managers.

- Makes recruiting of junior managers easier.

- Cost annual maximum of $250,000 (50 × $5,000) not extremely high.

    Disadvantages

- Almost eliminates salary gap between junior and senior managers.

- Raises all juniors indiscriminately.

- Will cause more disharmony in managerial ranks.

Summary: Does not meet criteria at all since it creates disharmony and does not solve problem for total personnel.

   2. For selected junior managers (90 percent).

    Advantages

- Reduces cost to $225,000 (90 percent of 50 × $5,000), $25,000 less than that of Alternative A.

- Does not raise indiscriminately.

    Disadvantages

- Does not help senior managers.

Summary: Does not sufficiently meet criteria, but is not so destructive as some other alternatives.

   3. For all senior members.

    Advantages

- Creates greater salary gap, which is good for manager motivation.

    Disadvantages

- Cost of $1,125,000 (225 × $5,000) is probably too high unless absolutely best alternative.

- Indiscriminate raises would reward the 60 percent of senior managers who are not mobile, some (or many) of whom do not deserve extra raises.

- Does not aid recruiting in that it keeps lower-level salaries below competitive levels and does nothing about the problem Thornton represents, nor about Thornton's personal concern.

Summary: Fails to meet any of criteria.

   4. For selected senior managers (40 percent).

    Advantages

- Creates salary gap without the cost of rewarding all senior managers. Approximate minimum cost of $450,000 (40 percent of 225 × $5,000) not absolutely prohibitive. (Some of those senior managers included in the non-mobile 60 percent might need also to be raised to create harmony and equity. Thus, cost would most likely end up being higher than $450,000.)

Disadvantages

- Does not aid recruiting of young people.
- Does not solve "Thornton problem."
- May create dissension in senior ranks.
- Cost is high.

Summary: High cost for fairly low satisfaction of criteria.

5. For all junior and senior managers.
   Advantages

   - Would make junior salaries competitive in market.
   - Would solve "Thornton problem."
   - Would create equitable and harmonious junior/senior salary structures.

   Disadvantages

   - Prohibitive cost.
   - Destroys reward system for merit by rewarding all indiscriminately.

   Summary: Strong disadvantages far outweigh advantages.

6. For all senior and selected junior managers.
   Advantages

   - Creates greater salary gap while aiding recruiting of good juniors.

   Disadvantages

   - Tremendous cost of $225,000 (90 percent of 50 × $5,000) for juniors and $1,125,000 (225 × $5,000) for seniors is prohibitive.
   - Indiscriminate raises to some undeserving seniors.

   Summary: Too costly and indiscriminate to meet objectives.

7. For all junior and selected senior managers.
   Advantages

   - Creates competitive salaries for attracting new recruits.
   - Solves "Thornton problem."
   - Rewards deserving and mobile seniors.
   - Cost may be minimum at which change can be made, amounting to $250,000 (50 × 5,000) annually for juniors and $450,000 (40% of 225 × $5,000) for selected seniors.

   Disadvantages

   - Costly, but a price that may have to be recommended.
   - Rewards the 10 percent of juniors who have not met standards.

Summary: <u>Best alternative up to this point in terms of meeting personnel, dollar, and time criteria.</u>

8. For selected junior and selected senior managers.
Advantages

- Same as Alternative 7 above, but does not reward the 10 percent of juniors who are undeserving.

Disadvantages

- Cost of rewarding even deserving senior managers is very high.

Summary: <u>About as good as Alternative 7. Choice is between these two.</u>

D. Give Graduated Raises
Give raises only to those two groups (all juniors and selected seniors, or selected juniors and selected seniors) where any action taken best meets the evaluation criteria. Such raises would amount to $5,000 but would be spread over a two-year period.
Advantages

- Spreads the dollar impact on company over a longer period, when profits and cash availability may be improved.
- Might achieve much of the same motivation as would a flat $5,000 upward salary adjustment in year one.

Disadvantages

- Runs risk of not being a quick enough adjustment.

Summary: <u>Nothing is ideal. But knowledge that the company is raising salaries may be enough to retain most managers and at the same time soften the impact on company cash outlays and profitability.</u>

VII. <u>Recommendations</u>

A. Point out first that recommendations are based on Hilton's estimates of managers in each group who might leave. Be sure to advise Hilton to double-check the accuracy of his estimates before accepting your recommendations. The following could be done:

1. Conduct an opinion survey, perhaps.
2. Check with key personnel, asking for their frank opinions.
3. Examine historical turnover figures to see whether there is a trend indicating a loss of desirable personnel from the company.
4. Examine absenteeism figures, to get tangible evidence of unrest.

B. If Hilton's estimates are accepted, the recommendation to advance is clearly to raise salary levels for selected juniors and seniors in two steps over a two-year period.

C. Costs of the recommended raises for <u>each</u> of the next two years would be:

1. $112,500 for selected junior managers, and

2. $225,000 for selected senior managers.

D. As a side issue, evaluate training program in light of general criticism by new MBA's.

SAMPLE WRITTEN REPORT BASED ON ANALYSIS

TO: Carl Hilton

FROM: Samuel Potnick

SUBJECT: Equitable and Competitive Salary Structure

DATE: March 1, 19— —

After analyzing all feasible alternatives, I recommend that Allgood Products, Inc. raise the salaries of selected junior and senior managers over a two-year period.

The report that follows

1. Defines the ramifications of the greater problem that is symbolized by John Thornton's complaint.

2. Considers four alternative courses of action to remedy the problem.

3. Sets objectives and evaluation criteria to be met by any alternative considered.

4. Evaluates each alternative in terms of how well it meets or fails to meet the evaluation criteria.

Statement of Problem

My conclusion is that this recommended action will best enable Allgood Products, Inc. to solve the following pressing problems:

1. How to maintain an equitable, yet competitive salary structure within Allgood without jeopardizing the company's profitability and its cash position.

2. How to retain the services of valuable junior managers like John Thornton, as well as Thornton himself.

As you have described the problems, Allgood's freedom of action is restricted not only by dollar but also by time and personnel limitations on Allgood's freedom of action. These are suggested not only by Thornton's threat of quitting, but also by your belief that similar unrest exists among both junior and senior managers in the company. Added to this is the feeling that inequities really do exist as a result of the salary floor for new recruits having been forced upward by $5,000 in the last two years.

The situation is complicated, finally, by a shortage of qualified managers at Allgood Products. A sizable number of resignations would only mean that these employees would have to be replaced by new people, probably at higher, more competitive salaries, thus adding to the dollar dilemma.

Moreover, the scope of the problem is large, since you estimate that 40 percent of the 225 senior managers and 90 percent of the junior managers might quit over a short period of time if nothing is done.

Check on Key Assumptions

The accuracy of the estimate as to the percentages of managers who might leave Allgood Products is critical to any analysis of this situation. Therefore, although I shall accept your estimate as a basis for my recommendations, I request that before you act, you direct that the following be undertaken as quickly as possible:

1. A confidential opinion survey to determine the extent of the unrest and the probable percentages of managers who might leave if no raises are forthcoming,

2. An examination of historical turnover figures to determine whether a trend exists toward leaving because of salary dissatisfaction (and not primarily because of other factors),

3. An analysis of absenteeism data, manager productivity, and other indexes of dissatisfaction.

If such investigations indicate that your estimates as to manager unrest are accurate, I would then urge that a double-check be made of competitive salaries paid in the industry, to make certain that your estimate of $5,000 is an accurate judgment of the across-the-board salary discrepancy between Allgood Products and its competitors.

Alternative Courses of Action

On the basis of your estimates of the situation, my analysis indicates that four alternatives seem feasible and worthy of consideration:

1. Defer action completely and wait to see if resignations do occur.
2. Give Thornton a raise and delay taking further action.
3. Raise salaries $5,000 for all or selected groups of managers.
4. Devise a system of step-raises for all or selected groups of managers, achieving a $5,000 increase over a period of time.

These alternatives have been evaluated in terms of how well each meets the following objective and criteria for decision:

Objective

To achieve salary harmony and equity within Allgood Products without jeopardizing the company's profitability and cash position.

Criteria

1. Personnel
   Any salary changes should reward deserving personnel, avoid perpetuation of any inequities, and lay the foundation for future hiring and retention of good personnel.
2. Time
   The situation seems to Carl Hilton to be urgent, so proposals should remedy the difficulties as soon as possible.
3. Dollar
   Recommended courses of action must be financially feasible.

Evaluation of Alternatives

In the section that follows, each alternative course of action has been measured to determine whether it achieves the objectives set and meets the necessary criteria.

Alternative 1. Defer action completely. This alternative fails to meet our goals. All that can be said in favor of it is that it obviously conserves needed cash and avoids what might possibly be considered precipitous action. However, the problem is clearly not going to go away. Needed junior managers like Thornton, plus a sizable number of the senior managers may well be lost. Thus, delaying action might cost Allgood Products more in the long run (in costs of recruiting plus inevitable higher salaries).

Alternative 2. Raise Thornton's salary and delay action on others. This alternative has the advantage only of satisfying Thornton and costing very little. Taking this action would produce the following disadvantages because it would

- create one more instance of salary inequity.
- not be fair to others in Thornton's situation.
- probably lead to the loss of other good young managers like Thornton.

Hence, this alternative falls far short of meeting our objectives.

Alternative 3. Raise salaries $5,000 for selected groups of managers. The recommendation that $5,000 raises be given to selected junior and senior managers was arrived at after a thorough consideration of giving $5,000 raises to the following eight categories of managers:

1. all junior managers

2. selected junior managers

3. all senior managers

4. selected senior managers

5. all junior and senior managers

6. all senior and selected junior managers

7. all junior and selected senior managers

8. selected junior and selected senior managers

The cost of each of these alternatives is shown in Table I:

TABLE I
Costs of Raise Alternatives

All junior managers	50 × $5,000		= $ 250,000
Selected junior managers (90 percent)	45 × $5,000		= $ 225,000
All senior managers	225 × $5,000		= $1,125,000
Selected senior managers (40 percent)	90 × $5,000		= $ 450,000
All junior and senior managers	$250,000	+ $1,125,000	= $1,375,000
All senior and selected junior managers	$1,125,000 +	$225,000	= $1,350,000
All junior and selected senior managers	$250,000 +	$450,000	= $ 700,000
Selected junior and senior managers	$225,000 +	$450,000	= $ 675,000

This table assumes the validity of your estimates of percentages of mobile managers, plus the $5,000 suggested level for raises.

Before you consider these alternatives, you need to answer two critical questions: (1) Should the salaries of all managers be raised, regardless of the managers' mobility, relative value to Allgood Products, and market value? (2) Can Allgood Products afford whatever action is chosen?

A negative answer to question 2 immediately eliminates those alternatives that are prohibitively expensive. It is also good management for us to refuse to raise the salaries of those whose market value, as well as worth to Allgood, is low. If these people were to leave and had to be replaced by higher salaried personnel, Allgood Products would at least have a chance of replacing them with people of greater competence. However, we should raise the salaries of those competent persons who, although highly mobile, have chosen to remain with Allgood through loyalty. Otherwise, the motivating effect of selected raises would be lost; in fact, continued unrest among valued personnel might result.

Offering raises only to senior managers who fall into the 40 percent desirable category amounts to $450,000 (as opposed to $1,125,000 for all seniors. And while raising the salaries of all junior managers would add only $25,000 per annum to costs (up from $225,000 for 90 percent to $250,000), the same logic as that applied to senior managers indicates that across-the-board indiscriminate raises are unjustifiable.

Now the only question that remains is whether only selected junior managers, selected senior managers, or both, should be given raises.

The cost of raising only selected junior managers would be low. Yet, it fails to meet the objective of an action aimed at producing harmony and a sense of equitable treatment in senior management. In fact, such an action might create a worse problem for Allgood Products.

Nor does raising the pay of only selected senior managers solve the problem symbolized by Thornton. The rising competition for new MBA's makes it obvious that desirable juniors are going to command higher salaries.

Consequently, the alternative of giving $5,000 raises to selected junior and senior managers, although costly, seems the only justifiable course of action to be recommended.

Cautions about Recommendation

Before making this recommendation to Mr. Allgood, you should, as suggested earlier, double-check the estimates as to the number of junior and senior managers who might leave, as well as your acceptance of $5,000 as being the "magic" figure that will settle unrest.

If these estimates prove to be approximately correct, you should then take special pains to determine whether or not this $5,000 raise to selected junior and senior managers could be spread over a two-year period and still retain its harmony- and equity-building power. If so, the cost to the company during the first year would be only $337,500 and the two-year cost $1,012,500 instead of $1,350,000.

If I can be of help in conducting the further research suggested, please let me know.

CASES

Case 1
Human Rights and Corporate Responsibility Revisited

To apply the problem-solving technique developed in this chapter, turn to the "Human Rights and Corporate Responsibility" case, Unit 10, Parts 1 through 6. However, instead of doing the assignments given at the end of each part of this case, focus now on the entire series of events related in all the case parts. Based on what you have read, decide the following:

1. Is there an underlying problem that is symbolized by the conflict between these disgruntled employees and Samuel Potnick? Is what we read here possibly just the tip of the iceberg? If so, how would you define this more long-range problem? Also, how would you define the more immediate problems?

2. What limitations are there on your freedom to act?

3. How would you define the best possible solution under the circumstances?

4. What alternative courses of action should be considered?

5. Which alternative best achieves the solution desired?

Assignment

Maxwell Allgood has asked you to report fully to him your analysis of this distressing situation. Do so.

Case 2
Fine's New Sales Bonus System Revisited

Now apply the problem-solving technique you have learned to "Fine's New Sales Bonus System" case, Unit 6, Parts 1 through 4. However, instead of doing the assignments given at the end of each part of this case, focus now on the entire series of events related in all the case parts. Based on what you have read, decide the following:

1. Is there an underlying problem that is symbolized by the conflict over Fine's bonus system? If so, what is possibly the basic problem which has caused this conflict?

2. What limitations are there on your freedom to act?

3. How would you define the best possible solution under the circumstances?

4. What alternative courses of action should be considered?
5. Which alternative best achieves the solution desired?

Assignment

Maxwell Allgood has asked you to report fully to him your analysis of this distressing situation. Do so.

Glossary

active voice   Refers to the form of a verb. The subject of the verb is the person or thing doing the action. *(chapter 9)*

audience and message analysis   Examination by a presenter of the audience and the effect the message will have on the audience. Specific concerns are relationship with the audience, power position relative to the audience, and likely audience response to the message. *(chapter 20)*

bar chart   A type of graphic that summarizes complex data and is used to show comparisons among different sizes and different amounts. *(chapter 7)*

bottom line   The message's statement of purpose; the statement that reveals why the writer sent the message. *(chapter 1)*

bottom-line organizational pattern   In this pattern you state the purpose of the message (bottom line) at the beginning of the message. Used in non-sensitive situations. *(chapter 1)*

bottom-lining   Organizing your thoughts so that they communicate directly, clearly, and forthrightly the gist, the very essence of what you have to say. *(chapter 1)*

chief executive officer (CEO)   The source of all power in a business organization, either the Chairman of the Board or the President. *(chapter 2)*

chief operating officer (COO)   Person responsible for the day-to-day operations of a company. Next in chain of command to the CEO. *(chapter 2)*

circuitous organizational pattern   In this pattern you withhold the bottom line, or purpose of your message, until you have had a chance to prepare your reader to accept the message. Used in sensitive situations where bottom-lining is inappropriate or too risky. *(chapters 1, 12)*

colorful style   A way of communicating that has a literary quality because of the use of adverbs, adjectives, similes, metaphors, and other figures of speech. *(chapters 14, 15, 20)*

colorless style   A way of communicating that results from a blending of the passive and impersonal styles and, hence, produces little emotional reaction in the reader. *(chapters 15, 20)*

complex sentence   Consists of at least one independent clause and one or more dependent clauses. *(chapter 9)*

compound sentence   Made up of two independent clauses joined together by *and*, *or*, or *but*. *(chapter 9)*

contract sentence or statement   A guiding statement that organizes, for both the reader and the writer, the direction a long document follows. *(chapter 6)*

cultural sensitivities   Rules of behavior that are so deeply ingrained that a member of a certain culture may become irritated or even insulted if you violate one or more of them. *(chapter 22)*

data management programs or databases   Computer software programs that help you manage and use long lists of data. *(chapter 2)*

dependent clause   Contains a subject and a verb but cannot stand alone. *(chapter 9)*

direct organizational pattern   See **bottom-line organizational pattern.** *(chapter 1)*

direct staff support   Refers to work performed by staff assistants who assist line managers, their bosses, in the performance of given tasks. *(chapter 2)*

direction   One of the situational factors of a message; refers to the fact that people within organizations must write up, down, or across the hierarchy. *(chapter 11)*

electronic mail (E-mail)   A computer-age message system that involves sending messages directly from computer to computer. *(chapter 2)*

environment   The setting that surrounds a businessperson and, therefore, influences the way messages are read and written. *(chapter 1)*

enunciation   Refers to the clarity and accuracy with which you pronounce your words. *(chapter 20)*

forceful style   A way of communicating that gives orders, avoids qualifying words, and uses an active voice sentence structure. *(chapters 14, 15, 20)*

function   A department within an organization, such as Finance, Accounting, Production, Marketing, or Personnel. *(chapter 2)*

high-context culture   An essentially oral culture based more on personal trust than on legally binding written agreements. *(chapter 22)*

high-impact writing   Writing that is clear and easy to read. Words and sentences appear to leap off the page and demand the reader's attention. Essential for effective non-sensitive messages. *(chapters 1, 8, 10)*

human support   Secretarial, clerical, and staff support provided to line managers. *(chapter 2)*

impact   The strength of the effect a message exerts on a reader or listener. *(chapter 1, unit 4)*

impersonal style   A way of communicating that avoids using person's names and personal pronouns and attributes responsibility for negative statements to faceless "others." *(chapters 14, 15, 20)*

independent clause   A sentence that can stand alone. *(chapter 9)*

indirect staff support   Refers to work performed by departments, such as Accounting and Personnel, that provide centralized services for the entire organization. *(chapter 2)*

informal organization   A secondary power system that does not show up on the formal organization chart but that may more accurately reflect the power structure of a company. *(chapter 11)*

international communication   Any communication taking place between two people of different countries. *(chapter 22)*

line chart   A type of graphic that summarizes complex data and is used to show trends. Should only be used when both sets of information are numerical and/or sequential. *(chapter 7)*

line managers   Persons whose positions lie in the direct line of delegated authority. These people have direct responsibility for implementing policies and plans set by executives in higher positions. *(chapter 2)*

low-context culture   A culture in which business deals are concluded by a specific written agreement between parties. *(chapter 22)*

low-impact writing   Writing that is difficult to read; the words are unfamiliar, the sentences complicated, and the paragraphs long. *(chapters 1, 8)*

message   *What* is said; that is, the information conveyed to a reader or listener. *(chapter 3)*

negative message   A communication that relays bad news, such as "No," evoking feelings of dismay, anger, and disappointment. *(chapter 11)*

negative-persuasive situation   A situation where the writer's task is to persuade readers to do something they don't want to do, something they perceive as of no benefit to them. *(chapter 11)*

non-sensitive message   A communication that causes little or no emotional reaction in the reader or listener. *(chapters 1, 3)*

organization   *When* in the body of a message the sender chooses to reveal the message's purpose. *(chapter 3)*

organization chart   Chart that shows the formal power structure of an organization. *(chapter 2)*

passive style   A way of communicating that avoids imperatives, uses the passive voice heavily, and uses qualifying words. *(chapters 14, 15, 20)*

passive voice   Refers to the form of a verb. The action is done to the subject. *(chapter 9)*

pausing   A moment or moments of silence used to build suspense and anticipation in a presentation and to draw attention to your topic and yourself. *(chapter 20)*

personal style   A way of communicating that sounds like one businessperson talking with another, uses the active voice, persons' names, personal pronouns, and questions. *(chapters 15, 20)*

persuasive message   A communication that attempts to cause someone to take an action desired by the sender. *(chapter 11)*

pie chart   A type of graphic that summarizes complex data and is used to show comparisons among proportions or percentages. *(chapter 7)*

pitch   The frequency level of the voice, which can range from high to low. *(chapter 20)*

positive message   A communication that conveys good news, evoking feelings of gladness and pleasure. *(chapter 11)*

positive-persuasive situation   A situation where the writer's task is to persuade readers to do something they know deep inside clearly benefits their ultimate interests. *(chapter 11)*

predominant message   The message that conveys the bottom line of the communication. *(chapter 19)*

projection   Refers to how you throw your voice toward the audience during a presentation. *(chapter 20)*

relationship   One of the situational factors of a message. Relationships between writer and reader can be classified as warm, neutral, or cold. *(chapter 11)*

report to   Means to be responsible to, and only to, your immediate superior. *(chapter 2)*

risk   One of the situational factors of a message. The risk associated with sending a given message ranges from being completely harmless to highly dangerous. *(chapter 11)*

semi-circuitous organizational pattern   In this pattern you use a contract sentence at the beginning of the message to tell the reader where the bottom line can be found. Used in sensitive situations where bottom-lining is inappropriate—or too risky. *(chapters 1, 12)*

sensitive message   A communication that evokes a favorable or a negative emotional reaction in a receiver. *(chapters 1, 11)*

simple sentence   Needs to contain a subject and a verb and needs to be able to stand by itself as an independent unit. *(chapter 9)*

situational factors   Certain environmental factors inherent in a communication situation over which we have no control. *(chapter 11)*

skeletal organization   The headings and subheadings in a message that derive from a contract statement and serve as guideposts for the reader. *(chapter 6)*

so-what? test   Test used to determine whether a message has a bottom-line organization. The reader asks of a sentence or passage, "So what? What's this all about?" *(chapter 4)*

speed   The rate at which you speak. During a presentation, that fastest speed should not exceed 175 words per minute. *(chapter 20)*

spreadsheet programs   Computer software programs that help handle tables of numbers. *(chapter 2)*

staff people   Persons who support line officers in business. This support may either be indirect or direct. *(chapter 2)*

staff professional   Refers to experts in various specialized areas brought into headquarters to perform the complex, analytical work required as background for sound decisions. *(chapter 2)*

style   The *way* something is said or written, as distinguished from the substance of what is conveyed. *(chapters 1, 14)*

sub-bottom-line statement   A bottom-line statement in a subsection of a report. *(chapter 6)*

subcontract sentence   This states what a subsection of a report is about, makes a transition from previous subsections to the present subsection, and specifies clearly the topics to be discussed in that particular subsection. *(chapter 16)*

synergism   Interaction of elements that produces an effect greater than that produced by the sum of the effects of each. *(chapter 18)*

table   Presents numerical information in a compact, readable form. Used when data contain so many points of information that a chart or graph would be unreadable, confusing, or unwieldy in size. *(chapter 7)*

technological support   The use of word processing centers, personal computers, and telephone and electronic mail as part of the communication process. *(chapter 2)*

telephone mail   Operates somewhat like a home answering machine. People are able to exchange information through tape-recorded messages without having to speak directly to each other. *(chapter 2)*

tone   The capacity a given document's style, organizational pattern, and visual display have for producing an emotional reaction in the reader. *(chapter 4)*

upgrade   Moving a message away from the negative and risky to the more positive, if possible. *(chapter 19)*

white space The area on a page not covered by type. Used in high-impact writing and often results from itemizing ideas. *(chapter 10)*

word processing programs Computer software programs that help you write and edit memos, letters, and reports. *(chapter 2)*

Index

Photo Credits

Table of Contents. Unit 1: Permission for use of photograph granted by The Coca-Cola Company. Unit 2: Four by Five, Inc. Unit 3: Courtesy of International Business Machines Corporation. Unit 4: Courtesy of Hewlett-Packard Company. Unit 5: Four by Five, Inc. Unit 6: Fern Logan/Monkmeyer Press Photo Service. Unit 7: Norman Mosallem/Bruce Coleman. Unit 8: Victor Serbin/Leo de Wys Inc. Unit 9: Tony O'Brien/Picture Group. Unit 10: Four by Five, Inc.

Page 16, *clockwise from left:* Susan Lapides 1981/Design Conceptions; Courtesy of Atlantic Richfield Company; Courtesy of International Business Machines Corporation. Page 20: Gerard Fritz/Monkmeyer Press Photo Service. Page 22: Courtesy of Wang Laboratories, Inc. Copyright © Wang Laboratories, Inc. 1989. Page 23: Christopher Brown/Stock, Boston. Page 46: Chester Higgins, Jr./Photo Researchers, Inc. Page 204: Comstock. Page 205: Gerard Fritz/Monkmeyer Press Photo Service. Page 207: Meri Houtchens-Kitchens/Picture Cube. Page 378: Robert George Gaylord/EKM-Nepenthe. Page 381: Art Stein/Photo Researchers, Inc. Page 388: Steven Baratz/Picture Cube. Page 400: Howard Dratch/The Image Works, Inc. Page 402: David M. Grossman/Photo Researchers, Inc. Page 415: Michael Kienitz/Picture Group. Page 418: Rene Burri/Magnum Photo. Page 423: Laima Druskis/Taurus Photos. Page 433: Robert A. Isaacs/Photo Researchers, Inc. Page 517: Joel Gordon 1986.

Photo Essay 1. Page 1: Courtesy of Texas Instruments. Page 2, *top:* Tony Stone/TSW; *bottom:* Courtesy of International Business Machines Corporation. Page 3: Courtesy of International Business Machines Corporation. Page 4, *top:* Courtesy of Unisys Corporation; *bottom:* Courtesy of Hewlett-Packard Company. Page 5, *top:* Courtesy of International Business Machines Corporation; *bottom:* Courtesy of Zenith. Page 6, *top:* Courtesy of Xerox Corporation; *bottom:* Courtesy of International Business Machines Corporation. Page 7, *top:* Courtesy of Apple Computer, Inc.; *bottom:* Courtesy of Hewlett-Packard Company. Page 8, *top:* Comstock; *bottom left:* Courtesy of Apple Computer, Inc.; *bottom right:* Courtesy of AT&T.

Photo Essay 2. Page 1: Courtesy of Agfa Matrix Division. Page 2, *top:* Joel Gordon/Joel Gordon Photography; *bottom:* Courtesy of Ashton-Tate Corporation. Page 3: Courtesy of International Business Machines Corporation. Page 4, *top:* Courtesy of Agfa Matrix Division; *bottom:* Courtesy of International Business Machines Corporation. Page 5, Courtesy of Agfa Matrix Division. Page 6: Courtesy of International Business Machines Corporation. Page 7, *top:* Courtesy of Hewlett-Packard Company; *bottom:* Courtesy of International Business Machines Corporation. Page 8: Courtesy of International Business Machines Corporation.

627